New Directions in German Studies

Vol. 2

Series Editor

IMKE MEYER

Professor of Germanic Studies, University of Illinois at Chicago

Editorial Board:

KATHERINE ARENS
Professor of Germanic Studies, University of Texas at Austin

ROSWITHA BURWICK
Distinguished Chair of Modern Foreign Languages Emerita,
Scripps College

RICHARD ELDRIDGE
Charles and Harriett Cox McDowell Professor of Philosophy,
Swarthmore College

ERIKA FISCHER-LICHTE
Professor Emerita of Theater Studies, Freie Universität Berlin

CATRIONA MACLEOD
Edmund J. and Louise W. Kahn Term Professor in the Humanities
and Professor of German, University of Pennsylvania

STEPHAN SCHINDLER
Professor of German and Chair, University of South Florida

HEIDI SCHLIPPHACKE
Associate Professor of Germanic Studies,
University of Illinois at Chicago

ANDREW J. WEBBER
Professor of Modern German and Comparative Culture,
Cambridge University

SILKE-MARIA WEINECK
Professor of German and Comparative Literature,
University of Michigan

DAVID WELLBERY
LeRoy T. and Margaret Deffenbaugh Carlson University Professor,
University of Chicago

SABINE WILKE
Joff Hanauer Distinguished Professor for Western Civilization and
Professor of German, University of Washington

JOHN ZILCOSKY
Professor of German and Comparative Literature, University of Toronto

Volumes in the series:

Vol. 1. *Improvisation as Art: Conceptual Challenges, Historical Perspectives*
by Edgar Landgraf

Vol. 2. *The German Pícaro and Modernity: Between Underdog
and Shape-Shifter*
by Bernhard Malkmus

Vol. 3. *Citation and Precedent: Conjunctions and Disjunctions
of German Law and Literature*
by Thomas O. Beebee

Vol. 4. *Beyond Discontent: 'Sublimation' from Goethe to Lacan*
by Eckart Goebel

Vol. 5. *From Kafka to Sebald: Modernism and Narrative Form*
edited by Sabine Wilke

Vol. 6. *Image in Outline: Reading Lou Andreas-Salomé*
by Gisela Brinker-Gabler

Vol. 7. *Out of Place: German Realism, Displacement, and Modernity*
by John B. Lyon

Vol. 8. *Thomas Mann in English: A Study in Literary Translation*
by David Horton

Vol. 9. *The Tragedy of Fatherhood: King Laius
and the Politics of Paternity in the West*
by Silke-Maria Weineck

Vol. 10. *The Poet as Phenomenologist: Rilke and the
New Poems*
by Luke Fischer

Vol. 11. *The Laughter of the Thracian Woman: A Protohistory of Theory*
by Hans Blumenberg, translated by Spencer Hawkins

Vol. 12. *Roma Voices in the German-Speaking World*
by Lorely French

Vol. 13. *Vienna's Dreams of Europe: Culture and Identity beyond
the Nation-State*
by Katherine Arens

Vol. 14. *Thomas Mann and Shakespeare: Something Rich and Strange*
edited by Tobias Döring and Ewan Fernie

Vol. 15. *Goethe's Families of the Heart*
by Susan E. Gustafson

Vol. 16. *German Aesthetics: Fundamental Concepts
from Baumgarten to Adorno*
edited by J. D. Mininger and Jason Michael Peck

Vol. 17. *Figures of Natality: Reading the Political in the Age of Goethe*
by Joseph D. O'Neil

Vol. 18. *Readings in the Anthropocene: The Environmental Humanities,
German Studies, and Beyond*
edited by Sabine Wilke and Japhet Johnstone

Vol. 19. *Building Socialism: Architecture and Urbanism
in East German Literature, 1955–1973*
by Curtis Swope

Vol. 20. *Ghostwriting: W. G. Sebald's Poetics of History*
by Richard T. Gray

Vol. 21. *Stereotype and Destiny in Arthur Schnitzler's Prose:
Five Psycho-Sociological Readings*
by Marie Kolkenbrock

Vol. 22. *Sissi's World: The Empress Elisabeth in Memory and Myth*
edited by Maura E. Hametz and Heidi Schlipphacke

Vol. 23. *Posthumanism in the Age of Humanism: Mind, Matter,
and the Life Sciences after Kant*
edited by Edgar Landgraf, Gabriel Trop, and Leif Weatherby

Vol. 24. *Staging West German Democracy: Governmental PR Films
and the Democratic Imaginary, 1953–1963*
by Jan Uelzmann

Vol. 25. *The Lever as Instrument of Reason:
Technological Constructions of Knowledge around 1800*
by Jocelyn Holland

Vol. 26. *The Fontane Workshop: Manufacturing Realism in the
Industrial Age of Print*
by Petra S. McGillen

Vol. 27. *Gender, Collaboration, and Authorship in German Culture:
Literary Joint Ventures, 1750–1850*
edited by Laura Deiulio and John B. Lyon

Vol. 28. *Kafka's Stereoscopes: The Political Function of a Literary Style*
by Isak Winkel Holm

Kafka's Stereoscopes

The Political Function
of a Literary Style

Isak Winkel Holm

BLOOMSBURY ACADEMIC
NEW YORK · LONDON · OXFORD · NEW DELHI · SYDNEY

BLOOMSBURY ACADEMIC
Bloomsbury Publishing Inc
1385 Broadway, New York, NY 10018, USA
50 Bedford Square, London, WC1B 3DP, UK
29 Earlsfort Terrace, Dublin 2, Ireland

BLOOMSBURY, BLOOMSBURY ACADEMIC and the Diana logo are
trademarks of Bloomsbury Publishing Plc

First published in the United States of America 2020
Paperback edition published 2021

Cover design: Andrea F. Bucsi

Bloomsbury Publishing Inc does not have any control over, or responsibility
for, any third-party websites referred to or in this book. All internet addresses
given in this book were correct at the time of going to press. The author and
publisher regret any inconvenience caused if addresses have changed or sites
have ceased to exist, but can accept no responsibility for any such changes.

Library of Congress Cataloging-in-Publication Data
Names: Holm, Isak Winkel, 1965– author.
Title: Kafka's stereoscopes: the political function of a literary style/Isak
Winkel Holm.
Description: New York, NY: Bloomsbury Academic, 2019. | Series: New
directions in German studies; vol. 28 | Includes bibliographical references
and index.
Identifiers: LCCN 2019011690 (print) | LCCN 2019016342 (ebook) |
ISBN 9781501347832 (ePub) | ISBN 9781501347849 (ePDF) |
ISBN 9781501347825 (hardback : alk. paper)
Subjects: LCSH: Kafka, Franz, 1883-1924—Criticism and interpretation. |
Imagery (Psychology) in literature.
Classification: LCC PT2621.A26 (ebook) | LCC PT2621.A26 Z746386 2019
(print) | DDC 833/.912—dc23
LC record available at https://lccn.loc.gov/2019011690

ISBN: HB: 978-1-5013-4782-5
         PB: 978-1-5013-7836-2
         ePDF: 978-1-5013-4784-9
         eBook: 978-1-5013-4783-2

Series: New Directions in German Studies

Typeset by RefineCatch Ltd, Bungay, Suffolk

To find out more about our authors and books, visit www.bloomsbury.com
and sign up for our newsletters.

For Runa.

Contents

List of Figures   xi
Acknowledgments   xii
List of Abbreviations   xiv

Introduction: Kafka and the Political: In the
Kaiserpanorama   1

PART I   **19**

1   We Don't Want to Accept Him: Content, Form, and
    Function of Kafka's Stereoscopes: "Fellowship"   21

2   They Are Not Human Beings: The Content of Kafka's
    Stereoscopes: The Prague Asbestos Works Hermann & Co   39

3   Simultaneously Also Nothing: The Form of Kafka's
    Stereoscopes: "The Judgment"   61

4   Storming the Border: The Function of Kafka's Stereoscopes:
    "Researches of a Dog"   85

PART II   **111**

5   A Construction of Chance and Laws: Kafka in the Yiddish
    Theater: *Der Meschumed*   113

6   A Weakness of Imagination: Kafka in China: "Building the
    Great Wall of China"   133

PART III   **165**

7   A Matter of Justice: Karl as Defense Lawyer: *Amerika*   167

8   I Speak for Them, Not for Myself: Josef K. as Popular
    Speaker: *The Trial*   195

x   Contents

9   As If the Whole of Existence Were Transformed:
    K. as Liberator of Girls: *The Castle*   221

    Conclusion: Worthy of the Law: "On the Question of
    the Laws"   247

    Bibliography   259
    Index   271

Figures

Figure 0.1:   The Kaiserpanorama   2
Figure 0.2:   Stereographic slide from a Kaiserpanorama   5
Figure 0.3:   *Monument to Tito Speri*   6
Figure 7.1:   "Broadway in the business district"   171
Figure 8.1:   Pornographic stereoscopic slides from the early
              twentieth century   203

Acknowledgments

In the fragmentary story "Researches of a Dog," Franz Kafka tells of a dog that spends the best years of its life on an endless and hopeless research project aiming to understand the innermost core of what it refers to as "Hundeschaft," or "dogdom." At times, during the years I have worked on this book, I have felt a close kinship to Kafka's canine researcher. Unlike the dog, however, I have not been working alone. I count myself fortunate that many generous, sharp, and intellectually honest friends and colleagues read and responded to this book as it evolved. First of all, I extend profound thanks to colleagues past and present at the University of Copenhagen: Michael Andersen, Jens Christian Borrebye Bjering, Christian Dahl, Anne Fastrup, Martin Hultén, Peer Illner, Runa Johannessen, Klemens Kappel, Tue Andersen Nexø, Niklas Olsen, Mikkel Bolt Rasmussen, Lilian Munk Rösing, Moritz Schramm, Devika Sharma, and Erik Steinskog. A very special thanks to my friend and colleague Frederik Tygstrup for more than two decades of close collaboration without which this book, and much more besides, would not have been the same. I am grateful to Frederik Stjernfelt, Drude von der Fehr, and Jakob Lothe for their careful and eye-opening responses to an earlier and more academic incarnation of this book. Thanks too to my students at the University of Copenhagen for contributing brilliant insights and thought-provoking questions to my courses on Kafka over the years. Niels Jager Nykrog and Christine Strandmose Toft were among those who offered invaluable feedback on the manuscript. I am obliged to researchers from other universities and other academic fields who have offered invaluable feedback, among them Ingvild Folkvord, Asbjørn Hróbjartsson, and Somogy Varga. Thanks to the poet Claus Handberg for reading the whole manuscript and teaching me why and how to avoid academic jargon, and to my mother, Merete Winkel Holm, for heroically and perpetually reading what I write about Kafka. I am appreciative to all those audiences who responded to my talks and papers on Kafka, among them NTNU, University of Trondheim, Norway, EHESS, Paris, University of

Aarhus, Denmark, University of Memphis, Tennessee, and Södertörn University, Sweden. My thanks also to Neil Bennun and Niels Davidsen-Nielsen for much-needed help with the English language. And, most of all, thanks to Runa for patience, support, and excellent suggestions. Without our life together with Eskild and Leonard, being a researcher dog would be neither possible, nor worthwhile.

Abbreviations

All works by Kafka are cited according to the pagination of Fischer's historical-critical edition of *Schriften Tagebücher Briefe*, edited by Gerhard Neumann, Malcolm Pasley, and Jost Schillemeit (1982–). The reference to the German edition is, after a semicolon, followed by a reference to an English translation where available.

A—*Amerika: The Missing Person.* Trans. Mark Harman. New York: Schocken, 2008.

AS—*Amtliche Schriften.* Ed. Klaus Hermsdorf and Benno Wagner. New York/Frankfurt am Main: Fischer, 2004.

B1—*Briefe 1900–1912.* Ed. Roger Hermes and Waltraud John. New York/Frankfurt am Main: Fischer, 1999.

B2—*Briefe 1913–März 1914.* Ed. Waltraud John. New York/Frankfurt am Main: Fischer, 2001.

B3—*Briefe April 1914–1917.* Ed. Waltraud John. New York/Frankfurt am Main: Fischer, 2005.

B4—*Briefe 1918–1920.* Ed. Waltraud John. New York/Frankfurt am Main: Fischer, 2013.

BF—*Briefe an Felice und andere Korrespondenz aus der Verlobungszeit.* Ed. Erich Heller and Jürgen Born. New York/Frankfurt am Main: Fischer, 1967.

BK—*Beschreibung eines Kampfes: Novellen, Skizzen, Aphorismen aus dem Nachlass.* Ed. Max Brod. Berlin: Schocken, 1936 (*Gesammelte Schriften,* vol. 5).

BM—*Briefe an Milena: Erweiterte und neu geordnete Ausgabe*. Ed. Jürgen Born and Michael Müller, unabridged edition. New York/Frankfurt am Main: Fischer, 1986.

BON—*The Blue Octavo Notebooks*. Trans. and ed. Max Brod, Ernst Kaiser, and Eithne Wilkins. Cambridge: Exact Change, 1991.

Br—*Briefe 1902–1924*, ed. Max Brod. New York/Frankfurt am Main: Fischer, 1958.

C—*The Castle*. Trans. Mark Harman. New York: Schocken, 1998.

CS—*Franz Kafka: The Complete Stories*. Ed. Nahum N. Glatzer. New York: Schocken, 1971.

D—*Diaries, 1910–1923*. Trans. Joseph Kresh and Martin Greenberg (with the assistance of Hannah Arendt). New York: Schocken, 1948.

DF—*Dearest Father*. Trans. Ernest Kaiser and Eithne Wilkins. New York: Schocken, 1954.

DzL—*Drucke zu Lebzeiten*. Ed. Wolf Kittler, Hans-Gerd Koch, and Gerhard Neumann. New York/Frankfurt am Main: Fischer 1994.

DzLA—*Drucke zu Lebzeiten. Apparatband*. Ed. Wolf Kittler, Hans-Gerd Koch, and Gerhard Neumann. New York/Frankfurt am Main, 1996.

GWC—*The Great Wall of China and Other Short Works*. Trans. Malcolm Pasley. London: Penguin Books, 1991.

HA—*A Hunger Artist and Other Stories*. Trans. Joyce Crick. Oxford: Oxford University Press, 2012.

LFFE—*Letters to Friends, Family, and Editors*. Trans. Richard and Clara Winston. New York: Schocken, 1977.

LF—*Letters to Felice*. Trans. James Stern and Elizabeth Duckworth. New York: Schocken, 1973.

LM—*Letters to Milena*. Trans. Philip Boehm. New York: Schocken, 1990.

M—*The Metamorphosis*. Trans. and ed. Stanley Corngold. New York: Norton, 1996.

MoS—*The Metamorphosis and Other Stories*. Trans. Joyce Crick, ed.
Ritchie Robertson. Oxford/New York: Oxford University Press, 2009.

NS1—*Nachgelassene Schriften und Fragmente 1*. Ed. Hans-Gerd Koch,
Michael Müller, and Malcom Pasley. New York/Frankfurt am Main:
Fischer, 1993.

NS1A—*Nachgelassene Schriften und Fragmente 1. Apparatband*. Ed.
Hans-Gerd Koch, Michael Müller, and Malcom Pasley. New York/
Frankfurt am Main: Fischer, 1993.

NS2—*Nachgelassene Schriften und Fragmente 2*. Ed. Jost Schillemeit.
New York/Frankfurt am Main: Fischer, 1992.

NS2A—*Nachgelassene Schriften und Fragmente 2. Apparatband*. Ed. Jost
Schillemeit. New York/Frankfurt am Main: Fischer, 1992.

OW—*The Office Writings*. Trans. Eric Patton with Ruth Hein, ed.
Stanley Corngold, Jack Greenberg, and Benno Wagner. Princeton, NJ:
Princeton University Press, 2009.

P—*Der Proceß. Schriften*. Ed. Malcom Pasley. New York/Frankfurt am
Main: Fischer, 1990.

PA—*Der Proceß. Apparatband*. Ed. Malcom Pasley. New York/Frankfurt
am Main: Fischer, 1990.

PGS—*Der Prozeß*. Ed. Max Brod and Heinz Politzer. Berlin: Schocken,
1935 (*Gesammelte Schriften*, vol. 3).

PFE—*Der Process. Faksimile-Edition*. Ed. Roland Reuß and Peter
Staengle. Frankfurt am Main/Basel: Strofeld/Roter Stern, 1997.

S—*Das Schloß*. Ed. Malcom Pasley. New York/Frankfurt am Main:
Fischer, 1982.

SA—*Das Schloß. Apparatband*. Ed. Malcom Pasley. New York/Frankfurt
am Main: Fischer, 1982.

SS—*Kafka's Selected Stories: New Translations, Backgrounds and Contexts,
Criticism*. Trans. Stanley Corngold. New York: W.W. Norton, 2006.

T—*Tagebücher*. Ed. Hans-Gerd Koch, Michael Müller, and Malcom
Pasley. New York/Frankfurt am Main: Fischer, 1990.

TA—*Tagebücher. Apparatband*. Ed. Hans-Gerd Koch, Michael Müller and Malcom Pasley, New York/Frankfurt am Main: Fischer 1990.

TK—*Tagebücher. Kommentar*. Ed. Malcom Pasley. New York/Frankfurt am Main: Fischer, 1993.

Tr—*The Trial*. Trans. Breon Mitchell. New York: Schocken, 1998.

V—*Der Verschollene*. Ed. Jost Schillemeit. New York/Frankfurt am Main: Fischer, 1983.

VA—*Der Verschollene. Apparatband*. Ed. Jost Schillemeit. New York/Frankfurt am Main: Fischer, 1983.

WPC—*Wedding Preparations in the Country, and Other Posthumous Prose Writings*. Trans. Ernst Kaiser and Eithne Wilkins. London: Secker and Warburg, 1954.

Introduction

Kafka and the Political: In the Kaiserpanorama

"Seen from the perspective of literature, my fate is very simple. The talent for presenting my dreamlike inner life has turned everything else into a matter of secondary importance," Franz Kafka wrote in a famous diary entry of August 6, 1914.[1] According to a tradition within Kafka research that began with his friend and publisher Max Brod, Kafka's talent for presenting that dreamlike inner life corresponds to a complete inability to present the factual outer life. The Kafka scholar Walter Sokel quotes the diary entry in his influential *Franz Kafka: Tragik und Ironie* (1964) as proof that the people and things described in Kafka's literary works are to be understood as "pure expression of the psyche, clothing of the inner, nothing but symbol."[2]

Yet biographical evidence contradicts this traditional picture of Kafka as an apolitical and solipsistic writer absorbed by his own inwardness and by timeless questions of religion, psychology, metaphysics, and high art. An insurance assessor in Prague at the Workmen's Accident Insurance Institute for the Kingdom of Bohemia before the First World War, Kafka gained first-hand knowledge of the struggles between employers and workers in the course of frequent visits to the booming industrial towns of northern Bohemia. During the war, Kafka took a central role in the establishment of a psychiatric hospital for shell-shocked soldiers returned from the front. In his off-duty hours, he attended political meetings, listened to lectures, and

---

1 "Von der Litteratur aus gesehen ist mein Schicksal sehr einfach. Der Sinn für die Darstellung meines traumhaften innern Lebens hat alles andere ins Nebensächliche gerückt" (T 546; D 302, translation modified).
2 Walter Sokel, *Franz Kafka: Tragik und Ironie* (Frankfurt am Main: Fischer, 1983), 110.

read articles and books by anarchists, social democrats, trade unionists, and Czech nationalists. A number of Kafka's closest friends, the perpetually enthusiastic Max Brod among them, were committed to the cause of Zionism, a political movement Kafka followed with profound interest. Inspired by the Balfour Declaration of November 1917 that supported "a national home for the Jewish people" in Palestine, Kafka even drafted a short constitution for a Kibbutz-like society of workers.[3] In short, Kafka had a keen interest in, and a comprehensive professional and intellectual knowledge of, the important political issues of his day.

Brod and Sokel's picture of the apolitical Kafka has been countered by a number of classic studies from, among others, Walter Benjamin, Theodor W. Adorno, Marthe Robert, and Gilles Deleuze and Félix Guattari. This book contributes to the tradition of political readings of Kafka by giving a detailed consideration of his stereoscopic literary style. By a "literary stereoscope," I mean a passage in a written work emulating the effect of the optical stereoscope: a visual apparatus creating the illusion of three-dimensional depth through the juxtaposition of two images of the same object seen from slightly different perspectives. I contend that this binocular setup plays a key role in the relationship between literature and the political in Kafka's authorship.

Figure 0.1 The Kaiserpanorama.

---

3   (NS2 105).

In February 1911, on one of his business trips to northern Bohemia, Kafka paid a visit to a Kaiserpanorama, or Imperial Panorama. Invented in 1880 by the German scientist and entrepreneur August Fuhrmann, the Kaiserpanorama was a stereoscopic spectacle in the form of a cylindrical box surrounded by as many as twenty-five seats or viewing stations, from which viewers watched pairs of backlit glass slides rotating inside at approximately two-minute intervals. Seen through binocular optics, the flat images of the juxtaposed slides combined to give the illusion of depth. On this particular day in 1911, the Kaiserpanorama in Friedland happened to be showing images of the cities of northern Italy where Kafka and Max Brod spent their summer holiday in 1909. While the emergence of silent film at the turn of the century had relegated the Kaiserpanorama to the status of an outdated visual attraction, Kafka writes enthusiastically about the experience in a letter to Max and, in greater detail, in his travel diary:

> Kaiserpanorama. Sole entertainment in Friedland. Don't feel properly comfortable in it because I hadn't been prepared for such a beautiful setup as I found there, had entered with snow-laden boots, and now, sitting in front of the eyepiece, barely touched the carpet with the tips of my toes. I had forgotten about the setup of panoramas, and for a moment I was afraid I would have to go from chair to chair. An old man at a lamp-lit table, who is reading a copy of the Illustrated World, directs everything. After a little while plays an Ariston for me. Later 2 old women also enter, sit down to my right, then another one to my left.[4]

In this passage, the word "setup" ("Einrichtung") is used twice: the Kaiserpanorama is a "beautiful setup" and, due to its obsolescence at that time, Kafka "had forgotten about the setup of panoramas." Yet the

---

4 "Kaiserpanorama. Einzige Vergnügung in Friedland. Habe keine rechte Bequemlichkeit darin, weil ich mich einer solchen schönen Einrichtung wie ich sie dort antraf, nicht versehen hatte, mit schneebehängten Stiefeln eingetreten war und nun vor den Gläsern sitzend nur mit den Fußspitzen den Teppich berührte. Ich hatte die Einrichtung der Panoramas vergessen und fürchtete einen Augenblick lang von einem Sessel zum andern gehn zu müssen. Ein alter Mann bei einem beleuchteten Tischchen, der einen Band Illustrierte Welt liest, führt das Ganze. Läßt nach einer Weile für mich ein Ariston spielen. Später kommen noch 2 alte Damen, setzen sich rechts von mir, dann noch eine links" (T 936–7; D 429–31). I have modified the English translation of the diaries substantially, gratefully taking a cue from the translation offered by Hanns Zischler, *Kafka Goes to the Movies* (Chicago and London: University of Chicago Press, 2003).

focus of the diary entry is not on the apparatus's technical configuration; it is on the aesthetic experience it provides. Comparing panorama to cinema, its successor, Kafka accentuates the former's realism:

> The images more alive than in the cinematograph, because they allow the eye the stillness of reality. The cinematograph lends the observed objects the agitation of their movement, the stillness of the gaze seems more important. Smooth floor of the cathedrals in front of our tongue [. . .] The distance between merely listening to a narrative and looking at a panorama is greater than the distance between the latter and looking at reality.[5]

Apparently, the sight of a panoramic image is not so different from the sight of unmediated reality. The stereoscopic illusion of three-dimensional depth makes the objects in the foreground of the stereographic images, for instance the smooth floor of the cathedrals, reach out toward the viewer as if they were palpable—almost as if we could taste them.

It is not only the hyper-realism of the Kaiserpanorama's three-dimensional image that interests Kafka, however, but also the artificial and uncanny aesthetic experience it offers. He began the entry in his travel diary by noting that he did not "feel properly comfortable" when entering the Kaiserpanorama, and it seems as if this discomfort characterizes both his approach to the panorama—entering with snow-laden boots and sitting so that he barely touches the carpet with the tips of his toes—and his perception of the stereographic slides that rotate inside it. Before comparing panorama to cinema, Kafka describes the way in which people and things show up on the stereographic images of the Italian cities:

> Brescia, Cremona, Verona. People inside like wax figures, their soles fixed to the ground on the pavement. Funerary monuments: a lady with a train trailing over a short flight of steps opens a door slightly ajar and looks back as she does so. A family, in the foreground a young man reads, one hand on his temple, a boy on the right draws a stringless bow. Monument to the hero Tito Speri:

---

5   "Die Bilder lebendiger als im Kinematographen, weil sie dem Blick die Ruhe der Wirklichkeit lassen. Der Kinematograph gibt dem Angeschauten die Unruhe ihrer Bewegung, die Ruhe des Blickes scheint wichtiger. Glatter Boden der Kathedralen vor unserer Zunge. [. . .] Die Entfernung zwischen bloßem Erzählenhören und Panorama sehn ist größer als die Entfernung zwischen letzterem und dem Sehn der Wirklichkeit" (T 937; D 430).

ragged and enthusiastic, his clothes waft around his body. Blouse, broad-brimmed hat.[6]

This passage does not celebrate the mimetic hyper-realism arising when the two flat images synthesize into the enchanting wholeness of a three-dimensional image, but rather describes the strange, wax doll-like anti-realism that emerges when the viewer cannot integrate the two juxtaposed images into a coherent, unified picture.

At the turn of the century, it was often observed that objects pictured in a stereoscope, especially those in the middle ground and in the far distance, appear strangely insubstantial and flat, as if they were cardboard cutouts separated by airless space. In 1893, for instance, the German critic and sculptor Adolf Hildebrand criticized the Kaiserpanorama by noting that it "supports the coarseness of sense by a perverse sensation and a falsified feeling of reality in precisely the same way that wax figures do!"[7] In a 1913 essay, Max Brod, the recipient

Figure 0.2 Stereographic slide from a Kaiserpanorama.

---

6   "Brescia, Kremona, Verona. Menschen drin wie Wachspuppen an den Sohlen im Boden im Pflaster befestigt. Grabdenkmäler: eine Dame mit über eine niedrige Treppe schleifender Schleppe öffnet ein wenig eine Tür und schaut noch zurück dabei. Eine Familie, vorn liest ein Junge eine Hand an der Schläfe, ein Knabe rechts spannt einen unbesaiteten Bogen. Denkmal des Helden Tito Speri: verwahrlost und begeistert wehen ihm die Kleider um den Leib. Bluse, breiter Hut" (T 937; D 430).

7   Adolf Hildebrand, "The Problem of Form in the Fine Arts," in *Empathy, Form, and Space: Problems in German Aesthetics, 1873–1893*, ed. Robert Vischer (Chicago: University of Chicago Press, 1994), 242. For further discussion, see Jonathan Crary, *Techniques of the Observer: on Vision and Modernity in the Nineteenth Century* (Cambridge, MA: The MIT Press, 1990), 295. Crary aptly sums up the comments upon the anti-realism of the stereoscope: "If perspective implied a homogenous and potentially metric space, the stereoscope discloses a fundamental disunified and aggregate field of disjunct elements." *Techniques of the Observer*, 125.

of Kafka's postcard from Friedland, described the slides of the Kaiserpanorama as "flat, dead, closed," not least when representing the interiors of churches and palaces: "In this glassy depth of the slides I find the beautiful, merry stylization of the world of the panorama, its distance from the earth."[8]

Kafka, too, is fascinated by the Kaiserpanorama's distance from the earth, as Brod wrote. Interestingly, the uncanny aesthetic experience of the Italian cities seems to blur the border between human beings and statues. At first reading, it is easy to overlook that the people resembling wax figures are living human beings and, conversely, that the lady

Figure 0.3 *Monument to Tito Speri* by Domenico Ghidoni (Brescia). Photo: Stefano Bolognini.

---

8   Max Brod, "Panorama," in *Über die Schönheit hässlicher Bilder* (Leipzig: K. Wolff, 1913), 63. For further discussion, see Carolin Duttlinger, "Die Ruhe des Blickes: Brod, Kafka, Benjamin and the Kaiserpanorama," in *Science, Technology and the German Cultural Imagination*, ed. Christian Emden and David R. Midgley (Oxford and New York: Peter Lang, 2005).

dragging a train over a short flight of steps, the young man reading a book, and the boy drawing a stringless bow are lifeless statues. In the prose of Kafka's diary entry, this dissolution of the order of things is brought about through the use of discreet figurative language: whereas the human beings are compared to dead wax figures ("*like* wax figures"), the non-human statues are described with active verbs that are, in the vocabulary of classical rhetoric, animations (the statues *open* a door, *read* a book, and *draw* a stringless bow).

Likewise, on the stereographic photograph of Tito Speri, a patriot from the Italian *Risorgimento*, the clothes, not the man, are "ragged, enthusiastic." The German word "begeistert," translated as "enthusiastic," comes from "Geist" ("spirit"), and conveys a sense approximate to "animated." Hence, it is as if the visual experience of the stereoscope serves to animate the dead statue by making the spirit jump from the man to the marble clothes draped around his body.

In both cases, then, the aesthetic experience of the Kaiserpanorama seems to dissolve the order of the human community by destabilizing the distinction between people and things, between human beings made of flesh and blood and monuments made of stone. Although Kafka does not stress the political dimension of the stereoscopic vision in this early diary entry, this "disfiguration" of the representation of communal life, in the literary theorist Paul de Man's sense of the term,[9] will soon become crucial to Kafka's literary stereoscopes.

After the Friedland trip, Kafka worked meticulously to recreate the wax doll-like aesthetic experience of the Kaiserpanorama in his literary sketches. In his notebooks and diaries, he started translating the stereoscope's "beautiful" setup into his literary prose by juxtaposing two dissimilar images of the same object. While Kafka had made experiments with dual vision even before February 1911,[10] it was only after his visit to Friedland that he started to develop the literary stereoscope as a means to present his dreamlike inner life, beginning with two diary entries from early October 1911.[11]

In general, Kafka was fascinated by the apparatuses of communication and perception of his day. In his notebooks, diaries, and letters, he comments not only on the stereoscope, but also on the typewriter, the phonograph, the telephone, the camera, the cinema, the tabulating

---

9   Paul de Man, *The Rhetoric of Romanticism* (New York: Columbia University Press, 1984), 110. I will return to the concept of disfiguration in Chapter 4.

10   See, for instance, Kafka's letter to Ernst Eisner from 1909 or 1910 (B1 116f; LFFE 61–2).

11   (T 56–7, 59–60; D 60–1, 63–4). I present an analysis of this letter and two related diary entries in *Stormløb mod grænsen: Det politiske hos Kafka* (Copenhagen: Gyldendal, 2015), Chapter 6.

machine, and even the so-called psychograph.[12] Compared to the other modern and not-so-modern technical devices that play a role in Kafka's oeuvre, however, the stereoscope stands out on account of the binocular style combining two images of the same object.[13]

To be sure, Kafka was not alone in his fascination with the device; this was something he shared with Charles Baudelaire, James Joyce, Robert Musil, Ernst Jünger, Walter Benjamin, and, as much research attests, with Marcel Proust.[14] Yet while the greater part of research on

---

12 The typewriter and the phonograph: Wolf Kittler, "Schreibmaschinen, Sprechmaschinen: Effekte technischer Medien im Werk Franz Kafkas," in *Franz Kafka: Schriftverkehr*, ed. Wolf Kittler and Gerhard Neumann (Freiburg im Breisgau: Rombach, 1990). The telephone: Gerhard Neumann, "Nachrichten vom 'Pontus': Das Problem der Kunst im Werk Franz Kafkas," in *Franz Kafka: Schriftverkehr*, ed. Wolf Kittler and Gerhard Neumann (Freiburg im Breisgau: Rombach, 1990); Avital Ronell, *The Telephone Book: Technology-Schizophrenia-Electric Speech* (Lincoln: University of Nebraska Press, 1989). The camera: Carolin Duttlinger, *Kafka and Photography* (Oxford: Oxford University Press, 2007). The movie theater: Peter Beicken, "Kafka's Visual Method: The Gaze, the Cinematic, and the Intermedial," in *Kafka for the Twenty-First Century*, ed. Stanley Corngold (Rochester, NY: Camden House, 2011); Zischler, *Kafka Goes to the Movies*. Hollerith's tabulating machine: Stanley Corngold and Benno Wagner, *Franz Kafka: The Ghosts in the Machine* (Evanston, IL Northwestern University Press, 2011), 31–2. The 'psychograph': Andreas B. Kilcher, "Geisterschrift: Kafkas Spiritismus," in *Schrift und Zeit in Franz Kafkas Oktavheften*, ed. Caspar Battegay, Felix Christen, and Wolfram Groddeck (Göttingen: Wallstein, 2010).
13 For further discussion of Kafka and the stereoscope, see Duttlinger, *Kafka and Photography*, 51–61; Andreas Huyssen, *Miniature Metropolis: Literature in an Age of Photography and Film* (Cambridge, MA: Harvard University Press, 2015); David Trotter, "Stereoscopy: Modernism and the 'Haptic'," *Critical Quarterly* 46, no. 4 (2004); Zischler, *Kafka Goes to the Movies*, 25–32; J.J. Long, "Photography," in *Franz Kafka in Context*, ed. Carolin Duttlinger (Cambridge: Cambridge University Press, 2018). These insightful accounts of Kafka's visit to the Kaiserpanorama in Friedland form part of explorations of Kafka's relation to other media, either photography (Duttlinger, Long), cinema (Zischler), or both (Huyssen). Consequently, they tend to downplay the unique setup of the binocular apparatus.
14 Baudelaire: Marit Grøtta, *Baudelaire's Media Aesthetics: The Gaze of the Flâneur and 19th Century Media* (New York: Bloomsbury Academic, 2015); Françoise Meltzer, *Seeing Double: Baudelaire's Modernity* (Chicago: University of Chicago Press, 2011). Joyce: Trotter, "Stereoscopy,"; Musil: Huyssen, *Miniature Metropolis*. Jünger: *Miniature Metropolis*; Carsten Strathausen, "The Return of the Gaze: Stereoscopic Vision in Jünger and Benjamin," *New German Critique* 80 (2000). Benjamin: Susan Buck-Morss, *The Dialectics of Seeing: Walter Benjamin and the Arcades Project* (Cambridge, MA, and London: The MIT Press, 1989); Esther Leslie, *Walter Benjamin: Overpowering Conformism* (London and Sterling, VA: Pluto Press, 2000); Proust: Roger Shattuck, *Proust's Binoculars: A Study of Memory, Time, and Recognition in* A la recherche du temps perdu (London: Chatto & Windus, 1964); Mieke Bal, *The Mottled Screen: Reading Proust Visually* (Stanford, CA: Stanford University Press, 1997); Sara Danius, *Prousts motor* (Stockholm:

the role of the stereoscope in modern literature focuses on questions of mediality and visuality, in Kafka's work, I contend, the stereoscope poses not only medial or visual but also political questions: Kafka's literary stereoscopes juxtapose two political, rather than perceptual, experiences. His two-fold vision is, first of all, a dual vision of a legal and political community.

Telling him at the same time . . .

The opening scene of the short story "The Judgment," written in September 1912, a year and a half after the visit to the Kaiserpanorama in Friedland, offers one of the earliest and clearest examples of Kafka's stereoscopic style. Georg Bendemann, a young and successful businessman, has just finished a letter to a boyhood friend who emigrated to Russia several years earlier. With the letter in his hand, Georg remains sitting at his desk for a long time, his face turned to the window, reflecting on his relationship to his friend abroad:

> What could one write to such a man, who had obviously become stuck and whom one could pity but not help? Should one perhaps advise him to come home again, to re-establish himself here, take up all the old friendly relations—there was nothing to prevent this—and for the rest put his trust in the help of his friends? But that meant nothing less than telling him at the same time—and the more one spared his feelings, the more hurtful it was—that so far his efforts had failed, that he should give them up once and for all, that he would have to come back and be gaped at by everybody as a man who had come back for good, that only his friends knew the score, and he was an overgrown baby who would simply have to do as he was told by his successful friends who had stayed at home.[15]

Bonnier, 2000); Roxanne Hanney, *The Invisible Middle Term in Proust's* A la recherche du temps perdu (Lewiston, ME, and Lampeter: Mellen, 1990).

15 "Was wollte man einem solchen Manne schreiben, der sich offenbar verrannt hatte, den man bedauern, dem man aber nicht helfen konnte. Sollte man ihm vielleicht raten, wieder nach Hause zu kommen, seine Existenz hierher zu verlegen, alle die alten freundschaftlichen Beziehungen wieder aufzunehmen— wofür ja kein Hindernis bestand—und im übrigen auf die Hilfe der Freunde zu vertrauen? Das bedeutete aber nichts anderes, als daß man ihm gleichzeitig, je schonender, desto kränkender, sagte, daß seine bisherigen Versuche mißlungen seien, daß er endlich von ihnen ablassen solle, daß er zurückkehren und sich als ein für immer Zurückgekehrter vor allen mit großen Augen anstaunen lassen müsse, daß nur seine Freunde etwas verstünden und daß er ein altes Kind sei und den erfolgreichen, zu Hause gebliebenen Freunden einfach zu folgen habe" (DzL 44–5; SS 3–4, translation modified).

What at first sight seems to be a thoughtful consideration of the advice one might give a friend is, in fact, a clash between two different images of the group of friends to which Georg and his bachelor friend in Russia both belong. To advise him to come home and re-establish himself in Prague, Georg speculates, would be to offer him two incompatible representations of the same community.

The first depicts the community as a circle of friends who help one another. According to this image of social life, "there was nothing to prevent" the friend in Russia from taking up "the old friendly relations." Thus, the advice would be that, since these amicable relations are still in force, he can safely put his trust in his friends.

But this very same advice, in the second of these irreconcilable representations, paints the image of a community not at all bound by friendly relations. In this version, the group of non-friends will not help their Russia-dwelling acquaintance but, rather, pity him; presumably they will even compete with him and regard him as a loser. If he were to return home, he would no longer be an equal member of the circle of friends but an "overgrown baby who would simply have to do as he was told." At the end of the passage, Georg concludes that there is, in fact, something that prevents the Russian friend from taking up with his old friends: "Under such circumstances, was it possible to believe that he could actually make any headway here?"

The word "gleichzeitig" ("at the same time") indicates the junction of the two different images of the community. To advise the friend to come home would indicate both that the group of people in Prague is a circle of friends and, at the same time, that they are a crowd of rivals. As we shall see in more detail in Chapter 3, the dual vision of communal life continues to structure Georg's reflections on the nature of his group of friends, beyond the opening passage into the rest of the short story. My contention is that this specific kind of dual vision is a recurrent and systematic feature in Kafka's authorship. What I call a stereoscopic style is a formal arrangement that pairs two dissimilar images of the same community—one orderly, the other disorderly.

In the orderly image, life in common is configured as a well-organized and well-defined collectivity composed of individual human beings (or individual living beings) bound together by shared rules, interests, and habits, thereby forming a homogeneous unity. In the disorderly image, by contrast, the community takes the shape of a disconnected and chaotic crowd of people who relate to each other as strangers. The word "community" derives etymologically from Latin *cum-munus*, where *cum* means "shared" and *munus* (or *munia*) hovers between a number of different meanings: "task," "obligation," "law," "gift," and "tribute."[16] Kafka's literary stereoscopes explores the nature of the common *munia*. By juxtaposing two conflicting images of a given community, they investigate the network of ties that bind the members together.

The Configuration of Communal Life

"Thoughts about Freud, of course,"[17] Kafka wrote in his diary the morning after having written "The Judgment" in one sitting from ten o'clock at night to six o'clock in the morning. Unsurprisingly, the story about Georg and his father has been interpreted as the first successful product of Kafka's talent for presenting his dreamlike inner life. But, as the opening scene makes clear, even in "The Judgment," Kafka also makes use of his talent for presenting the life of a specific group of people. As we shall see in the following chapters, his literary works teem with such representations of communities—social bodies composed of, say, the members of a family, the workers in a factory, the world's dogs, the people of China during the Ming dynasty, or the residents of an unnamed village below a castle. As these examples demonstrate, Kafka's literary works are not to be understood simply as pure expressions of the psyche, as Sokel suggested, but as careful explorations of the social.

Yet it might be more exact to say that Kafka's works blur the very distinction between subject and object altogether. The opening of "The Judgment"—Georg sitting alone at his desk thinking about his friend—is to be seen neither as a profound psychological analysis of the protagonist's dreamlike inner life nor as a detailed sociological analysis of the factual outer life of his group of friends. Rather, it is an investigation of the very intersection of inner and outer, a mapping of the intermediate zone where the social is mediated through and mixed up with the psyche. Investigating this zone, Kafka makes use of his talent for presenting what might be called "the dreamlike outer life": our common dreams about the basic shape of our communal life.

What I suggest calling the configuration of a community is an image of the basic form or shape of a given group of people (or, in Kafka's works, of a given group of dogs, mice, or jackals). A configuration is best defined as an arrangement of parts or elements in a particular form, figure, or combination. Often when we use the word—when we

---

16 While indebted to Roberto Esposito's etymological reflections on the word "community," I insist on the undecidable nature of the term *munia*. For further discussion, see Roberto Esposito, *Immunitas: The Protection and Negation of Life* (Cambridge and Malden, MA: Polity, 2011), 5; *Terms of the Political: Community, Immunity, Biopolitics* (New York: Fordham University Press, 2013), 14.

17 "Gedanken an Freud natürlich" (T 461; D 213).

refer to a configuration of the stars, for instance—the particular constellation of elements is the pattern that appears when those elements are perceived from a specific viewpoint. Thus, "configuration" is not just a name for the basic shape of things; it is also a term for the way this basic shape appears to a subject.

In Kafka's stories about groups of friends, family members, workers, dogs, Chinese people, and villagers, detailed information about the specific rules and norms of the communities in question is surprisingly sparse. Instead, Kafka explores the deeper level of order that determines the basic shape of the communal life to which those rules and norms are applied. In other words, Kafka focuses on the configuration rather than the constitution, if we understand a constitution as a body of rules and norms governing a community. At stake is how the individuals stand in relation to each other, how they fit together, how they are connected to other groups and to the surrounding world.

Expressed in the vocabulary of the political philosopher Jacques Rancière, Kafka's literary stereoscopes are dissensual devices. A dissensus "is not a conflict of interests, opinions, or values; it is a division put in the 'common sense': a dispute about what is given, about the frame within which we see something as given."[18] Rancière refers to this "common sense" as a "distribution of the sensible," that is, a "common *aisthesis*" or "configuration of the sensible world" that frames the specific way of being together in a given society.[19] In Rancièrian terms, Kafka's stereoscopic style does not juxtapose two opposed political ideas about the world but, more fundamentally, two incompatible sensory worlds in their own right.

Three Theses

In a heroic effort to offer an overview of the political readings of Kafka, the literary scholar Bill Dodd remarks that to pose the question about the relation between literature and the political in the case of a writer like Kafka "effectively means asking what we mean by 'the political'."[20] Indeed, different meanings of the concept of the political have opened diverse political dimensions of Kafka's oeuvre. In recent Kafka research, some scholars locate the political in his critical sensibility, a skeptical attitude toward patriarchal and bureaucratic hierarchies of power.[21]

---

18 Jacques Rancière, *Dissensus: On Politics and Aesthetics*, trans. Steve Corcoran (London: Continuum, 2009), 69.

19 *Dissensus*, 38, 133.

20 William John Dodd, "The Case of a Political Reading," in *The Cambridge Companion to Kafka*, ed. Julian Preece (Cambridge and New York: Cambridge University Press, 2002), 131.

21 Michael Löwy, *Franz Kafka: Rêveur insoumis* (Paris: Stock, 2004), 48.

Others find the political in his reaction to specific institutions and events such as workers' insurance, patriarchal society, or the war.[22] Others again look for the political Kafka in his rewriting and rearranging of the political discourses of his day.[23] I suggest using the term "the political" rather than "politics." In political philosophy after Hannah Arendt, especially in France, "politics" ("la politique") often denotes a social sub-system that sets the framework for the law-making process and for the debates that occur within the framework of this system; in Kafka's Austria-Hungary and later Czechoslovakia, for instance, "politics" took place in the parliament, in the political parties, in the workers' movements, in newspapers, and in the large number of Prague's reading and lecture groups. The concept of "the political" ("le politique"), meanwhile, is used as a name for an ephemeral political moment, an originary *fiat* in which a people recreate the foundation of their communal life. According to Arendt, this "acting in concert" or "acting together" exerts the world-building capacity of man by breaking with a petrified order of things and recreating the foundation of communal life.[24] What I am looking for is how Kafka uses the stereoscopic style to prompt a kind of political thinking endowed with this world-building force. In order to provide an account of Kafka and the political, in this Arendtian sense of the term, I put forward three theses concerning, respectively, the content, form, and function of his literary stereoscopes.

According to the first thesis, the content of Kafka's stereoscopes, the subject matter of the image shown us when we address ourselves to the apparatus, is the configuration of a community. In the opening scene of "The Judgment," Georg reflects not on the political, legal, or moral

---

22 For recent contributions, see, for instance, Howard Caygill, *Kafka: In Light of the Accident* (London and New York: Bloomsbury, 2017); Elizabeth Boa, *Kafka: Gender, Class and Race in the Letters and Fictions* (Oxford: Clarendon Press, 1996); Manfred Engel and Ritchie Robertson, *Kafka, Prag und der Erste Weltkrieg = Kafka, Prague and the First World War* (Würzburg: Königshausen & Neumann, 2012).

23 In Chapter 6, I will discuss the work of Benno Wagner, a prominent example of this approach to Kafka and the political.

24 Hannah Arendt, *On Revolution* (New York: Penguin Books, 2006), 175. The distinction between *politics* and *la politique* was suggested by the French philosopher Paul Ricoeur shortly after the invasion of Hungary by the Warsaw Pact countries; see "Le paradoxe politique," in *Histoire et vérité* (Paris: Éditions du Seuil, 1966), 249. The distinction plays a role, in different ways, in the works of Jean-Luc Nancy, Claude Lefort, Alain Badiou, Jacques Rancière, Ernesto Laclau, Chantal Mouffe, and Giorgio Agamben. For a fine overview of this recent tradition, see Oliver Marchart, *Post-Foundational Political Thought: Political Difference in Nancy, Lefort, Badiou and Laclau* (Edinburgh: Edinburgh University Press, 2007).

order but, rather, on what we might term the order of things, used in a deliberately extended sense. My exploration of this deeper-lying level of order in Kafka's work will draw, as a starting point, on the concept of the social imaginary. For the political philosopher Charles Taylor, a social imaginary is a way in which people "imagine their social existence, how they fit together with others, how things go on between them and their fellows."[25] I use the concept of imagination in the strong sense, comparable to Spinoza's concept of "imaginatio" and Kant's notion of "Einbildungskraft," both of which denote the ability of the human mind to create images of things that are not present in a given situation—in "The Judgment," for instance, the ability to imagine an adult person as an "overgrown baby." The social imaginary, then, is a repertoire of figures, metaphors, symbols, narratives, and other forms of imagination with which people represent the order of things. These figures, sensible in the Kantian meaning of "sinnlich"—that is, sensuous and non-conceptual—serve as conditions of possibility for the construction of images of communal life. In this way, a social imaginary is doubly social, consisting of our shared ways of imagining our shared life.

According to the second thesis, the form of Kafka's stereoscopes, the basic setup of the literary device, is defined by the juxtaposition of two dissimilar images of the same community. Sitting with his letter in hand, Georg shuttles back and forth between two representations of the same group of people seen as, alternately, a circle of friends and a crowd of non-friends. Seeing the friends from Georg's wavering perspective, the reader of the passage is also challenged to move back and forth between the orderly and the disorderly image of the same body of individuals in a process I would call "aesthetic reflection." According to Kant, to reflect is to compare two representations in order to find the features they have in common.[26] Thus, the aesthetic experience of Kafka's stereoscopic texts is reflective in so far as the disparity between the two images triggers a process of comparison.

According to the third thesis, finally, the function of Kafka's stereoscopes is to bring about a reconfiguration of a community. In Chapter 3, we shall see how the stereoscopic style of "The Judgment" prompts a kind of political thinking which restructures and reshapes the image of the communal life. I contend that this political thinking has the structure of a political moment as described by Arendt. To be sure,

25 Charles Taylor, *Modern Social Imaginaries* (Durham, NC: Duke University Press, 2004), 23.
26 Immanuel Kant, *Lectures on Logic*, trans. J. Michael Young (Cambridge and New York: Cambridge University Press, 1992), 592.

Kafka's stereoscopic style triggers political thinking in the reader, not political acting in concert, but it is important to note that this kind of thinking exerts what Arendt calls the world-building capacity of man by reconfiguring our shared ways of imagining social life.

Above I have suggested that the three theses regarding the content, form, and function of Kafka's literary stereoscopes should be approached as questions of social imaginaries, aesthetic reflection, and political moments respectively.

For the literary scholar Vivian Liska, similarly, the political is a question of the configuration of the community. In *When Kafka Says We: Uncommon Communities in German-Jewish Literature* (2009), Liska explores Kafka's ambivalence toward both the Jewish community, in particular, and toward communities in general. In Kafka's literary works, she writes, images of social unity and wholeness "constitute precisely the ground of ambiguity where the ideal of a homogeneous community is simultaneously an object of longing and an instance of terror."[27] According to Liska, then, Kafka's dual vision of community is to be understood as a superimposition of longing and terror, of attraction and repulsion. While this is no doubt true, I will approach Kafka's two-fold vision of community not as the symptom of an ambivalent attitude but rather as the setup of a technical apparatus. Georg's oscillation between orderly and disorderly images of the same group of friends is not only a token of the protagonist's, or of the author's, ambivalence toward communal life; it is also a task for the reader of the short story. The derivation of the word "apparatus," from the idea of making ready (*parare*) for something (*ad*), can help us see Kafka's stereoscopes as devices that make the reader ready for political thinking.

Literature's Creative and Beneficent Force

Kafka's most explicit meditations on the relation between literature and the political are found in a handful of diary entries on "the literature of small nations" written in December 1911. In these pages, made famous by Deleuze and Guattari,[28] Kafka compares German literature with contemporary Czech writing and that emerging from the Jewish community in Warsaw, which his Eastern Jewish friend Yitzhak Löwy had told him about. German literature, Kafka asserts, is so rich in great talents that no one within the literary field has to connect with the world outside of literature. But in Czech and Jewish literature, the

27   Vivian Liska, *When Kafka Says We: Uncommon Communities in German-Jewish Literature* (Bloomington, IN: Indiana University Press, 2009), 20.
28   Gilles Deleuze and Félix Guattari, *Kafka: Toward a Minor Literature*, trans. Dana Polan (Minneapolis, MN: University of Minnesota Press, 1986), 16–27.

narrowness of the literary field compels one to reach the "border with politics, indeed, one even strives to see this border before it is there, and often sees this shrinking border everywhere."[29]

According to Kafka, literature's function, its "creative and beneficent force,"[30] is to be found at its border with politics. Indeed, he draws up a long list of ways in which minor literatures can exert this creative and beneficent force:

> The narrowing down of the attention of a nation upon itself and the accepting of what is foreign only in reflection, the birth of a respect for those active in literature, the transitory awakening in the younger generation of higher aspirations, which nevertheless leaves its permanent mark, the acknowledgment of literary events as objects of political solicitude, the ennobling and the possibility of negotiation of the antithesis of fathers and sons.[31]

The list continues. In the last example quoted here, Kafka describes literature as a "Besprechungsmöglichkeit" (an opportunity to negotiate or discuss something). Remarkably, Kafka does not write that literature is *about* the debates concerning "the antithesis of fathers and sons" that actually took place in newspapers, cafés, and reading and lecture groups in Prague. Instead, he argues that literature is *in itself* a place where negotiation is possible. He asks us, in other words, to imagine the literary institution as a forum in which to debate public matters.

In this book, I approach Kafka's stereoscopes as "Besprechungs-möglichkeiten," as apparatuses constructed in order to effect political thinking in the reader. My concern, first and foremost, is the political import of Kafka's stereoscopic style. The book took root in a conviction that Kafka's literary apparatuses have not become obsolete in the way the Kaiserpanorama in Friedland became old-fashioned after the emergence of the silent movie, but that they still possess their creative

---

29 "am ehesten erreicht man die Grenze gegenüber der Politik, ja man strebt sogar danach, diese Grenze früher zu sehen als sie da ist und oft diese sich zusammenziehende Grenze überall zu finden" (T 321; D 150, translation modified).

30 "schöpferische und beglückende Kraft" (T 314, D 149, translation modified).

31 "die Einschränkung der Aufmerksamkeit der Nation auf ihren eigenen Kreis und Aufnahme des Fremden nur in der Spiegelung, das Entstehen der Achtung vor litterarisch tätigen Personen, die vorübergehende aber nachwirkende Erweckung höheren Strebens unter den Heranwachsenden, die Übernahme litterarischer Vorkommnisse in die politischen Sorgen, die Veredlung und Besprechungsmöglichkeit des Gegensatzes zwischen Vätern und Söhnen" (T 313; D 148, translation modified).

and beneficent force. My aim is to put Kafka's binocular apparatuses to use rather than to describe the way they were used 100 years ago when only a small number of his finished and published works attracted the attention of literary connoisseurs. When literature reaches its border with politics, as Czech and Jewish literature of the time repeatedly did, it is no longer an issue that can be entrusted to the few "experts in literary history" described by Kafka in his diary entries on the literatures of small nations, but a concern "of the people."[32] In the same way, I contend, Kafka's authorship is not just a concern for the closed circle of Kafka researchers; it is a concern for the people—for the reader as a political citizen.

The first part of the book explores the three theses concerning the content, form, and function of Kafka's literary stereoscopes. Chapter 1, "We Don't Want to Accept Him," fleshes out the three core theses in an analysis of "Fellowship," a short, parable-like text from the autumn of 1920. Chapter 2, "They Are Not Human Beings," focuses on the thesis concerning the content of Kafka's stereoscopes by offering a close reading of a little-known diary entry from 1912 in which Kafka describes a scene from the Kafka family's asbestos factory, the Prague Asbestos Works Hermann & Co. Chapter 3, "Simultaneously Also Nothing," examines the thesis regarding the form of Kafka's stereoscopes. The bulk of the chapter addresses the juxtaposition of orderly and disorderly image through a more detailed examination of "The Judgment" from 1912. Finally, Chapter 4, "Storming the Border," discusses the thesis concerning the function of Kafka's stereoscopes, using as the point of departure a detailed reading of "Researches of a Dog," a long and unfinished story written in 1922.

In the second part of the book, I take a look at two important events in Kafka's life that gave shape to his stereoscopic style. Chapter 5, "A Construction of Chance and Laws," is concerned with Kafka's diary entries on the formative experience of the visit to Prague of the Yiddish theater troupe lead by his friend Yitzhak Löwy in the autumn of 1911. And Chapter 6, "A Weakness of Imagination," tells the story of Kafka's work for the health care of disabled veterans returning from the First World War, and of the way in which he reflected on these professional tasks in the fictional story "Building the Great Wall of China."

The third and final part of the book explores Kafka's three novels as stereoscopic apparatuses. Chapter 7, "A Matter of Justice," offers a detailed analysis of "The Stoker," the opening chapter of *Amerika* (or *The Missing Person*), Kafka's first unfinished novel. Chapter 8, "I Speak

---

32 "Litteraturgeschichtskundige" and "Angelegenheit des Volkes" (T 315; D 149, translation modified).

for Them," focuses mainly on "Initial Inquiry," the third chapter of *The Trial*, Kafka's second unfinished novel. Chapter 9, "As If the Whole of Existence Were Transformed," considers *The Castle*, Kafka's third and last unfinished novel. The conclusion "Worthy of the Law," finally, draws to a close the investigation of Kafka's stereoscopes by analyzing the short parable "On the Question of the Laws," one of the most condensed articulations of political subject matter in his work.

Part I

One We Don't Want to Accept Him

Content, Form, and Function of Kafka's Stereoscopes: "Fellowship"

Over three chapters of Fyodor Dostoyevsky's novel *Notes from Underground* (1864), we read the story of a farewell dinner given for an officer, Zverkov, who is about to be transferred from St. Petersburg to a distant Russian province. The night before his departure, three former high-school friends meet to arrange the dinner to which the underground man, the protagonist of the novel, is explicitly not invited. "But this is our own narrow circle of friends," one of the high-school friends says to the underground man. "It's not an official gathering. Perhaps we don't want you at all . . ."[1] The protagonist's toe-curling efforts to gatecrash the dinner party lead, among other things, to problems of number. It is unclear how many dinner guests there will be the following evening and, hence, how many roubles the three friends (plus Zverkov) will have to spend: "With three of us that makes twenty-one altogether," and "What will the four of us do with half a dozen bottles?"[2]

Kafka, an enthusiastic reader of Dostoyevsky, offers an abstracted version of the conflict between the underground man and the narrow circle of Zverkov's friends in a short text from the autumn of 1920, published posthumously by Max Brod in 1936 under the title "Fellowship" ("Gemeinschaft"). I quote Kafka's text in its entirety:

> We are five friends, one day we came out of a house one after the other, first one came and placed himself beside the gate, then the second came or rather glided through the gate as gently as a little ball of quicksilver glides, and placed himself near the first one, then came

---

1   Fyodor Dostoyevsky, *Notes from Underground: A New Translation, Backgrounds and Sources, Responses, Criticism*, trans. Michael R. Katz (New York: Norton, 1989), 44, translation modified.

2   *Notes from Underground*, 43.

the third, then the fourth, then the fifth. Finally we all stood in a row. People began to notice us, they pointed at us and said: Those five just came out of that house. Since then we have been living together; it would be a peaceful life if it weren't for a sixth one constantly trying to meddle. He doesn't do us any harm, but it annoys us, and that is harm enough; why does he intrude where he is not wanted? We don't know him and don't want to accept him. There was a time, of course, when the five of us did not know one another, either; and one could say that we still don't know one another, but what is possible and can be tolerated by the five of us is not possible and cannot be tolerated with this sixth one. In any case, we are five and don't want to be six. And what is the meaning of this continual being together anyhow? It is also meaningless for the five of us, but here we are together and will remain together; a new union, however, we do not want, exactly because of our experiences. But how is one to make all this clear to the sixth one? Long explanations would almost amount to accepting him in our circle, so we prefer not to explain and do not accept him. No matter how he pouts his lips we push him away with our elbows, but however much we push him away, back he comes. People count us and say: Earlier there were 5, now it is 6. No, we say and stamp our foot in the ground, "we are only 5."[3]

---

3   "Wir sind fünf Freunde, wir sind einmal hintereinander aus einem Haus gekommen, zuerst kam der eine und stellte sich neben das Tor, dann kam oder vielmehr glitt so leicht wie ein Quecksilberkügelchen gleitet der zweite aus dem Tor und stellte sich unweit vom ersten auf, dann der dritte, dann der vierte, dann der fünfte. Schließlich standen wir alle in einer Reihe. Die Leute wurden auf uns aufmerksam, zeigten auf uns und sagten: Die fünf sind jetzt aus diesem Haus gekommen. Seitdem leben wir zusammen, es wäre ein friedliches Leben wenn sich nicht immerfort ein sechster einmischen würde. Er tut uns nichts, aber es ist uns lästig, das ist genug getan; warum drängt er sich ein, wo man ihn nicht haben will. Wir kennen ihn nicht und wollen ihn nicht bei uns aufnehmen. Wir fünf haben zwar früher einander auch nicht gekannt und wenn man will, kennen wir einander auch jetzt nicht, aber was bei uns fünf möglich ist und geduldet wird ist bei jenem sechsten nicht möglich und wird nicht geduldet. Außerdem sind wir fünf und wir wollen nicht sechs sein. Und was soll überhaupt dieses fortwährende Beisammensein für einen Sinn haben, auch bei uns fünf hat es keinen Sinn, aber nun sind wir schon beisammen und bleiben es, aber eine neue Vereinigung wollen wir nicht, eben auf Grund unserer Erfahrungen. Wie soll man aber das alles dem sechsten beibringen, lange Erklärungen würden schon fast eine Aufnahme in unsern Kreis bedeuten, wir erklären lieber nichts und nehmen ihn nicht auf. Mag er noch so sehr die Lippen aufwerfen, wir stoßen ihn mit dem Ellbogen weg, aber mögen wir ihn noch so sehr wegstoßen, er kommt wieder. Die Leute zählen uns und sagen: Früher waren es 5, jetzt sind es 6. Nein sagen wir und stampfen mit dem Fuss 'wir sind nur 5'" (NS2 313–14; CS 435–6); for the final sentences of the text, see (NS2A 295). In the following analysis of "Fellowship," I quote from these pages.

If we compare the two representations of an awkward situation, it is evident that in "Fellowship" Kafka has stripped the situation of social particularities such as education and profession, thereby turning the tight circle of friends into a non-specific and diagrammatic community. The six individuals outside the house are distinguished by their complete *lack of* distinguishing features. Instead of names, the narrator—one of the five friends standing in a row—offers us merely numbers. As alike as balls of mercury, they seem to be elements of a scientific experiment or characters in a parable rather than individual human beings. Unlike the realist and naturalist novels that Kafka enjoyed reading (among them those of Dickens and Flaubert), his literary works do not offer any detailed panorama of the specific social, ethnic, and political communities of his day. Although deeply concerned with questions of Jewishness, for instance, in his literary works Kafka does not characterize a single fictional person by the word "Jew."[4] Instead, the groups of friends, family members, workers, villagers, jackals, dogs, and mice that populate Kafka's literary works can be described as diagrammatic communities, and in that respect are similar to the five nameless friends standing outside a generic house.

Moreover, "Fellowship" also differs from *Notes from Underground* in its stereoscopic style. As we shall shortly see, the parable juxtaposes two disjunctive images of the tiny community outside the house, thereby offering the reader an unstable and uncanny aesthetic experience of the urban scene comparable to Kafka's experience of the Italian urban view presented by the Kaiserpanorama in Friedland. In a sense, the reader perceives the narrow circle of friends as three-dimensional shapes in the strange wax figure-like atmosphere of the stereoscopic peep show. The sexual connotations of the word "peep show" are not beside the point here. In Kafka's day, following the advent of silent movies, stereoscopic apparatuses were rendered obsolete and relegated to the field of pornography.[5] As we shall see in Chapter 8, pornographic stereographs serve as templates for a number of scenes in *The Trial*. In "Fellowship," the sexual connotations seem to be of a masturbatory nature. If we choose to see the five friends standing in a row as the five fingers of a hand and the sixth one as a penis or a pen, then the parable turns into a riddle, perhaps even a dirty joke, about the relationship between two kinds of solitary pleasure. Starting

---

4   With one single exception: the fragment "A Guest of the Dead" ("Bei den Toten zu Gast") from August 1920 does in fact mention a "Jewish girl" ("ein Judenmädchen" [NS2 227]).

5   See Crary, *Techniques of the Observer* and *Suspensions of Perception: Attention, Spectacle, and Modern Culture* (Cambridge, MA, and London: The MIT Press, 1999), 127.

out from the micro-sociological analyses in Dostoyevsky's *Notes from Underground*, however, I will approach "Fellowship" as an exploration of social life, and not a reflection on the relation between the sexual life and the literary life. I begin by expounding on the three theses put forward in the introductory chapter concerning the content, form, and function of Kafka's stereoscopes.

Living Together

According to my first thesis, the content of Kafka's stereoscopes is the configuration of a community. The subject matter of "Fellowship" is the community outside the house, or, to be more precise, in fact two different communities referred to, respectively, as a "living together" and as a "continual being together."[6] Even if these two designations, "Zusammenleben" and "Beisammensein," are nearly identical, they denote two different configurations of sociality.

The narrator claims that the five friends standing in a row are "living together." He also refers to this "Zusammenleben" as "the five of us," as "our circle," and as a "union." By hinting at "what is possible and can be tolerated by the five of us," the narrator implies that this union of friends is bound together by a shared set of rules and norms.

But the narrator also refers to the group of all six individuals outside the house (that is, the five friends plus the burdensome sixth) as a "continual being together." This "Beisammensein" is not a circle of friends but, rather, a crowd of non-friends. Speaking for his friends, the narrator is careful to point out that the rules and norms of the five do not apply to the sixth: "What is possible and can be tolerated by the five of us is not possible and cannot be tolerated with this sixth one." Thus, this continual being together takes place outside the jurisdiction of the community of friends. This is probably why the communal life in question seems to consist of childishly or rudely pouting lips, pushing away, and then returning.

Yet even if the narrator briefly mentions the community's social laws, he seems unconcerned with their content. Remarkably, he says nothing about what is, in fact, "possible and can be tolerated by the five of us." Rather than actually applying the laws by judging specific acts to be either legal or illegal, moral or immoral, he restricts himself to passing judgment on the applicability of these laws. Whatever their content, the laws do not apply to the interaction between the five friends and the interloping sixth.

As we have seen, the six outside the house have neither names nor individual features, only numbers: "then the second came or rather

---

6   "Seitdem leben wir zusammen" and "dieses fortwährende Beisammensein."

glided through the gate as gently as a little ball of quicksilver glides."
Even if the small balls of mercury connote scientific matter-of-factness,
they are in themselves figurative: the second friend glides through the
gate *as* a ball of mercury might glide.[7] If the social imaginary is to be
defined as the store of figures, metaphors, symbols, and narratives with
which a group of people conceive the basic shape of their own being
together, then it plays an important role in "Fellowship" as the
imaginative figuration of human beings as small balls of mercury.
Indeed, the rhetorical image of the chemical element organizes the
entire representation of communal life outside the house. The uniformity
of the balls of mercury underlines the homogeneity of the union of
friends, and the capacity for globules of quicksilver to easily merge into
a larger ball emphasizes the group's effortless formation.

Even if the mercury is mentioned only once at the beginning of the
text, the rhetorical figure is implicitly present in what follows. Three
times the narrator rejects the possibility of accepting the sixth individual
by using the word "Aufnahme": the five friends "don't know him and
don't want to accept him" ("bei uns aufnehmen"); if they were to offer
long explanations, it "would almost amount to accepting him in our
circle" ("Aufnahme in unsern Kreis"); and they prefer "not to explain
and do not accept him" ("nehmen ihn nicht auf"). Interestingly, the
German "aufnehmen" not only denotes the social process of integrating
an individual (or a group of individuals) into a larger community, but
also the chemical process of absorbing a substance into a solution.

Chemical imagery also plays a role when the narrator claims that the
sixth individual is constantly "trying to meddle." Here the German
"einmischen" (from "Mischung," "meddling" and "mixture") can be
understood as a reference to the blending of different substances.
Similar connotations can be found in the description of the second
friend's gliding movement as "leicht" ("gentle" or "light") and in the
characterization of the intrusion of the sixth one as "lästig" ("it annoys
us"). The German "lästig," etymologically derived from "Last"
("burden"), is a figuration of the difference between friend and non-
friend in terms of physical weight. All in all, the social imaginary of
"Fellowship" naturalizes the circle of friends by describing the
constitution of their community as a matter of chemical forces rather
than of collective decisions. In fact, the narrator offers only tautological
arguments for not accepting the sixth individual ("In any case, we are
five and don't want to be six"). Rather than rational argumentation, his
configuration of the community seems to be based on imaginative
figuration.

---

7   "wie ein Quecksilberkügelchen gleitet."

This first thesis on Kafka's stereoscopic style assumes a critical stance toward scholars who interpret his literary works as satires of bureaucratic organizations or critiques of legal systems.[8] As we have seen, the exploration of the diagrammatical community in "Fellowship" is not concerned with particular institutional practices or legal procedures, but rather with acts of imaginative figuration that shape the understanding of how individuals stand in relation to each other, how they fit together, and how they are connected to other groups and to the surrounding world.

What is the Meaning Anyhow?

According to my second thesis, the form of Kafka's stereoscopes—the basic arrangement of these literary devices— is a juxtaposition of two dissimilar images of the same community. Just like Georg in the opening scene of "The Judgment," the narrator of "Fellowship" seems to shuttle back and forth between two incompatible representations of the same circle of friends.

In the orderly image, the group of five friends appears to be a well-organized and well-defined community. As we have seen, this image of living together outside the house is supported by a social imaginary that invites us to perceive the friends as small, homogeneous balls of mercury and to imagine their interactions as chemical processes of absorption and blending. Understood this way, there are substantial and, as it were, ontological differences between the members and the non-members of the circle of friends.

In the disorderly image, conversely, the very same group of friends is understood as a number of random individuals, not bound together by any system of rules and norms. Indeed the five standing in a row are represented as a heterogeneous multitude of non-friends. This image, too, is supported by the chemical features of mercury, given that we do not think of how small balls of it merge into larger spheres, but rather of how they disintegrate into a multitude of smaller volatile balls. In German, the term "ein Quecksilber" can be used to describe an inconstant and fickle person.

Due to this juxtaposition of orderly and disorderly image, the narrator entangles himself in two contradictions. The first of these has to do with the five friends' knowledge of each other: "There was a time, of course, when the five of us did not know one another, either; and one

---

8   In *The Mirror of Justice*, for instance, Theodore Ziolkowski argues that *The Trial* should be interpreted as a critical portrait of the legal system as it was practiced during the Hapsburg *fin de siècle* period; Theodore Ziolkowski, *The Mirror of Justice: Literary Reflections of Legal Crises* (Princeton, NJ: Princeton University Press, 1997), 239.

could say that we still don't know one another." According to the first half of this quote, the five friends know each other in the present moment. At an earlier moment in time, presumably in some primordial state of nature, they did not yet know each other. But now, fortunately, they have entered into a minor social contract that has turned strangers into friends: a bunch of people has become a body politic. In the second half of the quote, however, the self-correction "and one could say" indicates the shift from orderly to disorderly image. One ("man") could say that the friends still do not know one another, that is, even in the present moment one could judge the five individuals standing in a row as being a non-community. According to the disorderly image, then, the chaotic state of nature has never been put behind; indeed, it is a permanent condition for the living together of the group of five.

A few lines later, the narrator contradicts himself once more, and this time the contradiction has to do with the meaning of the friends' communal life: "And what is the meaning of this continual being together anyhow? It is also meaningless for the five of us, but here we are together and will remain together; a new union, however, we do not want, exactly because of our experiences." In most cases, the logical conjunction "exactly because" ("eben auf Grund") suggests that a fact one would expect to support a particular line of argument does, in fact, support the opposing argument.[9] Even if the friends' experience of the meaninglessness of communal life could have served as a reason for founding a new and better union, the narrator cites it as an argument for *not* wanting a new union. Nevertheless, the narrator surprisingly admits that neither the continual being together with the sixth one nor the living together of the five friends makes any sense.

In *When Kafka Says We*, Vivian Liska puts forward a perceptive interpretation of "Fellowship" in which she distinguishes between an

---

9   This is the way in which Kafka tends to use the synonymous conjunctions "eben auf Grund," "eben weil," "eben deshalb," and "gerade deshalb." An instance similar to the one in "Fellowship" can be found in a short text from 1917. Here the narrator is a beggar who for years has been sitting at a busy junction but who "meddles" in nothing that goes on around him ("ich mische mich [. . .] in nichts ein"). One would expect that the beggar's abstention from meddling with street life would lead to a lack of understanding of the social situation and his own position in it, but in fact, he claims, the opposite is the case: "But for that very reason, because I bother with no one and in the tumult and absurdity of the street preserve the calmness of my outlook and the calmness of my soul, I understand better than anyone else everything that concerns me, my position, and what is rightfully my due." ("Eben deshalb aber weil ich mich um niemanden kümmere und in dem Lärm und Unsinn der Straße den ruhigen Blick und die ruhige Seele bewahre, verstehe ich alles, was mich, meine Stellung, meine berechtigten Ansprüche betrifft, besser als irgendwer" [T 817; D 376–7]).

affirmative and an undermining perspective on the union of friends: "These first lines of the text simultaneously affirm and undermine the 'founding myth' of the little *Gemeinschaft*."[10] In the affirmative perspective we understand there to be a quasi-natural law "holding the group together." The undermining perspective, meanwhile, "unmasks this pretense and reveals the cruel mechanism behind this seemingly natural cohesion." As mentioned in the previous chapter, I suggest interpreting this dual vision not as an expression of Kafka's ambivalent attitude toward closed communities, as Liska has it, but, rather, as a binocular device. As a literary apparatus, "Fellowship" makes ready for an aesthetic experience in which the reader is challenged to compare the two juxtaposed images of the same group of friends seen simultaneously as friends and non-friends, as known and not known to each other, as hoping for a meaningful living together and experiencing its meaninglessness.

I suggest the term "aesthetic reflection" for the process through which the reader compares the two juxtaposed images of the same body of individuals outside the house. It is through the juxtaposition of two dissimilar images that the parable's stereoscopic style orchestrates a reflective aesthetic experience.

This second thesis regarding Kafka's stereoscopic style is polemically directed toward scholars who interpret the aesthetic reflection in Kafka's literary works as self-referentiality, self-thematization, and metafiction—a turning-back, that is, from the literary image to the writer's construction of the literary image.[11] As I see it, the reflection set in motion by Kafka's literary stereoscopes is not a reflection on the literary work itself, but rather a reflection on the extra-literary world— on the social imaginary that frames the way we construct images of communal life.

Now It Is 6

According to my third thesis, the function of Kafka's stereoscopes is to make the reader reconfigure the community represented in the text. When trying to synthesize the two juxtaposed images of the group of people outside the house, the reader of "Fellowship" is challenged to restructure and reshape the representation of communal life.

---

10 Liska, *When Kafka Says We*, 23.
11 In a German context, this view was famously suggested by Hans-Thies Lehmann in an article from 1984. Literature presents itself in Kafka's literary works, Lehmann argued, "whereas all 'things' that are external in relation to writing glide away and recede into the background." Hans-Thies Lehmann, "Der buchstäbliche Körper: Zur Selbstinszenierung der Literatur bei Franz Kafka," in *Der junge Kafka*, ed. Gerhard Kurz (Frankfurt am Main: Suhrkamp, 1984), 220.

In the very last sentences of the parable, the friends angrily dispute their status with "people" ("die Leute"), apparently a larger group of individuals also present outside the house: "People count us and say: Earlier there were 5, now it is 6. No, we say and stamp our foot in the ground, 'we are only 5.'" Until this moment, as we have seen, the narrator has been shuttling back and forth between two incompatible images of the group of friends as either a community or a non-community. But "people" suggest a third image of communal life outside the house, in the light of which the five friends and the sixth individual together form a new community: "Earlier there were 5, now it is 6." The tiny word "now" ("jetzt") refers to the moment of a second constitutive act that reconfigures the order of things by incorporating the sixth into the community.

Before abandoning "Fellowship," Kafka chose to delete the sentences that describe the disagreement between friends and "people"; in the posthumous version, published by Brod in 1936, no "people" declare a new community. But it is my contention that the reconfiguration of a community can take place in both in the world of the fictional characters and in the mind of the reader. In "Fellowship," the incompatibility of orderly and disorderly image challenges the reader to exert what Hannah Arendt refers to as the world-building capacity of man to construct a new image, a third image, of the community outside the house. In other words, the text triggers a kind of political thinking that has the structure of a political moment—according to Arendt a collective act that exerts "the freedom to call something into being which did not exist before."[12] Thus, in the final version of "Fellowship," the political reconfiguration of the community is not depicted in the text but, rather, prompted by the stereoscopic style of the text.

This third thesis on Kafka's stereoscopes, finally, is aimed critically against scholars who paint an exclusively negative image of legal and political matters in his work.[13] It is widely supposed that Kafka's fictive machinery of moral and legal norms is nothing but a tool for the power structures that discipline and destroy the individual human body. As a consequence, the only kind of freedom relevant for the six individuals outside the house would be the negative freedom lying in escape from an oppressive community. As I see it, however, Kafka's literary works

---

12 Hannah Arendt, *Between Past and Future: Eight Exercises in Political Thought* (New York: Viking Press, 1968), 151.
13 See, for instance, Ulf Abraham's claim that the true face of law, in Kafka, is power; more specifically the disciplinary power that subjects the individual human being. Ulf Abraham, *Der verhörte Held: Verhöre, Urteile und die Rede von Recht und Schuld im Werk Franz Kafkas* (Munich: W. Fink, 1985), 20, 266.

are guided by a utopian idea of the political moment. In the miraculous *now* of the political moment, regardless of whether this moment takes the form of a political action pictured by the aesthetic representation or political thinking provoked by the aesthetic experience, the community is a site for the positive freedom that lies in exerting the world-building capacity of man.

Admittance to the Law

Seen from the perspective of political philosophy, the narrator's arbitrary judgments on the scope of the union of friends are in conflict with the principle of justice. If all six individuals outside the house resemble globules of mercury, there can be no rational ground for not accepting the sixth. In a sense, of course, all Kafka's literary works deal with matters of justice, not least in their numerous descriptions of judgments, interrogations, courtrooms, lawyers, punishments, and so on. As we shall see in the following chapters, abundant scholarly work convincingly demonstrates the crucial role of specific practices and concepts of justice in Kafka's oeuvre. Yet it is important to distinguish between different notions of justice.

According to Plato and Aristotle, justice is a matter of who deserves what. The classical maxim *suum cuique* defines justice as a question of giving "everyone his [or her] due" in so far as he or she is a member of a legal and political community. As Aristotle points out, there are basically two distinct questions about what everyone deserves, respectively a question of distributive or corrective justice (or retributive justice, as we tend to say today). This seminal distinction hinges on the difference between sharing and punishing. In *Nicomachean Ethics*, Aristotle writes that distributive justice "is found in the distributions of honor or money or any of the other things divisible among those who share in the regime (for in these things it is possible for one person to have a share that is either unequal or equal to another's). The other form of such justice is the corrective one involved in transactions."[14] We distinguish between political and legal justice in more or less the same way today. While matters of distributive justice are discussed in parliament, matters of retributive justice are handled by the police and the courts of law.

However, the notion of justice at issue in "Fellowship" is more fundamental than the distinction between distributive and retributive justice. The judgments passed by the narrator are not concerned with "honor or money or any of the other things" that can be piled up and

---

14   Aristotle, *Nicomachean Ethics*, trans. C. D. C. Reeve (Indianapolis, IN: Hackett, 2014), 1131a.

distributed among the six persons outside the house, and neither do they mete out punishment or reward to the sixth. Rather, they decide who counts as one deserving his due. In the vocabulary of modern justice theory, then, the text is concerned with the scope rather than the substance of justice.[15] Shifting the focus to "Before the Law," originally a part of the unfinished novel *The Trial*, on which Kafka worked in the second half of 1914, we are dealing not with the judge's practice of justice, but the doorkeeper's—the practice of deciding who gets "admittance to the law."[16]

Aristotle approaches the question of the scope of justice in his remarks on the large part of the population who lived outside the political sphere of the Greek city-state. In Aristotelian vocabulary, *polis* is a name for the political community in which the free male citizens meet to discuss the political matters. Within the walls of the *polis*, he argues, the male citizens, like Kafka's five friends, are bound together by a kind of "watered-down" version of friendship (*philein*).[17] *Oikos*, meanwhile, is the community of the household in which the male citizen rules over his wife, children, slaves, and animals. According to Aristotle, since these members of the household are completely preoccupied with matters of production and reproduction, they have no time to participate in the political community. The same applies to the large population of metics (resident aliens) who live and work in the city-state. Busy taking care of practical matters, these subordinate human beings exist in a void in the web of legal and political rights. Aristotle refers to the members of the *oikos* community as all those for whom justice "does not exist." Passing judgment on the applicability of the law, he argues that, for the women, children, and slaves in the *oikos*, "there is nothing politically just in relation to one another, but only something just in a certain sense and by way of a similarity. The just exists for those for whom there is also law pertaining to them."[18]

---

15 The political philosopher Nancy Fraser writes about a *who*-question as opposed to a *what*-question of justice: "At issue here is the scope of justice, the frame within which it applies: who counts as a subject of justice in a given matter? Whose interests and needs deserve consideration? Who belongs to the circle of those entitled to equal concern?" Nancy Fraser, "Abnormal Justice," in *Justice, Governance, Cosmopolitanism, and the Politics of Difference* (Berlin: Der Präsident der Humboldt-Universität zu Berlin, 2007), 123. For further discussion of the scope of justice, see Seyla Benhabib, *The Rights of Others: Aliens, Residents and Citizens* (Cambridge: Cambridge University Press, 2004); Charles Taylor, "The Nature and Scope of Distributive Justice," in *Philosophy and the Human Sciences* (Cambridge: Cambridge University Press, 1985).

16 "Eintritt in das Gesetz" (DzL 267; SS 68).

17 Aristotle, *Politics*, trans. Richard Kraut (Oxford: Clarendon Press, 1997), 1262b10.

18 *Nicomachean Ethics*, 1134a–b20.

Seen from today's perspective, Aristotle's reflections on slaves and other members of the household are a problematic part of his political philosophy, to say the least. He legitimates an unjust order of things by "drawing a border" (*dioristai*) between those who are "naturally free" and those who are "naturally slaves."[19] In other words, Aristotle plays the role of the doorkeeper: his dehumanization of the slave is a classic example of an act of judging which takes place before the law, understood as being prior to the law, and which determines who is granted admittance to the law.

Interestingly, Aristotle's judgment on the applicability of the law is not based on a chain of abstract concepts, but rather on a swarm of sensible images. The social imaginary of the city-state enables him to decide where justice exists and where it does not. The relation between free man and slave is analogous to the relations between soul and body, man and animal, man and woman, and man and tool, Aristotle imagines. And in the light of these imaginative figurations, it makes sense for him to metaphorically understand the slave as an "animate tool."[20] In other words, the judgment that categorizes human beings as either members or non-members of the legal and political community is evidently not based on a natural fact but instead on the cultural figurations of the social imaginary.

State of Nature/State of Exception

Even if his Altstädter Deutsche Gymnasium (Old Town German High School) education had meant that he could read the classics in Greek, Kafka is unlikely to have known the details of Aristotle's description of the Greek household as a community in which justice "does not exist." By contrast, it is evident that he was familiar with two well-known modern notions of a lacuna in the order of justice—the related concepts of the state of nature and the state of exception.

In *Leviathan* (1651), Thomas Hobbes describes the state of nature as a social situation in which the question of justice does not pertain: "the notions of right and wrong, justice and injustice, have here no place."[21] What Aristotle referred to as a *polis*, Hobbes calls a "commonwealth" when writing in English, and a *civitas* when writing in Latin. In the brutish manner of life before men form a commonwealth by entering into a covenant, Hobbes argues, there is no common or overarching

---

19 *Politics*, 1255b20.
20 *Politics*, 1253b4. For a cogent account of Aristotle's cultural imagination of the slave, see Iris Därmann, *Figuren des Politischen* (Frankfurt am Main: Suhrkamp, 2009), 52–79.
21 Thomas Hobbes, *Leviathan*, trans. J. C. A. Gaskin (Oxford: Oxford University Press, 1996), 63.

power to enforce civil laws, and therefore "just" and "unjust" simply do not exist as concepts. Summed up by one of the most famous formulations of modern political philosophy, the life of man, in this prepolitical condition, is "solitary, poor, nasty, brutish, and short."[22] One of the recurrent themes in *Leviathan*, written after the English Civil War, is that even after the institution of an orderly civil state, the political community is always threatened by a relapse into the disorderly natural condition. According to Hobbes, a people is then turned into a crowd, in Latin a *multitudo*, sometimes even a *dissoluta multitudo*, "that dissolute condition of masterless men, without subjection to laws, and a coercive power to tie their hands from rapine and revenge."[23] In this dissolute mode of being, the community is not a unified body politic but, rather, an irregular and tumultuous political organism, a "mere concourse of people, without union to any particular design, not by obligation of one to another."[24]

In *Römische Geschichte* (*The History of Rome*, 1864) and *Römisches Staatsrecht* (*Roman Constitutional Law*, 1876), the legal historian Theodor Mommsen defines emergency powers ("Nothfall" and "Nothstand") and state of war ("Kriegszustand") as temporary suspensions of the rule of law. In conformity with the Roman constitution, Mommsen writes, "all legal regulation of commanding and obeying, in which the commonwealth consists, is suspended where the immediate danger demands an immediate response."[25] *Tumultus* is the Latin term for the social disorder that occurs when, for instance, an enemy army stood outside the walls of Rome, or when civil war was about to break out. In a tumultuous situation, when formal legal rules were no longer applicable, the Roman constitution enabled the senate to appoint a magistrate, usually designated as a dictator, for a finite period of six months in order to restore order and safety to the republic. Bypassing the complicated system of checks and balances in the constitution, the dictator was able to revive a "regal" authority and rule with more or less unlimited power.[26] Thus, even if the authorities suspended the rule of law, the suspension was intended to ensure a minimal level of order and regularity which was the precondition for applying the law to the political community. In the words of the controversial legal theorist

---

22 *Leviathan*, 62.
23 *Leviathan*, 94.
24 *Leviathan*, 121. For further discussion of the distinction between people and multitude, see Hobbes, *On the Citizen* (Cambridge and New York: Cambridge University Press, 1998), 76–7, 137; Paolo Virno, *A Grammar of the Multitude: for an Analysis of Contemporary Forms of Life* (Cambridge, MA, and London: Semiotext(e), 2003), 21–5.
25 Theodor Mommsen, *Römisches Staatsrecht* (Basel: S. Hinzel, 1876), 662.
26 *The History of Rome*, trans. William P. Dickson (London: Macmillan & Co., 1908), 326.

Carl Schmitt, the decision about the state of exception is based on an interpretation of the configuration of the community:

> Every general norm demands a normal configuration of the living conditions to which it can be factually applied and which is subjected to its normative regulations. The norm requires a homogeneous medium [. . .]. There exists no norm that is applicable to chaos. The order [*die Ordnung*] must be established for a legal order to make sense. A normal situation must be created, and he is sovereign who definitely decides whether this normal situation actually exists.[27]

What is important here is that the state of exception is not in itself the disorderly social situation but, rather, a response to the threatening chaos. It is a constitutional means by which the authorities endeavor to recreate the normal situation where social life can again serve as the "homogeneous medium" which law requires. In the German original, Schmitt describes the homogeneous medium as "eine normale Gestaltung der Lebensverhältnisse"—literally a normal configuration or shape of living conditions. In both Mommsen and Schmitt, an important aspect of the state of exception is the act of judging that decides whether the configuration of living conditions can be categorized as either orderly or disorderly. Mommsen refers to the senate's decision as an "ascertainment" and a "declaration" of the emergency situation (a "Constatirung" and an "Erklärung des Nothstandes").[28] In the above quote, Schmitt claims that the sovereign is he who decides whether an orderly configuration of living conditions obtains in a given situation.

While there is nothing to document his reading Hobbes's *Leviathan* or other philosophical discussions of the state of nature, as we shall see in Chapter 6, a number of Kafka's later fictional texts appear to draw heavily on Hobbes's distinction between the orderly civil state and the disorderly natural state. By contrast, there is ample evidence of Kafka's acquaintance with the concept of the emergency powers in the Roman constitution. In the winter term of 1901–02, he attended the lectures on Roman legal history at the Charles University in Prague where Mommsen's *Römisches Staatsrecht* (*Roman Constitutional Law*) formed a part of the curriculum. Interestingly, the emergency powers, as

---

27 Carl Schmitt, *Political Theology: four Chapters on the Concept of Sovereignty*, trans. George Schwab (Cambridge, MA: The MIT Press, 1985), 13, translation modified; *Politische Theologie: Vier Kapitel zur Lehre von der Souveränität* (Munich: Duncker & Humblot, 1934), 20.
28 Mommsen, *Römisches Staatsrecht*, 663.

described by Mommsen, are a recurring theme in Kafka's literary works. In the 1914 story "In the Penal Colony," for instance, it seems as though the travelling researcher legitimizes the colony's horrendous policy of execution with a concept borrowed from Mommsen.[29]

Even so, the concepts of the state of nature and the state of exception should be used with great caution in the interpretation of Kafka's literary works. It goes without saying that abstract notions derived from state theory and constitutional law can be applied only analogically and metaphorically to the cases of a group of friends living in Prague and a narrow circle of friends standing in a row outside a house. The problem here is not just that these tiny communities are not proper political bodies; it is also that the disorder is not as extreme here as it is in the state of nature and the state of exception. Hobbes draws a sharp distinction between civil state and state of nature; in the condition of mere nature, he asserts, there are "no civil laws, nor commonwealth *at all*."[30] Mommsen suggests a similar binary of order and disorder when he writes, as quoted above, that the senate's declaration of the emergency situation suspends "*all* legal regulation of commanding and obeying." It is as if the concepts of the state of nature and the state of exception imply the idea of a switch with which the entire legal order can either be turned on or turned off.

Kafka's analysis of the configuration of fictional and non-fictional communities makes no sharp binary distinction between state of nature and civil state, or between state of exception and normal situation.[31] In

---

29 "The traveller looked at the harrow with his brow creased. The account of the legal procedure had not satisfied him. Nevertheless, he had to remind himself that this was a penal colony, that special measures [*Maßregeln*] were necessary here, and that military procedures had to prevail throughout" ("Der Reisende sah mit gerunzelter Stirn die Egge an, Die Mitteilungen über das Gerichtsverfahren hatten ihn nicht befriedigt. Immerhin mußte er sich sagen, daß es sich hier um eine Strafkolonie handelte, daß hier besondere Maßregeln notwendig waren und daß man bis zum letzten militärisch vorgehen mußte" [DzL 214; SS 41, translation modified]). When the enemy is 'ad portas' of Rome, Mommsen writes, it can occasion "measures [*Maßregeln*] that even conflict with the normal order." *Römisches Staatsrecht*, 663.

30 Hobbes, *Leviathan*, 110, 68, my italics.

31 Here I am inspired by William Connolly's critique of the binary of ordinary and extraordinary in Giorgio Agamben's Schmittian concept of the state of exception: "Politics and culture [. . .] do not possess as tight a logic as Agamben suggests. They are more littered, layered and complex than that. The dense materiality of culture ensures that it does not correspond neatly to any design, form, pattern of efficient causality, or ironclad set of paradoxes." William Connolly, *Pluralism* (Durham, NC: Duke University Press, 2005), 140. For further discussion, see Bonnie Honig, *Emergency Politics: Paradox, Law, Democracy* (Princeton, NJ: Princeton University Press, 2009), 106–11.

most cases, the two configurations of the community juxtaposed by Kafka's stereoscopic style differ only with regard to a tiny subset of social rules and norms. In the disorderly image offered by "The Judgment," for instance, the only rules not in force are the so-called "friendly relations" that stipulate how the members of the group of friends should help and respect each other. There is no reason to believe that the community depicted in the short story is completely unregulated by law; if Georg Bendemann abused or killed one of his friends, he would presumably be prosecuted on the basis of the 1873 *Austrian Code of Criminal Procedure*. In fact, things are fairly normal in this fictional Prague; the city has not relapsed into a brutish condition where man is wolf to man, and Hannibal's elephants do not stand outside the gates. And yet, even if the disorder does not cut very deep into the fabric of social laws, I contend that the juxtaposition of order and disorder plays an important role in Kafka's political thinking.

The Pawn of a Pawn

In a letter written in the summer of 1920, just a few months before the completion of "Fellowship," Kafka describes another conflict between a union of friends and an annoying intruder. This time, the question of justice is formed as a question of sex. Kafka tries to explain to Milena Jesenská the problems he has in relating to her as a girlfriend rather than as just a pen friend:

> The only thing I do fear [. . .] is this inner conspiracy against myself [. . .] which is based on the fact that I, who am not even the pawn of a pawn in the great chess game, far from it, now want to take the place of the queen, against the rules of the game and to the confusion of the whole game—I, the pawn of a pawn, that is, a piece which doesn't even exist, which isn't even in the game— and then perhaps also the king's place or even the whole board, and, if that were what I really wanted, it would have to happen in some other, more inhuman way.[32]

---

32   "Was ich fürchte [. . .] ist nur diese innere Verschwörung gegen mich [. . .] die sich etwa darauf gründet, daß ich, der ich im großen Schachspiel noch nicht einmal Bauer eines Bauern bin, weit davon entfernt, jetzt gegen die Spielregeln und zur Verwirrung alles Spiels auch noch den Platz der Königin besetzen will—ich der Bauer des Bauern, also eine Figur, die es gar nicht gibt, die gar nicht mitspielt—und dann vielleicht gleich auch noch den Platz des Königs selbst oder gar das ganze Brett, und daß wenn ich das wirklich wollte, es auf andere unmenschlichere Weise geschehen müßte" (B4 194; LM 56, translation modified).

If we map Kafka's and Milena's romantic relationship onto the diagrammatic community of "Fellowship," then Milena, her husband (the notoriously promiscuous writer Ernst Pollak), and his multitude of mistresses correspond to the five friends standing in a row outside a house; Kafka is the annoying sixth person who tries to get access to the amorous community that does not know him and does not want to accept him; and "the rules of the game" are equivalent to the social norms of the union of friends determining "what is possible and can be tolerated by the five of us."

Once again, however, Kafka does not go into detail with regard to the specific content of the rules of the game, focusing instead on the configuration of the community. According to the arrangement of pieces and sexual bodies, the rules of the game—here, chess—do not apply to Kafka. As the pawn of a pawn, he is so marginal a piece that he is not even in the erotic game, just as the sixth individual was not even in the row of friends outside the house. In Aristotle's terms, he is one of those for whom justice "does not exist."

Yet in spite of his marginal position, Kafka speculates about the anxiety-provoking possibility of taking the place of Milena's husband. According to the rule of promotion in chess, a pawn reaching the far side of the board is immediately changed into a piece of the player's choice, almost always a queen. In the letter to Milena, the pawn is promoted when it makes a precipitous move from the edge to the center of the board, from where it can exert its sovereign power. Although this movement disrupts the given order of things in so far as it entails a "confusion of the whole game," it also constructs a *new* order of things, given that it enables a reconfiguration of the community, this time with Kafka at the center of the board.

Dramatically underlining the distance between the humbleness of the pawn and the hubris of the king, Kafka, of course, can only reject the absurd idea of his usurping the place of the king and laying claim to Milena. Nevertheless, the last sentence from the letter intimates that the pawn promotion might, in fact, occur. Were Kafka to take the king's place, he suggests, the order of things could be rearranged not by making Milena move to Prague but "in some other, more inhuman way." If we interpret the letter according to my third thesis concerning Kafka's stereoscopes, this other, more inhuman way of reconfiguring communal life is literature's.

The Problem of Group Formation

Kafka's works found fame in the years after the Second World War. In the shadow of the short twentieth century, with its totalitarianism and the threat of nuclear war, it was natural and perhaps inevitable that his works should be interpreted as depictions of a struggle between powerless individuals and meaningless organizations. Regardless of whether these sinister organizations were interpreted as divine, bureaucratic, moral, existential, psychological, or disciplinary, they were understood as having something of the character of fate in that they were unpredictable, uncontrollable and, and, above all, unalterable. "Fate" comes from Latin *fatum*, "that which has been spoken," by implication by the gods, so that humans have no reason to talk with each other about it. And "destiny" comes from *destinare*, "make firm, establish," again by the gods, so that we have no possibility of changing it. According to the well-known "Kafkaesque" picture of Kafka, his literary works depict a dark, unfathomable world in which the order of things has been established and made firm by quasi-divine powers and in which political change is absent.

In a short text from 1979, the Kafka scholar Harmut Binder sketches out such a "Kafkaesque" reading of "Fellowship." According to Binder, the fact that the tiny group of people outside the house are neither five nor six is an aporia: "Indeed, this aporia has a tragic character. The problem of group formation is here nothing but an occasion."[33] As Binder has it, the scene outside the house is merely a pretext for demonstrating either that the five friends are guilty of inconsistent human behavior or, alternatively, that they are innocent victims of "people," who he seems to interpret as a sinister group that persecutes powerless individuals. In both cases, Binder suggests, "Fellowship" is concerned with tragic fate rather than with political justice, given that the problem of group formation is "nothing but an occasion." In other words, his reading is in line with Walter Sokel who, as noted in the Introduction, argued that people and things in Kafka's literary works are to be understood as "pure expression of the psyche, clothing of the inner, nothing but symbol."[34]

In this chapter, I have argued that the problem of group formation, far from being clothing of the inner, is the core issue of "Fellowship." In fact, Kafka's stories abound with group formations in which fictional characters become friends, decide to go for walks together, prepare for weddings, organize demonstrations, enter into covenants, found cities, build towers and, as it is said in *Amerika*, struggle to keep order among strangers who can think only of themselves.[35] Kafka's stereoscopes are literary apparatuses that reveal how these communities are anything but uncontrollable and unalterable facts. Thanks to the binocular style, the reader is made aware that the fictional communities have been constructed and can, therefore, be reconstructed.

---

33 Hartmut Binder, *Kafka-Handbuch in zwei Bänden* (Stuttgart: Kröner, 1979), 365–6.
34 Sokel, *Franz Kafka*, 110.
35 "zwischen fremden, nur auf sich selbst bedachten Leuten Ordnung schaffen" (V 283; A 192).

Two They Are Not Human Beings

The Content of Kafka's Stereoscopes: The Prague Asbestos Works Hermann & Co

In the autumn of 1911, the Kafka family bought a small asbestos factory in the Prague suburb of Žižkov, consisting of fourteen asbestos machines powered by a diesel motor and maintained by approximately twenty female employees. A year earlier, Franz Kafka's oldest sister, Elli (or Gabriele), had married the businessman Karl Hermann, who had persuaded the Kafka family to lend him the money as a kind of dowry to invest in the Prague Asbestos Works Hermann & Co. The discreet "& Co." in the firm's name refers to Franz Kafka who, more or less voluntarily, had invested in the project and taken on the role of unpaid co-manager and legal specialist. According to the plan, Kafka was to work at the asbestos factory after his working day at the insurance company. Soon, however, his commitment to the factory clashed with his commitment to literature, and he considered solving the problem by jumping out of a window.[1] In a diary entry of December 1911, Kafka writes: "The torment that the factory causes me. Why didn't I object when they made me promise to work there in the afternoons. No one used force to make me do it, but my father compels me by his reproaches, Karl by his silence, and I by my consciousness of guilt."[2]

The longest and most detailed account Kafka gives of the factory, a diary entry of February 7, 1912, is also concerned with the torment it caused him. Here, however, what torments him is not the guilt of his

---

1   Max Brod, *Franz Kafka: Eine Biographie: Erinnerungen und Dokumente* (New York: Schocken, 1946), 114.
2   "Die Qual, die mir die Fabrik macht. Warum habe ich es hingehen lassen als man mich verpflichtete, daß ich nachmittags dort arbeiten werde. Nun zwingt mich niemand mit Gewalt, aber der Vater durch Vorwürfe, Karl durch Schweigen und mein Schuldbewußtsein" (T 327; D 155).

failure to behave as he ought to toward his father and his brother-in-law
but, rather, the shame caused by his behavior toward his employees:

Yesterday at the factory. The girls in their absolutely unbearably
dirty and untailored clothing, their hair unkempt, as though they
had just got out of bed, their facial expressions set by the incessant
noise of the transmission belts and by the separate machine that is
automatic but unpredictable, stopping and starting; they are not
human beings—you don't say hello to them, you don't apologize
for bumping into them; when you call them over to do something,
they do it but go right back to the machine; with a nod of the head
you show them what to do; they stand there in petticoats; they are
at the mercy of the pettiest power and do not even have enough
calm to acknowledge this power and mollify it with glances and
bows. When six o'clock comes, however, and they call it out to
one another, they untie their kerchiefs from around their necks
and hair, dust themselves off with a brush that is passed around
the room and is demanded by the ones who are impatient, they
pull their skirts over their heads and clean their hands as well as
they can; they are women, after all; they can smile in spite of their
pallor and bad teeth, shake their stiff bodies; you can no longer
bump into them, stare at them, or ignore them; you squeeze
against the greasy crates to make room for them, hold your hat in
your hand when they say good night, and you do not know how
to react when one of them holds our winter coat for us to put on.[3]

---

3   "Gestern in der Fabrik. Die Mädchen in ihren an und für sich unerträglich
schmutzigen und gelösten Kleidern, mit den wie beim Erwachen zerworfenen
Frisuren, mit dem vom unaufhörlichen Lärm der Transmissionen und von der
einzelnen zwar automatischen aber unberechenbar stockenden Maschine
festgehaltenen Gesichtsausdruck sind nicht Menschen, man grüßt sie nicht, man
entschuldigt sich nicht, wenn man sie stößt, ruft man sie zu einer kleinen Arbeit,
so führen sie sie aus, kehren aber gleich zur Maschine zurück, mit einer
Kopfbewegung zeigt man ihnen wo sie eingreifen sollen, sie stehn in Unterröcken
da, der kleinsten Macht sind sie überliefert und haben nicht einmal genug ruhigen
Verstand, um diese Macht mit Blicken und Verbeugungen anzuerkennen und
sich geneigt zu machen. Ist es aber sechs Uhr und rufen sie das einander zu,
binden sie die Tücher vom Hals und von den Haaren los, stauben sie sich ab mit
einer Bürste, die den Saal umwandert und von Ungeduldigen herangerufen
wird, ziehn sie die Röcke über die Köpfe und bekommen sie die Hände rein so
gut es geht, so sind sie schließlich doch Frauen, können trotz Blässe und schlechten
Zähnen lächeln, schütteln den erstarrten Körper, man kann sie nicht mehr stoßen,
anschauen oder übersehn, man drückt sich an die schmierigen Kisten um ihnen
den Weg freizumachen, behält den Hut in der Hand, wenn sie guten Abend sagen
und weiß nicht, wie man es hinnehmen soll, wenn eine unseren Winterrock
bereithält, daß wir ihn anziehn" (T 373–4; D 179, translation modified).

Perhaps surprisingly, the bulk of the entry is a rehearsal of the basic rules of politeness prescribing how one should greet people, or make space for others with one's hat in one's hand, or apologize for bumping into them, and so on. Given what we know today about the carcinogenic properties of asbestos, the employees, protected only by a handkerchief, clearly had more serious problems to worry about than impoliteness.

It is important to realize, however, that the diary entry does not focus on the content of the laws of politeness but, rather, on the community to which these laws are applied. At issue, then, is not the definition of politeness but the social situation in which politeness as such is either relevant or irrelevant. Here I am restating this book's first thesis, according to which Kafka's stereoscopes afford us a dual image of the basic shape of a given community. Even if the diary entry offers a detailed overview of the laws of politeness, Kafka, in the provocative sentence "They are not human beings," does not apply a universal law of polite behavior to a particular case but, rather, passes judgment on the very applicability of the laws that define polite behavior. By categorizing the employees as "not human beings," he is neither describing them as polite nor as impolite but, rather, as a-polite, as *apolis*, as non-members of the civilized community.

The judgment on the applicability of laws is a recurring theme throughout Kafka's literary works. In the last chapter, we saw the narrator of "Fellowship" passing a judgment on the non-applicability of the laws of the five friends: "what is possible and can be tolerated by the five of us is not possible and cannot be tolerated with this sixth one."[4] The most famous example of this is probably the parable "Before the Law," in which this kind of judgment is made by the doorkeeper who guards the entrance to the law: "Before the law stands a doorkeeper. A man from the country comes to the doorkeeper and asks for admittance to the Law. But the doorkeeper says that he cannot grant admittance now."[5] Unlike the verdict of a judge, the judgment of the doorkeeper is not concerned with the substance of the law, but rather with admittance to the law, the "Eintritt in das Gesetz."

The diary entry about the asbestos factory is a good place to begin the exploration of this kind of judgment without a reversion to the "Kafkaesque" picture of Kafka's literary works. According to this well-known picture, judgments are nothing but arbitrary and absurd acts of violence decreed by sinister organizations and enacted by various

---

4   (NS2 313; CS 436).

5   "Vor dem Gesetz steht ein Türhüter. Zu diesem Türhüter kommt ein Mann vom Lande und bittet um Eintritt in das Gesetz. Aber der Türhüter sagt, daß er ihm jetzt den Eintritt nicht gewähren könne" (DzL 267; SS 68).

relatives of the doorkeeper. In the diary entry, however, the judgments are not a means by which evil bureaucratic powers persecute the innocent little man. Kafka is the manager of the factory. Neither are the judgments symptoms of some metaphysical problem located somewhere near the ahistorical core of human existence. Rather, the acts of judging are clearly concerned with the configuration of the community—that is, with the way in which a specific group of people fit together and how things are between them.

When Six O'clock Comes, However

Reading the diary entry about the asbestos factory, it's evident that its setup—its "Einrichtung," as Kafka wrote about the Kaiserpanorama—is stereoscopic. The text juxtaposes two disjunctive images of the same group of people, the female employees and their male manager, separated at the center of the text by the inconspicuous "however" or "but" ("Ist es aber sechs Uhr . . .").

The first half of the diary entry offers a disorderly image of communal life in the factory. During working hours, before six o'clock, Kafka the manager categorizes the employees as non-human: "They are not human beings."[6] This judgment on the civic status of the employees implies that Kafka is not obliged to interact with them as moral persons: he does not say hello to them, he bumps into them without apologizing, he shows them what to do with an impolite nod of the head, he stares at them, and he ignores them. The employees, too, are not bound by standard dress codes and do their work in dirty and untailored clothing, hair unkempt. They also seem unable to carry on a conversation, since the leather belts connecting the asbestos machines to the diesel motor emit a maddening noise, drowning their voices. Even their facial expressions and bodily gestures are impeded: "they are at the mercy of the pettiest power and do not even have enough calm to acknowledge this power and mollify it with glances and bows." In this case, "the pettiest power" is Kafka, who, one must assume, was no frightening manager. Even toward him, however, the employees are defenseless.

By contrast, the second half of the diary entry paints an orderly image of the factory community. After six o'clock, Kafka revises his judgment on the civic status of the employees: "they are women, after all."[7] This sudden change of status means that Kafka can no longer bump into them, stare at them, or ignore them. On his way out, in a demonstrative gesture of respect, he even squeezes against the greasy crates to make room for them and holds his hat in his hand when they

6   "Die Mädchen [. . .] sind nicht Menschen."
7   "so sind sie schließlich doch Frauen."

say good night. Likewise, the women begin to behave differently; they smarten themselves up and start to smile, in spite of their pallor and bad teeth. Now the employees seem to be autonomous subjects who, on their own initiative, put on skirts, wash hands, call out for the hairbrush, even hold the bewildered manager's coat. Thus, when six o'clock comes, the speechless and defenseless non-humans suddenly metamorphose into articulate and independent human beings. Incidentally, this ontological change also takes the shape of a grammatical change: in the disorderly image, the employees figure in the sentences only as grammatical objects; in the orderly image, by contrast, they are suddenly promoted to grammatical subjects.

Two months earlier, in November 1911, Kafka wrote another diary entry, also describing his relation to the female employees of the Kafka family, that can be viewed as a draft for the entry about the asbestos factory. This time the word "girls" ("Mädchen") does not refer to factory workers but to housemaids with whom the young Kafka seems to have sexual relations.[8]

The education of girls, their growing up, the habituation to the laws of the world, was always especially important to me. Then they no longer run so hopelessly out of the way of a person who knows them only casually and would like to speak casually with them, they have begun to stop for a moment, even though it be not quite in that part of the room in which you would have them, you need no longer hold them with glances, threats, or the power of love; when they turn away they do so slowly and do not intend any harm by it, then their backs have become broader too. What you say to them is not lost, they listen to the whole question without your having to hurry, and they answer, jokingly to be sure, but directly to the point. Yes, with their faces lifted up they even ask questions themselves, and a short conversation is not more than they can stand. They hardly ever let a spectator disturb them any more in the work they have just undertaken, and therefore pay less attention to him, yet he may look at them longer. They withdraw only to dress. This is the only time when

---

8   The sexual character of the diary entry is corroborated by a letter to Max Brod of July 1908 in which Kafka explicitly meditates on a sexual encounter with a maid at a hotel: "She is too old to still be melancholy, but feels sorry, though it doesn't surprise her, that people are not as kind to prostitutes as they are to a mistress. I didn't comfort her since she didn't comfort me either" ("Sie ist zu alt, um noch melancholisch zu sein, nur tut ihr leid, wenn es sie auch nicht wundert, daß man zu Dirnen nicht so lieb wie zu einem Verhältnis ist. Ich habe sie nicht getröstet, da sie auch mich nicht getröstet hat" [B1 87; LFFE 45]).

you may be insecure. Apart from this, however, you need no
longer run through the streets, lie in wait at house doors, and wait
over and over again for a lucky chance, even though you have
really long since learned that such chances can't be forced. But
despite this great change that has taken place in them it is no
rarity for them to come towards us with mournful faces when we
meet them unexpectedly, to put their hands flatly in ours and
with slow gestures invite us to enter their homes as though we
were a business acquaintance. They walk heavily up and down in
the next room; but when we penetrate there too, in desire and
spite, they crouch in a window-seat and read the paper without a
glance to spare for us.⁹

Like the entry about the asbestos factory, this earlier account juxtaposes
two different images of the same group of girls, divided by the "great

---

9   "Immer hatte die Erziehung der Mädchen, ihr Erwachsensein, die Gewöhnung
an die Gesetze der Welt einen besonderen Wert für mich. Sie laufen dann einem,
der sie nur flüchtig kennt und gern mit ihnen flüchtig reden möchte, nicht mehr
so hoffnungslos aus dem Weg, sie bleiben schon ein wenig stehn und sei es auch
nicht gerade an der Stelle des Zimmers wo man sie haben will, man muß sie
nicht mehr halten mit Blicken, Drohungen oder der Macht der Liebe, wenn sie
sich abwenden, tun sie es langsam und wollen damit nicht verwunden, dann ist
auch ihr Rücken breiter geworden. Was man ihnen sagt, geht nicht verloren, sie
hören die ganze Frage an, ohne daß man sich beeilen müßte und antworten,
zwar scherzhaft, jedoch genau auf die gestellte Frage. Ja sie fragen sogar selbst
mit erhobenem Gesicht und ein kleines Gespräch ist ihnen nicht unerträglich.
Sie lassen sich in der Arbeit, die sie gerade vorgenommen haben, durch einen
Zuschauer kaum mehr stören, berücksichtigen ihn also weniger, doch darf er sie
auch länger anschauen. Nur zum Ankleiden ziehn sie sich zurück. Es ist die
einzige Zeit, während der man unsicher sein kann. Sonst aber muß man nicht
mehr durch Gassen laufen, bei Haustoren abfangen und immer wieder auf
einen glücklichen Zufall warten, trotzdem man doch schon erfahren hat, daß
man die Fähigkeit nicht besitzt ihn zu zwingen. Trotz dieser großen Veränderung
aber die mit ihnen vorgegangen ist ist es keine Seltenheit, daß sie bei einer
unerwarteten Begegnung mit einer Trauermiene uns entgegenkommen, die
Hand flach in die unsere legen und mit langsamen Bewegungen uns wie einen
Geschäftsfreund zum Eintritt in die Wohnung laden. Schwer gehn sie im
Nebenzimmer auf und ab, wie wir aber auch dort eindringen aus Lüsternheit
und Trotz hocken sie in einer Fensternische und lesen die Zeitung ohne einen
Blick für uns zu haben" (T 277–8; D 129–30, translation modified). Remarkably,
the English translation of the diary entry complies with Brod's desexualized
image of Kafka by downplaying the text's erotic character. When Kafka writes,
ambiguously, that the girls "withdraw only to dress" ("Nur um zu Ankleiden
ziehn sie sich zurück"), the translator supplements: "They withdraw only to
dress *for dinner*" (my italics), thereby imagining a non-erotic situation of
dressing.

change" of the girls' "growing up, the habituation to the laws of the world." The disorderly image shows the interaction of the young man and the girls to be unregulated by the laws of the world. Unable to meet up with (or arrange to meet) a girl, for instance, the young man has to "run through the streets, lie in wait at house doors, and wait over and over again for a lucky chance." According to the orderly image, on the other hand, their interaction takes place in a predictable social space organized by rules and norms. Suddenly metamorphosed into autonomous subjects, the girls no longer run annoyingly (in his view) out of the way when the young man addresses them. "What you say to them is not lost," Kafka remarks, adding that they are even able to take the initiative themselves and start asking questions. When the young man, in the final lines of the diary entry, penetrates into the next room, most likely with insidious intent, he learns that the girls are busy informing themselves informed about public life: "they crouch in a window-seat and read the paper without a glance to spare for us." As in the diary entry about the asbestos factory, the male subject is overcome by bewilderment when the girls exert their new-won autonomy: "you do not know how to react when one of them holds our winter coat for us to put on."

A Swarm of Terms of Abuse

The asbestos factory never became a success economically and was sold when Karl Hermann was drafted for the First World War. As a consequence, the social status of the Kafka family continued to rely on Hermann Kafka's store selling haberdashery and ladies' accessories. In an unsent letter to his father from November 1919, Kafka describes his feeling of shame when, visiting the store as a little boy, he witnessed his father's lack of "ordinary polite behavior."[10] Kafka conceptualizes his father's brusqueness toward the staff as a matter of justice: "That was also where I learned the great lesson that you could be unjust." Both the concept of justice and its traditional image, the balance scales of Justitia, play a role in Kafka's letter: "And even if, insignificant as I was, I had licked their feet down below, still it would never have made up for [Ausgleich] the way you, as their master, hammered away at them from above."[11] The German "Ausgleich," from "gleichen," means balancing and making equal. As we saw in the discussion of Aristotle's

10   "gewöhnliches anständiges Benehmen" (NS2 174; MoS 116).
11   "Dort bekam ich auch die große Lehre, daß Du ungerecht sein konntest" and "Und hätte ich, die unbedeutende Person, ihnen unten die Füße geleckt, es wäre noch immer kein Ausgleich dafür gewesen, wie Du, der Herr, oben auf sie loshacktest" (NS2 173–4; MoS 116–7).

concept of justice in the previous chapter, however, Kafka's effort to make things equal has nothing to do with the distribution of material goods nor with the retribution for illegal acts; rather, it is concerned with the underlying configuration of communal life in the store.

According to Kafka, this kind of injustice is derived, among other things, from the way in which his father speaks to his employees: "But I heard you and saw you in the shop shouting abuse and raging in a way that, so I thought at the time, occurred nowhere else in the whole world. And not only shouting abuse—other kinds of tyranny."[12] Earlier in the letter, Kafka offers a detailed rhetorical analysis of Hermann's abusive language:

> I don't recall that you swore at me in expressly bad language. In any case, it wasn't necessary: you had so many other methods. Besides, in talk at home and especially in the shop the words of abuse [Schimpfwörter] were flying down on other people around me so that as a small boy I was sometimes almost stunned by them, and had no reason not to refer them to myself as well, for the people you were abusing were certainly no worse than I, and you were no more dissatisfied with them than you were with me.[13]

Among the examples Kafka gives of his father's abusive language are his calling a clerk with tuberculosis a "mangy dog" ("The sooner he dies the better, the mangy dog"),[14] referring to the employees at the store as "paid enemies,"[15] and comparing Kafka's friend Yitzhak Löwy, the leader of a troupe of Yiddish actors from Galicia, "terribly, in a way I've now forgotten, to some kind of vermin."[16] These are, according to

---

12 "Dich aber hörte und sah ich im Geschäft schreien, schimpfen und wüten, wie es meiner damaligen Meinung nach in der ganzen Welt nicht wieder vorkam. Und nicht nur schimpfen, auch sonstige Tyrannei" (NS2 172; MoS 116).

13 "Daß Du mich direkt und mit ausdrücklichen Schimpfwörtern beschimpft hättest, kann ich mich nicht erinnern. Es war auch nicht nötig, Du hattest so viele andere Mittel, auch flogen im Gespräch zuhause und besonders im Geschäft die Schimpfwörter rings um mich in solchen Mengen auf andere nieder, daß ich als kleiner Junge manchmal davon fast betäubt war und keinen Grund hatte, sie nicht auch auf mich zu beziehn, denn die Leute, die Du beschimpftest, waren gewiß nicht schlechter als ich und Du warst gewiß mit ihnen nicht unzufriedener als mit mir" (NS2 160–1; MoS 109, translation modified).

14 "Er soll krepieren, der kranke Hund" (NS2 172; MoS 116).

15 "bezahlte Feinde" (NS2 172; MoS 116).

16 "verglichst Du ihn in einer schrecklichen Weise, die ich schon vergessen habe, mit Ungeziefer" (NS2 154; MoS 106, translation modified).

Kafka, "rhetorical tactics."[17] The father's acts of abuse, that is to say, are acts of figuration, a kind of unjust behavior based on the capacity to evoke images independently of the reality of objects present in the store. The difficult-to-translate sentence "the words of abuse were flying down on other people around me" ("flogen ... auf andere nieder") invites us to imagine the invectives as swarms of birds or insects that aggressively swoop down on people, first of all on the employees. Each time Hermann Kafka applied a general word of insult to a particular individual, he passed a judgment on the configuration of communal life. Thus, in the haberdashery store, the manager Hermann Kafka made a dehumanizing judgment on a clerk by figuring him as a "mangy dog"; in the asbestos factory, many years later, the manager Franz Kafka passed a similar dehumanizing judgment on the employees by figuring them as non-human.

Maybe because of Hermann's "rhetorical tactics," terms of abuse play a crucial role in Kafka's literary works. His fictional characters have a propensity to call each other mangy dogs, annoying monkeys, mad cats, grass frogs, bugs, lazybones, layabouts, louts, rabble, scoundrels, and, in one particularly inspired moment, "useless loafers and breathers of air."[18] Just a year after Hermann Kafka's appalling comparison of Yitzhak Löwy to vermin,[19] Franz Kafka let the protagonist of "The Metamorphosis" wake up one fine morning transformed into some species of beetle-like "monstrous vermin."[20]

At first glance, the diary entry about the asbestos factory seems to be devoid of rhetorical figures. The two juxtaposed images of the social situation in the factory appear to be mere lists of micro-sociological observations unadorned by figural language. On closer inspection, however, the entry focuses on the "rhetorical tactics" on the basis of which the group of people is configured. First, the two central judgments on the community are metaphorical. In the sentence "They are not human beings," the word "human beings" ("Menschen") is not used in its literal meaning, as a designation of a member of the species *homo*

---

17 "rednerischen Mittel" (NS2 160; MoS 109).
18 "unnützen Eckensteher und Lufteinatmer" (DzL 331; CS 322, translation modified).
19 "Ungeziefer" (NS2 154; MoS 106, translation modified). In a diary entry from November 1911, when Löwy was still living in Prague, Kafka writes: "Löwy— My father about him: 'Whoever lies down with dogs gets up with fleas [*Wanzen*]'" ("Löwy—Mein Vater über ihn: Wer sich mit Hunden zu Bett legt steht mit Wanzen auf" [T 223; D 103]).
20 "einem ungeheuren Ungeziefer" (DzL 115; MoS 3).

sapiens, but in its figural meaning, as a metaphor for an autonomous subject. Likewise, in "They are women, after all," the word "women" ("Frauen") is used as a figural expression for a certain civic status. Literally and biologically, the employees are humans and women; metaphorically and ethically, however, they are spoken of as if they were non-humans and non-women.

Figurative meanings also play an important role in the detailed descriptions that surround the two central judgments. In the disorderly image, the employees are immature "girls" who are "unbearably dirty" and have "stiff bodies." In the orderly image, the same employees are grown-up "women" who are "clean" and capable of moving independently. These descriptions are not just literal observations of the two social situations before and after six o'clock; they are based on a web of metaphorical oppositions: adult/minor, clean/dirty, and living/ dead.

Rhetorical figuration also plays a role for the distinction between public and private which structures the diary entry. Before six o'clock, the employees do their work "in petticoats," in accordance with the formlessness of the private sphere. After six o'clock, as noted above, they are eager to dress up and brush their hair so that they come to look like the co-citizens that one might meet in the public sphere outside the factory. This is not only a no-nonsense sociological observation: during working hours, the employees have unkempt hair "as though they had just got out of bed." Literally, they have not just got out of bed; figuratively, they are spoken of *as if* they had.

According to Kant, the imagination, "die Einbildungskraft," is the faculty of sensible or sensuous presentation of absent objects, of "Darstellung."[21] Whereas the reproductive imagination calls forth the objects of past experience, the productive imagination produces images independently of the reality of objects.[22] Even if the diary entry about the asbestos factory seems to consist of two unadorned lists of empirical observations, the representation of the community is both a work of the reproductive imagination and of the productive imagination—the faculty of forming and transforming images.

Social Imaginaries

The "rhetorical tactics" in the haberdashery store and the asbestos factory are just two local examples of a general rhetoric that framed the

---

21 Immanuel Kant, *Critique of the Power of Judgment*, trans. Paul Guyer and Eric Matthews (Cambridge and New York: Cambridge University Press, 2000), 232.
22 Kant, *Lectures on Metaphysics*, trans. Karl Ameriks and Steve Naragon (Cambridge and New York: Cambridge University Press, 1997), 237.

way social life was perceived in Central Europe in the years before the First World War. The collective figuration of collective life is what I suggest calling a social imaginary. In the words of the philosopher Cornelius Castoriadis, we rely on social imaginaries whenever we answer questions about the fundamental features of the community: "Who are we as a collectivity? What are we for one another? Where and in what are we? What do we want; what do we desire; what are we lacking?"[23]

While it is easiest to grasp the concept of the social imaginary as a swarm of words of abuse and a web of metaphors, the idea cannot be wholly understood without a consideration of a number of other acts of imaginative figuration. Among these are invoking the spirits of the dead, purifying defiled objects, praying to divine beings, discussing metaphysical ideas, referring to mythical pasts, prophesying future disasters, writing about utopias, and revering sovereign kings. Such figurations are imaginative in so far as they are created by the productive imagination, the faculty of forming and transforming images. And they form a part of a *social* imaginary to the extent that they frame the way we think and act in communal life.

The concept of the social imaginary expands the scope of political analysis. When accounting for the "*common aisthesis*" according to which we see something as given, as Rancière suggested,[24] the discussion of the political community is no longer concerned only with constitutions, institutions, and interests. In recent political philosophy, cultural theory, and political anthropology, the concept of the social imaginary has been applied to a number of different aspects of social life. Researchers have explored how the imagination shapes our view on notions such as national identity,[25] sovereignty,[26] moral order,[27] humanitarianism,[28]

23 Cornelius Castoriadis, *The Imaginary Institution of Society*, trans. Kathleen Blarney (Cambridge: Polity, 1987), 146–7.
24 Rancière, *Dissensus*, 69.
25 Benedict Anderson, *Imagined Communities: Reflections on the Origin and Spread of Nationalism* (London: Verso, 1983).
26 Ernst Kantorowicz, *The King's Two Bodies: A Study in Medieval Political Theology* (Princeton, NJ: Princeton University Press, 1957); Kevin Olson, *Imagined Sovereignties: The Power of the People and other Myths of the Modern Age* (Cambridge and New York: Cambridge University Press, 2016).
27 Taylor, *Modern Social Imaginaries*.
28 Craig Calhoun, "The Idea of Emergency: Humanitarian Action and Global (Dis) Order," in *Contemporary States of Emergency: The Politics of Military and Humanitarian Interventions*, ed. Didier Fassin and Mariella Pandolfi (New York and Cambridge, MA: Zone Books, 2010); Didier Fassin, *Humanitarian Reason: A Moral History of the Present Times* (Berkeley, CA: University of California Press, 2012).

vulnerability,[29] and political participation.[30] Most often, however, researchers seem more eager to understand the object of a given social imaginary than to explore the acts of imagination in themselves. This is perhaps one of the reasons why the term social imaginary is currently used in a number of differing senses. While an overview of the uses and understandings of the concept of the social imaginary is beyond the scope of this chapter, I will here turn to three dichotomies to outline my use of it.

First, a social imaginary is not a social theory. Both social imaginaries and social theories are concerned with the fundamental features of a given community. But whereas social theories articulate an understanding of a community in the medium of abstract concepts and laws, social imaginaries belong to the medium of non-conceptual or pre-conceptual presentations. "What I'm trying to get at with this term," Charles Taylor writes when introducing his influential concept of the social imaginary, "is something much broader and deeper than the intellectual schemes people may entertain when they think about social reality in a disengaged mode."[31]

In the diary entry about the asbestos factory, Kafka does not use abstract concepts to describe his unpleasant behavior toward his employees; even the central concept of politeness ("Höflichkeit") is not mentioned in the text. Instead, the entry offers a detailed account of the imaginative figures that frame the communal life in the factory.

Second, a social imaginary should not be understand as a background understanding of community. Here I differ from those theorists who, like Charles Taylor, use the concept of the social imaginary as a label for all kinds of non-conceptual understandings of communal life.[32] As I see it, however, what might be called the broader notion of the social imaginary is problematic because it uses the term as a synonym for well-established concepts such as habitus, background understanding,

29 Judith Butler, *Precarious Life: The Powers of Mourning and Violence* (New York: Verso, 2004); *Frames of War: When is Life Grievable?* (London: Verso, 2009).
30 Jacques Rancière, *Disagreement: Politics and Philosophy*, trans. Julie Rose (Minneapolis, MN: University of Minnesota Press, 1999).
31 Taylor, *Modern Social Imaginaries*, 23.
32 According to Charles Taylor's broad concept, the social imaginary is "what contemporary philosophers have described as the 'background.' It is in fact that largely unstructured and inarticulate understanding of our whole situation, within which particular features of our world show up for us in the sense they have." *Modern Social Imaginaries*, 25. For related broad concepts of the social imaginary, inspired by Taylor, see, for instance, Paul W. Kahn, *Finding Ourselves at the Movies: Philosophy for a New Generation* (New York: Columbia University Press, 2013); Olson, *Imagined Sovereignties*.

and pre-understanding. Instead, I suggest a narrow concept of the social imaginary, one based firmly on the Kantian concept of the productive imagination understood as a capacity to evoke and rework sensible presentations. Building on Kant and Aristotle, Castoriadis proposes a similarly restricted version of the concept when he defines the social imaginary as "the unceasing and essentially undetermined [. . .] creation of figures/forms/images, on the basis of which alone there can ever be a question of 'something.' What we call 'reality' and 'rationality' are its works."[33]

The diary entry about the asbestos factory could be said to analyze a social imaginary in the broad, Taylorian, sense of the term. The shared background understanding shared by the tiny community in the factory is expressed, first of all, in the routine movements of Kafka and his employees. As outlined above, the text carefully describes how the individuals nod to each other, bump into each other, leave the machines, put on clothes, pass around the hairbrush, and so on. In the deafening noise of the machines, the production of asbestos comes into view as a silent choreography of bodily gestures and affective reactions based on a system of embodied norms.

The social imaginary in the narrow sense of the term is closely related to this idea of a non-conceptual background understanding. Still, in my view, there are good reasons to distinguish between a web of imaginative figures and a broader web of embodied meaning shared by a given community. Imagining obeys one set of unwritten rules; gesturing and feeling another. This means, among other things, that the acts of imaginative figuration are linked in a different way to the historical repertoire of prefigurations outside the walls of the factory.

Third and finally, a social imaginary is not an individual fantasy. In Kantian terms, both social imaginaries and individual fantasies are works of the productive imagination that forms and transforms images. Over the course of the eighteenth and nineteenth centuries, however, the capacity for fantasy came to be seen as something belonging to the gifted individual, the Romantic genius being a creator of an idiosyncratic imaginary world divorced from the social practices that constitute reality. The social imaginary, by contrast, is fantasy at work; here the imaginative figuration is not cut off from but, rather, immanent to the community. In the words of the anthropologist Arjun Appadurai, this

---

33 Castoriadis, *The Imaginary Institution of Society*, 3. For related narrow concepts of the social imaginary, see, for instance, Chiara Bottici, *Imaginal Politics: Images Beyond Imagination and the Imaginary* (New York: Columbia University Press, 2014); Butler, *Frames of War*.

kind of imagination is to be understood as "fuel for action," as "a staging ground for action, and not only for escape."[34]

In the diary entry about the asbestos factory, the web of metaphors should not be interpreted as the work of Kafka's fantasy—that is, as poetic images with which the literary writer communicates his observations of the factory scene. Instead, the figuration is part and parcel of the social practice itself; like the bodily gestures and the affective reactions, the acts of figuration set the stage for Kafka's interaction with his employees. In this case, then, the work of the literary writer does not consist of making up new metaphors but, rather, in making latent metaphors explicit.

Thus, what I call a configuration is a representation of communal life shaped on the basis of the rhetorical figures that make up the social imaginary. In this context, it is useful to point out that "configuration" comes from the Latin *configurare*, "shape after a pattern" (from *con* "together" and *figurare* "to shape").

In Kantian terms, this shaping after a pattern can be understood as a schematization. In a dense and much disputed paragraph of *Critique of Pure Reason*, Kant argues that the productive imagination plays a central role in human cognition. The transcendental schema, he writes, is "a product and as it were a monogram of pure *a priori* imagination" that enables the application of the concepts of the understanding to the manifold of sensible representations offered by the intuition.[35] A judgment applying the empirical concept of a dog, according to Kant's example, depends on some kind of pre-process in which "my imagination can specify the shape of a four-footed animal in general, without being restricted to any single particular shape that experience offers me or any possible image that I can exhibit in concreto."[36] Hence, this abstract shape or figure ("Gestalt") is not an image of a specific dog but, rather, a kind of pictogram of a dog in general. By producing such "mediating representations" midway between rationality and sensibility, the imagination contributes to the experiential judgment by making the chaotic sense data of the intuition compatible with the general concepts of the understanding. According to Kant's famous phrase, the schematism of our understanding is "a hidden art in the depths of the human soul, whose true operations we can divine from

34 Arjun Appadurai, *Modernity at Large: Cultural Dimensions of Globalization* (Minneapolis, MN: University of Minnesota Press, 1996), 7.

35 Immanuel Kant, *Critique of Pure Reason*, trans. Paul Guyer and Allen W. Wood (Cambridge and New York: Cambridge University Press, 1998), B177–87.

36 *Critique of Pure Reason*, 180.

nature and lay unveiled before our eyes only with difficulty."[37] In Kafka's literary works, the social imaginary is such a hidden art that schematizes the way we think and act in a community. The important difference, however, is that this hidden art is not buried in the depths of the human soul but, rather, in the depths of human culture.

Pre-Process

In Chapter 1, I discussed the inspiration Kafka took from the concepts of state of nature and state of exception. When analyzing the act of passing a judgment on the configuration of the community, however, Kafka seems to be drawing on a concept neither from political philosophy, nor from constitutional law, but, rather, from criminal law. In the Austro-Hungarian legal system of Kafka's day, criminal proceedings were divided into two stages. The trial itself was oral and public as in modern criminal law. Prior to the main process was a "pre-process" ("Vorprozess") or "pre-examination" ("Voruntersuchung"), the responsibility of the so-called examining magistrate ("Untersuchungsrichter"), whose task it was to procure and test the evidence that entered into the trial. Based on the interrogation methods of the inquisition, this pre-process was neither oral nor public.

The work of the examining magistrate was described in detail by the Prague criminologist Hans Gross who, at the same time Conan Doyle was writing his Sherlock Holmes stories, produced a number of influential and widely translated works about the technicalities of detective work. Gross's *Criminal Investigation* (*Handbuch für Untersuchungsrichter*, 1893) was a handbook for the first stage of the criminal proceeding, the pre-process, in which the examining magistrate had the duty of "weighing the evidence collected by the police, sifting further any points that have been missed or inadequately treated, hearing all that the accused has to say or adduce on his own behalf, and deciding the case in the interests of truth and justice."[38] The more theoretical work *Criminalpsychologie* (*Criminal Psychology*, 1898) describes the task of the examining magistrate as "a work of construction" ("eine Constructionsarbeit"), a duty that "belongs to the most difficult of our psychological tasks—but it must be performed unless we want to go on superficially and without conscience."[39]

---

37 *Critique of Pure Reason*, 180–1.

38 Hans Gross, *Handbuch für Untersuchungsrichter als System der Kriminalistik* (Munich: J. Schweitzer, 1904), VI; *Criminal Investigation: A Practical Handbook for Magistrates, Police Officers, and Lawyers*, trans. John Adam and J. Collyer Adam (London: The Specialist Press, 1907), 10.

39 *Criminalpsychologie* (Graz: Leuschner & Lubensky, 1898), 134, my translation.

The pre-process is a work of construction that takes place before the law. According to Gross, the examining magistrate cannot restrict himself "exclusively to study our twelve tables and their interpretations."[40] Rather, his task is to give a representation of the social situation to which the Law of the Twelve Tables, the Roman *Duodecim Tabulae*, can be applied. But even if the pre-process is pre-legal, it contains a kind of judgment, Gross asserts: "not the judgment of the court [*Urtheil im processualen Sinne*], but the more general judgment which occurs in any perception."[41] Thus, in order to corroborate his notion of the pre-legal judgment passed by the examining magistrate, Gross draws on Kant's discussion of the cognitive act as a legal judgment.

Gross was a professor of law at the Charles University in Prague, where Kafka attended his seminars on criminal procedure. Moreover, he knew the professor's son, Otto Gross, a prominent anarchist and Freudian, whom he met through Max Brod in 1917. Both critical of patriarchal power, Kafka and Otto Gross planned to publish a journal, *Blätter gegen den Machtwillen* (*Pages on Combating the Will to Power*). It is evident that the pre-process and, more specifically, Hans Gross's depiction of the examining magistrate as *profiler* play an important role in Kafka's literary works.[42] In *The Trial*, for instance, Joseph K.'s lawyer, Mr. Huld, distinguishes sharply between the "pre-proceedings" and the "main proceedings" in the trial against K.[43]

In the vocabulary of the Austro-Hungarian legal system, Kafka's two judgments on his employees in the asbestos factory ("They are not human beings" and "They are women, after all") can be described as belonging to a pre-process. At issue are pre-legal acts of judging that decide whether a specific social situation should be localized outside

---

40 *Criminalpsychologie*, 6, my translation.
41 *Criminalpsychologie*, 208, my translation.
42 For further discussion of Kafka's relation to Gross's criminal anthropology, see Mark Anderson, *Kafka's Clothes: Ornament and Aestheticism in the Habsburg fin de siècle* (Oxford: Oxford University Press, 1992).
43 "Vorverhandlungen" and "Hauptverhandlung" (P 164, 242; Tr 122, 178). The "pre-proceedings," as Mr. Huld patiently explains to K., are secret: "K. must not overlook the fact that the proceedings are not public, they can be made public if the court considers it necessary, but the Law does not insist upon it. As a result, the court records, and above all the writ of indictment, are not available to the accused and his defense lawyers" ("K. möge doch nicht außer acht lassen, daß das Verfahren nicht öffentlich sei, es kann, wenn das Gericht es für nötig hält, öffentlich werden, das Gesetz aber schreibt Öffentlichkeit nicht vor. Infolgedessen sind auch die Schriften des Gerichtes, vor allem die Anklageschrift dem Angeklagten und seiner Verteidigung unzugänglich" [P 151–2; Tr 113]).

the gates of law, in a community of non-humans, or inside the gates, in a community of women.

Recent research has explored the close relation between Kafka's literary works and the Austro-Hungarian legal system, demonstrating that many of the legal procedures previously described as "Kafkaesque" and "absurd" were, in fact, standard legal practice in early twentieth-century Central Europe.[44] Yet it would be a misunderstanding to interpret Kafka's literary works as a portrayal and a critique of the realm of criminal procedure of his day. Neither the diary entries about the asbestos factory nor "Fellowship" and "Before the Law" are concerned with the Austro-Hungarian legal system. In other words, it is important to keep in mind that the notion of the pre-process is used figuratively in Kafka's literary works: Austro-Hungarian criminal law is not just a theme; it also serves as a template for Kafka's political thinking.

The Intellectual Assertion of Existence

"Ever since I have been able to think, I have had such profound concerns about the intellectual assertion of existence that everything else was a matter of indifference to me," Kafka explains in the 1919 unsent letter to his father discussed above.[45] Literature was one of Kafka's many attempts at the intellectual assertion of existence, he explains a couple of pages earlier, even if, unfortunately, the attempt had not proved entirely successful: "Here I had in fact escaped from you some little way by my own efforts, even if it did rather remind me of the worm whose tail had been trampled by a foot, but tears itself free and drags itself aside with its front."[46]

---

44 See Arnold Heidsieck, "Kafka's Fictional and Non-Fictional Treatments of Administrative, Civil, and Criminal Law," http://www.usc.edu/dept/LAS/german/track/heidsiec/KafkaLawsources/KafkaLawsources.pdf; Wolf Kittler, "Heimlichkeit und Schriftlichkeit: Das österreichische Strafprozessrecht in Franz Kafkas Roman Der Proceß," *Germanic Review* 78 (2003); "In dubio pro reo: Kafkas "Strafkolonie"," in *Kafkas Institutionen*, ed. Oliver Simons Arne Höcker (Bielefeld: transcript, 2007); Ziolkowski, *Mirror of Justice*; Ziolkowski, "Law," in *Franz Kafka in Context*, ed. Carolin Duttlinger (Cambridge: Cambridge University Press, 2018).

45 "Ich hatte, seitdem ich denken kann, solche tiefste Sorgen der geistigen Existenzbehauptung, daß mir alles andere gleichgültig war" (NS2 194; MoS 127, translation modified).

46 "Hier war ich tatsächlich ein Stück selbständig von Dir weggekommen, wenn es auch ein wenig an den Wurm erinnerte, der, hinten von einem Fuß niedergetreten, sich mit dem Vorderteil losreißt und zur Seite schleppt" (NS2 192; MoS 126).

Two years later, Kafka wrote a handful of letters to his older sister Elli about the education of the eleven-year-old Felix, eldest son of Elli and Karl Hermann. Trying to persuade Elli to let Felix be educated at a boarding school, he finds an argument in Jonathan Swift's *Gulliver's Travels*:

This, then, is what Swift thinks:
Every typical family is first and foremost an animal assemblage [*tierischen Zusammenhang*], as it were, a single organism, a single circulation of blood. Cast back on itself, then, it cannot get beyond itself. From itself it cannot create a new human being and if it tries to do so through the education within the family it is a kind of intellectual incest.[47]

The opposition between intellectual assertion of existence and intellectual incest is a fundamental theme throughout Kafka's life and work. As a twenty-year-old law student, Kafka enthusiastically quoted the stoic Roman emperor Marcus Aurelius, who wrote that a man with prudent speech and a hard hammer can make himself "into a controlled, steely, upright person."[48] In his notebooks, diaries, and letters, Kafka never tired of creating sensible figures for everything that a worm whose tail has been trampled by a foot is lacking: to be human is to be justified, to be able to say a fundamental "yes" to oneself, to have firm ground under one's feet, to be consolidated, to be able to breathe, to have backbone, to hold one's head high, to be steadfast, and to be "absolutely solid, black and clear-cut."[49]

Interpreted as a philosophical concept, the intellectual assertion of existence is a concept of dignity with a peculiarly Kantian ring to it. According to Kant, dignity ("Würde") is a name for the moral worth possessed by an individual due to her "humanity" alone. It is a basic feature that grants the individual admittance to the law as a moral, legal, and political person. Kantian or not, dignity is a recurring concept in Kafka research. As early as 1924, Walter Benjamin wrote that Kafka

---

47 "Swift meint also:/ Jede typische Familie stellt zunächst nur einen tierischen Zusammenhang dar, gewissermaßen einen einzigen Organismus, einen einzigen Blutkreislauf. Sie kann daher, auf sich allein angewiesen, nicht über sich hinaus, sie kann aus sich allein keinen neuen Menschen schaffen, versucht sie es durch Familienerziehung, ist es eine Art geistiger Blutschande" (Br 339–47; LFFE 290–97, translation modified).
48 "zu einem beherrschten, ehernen, aufrechten Menschen machen möchte" (B1 33; LFFE 14).
49 "ganz fest, schwarz vor Umrissenheit" (DzL 18; MoS 8).

used his literary works in an attempt "to catch hold of himself,"[50] and the two latest and most ambitious biographies give a convincing presentation of Kafka's personal life as a struggle for independence and autonomy.[51]

All too often, however, Kafka's struggle for the intellectual assertion of existence is discussed as a mere family matter. Though it is true that Kafka is a ferocious critic of what he, in the letters to Elli, calls "the oppressive, poison-laden, child-consuming air of the nicely furnished family room,"[52] I contend that Kafka's profound concerns about the intellectual assertion of existence is not just a response to a psychological problem. It is a response to a political problem, too.

In the available English translations of the letter to his father, Kafka writes that he always had such profound concerns about asserting "*my* intellectual existence" or "*my* spiritual existence."[53] In the German original, however, Kafka writes of his concerns about "der geistigen Existenzbehauptung"—literally "the intellectual assertion of existence" and not the individualizing and psychologizing "my spiritual existence." Put differently, the profound concerns about the intellectual assertion of existence (as I choose to translate Kafka's sentence) reflect Kafka's concerns not only about his own status in the family but also his concerns about, for instance, the status of the employees in its two businesses. As we have seen, the factory staff are caught in an animal assemblage, a single organism, a single circulation of blood, which makes them unable to communicate and, in a general sense, unable to assert their intellectual existence.

Accordingly, when Kafka actually criticizes the animal assemblage of the family, he does so in political rather than psychological terms. In the letters to Elli, Kafka does not use psychological concepts to describe Felix's development toward independence and maturity. Instead, he uses political concepts such as "justice," "equality," "rights," "representation," and "organization." The passage about the family as an animal assemblage quoted above continues:

---

50 Walter Benjamin, *Illuminations*, trans. Harry Zohn (New York: Schocken, 2007), 138.

51 Peter-André Alt, *Franz Kafka: Der ewige Sohn. Eine Biographie* (Munich: Beck, 2005); Reiner Stach, *Kafka: The Decisive Years*, trans. Shelley Laura Frisch (Princeton, NJ: Princeton University Press, 2013); *Kafka: The Years of Insight*, trans. Shelley Laura Frisch (Princeton, NJ: Princeton University Press, 2013); *Kafka: The Early Years*, trans. Shelley Laura Frisch (Princeton, NJ: Princeton University Press, 2016).

52 "die dumpfe, giftreiche, kinderauszehrende Luft des schön eingerichteten Familienzimmers" (Br 347; LFFE 295).

53 (MoS 127; WPC 198, my italics).

The family, then, is an organism, but an extremely complex and
unbalanced one, and like every organism it continually strives for
equilibrium [. . .]. The reason for the absolute impossibility of
an immediate, just equilibrium (and only a just equilibrium is a
real one, only this has any stability) within this family animal is
the inequality of its parts, that is to say the monstrous superiority
in power of the parents vis-à-vis the children for so many years.
In consequence of this, the parents arrogate to themselves the
sole right, during the childhood of the children, to represent the
family, not only to the outside world but also within the inner
intellectual organization, and they therefore step by step deprive
the children of their personal right and from then on can make
them incapable of ever claiming this right in a healthy way, a
misfortune that later will weigh no less heavily on the parents
than on the children.[54]

In the terminology of this book, this quote passes judgment on the
configuration of a community: "The family, then, is an organism." What
Kafka here refers to as the inner intellectual organization of the family
is an example of a basic shape of communal life. Deprived of their
personal right, the children are exposed to the parents' bursts of
unmotivated love and blind rage. By contrast, the parents, thanks to
their monstrous sovereign power, are the only ones who can represent
the family to the outside world and within its inner intellectual
organization.

It is not difficult to see that the configuration of the community, in
the letters to Elli, is a figuration of it. Kafka's highly polemic depiction
of the elementary features of family life is conspicuously framed by the
metaphor of family as organism, a family animal, and, in the earlier

---

54 "Die Familie ist also ein Organismus, aber ein äußerst komplizierter und
unausgeglichener, wie jeder Organismus strebt auch sie fortwährend nach
Ausgleichung. [. . .] Der Grund der unbedingten Unmöglichkeit einer sofortigen
gerechten Ausgleichung (und nur eine gerechte Ausgleichung ist wirkliche
Ausgleichung, nur sie hat Bestand) innerhalb dieses Familientieres ist die
Unebenbürtigkeit seiner Teile, nämlich die ungeheuerliche Übermacht des
Elternpaares gegenüber den Kindern während vieler Jahre. Infolgedessen
maßen sich die Eltern während der Kinderzeit der Kinder das Alleinrecht an,
die Familie zu repräsentieren, nicht nur nach außen, sondern auch in der inneren
geistigen Organisation, nehmen also dadurch den Kindern das Persönlichkeitsrecht Schritt für Schritt und können sie von da aus unfähig machen,
jemals dieses Recht in guter Art geltend zu machen, ein Unglück, das die Eltern
später nicht viel weniger schwer treffen kann als die Kinder" (Br 345; LFFE 294).

quote, a single organism, a single circulation of blood ("Blutkreislauf"), and intellectual incest. In this chapter, I have described Kafka's stereoscopes as apparatuses that elicit the reader's reflection of such figurations of communal life. If the social imaginary, to distort Kant's famous formulation, is a hidden art in the depths of human culture, the aim of the literary stereoscope is to lay its true operations bare.

Three Simultaneously Also Nothing

The Form of Kafka's Stereoscopes: "The Judgment"

In the winter of 1920, Franz Kafka had more or less abandoned the idea of being a writer. He had not written a literary text of any significant length in the two-and-a-half years since his first attack of tuberculosis, completing only a small number of aphoristic texts published posthumously in 1931 by Max Brod. In a diary entry of February 1920, the 36-year-old Kafka describes how as a young man he sat on Laurenziberg, a hill on the left bank of the Vltava River in Prague, and dreamt about his future authorship:

> This is the problem: many years ago I sat one day, in a sad enough mood, on the slopes of Laurenziberg. I went over the wishes that I wanted to realize in life. I found that the most important or the most delightful was the wish to attain a view of life (and—this was necessarily bound up with it—to be able to convince others of it in writing), in which life, while still retaining its natural, heavy rise and fall, would simultaneously be recognized no less clearly as a nothing, a dream, a hovering. A beautiful wish, perhaps, if I had wished it rightly. Something like the wish to hammer together a table with meticulous and orderly craftsmanship, and simultaneously to do nothing at all, and not in such a way that one could say: "Hammering is nothing to him," but rather, "Hammering is a real hammering to him, but simultaneously also nothing," whereby certainly the hammering would have become still bolder, still more determined, still more real and, if you will, still more insane.[1]

---

1   "Es handelt sich um folgendes: Ich saß einmal vor vielen Jahren, gewiß traurig genug, auf der Lehne des Laurenziberges. Ich prüfte die Wünsche, die ich für

Sitting on Laurenziberg, the young Kafka's most important or most desired wish was to attain "eine Ansicht des Lebens," a view of, or a perspective on, life. In the parenthesis, Kafka adds that this wish was necessarily bound up with the wish to be able to convince others of this view in writing; in other words, the aphoristic text describes a specific aesthetic experience which the young Kafka was to attain by help of his literary style.

This vision of life is clearly a dual vision. It juxtaposes an image in which life retains its natural rise and fall and, simultaneously, an image in which life would be recognized no less clearly as "a nothing, a dream, a hovering." The distinction between order and disorder seems here to be based on both human laws and on the laws of nature. Applying to the fall as well as to the rise, the adjectives "natural" and "heavy" suggest that both the downward and the upward movement follow the universal law of gravitation. The disorderly image, by contrast, seems to be characterized by a suspension of the force of gravity.

In the second half of the quote, Kafka makes the point more specifically, describing not a view of life in general but a view of a tiny subset of life: a person hammering together a table. In this case, the content of Kafka's stereoscopes is not the configuration of community but, rather, the configuration of a specific practice. In a sense, hammering together a table is equivalent to the process of working together in the asbestos factory and standing together in a row outside a house.

Seen through the orderly lens of the stereoscope, the hammering would be recognized as "a real hammering," a practice following the rules of "meticulous and orderly craftsmanship." Seen through the disorderly lens, on the other hand, the hammering is not a rule-bound social practice but, rather, a "nothing."[2]

---

das Leben hatte. Als wichtigster oder als reizvollster ergab sich der Wunsch, eine Ansicht des Lebens zu gewinnen (und—das war allerdings notwendig verbunden—schriftlich die andern von ihr überzeugen zu können) in der das Leben zwar sein natürliches schweres Fallen und Steigen bewahre aber gleichzeitig mit nicht minderer Deutlichkeit als ein Nichts, als ein Traum, als ein Schweben erkannt werde. Vielleicht ein schöner Wunsch, wenn ich ihn richtig gewünscht hätte. Etwa als Wunsch einen Tisch mit peinlich ordentlicher Handwerksmäßigkeit zusammenzuhämmern und dabei gleichzeitig nichts zu tun undzwar nicht so daß man sagen könnte: 'ihm ist das Hämmern ein Nichts' sondern 'ihm ist das Hämmern ein wirkliches Hämmern und gleichzeitig auch ein Nichts', wodurch ja das Hämmern noch kühner, noch entschlossener, noch wirklicher und wenn Du willst noch irrsinniger geworden wäre" (T 854–5; GWC 108–09, translation modified).

2   In fact, the formulation "Something like the wish to hammer together a table ..." ("Etwa als Wunsch einen Tisch ...") is unclear about whether the hammering together is the object of the view of life or the process of creating this view—in other words, whether it is a question of a metaphor for a represented

Even in this brief example, Kafka introduces an outside observer, an anonymous "one" ("man"), who passes what seems to be a neutral judgment on the nature of the practice of hammering: "and not in such a way that one could say . . ." We have met this kind of external judgment a number of times in the preceding chapters. In the diary entry on the asbestos factory, for instance, it was Kafka himself who passed judgment on the civic status of the employees by categorizing them as non-human and human, respectively ("They are not human beings" and "They are women, after all").

In this chapter, I focus on the second thesis of this book, according to which the form of Kafka's stereoscopes is a juxtaposition of two dissimilar images of communal life as, simultaneously, orderly and disorderly. In order to understand the literary techniques with which he attains this dual vision of life, I will return to "The Judgment," discussed briefly in the Introduction.

No Real Connections
In the first pages of "The Judgment," the young businessman Georg Bendemann has just finished a letter to a boyhood friend who emigrated to Russia several years earlier. The business Georg shares with his father is flourishing and he has just become engaged to a young woman from a well-to-do family; by contrast, the friend in Russia complains that neither his professional nor his private life is going well. As the friend has told Georg in his letters, "he had no real connections with the colony of his countrymen there, but he also had almost no social intercourse with local families either, and so was settling into a terminal bachelorhood."[3] The German "keine rechte Verbindung" has been translated as "no real connections," "no proper connections," and "no regular connections." As noted in the Introduction, Georg shuttles back and forth between an orderly and a disorderly image of the same circle of friends. This stereoscopic setup poses a question about the authenticity of the Russian friend's connections with his old group of friends in Prague too. According to the orderly image, he does indeed have real connections with the circle of friends; according to the

---

practice or a metaphor for the practice of representation itself; see Stanley Corngold, *Lambent Traces: Franz Kafka* (Princeton, NJ: Princeton University Press, 2004), 129. I am minded to interpret the hammering together as the object of literature, considering it analogous to the first half of the text which clearly deals with the object of the view of life (how life "would . . . be recognized").

3   "Wie er erzählte, hatte er keine rechte Verbindung mit der dortigen Kolonie seiner Landsleute, aber auch fast keinen gesellschaftlichen Verkehr mit einheimischen Familien und richtete sich so für ein endgültiges Junggesellentum ein" (DzL 44; SS 3).

disorderly image, though, he has "keine rechte Verbindung"; seen this
way, the "old friendly relations" are, in fact, not friendly at all. This
time, I will quote the entire passage about Georg's reflections on the
letter:

> What could one write to such a man, who had obviously become
> stuck and whom one could pity but not help? Should one perhaps
> advise him to come home again, to re-establish himself here, take
> up all the old friendly relations—there was nothing to prevent
> this—and for the rest put his trust in the help of his friends? But
> that meant nothing less than telling him at the same time—and
> the more one spared his feelings, the more hurtful it was—that so
> far his efforts had failed, that he should give them up once and for
> all, that he would have to come back and be gaped at by everybody
> as a man who had come back for good, that only his friends knew
> the score, and he was an overgrown baby who would simply
> have to do as he was told by his successful friends who had stayed
> at home. Besides, was it even certain that all the torment you
> would have to put him through would serve any purpose?
> Perhaps it would not even succeed in bringing him back—after
> all, he himself had said that he no longer understood the
> conditions at home—and so, despite everything, he would remain
> abroad, embittered by the suggestions and alienated even further
> from his friends. But if he really did take this advice and was
> brought low here—of course, not from anyone's doing but
> because of the situation—if he could not make a go of it either
> with his friends or without them, felt disgraced, and now really
> no longer had either home or friends, would it not be much better
> for him to have stayed abroad, just as he was? Under such
> circumstances, was it possible to believe that he could actually
> make any headway here?[4]

---

4   "Was wollte man einem solchen Manne schreiben, der sich offenbar verrannt
    hatte, den man bedauern, dem man aber nicht helfen konnte. Sollte man ihm
    vielleicht raten, wieder nach Hause zu kommen, seine Existenz hierher zu
    verlegen, alle die alten freundschaftlichen Beziehungen wieder aufzunehmen—
    wofür ja kein Hindernis bestand—und im übrigen auf die Hilfe der Freunde zu
    vertrauen? Das bedeutete aber nichts anderes, als daß man ihm gleichzeitig, je
    schonender, desto kränkender, sagte, daß seine bisherigen Versuche mißlungen
    seien, daß er endlich von ihnen ablassen solle, daß er zurückkehren und sich als
    ein für immer Zurückgekehrter von allen mit großen Augen anstaunen lassen
    müsse, daß nur seine Freunde etwas verstünden und daß er ein altes Kind sei
    und den erfolgreichen, zu Hause gebliebenen Freunden einfach zu folgen habe.

Georg's reflections end with two possible future scenarios. If the Russian friend does not take the advice, he will remain in St. Petersburg, "embittered by the suggestions and alienated even further from his friends." The words "even further" ("noch ein Stück mehr") hint that he is already estranged from his friends, and that the advice will only risk worsening that loosening of ties. If, on the other hand, the friend does indeed take the advice, and if his return to Prague turns out to be a failure, he will "now really no longer [have] either home or friends." The word "really" ("wirklich"), which, for some reason, tends to disappear in English translations, implies a threat of social exclusion. If it *seems* to the Russian friend as though he has neither home nor friends, this potential outcome may become a reality if he does return home.

According to this disorderly image, the transactions between the members of the community do not mean that they help each other, but rather that they compete with each other, gape at each other, ordering each other about, bringing each other low, and feeling contempt and shame for each other. A little later in the story, Georg expounds on the second future scenario, explaining to his fiancée that his friend, should he decide to return to Prague for the wedding, "would feel constrained and at a disadvantage, perhaps envious of me and certainly dissatisfied and incapable of ever shaking off his dissatisfaction."[5] At the end of the story, Georg's father contributes with a vulgar version of this bleak image of a communal life characterized by constraint, disadvantage, and dissatisfaction: "And now, when you thought you'd got him on his back, so flat on his back that you could plant your behind on him and he wouldn't budge."[6]

Und war es dann noch sicher, daß alle die Plage, die man ihm antun müßte, einen Zweck hätte? Vielleicht gelang es nicht einmal, ihn überhaupt nach Hause zu bringen—er sagte ja selbst, daß er die Verhältnisse in der Heimat nicht mehr verstünde—, und so bliebe er dann trotz allem in seiner Fremde, verbittert durch die Ratschläge und den Freunden noch ein Stück mehr entfremdet. Folgte er aber wirklich dem Rat und würde hier—natürlich nicht mit Absicht, aber durch die Tatsachen—niedergedrückt, fände sich nicht in seinen Freunden und nicht ohne sie zurecht, litte an Beschämung, hätte jetzt wirklich keine Heimat und keine Freunde mehr; war es da nicht viel besser für ihn, er blieb in der Fremde, so wie er war? Konnte man denn bei solchen Umständen daran denken, daß er es hier tatsächlich vorwärts bringen würde?" (DzL 44–5; SS 3–4, translation modified).

5   "er würde sich gezwungen und geschädigt fühlen, vielleicht mich beneiden und sicher unzufrieden und unfähig, diese Unzufriedenheit jemals zu beseitigen" (DzL 47; SS 5).

6   "Wie du jetzt geglaubt hast, du hättest ihn untergekriegt, so untergekriegt, daß du dich mit deinem Hintern auf ihn setzen kannst und er rührt sich nicht" (DzL 56; SS 9).

Confronted with the dual vision of the circle of friends, Georg comes to a standstill.[7] He puts the letter in the envelope slowly, "toying with it." Afterwards he sits at the desk for a long time, his face turned to the window, and when an acquaintance passes by and greets him from the street, he responds only with an absentminded smile. Later, he refers to this process of reflection by saying that he had "hesitated" telling his friend about the engagement.[8] Finally, however, Georg leaves his private room, crosses a small corridor and enters his father's room in order to inform him that he has "sent news of my engagement to St. Petersburg after all."[9]

Surprisingly, the father quickly jumps from the news of Georg's engagement to his relationship with the friend in Russia. After lamenting his own situation as a lonely widower, the father asks: "But since we're now on this subject, this letter, I'm pleading with you, Georg, don't fool me. It's just a trifle, it's not even worth mentioning, so don't fool me. Do you really have this friend in St. Petersburg?"[10] The father, of course, knows very well that Georg has a friend in St. Petersburg; at the end of the story, the elder Bendemann explains that he himself has even corresponded with him for several years. Thus, the question is not whether Georg has a friend in St. Petersburg; it is whether this friend can be characterized as a real friend. In the German "Hast du wirklich diesen Freund in Petersburg?" the word "wirklich" ("real") is used in the same way as in Georg's second future scenario according to which the man in Russia "now really no longer had either home or friends." Where Georg makes a distinction between really and

---

7   Uta Degner has made a similar point about Georg's letter to his friend. According to Degner, Georg's ambivalence is a collision between two different approaches to writing, one realist and the other aestheticist: "Georg's digressions perform the anti-logical 'logic' of the aestheticist artwork, which does not admit reality but subverts it by establishing its own mode of perception." Uta Degner, "What Kafka Learned from Flaubert: 'Absent-Minded Window-Gazing' and 'The Judgement'," in *Kafka for the Twenty-First Century*, ed. Stanley Corngold (Rochester, NY: Camden House, 2011), 83. Degner rightly connects this dual vision to Flaubert, but as I see it, she misses the connection between stereoscope and politics. "The Judgment" not only juxtaposes two different approaches to literary writing; it also juxtaposes two different approaches to the configuration of a community.

8   "gezögert" (DzL 51; SS 7).

9   "daß ich nun doch nach Petersburg meine Verlobung angezeigt habe" (DzL 50; SS 7).

10   "Aber weil wir gerade bei dieser Sache sind, bei diesem Brief, so bitte ich dich Georg, täusche mich nicht. Es ist eine Kleinigkeit, es ist nicht des Atems wert, also täusche mich nicht. Hast du wirklich diesen Freund in Petersburg?" (DzL 52; SS 7).

seemingly lacking home or friends, his father distinguishes between really and seemingly having a friend.

True, but Truer Still

In February 1913, while reading the proofs of "The Judgment," Kafka wrote down "all the relationships which have become clear to me in the story as far as I now remember them."[11] Researchers have made much of Kafka's remarks about the similarities between his own name and the protagonist's name, and between the names Felice Bauer and Frieda Brandenfeld, Georg's fiancée: "Georg has the same number of letters as Franz. [. . .] Bende has exactly the same number of letters as Kafka, and the vowel e occurs in the same places as does the vowel a in Kafka."[12] Much less has been made of the diary entry's somewhat enigmatic sketch of an analysis of the short story. The equivocal character of this analysis is owed to Kafka's focus on the configuration of a community, not on the situation of a single individual. Once again, his perspective is sociological rather than psychological:

> The friend is the link between father and son, he is their largest commonality. Sitting alone at his window, Georg rummages voluptuously in this thing in common, believes he has his father within him, and finds everything peaceful if it were not for a fleeting, sad thoughtfulness. In the course of the story the father rises up from the thing in common, from the friend, and sets himself up as Georg's antagonist, with the strength that other, lesser commonalities give him, namely love, devotion to the mother, loyalty to her memory, the clientele that the father had been the first to acquire for the business.[13]

---

11   "Anläßlich der Korrektur des 'Urteils' schreibe ich alle Beziehungen auf, die mir in der Geschichte klar geworden sind, soweit ich sie gegenwärtig habe" (T 491; D 214, translation modified).

12   "Georg hat soviel Buchstaben wie Franz [. . .] Bende aber hat ebensoviele Buchstaben wie Kafka und der Vokal e wiederholt sich an den gleichen Stellen wie der Vokal a in Kafka" (T 492; D 215); see also the letter to Felice from June 2, 1913 (BF 394; LF 265).

13   "Der Freund ist die Verbindung zwischen Vater und Sohn, er ist ihre größte Gemeinsamkeit. Allein bei seinem Fenster sitzend wühlt Georg in diesem Gemeinsamen mit Wollust, glaubt den Vater in sich zu haben und hält alles bis auf eine flüchtige traurige Nachdenklichkeit für friedlich. Die Entwicklung der Geschichte zeigt nun, wie aus dem Gemeinsamen, dem Freund, der Vater hervorsteigt und sich als Gegensatz Georg gegenüber aufstellt, verstärkt durch andere kleinere Gemeinsamkeiten nämlich durch die Liebe, Anhänglichkeit der Mutter durch die treue Erinnerung an sie und durch die Kundschaft, die ja der Vater doch ursprünglich für das Geschäft erworben hat" (T 491; D 214, translation modified).

The central concepts of this literary analysis are "Gemeinsamkeit" and "das Gemeinsame," for which I suggest the translations "commonality" and "thing in common." Unlike "Gemeinschaft," the words "Gemeinsamkeit" and "das Gemeinsame" here do not refer to the group of people constituting the community, but rather to the network of ties that bind the members of the community together—the *munia*, that is, of the Latin *cum-munus*. According to Kafka's interpretation of his own short story, the tiny community of the Bendemann family, consisting only of Georg and his father, is bound together by a number of different bonds: "love, devotion to the mother, loyalty to her memory, the clientele," and, most importantly, their many encounters and discussions with and about the friend in Russia. Later on in the diary entry, Kafka calls this specific "Gemeinsamkeit" a "circle of blood that is drawn around father and son."[14] The German "Blutkreis" here points ahead to the word "circulation of blood" ("Blutkreislauf") with which, as we saw in the last chapter, Kafka described the animal assemblage of the family in the letters to Elli in 1921.[15]

"The Judgment," too, is careful to underline the commonality of father and son. They are said to be living in "a shared household" and to be reading their newspapers in "the shared living room."[16] The important thing to realize, however, is that the short story juxtaposes two dissimilar images of this commonality. The shift between orderly and disorderly image is easiest to detect in a passage where Georg undresses his father in order to put him to bed:

At the sight of the not especially clean underwear, he blamed himself for having neglected his father. It would certainly have been his duty to supervise his father's change of underwear. He had not yet expressly spoken to his fiancée about how they proposed to arrange for his father's future, for they had assumed without further discussion that his father would live by himself in the old apartment. Yet now in an instant he resolutely made up his mind to take his father along into his future household. On closer inspection, it looked almost as if the care his father would receive there might come too late.[17]

14 "den Blutkreis, der sich um Vater und Sohn zieht" (T 491; D 214).
15 (Br 344; LFFE 294).
16 "in gemeinsamer Wirtschaft" and "im gemeinsamen Wohnzimmer" (DzL 45, 49; SS 4, 6, translation modified).
17 "Beim Anblick der nicht besonders reinen Wäsche machte er sich Vorwürfe, den Vater vernachlässigt zu haben. Es wäre sicherlich auch seine Pflicht gewesen, über den Wäschewechsel seines Vaters zu wachen. Er hatte mit seiner Braut darüber noch nicht ausdrücklich gesprochen, wie sie die Zukunft des Vaters

The words "Yet now" indicate this shift. According to the orderly image, the Bendemann family is a true family, the members of which live together in a shared household, taking care of each other. When Georg views their commonality this way, he is conscious of his obligation to comply with the laws of piety regulating family life: "It would certainly have been his duty to supervise his father's change of underwear." In so far as the being together of the young and the old Bendemann is configured as a family, filial duty ("Pflicht") is in force. Indeed, complying with rules seems to be an important feature of this orderly image of community: "I will call the doctor, and we will follow his orders," the good son Georg announces a little earlier.[18]

According to the disorderly image, by contrast, the Bendemann "family" is a non-family where the son, without giving it a second thought, leaves his father behind in the old apartment and neglects his poor health. The father points out that Georg has also neglected the memory of his late mother by saying that her death "has taken a lot more out of me than of you" and, more aggressively at the end of the story, that he has disgraced her memory altogether.[19]

The binocular style of "The Judgment" finds its most extreme expression in the father's verdict, which ends the story. After having told Georg that he does indeed know the man in Russia and that he has even corresponded with him over the last three years, the father passes the judgment that has given the story its name: "So now you know what else there was in the world beside you, until now you knew only about yourself! True, you were an innocent child, but truer still, you were a devilish man!—And therefore know this: I now sentence you to death by drowning!"[20]

The judgment that sentences Georg to death by drowning is based on an underlying judgment on Georg's social existence. This fundamental kind of judgment is concerned with the configuration of the community in which Georg is a member. It is a recurring stylistic

---

einrichten wollten, aber sie hatten stillschweigend vorausgesetzt, daß der Vater allein in der alten Wohnung bleiben würde. Doch jetzt entschloß er sich kurz mit aller Bestimmtheit, den Vater in seinen künftigen Haushalt mitzunehmen. Es schien ja fast, wenn man genauer zusah, daß die Pflege, die dort dem Vater bereitet werden sollte, zu spät kommen könnte" (DzL 54–5; SS 9).

18   "Ich werde den Arzt holen und seine Vorschriften werden wir befolgen" (DzL 53; SS 8).

19   "hat mich der Tod unseres Mütterchens viel mehr niedergeschlagen als dich" and "hast du unserer Mutter Andenken geschändet" (DzL 52, 57; SS 7, 10).

20   "Jetzt weißt du also, was es noch außer dir gab, bisher wußtest du nur von dir! Ein unschuldiges Kind warst du ja eigentlich, aber noch eigentlicher warst du ein teuflischer Mensch!—Und darum wisse: Ich verurteile dich jetzt zum Tode des Ertrinkens!" (DzL 60; SS 12).

feature of the story that such judgments are followed by a reflection on their logical consequences. Frieda: "Georg, if you have such friends, you should never have become engaged."[21] And Georg: "If he is a good friend, I said to myself, then my being happily engaged will make him happy too."[22] This conditional "if . . . then" structure ("wenn . . . dann") is repeated in the father's ultimate judgment on Georg: if you are a devilish man, then you should be sentenced to death by drowning.

Thanks to Kafka's stereoscopic style, however, the judgment on the basic shape of the communal life is doubly exposed: it establishes both what is true about Georg's social existence, and what is "truer still." The German "eigentlich . . . aber noch eigentlicher" may be directly translated as "properly . . . but more properly" or "truly . . . but more truly." Normally, of course, one would say "apparently . . . but really." Stereoscopically, however, both images are equally real. Thus, the syntagm "eigentlich . . . aber noch eigentlicher" can be understood as the most condensed formula for Kafka's stereoscopes. *Eigentlich*, in the orderly image, Georg has real friendly relations with friends and family members. *Aber noch eigentlicher*, in the disorderly image, he interacts with the very same friends and family members as if they were competitors and enemies. In the words of the Laurenziberg text, Georg is simultaneously an innocent child and a devilish man.

In German, however, the words "eigentlich" and "uneigentlich" also name the difference between literal and figurative language ("uneigentliche Rede"). From a rhetorical point of view, both judgments ("You were an innocent child" and "You were a devilish man") are examples of a metaphorical use of language.

In general, the story's images of communities are shaped by a web of metaphorical oppositions. While a detailed analysis of the figurative language is beyond the scope of this chapter, in brief the short story maps out the space of communal life with a set of metaphorical axes. The center/periphery axis: Georg lives in the "front room" whereas his father is exiled to the dark "back room" of the flat;[23] Georg lives in Prague whereas his friend is exiled in far-away Russia. The up/down axis: Georg manages to get his father "to sit back down" and put him to bed;[24] the father later jumps up and stands "upright in the bed;"[25] the

---

21 "Wenn du solche Freunde hast, Georg, hättest du dich überhaupt nicht verloben sollen" (DzL 48; SS 5).

22 "Wenn er mein guter Freund ist, sagte ich mir, dann ist meine glückliche Verlobung auch für ihn ein Glück" (DzL 51; SS 7).

23 "Vorderzimmer" and "Hinterzimmer" (DzL 53, 58; SS 8, 10).

24 "niederzusetzen" (DzL 54; SS 8).

25 "stand aufrecht im Bett" (DzL 56; SS 10).

friend would maybe be "brought low" if he returned from Russia;[26] Georg has, according to his father, got him on his back and sat on him.[27] The light/darkness axis: Georg's front room is sunny; the father's back room is "unbearably dark."[28] The grown-up/child axis: Georg tucks his father in as if he were a helpless little child;[29] the friend in Russia would be "an overgrown baby" if he returned to Prague. Similar examples could be drawn up to demonstrate the metaphorical axes between healthy/sick, living/dead, young/old, eating/not eating, and so on.

As I suggested in Chapter 2, this figuration is a part of a social imaginary in so far as it enables the construction of images of communal life. In both the orderly and the disorderly image, the configuration of the community is *figuration*, by which I mean that the representation of social life is made possible through a swarm of imaginative figures. It is worth noting here that the social imaginaries are immanent to the fictional community: it is Georg and his father, and not the anonymous narrator of the story, who imagine their communal life mediated through the hidden art of the social imaginary.

Aesthetic Reflection

The stereoscopic style of "The Judgment," which juxtaposes two dissimilar images of the same community, orchestrates an aesthetic experience characterized by aesthetic reflection. After having written the letter, Georg remains seated at his desk for a long time, slowly and absentmindedly putting it in the envelope. My contention is that the reader of Georg's letter, and of "The Judgment" in general, contemplates and hesitates in a similar way when confronted with the two dissimilar images of the community of friends and the two contrasting descriptions of Georg as innocent child and devilish man.

According to Kant, reflection consists of comparing two given representations in order to find commonalities. When I see a spruce, a willow, and a linden, Kant writes in his *Jäsche Logic*, one of his pre-critical writings, I start out by comparing these representations and noting any differences. Hereafter, "I reflect on that which they have in common among themselves, trunk, branches, and leaves themselves, and I abstract from the quantity, the figure, etc., of these; thus I acquire a concept of a tree."[30] Here, Kant sees reflection as a process of thought

---

26 "niedergedrückt" (DzL 45; SS 4).
27 "untergekriegt" and "mit deinem Hintern auf ihn setzen kannst" (DzL 45, 56; SS 4, 9).
28 "unerträglich dunkel" (DzL 50; SS 6).
29 (DzL 53; SS 8).
30 Kant, *Lectures on Logic*, 592.

in which universal empirical concepts are generated from sensible particulars such as individual intuitions of trunks, branches, and leaves. The concept of reflection also plays a central role in Kant's aesthetic theory in *Critique of Judgment*. Here, too, reflection is a thought process that begins with a manifold of sensible particulars. According to Kant, the aesthetic experience (in Kantian terms, "the judgment of taste") begins as a normal judgment of experience that is meant to subsume the manifold of intuition under pre-given concepts. For some reason, however, the process of thought loses its way and embarks on a search for a way to unify the sensible particulars. Thus, whereas the "determinative judgment" of the judgment of experience leads to subsumption of particular intuitions under the previously established universal concepts of understanding, the so-called "reflective judgment" of the aesthetic experience does not supply a determination of the intuition, but rather ends up in a free and harmonious interplay of the imagination and the understanding—that is, of the capacity to synthesize in sensible forms and the capacity to synthesize according to rules or concepts.

Within the confines of *Critique of Judgment* it is, in fact, difficult to explain in what sense the process of reflection immanent to the aesthetic experience can be said to be a comparison.[31] In Kafka's stereoscopes, however, the process of comparison is straightforward, given that the reader is challenged to compare the two dissimilar images of the same community. To arrive at a more detailed understanding of this reflective thought process, I will take a brief look at the two most well-known concepts of aesthetic reflection since Kant and, more specifically, since the Kantian influence on the German *Frühromantik*.

First, aesthetic reflection is often discussed as irony. According to Kenneth Burke's classic definition, irony gives us "a representation by the use of mutually related or interacting perspectives."[32] In the voluminous literature on the subject, irony is frequently characterized as a double meaning, a double gaze, a double exposure, and a dual image.[33]

---

31 A good explanation for this is offered by Henry E. Allison, *Kant's Theory of Taste: A Reading of the Critique of Aesthetic Judgment* (Cambridge and New York: Cambridge University Press, 2001), Chapter 2.

32 Kenneth Burke, *A Grammar of Motives* (Berkeley, CA: University of California Press, 1969), 503.

33 See, respectively: Claire Colebrook, *Irony* (London and New York: Routledge, 2004), 14; Donna Haraway, "A Manifesto for Cyborgs: Science, Technology, and Socialist Feminism in the 1980s," in *Feminism/Postmodernism*, ed. Linda J. Nicholson (New York: Routledge, 1990), 196; Allan Rodway, "Terms for Comedy," *Renaissance and Modern Studies* 6, no. 1 (1962): 113; Linda Hutcheon, *Irony's Edge: The Theory and Politics of Irony* (London and New York: Routledge, 1994), 64.

In so-called tragic irony, the contradiction between opposing perspectives creates an ominous "double meaning" of the sentences uttered by the tragic hero on stage.[34] In order to interpret this double meaning, the reader (or the audience of the tragedy) must engage in a process in which thought shuffles back and forth between the two opposed images. Kafka's literary works are frequently described as ironic. Walter Sokel, in his *Franz Kafka: Tragik und Ironie* (1964), also discussed in the Introduction to this book, claims that irony and tragedy constitute the structuring principles of Kafka's late and early literary works respectively. According to Sokel, we may understand Kafka's irony to be derived from a conflict between the perspective of the protagonist, who insists on ideals of purity and autonomy, and the perspective of the narrator and of the reader, who witness how the actions of the protagonist constantly undermine his limited perspective.[35]

In the context of Kafka's stereoscopic style, however, the problem with most concepts of irony, tragic or otherwise, is that they locate the conflicting images at two different levels of insight. Seen this way, reflection is not just a cognitive movement back and forth between juxtaposed images but also a movement vertically up and down between, on the one hand, the limited perspective of the protagonist or the tragic hero and, on the other, the greater insight of the narrator, the reader, or the theater audience. Accordingly, irony tends to be associated with the affective tones of mockery, derision, and contempt.[36] A still unsurpassed description of irony's condescending mood is found in Søren Kierkegaard's *The Concept of Irony* (1841): "it travels around, so to speak, in an exclusive incognito and looks down pitying from this high position on ordinary, prosaic talk."[37]

In "The Judgment," however, and in Kafka's literary stereoscopes in general, the orderly and the disorderly image differ in terms of the applicability of the law—not in terms of the superiority of knowledge.

---

34 Arnold Hug, "Der Doppelsinn in Sophokles Oedipus König," *Philologus*, no. 31 (1872); for an overview of the theory of tragic irony, see Christoph Menke, "Ästhetik der Tragödie: romantische Perspektiven," in *Tragödie – Trauerspiel – Spektakel*, ed. Christoph Menke and Bettine Menke (Berlin: Theater der Zeit, 2007).

35 Sokel, *Franz Kafka*, 21. For Sokel's own modification of this view, see "Beyond Self-Assertion: A Life of Reading Kafka," in *A Companion to the Works of Franz Kafka*, ed. James Rolleston (Rochester, NY: Camden House, 2002).

36 For a historical overview of the affective dimension of irony, see Hutcheon, *Irony's Edge*, 35–41.

37 Søren Kierkegaard, *The Concept of Irony, with Continual Reference to Socrates*, trans. Howard V. Hong and Edna H. Hong (Princeton, NJ, and Oxford: Princeton University Press, 1989), XIII 323.

Here reflection is a process in which thought moves horizontally back and forth between two images at the same level of insight. To be sure, Bendemann Senior says "true, but truer still" when juxtaposing the two images of Georg's social existence, but the prioritizing of the disorderly image as "truer still" appears to be a strategic move on the part of the father, not a defining feature of the two images. Generally, the condescending affective tone often associated with irony sits badly with Kafka's prose style.

Nevertheless, aesthetic reflection in Kafka might well be described as ironic on the premise that we clarify what we mean by a "limited perspective" as described above. In the stereoscopic style, the perspective of the protagonist is not shown to be limited in comparison to the superior perspective of the narrator or the reader, I would argue. Rather, the two images mutually limit each other simply by being juxtaposed. By comparing two disjunctive images of the same community, the process of reflection produces an awareness of the limitedness of *both* images in so far as they can have only partial access to truth. The figuration of Georg as an innocent child is exposed as having only limited validity when juxtaposed with the figuration of the same Georg as a devilish man, and vice versa.

Second, aesthetic reflection is also often thought of as self-reflection, self-reference, and metafiction. According to the German *Frühromantiker* Friedrich Schlegel's influential theory about "transcendental poetry," artistic reflection allows the work of literature to "present the productive together with the product" and thus to be "simultaneously poetry and poetry of poetry."[38] Viewed via this lens, reflection is a process in which thought turns back from the literary image to the act of writing that constructed the image. The idea of the artwork's turn back upon itself is supported by the mixed Greek and Latin etymology of the word *re-flectio*—originally a reference to the bent shape of the shepherd's crook.[39] Thus, this kind of reflective process draws attention to the constructedness of the literary representation.

Kafka researchers have rightly described Kafka's literary works as self-reflective in this way. "The Judgment" starts out with a young man—whose name, according to Kafka, is strangely similar to his own—sitting at his desk thinking about his writing. In general, writing scenes, writing desks, and typewriters are frequent motifs in Kafka's works. Sometimes Kafka even refers obliquely to his own

---

38 Friedrich von Schlegel, *Philosophical Fragments* (Minneapolis, MN: University of Minnesota Press, 1991), 50, translation modified.
39 Robert Siegle, *The Politics of Reflexivity: Narrative and the Constitutive Poetics of Culture* (Baltimore, MD, and London: Johns Hopkins University Press, 1986), 1.

earlier literary works, turning his writing into "semi-private games" of some kind.[40]

To understand Kafka's stereoscopic style according to this concept of reflection, however, we must be certain to fully understand the process of construction this reflection is said to turn back upon. Indeed, "The Judgment" can be interpreted as a self-reflective text inviting the reader to turn back from the images of specific communities to the act of writing by which Kafka constructed these images.[41] It is evident, however, that this narrow concept of reflection is of no use in an investigation of Kafka and the political. All too often, in fact, aesthetic reflection is discussed as if the literary work were either self-reflectively directed toward the construction of the representation or mimetically directed toward the content of the representation—in short, as if reflection and representation were mutually exclusive.[42]

Nonetheless, it is possible to describe aesthetic reflection in Kafka as self-reflection on the condition that we clarify what we mean by "constructing an image." The stereoscopic style not only makes the reader turn back to the writer's construction of images, in this case Kafka's writing of "The Judgment." Posing a broader question, it also makes the reader turn back to the conditions of possibility for forming images of communal life in general. These are the preconditions for imaging sociality shared by the writer, the narrator, the fictional characters, and even the reader of the story. To put it another way, the aesthetic reflection draws attention to the social imaginary on the basis of which a world is configured and not just to the literary imaginary on the basis of which a work is constructed.

Closing in on Schizophrenia

In a sense, there is nothing new about what I am saying about Kafka's stereoscopic style, given that the stereoscope has been a hidden metaphor in a century of Kafka research. One of the first critical texts written about Kafka, published by the Austrian author Robert Musil in August 1914, is a literary review of "The Stoker," the introductory chapter of *Amerika* (or *The Missing Person*), published separately as a short story in May 1913. In this literary review, Kafka's style is characterized as a conflict between disintegration and reserve: "This

---

40 Malcolm Pasley, "Semi-Private Games," in *The Kafka Debate: New Perspectives for Our Time*, ed. Angel Flores (Staten Island, NY: Gordian Press, 1977).

41 Uta Degner's article on "The Judgment," mentioned above, is a fine example of this kind of reading.

42 In Chapter 1, I quoted an influential example of this tendency from Lehmann, "Der buchstäbliche Körper: Zur Selbstinszenierung der Literatur bei Franz Kafka," 220.

narrative is entirely disintegration and entirely reserve,"[43] Musil writes. The German phrase ("Diese Erzählung ist ganz Zerflattern und ganz Gehaltenheit") fleshes out the abstract conflict between disorder and order: "flattern" connotes a "fluttering" or "flapping" movement; "gehalten" implies both the body posture of holding back and the idea of being bound by legal or moral obligations.

In 1915, a year after Musil's review, the expressionist Kasimir Edschmid pointed to a similar conflict in Kafka's story "The Metamorphosis." According to Edschmid, Kafka "forces the miracle down to earth and weaves it, matter-of-factly as something entirely habitual, into the course of his story 'The Metamorphosis,' which is perceived all but drily-humanly."[44] In 1916, the literary scholar Oskar Walzel followed up by asserting that Kafka narrates the strange and incredible content as if it were "a part of reality."[45] And in 1921, the writer and essayist Kurt Tucholsky elegantly diagnosed Kafka's images as "closing in on schizophrenia" because they are "blossoming with the fantastic, but at the same time are firm and factual."[46]

In general, many Kafka readers and researchers have described his literary style as a mixture of reserve and disintegration, the habitual and the miraculous, the factual and the fantastic, the real and the unreal, the natural and the supernatural, the quotidian and the mystical, and so on. In 1955, the German philosopher Theodor W. Adorno made explicit the implicit metaphor by writing that Kafka's texts are designed to agitate the reader's feelings "to a point where he fears that the narrative will shoot toward him like a locomotive in a three-dimensional film."[47]

Where I differ from most descriptions of Kafka's style, however, is when it comes to the understanding of the two juxtaposed images. According to Edschmid, for instance, "The Metamorphosis" "interlaces" an image that depicts the miracle, the uncommon and the ungraspable with an image that "drily-humanly" represents reality as we know it. In its general outline, I agree with this description of Kafka's style as an interlacement of incompatible images. But when Edschmid writes that Kafka "forces the miracle down to earth," he draws a border between up

---

43 Robert Musil, "Literarische Chronik," in *Gesammelte Werke* (Reinbek bei Hamburg: Rowohlt, 1978), 1468.

44 Kasimir Edschmid, "Deutsche Erzählungsliteratur," in *Franz Kafka: Kritik und Rezeption zu seinen Lebzeiten 1912–1924*, ed. Jürgen Born (Frankfurt am Main: Fischer, 1979), 61.

45 Oskar Walzel, "Logik im Wunderbaren," in *Franz Kafka: Kritik und Rezeption zu seinen Lebzeiten 1912–1924*, ed. Jürgen Born (Frankfurt am Main: Fischer, 1979).

46 Kurt Tucholsky, *Gesammelte Werke* (Reinbek bei Hamburg: Rowohlt, 1975), 3,91.

47 Theodor W. Adorno, *Prisms*, trans. Samuel Weber and Shierry Weber (Cambridge, MA: The MIT Press, 1981), 245.

and down, between heaven and earth, and this well-known metaphysical architecture invites us to understand the disorderly image as an image of some transcendent or supernatural phenomenon. According to Edschmid, the strangeness in Kafka's literary works is a "Wunder": a miracle that contradicts the rule-bound everyday order of nature.

A similar understanding of the two images in Kafka's style can be found in Tzvetan Todorov's *The Fantastic: A Structural Approach to a Literary Genre* (1968), probably the most influential exploration of Kafka's dual vision. Todorov's description of the fantastic and its neighboring genres of the marvelous and the uncanny hinges on a distinction between the natural and the supernatural. In the marvelous ("le merveilleux"), the strange phenomenon is viewed as a matter of routine that does not elicit any wonder in the fictional characters or in the reader. In the uncanny ("l'étrange"), the strange phenomenon is perceived as something that, at first sight, does not fit into a realistic universe but turns out to be explicable by the familiar laws of reality. The fantastic, however, is midway between the marvelous and the uncanny. When the status of the strange phenomenon is uncertain, the ambiguous vision ("vision ambigue") makes the reader hesitate:

> In a world which is indeed our world, the one we know, a world without devils, sylphides, or vampires, there occurs an event which cannot be explained by the laws of this same familiar world. The person who experiences the event must opt for one of two possible solutions: either he is the victim of an illusion of the senses, of a product of the imagination—and laws of the world then remain what they are; or else the event has indeed taken place, it is an integral part of reality—but then this reality is controlled by laws unknown to us [. . .]. The fantastic is that hesitation experienced by a person who knows only the laws of nature, confronting an apparently supernatural event.[48]

This description of Kafka's stereoscopic style highlights the reader's reflective interpretation process. According to Todorov, the fantastic is defined by this moment of hesitation in which the fictional character and the reader reflect on whether or not the strange phenomenon is real: "I nearly reached the point of believing . . ." ("j'en vins presque à croire . . .").[49]

---

48 Tzvetan Todorov, *The Fantastic: A Structural Approach to a Literary Genre*, trans. Richard Howard (Cleveland, OH: Press of Case Western Reserve University, 1973), 25.
49 *Introduction à la littérature fantastique* (Paris: Éditions du Seuil, 1970), 35; *The Fantastic*, 31.

As I see it, the problem with Todorov's account is that he, like Edschmid, describes Kafka's literary stereoscope as a juxtaposition of the natural and the supernatural. In so doing, he turns the question of the status of the strange phenomenon into one of metaphysics. Todorov, in other words, ignores the distinction between natural laws and social laws. For him, "the laws of the world" seem to be identical to "the natural laws,"[50] and "the strange phenomenon" is synonymous with "the supernatural phenomenon."[51] Seen this way, only supernatural phenomena violate the established rules of the given reality—not, for instance, impolite behavior in an asbestos factory or unkind attitudes in a group of old friends.

Todorov's distinction between the natural and the supernatural prevents him from giving a satisfying account of the binocular style of Kafka's "The Metamorphosis," which he analyzes in the ultimate chapter of *The Fantastic*. "With Kafka," Todorov argues, "we are [. . .] confronted with a generalized fantastic which swallows up the entire world of the book and the reader along with it."[52] The strange phenomenon, Gregor's metamorphosis into vermin, is not stranger than the fictional world which makes up its background. Indeed, neither Gregor nor any of his family members seem to wonder the least about the metamorphosis. But since Todorov fails to distinguish between natural laws and human laws, he is not able to describe the kind of hesitation and reflection elicited when a phenomenon violates the laws that regulate the *social* reality.

In fact, there are few supernatural events in Kafka's literary works. In "The Judgment," for instance, the reflection process is not set in motion by a supernatural event. The stereoscopic style does not juxtapose natural and supernatural, earth and heaven but, rather, two very mundane images of the communities in question. The laws suspended in the disorderly image are the human laws of friendship and piety, not the laws of nature. To sum up, I contend that Kafka's stereoscopic style should not be understood metaphysically (based on the distinction between the natural and the supernatural) but, rather, politically (based on the distinction between the orderly and the disorderly configuration of community).

Edschmid was one of Kafka's first reviewers, so of course he read the appraisal carefully. According to Gustav Janouch's somewhat unreliable book about his conversations with Kafka, a book published many years

---

50 In the French original, Todorov writes about "les lois du monde" and "les lois naturelles," *Introduction à la littérature fantastique*, 29.
51 Todorov, *The Fantastic*, 32.
52 *The Fantastic*, 174.

after Kafka's death and even after the publication of Kafka's diaries, Kafka was annoyed by Edschmid's drawing of a border between heaven and earth. "The young Prague citizen Franz Kafka forces the miracle down to earth," Edschmid wrote. As Janouch has it, Kafka comments:

Edschmid speaks of me as if I were a constructor [*Konstrukteur*]. Whereas I am only a very mediocre, clumsy draughtsman [*Abzeichner*]. Edschmid claims that I introduce miracles into everyday events. That is, of course, a serious error on his part. The everyday is itself a miracle! All I do is reproduce it. Possibly, I also illuminate matters a little.[53]

Kafka probably never said this, but the phrasing is useful anyway: Kafka does not construct miracles or call them down from some kind of supernatural beyond; he merely depicts—literally "traces up" (and maybe also illuminates)—a disorder that already exists in everyday life.

Constructive Destruction

Kafka's numerous letters and aphorisms on Søren Kierkegaard take issue with the ethical and political content of his works, especially *Fear and Trembling*, as we shall see in Chapter 9. A single aphorism from February 1918, however, addresses the aesthetic experience of Kierkegaard's prose:

There is a magic spell accompanying his argument of the case. One can escape from an argument into the world of magic, from a magic spell into logic, but both simultaneously are crushing, all the more since they constitute a third entity, a living magic or a destruction of the world that is not destructive but constructive.[54]

---

53 "Edschmid spricht von mir so, als ob ich ein Konstrukteur wäre. Dabei bin ich nur ein sehr mittelmäßiger, stümperhafter Abzeichner. Edschmid behauptet, daß ich Wunder in gewöhnliche Vorgänge hineinpraktiziere. Das ist natürlich ein schwerer Irrtum von seiner Seite. Das Gewöhnliche selbst ist ja schon ein Wunder! Ich zeichne es nur auf. Möglich, daß ich die Dinge auch ein wenig beleuchte." Gustav Janouch, *Gespräche mit Kafka: Aufzeichnungen und Erinnerungen* (Frankfurt: Fischer, 1981), 90; *Conversations with Kafka*, trans. Goronwy Rees (New York: New Directions, 2012), 74, translation modified.

54 "Neben seiner Beweisführung geht eine Bezauberung mit. Einer Beweisführung kann man in die Zauberwelt ausweichen, einer Bezauberung in die Logik, aber beide gleichzeitig erdrücken zumal sie etwas drittes sind, lebender Zauber oder nicht zerstörende sondern aufbauende Zerstörung der Welt" (NS2 105: DF 103, translation modified).

It is an aphorism paradoxical to the verge of incomprehensibility. Accordingly, this abstract statement about the constructive destruction of the world is taken by Kafka scholars to refer to practically any kind of destruction.[55] Yet I will argue that the paradox makes sense when viewed in the context of Kafka's stereoscopic style. In this light, the indefinite pronoun "one" ("man") refers to the reader who tries to maneuver between the two different modes of presentation that characterize Kierkegaard's hybrid works.[56] One stereoscopic image represents a logical world ordered by philosophical and theological concepts, in particular the Hegelian conceptuality that gives shape to Kierkegaard's prose. By contrast, the other image represents the world of magic created by Kierkegaard's literary devices, not least the multitude of rhetorical images, short narratives, everyday observations, jokes and puns. On the title page of *Fear and Trembling*, Kierkegaard himself describes this characteristic mixture of philosophy and literature as "A Dialectical Lyric."[57]

According to Kafka, then, Kierkegaard's oeuvre offers a mixed aesthetic experience in so far as the literary magic accompanies (literally, "goes along with") the philosophical argument.[58] If Kierkegaard's prose style were structured only by philosophical concepts, the reader could have escaped into some imaginary world; if the style consisted only in literary imaginations, the reader could have sidestepped it into sober-minded conceptual cogency. But the concurrence of philosophical argument and literary magic traps the reader, causing the reading process to become a crushing, oppressing, or suffocating aesthetic experience ("erdrücken").[59]

---

55 See, for instance, Richard T. Gray, *Constructive Destruction: Kafka's Aphorisms, Literary Tradition, and Literary Transformation* (Tübingen: M. Niemeyer, 1987), 19; Dieter Hasselblatt, *Zauber und Logik: Eine Kafka-Studie* (Cologne: Wissenschaft und Politik, 1964), 95; Doris Kolesch, *Aufbauende Zerstörung: Zur Paradoxie des Geschichts-Sinns bei Franz Kafka und Thomas Pynchon* (Frankfurt am Main and New York: P. Lang, 1996).

56 In this, I follow the interpretations of Richard T. Gray et al., *A Franz Kafka Encyclopedia* (Westport, CT: Greenwood Press, 2005), 159–60; Wolfgang Lange, "Über Kafkas Kierkegaard-Lektüre und einige damit zusammenhängende Gegenstände," *Deutsche Vierteljahrsschrift für Literaturwissenschaft und Geistesgeschichte* 60, no. 60 (1986): 302.

57 For a discussion of Kierkegaard's mixture of styles, see my own *Tanken i billedet: Søren Kierkegaards poetik* (Copenhagen: Gyldendal, 1998); an English excerpt can be found in "Monstrous Aesthetics: Literature and Philosophy in Søren Kierkegaard," *Nineteenth-Century Prose* 32, no. 1 (2005).

58 "geht eine Bezauberung mit."

59 This interpretation of Kafka's aphorism finds support in a letter written by the author to Brod one month earlier. Here he describes Kierkegaard's works *Either/ Or* from 1843 and *The Instant* from 1855 as the two lenses of a stereoscope

According to the above interpretation of Kafka's aphorism on Kierkegaard, the paradoxical concluding sentence about the "destruction of the world that is not destructive but constructive" describes the reflective aesthetic experience orchestrated by Kierkegaard's stereoscopic style. In the next chapter, I will explore how the reader's difficulties in dealing with the simultaneity of philosophical argument and literary magic, of orderly and disorderly image, can be said to be both crushing and, somehow, creative.

Bourgeoisification of Nothingness

"Something like the wish to hammer together a table with meticulous and orderly craftmanship, and simultaneously to do nothing at all," Kafka wrote in the Laurenziberg text. In the years in which he did not write any fictional texts, the years before and after this short text, he had, among other things, taken lessons in a carpenter's shop, which is possibly why he chose to exemplify his reflections on literature by turning to woodwork. But the example also refers to Plato's theory about literature's function in society. In *The Republic*, Socrates, who Plato uses as his spokesman, argues that literature, and mimetic art in general, is not a good thing for the Greek city-state and for the individual Greek citizen. To drive home his argument, Socrates mentions a number of different craftsmen, among them a carpenter, a shoemaker, and a general, each with deep knowledge of their craft. In the words of the Laurenziberg text, these craftsmen are indeed capable of doing their work "with meticulous and orderly craftsmanship." On the other hand, the poet, when he depicts shoemaking, or generalship, or anything else in his literary work, knows nothing of the rules of these crafts; "the only thing he knows anything about is imitation."[60] That the creator of images lacks knowledge is expressed in the famous analysis of the three kinds of beds. God makes the idea of the bed, the bed that really is; the carpenter makes the material bed, a likeness of the idea of the bed; and the painter makes only a mere image of a material bed as it appears, a *phantasmaton* "at a third remove from the truth."[61]

("Gläser"): "*Either/Or* and *The Instant* are certainly two very different lenses through which one can examine this life forwards or backwards and of course also in both directions at the same time" ("es sind das wirklich zwei sehr verschiedene Gläser (Entw.-Oder und Augenblick) durch die man dieses Leben nach vorwärts oder rückwärts und natürlich auch nach beiden Richtungen zugleich untersuchen kann" [B4 31; LFFE 200]).

60 Plato, *The Republic*, trans. Tom Griffith (Cambridge: Cambridge University Press, 2000), 601b.

61 *The Republic*, 597a.

Later in the same chapter, Plato generously lets Socrates create space for the defenders of literature: "I suppose we might allow those of her defenders who have no gift for poetry, but are lovers of poetry, to speak in prose on her behalf, and tell us she is not only pleasurable but also a good thing—for political regimes and individual human lives. We'll be good listeners."[62]

The Laurenziberg text can be understood as Kafka accepting Socrates's challenge to defend literature. Thanks to his classical education from the Altstädter Gymnasium (Old Town High School), Kafka was able to read the works of Plato in Greek. And according to Janouch, he and Kafka even had a conversation about Plato's critique of the poet in *The Republic*.[63] Kafka not only reuses Plato's carpenter but, as we shall see below, draws on the Platonic distinction between the worlds of ideas and the world of appearances, the "Scheinwelt."

In spite of the Platonic framework, however, Kafka offers an entirely different account of the function of literature. According to Plato, it is a problem that the poet has no knowledge of the craftsmanship which he depicts; due to this lack of knowledge, "the art of imitation is a far cry from truth."[64] But for Kafka, the suspension of the rules of meticulous and orderly craftsmanship is not a problem; it is a possibility. In a stereoscopic view of life, we would be able to recognize the hammering as, simultaneously, complying and not complying with the rules of craftsmanship, "whereby certainly the hammering would have become still bolder, still more determined, still more real and, if you will, still more insane [*noch irrsinniger*]." Here the suspension of the rules does not take us a step away from the reality, as Plato would argue, but rather takes us a step closer to reality ("still more real"). The important word in the quote is "whereby" ("wodurch"), linking the increase in boldness, determination, and reality to the preceding sentence about the stereoscopic view of the hammering.

In other words, while Plato's argument about the function of literature hinges on a concept of knowledge, Kafka's argument hinges

---

62 *The Republic*, 607d.
63 In Janouch's opinion, Kafka argued that Plato's exclusion of the poet from the community of the state was perfectly reasonable: "Poets try to give men a different vision, in order to change reality. For that reason, they are politically dangerous elements, because they want to make a change. For the State, and all its devoted servants, wants only one thing, to persist." ("Die Dichter versuchen es, dem Menschen andere Augen einzusetzen, um dadurch die Wirklichkeit zu verändern. Darum sind sie eigentlich staatsgefährliche Elemente, denn sie wollen ändern. Der Staat und mit ihm alle seine ergebenen Diener wollen nämlich nur dauern.") Janouch, *Conversations with Kafka*, 140. *Gespräche mit Kafka: Aufzeichnungen und Erinnerungen*, 158.
64 Plato, *The Republic*, 598b.

on aesthetic reflection. For Kafka, literature is not meant to make the reader knowledgeable about the laws of reality; its task, rather, is to prompt the reader to think about these laws in the reflective process of comparing an orderly image with its disorderly version.

If this is a defense of literature, however, it is a defense toward which Kafka himself expresses skepticism. According to the 36-year-old author of the Laurenziberg text, there was something wrong with his own wish to create a stereoscopic style: "A beautiful wish, perhaps, if I had wished it rightly." Apparently, the problem is not the wish in itself but, rather, the way in which he wished it as a young man. In the passage's final lines, Kafka returns to his own erroneous way of wishing:

> [. . .] still more determined, still more real and, if you will, still more insane. But he could not wish in this way, for his wish was no wish, it was merely a defense, a bourgeoisification of nothingness, a touch of liveliness that he wanted to give to nothingness, to that empty space in which he had by then scarcely taken his first conscious steps, but which he already felt as his element. It was at that time a sort of farewell that he took from the illusory world of youth [*Scheinwelt der Jugend*]; although it had never directly deceived him, but only caused him to be deceived by the speeches of all the authorities around him. Thus had the necessity of his "wish" arisen.[65]

The orderly image of the world of youth represents life as regulated by laws formulated in the speeches of the authorities around the young Kafka. The disorderly image, on the other hand, represents a nothingness, an empty space of literature "in which he had by then scarcely taken his first conscious steps." At that time, the wish to attain a stereoscopic view of life, juxtaposing rule-bound space and empty space, liveliness and nothingness, appeared to be necessary because of the need to leave behind the illusory world of youth.

---

65 "wodurch ja da Hämmern noch kühner, noch entschlossener, noch wirklicher und wenn Du willst noch irrsinniger geworden wäre. Aber er konnte gar nicht so wünschen, denn sein Wunsch war kein Wunsch, er war nur eine Verteidigung, eine Verbürgerlichung des Nichts, ein Hauch von Munterkeit, den er dem Nichts geben wollte, in das er zwar damals kaum die ersten bewußten Schritte tat, das er aber schon als sein Element fühlte. Es war damals eine Art Abschied, den er von der Scheinwelt der Jugend nahm; sie hatte ihn übrigens niemals unmittelbar getäuscht, sondern nur durch die Reden aller Autoritäten rings herum täuschen lassen. So hatte sich die Notwendigkeit des 'Wunsches' ergeben" (T 854; GWC 109, translation modified).

This is why it was a beautiful wish—even if, according to the mature Kafka, the defensive fashion in which it was wished was not right. In a sense, the problem is that Kafka accepted Socrates's challenge to step up as a defender of literature in the manner of, say, Philip Sidney, Percy Bysshe Shelley, and Martha Nussbaum. Interestingly, Kafka uses the word "defense" as a parallel to "bourgeoisification" or "embourgeoisement." In German, this parallelism is underlined by an alliteration: "eine Verteidigung, eine Verbürgerlichung des Nichts." According to the Grimms' *Deutsches Wörterbuch*, the word "Verbürgerlichung" has both a sociological and a legal meaning. It refers to the integration of a social class such as the working class or the nobility into the social norms of the bourgeoisie ("bürgerliche sitten annehmen"). As a synonym to "Einbürgerung," it also denotes the process of naturalization through which a foreigner is granted citizenship of a political community ("das bürgerrecht erwerben"). In both meanings of the word, however, the juxtaposition of order and disorder is understood as an integration or domestication of disorderliness into a pre-given order. To defend and domesticate the nothingness of literature is to make it admissible to the order of things.

Unfortunately, Kafka says nothing about how to wish for a stereoscopic style in a non-domesticating way. In February 1920, he had not written any fictional texts since his first attack of tuberculosis in the autumn of 1917, so maybe he had good reasons for not articulating a literary strategy. In the next chapter, however, I want to show that the right way in which to wish for a stereoscopic style, according to Kafka, is offensive rather than defensive. One should not wish for a bourgeois integration of disorder into the pre-given order of things but, rather, for a revolutionary reconfiguration of the well-ordered community by means of aesthetic reflection.

Four Storming the Border

The Function of Kafka's Stereoscopes:
"Researches of a Dog"

"This past week I suffered something very like a breakdown; the only one to match it was on that night two years ago; apart from then I have never experienced its like. Everything seemed over with, even today there is no great improvement to be noticed."[1] In a famous diary entry of January 16, 1922, Franz Kafka describes a serious physical and nervous breakdown as a pursuit or a hunt ("ein Jagd") driven forward by incessant self-observation ("Selbstbeobachtung"). Self-observation, we are led to understand, can become a pursuit when, unable to produce stable images of the self, it becomes a never-ending matter of hunting down any image at all:

This pursuit takes the direction away from humanity. The solitude that for the most part has been forced on me, in part voluntarily sought by me—but what was this if not also by force?—is now losing all its ambiguity and goes to the utmost. Where is it leading? The strongest likelihood is that it may lead to madness; there is nothing more to say, the pursuit goes right through me and rends me asunder. Or I can—I can?—manage to keep my feet, if only to the tiniest part, and thus let myself be carried along by the pursuit. Where, then, shall I be brought? "Pursuit," indeed, is only an image, I can also say, "a storming of the last earthly border," a storming, moreover, launched from below, from the

---

1 "Es war in der letzten Woche wie ein Zusammenbruch, so vollständig wie nur etwa in der einen Nacht vor 2 Jahren, ein anderes Beispiel habe ich nicht erlebt. Alles schien zuende und scheint auch heute durchaus noch nicht ganz anders zu sein" (T 877; D 398).

humans, and since this too is an image, I can replace it by the image of a storming from above, aimed at me from above.[2]

In this dense passage, Kafka twice asks a question about the direction of the wild pursuit of self-observation ("Where is it leading?" and "Where, then, shall I be brought?"). Most likely, it is leading nowhere; the pursuit will end up in madness. It will probably go right through him, rendering him asunder. This seems so likely that there is, in a sense, nothing more to say· "Everything seemed over with." Yet even so, Kafka also remarks on the possibility that this uncontrollable self-observation might, in fact, lead somewhere, provided that he can manage to keep his feet and let himself be carried along by the pursuit. In order to grasp this second possibility, Kafka switches the metaphor from "Jagd" to "Ansturm": "'Pursuit,' indeed, is only an image," Kafka meditates, "I can also say, 'a storming of the last earthly border.'"

In the last paragraph of the diary entry, Kafka suddenly shifts the focus from suffering a breakdown to writing literature. When describing the wild pursuit, it seems, he was giving not only an account of his psychological condition; he was also taking stock of his entire literary project, in a sense looking back at his oeuvre a couple of years before his death:

This entire literature is a storming of the border and it would have—if only Zionism had not gotten in the way—easily been able to develop into a new secret teaching, a Cabala. There are intimations of this. Though of course it would require genius of an unimaginable kind to strike root again in the old centuries, or create the old centuries anew and not spend itself withal, but only then begin to flower forth.[3]

---

2 "Dieses Jagen nimmt die Richtung aus der Menschheit. Die Einsamkeit, die mir zum größten Teil seit jeher aufgezwungen war, zum Teil von mir gesucht wurde—doch was war auch dies anderes als Zwang—wird jetzt ganz unzweideutig und geht auf das Äußerste. Wohin führt sie? Sie kann, dies scheint am Zwingendsten, zum Irrsinn führen, darüber kann nichts weiter ausgesagt werden, die Jagd geht durch mich und zerreißt mich. Oder aber ich kann—ich kann?—sei es auch nur zum winzigsten Teil mich aufrechterhalten, lasse mich also von der Jagd tragen. Wohin komme ich dann? 'Jagd' ist ja nur ein Bild, ich kann auch sagen 'Ansturm gegen die letzte irdische Grenze' undzwar Ansturm von unten, von den Menschen her und kann, da auch dies nur ein Bild ist, es ersetzen durch das Bild des Ansturmes von oben, zu mir herab" (T 877–8; D 399).

3 "Diese ganze Litteratur ist Ansturm gegen die Grenze und sie hätte sich, wenn nicht der Zionismus dazwischen gekommen wäre, leicht zu einer neuen Geheimlehre, einer Kabbala entwickeln können. Ansätze dazu bestehn.

Clearly writing to himself rather than to the literary public, Kafka does not feel the need to explain what he means by "storming," "border," and "Cabala." Understandably, this hermeticism has troubled Kafka researchers.[4] In this context, however, I will not put forward an interpretation of the diary entry but restrict myself to some comments on its metaphors. Even if Kafka writes that the idea of a pursuit is "only an image" ("nur ein Bild"), his use of metaphorical images offers important insights into his ideas about the function of literature.

In fact, the final passage uses two incompatible metaphors, one military and one organic. First, literature is depicted as a storming of the border (or, in a more direct translation, without the indefinite article: "this entire literature is storming of the border.") The German word "Ansturm," designating an assault or an onslaught, suggests a positive answer to the question about the probable outcome of the wild pursuit. The storming of a city or a fortress, for instance, is a kind of event that does not only lead to destruction and madness; in some cases, a successful military assault might even bring about a reconfiguration of a political situation.

Second, literature is also pictured as the work of a genius able to "strike root again in the old centuries, or create the old centuries anew." Once again, Kafka's image implies an idea of a reconfiguration of the order of things, even if the recreating and rejuvenating moment would demand genius of an unimaginable kind.

In this chapter, I want to consider what Kafka might mean when he depicts this entire literature as storming the border and striking root in the old centuries. It is my contention that he uses these incompatible metaphors in an effort to grasp the function of literature: to storm the border and to create old centuries anew is to bring about a political moment in which the foundation of communal life is transformed. In other words, I have now reached the third and last of my three theses, according to which the function of Kafka's stereoscopic style is to challenge the reader to reconfigure the order of things. As I see it, this

---

Allerdings ein wie unbegreifliches Genie wird hier verlangt, das neu seine Wurzeln in die alten Jahrhunderte treibt oder die alten Jahrhunderte neu erschafft und mit dem allen sich nicht ausgibt, sondern jetzt erst sich auszugeben beginnt" (T 878; D 399).

4   Too many Kafka researchers have interpreted this diary entry based on what the word "border" means to them. For a cabbalistic interpretation, see Harold Bloom, *Ruin the Sacred Truths: Poetry and Belief from the Bible to the Present* (Cambridge, MA: Harvard University Press, 1989); for a Christian interpretation, see Hulda Göhler, *Franz Kafka: Das Schloss, "Ansturm gegen die Grenze", Entwurf einer Deutung* (Bonn: Bouvier, 1982); for an avant-garde aesthetic interpretation, see Maurice Blanchot, *La part du feu* (Paris: Gallimard, 1949), 25.

particular kind of political thinking has the structure of a political moment in the Arendtian sense of the term: an act of world-building that reshapes the foundation of communal life.

Bulwarks of Silence That We Are

Prior to his breakdown in January 1922, Kafka had written nothing for five years other than a number of aphoristic texts, among them the Laurenziberg text discussed in the last chapter. Two weeks after writing it, however, against all odds he suddenly started to write again, embarking on his third and final novel *The Castle*, the uncompleted story of K., a man who struggles to be recognized as a land surveyor in a foreign village, storming (as it were) the last earthly border (as it is phrased in the diary entry discussed above) between the village and the castle.

In July 1922, Kafka took a short break from work on *The Castle* to write a long fragment of a story which Max Brod published posthumously as "Researches of a Dog." The narrator is an ageing dog taking stock of a hopeless research project on which it has spent its entire life. The aim of the project has been to understand the community of the dogs, to "penetrate" into their nature.[5] In the terminology of the narrating dog, the canine community is referred to, with what seems to be demonstrative awkwardness, as "dogdom" ("die Hundeschaft").

Interestingly, Kafka takes up the metaphor from the breakdown diary entry and lets the researcher dog describe its own scientific endeavours as a storming of the border. Its intention, on one hand, is to gain access; as it explains, it has always felt that it was "cast out and had to run up against the walls of my species like a savage."[6] On the other hand, the dog also wants to escape. "I could have remained quietly among the others," the dog says, and "would not, like some badly behaved child, have had to force my way out of the ranks of grownups."[7] In both cases, however, the walls of dogdom are strong enough to resist the assault: "we stand fast against all questions even our own, bulwarks of silence that we are."[8]

It would seem that the bulwarks of dogdom are built from both blindness and silence. The story's implicit premise is that the race of dogs suffers from a kind of tunnel vision that makes them unable to see

---

5   "In das Wesen der Hunde einzudringen" (NS2 481; SS 160).
6   "während ich mich bisher im Innersten ausgestoßen fühlte und die Mauern meines Volkes berannte wie ein Wilder" (NS2 469; SS 154).
7   "Dann hätte ich mich aber auch gar nicht absondern müssen, hätte ruhig unter den anderen bleiben können, hätte nicht wie ein unartiges Kind durch die Reihen der Erwachsenen mich hinausdrängen müssen" (NS2 459; SS 150).
8   "wir widerstehen allen Fragen, selbst den eigenen, Bollwerk des Schweigens, das wir sind" (NS2 444; SS 142).

their human masters. "Besides us dogs there are many different kinds of creatures all around—poor, meager, mute beings, whose speech is limited only to certain cries," the researcher dog explains at the beginning of the story.[9] The peculiar blindness to human beings creates philosophical problems. The dogs dance and sing to make food come flying mysteriously down from above and they narrate stories about the "air dogs" ("Lufthunde"), artificial, immature, over-carefully coiffed creatures "supposed to move about most of the time high in the air while doing no visible work just resting."[10] Since humans are invisible, lap dogs seem as if they are flying calmly around high in the air.

Even if the researcher dog suffers from the same blindness as its fellow dogs, it does at least have a feeling that something is not quite right. As a young dog, it runs around annoying its fellow dogs with never-ending questions about the nature of dogdom. Later in life, it sets up complicated experiments in order to solve the mystery of where food comes from. Finally, at the end of its life, it launches into an ambitious project of starving itself in order to gain access to the hidden truth about dogdom.

In the opening lines of the story, the old researcher dog looks back at its happy days as a puppy in order to understand why it chose to embark on this research project:

How my life has changed, and yet how, at heart, it has not! If I now think back and summon up remembrance of the times when I was still living in the midst of dogdom, taking part in all its concerns, a dog among dogs, on closer scrutiny however I soon find that something was not quite right from the very beginning, that a little fracture was in place, a slight discomfort would come over me in the midst of the most venerable of public arrangements, sometimes even in the closest circle of friends; no, not sometimes, but actually quite often, the mere sight of another dog, someone dear to me—the mere sight of it, as if I were seeing it for the first time somehow filled me with embarrassment, fright, helplessness, even despair.[11]

---

9 "Es gibt außer uns Hunden vierlei Arten von Geschöpfen ringsumher, arme, geringe, stumme, nur auf gewisse Schreie eingeschränkte Wesen" (NS2 425; SS 132).

10 "dieser Hund sollte wie man erzählte, meistens hoch in der Luft sich fortbewegen, dabei aber keine sichtbare Arbeit machen sondern ruhen" (NS2 447; SS 143).

11 "Wie sich mein Leben verändert hat und wie es sich doch nicht verändert hat im Grunde! Wenn ich jetzt zurückdenke und die Zeiten mir zurückrufe, da ich noch inmitten der Hundeschaft lebte, teilnahm an allem was sie bekümmert, ein

The first sentence of this opening passage compares the dog's past (young) life to its present (old) life—"How my life has changed, and yet how, at heart, it has not!"—where the junction of the two interpretations is indicated by a discreet "and yet" ("doch nicht"). A similar shift of perspective is later registered by another "doch"—"on closer scrutiny however" ("bei näherem Zusehen doch").

If we look at the orderly image of the young researcher dog's life, there has been an important change since the time when the dog lived happily "in the midst of dogdom, taking part in all its concerns, a dog among dogs." Seen this way, the young dog was a member of a well-organized community. The dog even describes itself as an "admittedly somewhat cold, reserved, calculating dog but, all in all, a regular dog." "Ein regelrechten Hund": a dog that complies with the rules and norms of the dog community.

Yet if we look at the disorderly image of the young researcher dog, its life has not changed "at heart" or "after all" ("im Grunde"). Viewed this way, it has been alienated from the community of dogs since its youth. Even when the researcher dog lived in the midst of dogdom, it had a feeling that there was "a little fracture" or "a little breakage" in the communal life of dogs. A slight discomfort would sometime come over it "in the midst of the most venerable of public arrangements." In these moments of alienation, the young dog would perceive a dear friend as a foreigner, as if "seeing it for the first time." Looking at a friend as a non-friend, the young dog was filled not with feelings of friendship, lust, or love but, rather, with "embarrassment, fright, helplessness, even despair."

Thus, just like Gregor in "The Judgment," who was, according to his father's sentence, simultaneously an innocent child and a devilish man, the young researcher dog was, simultaneously, a regular dog and a peculiar dog.[12]

What Difficult Things These Are

A couple of pages later, the researcher dog offers another example of the dual vision, this time directing the binocular optics not toward itself as

---

Hund unter Hunden, finde ich bei näherem Zusehen doch, daß hier seit jeher etwas nicht stimmte, eine kleine Bruchstelle vorhanden war, ein leichtes Unbehagen inmitten der ehrwürdigsten volklichen Veranstaltungen mich befiel, ja manchmal selbst im vertrauten Kreise, nein, nicht manchmal, sondern sehr oft, der bloße Anblick eines mir lieben Mithundes, der bloße Anblick, irgendwie neu gesehen, mich verlegen, erschrocken, hilflos, ja mich verzweifelt machte" (NS2 423; SS 132, translation modified).

12   "regelrechten Hund" and "meine Sonderbarkeiten" (NS2 424; SS 132).

an individual dog, but rather toward the entire community of dogs. At the beginning of this passage, the dog affirms its total lack of interest for the poor beings whose speech is limited only to certain cries. I quote the passage at some length because it is crucial to the political thinking of the researcher dog:

> they [the poor, meager, mute beings] leave me cold, I mix them up, I look right through them; but one thing is too striking to have escaped me—namely how little, compared with dogs, they stick together, how they pass each other by in so foreign a way, how neither a high nor a base common interest bind them together, and how every interest rather keeps them more away from each other than what is entailed by the habitual peaceful state of things. We dogs, on the other hand! One can safely say that we live together literally in one single heap, all of us, however much we may differ in other ways as a result of the countless and profound differences that have arisen over time. All in one heap! Something urges us toward one another, and nothing can prevent us from expressing this urge, over and over again; all our laws and institutions, the few that I still know and the countless ones that I have forgotten or never knew, go back to the longing for the greatest happiness we are capable of: warm togetherness. But now the other side of the coin. No species, to my knowledge, lives so widely dispersed as we dogs do, none has so many differences of class, of kind, of vocation—so many that they cannot be surveyed. We who want to hold together—and again and again, in spite of everything, we do succeed, if only on a small scale and even then only in exuberant moments—it is precisely we who live far apart from one another, in peculiar professions often incomprehensible to the next dog, clinging to rules that are not those of dogdom, indeed, are more truly opposed to it. What difficult things these are, things that one would do better to leave unexamined [. . .] and yet these are things that completely fascinate me. Why won't I behave like the others, live in harmony with my people, silently accept whatever disturbs that harmony, overlook it as a little mistake in the great reckoning, and turn forever toward what binds us happily together and not toward what, time and time again, irresistibly, admittedly, tears us out of the circle of the people?[13]

---

13 "mir sind sie, wenn sie mich nicht etwa zu stören versuchen, gleichgültig, ich verwechsle sie, ich sehe über sie hinweg, eines aber ist zu auffallend, als daß es mir hätte entgehen können, wie wenig sie nämlich, mit uns Hunden verglichen, zusammenhalten, wie fremd sie aneinander vorübergehen, wie sie weder ein

The difficult things that completely fascinate the researcher dog can, of course, be interpreted as Jewish matters. It is easy to recognize the Jewish diaspora in the description of the dogs living "widely dispersed" and according to rules that are not those of their own community.[14] Yet such difficult things are peculiar neither to the dog community nor to the Jewish community, pertaining to communal life in general. In "Fellowship," for instance, Kafka approaches similar things without alluding to the Jewish people.

Moreover, as in "Fellowship," the stereoscopic style offers two incompatible images of the community of dogs. In a sense, then, the difficult things only come to light when communal life is seen in binocular vision. This time the junction of the two juxtaposed images of dogdom is indicated by the words "Nun aber das Gegenspiel hierzu." The German "Gegenspiel," a countermove in a game, is often used abstractly as a synonym of "counterpart" or "opposite." The available English translations of the story, however, insist on recreating the intuitive dimension of the sentence by substituting the untranslatable image with sensible figures of coins and pictures: "But now the other side of the coin" and "But now the other side of the picture."[15]

---

hohes noch ein niedriges Interesse verbindet, wie vielmehr jedes Interesse sie noch mehr von einander abhält, als es schon der gewöhnlichen Zustand der Ruhe mit sich bringt. Wir Hunde dagegen! Man darf doch wohl sagen, daß wir alle förmlich in einem einzigen Haufen leben, alle, so unterschieden wir sonst durch die unzähligen und tief gehenden Unterscheidungen, die sich im Laufe der Zeiten ergeben haben. Alle in einem Haufen! Es drängt uns zueinander und nichts kann uns hindern, diesem Drängen genugzutun, alle unsere Gesetze und Einrichtungen, die wenigen die ich noch kenne und die zahllosen, die ich vergessen habe, gehen zurück auf dieses höchste Glück dessen wir fähig sind, das warmen Beisammensein. Nun aber das Gegenspiel hierzu. Kein Geschöpf lebt meines Wissens so weithin zerstreut wie wir Hunde, keines hat so viele, gar nicht übersehbare Unterschiede der Klassen, der Arten, der Beschäftigungen, wir, die wir zusammenhalten wollen—und immer wieder gelingt es uns trotz allem, in überschwänglichen Augenblicken—gerade wir leben weit von einander getrennt, in eigentümlichen, schon dem Nebenhund oft unverständlichen Berufen, festhaltend an Vorschriften, die nicht die der Hundeschaft sind, ja eher gegen sie gerichtet. Was für schwierige Dinge das sind, Dinge, an die man lieber nicht rührt [. . .] und doch Dinge, denen ich ganz und gar verfallen bin. Warum tue ich es nicht wie die anderen, lebe einträchtig mit meinem Volke und nehme das was die Eintracht stört, stillschweigend hin, vernachlässige es als kleinen Fehler in der großen Rechnung und bleibe immer zugekehrt dem was glücklich bindet, nicht dem, was uns immer wieder unwiderstehlich aus dem Volkskreis zerrt" (NS2 425; SS 133, translation modified).

14   This important relation between "Hundeschaft" and "Judentum" has been explored among others by Giuliano Baioni, *Kafka: Literatur und Judentum*, trans. Gertrud Billen and Josef Billen (Stuttgart: Metzler, 1994), 144–67.

15   (SS 133; GWC 142; CS 279).

The "Spiel," on the one hand, is an orderly image according to which dogdom is seen in "the habitual peaceful state of things." According to the researcher dog, communal dog life is characterized by "warm togetherness" and, a couple of pages further down, by "the good, familiar doggish connection" and by "comradeship."[16] In *Political Theology*, written in the same year as "Researches of a Dog," Carl Schmitt, as discussed in Chapter 2, refers to this peaceful state of things as the "normal configuration of the living conditions" to which law can be applied.[17] As is often the case with Kafka's stereoscopic style, the judgment on the configuration of the community is passed by a neutral observer, in the above quotation referred to by the indefinite pronoun "one" ("man"): "One can safely say that we live together literally in one single heap."

The "Gegenspiel," on the other hand, is a disorderly image that represents the dogs not as fellows but as foreigners. In this dissolute mode of being of dogdom, the dogs are very much like the poor, meager, mute beings outside the confines of the dog people. Just like the orderly image, this disorderly image is centered around a judgment on the configuration of the community; this time, however, the judgment has the opposite outcome: "No species, to my knowledge, lives so widely dispersed as we dogs do." In order to support this judgment, the researcher dog offers a detailed sociological description of the reasons why the dogs pass each other by in so foreign a way. Of the "countless and profound differences" between dogs, he offers "differences of class, of kind, of vocation" to explain why dogs live "in peculiar professions often incomprehensible to the next dog."

The social imaginary that shapes the two dissimilar images of dogdom consists in a web of spatial metaphors. The difficult things are difficult because they are abstract, having to do with the nature of the ties that bind together the members of the dog community. While the orderly and the disorderly character of communal life are equally invisible, the researcher dog's figuration renders these abstract things concrete.

First, the metaphor of the heap visualizes the difficult things as an opposition between spatial closeness and spatial distance. "One can safely say that we live together literally in one single heap [*in einem einzigen Haufen*]," the narrator dog asserts, thereby introducing a distinction between lying in one single mass and living widely dispersed. This rhetorical figure, in which, by the way, the figurative

---

16 "die gute vertraute hündische Verbindung" and "Genossenschaft" (NS2 430, 454; SS 135, 139).
17 Schmitt, *Political Theology*, 13, translation modified.

meaning is paradoxically underlined by the word "literally" ("förmlich"),[18] is insisted on a couple of lines further down: "All in one heap!" At a literal level, of course, the orderly and the disorderly image do not differ in terms of the spatial organization of the dogs. Likewise, the "warm togetherness" in the heap is a figurative warmth, not the kind of physical warmth that one can measure with a thermometer.

Second, the metaphor of the circle illustrates the difficult things as a tension between centripetal and centrifugal forces. "Something urges us toward one another," the researcher dog writes, alluding to some unnamed and compelling agency. At the end of the quote, the dog expands on this metaphor by distinguishing between a centripetal force that "binds us happily together" and a centrifugal force that, "time and time again, irresistibly, admittedly, tears us out of the circle of the people."

This contrast between centripetal and centrifugal forces is also a question of law. On the one hand, the researcher dog claims that "all our laws and institutions" go back to a longing for warm togetherness; on the other hand, it concedes that the dogs are clinging to rules or precepts ("Vorschriften") that are not those of dogdom. Later, the dog continues to reflect on questions of "dog law," "good manners," and "principles."[19] Yet, like the narrators in "Fellowship" and in the diary entry about the asbestos factory, the researcher dog is concerned with the form rather than the content of law. We learn that the laws of the dogs "always unconditionally require" that dogs respond when they are called,[20] but apart from that, very little is said about the substance of the laws. The two central judgments of the above passage ("One can

---

18 "Förmlich," a frequent adverb in Kafka's prose, is a tricky word when it comes to figuration. On the one hand, it can be used to stress the literal meaning of a proposition; on the other hand, inversely, it can serve to underline the figurative meaning of a proposition. In fact, a similar ambiguity characterizes the English translation of "förmlich." According to the *Oxford English Dictionary*, "literal" can mean "in a literal manner or sense; exactly," but the word is also more and more frequently "used for emphasis while not being literally true: *I have received literally thousands of letters.*" In Kafka's prose, "förmlich" tends to hover between "really" and "really as if." This tropological ambiguity is a characteristic feature of the social imaginary in his literary works: while the imaginative figures are not literally true, they contribute to the construction of a truth about a given community. For a discussion of Kafka's frequent use of the adverb "förmlich," see my "Verkörperlichung der Symbole: Franz Kafkas Metaphern zwischen Poetik und Stilistik," *Hoffmansthal-Jahrbuch*, no. 10/2002 (2002); Holm, *Stormløb mod grænsen*, Chapter 8.

19 "Hundegesetz," "die guten Sitten" and "Grundsätzen" (NS2 439, 431, 460; SS 140, 136, 150).

20 "was unsere Gesetze bedingungslos immer verlangen" (NS2 431; SS 136).

safely say that we live together literally in one single heap" and "No species, to my knowledge, lives so widely dispersed as we dogs do") do not apply the abstract rules to concrete cases. Rather, they pass judgment on the configuration of dogdom to which dog law could be applied. Thus, the "little fracture" that the young researcher dog perceived in the communal life of dogs is, in legal terms, a fracture that separates dog law from dog life.

Miracles in the Street

Interestingly, the researcher dog has not only an unsettling feeling that something is not quite right in the configuration of the community of dogs; it also has an urge to make things right again. If the dogs would just collaborate, it imagines, they might be able to repair the fissure separating law and life. In the vocabulary of Hannah Arendt, the dog fable articulates a dream of a political moment as the originary *fiat* that would reshape the very foundation of communal life.

In Central Europe in the first decades of the twentieth century, dreams of founding moments and revolutionary beginnings were ubiquitous, not only among Czech and German nationalists, who were beginning to rally in the streets, but also among Kafka's Zionist friends who worked to make real the dream formulated in Theodor Herzl's *The Jewish State* of 1896. In 1918, for instance, Kafka read the manuscript of a novel written by Max Brod, *Das grosse Wagnis* (*The Great Risk*), in which a party of soldiers fighting the First World War found the free state Liberia in the middle of no-man's-land. And in 1920, Kafka read the proofs of his and Max's friend Felix Weltsch's philosophical dissertation *Gnade und Freiheit* (*Grace and Freedom*) in which faith is defined as a founding act, "a free decision, a settlement" ("eine Setzung").[21]

According to the political imagination of the researcher dog, an imagination fueled by the multitude of canine legends, in the time of the first generations of dogs this political moment was imminent. The patriarchs of dogdom were more youthful than the present generation, not yet overburdened by the weight of memory, and thus had a greater opportunity to change the order of things, even if none of them ever succeeded in doing so:

> Even then, of course, miracles did not run freely through the streets for just anyone to catch, but dogs were—I cannot put this any differently—not so doggish as today; the edifice of dogdom was still slack; at that time the true word could still have

---

21 Felix Weltsch, *Gnade und Freiheit: Untersuchungen zum Problem des schöpferischen Willens in Religion und Ethik* (Munich: Kurt Wolff, 1920), 13, my translation.

intervened, determined the build, changed its tune, changed it at will, turned it into its opposite, and that word was there, or at least was near, hanging on the tip of everyone's tongue, everyone could receive it; where has it gone today? Today you could dig into your bowels and still not find it. Our generation may be lost, but it is more innocent than the former one. I can understand the hesitation of my generation; indeed, it is no longer hesitation, it is the forgetting of a dream dreamed a thousand nights ago and forgotten a thousand times: who will scold us merely for forgetting for the thousandth time?[22]

Here the researcher dog, like a number of its fellow narrators from Kafka's late stories, imagines the political community as a building or as the build or frame of a body.[23] According to *Complete Stories*, the researcher dog refers to "the edifice of dogdom;" *Selected Stories* and *The Great Wall of China and Other Short Stories*, on the other hand, has the dog talking more abstractly about "the structure of dogdom" and "the fabric of the dog community."[24] This disagreement derives from an ambiguity in the German word "Gefüge" ("das Gefüge der Hundeschaft"). According to the Grimm brothers' *Deutsches Wörterbuch*, "Gefüge," deriving etymologically from "fügen" ("to join together"), can either mean a building (understood as a joined-together construction) or a build (the proportions, composition, and structure of something such as a body). In this second sense, the concept of the "Gefüge" of dogdom is more or less synonymous with what I call the configuration of the community.

For the present generation of dogs, the narrator imagines, the configuration of the dog community is unalterable. Today the dogs

---

22   "Die Wunder gingen freilich auch damals nicht frei über die Gassen zum beliebigen Einfangen, aber die Hunde waren, ich kann es nicht anders ausdrücken, noch nicht so hündisch wie heute, das Gefüge der Hundeschaft war noch locker, das wahre Wort hätte damals noch eingreifen, den Bau bestimmen, umstimmen, nach jedem Wunsche ändern, in sein Gegenteil verkehren können und jenes Wort war da, war zumindest nahe, schwebte auf der Zungenspitze, jeder konnte es erfahren; wo ist es heute hingekommen, heute könnte man schon ins Gekröse greifen und würde es nicht finden. Unsere Generation ist vielleicht verloren, aber sie ist unschuldiger, als die damalige. Das Zögern meiner Generation kann ich verstehen, es ist ja auch gar kein Zögern mehr, es ist das Vergessen eines vor tausend Nächten geträumten und tausendmal vergessenen Traumes, wer will uns gerade wegen des tausendsten Vergessens zürnen?" (NS2 456; SS 148, translation modified).
23   As we shall see in Chapter 6, the most important example of this is the Chinese narrator of "Building the Great Wall of China" written in 1917.
24   (CS 300; SS 148; GWC 161).

could dig into their bowels (as phrased so strikingly in the quote above) and still not uncover the true word that would change the build of communal life. A couple of pages earlier, the narrator dog concedes that the present generation of dogs have given up their dreams of changing the edifice of dogdom: "Can I see the foundations of our life, intuit their depth, see the workers engaged in building, laboring in the dark, and still expect that all this will be brought to an end, destroyed, abandoned in answer to my questions? No, I truly no longer expect this."[25] Since the important layers of the order of things are situated outside the light of consciousness, in the bowels of the dogs or in the deep foundations of the edifice of dogdom, it is vain to hope for a transformation. At best, one can get a glimpse of the "deep-rootedness of the lie."[26]

The unalterable character of dogdom activates a third meaning of the word "Gefüge." In classical German, "Gefüge" and "Fügung" means "fate" or "destiny," understood as that which the gods have joined together. Given that the canine order of things is fate-like and fixed by transcendent powers, the present generation of dogs are, in a sense, more innocent than the former.

In the days of the forefathers, by contrast, the dog community was somehow changeable. At that time, the researcher dog imagines, the edifice of dogdom was "noch locker," that is, "still slack," "still loose," or "still loosely put together."[27] Given the flexible configuration of community, the possibility of a political moment was still there. The first dogs could have intervened and have "determined the build [den Bau bestimmen], changed its tune [umstimmen], changed it at will, turned it into its opposite tune." The nature of this dreamt-of political moment is defined by the tension between the two near-rhyming words "bestimmen" and "umstimmen." To "bestimmen" is a rational act of determining something; seen in this light, the community of dogs could have made a decision concerning the abstract principles of their shared life. To "umstimmen," on the other hand, is the much more intuitive act of changing the tuning of an instrument to another key, a meaning underlined by the musical metaphor recurring throughout the fable. Regarded as the changing of a tuning, the political moment would not have been a reconstitution of the legal and political order but, rather, a transformation of the deeper-lying configuration of communal life.

---

25   "Sehe ich die Fundamente unseres Lebens, ahne ihre Tiefe, sehe die Arbeiter beim Bau, bei ihrem finstern Werk und erwarte noch immer, daß auf meine Fragen hin alles dies beendigt, zerstört, verlassen wird? Nein, das erwarte ich wahrhaftig nicht mehr" (NS2 443; SS 142).
26   "etwas von der tiefen Verwurzelung der Lüge" (NS2 448; SS 144).
27   (CS 300; GWC 161).

The researcher dog suggests the miracle as a metaphor for a foundational act that could have recreated dogdom with a new "bestimmen" and "umstimmen." While, even at the time of the first generations of dogs, this kind of miracle did not run freely through the streets, the researcher dog concedes, at least the political moment was possible. In other words, the miracle plays the same role for the researcher dog as it does for Hannah Arendt, who, on several occasions, uses it as a metaphor for the political moment as an acting in concert. In *The Human Condition* (1958), Arendt describes the miracle as "the birth of new men and the new beginning, the action they are capable of by virtue of being born."[28] In "Introduction *into* Politics," a manuscript from the same year, she expands on the metaphor: "If the meaning of politics is freedom, that means that in this realm—and in no other—we do indeed have the right to expect miracles. Not because we superstitiously believe in miracles, but because human beings, whether or not they know it, as long as they can act, are capable of achieving, and constantly do achieve, the improbable and unpredictable."[29]

A Common Bite

The present generation of dogs are probably lost, the researcher dog imagines, because they no longer dream of the political moment, today reduced to a dream "dreamed a thousand nights ago and forgotten a thousand times." It should be noted, however, that the researcher dog's dream of a miracle is turned not only backward toward the first generations of dogs but also forward, toward a future moment the dog hopes to bring about. Indeed, this utopian dream underlies the research project and thereby the entire life of the researcher dog.

The forward-directed nature of the dream comes into view in three metaphors that have, more or less, the same tenor as the miracle metaphor. Of these, the last two are hidden in the fable's deleted passages:

> All knowledge, the totality of all questions and all answers, resides in dogs. If only this knowledge could be made effective, if only it could be brought into the light of day, if only dogs did not know so infinitely much more than they admit, than they admit to themselves![30]

28 Hannah Arendt, *The Human Condition* (Chicago: University of Chicago Press, 1998), 247.

29 "Introduction *into* Politics," in *The Promise of Politics* (New York: Schocken, 2005), 114.

30 "Alles Wissen, die Gesamtheit aller Fragen und aller Antworten ist in den Hunden enthalten. Wenn man nur dieses Wissen wirksam, wenn man es nur an den hellen Tag bringen könnte, wenn sie nur nicht so unendlich viel mehr wüßten, als sie zugestehen, als sie sich selbst zugestehen" (NS2 441; SS 141).

[. . .] not only the blood we have in common, also our knowledge, and not only this knowledge, but also the key to it. Without the others I do not have it, I cannot get it without their help, this bone that contains the finest marrow can only be approached in a common bite, with every tooth of every dog.[31]

I do not look at what I am doing myself, only back at my people in order to see if they should perhaps wish to move themselves, if my research should perhaps mind them to move. Am I getting any further with them? I do not know, the all too vital dog people lie, seen with my eyes, in rigor mortis.[32]

Becoming visible, becoming edible, becoming alive—the three parallel metaphors describe the political moment as a kind of *biting in concert*. What is important to realize is that the political moment is imagined as a future event which the dog hopes to bring about through its research project. In a sense, the researcher dog wishes to perform miracles: *if only* the latent knowledge of the dogs could be brought into the light of day, *if only* the fine bone marrow could be accessed, *if only* the research could give the dog people the mind to move themselves.

It is easy to see that the researcher dog is one of the many semi-autobiographical characters that people Kafka's literary works. At the end of his life, the weak, tubercular, and anorexic Kafka takes stock of his authorship by letting a "weak, skinny dog, malnourished and too little concerned about food" look back at its life-long research project.[33] In this portrait of the artist as a young dog, Kafka goes over a number of important events in his own career as a writer, transposing them from human to canine experience. For instance, as we shall see in the next chapter, the story about the young researcher dog's formative meeting with a small group of "music dogs" is also a story about the young Kafka's own formative meeting with Yitzhak Löwy's little troupe

---

31 "[. . .] nicht nur das Blut haben wir gemeinsam, sondern auch das Wissen und nicht nur das Wissen, sondern auch den Schlüssel zu ihm. Ich besitze es nicht ohne die andern, ich kann es nicht haben ohne ihre Hilfe, diesem Knochen, enthaltend das edelste Mark, kann man nur beikommen durch ein gemeinsames Beissen aller Zähne aller Hunde" (NS2A 358, my translation).

32 "ich sehe förmlich gar nicht darauf, was ich tue, sondern immer nur zurück auf mein Volk, ob es sich vielleicht schon rühren mag, ob ihm meine Forschungen schon ein wenig Mut dazu geben./ Komme ich weiter mit ihnen? Ich weiss es nicht, dieses überlebendige Hundevolk liegt, mit meinem Blick gesehen, totenstarr." (NS2A 372, my translation).

33 "Weil ich ein magerer schwacher Hund war, schlecht genährt und zu wenig um Nahrung besorgt" (NS2 439; SS 140).

of Yiddish actors from the Austro-Hungarian province of Galicia in the autumn of 1911.[34]

If we insist on the analogy between the dog's research project and Kafka's writing project, the function of literature—if literature has any function at all—is to bring about a miraculous political moment: to make the people wish to move themselves. In accordance with the third thesis of this book, the stereoscopic style is an apparatus with which to achieve this political aim. By making the reader occ what binds us happily together while simultaneously making her aware of the forces that tear us out of the human circle, the stereoscopic setup might succeed in generating a kind of political thinking that fundamentally restructures and reshapes the configuration of the community.

Reflective Reconfiguration

To grasp how, orchestrated by the binocular format of Kafka's literary works, the reader's reflective aesthetic experience is able to reconfigure the image of community, we may briefly return to Kant's general definition of the concept of reflection.

When I see a spruce, a willow, and a linden, Kant taught us in the last chapter, "I reflect on that which they have in common among themselves, trunk, branches, and leaves themselves, and I abstract from the quantity, the figure, etc., of these; thus I acquire a concept of a tree."[35] According to this definition from the *Jäsche Logic*, reflection is a comparison directed toward a universal concept. Starting out from representations of sensible particulars (in this case trunk, branches, and leaves), we seek to generate a universal empirical concept (a tree). Similarly, Kant, at the very beginning of *Critique of Pure Reason*, describes comparison as a process that aims "to work up the raw material of sensible impressions into a cognition of objects that is called experience."[36]

On a closer look, however, Kant's description of the process of reflection in the *Jäsche Logic* seems a little odd. It is hard to understand how we are to work up the raw materials of sensible impressions if we do not begin the process already holding a universal concept. Without the universal concept of a tree, we would be unable to select three different types of trees for comparison, rather than, for instance, a willow, a brook, and a blackbird. Likewise, we would not be able to focus on the defining features of trees such as trunk, branches, and leaves.

---

34 For a thorough discussion of more or less relevant parallels between the researcher dog's life and Kafka's, see Hartmut Binder, *Kafka-Kommentar zu sämtlichen Erzählungen* (Munich: Winkler, 1975).

35 Kant, *Lectures on Logic*, 592.

36 *Critique of Pure Reason*, B 1.

Scholars have sought to solve this problem by referring to the various accounts of the process of reflection given by Kant outside the *Jäsche Logic*. In some of these, he states that the universal concept must in fact already be present in the process of reflection, if only in an undetermined and intuitive state.[37] In Kantian vocabulary, a universal concept in an undetermined and intuitive state is a "schema." As we saw in Chapter 2, the schema, according to Kant, is "a product and as it were a monogram of pure *a priori* imagination" that enables the application of the concepts of the understanding to the manifold of intuition.[38] In other words, the schema of the imagination is a "mediating representation" halfway between the intellect and the sensible. According to Kant's alternative accounts of the process of reflection, then, the schema plays a central role in both the application and the formation of concepts. The process of reflection that works up the raw material of sensible impressions is, first of all, a working through of the hidden art in the depths of the human soul.

The reflection provoked by Kafka's literary stereoscopes is a thought process in which two juxtaposed images of the community are compared, much like Kant's reflection compared two (or more) images of, for instance, a willow and a linden, and reflected on that which they have in common. The important thing to note is that the reader's reflective work is a working through of the imaginative figures of the community. Social imaginaries are, precisely, cultural repertoires of "mediating representations," swarms of general shapes and figures that mediate between the universal concept of the community and the particular details of human life. Put differently, Kafka's stereoscopic style triggers the reader's reflective work on the hidden art in the depths not of the human soul, but of human culture.

As we have seen above, the process of reflection has destructive and constructive sides; I suggest calling these disfiguration and transfiguration, respectively. First, according to the literary theorist Paul de Man, a disfiguration of a literary text can be defined as "the possibly disruptive mediation of its own figuration."[39] A text is

---

37 This argument has been proposed in Béatrice Longuenesse, *Kant and the Capacity to Judge: Sensibility and Discursivity in the Transcendental Analytic of the Critique of Pure Reason* (Princeton, NJ: Princeton University Press, 1998), 107–30. For further discussion, see Allison, *Kant's Theory of Taste*, Chapters 1 and 2; Robert B. Pippin, *Kant's Theory of Form: An Essay on the Critique of Pure Reason* (New Haven, CT, and London: Yale University Press, 1982), 108–19.

38 Kant, *Critique of Pure Reason*, B177–87.

39 de Man, *The Rhetoric of Romanticism*, 110.

mediating its own figuration, de Man argues, when it is unmasking the mechanisms of its figurative language, thereby undoing the text's mimetic representation of reality by returning it to its status as a figure. In Kafka's stereoscopic style, more specifically, the disfiguration is to be understood as a disruptive mediation on the figuration of the community. The reader's reflective comparison of the two juxtaposed images of the community undoes these images by making them come into view as imaginative figurations.

In Kantian terms, then, the reader's reflective awareness is destructive in so far as it undoes the mediating representations halfway between the intellect and the sensible. The disruptive mediation of the figuration disconnects the universal concept of the community from the particular intuitions of social life. By doing this, it reopens the question of how to apply the concept of the community to a specific group of people or (say) dogs.

As seen above, the miracle of the political moment, according to the researcher dog, would only be possible when deep foundations of the edifice of dogdom were "brought to an end, destroyed, abandoned."[40] Thus, the destructive work on the bulwarks of silence is a prerequisite for making the order of things "slack" or "loose" or, less metaphorically, replaceable by new acts of figuration.

Second, the philosopher Paul Ricoeur explores the ability of a work of fiction "to transform or transfigure reality."[41] In this strictly secular meaning of the concept of transfiguration, it denotes the way in which the world of the text intervenes in the world of action "in order to give it a new configuration or, as we might say, in order to transfigure it."[42] In the context of Kafka's stereoscopic style, his literary works are apparatuses constructed in order to transform or transfigure the reader's experience of the communities in question.

Formulated after Kant, the reader's reflective work is a work of construction in so far as it suggests alternative mediating representations that could link the universal concept of the community to the particular details of social life. The stereoscopic style challenges the reader to plunge into the text's swarm of shapes and figures in order to search out alternative ways of imagining common life—to work up the raw material of sensible impressions of a specific social situation into a cognition that is called experience, as Kant had it. To put it another way, the reader of Kafka's literary stereoscopes is not just a passive spectator to a number

---

40 "beendigt, zerstört, verlassen" (NS2 443; SS 142).
41 Paul Ricoeur, "The Function of Fiction in Shaping Reality," *Man and World* 12, no. 2 (1979): 134.
42 Paul Ricoeur, *From Text to Action: Essays in Hermeneutics II* (London: Continuum, 2008), 10.

of failed attempts to construct coherent images of the community; she is also actively responsible for constructing a more adequate representation of how the individuals stand to each other and where to draw the line between members and non-members of the community.

Formulated with the metaphors of the researcher dog, rather than Kant, transfiguring is "umstimmen." The reader is challenged to do what the first generations of dogs were allegedly on the verge of doing: experiencing a political moment in which it is possible to "bestimmen" and to "umstimmen," to determine the build of the community and to re-tune it.

Thus, the reader's reflective comparison of the two juxtaposed images of the community leads to both the undoing of these images and their redoing. In saying this, I am aware that I have offered only an abstract account of the destructive and the constructive sides of the reflective reconfiguration of the life in common. In the following section, I will continue the reading of "The Judgment" begun in Chapter 3 in order to flesh out how the stereoscopic style disfigures and transfigures the social imaginaries of the short story.

The Political Moment in "The Judgment"

After the publication of "The Judgment" in June 1913, Kafka sent a copy to Felice along with a brief account of how it came into being: "When I sat down to write, after a Sunday so miserable I could have screamed [. . .], I meant to describe a war; from his window a young man was to see a vast crowd advancing across the bridge, but then the whole thing turned in my hands into something else."[43] A description of a vast crowd advancing across a bridge during wartime might well qualify as a description of the storming of a border. But then the whole thing "turned" in Kafka's hands and the advancing mob ended up as a marginal motif. The protagonist Georg Bendemann, trying to make his father remember his friend in Russia, recalls the last time he visited the two of them in Prague, three years earlier, and told them incredible stories about the first Russian Revolution in 1905: "How, for example, on a business trip in Kiev, during a riot he had seen a priest on a balcony cut a broad, bloody cross into the palm of his hand, raise this hand, and appeal to the crowd."[44]

---

43 "Als ich mich zum Schreiben niedersetzte, wollte ich nach einem zum Schreien unglücklichen Sonntag [. . .] einen Krieg beschreiben, ein junger Mann sollte aus seinem Fenster eine Menschenmenge über die Brücke herankommen sehn, dann aber drehte sich mir alles unter den Händen" (BF 394; LF 265).

44 "Wie er z. B. auf einer Geschäftsreise in Kiew bei einem Tumult einen Geistlichen auf einem Balkon gesehen hatte, der sich ein breites Blutkreuz in die flache Hand schnitt, diese Hand erhob und die Menge anrief" (DzL 54; SS 8).

If this political crowd, whether revolutionary or anti-Semitic, is only a marginal motif in the story, the reconfiguration of the order of things is a central issue. Interestingly, the fictional characters are keen on discussing how to organize their shared life. As Georg enters his father's room with the letter to his friend in his pocket, the father says: "You've come to me about this matter in order to talk it over with me."[45] Even if Georg and his father work together every day in the business and have lunch every day "at the same time in a restaurant,"[46] they apparently don't have time to talk over or discuss ("beraten") the arrangement of their common life.

In the father's room, however, father and son discuss not only whether Georg should send the letter to his friend concerning the engagement, but also whether the two of them should switch rooms. At the sight of his father's dark room, Georg exclaims: "That won't do. We are going to have to introduce a whole new way of life for you. And I mean from the ground up. You sit here in the dark and in the living room you'd have a nice light."[47] And at the sight of his father's unclean underwear, Georg suddenly decides how to "arrange for" or "organize" ("einrichten") his father's future, as we saw in the previous chapter: "Yet now in an instant he resolutely made up his mind to take his father along into his future household."[48] Likewise, Georg and his friend in Russia discuss in their correspondence the possibility of the former's moving back to Prague to enjoy a whole new way of life and, some years earlier, the possibility of a whole new way of life for Georg in St. Petersburg.

In all three cases, the discussions of the fictional characters deal with the reconfiguration of communal life from the ground up ("von Grund aus"). Yet none of these discussions lead to an actual reorganization of the community. No change occurs in the story, if by "change" we understand an operation in which human beings rearrange themselves in physical and social space by switching rooms, for instance, or moving to foreign cities.

According to the third thesis of this book, however, the political moment not only takes place in the world of the fictional characters but also in the mind of the reader. In the preceding chapter, we saw how

45 "Du bist wegen dieser Sache zu mir gekommen, um dich mit mir zu beraten" (DzL 51; SS 7, translation modified).
46 "Das Mittagessen nahmen sie gleichzeitig in einem Speisehaus ein" (DzL 49; SS 6).
47 "Das geht nicht. Wir müssen da eine andere Lebensweise für dich einführen. Aber von Grund aus. Du sitzt hier im Dunkel, und im Wohnzimmer hättest du schönes Licht" (DzL 52; SS 8).
48 "Doch jetzt entschloß er sich kurz mit aller Bestimmtheit, den Vater in seinen künftigen Haushalt mitzunehmen" (DzL 55; SS 9).

Georg and his father map out the configuration of communal life with a set of metaphorical axes. In the words of the researcher dog, the two Bendemanns can be described as "workers engaged in building, laboring in the dark," in so far as both of them are busy constructing an image of the community with the tools of a dense web of metaphors (center/periphery, up/down, light/darkness, grown-up/child, and so on). The political thinking prompted by the stereoscopic style of the text can be understood as, at the same time, a destruction and a reconstruction of this collective repertoire of sensible images.

First, the aesthetic reflection is destructive in so far as it disfigures the images of communal life offered by the short story. This disfiguration undoes the short story's mimetic representation of reality by revealing its dependence on the mechanisms of figurative language. In Chapter 3, I distinguished between two dimensions of the process of aesthetic reflection and, hence, two dimensions of the disfiguration.

On the one hand, based on the concept of irony, aesthetic reflection can be understood as a process in which thought shuttles back and forth between the two opposed images of the same community. In this light, the activity of reflection yields an awareness of the *limitedness* of both images, since, for instance, the figuration of Georg as an innocent child undermines the figuration of Georg as a devilish man, and vice versa. In other words, the reader's reflective work can be understood as a de-centering of the images of communal life, exposing them not as objective and absolute truths to be taken at face value but, rather, as contingent interpretations conditioned by limited points of view.[49]

On the other hand, inspired by the concepts of self-reflection, metafiction, and transcendental poetry, I described aesthetic reflection as a process in which thought turns back from images of communal life to the conditions that make the construction of such images possible. In the process of reflection, the reader becomes aware of the *constructedness* of the images of the community, in the case of "The Judgment" by highlighting the swarm of imaginative figures with which Georg, his father, and the narrator of the story represent the social world. Put differently, the reader's reflective work can also be interpreted as a

---

49   In my use of the concept of limitedness, I am inspired by Theodor W. Adorno, who describes the awareness of limitedness ("Beschränktheit") as an important feature of aesthetic experience: "by the strength of insight into the artwork as artwork, these experiences are those in which the subject's petrification in his own subjectivity dissolves and the limitedness [*Beschränktheit*] of his self-positedness is revealed." See Theodor W. Adorno, *Aesthetic Theory*, trans. Robert Hullot-Kentor (Minneapolis, MN: University of Minnesota Press, 1997), 269, translation modified.

denaturalization of the images of communal life because this work makes them appear as the result of a process of construction rather than as natural and unalterable facts.[50]

Second, as we stressed earlier, the aesthetic reflection is not only destructive but also constructive in so far as it transfigures the social imaginary of the short story. When Georg has undressed his father and put him to bed, Bendemann Senior, forcefully throwing the blanket off and standing upright in the bed, exclaims that he, of course, knows the friend in Russia very well. Georg's reaction is surprising:

> Georg looked up at the nightmare image of his father. The St. Petersburg friend, whom his father suddenly knew so well, moved him as never before. He saw him lost in far-off Russia. He saw him at the door of his empty, plundered establishment. He was just barely able to stand among the wreckage of his shelves, the ransacked goods, the collapsing gas brackets. Why had he had to go so far away![51]

At this moment, Georg identifies with his friend in Russia. Suddenly, their distant "relationship of correspondence" is transformed into a much more intimate correspondence.[52] George is moved by his friend as never before, and this newfound affective closeness has consequences for the use of pronouns in the passage.

The pronoun "he" ("er") is used four times. In the first two instances, it refers to Georg, who imagines his friend in far-off Russia; in the third instance, "he" refers to the friend as Georg imagines him; but in the

---

50 In my discussion of the reader's awareness of constructedness, I am inspired by Hegel's famous reading of the Greek tragedies. Building on theories of tragic irony, Hegel describes the unity of the world represented by the Greek tragedy as not a natural unity, but rather "a constructed unity [als eine gemachte], forged by the subjective spirit," that is, as something "belonging to the subject." See Georg Wilhelm Friedrich Hegel, Aesthetics: Lectures on Fine Art, trans. T. M. Knox (Oxford: Clarendon Press, 1975), 1038. My use of Hegel's theory of aesthetic reflection draws heavily on the work of Christoph Menke; see, for instance, Christoph Menke, Tragödie im Sittlichen: Gerechtigkeit und Freiheit nach Hegel (Frankfurt am Main: Suhrkamp, 1996); "The Presence of Tragedy: An Aesthetic Enlightenment," Neue Rundschau 111, no. 1 (2000); "Ästhetik der Tragödie," Tragödie – Trauerspiel – Spektakel (Berlin: Theater der Zeit, 2007).

51 "Georg sah zum Schreckbild seines Vaters auf. Der Petersburger Freund, den der Vater plötzlich so gut kannte, ergriff ihn, wie noch nie. Verloren im weiten Rußland sah er ihn. An der Türe des leeren, ausgeraubten Geschäftes sah er ihn. Zwischen den Trümmern der Regale, den zerfetzten Waren, den fallenden Gasarmen stand er gerade noch. Warum hatte er so weit wegfahren müssen!" (DzL 56; SS 10).

52 "Korrespondenzverhältnis" (DzL 47; SS 5).

final sentence, "Why had he had to go so far away!", the pronoun "he" can refer both to the friend in Russia and to Georg. Interpreted literally, Georg's friend has had to go far away, being lost far from the narrow circle of friends. Interpreted figuratively, however, Georg, too, has had to go far away by alienating himself from his friend and from his father. Thus, being miserably lost to the community, being "Verloren," is a feature Georg and his friend have in common. By way of this grammatical ambivalence, a figure of isolation is suddenly transformed into a figure of commonality. In other words, the text suggests a movement of inversion in which the metaphorical axis center/periphery is turned on its head: the figures of exile and disconnection move into the very center of a new community.

The short story emphasizes this movement of inversion by alluding to the Christian notion of transfiguration. As Georg races down the stairs to execute his father's death sentence by drowning himself in the river, he meets the cleaning woman who, coming upstairs, shouts "Jesus!"[53] During the New Testament's account of the Transfiguration, Jesus, a despised and rejected human being, becomes radiant with glory and a voice from the cloud states: "This is my Son, the Beloved; listen to him!"[54] In the section above, I referred to Ricoeur's secular concept of transfiguration in order to keep a distance from the weighty religious and metaphysical connotations of this term. I wish to carefully retain, however, the subset of its religious connotations that stage the transfiguration as a miraculous movement of inversion in which a marginal figure suddenly becomes a figure for the entire community.

To sum up, "The Judgment" can be seen as literary apparatus constructed in order to bring about a reconfiguration of the representation of the communities portrayed. More specifically, as we have seen, there are two sides to this reflective reconfiguration: disfiguration and transfiguration. Destructively, the reader is made aware of the limitedness and constructedness of the images of the short story, thereby decentering and denaturalizing the representation of life in common. Constructively, the reader is charged with the task of establishing an alternative figuration able to link together the universal concept of the community and the particular details of social life. In this sense, the aesthetic reflection orchestrated by Kafka's stereoscopic style entails both an undoing and a redoing of the image of community.

---

53   (DzL 60; SS 12).
54   Mark 9:7 (NRSV).

The Clocks Are Not in Unison

At the beginning of this chapter, I discussed Kafka's famous diary entry concerning his breakdown in January 1922. The only sentences on which I did not comment describe the structure of the breakdown as a technical apparatus. In this instance the device is not optical but chronometric:

> [. . .] impossible to sleep, impossible to stay awake, impossible to endure life, or, more exactly, the sequence of life. The clocks are not in unison; the inner one runs crazily on at a devilish or demoniac or in any case inhuman pace, the outer one goes along in jerks at its usual speed. What else can happen but that the two worlds split apart, and they do split apart, or at least grind against each other in a frightful manner.[55]

While the outer clock follows the normal sequence or temporal order of human life ("Aufeinanderfolge des Lebens"), continuing at its usual pace, the inner clock shatters the expectation of well-ordered human temporality by moving at its hellish speed. Kafka turns to the remarkable metaphor of "grinding" or "tearing" ("reißen [. . .] an einander") to describe the experience of the ensuing split between the inner and outer worlds.

In the entry's last paragraph, the clash between interior and exterior takes shape as a confrontation between two kinds of Jewishness: "This entire literature is a storming of the border and it would have—if only Zionism had not gotten in the way—easily been able to develop into a new secret teaching, a Cabala." Whereas Zionism is directed outward toward actions in the political reality, Cabala is directed inward toward the religious experience of the individual.

However, it is important to note that Kafka approaches the result of the grinding of outer and inner worlds by posing a question: "What else can happen but . . ." The remaining part of the diary entry shows that this question is not rhetorical. A few lines further down, he poses similar questions to the pursuit that leads away from humanity: "Where is it leading?" and "Where, then, shall I be brought?" As we saw at the beginning of this chapter, Kafka offers both negative and positive

---

55 "[. . .] Unmöglichkeit zu schlafen, Unmöglichkeit zu wachen, Unmöglichkeit
das Leben, genauer die Aufeinanderfolge des Lebens zu ertragen. Die Uhren
stimmen nicht überein, die innere jagt in einer teuflischen oder dämonischen
oder jedenfalls unmenschlichen Art, die äußere geht stockend ihren
gewöhnlichen Gang. Was kann anderes geschehn, als daß sich die zwei
verschiedenen Welten trennen und sie trennen sich oder reißen zumindest an
einander in einer fürchterlichen Art" (T 877; D 398–99).

answers to these questions. It is most likely is that the pursuit will only lead to madness: "there is nothing more to say." Nothing else can happen but that the two worlds will grind against each other in a frightful manner.

Yet Kafka also intimates a positive answer: "Or I can—I can?—manage to keep my feet, if only to the tiniest part, and thus let myself be carried along by the pursuit." Seen this way, the grinding of the two worlds is not just frightful; it may also be fruitful. In the words of the aphorism on Kierkegaard's style discussed in the last chapter, the grinding of worlds would become "a destruction of the world that is not destructive but constructive."[56] In the metaphors of the breakdown diary entry, then, this grinding is a necessary precondition for the foundational act (possible, of course, only for a genius of an unimaginable kind) which strikes root again in the old centuries or creates the old centuries anew.

---

56   (NS2 105; DF 103, translation modified).

Part II

.

Five A Construction of Chance and Laws

Kafka in the Yiddish Theater: Der Meschumed

In his autobiography *Streitbares Leben* (*Embattled Life*, 1960), Max Brod narrates how he and his friend Kafka (in that order) were inspired by the Eastern European Jewish theater companies performing in Prague in the years before the First World War: "A poor, travelling company that wound up in the West and happened to perform in a little café in Prague became [. . .] a turning point in my transformation. Everything shown there was wrong and miserable, but everywhere the right thing shone through, the traditional, venerable, affectionate, and powerful, the Shakespearean insolence, the new which I (and shortly thereafter also Kafka) was absorbed in."[1] The traveling theater troupe, headed by the actor Yitzhak Löwy, came from Lemberg in the Austro-Hungarian province of Galicia, today Lviv in Ukraine. Everything was indeed "wrong and miserable," as Brod writes: the stage of only ten square meters was situated in the back of a café, the doorman used to work in a brothel and was now a pimp, the scenery was made of cardboard, the extras couldn't help giggling, the wigs were slipping off, and on one occasion, two of the actors even started fighting during a performance.[2]

All the same, Brod describes the encounter with Löwy's troupe as a turning point in his own transformation from apolitical aesthete to Zionist activist. For Kafka, too, the experience at Café Savoy on Ziegenplatz was a turning point. He watched at least eleven of the troupe's performances, some of them more than once, became close friends with Löwy, fell in love with one of the actresses, and even started to do some impresario work for the troupe. More than ten years later, in

---

1   Max Brod, *Streitbares Leben* (Munich: Kindler, 1960), 354, my translation.
2   (T 100; D 87).

the autobiographical fable "Researches of a Dog," Kafka describes his encounter with Löwy's troupe allegorically as the young researcher dog's encounter with seven enigmatic music dogs: "In itself it was nothing extraordinary—since then I have often enough seen such things, and even more remarkable ones—but at that time it made a strong, original, indelible impression that set the direction for many later impressions."[3]

After having watched the troupe for the first time on October 5, 1911, Kafka tried to capture the strong, original, indelible impression, as Brod wrote, in his diary: "Some songs, the expression 'yiddische kinderloch,' some of this woman's acting (who, on the stage, because she is a Jew, draws us listeners to her because we are Jews, without any longing for or curiosity about Christians) made my cheeks tremble."[4] In a sense, Kafka's turn to the Jewish tradition started with this trembling of the cheeks at Café Savoy.[5] Prior to October 1911, he had a rather distant relationship with his Jewish background. By the end of the month, however, he was able to name himself in Hebrew: "In Hebrew my name is Amschel, like my mother's maternal grandfather."[6] He began also, "eagerly and happily," to read a number of voluminous scholarly works on Judaism and Yiddish culture, taking detailed notes in his diaries.[7] The first time Kafka met Felice Bauer, in August 1912, they talked about Löwy's company and even flirtatiously agreed to emigrate to Palestine together.[8]

---

3   "An sich war es nichts Außerordentliches, später habe ich solche und noch merkwürdigere Dinge oft genug gesehen, aber damals traf es mich mit dem starken ersten unverwischbaren, für vieles folgende richtunggebenden Eindruck" (NS2 427; SS 134, translation modified).

4   "Bei manchen Liedern, der Aussprache 'jüdische Kinderloch', manchem Anblick dieser Frau, die auf dem Podium, weil sie Jüdin ist uns Zuhörer weil wir Juden sind an sich zieht, ohne Verlangen oder Neugier nach Christen, gieng mir ein Zittern über die Wangen" (T 59; D 65).

5   In this very moment, Kafka takes his place "among the Jewish children of the big family he has deserted," Marthe Robert writes; *Seul, comme Franz Kafka* (Paris: Calmann-Lévy, 1979), 74. For further discussion, see Baioni, *Kafka*; Iris Bruce, *Kafka and Cultural Zionism: Dates in Palestine* (Madison, WI: University of Wisconsin Press, 2007), 36; Guido Massino, *Kafka, Löwy und das Jiddische Theater* (Frankfurt am Main: Stroemfeld, 2007); Pascale Casanova, *Kafka: Angry Poet*, trans. Chris Turner (London and New York: Seagull Books, 2015).

6   "Ich heiße hebräisch Anschel wie der Großvater meiner Mutter von der Mutterseite" (T 318; D 152).

7   "gierig" and "mit solcher Gründlichkeit, Eile und Freude" (T 215; D 98). Kafka read first Heinrich Graetz, *Volkstümliche Geschichte der Juden in drei Bänden* (1888), followed by Meyer Isser Pinès, *Histoire de la littérature judéo-allemande* (1911), and finally Jakob Fromer, *Organismus des Judentums* (1909).

8   (BF 43, 77; LF 5, 16).

Yet Kafka's many diary entries about Löwy's troupe are not concerned with just the plays' cultural and religious content. What made his cheeks tremble was also the aesthetic experience at Café Savoy, an experience orchestrated by the dramatic form of the plays: the actors' way of singing, their way of pronouncing words like "jüdische Kinderloch" and their way of moving their bodies on stage. In his diary, Kafka analyzes the dramatic techniques Löwy's troupe employed on the narrow podium. Less than a month after watching his first performance, he also wrote down a complex reflection on dramatic theory (to which I return at the end of this chapter). In short, the encounter with Löwy's company was decisive for Kafka's relation both to Judaism and literature.

Although Kafka was influenced as a young writer by literary masters such as Goethe, Kleist, and Flaubert, his encounter with an amateur theater company was pivotal to the development of his oeuvre. In this chapter, I will try to explain why this was. My contention is that this encounter was so influential for Kafka's writing because it confirmed, to a certain extent, the direction in which he was already moving. In February that same year, he experienced the stereoscopic setup of the Kaiserpanorama in Friedland; in early October, only a couple of days before he saw his first performance of Löwy's troupe, Kafka made two diary entries clearly inspired by the stereoscope.[9] Now, quite suddenly, he saw his own—still vague—ideas of a stereoscopic style take shape on a stage in the back room of Café Savoy.

Der Meschumed

The first play Kafka saw at Café Savoy was *Der Meschumed: Komisches Lebensbild mit Gesang und Tanz* (*The Apostate: A Comic Picture of Life with Song and Dance*) by Abraham Scharkansky. In the days after the performance on October 5, 1911, Kafka wrote his first and longest diary entry about Löwy's troupe, offering among other things a detailed summary of the play's plot. The *Meschumed* of the title is the rich Jew Seidemann; he has converted to Christianity and murdered his wife, who had remained faithful to her Jewish faith. At the beginning of the play, Seidemann attempts to marry his daughter to a Christian officer even though the girl is in love with the Jewish Edelmann. In order to fulfil his goal, Seidemann now also murders Edelmann's father and tries to frame the younger man for the crime. In Act Three, the play turns into a legal drama in which Seidemann, seeing his deceit revealed, kills himself by taking poison.

---

9   (T 49–50, 55–56; D 60–61, 63–64).

Kafka's summary of the plot first begins only halfway into the diary entry, however. In the first pages of the entry, he describes two performers, the "male impersonator" Frau Klug and her husband, who, dancing at the front of the stage, hide the plot upstage with extended arms and snapping fingers. As I will go into detail with Kafka's reflections on these two performers, whom he refers to as "the two in caftans," I will take the liberty of quoting the passage at some length:

I really don't know what sort of person it is that she and her husband represent. If I wanted to explain them to someone to whom I didn't want to confess my ignorance, I should find that I consider them sextons, employees of the temple, notorious lazybones with whom the community has come to terms, privileged *shnorrers* for some religious reason, people who, precisely as a result of their being set apart, are very close to the centre of the community's life, know many songs as a result of their useless wandering about and spying, see clearly to the core the relationship of all the members of the community, but as a result of their lack of relatedness to the workaday world don't know what to do with this knowledge, people who are Jews in an especially pure form because they live only in the religion, but live in it without effort, understanding, or distress. They seem to make a fool of everyone, laugh immediately after the murder of a noble Jew, sell themselves to an apostate, dance with their hands on their earlocks in delight when the unmasked murderer poisons himself and calls upon God, and yet all this only because they are as light as a feather, sink to the ground under the slightest pressure, are sensitive, cry easily with dry faces (they cry themselves out in grimaces), but as soon as the pressure is removed haven't the slightest specific gravity but must bounce right back up in the air. They must have caused a lot of difficulty in a serious play, such as *Der Meschumed* by Lateiner [Abraham Scharkansky] is, for they are forever—large as life and often on tiptoe or with both feet in the air—at the front of the stage and do not untie but rather cut to pieces the suspense of the play. The seriousness of the play spins itself out, however, in words so closed, even where possibly improvised so carefully considered and so tightened up by a unified emotion that even when the plot is going along only at the rear of the stage, it always keeps its meaning. Rather, the two in caftans are suppressed now and then which befits their nature, and despite their extended arms and snapping fingers one sees behind them only the murderer, who, the poison in him, his hand at his really too large collar, is staggering to the door. The melodies are long, one's body is glad

to confide itself to them. As a result of their long-drawn-out
forward movement, the melodies are best expressed by a swaying
of the hips, by raising and lowering extended arms in a calm
rhythm, by bringing the palms close to the temples and taking
care not to touch them.[10]

Considering that Kafka really doesn't know what sort of person the two
in caftans represent, he makes astonishingly detailed conjectures about
their identity. Kafka imagines them to be sextons, notorious lazybones,
privileged *shnorrers* (a Hebrew word for a kind of beggar in the
synagogue), and Jews of an especially pure form—people somehow
exempt from the orderly workaday world. As Kafka understands them,

---

10 "Eigentlich weiß ich nicht, was für Personen das sind, die sie und ihr Mann
   darstellt. Wollte ich sie jemandem erklären, dem ich meine Unwissenheit nicht
   eingestehen will, würde ich sehn, daß ich sie für Gemeindediener halte, für
   Angestellte des Tempels, bekannte Faulenzer, mit denen sich die Gemeinde
   abgefunden hat, irgendwie aus religiösen Gründen bevorzugte Schnorrer,
   Leute, die infolge ihrer abgesonderten Stellung gerade ganz nahe am Mittelpunkt
   des Gemeindelebens sind, infolge ihres nutzlosen aufpasserischen Herumziehns
   viele Lieder kennen, die Verhältnisse aller Gemeindemitglieder genau durch-
   schauen aber infolge ihrer Beziehungslosigkeit zum Berufsleben nichts mit
   diesen Kenntnissen anzufangen wissen, Leute, die in einer besonders reinen
   Form Juden sind, weil sie nur in der Religion aber ohne Mühe, Verständnis und
   Jammer in ihr leben. Sie scheinen sich aus jedem einen Narren zu machen,
   lachen gleich nach der Ermordung eines edlen Juden, verkaufen sich einem
   Abtrünnigen, tanzen die Hände vor Entzücken am Wangenhaar, als der
   entlarvte Mörder sich vergiftet und Gott anruft, und doch alles nur weil sie so
   federleicht sind, unter jedem Druck auf dem Boden liegen empfindlich sind,
   gleich mit trockenem Gesicht weinen (sie weinen sich in Grimassen aus), sobald
   der Druck aber vorüber ist, nicht das geringste Eigengewicht aufbringen
   sondern gleich in die Höhe springen müssen. Sie müßten daher einem ernsten
   Stück wie es der 'Meschumed' von Lateiner ist, eigentlich viel Sorge machen, da
   sie immer in ganzer Größe und oft auf den Fußspitzen oder mit beiden Beinen
   in der Luft vorn auf der Bühne sind und die Aufregung des Stückes nicht lösen,
   sondern zerschneiden. Nun wickelt sich aber der Ernst des Stückes in so
   geschlossenen, selbst in der möglichen Improvisation abgewogenen, von
   einheitlichem Gefühl gespannten Worten ab, daß selbst wenn die Handlung nur
   im Hintergrund der Bühne vor sich geht, sie sich ihre Bedeutung immer wahrt.
   Eher werden hie und da die 2 im Kaftan unterdrückt, was ihrer Natur entspricht
   und man sieht trotz ihrer ausgebreiteten Arme und schnippenden Finger nur
   hinten den Mörder, der das Gift in sich, die Hand an seinem eigentlich zu weiten
   Kragen zur Türe wankt.—Die Melodien sind lang, der Körper vertraut sich
   ihnen gerne an. Infolge ihrer gerade verlaufenden Länge wird ihnen am besten
   durch das Wiegen der Hüften, durch ausgebreitete in ruhigem Atem gehobene
   und gesenkte Arme, durch Annäherung der Handflächen an die Schläfen und
   sorgfältige Vermeidung der Berührung entsprochen" (T 57–9; D 64–5, translation
   modified).

they move about in a local state of exception in which the laws of the village community, and even the laws of nature, are suspended: they dance around as light as a feather, often on tiptoe or with both feet in the air.

Evidently, the two in caftans have inspired a number of important fictional characters in Kafka's late oeuvre, among them the two conscientious and annoying balls of celluloid in the story "Blumfeld, an Elderly Bachelor," written in 1915, and the two childish assistants in *The Castle*, written in 1922. When Kafka, in "Researches of a Dog," looked back at his encounter with Löwy's troupe ten years later, he emphasized the disorderly character of the dancers. The little company of dancing dogs do not answer the calls of the researcher dog, and it is as if they have been exempted from the good manners of dogdom: "why wasn't the thing that our laws always unconditionally require not allowed this time? My heart rebelled, I almost forgot the music. These dogs before me were violating the law."[11]

According to Kafka's diary entry, the narrow stage of Café Savoy was divided in two: upstage, the audience could follow the actors performing Scharkansky's plot about Seidemann; at stage front, the audience was distracted by the two in caftans dancing around and hiding the plot with their extended arms and snapping fingers. In other words, the stage is a stereoscope. Löwy's troupe offers two dissimilar images of communal life in a Jewish village in Galicia, located at the rear and the front of the stage respectively.

In the orderly image, moral and legal rules are in force and the conflicts between the dramatic characters end before the court. In the disorderly image, the weightlessness of the two in caftans is another example of the tumultuous world to which the laws of the community do not apply. Among other things, the difference between orderly and disorderly image comes to light when the actions of the two in caftans at the front of the stage are out of sync with the dramatic events at the rear: light as a feather, they laugh immediately after the murder of old Edelmann, sell themselves to the treacherous Seidemann, and dance with their hands on their earlocks when Seidemann poisons himself in the last act.

In the words of the Laurenziberg text, the life of the Galician village, while still retaining its natural, heavy rise and fall, is simultaneously recognized no less clearly "as a nothing, a dream, a hovering." What

---

11 "warum durfte denn das, was unsere Gesetze bedingungslos immer verlangen, diesmal nicht sein? Das Herz empörte sich in mir, fast vergaß ich die Musik. Diese Hunde hier vergingen sich gegen das Gesetz" (NS2 431; SS 136).

Kafka experienced at Café Savoy, then, was a dramatic stereoscope incarnating, with decisive consequences for his work and for his understanding of his own Jewishness, his still vague ideas of a stereoscopic style.

Cutting Up the Plot

In the long quotation above, Kafka speculates that the two in caftans "must have caused a lot of difficulty in a serious play, such as *Der Meschumed*," because they "do not untie but rather cut to pieces the suspense of the play." Here Kafka draws on Aristotle's *Poetics*, according to which the plot of the tragic drama is to be understood as a knot first bound (*desis*) and then loosened (*lusis*).[12] Likewise, the Aristotelian notion of a unified causal plot (*mythos*) lies behind the subsequent description of the events taking place at the rear of the stage: "The seriousness of the play spins itself out, however, in words so closed, even where possibly improvised so carefully considered and so tightened up by a unified emotion that even when the plot is going along only at the rear of the stage, it always keeps its meaning." Put differently, the orderly image shows us a plot in which the individual lines by the dramatic characters are tied so closely together by the narrative causality of the play that there are no cracks in the aesthetic form.

However, the two in caftans do not untie or explicate the dramatic knot the way it should be done according to Aristotle. Rather, they cut it to pieces or cut it in two ("zerschneiden"), just as Alexander the Great sliced the Gordian knot in half with a stroke of his sword. This is another example of the violent nature of the aesthetic experience in which orderly and disorderly image, upstage and front stage, laws and chance grind against each other.

This is all still rather abstract, however, so I will focus in on Kafka's idea of cutting to pieces the plot by exploring his detailed summary of Scharkansky's play. What interests me is the way in which Kafka's paraphrases of two scenes in particular flesh out his abstract idea of somehow undoing the play's tight plot without untying it.

In the first of the two scenes, Seidemann and the two in caftans rehearse what to say and what to do in the future courtroom scene. For a while, the two in caftans leave stage front and intervene in the plot by bearing false witness against the young Edelmann: "For a whole act Seidemann, with great patience and very well-stressed little asides ('Yes, yes, very good.' 'No, that's wrong.' 'Yes, now that's better.' 'Of course, of course.'), instructs the two in caftans how they are to testify

---

12 Aristotle, *Poetics*, trans. Anthony Kenny (Oxford: Oxford University Press, 2013), 1455b.

in court concerning the alleged enmity that has existed between old and young Edelmann for years."[13] Accordingly, in the last act of the play, Seidemann goes on to direct the two as they appear before the court by tugging at their clothes.[14]

However, the two in caftans represent not only the false narrative about the enmity between the young and the old Edelmann, but also the way in which Seidemann wants them to represent this story: "They get going with difficulty, there are many misunderstandings (they come forward at an improvised rehearsal of the court scene and declare that Seidemann had commissioned them to represent the affair in the following way)."[15] When the two break the dramatic illusion and step forward in what, in classical comedy and German Romanticism, is called a parabasis, Seidemann's secret plans are exposed before the audience and the future court. His ambition is to use the bodily movement of the two in caftans to represent his false story about the murder; but when they reveal both the intention behind these movements and the fact that they have been commissioned to represent the affair in this way, their performance becomes useless.

In general, there is something spy-like ("aufpasserisch") and revealing in the way the two in caftans dance about at stage front. In the long quotation above, Kafka imagines that they "see clearly to the core the relationship of all the members of the community, but as a result of their lack of relatedness to the workaday world don't know what to do with this knowledge." Apparently, the two in caftans have a thorough knowledge of the rules and norms of the community (or the congregation, "Gemeinde"), but they do not apply this knowledge in goal-oriented social practices; they just use it to make fun of the other actors by miming their bodily gestures.

The second of the two scenes is the courtroom scene in the last act of the play. Der Meschumed ends with a classical example of poetic justice in which the playwright unties the conflict by punishing the wicked Seidemann and rewarding the young lovers. The court consists of a presiding judge and a defending lawyer "with great display of hair and

---

13 "Einen ganzen Akt lang instruiert Seidemann mit großer Geduld und sehr gut betonten kleinen Zwischenbemerkungen (Ja, ja. Ganz gut. Also das ist falsch. Ja das ist schon besser. Allerdings allerdings) die beiden im Kaftan wie sie vor Gericht die angebliche jahrelange Feindschaft zwischen dem alten und dem jungen Edelmann bezeugen sollen" (T 64; D 68).

14 (T 65; D 69).

15 "Sie kommen schwer in Gang, es gibt viele Mißverständnisse, so treten sie bei einer improvisierten Probe der Gerichtszene vor und erklären, Seidemann habe ihnen aufgetragen die Sache in folgender Weise darzustellen" (T 64; D 68).

moustache."[16] Behind the disguise, you recognize at once Seidemann's daughter, Kafka writes, but since the troupe is so small, you assume for a long time that she is just playing a second part. The turning point in the legal case occurs when the last witness, Seidemann's servant, says that he has seen Seidemann buy the knife, that he knows that at the crucial time Seidemann was at Edelmann's, and that Seidemann hates the Jews and especially Edelmann. *Der Meschumed*, and Kafka's voluminous summary, ends with the revelation of Seidemann's wickedness:

> Seidemann defends himself as a somewhat confused man of honour. Then the discussion turns to his daughter. Where is she? At home, naturally, and she'll bear him out. No, that she won't do, insists the defending lawyer, and will prove it, turns to the wall, takes off the wig, and turns toward the horrified Seidemann as his daughter. Punishing is the look of the clean whiteness of her upper lip when she takes off the moustache. Seidemann has taken poison in order to escape the justice of this world, confesses his misdeeds, but hardly any longer to the humans, rather to the Jewish God whom he now professes. Meanwhile the piano player has struck up a tune, the two in caftans feel moved by it and must start dancing. In the background stands the reunited bridal pair, they sing the melody, especially the serious bridegroom, in the customary old way.[17]

The model for this scene is the court drama at the end of *The Merchant of Venice*. In Shakespeare, Portia disguises herself as a young male doctor of the law in order to save her beloved, the merchant Antonio, from Shylock's demand of a pound of his flesh. In Scharkansky, Seidemann's daughter cross-dresses as a lawyer in order to clear her beloved Edelmann from the murder charge.

---

16 "mit großem Haar und Schnurrbartaufwand" (T 65; D 68).
17 "Seidemann wehrt sich als ein etwas verwirrter Ehrenmann. Da kommt die Rede auf seine Tochter. Wo ist sie? Zuhause natürlich und gibt ihm recht. Nein, das tut sie aber nicht, behauptet der Verteidiger und will es beweisen, wendet sich zur Wand, nimmt die Perücke ab und kehrt sich dem entsetzten Seidemann als seine Tochter zu. Strafend sieht das reine Weiß der Oberlippe aus, als sie auch den Schnurrbart entfernt. Seidemann hat Gift genommen, um der irdischen Gerechtigkeit zu entgehn, gesteht seine Übeltaten aber kaum mehr den Menschen, sondern dem jüdischen Gott, zu dem er sich jetzt bekennt. Inzwischen hat der Klavierspieler eine Melodie angeschlagen, die 2 im Kaftan fühlen sich von ihr ergriffen und müssen lostanzen. Im Hintergrund steht das vereinigte Brautpaar, sie singen, besonders der ernste Bräutigam die Melodie nach alter Tempelgewohnheit mit" (T 66–7; D 69, translation modified).

The important difference between the two scenes that end *The Merchant of Venice* and *Der Meschumed* is that Shakespeare's Portia remains disguised throughout the entire scene and thus stays within the confines of the legal institution. Dressed as, and taking the role of, a male lawyer, she simply solves the legal problem with a shrewd sentence. In the vocabulary of the Aristotelian theory of drama, she is able to untie the dramatic knot because she has a more detailed knowledge of its complications than her opponent. By contrast, Seidemann's daughter does not go through with the legal process but interrupts it by suddenly removing the great display of hair and moustache that underpinned her legal authority. Thus, Seidemann is punished extra-legally rather than legally. Thanks to Kafka's remarkable formulation—"Punishing is the look of the clean whiteness of her upper lip when she takes off the moustache"—it seems as if the punishment radiates from the white, hairless absence of a moustache, as it were from the sudden lack of a symbol of legal and patriarchal authority.

Aristotle is critical toward tragedies in which the untying of the knot comes from a *deus ex machina* rather than from the story itself.[18] Yet this is exactly what is going on in *Der Meschumed* where the turning point, as Kafka has it, is a shift from human to divine justice. In Kafka's description, the moment of divine intervention is characterized by two features.

First, the shift from human to divine justice is a shift from the practice of justice to the underlying configuration of the community. Rather than ask what the individuals have done, the scene suddenly poses a question about who they are and where they are located in the community. In the peripeteia, the lawyer "takes off the wig, and turns toward the horrified Seidemann *as* his daughter [*als seine Tochter*]." The daughter's sudden transformation from Christian man to Jewish woman changes her position in the community. Seidemann, too, radically alters his position in the order of things when, at death's door, he confesses his misdeeds "to the Jewish God whom he now professes." Thus, in Kafka's account of the final scene in Scharkansky's play, divine justice is linked to the configuration of communal life. The *deus* that intervenes from the machine is to be understood as a metaphorical *deus*, a figure from the repertoire of political theology.

Second, the shift from human to divine justice also entails a reconfiguration of the community. In *The Merchant of Venice*, the Christians win the case while the Jewish Shylock is sentenced to hand over half of his property and to convert to Christianity. In *Der Meschumed*, by contrast, by metamorphosing from Christian defense attorney into

---

18   Aristotle, *Poetics*, 1454b.

Jewish family member, Seidemann's daughter redraws the ethnical and cultural borders that underpin the entire play. Before the turning point, the play was about a Christian court passing judgment on a criminal Jew; after the turning point, it is about a Jewish court sentencing an apostate. Seen in this way, the divine intervention is not a theological moment in which a god interferes in human matters by punishing the evildoers who have evaded human justice; it is, rather, a political moment in which the community is, miraculously, reconfigured.

Consequently, just like the scene in which Seidemann instructs the two in caftans, the courtroom scene cuts the suspense of Scharkansky's play to pieces. When paraphrasing the play, Kafka hones in on a literary technique that, rather than driving the plot forward based on the legal and dramatic rules which are in force at the backstage, disrupts the social imaginary underlying the play.

Loosened, Shredded, Wafting About Him

In a short meditation on dramatic theory from October 29, 1911, some three weeks after the diary entry about *Der Meschumed*, Kafka gives a more condensed and conceptual version of his ideas about the aesthetic experience offered by the Yiddish theater. The passage has only played a marginal role in Kafka research, probably because of its complexity. Yet it does, in fact, make sense if understood in the context of Kafka's description of *Der Meschumed* as aesthetic experience and, more generally, in the context of his stereoscopic style. The immediate occasion for the meditation is the essay "Axiome über das Drama" ("Axioms for Drama") which Brod, also enthusiastic about Löwy's troupe, had just published in the journal *Die Schaubühne* (*The Stage*). However, Kafka's response to his friend's essay on dramatic form is strikingly detached: "'Axioms for the Drama' by Max in the *Schaubühne*. Has quite the character of a dream truth, which the expression 'axioms' suits too. The more dreamlike it inflates itself, all the more coolly must you seize it."[19]

In his very short and stylized essay, Brod discusses the ways in which the novel and the drama make things visible to the reader and the spectator. Initially, one might assume that the drama would side with sensible intuition whereas the novel would side with abstraction and, perhaps, with the indirect and mediated intuition that comes from seeing things with the "inner eye." But Brod asserts that the opposite is the case, in fact. An excess of visuality is not necessarily a good thing:

---

19 "'Axiome über das Drama' von Max in der Schaubühne. Hat ganz den Charakter einer Traumwahrheit, wofür auch der Ausdruck 'Axiome' paßt. Je traumhafter sie sich aufbläst, desto kühler muß man sie anfassen" (T 203; D 93–4).

"The stage offers too much, without selection [. . .]. While the novelist can open the shutter as much or as little as he wishes, on stage, we are offered the entire infinity of the event, the reality—and thus, in one word, 'nothing at all.'"[20] In support of his thesis about the visual overkill of the drama, Brod puts forward two arguments, of which the first has to do with authorial control and the second with aesthetic meaning.

In order to understand the problematic nature of the visuality of the stage, Brod argues, "it is sufficient to realize that any living being on the stage, any forest magic, any emotion created by facial expressions and bodily gestures, does not fall within the realm of power of the dramatic poet but is borrowed from two foreign art forms, the art of acting and the art of decoration." Since the dramatic poet is unable to control the spectacle, drama is not "a purely volitional art" ("eine reine gewillkürte Kunst"); in other words, visuality is not a part of the poet's sovereign poetic capacity.

Brod's second argument is that this lack of control brings about a lack of meaning in the dramatic work. If you do not control the visuality of the stage, you're not able to select the meaningful sensible details ("The stage offers too much, without selection"). By contrast, the novelist can restrict himself to visualizing what is expedient for the meaning of the work: "In short, it lies in my hand whether to expand or to reduce the horizon of the reader at my discretion, and thus to show my heroes at the level of detailing, of liveliness or lack of liveliness that I deem to be useful for the development of plot."

Evidently, Brod's reflections on the meaning of the work are guided by a rather traditional opposition between spirit and matter, the ideal and the real, up and down. If the dramatic poet, against all odds, should be able to create a successful drama without too much meaningless visuality, he would have found an aesthetic form with which he could "rise above the individual particularities in time and space and let his piece play out in a poetic way, emancipated from history, from spatial localization, in other words, without environment, without specific knowledge."

Kafka loyally reproduces his friend's ideas about an anti-theater devoid of uncontrolled visuality: "From the point of view of the novel, therefore, the best drama would be entirely unstimulating, for example, a philosophical drama that would be read by seated actors in any set at all that represented a room."[21] After a short summary of Brod's argument, however, Kafka points out its fallacy: "Error in this chain of

---

20 Max Brod, "Axiome über das Drama," *Die Schaubühne* 7, no. 2 (1911): 228, my translation. The following quotations are all taken from this short essay, 227–9.

21 "Im Sinne des Romans wäre daher das beste Drama ein ganz anregungsloses z. B. philosophisches Drama, das von sitzenden Schauspielern in einer beliebigen Zimmerdekoration vorgelesen würde, *Gesammelte Werke* (Jazzybee Verlag, 2012)."

reasoning: It changes its point of view without indicating it, sees things now from the writer's room, now from the audience."[22] To see things from the writer's study is to discuss what is normally called aesthetics of production; this is what Brod does when, for instance, he addresses the question of the poet's capacity to control his work. To see things from the audience, on the other hand, is to discuss aesthetics of reception; here, for example, Brod writes about the spectators who are offered "the entire infinity of the event."

In the last half of the short meditation, Kafka puts forward his own contribution to the discussion of dramatic theory. Until this point, Kafka's meditation is rather easy to understand, at least if interpreted in the light of Brod's essay, but when he starts moving forward on his own account, he becomes much more difficult to follow. In any case, it is evident that Kafka stays within the confines of an aesthetics of production (as opposed to an aesthetics of reception) by focusing on the work of the poet and of the actor:

Given that the audience does not see everything as the author intended, that even he is surprised by the performance [. . .], it is still the author who had the play with all its details within himself, who moved along from detail to detail, and who only because he assembled all the details in the speeches has given them dramatic weight and force. Because of this the drama in its highest development achieves an unbearable humanization which it is the task of the actor to draw down, to make bearable wearing his role loosened, shredded, wafting about him [*gelockert zerfasert, wehend um sich*]. The drama therefore hovers in the air, but not like a roof carried along on a storm, rather like a whole building whose foundation walls have been torn up out of the earth with a force which today is still close to madness.[23]

---

22 "Fehler dieser Schlußfolgerung: Sie wechselt ohne es anzuzeigen, den Standpunkt, sieht einmal die Dinge vom Schreibzimmer, einmal vom Publikum."

23 "Zugegeben, daß das Publikum nicht alles im Sinne des Dichters sieht, daß ihn selbst die Aufführung überrascht [. . .] so hat er doch das Stück mit allen Details in sich gehabt, ist von Detail zu Detail weitergerückt und nur weil er alle Details in den Reden versammelt, hat er ihnen die dramatische Schwere und Gewalt gegeben. Dadurch geräth das Drama in seiner höchsten Entwicklung in eine unerträgliche Vermenschlichung, die herabzuziehn, erträglich zu machen Aufgabe des Schauspielers ist, der die ihm vorgeschriebene Rolle gelockert zerfasert, wehend um sich trägt. Das Drama schwebt also in der Luft, aber nicht als ein vom Sturm getragenes Dach, sondern als ein ganzes Gebäude, dessen Grundmauern mit einer heute doch dem Irrsinn sehr nahen Kraft aus der Erde hinaufgerissen worden sind." (Translation modified).

One reason for the difficulty of the passage is Kafka's assertion that the drama in its highest development achieves "an unbearable humanisation" or "an insupportable humanification" ("eine unerträgliche Vermenschlichung"). At first glance, one could be tempted to think that a humanization would be something good—but this is clearly not the way Kafka thinks about it. Here, the humanization is unbearable, and it is the task of the actor to make it tolerable.

Kafka continues Brod's theoretical discussions of authorial control and aesthetic meaning but turns his conclusions upside down. First, with regard to control, Brod argued that the dramatic poet was dependent on both the art of acting and the art of decoration, two foreign and heteronomous art forms in relation to poetry. While Kafka also describes the drama as a power struggle between poet and actor, he sides with the actor against the poet's sovereign control over the poetic creation. Here Kafka seems to be drawing on the classical theory of inspiration, about which he had written a long diary entry only a couple of weeks earlier.[24] As Plato's spokesman Socrates says in *Ion*, "lyric poets do not compose these beautiful songs in their right minds [. . .], but when they are filled with Bacchic frenzy and possessed."[25] According to Brod, poetic creation is a controlled and goal-oriented practice. In a deleted passage of the meditation on dramatic theory, Kafka writes that the dramatic poet "hammers" together ("gehämmert") the unity of the drama,[26] as if poetic creation consisted in hammering a table together, in parallel to the Laurenziberg text discussed in Chapter 3.[27] Yet, to Kafka, this goal-oriented practice is only a part of the poetic creation. Presumably drawing on Plato, he describes the poet's loss of control not as a problem but, rather, as a premise for literary production, given the fact that poets cannot compose their beautiful songs when they are in full control of their mental faculties. In other words, the unbearable humanization takes place when the poet hammers together the drama *without* being carried away by the creative madness of inspiration.

The power struggle between poet and actor is anticipated in Kafka's description of the wicked Seidemann in *Der Meschumed*. As we saw, Seidemann steps up as both dramatic poet and director when he tries to make the two in caftans perform his little play but fails because they repeatedly thwart his treacherous intentions. The way the two obstruct Seidemann's dramatic intentions corresponds to the way the actor,

---

24 (T 59–60; D 63–4).
25 Plato, *Ion, Hippias Minor, Laches, Protagoras*, trans. Reginald E. Allen, *The Dialogues of Plato* vol. 3 (New Haven, CT: Yale University Press, 1984), 534a.
26 (TA 235).
27 (T 854; GWC 108–09).

according to Kafka's meditation on dramatic theory, seeks to "draw down" the unbearable humanization of the play. In both cases, the audience "does not see everything as the author intended," and even the author himself "is surprised by the performance."

Second, with regard to dramatic meaning, Brod asserted that the novelist, unlike the dramatic poet, was able to select the visuality that he deemed to be "useful for the development of plot." In other words, all material particularities of the drama are to be subordinated to the overall meaning of the narrative. Kafka addresses the same problem when he writes that it was the author "who had the play with all its details within himself, who moved along from detail to detail, and who only because he assembled all the details in the speeches has given them dramatic weight and force." Seen this way, the humanization is produced when the dramatic poet assembles—hammers together—all the material details of the play into a meaningful aesthetic totality. Unlike Brod, however, Kafka characterizes this totalizing humanization as unbearable and assigns the actor the task of undoing it.

This opposition between totality and fragmentation is anticipated in the diary entry about *Der Meschumed* too. The meaningful and uniform drama is the story that the actors perform at the rear of the stage. I have already twice quoted Kafka's description of the aesthetic totality, without cracks or fissures, and I am delighted to do it once more: "The seriousness of the play spins itself out, however, in words so closed, even where possibly improvised so carefully considered and so tightened up by a unified emotion that even when the plot is going along only at the rear of the stage, it always keeps its meaning." Thus, the way the two in caftans cut to pieces the plot of the drama corresponds to the way the actor, according to Kafka, should wear his role "loosened, shredded, wafting about him."

In short, I suggest interpreting humanization as the opposite of defamiliarization.[28] The "humanizing" poetic creation brings about an aesthetic totality based on the resources of meaning available in the forms and norms of society. The task of the defamiliarizing aesthetic experience, by contrast, is to cut to pieces and to shred ("zerschneiden" and "zerfasern") the order of human meaning. The forceful cutting and shredding undo the narrative fabric of the play. In the final sentence of Kafka's meditation on dramatic theory, a violent act of this kind undermines the edifice of the drama: "The drama therefore hovers in the air, but not like a roof carried along on a storm, rather like a whole

---

28 In this, I differ from Puchner's perceptive interpretation of Kafka's reflection on dramatic form; see Martin Puchner, "Kafka's Antitheatrical Gestures," *Germanic Review* 78, no. 3 (2003).

building whose foundation walls have been torn up out of the earth with a force which today is still close to madness." According to Kafka's metaphor, the drama is an edifice which is neither hammered together by the goal-oriented dramatic poet nor carried along by the non-human forces of a storm; rather, the edifice is to take shape in a gray zone between human intention and divine inspiration: someone has to actively tear out the foundation walls of the earth.

To sum up, Kafka's meditation on dramatic theory is one of his most advanced formulations about his defamiliarizing stereoscopic style. In the Laurenziberg text, the mature author looks back at his wishes, as a young man, to create a literary style "in which life, while still retaining its natural, heavy rise and fall, would simultaneously be recognized no less clearly as a nothing, a dream, a hovering." This style would make life "still bolder, still more determined, still more real and, if you will, still more insane [noch irrsinniger]."[29] I contend that these youthful wishes for a literary style took shape in Café Savoy. A similar madness of inspiration, a similar poetic "Irrsinn," is requested when the task is to tear out of the earth the foundational walls of the dramatic work "with a force which today is still close to madness [Irrsinn]."

Confused Jargon

A couple of months after the performance of Der Meschumed at Café Savoy, the Yiddish troupe had moved on, leaving Yitzhak Löwy in Prague. Taking the role of impresario, Kafka arranged a recitation of three Yiddish poems at the student Zionist organization Bar Kochba in February 1912. Tormented by anxiety, he prepared a short introductory lecture, "Speech on the Yiddish Language," in order to introduce the Eastern Jewish poems to an audience of assimilated and German-speaking Western Jews. In this lecture, Kafka focuses on the aesthetic experience rather than on the content of the poem: "Not that I am worried for the impression that will be made on each one of you this evening," Kafka starts by assuring his audience.[30] But he is soon to add that he does in fact worry that their "fear of Yiddish, fear with a certain amount of distaste at bottom,"[31] might obstruct the audience's experience of the poems:

---

29 (T 854; GWC 108–09, translation modified).
30 "Ich habe nicht eigentlich Sorge um die Wirkung, die für jeden von Ihnen in dem heutigen Abend vorbereitet ist" (NS1 188); I thankfully draw on Martin Chalmers's English translation in Liska, When Kafka Says We, 27–9.
31 "Aber Angst vor dem Jargon, Angst mit einem gewissen Widerwillen auf dem Grunde" (NS1 188).

Our western European circumstances are, if we consider them
with a cautious fleeting glance, ordered in this way: everything
takes its quiet course. We live in a virtually joyful harmony,
understand one another when it is necessary, get by without
one another when it suits us, and understand one another even
then. Who, from within such an order of things, could understand
the confused jargon of Yiddish or who would even wish to do
so? [. . .]

It has no grammar books. Admirers try to write such grammar
books, but Yiddish goes on being spoken; it doesn't come to rest.
The people don't leave it to the grammarians.

It consists only of foreign words. These, however, are not at rest
in it, but retain the urgency and liveliness with which they were
taken in. Migrations pass through Yiddish from one end to the
other. Within Yiddish all this German, Hebrew, French, English,
Slav, Dutch, Romanian, and even Latin is marked by curiosity and
frivolity, and it takes some strength to hold the languages together
in this state.[32]

As has frequently been noted, Kafka's speech is about both the Yiddish
language and the function of literature and art in a well-ordered modern
world where everything takes its quiet course.[33] More specifically, I
would like to add that Kafka's description of the curious and frivolous
Yiddish is modeled on his experience of the two curious and frivolous
performers in caftans at Café Savoy. Just like the Löwy troupe's
performance of *Der Meschumed*, Yiddish is a "construction of chance

---

32 "Unsere westeuropäischen Verhältnisse sind, wenn wir sie mit vorsichtig flüch-
    tigem Blick ansehn, so geordnet: alles nimmt seinen ruhigen Lauf. Wir leben in
    einer geradezu fröhlichen Eintracht; verstehen einander, wenn es notwendig ist,
    kommen ohne einander aus, wenn es uns paßt und verstehen einander selbst
    dann; wer könnte aus einer solchen Ordnung der Dinge heraus den verwirrten
    Jargon verstehen oder wer hätte auch nur die Lust dazu [. . .]/ Er hat keine
    Grammatiken. Liebhaber versuchen Grammatiken zu schreiben aber der Jargon
    wird immerfort gesprochen; er kommt nicht zur Ruhe. Das Volk läßt ihn den
    Grammatikern nicht./ Er besteht nur aus Fremdwörtern. Diese ruhen aber nicht
    in ihm, sondern behalten die Eile und Lebhaftigkeit, mit der sie genommen
    wurden. Völkerwanderungen durchlaufen den Jargon von einem Ende bis zum
    anderen. Alles dieses Deutsche, Hebräische, Französische, Englische, Slawische,
    Holländische, Rumänische und selbst Lateinische ist innerhalb des Jargon von
    Neugier und Leichtsinn erfaßt, es gehört schon Kraft dazu, die Sprachen in
    diesem Zustande zusammenzuhalten" (NS1 188–9).
33 See, for instance, Gerhard Neumann, "Wahrnehmung und Medialität," in *Franz
    Kafka: Eine ethische und ästhetische Rechtfertigung*, ed. Beatrice Sandberg and
    Jakob Lothe (Freiburg: Rombach, 2001), 54.

and laws." Kafka imagined that the two in caftans moved about in a zone of chaotic disorder in the midst of the well-ordered life of the Eastern Jewish village. In the same way, he claims, the confusing Yiddish forms a pocket of linguistic lawlessness in the midst of law-abiding Europe. Allegedly, it is a language that consists only of foreign words, has no grammar books, and is as unruly as a migrating crowd of people.

After summarizing the three poems Löwy is about to perform, Kafka returns to the theme of the audience's aesthetic experience of Yiddish, and hence of literature:

> You come very close to Yiddish, nevertheless, when you consider that within you, apart from knowledge, there are also forces at work and points of contact with forces which enable you to understand Yiddish affectively [. . .]. But sit still, and then you are suddenly in the midst of Yiddish. But once Yiddish has taken hold of you—and Yiddish is everything, word, Hassidic melody and the very being of this Eastern Jewish actor himself—then you will no longer recognize your earlier tranquility. Then you will feel the true unity of Yiddish so powerfully that you will be afraid, though no longer of Yiddish, but of yourself.[34]

According to Kafka, the experience of Yiddish is capable of triggering an inversion in which something marginal moves into the center. While the assimilated Jews in the lecture hall find themselves at the very center of Europe, Yiddish is located in the periphery, geographically, culturally, and socially. Suddenly, however, Kafka turns this figuration of social and geographical space inside out by describing Yiddish as something that you can be in the middle of: "sit still, and then you are suddenly in the midst of Yiddish."

This radical reconfiguration of communal life is possible because the assimilated audience are in fact closer to Yiddish than they themselves know. As Kafka tells his audience, there are "forces at work and points

---

34 "Ganz nahe kommen Sie schon an den Jargon, wenn Sie bedenken, daß in Ihnen außer Kenntnissen auch noch Kräfte tätig sind und Anknüpfungen von Kräften, welche Sie befähigen, Jargon fühlend zu verstehen. [. . .] Bleiben Sie aber still, dann sind Sie plötzlich mitten im Jargon. Wenn Sie aber einmal Jargon ergriffen hat—und Jargon ist alles, Wort, chassidische Melodie und das Wesen dieses ostjüdischen Schauspielers selbst,—dann werden Sie Ihre frühere Ruhe nicht mehr wiedererkennen. Dann werden Sie die wahre Einheit des Jargon zu spüren bekommen, so stark, daß Sie sich fürchten werden, aber nicht mehr vor dem Jargon, sondern vor sich" (NS1 193).

of contact with forces which enable you to understand Yiddish affectively." Even while the German-speaking Prague Jews are well integrated and well consolidated in Central European culture, the poems reveal the unacknowledged forces they share with Eastern Jewry. It may be difficult to see, but the Western and the Eastern Jews do have something in common, in fact. This is why Löwy's recital of the poems might make the Western Jews afraid, no longer of Yiddish, but of themselves. Just like the concluding scene in *Der Meschumed*, the Yiddish poems bring about a political moment, a pawn promotion, as it were, that reverses the audience's figuration of communal life by turning the marginal *Yiddischkeit* into a figure for a new community.

Six A Weakness of Imagination

Kafka in China: "Building the Great Wall of China"

On December 10, 1916, two years into the First World War, a patriotic article in the *Prager Tagblatt* newspaper urged its readers to donate toward the health care costs of returning injured soldiers, at the time somewhat bluntly called "war cripples" ("Kriegskrüppeln"):

> Let this appeal be heard everywhere, and let everyone respond! Our disabled veterans have suffered and are suffering for all of us, and they have the right to ask all of us to help alleviate as much as possible a very painful and worrisome future. Every day the war claims new victims, every day the trains carrying the wounded roll into the hinterland, and every day the hospitals accept new patients as they discharge the earlier ones. Of course, the physicians' skill manages to heal wounds inflicted by war entirely for many thousands, but for a great many more, the wounds go too deep, the bones are too shattered, the destruction wrought by shrapnel and grenade is too great. These unfortunate, needy men are maimed for life. The number of the maimed, crippled, blind, and deaf increases with every day of this long and harsh war.[1]

---

1   "Möge dieser Aufruf überall gehört werden, mögen alle ihn befolgen. Für uns alle litten und leiden unsere Kriegsinvaliden und sie haben ein Recht, von allen zu verlangen, daß ihr sehr schmerzliches und sorgvolles Schicksal—so weit es geht—entlastet werde. Täglich fordert der Krieg neue Opfer, täglich rollen die Verwundetenzuge ins Hinterland, täglich wechseln die Patienten der Hospitäler. Freilich, bei vielen tausenden gelingt es der Kunst des Arztes, die Kriegswunden vollkommen zu heilen, aber bei sehr vielen anderen ging die Wunde zu tief, splitterte der Knochen zu stark, waren die Zerstörungen zu groß, die das Schrapnell oder die Granate riß. Diese Bedauernswerten und Hilfsbedürftigen bleiben zeitlebens verstummelt. Die Zahl der Verstümmelten, der Krüppel, der Blinden und der Tauben wächst mit jedem Tage dieses langen und harten Krieges" (AS 506; OW 346).

The newspaper article "Help Disabled Veterans! An Urgent Appeal to the Public"[2] was unsigned, but it is highly probable that it was authored by Franz Kafka. Founded in 1889, the Workmen's Accident Insurance Institute for the Kingdom of Bohemia was commissioned to protect workers injured in the region's rapidly growing industries, but in 1915, the Ministry of the Interior commanded the Institute to offer care for soldiers maimed in the long and harsh conflict. The article in the *Prager Tagblatt* appeals for donations to the "The Public Crownland Agency of the Kingdom of Bohemia for Returning Veterans," a coordinating and organizing agency run by the insurance institute. As a *Concipist* at the insurance institute, a legal clerk entrusted with the drafting of official statements and petitions, Kafka played an important role in this agency by, among other things, writing a handful of newspaper articles mobilizing the German-speaking Bohemian public to donate. Kafka did not sign any of these articles—"A Major War Relief Plan Demands Realization" (October 1916), "Fellow Countrymen!" (November 1916), "Help Disabled Veterans! An Urgent Appeal to the Public" (December 1916), and "Help Disabled Veterans!" (May 1917)—but researchers agree that he either wrote them single-handedly or played an important role in the writing process.[3]

The introductory paragraph in the article in the *Prager Tagblatt* quoted above condenses the two most important themes of Kafka's wartime writings. On the one hand, Kafka describes the medical situation as being so severe that an appeal being made to the Bohemian public seems appropriate. Many thousands of veterans are taken care of in existing medical facilities, the article acknowledges, "but for a great

---

2   "Helfet den Kriegsinvaliden! Ein dringender Aufruf an die Bevölkerung."
3   In a letter to Felice Bauer of October 30, 1916, Kafka enclosed a newspaper cutting of "Fellow Countrymen!", adding that "the text (like that of so many others) is also mine. Well, no more about this" ("Auch der Text (wie so vieler anderer) ist von mir. Nun, darüber nichts weiter" [BF 737]). For the Workmen's Accident Insurance Institute for the Kingdom of Bohemia and Kafka's work at the institute, see Caygill, *Kafka: In Light of the Accident*; Klaus Hermsdorf, "Franz Kafka und die Arbeiter-Unfall-Versicherungs-Anstalt," in *Kafkas Fabriken*, ed. Hans-Gerd Koch and Klaus Wagenbach (Marbach am Neckar: Deutsche Schillergesellschaft, 2002); Klaus Hermsdorf and Benno Wagner, "Schreibanlässe und Textformen der amtlichen Schriften Franz Kafkas," in *Amtliche Schriften: Schriften, Tagebücher, Briefe* ed. Klaus Hermsdorf and Benno Wagner (Frankfurt am Main: Fischer, 2004); Benno Wagner, "Kafka's Office Writings: Historical Background and Institutional Setting," in *Franz Kafka: The Office Writings*, ed. Stanley Corngold, Jack Greenberg, and Benno Wagner (Princeton, NJ, and Oxford: Princeton University Press, 2009); Burkhardt Wolf, "Die Nacht des Bürokraten: Franz Kafkas statistische Schreibweise," *Deutsche Vierteljahrsschrift für Literaturwissenschaft und Geistesgeschichte* 80, no. 1 (2006).

many more, the wounds go too deep, the bones are too shattered, the destruction wrought by shrapnel and grenade is too great." The sheer scale of the health care problem calls for immediate action: *"The first order of business is procuring the resources.* To this end we request you most respectfully to participate in this great German Bohemian undertaking, to which there is nothing yet similar in Austria."[4] "Undertaking" is one English translation of the German "Werk," which can also be rendered as "work," "product," "deed" or "act." As a professional insurance "propagandist," Kafka mobilizes his readers to join forces in a communal "Werk."

On the other hand, Kafka discusses the social imaginary serving as the precondition for hearing and responding to the public appeal. At stake is the Bohemian citizens' "sense of patriotism" or "feeling of patriotism."[5] According to Kafka, the questions of whether the appeal will be heard everywhere, and whether everyone will respond to it, hinge on a power struggle between personal selfishness and love of one's home country: "Can it really be true that selfishness remains so strong in these times, which teach us love of fatherland, that an appeal on behalf of disabled veterans goes unheard? We hope not."[6]

Interestingly, Kafka appeals to the readers' love of fatherland, not to their love of the individual fellow human being. In the article's second sentence, the disabled veterans are presented as right-bearers rather than objects of moral compassion: "Our disabled veterans have suffered and are suffering for all of us, and they have the *right* to ask all of us to help alleviate as much as possible a very painful and worrisome future." The distinction between right and grace is the reason why, as Kafka underlines, "this article is not a request to the charitable, it is an appeal to duty."[7] As we shall see in the following chapters, however,

---

4   *"Die erste Arbeit ist die Beschaffung der Mittel.* Zu diesem Zwecke ergeht an Sie die ergebene Bitte, sich an diesem großem deutschböhmischen Werk, dem in Österreich noch nichts ähnliche der Seite steht, soweit nur möglich, zu beteiligen und in ihren Kreis dafur einzutreten" (AS 500; OW 346, Kafka's italics).

5   "patriotische Empfindung" (AS 508; OW 347).

6   "Sollte wirklich in dieser zur Vaterlandsliebe erziehenden Zeit die Ichsucht noch so stark geblieben sein, daß ein Appell für die Kriegsinvaliden ungehört bleibt? Wir hoffen es nicht" (AS 507; OW 347).

7   "dies soll keine Bitte an Mildtätige sein, dies ist ein Aufruf zur Pflichterfüllung" (AS 508; OW 347). Here Kafka follows his director at the Workmen's Accident Insurance Institute, Robert Marschner, who, earlier the same year, had argued that the care of the disabled veterans was to be understood as a legal claim and not as a charity. See Hermsdorf and Wagner, "Schreibanlässe und Textformen der amtlichen Schriften Franz Kafkas," 79, my translation.

the distinction between right and mercy is also an important theme in Kafka's literary authorship, from *Amerika* (or *The Missing Person*), written two years before the war, to *The Castle*, written several years after.

Since the precondition for hearing and responding to the appeal is a sense of political justice rather than an intuition of individual ethics, Kafka looks to the field of political philosophy for answers. Somewhat surprisingly for a newspaper article intended to mobilize the public, he addresses the complicated philosophical question of the relationship between the state and the citizen:

> We must not keep the concept of the state and the totality of its citizens in separate categories. The war has clearly shown that all of us are the state, that none of us stands outside the concept of the state, that the state's success is success for each one of us, and that a blow against the state is felt by each of us with equal force.[8]

Even if Kafka refers to "the concept of the state," his concern here is not the Bohemian people's conceptual understanding of their relation to the state, but rather their sensible imagination of it. According to Kafka, the war "has clearly shown" ("klar gezeigt") that all of his fellow citizens are the state. What I call a social imaginary is the sensible medium in which an abstract concept such as this can be presented intuitively. Thanks to this kind of non-conceptual figuration, a blow against the state is felt ("empfunden") by each member of the German-speaking Bohemian community with equal force. In other words, the sentence "The war has clearly shown that all of us are the state" is a judgment on the configuration of life in common, according to which the community is a political body organized by the bonds of citizenship. This is not the only possible judgment, however. As we have seen, it might also be true that selfishness has remained so strong in these times that the appeal on behalf of disabled veterans could go unheard. Seen this way, the members of the German-speaking Bohemian community are *not* the state, or at least not *only* the state; instead, they are configured as a disconnected and chaotic crowd of selfish individuals who relate to each other as strangers.

---

8   "Man soll den Begriff des Staats nicht von dem der Gesamtheit seiner Bürger trennen. Der Krieg hat uns klar gezeigt, daß wir alle der Staat sind, daß keiner von uns fremd gegen den Staatsbegriff steht, daß ein Erfolg des Staates ein Erfolg jedes einzelnen von uns ist, daß ein Schlag, der ihn trifft, von jedem von uns gleich eindringlich empfunden wird" (AS 507; OW 347, translation modified).

This chapter explores how the imaginative and affective pre-conditions for hearing and responding to a public appeal play a vital role in the literary works Kafka produced in the months following the publicity campaigns for disabled veterans. This question entails a more fundamental question about the relationship between the state and the citizen: whether and to what extent all of us are the state. In the fragmentary story "Building the Great Wall of China," written in March 1917, the Chinese empire appears in the uncanny dual vision of the stereoscope, just like the Italian cities represented by the Kaiserpanorama in Friedland. Focusing on this story, the chapter will show how Kafka employs his stereoscopic style to investigate the border between the political and the extra-political, between a group of individuals who do not stand outside the concept of the state, and a group of individuals who do.

"China Complex"

In early March 1917, three months after the article in the *Prager Tagblatt*, Kafka received a letter from the "k.u.k. Kriegspressequartier," the headquarters of the Austro-Hungarian press service during the war, inviting him to join a newly established artists' association for "Greater Austria." Hundreds of prominent writers and painters, among them Franz Werfel, Robert Musil, Oskar Kokoschka, and Alfred Kubin, contributed to the imperial war propaganda. Kafka, however, politely refused the invitation by writing that he was "incapable of envisaging a homogeneous Greater Austria and even less capable of imagining myself completely integrated into that spiritual whole; from such a decision I shrink back."[9] The German expression "im Geiste klarzumachen" means "envisaging" or, literally, "making clear in the mind." In the case of the political community of German Bohemia, Kafka the insurance lawyer argued that the war had "clearly shown" ("klar gezeigt") that all of us are the state. In the case of the vast Austro-Hungarian empire, however, Kafka the literary writer demurs from joining the propaganda machine on the grounds that he cannot "make clear" the idea of this much larger body politic.

---

9   "ich bin nämlich nicht imstande, mir ein im Geiste irgendwie einheitliches Groß-Österreich klarzumachen und noch weniger allerdings, mich diesem Geistigen ganz eingefügt zu denken, vor einer solchen Entscheidung schrecke ich zurück" (NS1 336–7); I draw gratefully on Benno Wagner's English translation of Kafka's reply letter; see Benno Wagner, "'Lightning No Longer Flashes': Kafka's Chinese Voice and the Thunder of the Great War," in *Franz Kafka: Narration, Rhetoric, and Reading*, ed. Jakob Lothe, Beatrice Sandberg, and Ronald Speirs (Columbus, OH: Ohio State University Press, 2011), 63.

In other words, even if the concepts of configuration and constitution describe two different levels of communal life, the sheer scale of the imperial constitution seems to play a role for the ability to configure political life.

On the very next page of the octavo notebook, Kafka begins work on "Building the Great Wall of China," a fragmentary story not about the defense of the twentieth-century Austro-Hungarian empire from the armies of the allied powers, but the defense of a fifteenth-century Chinese empire from nomads. One of the reasons Kafka turns to the Ming Dynasty is that China, in the European social imaginary of the eighteenth and early nineteenth century, served as the symbol of a petrified political system. In opposition to the dynamic Western culture, China was perceived as an unalterable world devoid of political moments. In the introduction to *Chinesische Lyrik vom 12. Jahrhundert v. Chr. bis zur Gegenwart* (*Chinese Poetry from the Twelfth Century* BCE *to the Present*, 1905), evidently an important source for Kafka's image of China, the editor and translator Hans Heilmann writes about the "strong continuity of the Chinese culture throughout all epochs and regions."[10] Even the sociologist Max Weber, in the early version of his *Protestant Ethic* (1904), drew on this political metaphor when talking about the "'Chinese' petrifaction" of modern culture.[11]

"Building the Great Wall of China" is the first and longest story in the so-called "China complex," a group of texts that deal with political issues, some of them set in China, some of them in a generic archaic world. The first cluster of texts that make up the "China complex," first of all "Building the Great Wall of China" and "A Page from an Old Document," was written in early 1917. The pressure of work at the insurance institute prevented Kafka from writing any literary

---

10   Hans Heilmann, *Chinesische Lyrik vom 12. Jahrhundert v. Chr. bis zur Gegenwart* (Munich: Piper, 1905), xx, my translation. Kafka mentions Heilmann's anthology in a letter to Felice from November, 24, 1912 (BF 118–19). For further discussion of Kafka's China image, see Manfred Engel, "Entwürfe symbolischer Weltordnungen: China und China Revisited. Zum China-Komplex in Kafkas Werk 1917–1920," in *Kafka, Prag und der Erste Weltkrieg = Kafka, Prague and the First World War*, ed. Ritchie Robertson (Würzburg: Königshausen & Neumann, 2012); Rolf J. Goebel, *Constructing China: Kafka's Orientalist Discourse* (Columbia, SC: Camden House, 1997); Weiyan Meng, *Kafka und China* (Munich: Iudicium Verlag, 1986).

11   Max Weber, "Die protestantische Ethik und der Geist des Kapitalismus," *Archiv für Sozialwissenschaft und Sozialpolitik* 21, no. 1 (1904/5): 109. For further discussion of the trope of "Chinese petrification," see Wagner, "Lightning No Longer Flashes," 64–5.

texts during the years of 1915 and 1916, but in November 1916, his sister Ottla rented one of the miniscule houses in Alchimistengasse close to Hradschin, Prague's medieval castle; here Kafka embarked on one of the most intense creative periods of his entire authorial career, writing (among other things) the stories published following the war in *A Country Doctor*. The second group of China stories were written four years later in late August 1920, a less prolific creative period during which Kafka wrote a number of short aphorisms and fables. In 1920, the political subject matter of the China stories was developed further in "The Refusal," "The Conscription of Troops," and "On the Question of the Laws," the last of which I will return to in the concluding chapter.

Taken together, the "China complex" is the strongest argument against the standard picture of Kafka as an apolitical writer whose works are, as Walter Sokel claimed, "pure expression of the psyche, clothing of the inner, nothing but symbol."[12] In these fictional texts, Kafka explicitly takes issue with the problem of constituting a unified political community. Hans Heilmann addresses this problem in his introduction to the anthology of Chinese poetry when writing that, in the third century, "the last emperor of the Qin Dynasty, the autocrat Qin Shi Huang, tried to violently impose unity on the shattered empire."[13] In the words of the narrator of "Building the Great Wall of China," imposing unity involves seeking to come together: "so many people were seeking to come together as much as possible around a single purpose."[14] In Kafka's China stories, as we shall see, the unification of a shattered and unalterable empire creates problems concerning the relationship between state and citizen, between authoritarian obedience and democratic participation, between state of nature and civil state, and between legal norms and social imaginaries.

Interestingly, Kafka approaches these well-known political problems in an ongoing dialogue with the political debates of his day. In recent research, "Building the Great Wall of China" has been interpreted convincingly as Kafka's reflection on the contemporary discourses about the health care for returning soldiers and, more generally, the political discourses concerning the construction of the welfare

---

12 Sokel, *Franz Kafka*, 110.
13 Heilmann, *Chinesische Lyrik*, xv, my translation.
14 "weil sich so viele möglichst auf einen Zweck hin zu sammeln suchten" (NS1 344; SS 116). In the following quotations from the story, I supplement Stanley Corngold's excellent translation with the translations by Malcolm Pasley in GWC and Joyce Crick in HA.

state.[15] It has been read as a response to the war propaganda that aimed to mobilize the Austro-Hungarian "Volkskraft" ("national power" or "people's power") for the defense of the empire against its barbarous enemies.[16] It has also been interpreted as a reaction to the Zionist dreams of the establishment of a Jewish state, understood as a bulwark against the barbaric East.[17] And it has been perceived as Kafka's engagement with major European philosophers who, in the words of Thomas Hobbes, reflect on the process in which a multitude of men "unite by their own decision in a single commonwealth."[18]

The Kafka scholar Benno Wagner, a driving force in the recent exploration of the discursive context of the "China complex," argues that Kafka's way of writing intervenes in the contemporary political discourses in that it "opens up and manages a trans-textual space of polyphony."[19] The important word in this quote is "manages" (or "administers": "bewirtschaftet"). Even if Kafka commented on his own "urge to imitate,"[20] his literary works do more than passively mimic the discourses of his day. The China story, for instance, is to be understood as "Kafka's reaction to and intervention in political

---

15 See among others Caygill, *Kafka: In Light of the Accident*; Hermsdorf, "Franz Kafka und die Arbeiter-Unfall-Versicherungs-Anstalt"; Benno Wagner, "'Zuerst die Mauer und dann den Turm': Der Widerstreit zwischen Biopolitik und Ethnopolitik als berufliches Problem und schriftstellerischer Einsatz Franz Kafkas," *brücken: Germanistisches Jahrbuch* 15 (2007); "Kafkas 'vergleichende Völkergeschichte': Eine Skizze zum Verhältnis von Litteratur und kulturellem Wissen," *Aussiger Beiträge* 2 (2008); Wolf, "Die Nacht des Bürokraten," *Deutsche Vierteljahrsschrift für Literaturwissenschaft und Geistesgeschichte* 80, no. 1 (2006): 97–127.

16 The word "Volkskraft" is used in "Building the Great Wall of China" as well as in Kafka's wartime journalism (NS1 344; SS 116 and AS 499; OW 340). For a fine example of this kind of reading, see Hermsdorf and Wagner, "Schreibanlässe und Textformen der amtlichen Schriften Franz Kafkas."

17 Baioni, *Kafka*; Ritchie Robertson, *Kafka: Judaism, Politics, and Literature* (Oxford: Clarendon Press, 1985); Benno Wagner, "'No one indicates the direction': The Question of Leadership in Kafka's Later Stories," in *Kafka's Selected Stories: New Translations, Backgrounds and Contexts, Criticism*, ed. Stanley Corngold (New York: W.W. Norton, 2007).

18 For the role of Hobbes in "Building the Great Wall of China," see Benno Wagner, "Beim Bau der chinesischen Mauer," in *Kafka-Handbuch: Leben, Werk, Wirkung*, ed. Manfred Engel and Bernd Auerochs (Stuttgart: Metzler, 2010), 254–5; for the role of Rousseau, see Joseph Vogl, *Ort der Gewalt: Kafkas literarische Ethik* (Munich: Fink, 1990), 203–15; for the role of Nietzsche, see Benno Wagner, "Insuring Nietzsche: Kafka's Files," *New German Critique*, no. 99 (2006).

19 Wagner, "Beim Bau der chinesischen Mauer," 257.

20 "Nachahmungstrieb" (T 329; D 157); see "Lightning No Longer Flashes," 72.

discourse by the aesthetic means of narration."[21] According to Wagner, Kafka's literary works intervenes in contemporary political discourses by opening up "virtual conference spaces" or "crypto-conferences."[22] In other words, Wagner and I agree that Kafka's works should be approached as "possibilities of negotiation," as "Besprechungsmöglichkciten." The question is how one is to understand the virtual conference spaces opened up by Kafka's literary works.[23]

The Preconditions for the Work

Like Kafka's wartime writings, "Building the Great Wall of China" explores the imaginative and affective preconditions for hearing and responding to an appeal, in this case the appeal to build a wall meant to protect the Chinese from the nomads. The narrator of the China story is a relatively low-ranking architect who, prior to his retirement, worked on the construction of the wall.[24] As a mid-level security professional,

---

21 Benno Wagner, "'Ende oder Anfang?': Kafka und der Judenstaat," in *Kafka, Zionism, and Beyond*, ed. Mark H. Gelber (Tübingen, Germany: Niemeyer, 2004), 223; "Lightning No Longer Flashes," 64.

22 "'Ende oder Anfang?': Kafka und der Judenstaat," 230; "No one indicates," 319; "Beim Bau der chinesischen Mauer," 259.

23 There seems to be a difference of nuances between the way Wagner and I understand literature's "possibility of negotiation." Wagner departs from a distinction between, on the one hand, the matrix text, understood as Kafka's inalterable literary text, in this case the printed pages of "Building the Great Wall of China"; and, on the other hand, the echo texts, understood as the polyphonic choir of contemporary discourses which the matrix text calls forth in the mind of the reader. The important thing, Wagner argues, is that Kafka's way of writing resuscitates not one single echo text but a large number of echo texts: "When, instead of the reflexive movement from matrix text to echo text and back again, the movement between the echo texts comes into view; when, in other words, the virtual conference space opened up by Kafka's texts is filled up again with speeches—it becomes possible to perceive and to experience the peculiar short circuit between aesthetics and politics made by Kafka's literature." "Beim Bau der chinesischen Mauer," 259. Here Wagner locates the virtual conference spaces at the level of discourses. To him, the thought process going on in the conference space is a movement back and forth between linguistic texts. By contrast, I focus on a cognitive movement that oscillates between sensible images. In the terminology of Jacques Rancière, in other words, we have to do with a difference between discussion and dissensus; see, for instance, *Dissensus*, 69. As I see it, the stereoscopic setup does not juxtapose two conflicting verbal propositions about the world but, more fundamentally, two incompatible sensory worlds.

24 (NS1 340; SS 114).

he happens to be a colleague of the insurance officer Franz Kafka. On the very last pages of the story, he tells a story about the day when he, as a young boy, first heard of the proclamation announcing the building of the wall:

> Into this world news of the building of the wall now penetrated. It, too, was delayed by some thirty years since its proclamation. It was on a summer evening. I, ten years old, was standing with my father on the riverbank [. . .]. At that moment a sailboat came to a halt before us; the boatman signaled to my father to come down the embankment; he himself climbed up toward him. They met halfway; the boatman whispered in my father's ear; to get close enough, he put his arms around him. I could not understand what they were saying; saw only that my father did not seem to believe it; the boatman tried to corroborate its truth; my father still could not believe it; then, with a sailor's passion, he practically tore his gown to shreds at his chest to warrant the truth; my father became quieter and the boatman leaped with a thump into the boat and sailed away.[25]

The first sentence of the quotation ("Into this world news of the building of the wall now penetrated") marks the junction of the two main parts of the story. Whereas the first and by far the longest part describes the world into which the news of the building of the wall penetrated, the second part is a brief narrative of the "now"—the moment in which the news penetrated into this world.

Interestingly, the short narrative of this extraordinary summer evening is not concerned with the content of the proclamation. The narrator stresses that he, as a young boy, could not understand what the sailor and the father were saying to each other, and a couple of lines further down he adds that he, as a retired architect, does not remember

---

25 "In diese Welt drang nun die Nachricht vom Mauerbau. Auch sie verspätet etwa dreißig Jahre nach ihrer Verkündigung. Es war an einem Sommerabend. Ich, zehn Jahre alt, stand mit meinem Vater am Flußufer. [. . .] Da hielt eine Barke vor uns, der Schiffer winkte meinem Vater zu, er möge die Böschung herabkommen, er selbst stieg ihm entgegen. In der Mitte trafen sie einander, der Schiffer flüsterte meinem Vater etwas ins Ohr; um ihm ganz nahezukommen umarmte er ihn. Ich verstand die Reden nicht, sah nur wie der Vater die Nachricht nicht zu glauben schien, der Schiffer die Wahrheit zu bekräftigen suchte, der Vater noch immer nicht glauben konnte, der Schiffer mit der Leidenschaftlichkeit des Schiffervolkes zum Beweise der Wahrheit fast sein Kleid auf der Brust zerriß, der Vater stiller wurde und der Schiffer polternd in die Barke sprang und weg fuhr" (NS1 356–7; SS 123).

the exact words his father said when he returned to their home, only that he "said something like: A strange boatman—I know all those who usually sail by here, but this one was a stranger—has just told me that a great wall is going to be built to protect the emperor."[26]

Rather than the proclamation itself, the narrative focuses on the way in which the proclamation penetrates into the childhood world of the narrator. Earlier in the story, he has related the old Chinese legend of the imperial message, published separately in *A Country Doctor*, according to which the emperor's messenger, "a strong man, a tireless man, a swimmer without equal,"[27] will always be obstructed by the imperial palace and the imperial capital, "heaped to the top with its sediment. No one can penetrate this."[28] In the narrative that ends the China story, the boatman must whisper in the father's ear, put his arms around him, try to corroborate the truth of the message, and finally tear his gown to shreds at his chest before the father finally believes the news.

The first part of "Building the Great Wall of China," on the other hand, is concerned with the world into which the news of the building of the wall penetrated. As it occurs, the narrator is not only an architect of the lower ranks but also an amateur historian or ethnographer who, already while the wall was being built, but especially after its conclusion, has been "occupied almost exclusively with the comparative history of peoples."[29] Thus, the bulk of the story consists of the narrator's reflections on the social and political life of China, highlighting first the construction of the wall and then the institution of the emperor.

At the very beginning of the story, the narrator offers a detailed discussion of the so-called "system of partial construction."[30] According to this building method, gangs of about twenty workers each completed a part of the wall of about five hundred yards while adjoining work gangs constructed a wall of equal length to meet it. As a consequence,

---

26 "Mein Vater sagte also etwa: [Ein fremder Schiffer—ich kenne alle, die gewöhnlich hier vorüberfahren, dieser aber war fremd—hat mir eben erzählt, dass eine grosse Mauer gebaut werden soll um den Kaiser zu schützen]" (NS1 357, NS1A 302; SS 123–4). Kafka deleted the father's utterance in the manuscript before abandoning the story completely.

27 "ein kräftiger, ein unermüdlicher Mann, ein Schwimmer sondergleichen" (NS1 351; SS 120).

28 "hochgeschüttet voll ihres Bodensatzes. Niemand dringt hier durch" (NS1 352; SS 120).

29 "fast ausschließlich mit vergleichender Völkergeschichte beschäftigt" (NS1 348; SS 118).

30 "System des Teilbaues" (NS1 337; SS 113).

numerous large gaps came about at the ends of these pieces of a thousand yards of wall—gaps that were only "gradually and slowly filled in."[31] Evidently, building a permeable wall is inconsistent with the need to protect the Chinese people from the nomads. "After all," the narrator writes, "the wall was conceived of as a defense against the peoples of the north. But how can a wall that is not a continuous structure offer protection? Indeed, not only can such a wall not protect, but the construction itself is in perpetual danger."[32]

Nevertheless, the construction could probably not have proceeded by any other method, the narrator asserts. His argument does not hinge on the idea of the function of the wall but, rather, on the idea of the preconditions allowing its erection:

> To understand this, one has to consider the following: the wall is supposed to provide protection for centuries; hence the most painstaking construction, the application of the architectural wisdom of all known ages and peoples, and the permanent feeling of personal responsibility in the builders were indispensable preconditions for the work.[33]

It is worth noting that the "indispensable preconditions for the work" are not only technical but also affective and imaginative. Without a permanent "feeling" ("Gefühl") of personal responsibility among the builders, it is impossible to pursue this sort of collaborative work. To supervise as few as four day laborers, the narrator adds a couple of lines further down, a man was needed who was "able to feel in the depths of his heart the purpose of this undertaking."[34] According to the narrator, those who felt the purpose of this undertaking were able to visualize themselves as being grown together with the wall:

---

31 "nach und nach langsam ausgefüllt wurden" (NS1 338; SS 113).

32 "Die Mauer war doch, wie allgemein verbreitet wird und bekannt ist, zum Schutz gegen die Nordvölker gedacht. Wie kann aber eine Mauer schützen die nicht zusammenhängend ist. Ja eine solche Mauer kann nicht nur nicht schützen, der Bau selbst ist in fortwährender Gefahr" (NS1 338; SS 113).

33 "Um das zu verstehn, muß man folgendes bedenken: Die Mauer sollte ein Schutz für die Jahrhunderte werden, sorgfältigster Bau, Benützung aller bekannten Zeiten und Völker, dauerndes Gefühl der persönlichen Verantwortung der Bauenden waren deshalb unumgängliche Voraussetzungen für die Arbeit" (NS1 339; SS 113–4).

34 "ein Mann der imstande war, bis in die Tiefe des Herzens mitzufühlen um was es hier gieng" (NS1 339; SS 114).

those who finally came in to lead the construction, even those at the bottom, were truly worthy of their responsibilities; these were men who had given a great deal of thought to the wall and never stopped thinking about it, who, on sinking their first stone into the ground, felt that they were, to a certain extent, grown together with the wall.[35]

Yet this feeling of purpose petered out during the roughly five years it took to finish 500 yards of wall: "by that time, of course, the leaders were generally exhausted and had lost all confidence in themselves, the construction, and the world."[36] Therefore, after the festival held when the sections of the thousand-yard wall were joined together, the leading builders were sent on celebratory tours through the whole country, were given medals, were cheered by new armies of workers, and spent some time at home. After this revitalization of the builders' social imaginary, they regained the desire to work on the wall: they "left home sooner than necessary, half the village accompanied them for long stretches; on all the roads, greetings, pennants, and flags: never before had they seen how great and rich and beautiful and lovable their country was."[37]

In his wartime writings, Kafka discussed the social imaginary as a precondition for donating to "this great German Bohemian *Werk*."[38] In "Building the Great Wall of China," his Chinese narrator reflects on the social imaginary as a precondition for building "this future *Werk*."[39] Thus, in the terminology of the *Prager Tagblatt* article, the point of the system of partial construction is to clearly show the Chinese builders that all of them are the empire, and that none of them—not even in their moments of despair—stands outside the concept of the empire.

---

35 "Aber diejenigen, die endlich als Bauführer sei es auch untersten Ranges zum Baue kamen, waren dessen tatsächlich würdig, es waren Männer die viel über den Bau nachgedacht hatten und nicht aufhörten darüber nachzudenken, die sich mit dem ersten Stein, den sie in den Boden einsenken ließen, dem Bau gewissermaßen verwachsen fühlten" (NS1 340; SS 114).

36 "dann waren zwar die Führer in der Regel zu Tode erschöpft, hatten alles Zutrauen zu sich, zum Bau, zur Welt verloren" (NS1 341; SS 115).

37 "sie reisten früher von zuhause fort als es nötig gewesen wäre, das halbe Dorf begleitete sie lange Strecken weit, auf allen Wegen Grüße, Wimpel und Fahnen, niemals hatten sie gesehn wie groß und reich und schön und liebenswert ihr Land war" (NS1 342; SS 115).

38 "an diesem großen deutschböhmischen Werk" (AS 500; OW 346).

39 "zu dem künftigen neuen Werk" (NS1 344; SS 116).

Stereoscopic China

While Kafka's reading of Hobbes's *Leviathan* and Rousseau's *Social Contract* is not documented, the contrast between the Chinese and the nomads that informs the entire "China complex" appears to draw heavily on the classical philosophical distinction between civil state and natural state. On the one hand, the Chinese live in a well-ordered society organized institutionally by the hierarchic imperial bureaucracy and spatially by the imperial capital, "the center of the world."[40] On the other hand, the nomads live a lawless and centerless life which, according to the social imaginary of the China stories, barely counts as human. According to the narrator, the nomads "changed their dwelling places with incomprehensible rapidity, like locusts."[41]

It goes without saying that this fundamental opposition between the orderly configuration of the Chinese community and the disorderly configuration of the nomad community is not a stereoscopic juxtaposition. If two images of different objects are placed side by side in an optical stereoscope—say, a photo of an Italian city and a photo of an Abyssinian village—the viewer will not be able to fuse them into a unified picture that offers an illusion of three-dimensional depth. According to the second thesis of this book, the form of Kafka's stereoscopes is a juxtaposition of two dissimilar images of the *same* community, in this case the Chinese community.

The stories that we have analyzed in the previous chapters all contain two disjunctive judgments on the same community, be it the group of friends to which Georg Bendemann and his Russian friend belong, the five or six individuals standing in a row outside a house, or the female workers attending the noisy machines of an asbestos factory. Similarly, in "Building the Great Wall of China," we find two different judgments on the configuration of the Chinese community. According to the narrator, those who lead the construction of the wall, even those at the lowest levels of leadership like himself, were "really" or "truly" ("tatsächlich") worthy of the job. Yet if we take another look at the passage in question, it reveals that they were also truly *not* worthy of it. Like old Bendemann's final verdict about Georg Bendemann in "The Judgment," the narrator juxtaposes "true" and "truer still":

> those who finally came in to lead the construction, even those at the bottom, were truly worthy of their responsibilities; these were men who had given a great deal of thought to the wall and never

---

40   "die Mitte der Welt" (NS1 352; SS 120).
41   "mit unbegreiflicher Schnelligkeit wie Heuschrecken ihre Wohnsitze wechselten" (NS1 339; SS 113).

stopped thinking about it, who, on sinking their first stone into the ground, felt that they were, to a certain extent [*gewissermaßen*], grown together with the wall.[42]

Accidentally, the German "gewissermaßen"—"to a certain extent" or "in a certain sense"—has been omitted in Brod's original edition of the story,[43] and hence also in most translations of it. This is probably one of the reasons why the stereoscopic setup of the China story is rarely commented on in the research.[44] The leading builders felt that they had "grown together" or become part of the wall—*to a certain extent*. Thus, the outcome of the judgment seems to depend on the measure on which the act of judging is based ("gewissermaßen" contains the word "Maß", or "measure").

On the orderly image, the Chinese community is represented as a unified body politic in which the individuals are bound together by the strong ties of brotherhood and blood. This is how the builders view society when they leave their homeland after a well-deserved holiday and half the village accompanies them for long stretches with greetings, pennants, and flags:

> never before had they seen how great and rich and beautiful and lovable their country was; every fellow countryman was a brother for whom they were building a protective wall and who was thankful all his life, thankful with everything that he had and was: unity! unity! breast on breast, a round dance of the people, blood no longer confined in the meager circulatory system of the body but rolling on sweetly and yet ever returning through the infinity of China.[45]

---

42   (NS1 340; SS 114).

43   (BK 69).

44   An exception is Siegfried Kracauer's perceptive essay from 1931 in which he distinguishes between two different configurations of the Chinese society: "what is most important for him [Kafka] is to play off the dense structure of the present against the looseness of the earlier moment." Siegfried Kracauer, *The Mass Ornament: Weimer Essays*, trans. Thomas Y. Levin (Cambridge, MA, and London: Harvard University Press, 1995), 275. To my knowledge, however, this important distinction between a dense and a loose structure of Chinese society has played a small role in the following years of Kafka research.

45   "niemals hatten sie gesehn wie groß und reich und schön und liebenswert ihr Land war, jeder Landsmann war ein Bruder, für den man eine Schutzmauer baute und der mit allem was er hatte und war sein Leben lang dafür dankte, Einheit! Einheit! Brust an Brust, ein Reigen des Volkes, Blut, nicht mehr eingesperrt im kärglichen Kreislauf des Körpers, sondern süß rollend und doch wiederkehrend durch das unendliche China" (NS1 342; SS 115).

This image of the Chinese community is a precursor of the dream vision of "warm togetherness" in "Researches of a Dog," written five years later. As we saw in Chapter 4, the researcher dog's imagining of the canine community was structured by a web of spatial metaphors, not least a tension between centripetal and centrifugal forces. "One can safely say that we live together literally in one single heap, all of us [. . .]. Something urges us toward one another," the dog claimed, imagining a centripetal force or "urge" ("Drängen") that "binds us happily together."[46] In the above quote from "Building the Great Wall of China," the imaginary blood is not only rolling on sweetly through the infinity of China but is also, thanks to a centripetal force, "returning" to its source ("und doch wiederkehrend"). The image of the circulation of blood ("Blutkreis") is repeated in the image of the people arranged in "a round dance" ("ein Reigen des Volkes").[47]

By contrast, the disorderly image depicts the Chinese community as a community that has never really left the natural state for the civil state. A couple of pages above, the narrator stated that the builders were, to a certain extent, "grown together with the wall."[48] Yet now he asserts that all Chinese citizens, in fact, all human beings, cannot endure being fettered to a wall and therefore violently tear themselves away from it:

> There was a great deal of confusion in people's minds at that time [. . .] perhaps precisely because so many people were seeking to come together as much as possible around a single purpose. Human nature, flighty in its essence, made like dust flying up, cannot endure being fettered; if it fetters itself, it will soon go mad, begin to rattle its chains, and tear to pieces

---

46   "Man darf doch wohl sagen, daß wir alle förmlich in einem einzigen Haufen leben [. . .] Es drängt uns zueinander" (NS2 425; SS 133).

47   As Scott Spector has cogently shown, Kafka was not alone in imagining the political community in the image of a circle. In the figuration of social life, Spector argues, the image of a circle played an important role in the so-called Prague circle to which Kafka belonged, together with a number of German-speaking Jews of the same age, among them Max Brod, Franz Werfel, Hugo Bergmann, Otto Pick, and Egon Erwin Kisch: "the rhetorical form of the circle has a number of functions. The first is the quality of circumscription, a gesture that at once effects a charting of inclusion and of exclusion, a dichotomy of internality and externality." Scott Spector, *Prague Territories: National Conflict and Cultural Innovation in Franz Kafka's Fin de Siècle* (Berkeley, CA: University of California Press, 2000), 19.

48   (NS1 340; SS 114).

wall, chain, and itself, scattering them to the four quarters of heaven.[49]

This depiction of human nature prefigures the researcher dog's image of the dog community as consisting of foreigners rather than fellow dogs: "But now the other side of the coin. No species, to my knowledge, lives so widely dispersed as we dogs do."[50] In this disorderly state, the dogs are driven by a centrifugal force that, "time and time again, irresistibly, admittedly, tears us out of the circle of the people."[51] In the disorderly image from "Building the Great Wall of China," the centrifugal thrust is given material shape in images of dust and rubble. Whereas the blood moves inward toward the heart, the particles of dust and rubble move chaotically outward: human nature is made like dust flying up ("auffliegenden Staubes"), and the pieces of wall, chain, and human beings are scattered "to the four quarters of heaven" ("in alle Himmelsrichtungen").

By the way, this image of a dispersive movement is also used to characterize the unruly and unbiddable Chinese people elsewhere in the story.[52] Two pages further down, the narrator uses an often-repeated Chinese parable to explain to what extent a Chinese citizen should think about the decrees of the leadership. "You will be as the river in spring," the narrator writes, which "keeps its own essence intact as it runs into the sea."[53] By contrast, excessive independent thinking sets in motion a destructive centrifugal force:

> But then the river overflows its banks, loses its outline and its shape, slows in its downward course, tries to run counter to its

---

49 "Es gab [. . .] viel Verwirrung der Köpfe damals, vielleicht gerade deshalb weil sich so viele möglichst auf einen Zweck hin zu sammeln suchten. Das menschliche Wesen, leichtfertig in seinem Grunde, von der Natur des auffliegenden Staubes, verträgt keine Fesselung, fesselt es sich selbst, wird es bald wahnsinnig an den Fesseln zu rütteln anfangen und Mauer Kette und sich selbst in alle Himmelsrichtungen zerreißen" (NS1 344; SS 116).

50 "Nun aber das Gegenspiel hierzu. Kein Geschöpf lebt meines Wissens so weithin zerstreut wie wir Hunde" (NS2 425–6; SS 133).

51 "was uns immer wieder unwiderstehlich aus dem Volkskreis zerrt" (NS2 426; SS 133).

52 At one instance, the small children are "scattered in all directions, sobbing"; in another scene, "everyone scattered and ran off into the beautiful day" ("heulend uns nach allen seiten zu unsern Eltern verliefen" and "alles zerstreute sich und lief in den schönen Tag" [NS1 340, NS1A 298; SS 113, 121]).

53 "Es wird Dir geschehn wie dem Fluß im Frühjahr. Er steigt, wird mächtiger, nährt kräftiger das Land an seinen langen Ufern, behält sein eigenes Wesen weiter ins Meer hinein" (NS1 346; SS 117).

destiny by forming little inland seas, damages the fields, and yet, since it cannot continue spreading itself so thin, instead runs back into its banks and in the hot season that follows even dries out dismally. Do not think this far about the decrees of the leadership.[54]

According to this parable, a centrifugal force spreads the river thin and dissolves its outline and its shape. This force is, of course, also exerted by the nomads that roam outside the confines of the Chinese empire. In other words, the disorderly image depicts the Chinese *as if* they were nomads. In Hobbes's terminology, the narrator does not claim that the Chinese commonwealth is actually dissolved into swirling particles of dust, rubble, and water; he considers the Chinese people "as if they were dissolved" (*ut tanquam dissoluta consideretur*).[55]

This way of envisioning China transports the disorder from the periphery to the center of the empire, thereby complicating the neat opposition between inside and outside, between civil state and natural state. At the emperor's court, the innermost center of the Chinese society, the narrator imagines a pre-legal and pre-moral state of nature that even trumps the fierceness of the nomads: "The emperor's wives—overfed among their silk cushions, estranged from noble custom by cunning courtiers, swollen with lust for power, irascible in their greed, expansive in their lust—commit their villainies again and again anew."[56]

An Obscure Concept

To the Chinese people, Hans Heilmann writes in the introduction to his anthology of Chinese poetry, "love of fatherland is alien or an obscure concept [*ein unklarer Begriff*]: the greater the love of home, of a closer-knit fatherland."[57] One reason for the lack of patriotism in the Chinese

---

54 "Dann aber übersteigt der Fluß seine Ufer, verliert Umrisse und Gestalt, verlangsamt seinen Abwärtslauf, versucht gegen seine Bestimmung kleine Meere im Binnenland zu bilden, schädigt die Fluren, und kann sich doch für die Dauer in dieser Ausbreitung nicht halten, sondern rinnt wieder in seine Ufer zusammen, ja trocknet sogar in der folgenden heißen Jahreszeit kläglich ein. Soweit denke den Anordnungen der Führerschaft nicht nach" (NS1 346; SS 117).

55 Hobbes, *On the Citizen*, 10, translation modified; *Elementa philosophica de cive* (Amsterdam and Lausanne: Franciscum Grasset, 1760), 21.

56 "Die kaiserlichen Frauen, überfüttert in den seidenen Kissen, von schlauen Höflingen der edlen Sitte entfremdet, anschwellend in Herrschsucht, auffahrend in Gier, ausgebreitet in Wollust, verüben ihre Untaten immer wieder von Neuem" (NS1 353; SS 121).

57 Heilmann, *Chinesische Lyrik*, ix, my translation.

people is their robust practical mindset oriented toward business and material well-being in the local *Heimat*.[58] Another reason is their characteristic "way of thinking and perceiving" ("Denk- und Anschauungsweise"), which can grasp the idea of the fatherland only as an obscure concept.[59] According to Heilmann, the "weak spot of the Chinese nature religion" was the "lack of sensible imaginative content."[60]

Kafka takes up this theme by letting his narrator offer a detailed discussion of the Chinese people's poor imagination. In the second half of his historical reflection on the world into which the news of the wall penetrated, the narrator shifts his focus from the system of the partial construction to the institution of the empire: "I have found that we Chinese possess certain public and state institutions that are uniquely clear and still others that are uniquely obscure [*in einzigartiger Unklarheit*]," the narrator asserts, and hastens to add that the empire is certainly among "our most obscure institutions."[61]

The "confusion in people's minds" makes it impossible for them to envisage (or to "make clear in the mind," as Kafka wrote in his answer to the Austro-Hungarian press service) the spiritual whole of the Chinese political community. Thus, the weak spot of the Chinese people is their lack of ability to imagine abstract political entities such as the imperial institution and the imperial capital: "It is harder for us to imagine such a city than to believe that Peking and its emperor are one single thing, say, a cloud peacefully changing shape under the sun in the course of the ages."[62]

In most cases, the narrator uses the German word "Auffassung" when referring to the way of thinking and perceiving enjoyed by the Chinese people. Even if the existing English translations render "Auffassung" as "attitude,"[63] I would suggest "perception," "apprehension," or "view," since these are words connoting a nonconceptual relation to the political community. What the narrator

---

58 *Chinesische Lyrik*, xi, my translation.
59 *Chinesische Lyrik*, xviii, my translation.
60 *Chinesische Lyrik*, xi, my translation.
61 "ich habe dabei gefunden, daß wir Chinesen gewisse volkliche und staatliche Einrichtungen in einzigartiger Klarheit, andere wieder in einzigartiger Unklarheit besitzen" and "unsern allerundeutlichsten Einrichtungen" (NS1 348–9; SS 118).
62 "Leichter als solche Stadt sich vorstellen ist es zu glauben, Peking und sein Kaiser wären eines, etwa eine Wolke, ruhig unter der Sonne sich wandelnd im Laufe der Zeiten" (NS1 354; SS 122).
63 (SS 122; GWC 69; CS 247).

calls "the dominant *Auffassung* concerning the Emperor" is, as I see it, a social imaginary: the repertoire of collective acts of figuration that supply sensible presentations of an abstract and absent political entity. In Rancièrian terms, it is a matter of the "common *aisthesis*" by which the Chinese perceive their political order:[64]

> I may perhaps be permitted to say that the dominant perception concerning the emperor again and again and everywhere exhibits certain features in common with the perception in my homeland. Now, I have no intention of accepting this perception as a virtue, on the contrary. And while it is mainly the fault of the regime, which in this most ancient empire on earth has always been unable, perhaps through neglect of this concern in favor of other matters, to develop the institution of empire with such clarity that it would exercise its influence immediately and incessantly as far as the realm's most distant frontiers. Nevertheless, it is on the other hand a weakness of imagination or conviction among the people, who are unable to embrace the empire obediently, in all its liveliness and presence, raising it from its submersion in Peking; and yet the subjects wish nothing more than just for once to feel this connection and drown in it.[65]

According to the narrator, the fault is to be attributed to the constitution as well as to the configuration of the community. On the one hand, the regime has been unable to develop the institution of empire with sufficient clarity; on the other, the Chinese people, due to their paucity of imagination or conviction, have been unable to "clearly show" to themselves that together they make up the empire. Thus, the sheer size of the imperial constitution seems to impede the people's sensible figuration of their communal life.

---

64 Rancière, *Dissensus*, 38, 133.

65 "[. . .] auf Grund alles dessen darf ich vielleicht sagen, daß die Auffassung die hinsichtlich des Kaisers herrscht, immer wieder und überall einen gewissen gemeinsamen Grundzug mit der Auffassung in meiner Heimat zeigt. Diese Auffassung will ich nun durchaus nicht als eine Tugend gelten lassen, im Gegenteil. Zwar ist sie in der Hauptsache von der Regierung verschuldet, die im ältesten Reich der Erde bis heute nicht imstande war oder dies über anderem vernachlässigte, die Institution des Kaisertums zu solcher Klarheit auszubilden, daß sie bis an die fernsten Grenzen des Reiches unmittelbar und unablässig wirke. Andererseits aber liegt doch auch darin eine Schwäche der Vorstellungs oder Glaubenskraft beim Volke, welches nicht dazu gelangt, das Kaisertum aus der Pekinger Versunkenheit in aller Lebendigkeit und Gegenwärtigkeit an seine Untertanenbrust zu ziehn, die doch nichts besseres will, als einmal diese Berührung zu fühlen und an ihr zu vergehn" (NS1 355; SS 122–3).

Once again, Kafka focuses on the sensible medium in which the political community is shown to the Chinese, be it in a clear or a confused way. Interestingly, the narrator offers a detailed rhetorical analysis of the confused social imaginary. In the passages preceding the one quoted above, he addresses the collective web of tropes and figures that frame the way the Chinese view their communal life. Thus, the dominant perception of the emperor is a figuration of the community, understood as a representation of communal life shaped according to prevailing patterns of rhetorical figures:

> Just so, as hopelessly and hopefully, our people view the emperor. They do not know which emperor is reigning, and there is even doubt about the name of the dynasty. A lot of this sort of thing is learned by rote at school, but the general uncertainty in this respect is so great that even the best students are drawn into it. In our villages, long-dead emperors are set on the throne, and one who lives on only in song has recently issued a decree that the priest reads aloud in front of the altar. Battles from our most ancient history are just now being fought, and with glowing cheeks your neighbor bursts into your house with the news.[66]

On the basis on the narrator's rhetorical analysis, the Chinese people's weak imagination—their "general uncertainty," as it is dubbed in the quotation—can be described as prosopopoeic. "Prosopopoeia" is a Greek rhetorical term closely related to the more well-known Latin term "personification," the trope in which an inanimate object or an abstract concept is spoken of as if endowed with life or with human attributes. Prosopopoeia is a specific kind of personification in that it presents an imaginary or absent person as speaking or acting. In a typical prosopopoeia, the corpse speaks. Etymologically, prosopopoeia means making a face—a *prosōpon* is a mask (like the Latin "persona"), and *poien* comes from *poiesis* ("making"). In other words, this rhetorical

---

66 "Genau so, so hoffnungslos und hoffnungsvoll sieht unser Volk den Kaiser. Es weiß nicht welcher Kaiser regiert und selbst über den Namen der Dynastie bestehen Zweifel. In der Schule wird vieles dergleichen der Reihe nach gelernt, aber die allgemeine Unsicherheit in dieser Hinsicht ist so groß daß auch der beste Schüler mit in sie gezogen wird. Längst verstorbene Kaiser werden in unseren Dörfern auf den Tron gesetzt und der nur noch im Liede lebt, hat vor Kurzem eine Bekanntmachung erlassen, die der Priester vor dem Altare verliest. Schlachten unserer ältesten Geschichte werden jetzt erst geschlagen und mit glühendem Gesicht fällt der Nachbar mit der Nachricht Dir ins Haus" (NS1 352–3; SS 120–1).

play with masks blurs the boundary between life and death, between animated and inanimate.

In the narrator's analysis of the weak spot in the Chinese power of imagination, however, the boundary between life and death is crossed in both directions. If all instances of prosopopoeia are "giving face," there is still a crucial difference between giving a dead person the face of a living person and, inversely, furnishing a living person with a death mask.

On the one hand, an animating type of prosopopoeia endows a dead or absent person with life. This is the trope which gives a living face "with glowing cheeks" to the stories of battles from the most ancient history and, in the above quote, which sets long-dead emperors on the throne.

On the other hand, a deanimating type of prosopopoeia presents a living person as if she were dead. In our villages, the narrator remarks, not only are long-dead emperors set on the throne, living emperors are put in the grave: "one who lives on only in song has recently issued a decree that the priest reads aloud in front of the altar." This rarer type of prosopopoeia is a figurative process that hides a living person behind a death mask. To see a living emperor as "one who lives on only in song"[67] is to see him as living on as dead.[68]

When the narrator writes that, in the villages of China, long-dead emperors are "set on the throne," the word "set" reveals the positing power of this specific process of figuration. Hereby it is important to note that this power not only transports the dead emperor into the world of the living; it also puts him in a position in which he has the authority to make decisions about Chinese societal life. The prosopopoeia is performative: the imaginative figure intervenes into the social and political reality.

A few paragraphs later, the narrator continues his rhetorical analysis of the confused minds of the Chinese people. This time he offers a description of a fairly straightforward situation in which an imperial official on a tour of inspection comes to the village and exerts political power authorized by the emperor in Peking.[69] Yet, due to their

---

67   "nur noch im Liede lebt."
68   It is important not to misconstrue this deanimating type of prosopopoeia as a disfiguration of prosopopoeia. As we saw in Chapter 4, the literary theorist Paul de Man defined a disfiguration as a disruptive unmasking of the mechanisms of figurative language; see de Man, *The Rhetoric of Romanticism*, 110. The deanimating prosopopoeia is a figurative process, not a debunking of a figurative process: to give someone a death mask is not to demask her.
69   The tour of inspection is also prefigured in Heilmann's preface; see Heilmann, *Chinesische Lyrik*, xii.

dysfunctional imagination, the villagers manage to turn this simple bureaucratic event into a political conundrum:

> This, then, is how the people deal with past emperors, although they mix up the current ones with the dead ones. If once, once in a lifetime, an imperial official touring the provinces accidentally comes into our village, makes certain demands in the name of the ruler, examines the tax rolls, visits schools, questions the priest about our doings, and then, before climbing back into his sedan chair, summarizes everything in long admonitions to the community rounded up there to hear him, a smile flickers across all our faces, each man looks furtively to the next and bends down to the children so as not to be observed by the official. What, one thinks, he is speaking about a dead man as if he were a living man, this emperor died a long time ago, the dynasty was wiped out, the official is making fun of us, but we will act as if we did not notice, so as not to hurt his feelings. But we will seriously obey only our present ruler, for to do otherwise would be a sin. And behind the sedan chair of the official, as it races off, someone who has been arbitrarily elevated climbs out of his already crumbling urn and stamps his foot as master of the village.[70]

Here the narrator analyzes the villagers' reflective knowledge of a process of figuration. In the narrator's village, "one thinks" ("denkt man") that the official is speaking in rhetorical figures. More specifically, the villagers seem to be able to identify an instance of prosopopoeia: "he is speaking about a dead man as if he were a living man." This kind of reflective knowledge leads to a disfiguration or debunking of the

---

70 "So verfährt also das Volk mit den Vergangenen, die Gegenwärtigen aber mischt es unter die Toten. Kommt einmal, einmal in einem Menschenalter, ein kaiserlicher Beamter, der die Provinz bereist, zufällig in unser Dorf, stellt im Namen des Regierenden irgendwelche Forderungen, prüft die Steuerlisten, wohnt dem Schulunterrichte bei, befragt den Priester über unser Tun und Treiben und faßt dann alles, ehe er in seine Sänfte steigt, zu langen Ermahnungen an die herbeigetriebene Gemeinde zusammen, dann geht ein Lächeln über alle Gesichter, einer blickt verstohlen zum andern, man beugt sich zu den Kindern herab, um sich vom Beamten nicht beobachten zu lassen. Wie, denkt man, er spricht von einem Toten wie von einem Lebendigen, dieser Kaiser ist doch schon längst gestorben, die Dynastie ausgelöscht, der Herr Beamte macht sich über uns lustig, aber wir tun so als ob wirs nicht merkten, um ihn nicht zu kränken. Ernstlich gehorchen aber werden wir nur unserm gegenwärtigen Herrn, alles andere wäre Versündigung. Und hinter der davoneilenden Sänfte des Beamten steigt irgendein willkürlich aus schon zerfallener Urne Gehobener aufstampfend als Herr des Dorfes auf" (NS1 353–4; SS 121).

power of the rhetorical figure; rather than obeying the long admonitions of the official, smiles flicker across the faces of the crowd, a sign of their ironic awareness of the tricks of the figurative process taking place in front of them. It is worth noting here that the reflective knowledge of the villagers sets in motion a centrifugal force. In German, the official addresses a "herbeigetriebene Gemeinde," a community "rounded up" or "driven together" in order to hear his admonitions. After the ironic insight, though, the centripetal force that urges the community toward the imperial sedan chair is countered by a centrifugal force driving them away from the center. Now "each man looks furtively to the next"—that is, no longer to the official—"and bends down to the children so as not to be observed by the official."

To be sure, the reflective knowledge of the villagers is a false knowledge. If we are to believe the narrator, the official is indeed an envoy of the present emperor. By consequence, his language is literal rather than figurative: he speaks plainly about a living man as if he were a living man. The villagers' ironical demystification of the official's speech in fact hinges on a deeper-lying mystification of which they are unaware. In this game of "properly . . . but more properly," the figurative sentence is in fact the one that the Chinese perceive as literal and demystifying: "this emperor died a long time ago, the dynasty was wiped out." This sentence is an instance of a deanimating or deadening prosopopoeia in which a living man is given the face of one deceased. Thus, in Hans Heilmann's terms, the narrator offers a rhetorical analysis of the way in which "skepticism and harsh superstition rule in close co-operation" in the Chinese people.[71]

Moreover, at the end of the quote, the villagers, in spite of their reflective knowledge, make precisely the kind of animating prosopopoeia they think they had exposed in the official's speech. As the sedan chair races off from the village, "someone who has been arbitrarily elevated climbs out of his already crumbling urn and stamps his foot as master of the village." Literally, this sentence speaks about a dead man who dwells in an already crumbling urn; figuratively, however, the sentence presents him as a living man. In German, this resuscitated man is referred to as a "Gehobener," as someone elevated or lifted up out of the urn, a remarkable word that points out the prosopopoeic act of figuration that sets the dead emperors on the throne.

Yet the "Gehobener" is not an emperor of the infinite China but, instead, an ancestor from the village. As Heilmann notes, the religion of ancient China was fundamentally one of ancestor-worship: "the spirits

---

71 Heilmann, *Chinesische Lyrik*, ix.

of the ancestors were the connecting link between the common mortals and the higher powers."[72] In the vocabulary of Hobbes's *Leviathan*, what Heilmann describes here is an example of "ghostly power." As opposed to the civil power of the present political sovereign, the ghostly power, according to Hobbes, is the extra-political power pertaining to bishops and religious persons "that moveth the members of a commonwealth, by the terror of punishments."[73] Thus, in "Building the Great Wall of China," the weakness of their imagination makes the Chinese people obey the ghostly power of the local ancestors rather than the political power of distant emperors.

Subject to No Current Law
In the last paragraphs of the historical and ethnographical reflections on the Chinese world, just before the brief description of his childhood memory about the proclamation of the wall, the narrator shifts his focus away from the way in which people's minds are confused to the way in which they manage to live with this confusion. The point he is making here is that the weakness of imagination among the people, as described in the previous paragraphs, is simultaneously a virtue and a vice:

> Thus this perception [*Auffassung*] is unlikely to be a virtue. It is all the more striking that precisely this weakness appears to be one of the most important means of unifying our people; indeed, if one may be so forward as to employ such an expression, it is the very ground on which we live.[74]

Paradoxically, the weakness of the social imaginary makes up the very ground on which the Chinese people live. On the one hand, by making them unable to imagine the political unity of the people, their prosopopoeic confusion is a vice; on the other, the confusion is also a virtue because it appears to be "one of the most important means of unifying our people." In a much-quoted paragraph, the narrator analyzes this political double bind:

> Now, the result of such opinions is, to a certain extent, a free, ungoverned life. By no means immoral; on my travels I have

---

72 *Chinesische Lyrik*, ix.
73 Hobbes, *Leviathan*, 172.
74 "Eine Tugend ist also diese Auffassung wohl nicht. Umso auffälliger ist es, daß gerade diese Schwäche eines der wichtigsten Einigungsmittel unseres Volkes zu sein scheint, ja wenn man sich im Ausdruck soweit vorwagen darf, geradezu der Boden auf dem wir leben" (NS1 356; SS 123).

hardly ever encountered such purity of morals as in my homeland. But still, a life that is subject to no current law and follows only directives and warnings that extend to us from ancient times.[75]

Perhaps due to the words "free" and "ungoverned," this passage has fallen victim to a large number of enthusiastic misreadings. In *Ort der Gewalt* (*Locus of Violence*, 1990), the literary scholar Joseph Vogl puts forward a seminal reading of the passage in the context of a discussion of Kafka's "question about the community."[76] According to Vogl, the free, ungoverned life that only follows "directives and warnings"—as opposed to complying to laws and imperatives—must be understood as a figure of a utopian community. Inspired by Jean-Luc Nancy's idea of an inoperative community, Vogl analyzes the passage as a rare and fleeting glimpse in Kafka's work of a communal life "without reference to representative incarnations such as state, God, emperor, law; a constitution of a communal being together unmediated by totality."[77]

Yet this way of reading the passage, once again, omits the word "gewissermaßen" ("to a certain extent"). To a certain extent, the Chinese people live a free, ungoverned life, namely, in so far as they do not obey the legal prescriptions of the distant emperor. To another extent, however, they live an unfree, governed life. In trying to squeeze out a progressive political vision of Kafka's text, Vogl and his many followers disregard its stereoscopic style. Vogl idealizes the villagers' "morals" (or "mores", "Sitten") and "directives and warnings" ("Weisung und Warnung") because this kind of normativity can be seen as an alternative to universal imperial law. But what he fails to see, I contend, is the other side of the coin according to which this extra-political normativity is also a kind of domination. A life that is subject to no current law is a life that is subject to a law of the past.

Two features characterize this extra-political normativity in force in the Chinese villages. First, this type of normative claims derive their

---

75   "Die Folge solcher Meinungen ist nun ein gewissermaßen freies, unbeherrschtes Leben. Keineswegs sittenlos, ich habe solche Sittenreinheit wie in meiner Heimat kaum jemals angetroffen auf meinen Reisen. Aber doch ein Leben, das unter keinem gegenwärtigen Gesetze steht und nur der Weisung und Warnung gehorcht, die aus alten Zeiten zu uns herüberreicht" (NS1 354–5; SS 122).

76   Vogl, *Ort der Gewalt*, 204.

77   *Ort der Gewalt*, 214, my translation. Also in recent research, the paragraph is interpreted in ways similar to that of Vogl; see, for instance, Caygill, *Kafka: In Light of the Accident*, 162–70; Engel, "Entwürfe symbolischer Weltordnungen," 227–8.

validity not from the authority of the present political sovereign but from tradition. According to the narrator, the directives and warnings "extend to us from ancient times." The German word for "extend" ("herüberreichen") means to hand over something, like the Latin *tradere*, the root of the word "tradition." Thus, we must assume that the master of the village who has been arbitrarily elevated out of his already crumbling urn exerts his ghostly power through a traditional kind of normativity.

Second, the extra-political normative claims are particular rather than universal. The German "Weisung" ("direction" or "instruction"), like "Zurechtweisung" and "Wegweisung" ("reproof" and "showing the way"), is a word of advice given to an individual human being—a father's instruction to his son, for example.[78] The above-mentioned parable admonishing the Chinese citizen to be as the river in spring can serve as an example of this kind of normative principle addressed to an individual "you": "In those days the secret principle held by many, even the best, was: Try with all your might to understand the decrees of the leadership, but only up to a certain point; then stop thinking about the subject."[79]

Likewise, a warning ("Warnung") is not a general rule but a threatening message given to an individual. According to the narrator, for the Chinese the raising of children hinges on this kind of normativity. "In artists' paintings, faithful to the truth," he explains, the Chinese can see the faces of the nomads as "faces of damnation, the gaping maws, the jaws equipped with long, pointed teeth, the scrunched-up eyes that seem to squint at the victim whom their maws will crush and rend." These horrific paintings are used as warnings to discipline the children: "When the children misbehave, we show them these pictures, and at once they fly, weeping, into our arms."[80]

---

78 In the unsent letter to the father from 1919, for instance, Kafka writes: "And those reproofs were so infuriating: when one was treated as a third person, not worth addressing in anger directly" ("Aufreizend waren auch jene Zurechtweisungen, wo man als dritte Person behandelt, also nicht einmal des bösen Ansprechens gewürdigt wurde" [NS2 162; MoS 101]).

79 "Damals war es geheimer Grundsatz vieler und sogar der Besten: Suche mit allen Deinen Kräften die Anordnungen der Führerschaft zu verstehn, aber nur bis zu einer bestimmten Grenze, dann höre mit dem Nachdenken auf" (NS1 345; SS 117).

80 "auf den wahrheitsgetreuen Bildern der Künstler sehen wir diese Gesichter der Verdammnis, die aufgerissenen Mäuler, die mit hoch zugespitzten Zähnen besteckten Kiefer, die verkniffenen Augen, die schon nach dem Raub zu schielen scheinen, den das Maul zermalmen und zerreißen wird. Sind die Kinder böse, halten wir ihnen diese Bilder hin und schon fliegen sie weinend an unsern Hals" (NS1 347; SS 118).

Until now, I have approached "Building the Great Wall of China" as Kafka's reaction to his own professional tasks for the Workmen's Accident Insurance Institute during the war. But, as I briefly touched upon at the beginning of this chapter, the political context of the story is not restricted to questions of insurance. In November 1916, four months before Kafka began writing the story, Franz Joseph I died after ruling the Austro-Hungarian empire for almost seventy years. And on March 8, 1917, the "February revolution"—the ostensible date discrepancy is down to Russia following the Julian calendar—erupted in Russia, bringing about the downfall of the Tsar.[81] Kafka seems to hint at these historical events when, in a deleted passage, he makes the narrator claim that "as a rule our people are scarcely affected by political upheavals, by contemporary wars."[82]

Seen in this wider context, hearing and responding to an appeal must be understood as being affected by political upheavals, that is, as participating in a political moment that breaks with an immobilized order of things and reshapes the foundation of communal life. Thus, to idealize the free, ungoverned life only subject to traditional directives and warnings is, in a sense, to side up with the authoritarian master of the village and ignore the freedom of the political moment. As quoted earlier, the political freedom of acting together is, according to Arendt, "the freedom to call something into being which did not exist before, which was not given, not even as an object of cognition or imagination."[83]

We Cannot Go Forward

"Let this appeal be heard everywhere, and let everyone respond!," Kafka began his article in the *Prager Tagblatt*. One or two months later, he wrote a short fictional text that tells the sad story of an appeal which is heard nowhere, and to which no-one responds. Max Brod published this text from Kafka's octavo notebooks in 1937 under the title "The Appeal" ("Der Aufruf"). Whereas one of Kafka's journalistic appeals to the Bohemian public was given the heading "Fellow Countrymen!",[84] "The Appeal" relates the story of a printed request distributed in a tenement house under the heading "To all my fellow lodgers" ("An alle meine Hausgenossen"). I quote the first half of the text:

81   For the contours of the Russian revolution in the China story, see William John Dodd, "Kafka's Russia and Images of War in 1912 and 1914," in *Kafka, Prag und der Erste Weltkrieg = Kafka, Prague and the First World War*, ed. Manfred Engel and Ritchie Robertson (Würzburg: Königshausen & Neumann, 2012).

82   "Ähnlich werden die Leute bei uns von staatlichen Umwälzungen von zeitgenössischen Kriegen in der Regel wenig betroffen" (NS1A 298; SS 121).

83   Arendt, *Between Past and Future*, 151.

84   "Volksgenossen!" (AS 498; OW 339).

In our house, this immense building in an outer suburb, a tenement house the fabric of which is interspersed with indestructible medieval ruins, the following appeal [*Aufruf*] was distributed today, on this foggy, icy winter morning.

To all my fellow lodgers:

I am in possession of five toy rifles. They are hanging in my wardrobe, one on each hook. The first belongs to me, and the others can be claimed by anyone who wishes to send in his name. If more than four people send in their names, the supernumerary claimants must bring their own rifles with them and deposit them in my wardrobe. For uniformity must be maintained; without uniformity we cannot go forward. Incidentally, I have only rifles that are quite useless for any other purpose, the mechanism is broken, the corks have got torn off, only the cocks still click. So it will not be difficult, should it prove necessary, to provide more such rifles. But fundamentally I am prepared, for a start, to accept even people without rifles. At the decisive moment we who have rifles will group ourselves round those who are unarmed. Why should not tactics that proved successful when used by the first American farmers against the Red Indians not also prove successful here, since after all the conditions are similar?[85]

It is evident that the unnamed person who writes a futile appeal to his fellow lodgers is in a situation parodically similar to that of Kafka who writes the unsigned appeals to his fellow Bohemian countrymen. The *Prager Tagblatt* article concludes by letting the reader know how to donate: "The Public Crownland Agency's postal checking-account

---

85 "In unserm Haus, diesem ungeheuern Vorstadthaus, einer von unzerstörbaren mittelalterlichen Ruinen durchwachsenen Mietskaserne, wurde heute am nebligen eisigen Wintermorgen folgender Aufruf verbreitet./ An alle meine Hausgenossen./ Ich besitze fünf Kindergewehre, sie hängen in meinem Kasten, an jedem Haken eines. Das erste gehört mir, zu den andern kann sich melden wer will, melden sich mehr als vier, so müssen die überzähligen ihre eigenen Gewehre mitbringen und in meinem Kasten deponieren. Denn Einheitlichkeit muß sein, ohne Einheitlichkeit kommen wir nicht vorwärts. Übrigens habe ich nur Gewehre, die zu sonstiger Verwendung ganz unbrauchbar sind, der Mechanismus ist verdorben, der Pfropfen abgerissen, nur die Hähne knacken noch. Es wird also nicht schwer sein, nötigenfalls noch weitere solche Gewehre zu beschaffen. Aber im Grunde sind mir für die erste Zeit auch Leute ohne Gewehre recht, wir die wir Gewehre haben werden im entscheidenden Augenblick die Unbewaffneten in die Mitte nehmen. Eine Kampfesweise die sich bei den ersten amerikanischen Farmern gegenüber den Indianern bewährt hat, warum sollte sie sich nicht auch hier bewähren, da doch die Verhältnisse ähnlich sind" (NS1 329–30; BON 54–5, translation modified).

number is 119516;"[86] the article "Fellow Countrymen!" ends with a long list of the prominent people that make up the "founding committee."[87] In "The Appeal," the list of names is mentioned in a second appeal distributed in the tenement house:

> No one has yet sent in his name to me. Apart from the hours during which I have to earn my living, I have been at home all the time, and in the periods of my absence, when the door of my room has always been left open, there has been a piece of paper on my table, for everyone who wished to do so to put down his name. Nobody has done so.[88]

Like "Building the Great Wall of China," "The Appeal" investigates the border between the political and the extra-political, between standing inside and standing outside the concept of the state. In his second appeal, the anonymous writer explains that he has been at home all the time, hoping for a political community to assemble, "apart from the hours during which I have to earn my living." According to Aristotle, as we saw in Chapter 1, the members of the Greek household, the extra-political *oikos*, were so busy with matters of production and reproduction that they had no time left in which to participate in the political community. In "The Appeal," the border between *polis* and *oikos* cuts right through the schedule of the appeal's writer, who dreams of a political moment but also has to earn some money.

At a closer look, this border between the political and the extra-political cuts through the entire text of the first appeal, turning it into a literary stereoscope. Trying to mobilize his fellow lodgers, the writer uses the collective pronoun "we" while insisting that "uniformity must be maintained; without uniformity we cannot go forward." Political uniformity ("Einheitlichkeit") is necessary if the lodgers are to change the order of things and go forward. On the other hand, however, the writer is also caught in the language of the *oikos*, in this case the private property rights that regulate economic transactions: "I am in *possession* of five toy rifles. They are hanging in *my* wardrobe, one on each hook. The first *belongs* to me, and the others can be *claimed* by anyone." This is

---

86   "Nummer des Postchekkontos der Landeszentrale: 119516" (AS 512; OW 352).
87   "Die gründende Versammlung" (AS 502).
88   "Es hat sich bisher niemand bei mir gemeldet. Ich war, soweit ich nicht meinen Lebensunterhalt verdienen muß, fortwährend zuhause und für die Zeit meiner Abwesenheit, während welcher meine Zimmertür stets offen war, lag auf meinem Tisch ein Blatt, auf dem sich jeder der wollte einschreiben konnte. Niemand hats getan" (NS1 329; BON 55).

a linguistic example of how, as Kafka wrote in the article in the *Prager Tagblatt*, "selfishness remains so strong in these times, which teach us love of fatherland."[89]

Compared to "Building the Great Wall of China," the boundary between the political and the extra-political has been displaced in "The Appeal," in Arendt's terms causing a "withering away" of the political realm in which the free citizens can meet and make collective life move forward.[90] In the China story, the narrator offered a detailed rhetorical analysis of the weakness of imagination that made the Chinese people unable to hear and respond to the appeals issued from the political sphere. Yet, in spite of a seemingly unalterable order of things, the Chinese empire in fact ended up "surrounded by a wall,"[91] even if the wall was perforated by large gaps. In "The Appeal," no stone wall is built, not even a perforated one. The anonymous writer can only fantasize about a future decisive moment in which the fellow lodgers with rifles "will group ourselves round those who are unarmed," a tactic he seems to have learned from a children's book about the first American farmers and the people they termed "Red Indians." The tenement house is protected not with a wall of stone, but with toy rifles with broken mechanisms and torn-off corks.

In the opening sentence of "The Appeal," the mix of the political and the extra-political is illustrated by the hybrid fabric of the house, a modern tenement house "interspersed with" or rather "grown through with" ("durchwachsenen") indestructible medieval ruins. This mixture of modernity and tradition, of uniformity and heterogeneity, of political decision and organic growth, is given material shape—as in "Building the Great Wall of China"—as a field of tension between centripetal and centrifugal forces: "Nobody in our house has either time or inclination to read appeals, far less to think about them. Before long the little sheets of paper were floating in the stream of dirty water that, beginning in the attics and fed by all the corridors, pours down the staircase and there collides with the other stream mounting up from below."[92]

---

89   (AS 508; OW 347).

90   Arendt, *The Human Condition*, 60.

91   "ummauert" (NS1 339; SS 114).

92   "In unserm Haus hat man keine Zeit und keine Lust Aufrufe zu lesen oder gar zu überdenken. Bald schwammen die kleinen Papiere in dem Schmutzstrom der vom Dachboden ausgehend, von allen Korridoren genährt, die Treppe hinabspült und dort mit dem Gegenstrom kämpft der von unten hinaufschwillt" (NS1 330; BON 55, translation modified).

Part III

Seven A Matter of Justice

Karl as Defense Lawyer: Amerika

In "Little Ahasuerus," a short story from 1909, the Danish author Johannes V. Jensen describes the so-called Mourning March, a Jewish demonstration held in New York on December 5, 1905 in response to the bloody pogroms made during the first Russian revolution.[1] Having visited New York during the winter of 1905, Jensen is able to describe the demonstration in detail:

> On that day, one hundred and fifty thousand exiled Jews marched in procession through the streets of New York, a historical spectacle that should petrify the world and that only formed another eddy in the human whirlpool of Manhattan. They gathered in the most wretched neighborhoods of dark Brooklyn, crossed Williamsburg Bridge and entered Eastern New York, along the way nourished by participants from the ghetto, until they, as an immeasurable flood, turned down the corner of Broadway and marched North through the city as a closed group.
>
> At intervals, brass bands played funeral music in the procession, so close to each other that one muffled psalm mixed its lamentation with the next in shrill disharmony. Old Jewish hymns, strangely dark and heavy, dragged by in a jarring din without mercy together with Chopin's inevitable funeral tune. [. . .]
>
> And as ever when music is thrown together, free and wild notes burst out by themselves in the air, screams from up in the air, as though they came from invisible beings, loud flute parts

---

1   See C. S. Monaco, *The Rise of Modern Jewish Politics: Extraordinary Movement* (New York: Routledge, 2013), 171–3.

that did not come from the instruments but came into being by
interference, queer naked shrieks that hinted at dead bodies close
by, the air full of crying souls.[2]

Franz Kafka read the German translation of Jensen's story published in
1909 in the journal *Neue Rundschau*. Presumably, it caught his interest
because the Mourning March was a response to pogroms that had taken
place not far from Prague only a couple of years earlier; as we saw in
Chapter 4, Kafka also hinted at these bloody events in "The Judgment."[3]
It is evident that Kafka uses "Little Ahasuerus" as a source of the
unfinished novel *Amerika* (or *The Missing Person*). In the last existing
chapter of the novel, the protagonist Karl Rossmann is hired by the so-
called Nature Theater in Oklahoma (as Kafka spells the state). When
asked to give his name to the authorities, however, he does not say
"Karl" but, surprisingly, "Negro" and, in the first draft for the novel,
"Leo"[4]—which happens also to be the first name of Johannes V. Jensen's
little Ahasuerus. In the Danish writer's short story, the four-year-old
Jewish newspaper boy Leo is orphaned when his father disappears
during the chaotic demonstration and his mother dies from tuberculosis
very shortly after. In Kafka's novel, it is Therese, Karl's colleague at the

---

2   "Et hundrede halvtredsindstyve Tusinde landflygtige Jøder gik den Dag i
    Procession gennem New Yorks gader, et historisk Skuespil der skulde forstene
    Verden og som kun dannede en Hvirvel mere i Manhattans Strømkogning af
    Mennesker. De samlede sig ovre i det mørke Brooklyns elendigste Kvarterer og
    gik over Williamsbourg Bridge ind i Øst New York, stadig nærende sig med
    Deltagere fra Ghettoen undervejs, til de som en uoverskuelig strøm bøjede ind
    paa Broadway og defilerede i sluttet Marsch nordpaa og gennem byen./ Med
    Mellemrum gik Hornorkestre i Optoget og spillede Sørgekoraler, ikke længere
    fra hinanden end at den ene dumpe Salme blandede sin Jammer i skærende
    Disharmoni med den anden. Gammeljødiske, underlig sorte og svangre Hymner
    slæbte sig i en Mislyd uden Naade sammen med Chopins uundgåelige
    Begravelsestoner [. . .]./ Og som altid naar Musik bliver mænget sammen
    sprang der frie og vilde Toner ud af sig selv i Luften, Skrig oppe fra Luften som
    af Usynlige, høje Fløjtestemmer der ikke kom fra Instrumenterne, men blev til
    ved Interferens, sære nøgne Hvin der lod ane Lig nær ved, Luften fuld af
    grædende Sjæle." Johannes V. Jensen, *Hos fuglene* (Copenhagen: Gyldendal,
    2001), 173–4, my translation.
3   In October 1911, Kafka heard Yitzhak Löwy reciting Haim Nahman Bialik's
    famous poem about an earlier Russian pogrom in 1903. According to Kafka's
    diary, this poem, "making capital out of the Kishinev pogrom, sought to further
    the Jewish cause" ("nur hier hat sich der Dichter um sein den Kischenewer
    Pogrom für die jüdische Zukunft ausbeutendes Gedicht zu popularisieren" [T
    89; D 81]). For Kafka's interest in Russian pogroms, see Bruce, *Kafka and Cultural
    Zionism*, 58, 139.
4   (V 402, VA 264; A 278).

hotel, who narrates the sad story about how she lost her mother to tuberculosis when she was only five.[5]

Moreover, Jensen's description of the demonstration itself plays an important role in Kafka's novel. At the end of the second chapter, Karl's car journey with a certain Mr. Pollunder is slowed by a demonstration of metal workers. Suddenly "the pavements seemed inundated with a mass of people moving forward only one tiny step at a time and singing songs that sounded even more uniform than if only one person were singing."[6]

Kafka of course knew about the political situation in the United States from a number of books, newspapers, and lectures, and not only from Jensen's short story.[7] The most important source for his image of the country seems to have been Arthur Holitscher's travelogue *Amerika heute und morgen* (*America Today and Tomorrow*, 1912) which, in a chapter named "American Unrest," gives an engaged account of the demonstrations arranged by the American workers' movement and of other kinds of political unrest during the first years of the century. In America, the ruling class of corporate leaders, the socialist Holitscher comments, would "like to own a standing army (naturally not in order to protect their borders, but in order to fire at the striking workers)."[8]

Characteristically, Karl is an onlooker rather than a participant in the demonstrations depicted in the novel. Far from being a political activist, he is a good and somewhat naïve boy who, in spite of his conscientious character, gradually sinks in the American whirlpool. It is tempting to say that the political unrest is only a marginal motif, and that the main plot is concerned with the psychological dramas that go on between Karl and the many tyrannical and hysterical father figures that crowd the novel. Seen this way, the important things take place inside the car where Karl, at the end of Chapter 2, is sitting hand in hand with Mr. Pollunder, and not out on the street where the metal workers demonstrate.

---

5   (V 196–202; A 131–6).

6   "dann erschienen [. . .] die Trottoire angefüllt mit einer in winzigen Schritten sich bewegenden Masse, deren Gesang einheitlicher war als der einer einzigen Menschenstimme" (V 74; A 49).

7   For a discussion of Kafka's knowledge of American demonstrations and the similarities between Johannes V. Jensen's short story and Kafka's *Amerika*, see Hartmut Binder, *Kafka: Der Schaffensprozess* (Frankfurt am Main: Suhrkamp, 1983), 75–7.

8   Arthur Holitscher, *Amerika heute und morgen: Reiseerlebnisse* (Berlin: S. Fischer Verlag, 1912), 382.

Yet I contend that the "American unrest" plays a crucial role for the stereoscopic style of the novel. Johannes V. Jensen noticed the "shrill disharmony" and (with one of Jensen's favorite words) the "interference" which emerged when the tunes of different brass bands were "thrown together." As we have seen, such a dissonant experience is a characteristic feature of Kafka's literary stereoscopes. In other words, the political turmoil of the demonstration should not be seen as a marginal motif in the novel's aesthetic representation alone; it also plays an important role at the level of aesthetic experience.

Karl on the Balcony I

Kafka worked thoroughly with his travel diaries, making fair copies once he had returned to Prague and drawing on them for fictional texts.[9] This is also the case with the diary entry about the Kaiserpanorama from February 1911, discussed in the Introduction. In the autumn of 1912, roughly the time of the breakthrough short story "The Judgment," Kafka started working on *Amerika*, where a number of passages more or less directly allude to the Kaiserpanorama in Friedland. Kafka takes as a starting point the photographs he found in Arthur Holitscher's *Amerika heute und morgen*, which had just been published as he started working on the novel.[10] Interestingly, however, he tends to transform Holitscher's two-dimensional photographs into three-dimensional stereographs. *Amerika* tells the story of a journey, as it were, through binocular glasses into the distorted world of the stereoscope.

In his travelogue, for instance, Holitscher shows a photograph with the legend "Bridge to Brooklyn."[11] Kafka evidently turned to this picture as a model when narrating how Karl, together with his dubious acquaintances Robinson and Delamarche, leaves New York and stops for a while to enjoy what they refer to as the "panorama" of the Brooklyn bridge, which, according to the novel, connects New York with Boston.[12]

---

9 For further discussion, see Hans-Gerd Koch, "Nachbemerkung," in *Reisetagebücher, Kritische Kafka Ausgabe* (Frankfurt am Main: Fischer, 1994), 246.

10 Kafka's library contains the 1913 edition of Holitscher's travelogue only, but the many parallels between Kafka's *Amerika* and Holitscher's *Amerika heute und morgen* make it difficult to imagine that Kafka had not studied Holitscher's travelogue before September 1912. For further discussion of the relation between the two books, see Duttlinger, *Kafka and Photography*; Sophie von Glinski, *Imaginationsprozesse: Verfahren phantastischen Erzählens in Franz Kafkas Frühwerk* (Berlin and New York: De Gruyter, 2004); Wolfgang Jahn, *Kafkas Roman "Der Verschollene" ("Amerika")* (Stuttgart: Metzler, 1965); Alfred Wirkner, *Kafka und die Aussenwelt: Quellenstudien zum "Amerika"-Fragment* (Stuttgart: Klett, 1976).

11 Holitscher, *Amerika*, 55.

12 (V 144; A 96).

Figure 7.1 "Broadway in the business district." Photo and caption from Alfred Holitscher, *Amerika heute und morgen: Reiseerlebnisse* (Berlin: Fischer, 1912), p. 49.

Another photograph from Holitscher's book, showing "Broadway in the business district," provides Kafka with the model for the description of Karl's view of New York as he stands on the balcony outside the flat of his wealthy uncle. Once again, Kafka transforms the image from a two-dimensional photograph into a three-dimensional stereograph:

A narrow balcony ran along the full length of his room. In his native city it would surely have been the highest lookout, yet here it offered little more than the view of a single street that ran in a straight line between two rows of veritably truncated buildings and therefore seemed to flee into the distance, where the outlines of a cathedral loomed monstrously out of a great haze. In the morning and in the evening and at night in his dreams, this street was filled with constantly bustling traffic, which seen from above seemed like a mixture, thrown together in ever new beginnings, of distorted human figures and of the roofs of all sorts of vehicles, out of which there arose a new, stronger, wilder mixture of noise, dust, and smells, and, catching and penetrating it all, a powerful light that was continually dispersed, carried away, and avidly refracted by the mass of objects that made such a corporeal impression on one's dazzled eye that it seemed as if a glass pane, hanging over the street and covering everything, were being smashed again and again with the utmost force.[13]

As in the diary entry about the Kaiserpanorama in Friedland, Kafka here describes an aesthetic experience. At issue is not only *what* Karl perceives from the balcony but also, first of all, *how* he perceives the city with his "dazzled eye." In the Kaiserpanorama, the smooth floor of the Italian cathedrals reached out toward the spectator, giving a visceral illusion of tactility as if located "in front of our tongue." While no cathedral is depicted in Holitscher's photography, Kafka adds an impressive American church whose outlines "loomed monstrously out of a great haze," offering a "corporeal impression" ("so körperlich") to the dazzled eye of the spectator.[14] Inside the Kaiserpanorama, the pairs

---

13   "Ein schmaler Balkon zog sich vor dem Zimmer seiner ganzen Länge nach hin. Was aber in der Heimatstadt Karls wohl der höchste Aussichtspunkt gewesen wäre, gestattete hier nicht viel mehr als den Überblick über eine Straße, die zwischen zwei Reihen förmlich abgehackter Häuser gerade und darum wie fliehend in die Ferne sich verlief, wo aus vielem Dunst die Formen einer Kathedrale ungeheuer sich erhoben. Und morgen wie abend und in den Träumen der Nacht vollzog sich auf dieser Straße ein immer drängender Verkehr, der von oben gesehen sich als eine aus immer neuen Anfängen ineinandergestreute Mischung von verzerrten menschlichen Figuren und von Dächern der Fuhrwerke aller Art darstellte, von der aus sich noch eine neue vervielfältigte wildere Mischung von Lärm, Staub und Gerüchen erhob, und alles dieses wurde erfaßt und durchdrungen von einem mächtigen Licht, das immer wieder von der Menge der Gegenstände verstreut, fortgetragen und wieder eifrig herbeigebracht wurde und das dem betörten Auge so körperlich erschien, als werde über dieser Straße eine alles bedeckende Glasscheibe jeden Augenblick immer wieder mit aller Kraft zerschlagen" (V 55; A 33–4, translation modified).

14   In the same chapter, however, Holitscher, standing on the top of the Singer building, describes Trinity Church in Manhattan; Holitscher, *Amerika*, 49.

of stereographic slides were penetrated by light from the bulb at the center of the box. In Karl's visual experience, a powerful light is "catching and penetrating it all [. . .], continually dispersed, carried away, and avidly refracted by the mass of objects."

The stereoscopic style creates a defamiliarizing aesthetic experience characterized by a perpetual destruction and reconstruction of the represented world. To Karl's dazzled eye, it feels "as if a glass pane [. . .] were being smashed again and again with the utmost force." In a nearly untranslatable phrase, the cityscape, seen this way, is described as "a mixture, thrown together in ever new beginnings, of distorted human figures and of the roofs of all sorts of vehicles." It is worth noting that the visual chaos consists of "ever new beginnings" ("immer neuen Anfängen"), as if the world were being constantly recreated in this aesthetic experience. In the following sections, I will show that this ever beginning anew plays a central role for the political import of the novel's stereoscopic style.

Karl at the Head Cashier's Office

"The Stoker," the first chapter of the novel, tells the story of Karl's arrival in New York. Ready to disembark, however, he remembers that he has left his umbrella behind. Therefore, instead of leaving the ship, he runs back into its bowels where he soon loses his way in the maze of corridors. In his confusion, he knocks on a random door. Inside the cabin, he meets a stoker who narrates a story about the injustice he has suffered:

> "Look, we're on a German ship, right? It belongs to the Hamburg–America Line, so why aren't we all Germans here? Why is the chief engineer a Romanian? His name is Schubal. It's unbelievable. And this dirty dog slave-drives us Germans on a German ship! Don't think"—he ran out of breath, his hand went flying in the air—"that I'm complaining just for the sake of complaining. I know that you have no influence, and that you're only a poor kid yourself. But it's really too much!" And he pounded on the table repeatedly with his fist, never taking his eye off his fist as he pounded.[15]

---

15 "'Sehen Sie, wir sind doch auf einem deutschen Schiff, es gehört der Hamburg-Amerika-Linie, warum sind wir nicht lauter Deutsche hier? Warum ist der Obermaschinist ein Rumäne? Er heißt Schubal. Das ist doch nicht zu glauben. Und dieser Lumpenhund schindet uns Deutsche auf einem deutschen Schiff! Glauben Sie nicht,' ihm ging die Luft aus, er fackelte mit der Hand—'daß ich klage, um zu klagen. Ich weiß, daß Sie keinen Einfluß haben und selbst ein armes Bürschchen sind. Aber es ist zu arg!' Und er schlug auf den Tisch mehrmals mit der Faust und ließ kein Auge von ihr, während er schlug" (DzL 71; SS 15–16).

The driving force of the entire chapter is the stoker's strong feeling of injustice, his "uncontainable feeling of outrage."[16] The stoker's mood quickly communicates itself to Karl: "'You mustn't put up with it,' said Karl excitedly,"[17] whereafter Karl attempts to convince his new friend that he must obtain justice: "Have you gone to see the captain yet? Have you pleaded with him for your rights?"[18] As a consequence, Karl and the stoker walk from the private cabins at the bottom of the ship to the public sphere in the head cashier's office where, for some reason, the captain of the ship and a number of other authorities are present. Here, however, they are twice turned away by an orderly and, later, by the head cashier himself. The orderly gives the stoker a look "as if he did not belong here."[19] To be on the safe side, he consults the head cashier, who confirms the orderly's judgment:

> This man—one could see this clearly—practically went rigid on hearing the words of the orderly but finally turned to face the man who wanted to speak to him and began waving his hands at the stoker in a gesture of strict refusal and, to be on the safe side, at the orderly too. Whereupon the orderly turned back to the stoker and said in the tone of someone passing on a confidential message, "Clear out at once!"[20]

It is at this juncture that the first of three turning points in the chapter occurs. While the stoker surrenders, Karl takes action: "Without further thought Karl broke loose and ran straight across the room."[21] After having shown his passport at the head cashier's desk, he steps up as a spokesperson for the stoker: "'May I take the liberty of saying,' he began, 'that in my opinion the stoker has been done an injustice.'"[22] At Karl's unexpected intervention, everyone in the office pricks up their

---

16 "aus seinem grenzenlos empörten Innern heraus" (DzL 86; SS 23).

17 "Das dürfen Sie sich nicht gefallen lassen" (DzL 72; SS 16).

18 "Waren Sie schon beim Kapitän? Haben Sie schon bei ihm Ihr Recht gesucht?" (DzL 72; SS 16).

19 "als gehöre er nicht hierher" (DzL 79; SS 19).

20 "Dieser Herr—das sah man deutlich—erstarrte geradezu unter den Worten des Dieners, kehrte sich aber endlich nach dem Manne um, der ihn zu sprechen wünschte, und fuchtelte dann, streng abwehrend, gegen den Heizer und der Sicherheit halber auch gegen den Diener hin. Der Diener kehrte darauf zum Heizer zurück und sagte in einem Tone, als vertraue er ihm etwas an: 'Scheren Sie sich sofort aus dem Zimmer!'"(DzL 79; SS 19).

21 "Ohne weitere Besinnung machte sich Karl los, lief quer durchs Zimmer" (DzL 79; SS 19).

22 "'Ich erlaube mir zu sagen', begann er dann, 'daß meiner Meinung nach dem Herrn Heizer Unrecht geschehen ist'" (DzL 80; SS 20).

ears. The head cashier, for instance, makes "a great turn to the right."[23] The German "Rechtswendung" indeed means a right turn, but also a turn of the notion of what is right: the first turning point of the chapter is a transformation of the practice of justice in which human beings who have no right to speak are suddenly granted this right.

According to Karl's interpretation of the captain, he had "evidently already made up his mind to hear the stoker's complaint. For he stretched out his hand and called to the stoker: 'Come here,' in a voice so firm you could hit it with a hammer."[24] "Give this man a chance to speak,"[25] the captain adds a little later as the head cashier tries to prevent the stoker from talking. Unfortunately, it soon becomes evident that the stoker is unable to present his case, mixing all his arguments up in "a whirling hodge-podge."[26] Karl tries to play the role of a legal advisor giving rhetorical advice in order to adjust the stoker's complaints to the legal context ("You have to explain things more simply, more clearly").[27] While this doesn't prevent his audience quickly becoming distracted, the captain maintains his decision to give the stoker a chance to speak; he "looked straight ahead—his eyes expressing his determination to hear the stoker out this one time."[28]

The captain's decision is not a judgment in which the laws of the ship are applied to the "trivial squabble between two engineers."[29] Rather, it is a judgment on the very applicability of these laws and, more specifically, about the right to speak in a matter of justice. In other words, the orderly, the head cashier, and the captain are all prefigurations of the doorkeeper, described two years later in "Before the Law," who passes a judgment on the admittance to the law.

The Stereoscopic Passport
The second turning point in the chapter occurs when a gentleman with a bamboo cane, who hitherto had been standing in the background by a large window together with the captain, suddenly recognizes Karl as his nephew. Since Mr. Jakob is a millionaire and a senator, this familial

---

23 "eine große Rechtswendung" (DzL 80; SS 20).
24 "der Kapitän [war] offenbar mit sich bereits übereingekommen [. . .], den Heizer anzuhören. Er streckte nämlich die Hand aus und rief dem Heizer zu: 'Kommen Sie her!' mit einer Stimme, fest, um mit einem Hammer darauf zu schlagen" (DzL 81; SS 21).
25 "Hören wir den Mann doch einmal an" (DzL 83; SS 21).
26 "ein trauriges Durcheinanderstrudeln" (DzL 85; SS 22).
27 "Sie müssen das einfacher erzählen, klarer" (DzL 86; SS 23).
28 "wenn auch der Kapitän noch immer vor sich hinsah, in den Augen die Entschlossenheit, den Heizer diesmal bis zu Ende anzuhören" (DzL 83; SS 22).
29 "diese geringfügige Zänkerei zweier Maschinisten" (DzL 106; SS 33).

link dramatically changes Karl's social status and facilitates his integration into American society; we later learn that the alternatives were either being turned back at the border or going to the bad in the streets of New York. This turning point, too, involves a shift based on the notion of "right," but this time a shift from a legal to a familial context. The uncle, Mr. Jakob (here referred to as "the senator"), makes this very clear: "'Gentlemen!' repeated the senator. 'You are taking part, against my wishes and yours, in a little family scene.'"[30]

Karl imagines that, given his newly won status, "he could say whatever occurred to him,"[31] and he therefore asks what is going to happen with the stoker. As it soon turns out, however, the principle of justice does not apply to the community in question: "'Don't misunderstand the situation,' said the senator to Karl, 'it may be a matter of justice, but at the same time it's a matter of discipline.'"[32] According to the uncle, Karl misjudges "die Sachlage," a legal term that refers not to a particular case but rather to the specific situation or context which gives meaning to the case. In other words, a "Sachlage" is more or less synonymous with a configuration of the community. The uncle juxtaposes two dissimilar judgments on the configuration of the stoker's case by proclaiming that it is simultaneously a matter of justice ("eine Sache der Gerechtigkeit") and a matter of discipline ("eine Sache der Disziplin").

In fact, the disorderly image of "die Sachlage" as a matter of discipline arrives in two different forms. In Karl's case, it is an image of a family scene where the underlying intent is the edification of youngsters. For instance, the uncle suggests that Karl should read a letter from the housemaid, who Karl made pregnant, causing his expulsion to America, "for his own edification in the quiet of the room that already awaits him."[33] In the stoker's case, on the other hand, the disorderly image discloses a workplace where the intent is rather to bring recalcitrant workers to order, by suspending the law if necessary. When Karl imagines how the captain will judge the stoker's case, he seems to be drawing on Theodor Mommsen's description of the concept

---

30 "'Meine Herren', wiederholte der Senator, 'Sie nehmen gegen meinen und gegen Ihren Willen an einer kleinen Familienszene teil'" (DzL 95; SS 28, translation modified).

31 "Er glaubte in seiner neuen Stellung alles, was er dachte, auch aussprechen zu können" (DzL 104; SS 32).

32 "'Mißverstehe die Sachlage nicht', sagte der Senator zu Karl, 'es handelt sich vielleicht um eine Sache der Gerechtigkeit, aber gleichzeitig um eine Sache der Disziplin'" (DzL 105; SS 32).

33 "in der Stille seines ihn schon erwartenden Zimmers zur Belehrung lesen kann" (DzL 99; SS 29).

of emergency powers in Roman law, where a threat to the existence of the state can occasion "measures that even conflict with the normal order."[34] "In dealing with someone like the stoker, no measure was too harsh," the captain is probably thinking, according to Karl, "and if there was anything to reproach Schubal for, it was for his not having been able to tame the recalcitrance of the stoker over time enough to keep the latter from daring to show up today before the captain."[35]

The double exposure of order and disorder, of a public and a private image of the same case, comes into view in the many references to Karl's passport. As if some kind of immigration control, the cashier's office seems to be located on a border between two countries. In any case, the first thing Karl does after breaking loose and running straight through the room is presenting his passport:

> Karl rummaged in his secret pocket, which he had no hesitation in betraying to these people, took out his passport, and in lieu of further introduction laid it open on the table. The head cashier seemed to consider the passport beside the point, for he flicked it to one side with two fingers, whereupon Karl, as if this formality had now been satisfactorily concluded, put his passport back in his pocket.
>
> "May I take the liberty of saying," he began, "that in my opinion the stoker has been done an injustice [. . .]."[36]

In a later chapter, we learn that Karl and his father, back in Prague, had to suffer the "useless questions" the authorities had asked when they were applying for the passport.[37] However, this official document is flicked to one side by the head cashier who, clearly, does not interpret it as allowing Karl to speak in the community.

---

34 Mommsen, *Römisches Staatsrecht*, 663.

35 "Gegen einen Mann, wie den Heizer, konnte man nicht streng genug verfahren, und wenn dem Schubal etwas vorzuwerfen war, so war es der Umstand, daß er die Widerspenstigkeit des Heizers im Laufe der Zeit nicht so weit hatte brechen können, daß es dieser heute noch gewagt hatte, vor dem Kapitän zu erscheinen" (DzL 90; SS 25).

36 "Karl kramte aus seiner Geheimtasche, die er den Blicken dieser Leute zu zeigen keine Bedenken hatte, seinen Reisepaß hervor, den er statt weiterer Vorstellung geöffnet auf den Tisch legte. Der Oberkassier schien diesen Paß für nebensächlich zu halten, denn er schnippte ihn mit zwei Fingern beiseite, worauf Karl, als sei diese Formalität zur Zufriedenheit erledigt, den Paß wieder einsteckte./ 'Ich erlaube mir zu sagen', begann er dann, 'daß meiner Meinung nach dem Herrn Heizer Unrecht geschehen ist'" (DzL 80; SS 20).

37 "nutzlose Fragen" (V 278; A 189).

As it happens, this is not the only passport in "The Stoker." While the stoker is losing his way in his "senseless racket,"[38] the uncle, totally inured to the chaotic speech, "took out a little notebook and, evidently occupied with entirely different matters, let his eyes wander back and forth between the notebook and Karl."[39] A little further down, the uncle explains that, without Karl's knowledge, Johanna Brummer, the housemaid who seduced Karl back in Prague, wrote a letter in which she narrates "the whole story" about the seduction and the pregnancy and even offers a "description of the person"—Karl.[40] As we learn, the uncle has transcribed Karl's most prominent features into his own little notebook, and this description enables him to identify Karl as his nephew.

In a brief flashback, Karl remembers how the housemaid carefully recorded his features as if she were some kind of passport official or police spy:

In the crush of images from the past that was growing ever remoter, she sat in the kitchen next to the cupboard, her elbows propped on its shelf. She would look at him whenever he occasionally came into the kitchen to get a glass of water for his father or to tell her something his mother wanted done. Sometimes she would be writing a letter, sitting in a convoluted posture to one side of the cupboard and would draw her inspiration for it from Karl's face.[41]

Thus, each of the two juxtaposed images of the community is furnished with its own passport authority. Whereas the public passport is issued by state authorities and controlled on an official's writing desk, the "private passport" is issued in the kitchen by members of the household and controlled by an uncle.

---

38 "nutzlosen Lärm" (DzL 87; SS 23).
39 "ein kleines Notizbuch hervorzog und, offenbar mit ganz anderen Angelegenheiten beschäftigt, die Augen zwischen dem Notizbuch und Karl hin und her wandern ließ" (DzL 88; SS 24).
40 "die ganze Geschichte" and "Personenbeschreibung" (DzL 98; SS 29).
41 "Im Gedränge einer immer mehr zurücktretenden Vergangenheit saß sie in ihrer Küche neben dem Küchenschrank, auf dessen Platte sie ihren Ellbogen stützte. Sie sah ihn an, wenn er hin und wieder in die Küche kam, um ein Glas zum Wassertrinken für seinen Vater zu holen oder einen Auftrag seiner Mutter auszurichten. Manchmal schrieb sie in der vertrackten Stellung seitlich vom Küchenschrank einen Brief und holte sich die Eingebungen von Karls Gesicht" (DzL 99; SS 29–30).

With Only the Slightest Pressure

In his letters to his sister Elli on the education of her son Felix, discussed in Chapter 2, Kafka described the bourgeois family as "a single organism, a single circulation of blood" in which the parents, through bursts of unmotivated love and blind rage, step for step deprive the children of their "personal right."[42] After the shift from legal scene to family scene in the head cashier's office, Karl involuntarily becomes party of such a circulation of blood. Deeply moved, the uncle embraces his nephew and exclaims his joy over having found him, and on one occasion, even has to turn away and dab his face with a handkerchief in order to keep the others from seeing his emotion.

I will explore the contrast between legal scene and family scene, between the circulation of rules and the circulation of blood, by focusing on a short passage toward the end of the chapter. Shortly before Karl leaves the head cashier's office together with his uncle, he takes leave of the stoker as if of a dying person:

> And now Karl wept as he kissed the stoker's hand and took that almost lifeless hand with its cracked skin and pressed it to his cheek, like a treasure that one must forego.—But there was his uncle the senator, already at his side and drawing him away, though with only the slightest pressure.
>
> "The stoker seems to have bewitched you," he said, casting a knowing look at the captain over Karl's head. "You felt abandoned, whereupon you fond the stoker, and you are grateful to him: that is entirely praiseworthy. But don't go to extremes, if only to do me a favor, and do begin to realize your position."[43]

In this short description of the uncle's gesture of understanding, one can find three features that distinguish Karl as a member of a private community (as depicted in the disorderly image) from Karl as a member of a political community (as depicted in the orderly image).

---

42 "Persönlichkeitsrecht" (Br 345; LFFE 294).

43 "Und nun weinte Karl, während er die Hand des Heizers küßte, und nahm die rissige, fast leblose Hand und drückte sie an seine Wangen, wie einen Schatz, auf den man verzichten muß.—Da war aber auch schon der Onkel Senator an seiner Seite und zog ihn, wenn auch nur mit dem leichtesten Zwange, fort./ 'Der Heizer scheint dich bezaubert zu haben', sagte er und sah verständnisinnig über Karls Kopf zum Kapitän hin. 'Du hast dich verlassen gefühlt, da hast du den Heizer gefunden und bist ihm jetzt dankbar, das ist ja ganz löblich. Treibe das aber, schon mir zuliebe, nicht zu weit und lerne deine Stellung begreifen'" (DzL 107; SS 33–4, translation modified).

First, the uncle is drawing Karl away from the stoker by using power, even if it is only the slightest pressure or the slightest constraint. In the following sentences, the uncle casts a knowing look at the captain "over Karl's head," thereby avoiding having to look Karl in the face. Based on these formulations, the opposition between orderly and disorderly image can be understood as an opposition between freedom and submission. Prior to the shift from legal scene to family scene, Karl acts as an independent subject who participates in a legal debate. Defending the case of the stoker, Karl is able to break loose and run straight across the room, and during the proceedings, he even feels "more powerful and alert than he had perhaps ever felt at home."[44] Moreover, he is convinced that he has a say in the discussion of the stoker's case, imagining "that he had the decision in his hand."[45] Borrowing a phrase from Kafka's letters to Elli, Karl, at this stage, believes in his own "intellectual assertion of existence" ("geistige Existenzbehauptung").

After the shift from legal scene to family scene, however, Karl seems to lose his status as an autonomous subject and is transformed into the passive object of his uncle's emotional outbursts. From now on, the form of address shifts from the formal "Sie" to the informal "du," and Karl is no longer able to assert his existence by having a say in the decisions being made in the office. "'And now,' cried the senator, 'I want you to state very clearly whether I am your uncle or not.'"[46] To this interpellation, Karl replies with a subordinate gesture that, seeming to belong to an absolute monarchy, sits awkwardly with the modern democratic America: "'You are my uncle,' said Karl, kissing the senator's hand and receiving a kiss on the forehead in return."[47] At the end of the chapter, when uncle and nephew leave the ship together, there is no longer any distance between their bodies: the senator hugs him tight, and "in close embrace" or "closely interlinked" they get into the dinghy.[48]

The lack of freedom Karl experiences in the family relation to the uncle repeats the lack of freedom he felt in the sexual relation to the housemaid back in Prague. In Karl's recollections, the woman is represented as the only agential subject in the encounter, laying him in

---

44   "Karl allerdings fühlte sich so kräftig und bei Verstand, wie er es vielleicht zu Hause niemals gewesen war" (DzL 91; SS 25).
45   "die Entscheidung in der Hand zu haben" (DzL 104; SS 32, translation modified).
46   "'Und jetzt,' rief der Senator, 'will ich von dir offen hören, ob ich dein Onkel bin oder nicht'" (DzL 101; SS 30).
47   "'Du bist mein Onkel,' sagte Karl und küßte ihm die Hand und wurde dafür auf die Stirne geküßt."
48   "engverbunden" (DzL 110; SS 35).

her bed, undressing him, pressing her naked belly against his body, and fumbling disgustingly between his legs.[49] I have already quoted the passage that describes how Johanna Brummer issued the private passport at the kitchen cupboard, drawing her inspiration from Karl's face. The passage continues: "Sometimes she covered her eyes with her hand, then it was impossible to get through to her."[50] Here Johanna plays the role of a blindfolded Justitia. While the classic Justitia is blind toward the particularities of the individual who stands before the law, this kitchen Justitia is impervious to Karl's efforts to speak to her or engage her in discussion (the German "anreden" can also mean to argue with someone).

Second, while drawing Karl away from the stoker, the uncle explains Karl's tears by referring to his feelings: "You felt abandoned." In the light of this formulation, the opposition between orderly and disorderly image is an opposition between the universal and the particular. Before the turn from legal scene to family scene, the discussion in the head cashier's office is based on universal principles. Karl explicitly looks away from particular details and focuses solely on the principles at stake: "I have stated the matter in only the most general terms," he says in his short defense speech for the stoker, "he will present his specific complaints to you himself."[51] In a discussion of a matter of justice, the only valid arguments are based on universal reasons applicable to any given individual in a similar situation.

After the shift from equity to affect, however, what is at stake are no longer universal principles but, rather, particular individuals. The uncle is casting a "knowing look" at the captain over Karl's head, and the rare German word "verständnisinnig," a compound of "Verständnis" ("understanding") and "innig" ("intimate" or "profound"), seems to imply a kind of understanding that does not explain Karl's behavior on the basis of universal and rational reasons (things that could be discussed in public), but rather on the basis of particular and affective reasons ("You *felt* abandoned"). Seen this way, Karl did not act in accordance with his rational insight into the principles of justice but only because the stoker "bewitched" him. Likewise, the uncle summons his nephew to change his behavior "to do me a favour," that is, out of regard for one single individual and not out of respect for the universal rules of justice.

---

49 (DzL 100; SS 30).

50 "Manchmal hielt sie die Augen mit der Hand verdeckt, dann drang keine Anrede zu ihr" (DzL 99; SS 29–30).

51 "Ich habe nur das Allgemeine über diese Sache gesagt, seine besonderen Beschwerden wird er Ihnen selbst vorbringen" (DzL 81; SS 20).

This contrast between universal and particular is also staged by the relation between the two different passports. It can be surmised that Karl's public passport contains a short list of general information about him. At least, it is evident that he himself imagines that the document will secure his universal right to be present and to speak up in the head cashier's office. The private passport, by contrast, has the shape of a narrative and mentions a number of specific details from Karl's life; as if to underline the amount of detail, the uncle is even brandishing the two gigantic and closely written pages that the housemaid sent him. Immediately after the recognition scene, Karl reflects: "I don't want him to tell the whole story to everyone. And he can't possibly know what happened. Who could have told him?"[52] But, of course, the uncle immediately continues by describing the events in the housemaid's bedroom to the tiniest, most embarrassing detail: "he was, in a word, seduced by a housemaid, one Johanna Brummer, a person of about thirty-five."[53] Whereas the public passport gives a general and pared-back representation of a human being as a political subject with a small bundle of universal rights and duties, the private passport depicts the individual human being with its multitude of particular habits and needs. In other words, all the details that Justitia was blindfolded in order not to pay attention to.

Third and finally, while drawing Karl away, the uncle's gesture is somewhat overexcited: "that is entirely praiseworthy," he exclaims, even if Karl's feelings for the stoker seem to be so feeble that he can be drawn away with only the slightest pressure. On the basis of this exclamation, the opposition between orderly and disorderly image is an opposition between right and grace. Before the turning point, Karl wants the stoker to get what is rightfully his and not to be paid "out of mercy."[54] After the shift to the family scene, the community of the uncle and Karl is defined by groundless and exaggerated gifts of grace. The uncle keeps referring to Karl as his "dear nephew" and "splendid nephew,"[55] even if he has never met him before and has no chance of knowing whether he is, in fact, dear and splendid. These groundless acts of grace continue in the next chapter where Karl has moved into his uncle's house in New York and where the uncle, among other things, donates a piano as an act of charity. (We shall return to Kafka's understanding of grace in the reading of *The Castle* in chapter 9.)

---

52 "ich will nicht, daß er es allen erzählt. Übrigens kann er es ja auch nicht wissen. Woher denn?" (DzL 96–7; SS 28).
53 "er wurde nämlich von einem Dienstmädchen, Johanna Brummer, einer etwa 35jährigen Person, verführt."
54 "aus Gnade" (DzL 72; SS 16, translation modified).
55 "meinen lieben Neffen" and "einen prächtigen Neffen" (DzL 94, 101; SS 27, 31).

During their ill-fated coupling, the housemaid identifies Karl in the same specific, and inaccurate, way. "Karl, oh you, my Karl," she exclaims,[56] even if Karl, as it seems, is busy fighting his own feeling of disgust and probably does nothing to merit her outbursts of tenderness. Like the stoker on the ship, Karl, in the arms of the uncle and the housemaid, receives an ungrounded and unmerited gift of grace.

Thus, the disorderly image not only depicts the particular identity of a human being; it also constructs that identity. Karl is pictured as the dearly beloved nephew who lives in the uncle's flat and takes lessons in English and horse-riding, and, paradoxically, this construction of his identity presupposes a certain inattentiveness toward Karl's actual personality on the part of the uncle. In general, the uncle's relation to his nephew is curiously imprecise; after the wordy monologue about the embarrassing sexual and familial issues, Karl feels called upon to correct the errors: the uncle's account is blemished by "a few other mistakes [. . .], that is to say, I mean, not everything actually happened the way you said it did."[57] If the family image offers a detailed representation of a human being, it is an image constructed without much sense for the actual character of the individual in question. "In the family, clutched in the tight embrace of the parents," Kafka wrote in his letters to Elli, "there is room only for certain kinds of people who conform to certain kinds of requirements."[58]

The Stereoscopic Head Cashier's Office

In summary, the stereoscopic style of "The Stoker" juxtaposes two images of the events in the head cashier's office viewed as, respectively, a matter of justice and a matter of discipline. The group of people present in the office are configured, on the one hand, as a public forum and, on the other, as a private company or a private family. In the vocabulary of constitutional law, the stereoscopic vision juxtaposes metaphorical versions of the state of normalcy and state of exception. Thus, the second and most important of the chapter's turning points is the moment of recognition in which the uncle takes a step back and, with a smile of near disbelief, identifies Karl as his nephew, triggering a change of scene from legal to familial.

The aesthetic experience of "The Stoker" is reflective in so far as the stereoscopic style challenges the reader to compare the two images of the head cashier's office before and after the turning point. As I use the

---

56 "Karl, o du mein Karl!" (DzL 100; SS 31).
57 "sind in deiner Rede einige Fehler enthalten gewesen, das heißt, ich meine, es hat sich in Wirklichkeit nicht alles so zugetragen" (DzL 101; 30–31).
58 (Br 345, LFFE 295).

concept of aesthetic reflection, however, it refers both to a process in which thought moves back and forth between two dissimilar images and another process in which thought turns back from the images to the construction of these images.

Indeed, the construction of images of communal life is an important theme in the chapter. When the uncle reveals to everybody that Karl was, in a word, seduced by Johanna Brummer, Karl turns around "in order to read the faces of the others for the impression that the story had made on them."[59] Throughout the entire chapter, he makes constant efforts to read the faces of the others in order to see how they view the events taking place at the head cashier's office. In this way, Kafka highlights Karl's laborious reconstruction of the shared images of shared life. In most of the decisions quoted above, for instance, the image of the underlying situation is formed of conjecture: "The head cashier *seemed* to consider the passport beside the point, for he flicked it to one side with two fingers."[60] The captain had "*evidently* already made up his mind to hear the stoker's complaint."[61]

Imaginative figures play a crucial role in Karl's reconstruction of the images of communal life. When Karl breaks loose and runs straight through the room, the orderly runs after him, "bent over, arms outstretched, to catch him as if he were chasing some vermin [*ein Ungeziefer*]."[62] Although not uttered by the orderly himself, the analogy of vermin is suggested by the narrator, probably colored by Karl's interpretation of the situation, in order to describe the impression that Karl's actions make on the orderly.

And when the chief engineer Schubal finally shows up at the head cashier's office and delivers a "beautiful" speech that contrasts greatly to the stoker's whirling hodge-podge, Karl, once again, reads the faces of the others: "It was certainly a lucid, manly speech; and to judge from the changed expressions of the listeners, one might have thought that these were the first human sounds they had heard in a long time."[63] Again, the metaphorical oppositions between manly and unmanly

---

59 "um den Eindruck der Erzählung von den Gesichtern der Anwesenden abzulesen" (DzL 97; SS 29).

60 "Der Oberkassier *schien* diesen Paß für nebensächlich zu halten, denn er schnippte ihn mit zwei Fingern beiseite" (DzL 80; SS 20, my italics).

61 "wenn nicht der Herr [. . .] *offenbar* mit sich bereits übereingekommen wäre, den Heizer anzuhören" (DzL 81; SS 21, my italics).

62 "der Diener lief gebeugt mit zum Umfangen bereiten Armen, als jage er ein Ungeziefer" (DzL 79; SS 19).

63 "Das war allerdings die klare Rede eines Mannes und nach der Veränderung in den Mienen der Zuhörer hätte man glauben können, sie hörten zum erstenmal nach langer Zeit wieder menschliche Laute" (DzL 92; SS 26).

speech and between human and inhuman sounds are suggested by Karl, and mediated by the narrator, in the effort to reconstruct the listeners' impression of Schubal's speech. These figures exclude the stoker from the human community and frame him as a kind of animal able only to emit a "senseless racket," not human sounds.[64]

In his *Politics*, Aristotle characterizes the community of the household by arguing that those for whom the just does not exist are unable to speak. To be sure, they do have a "voice" (*phonē*) with which to signify what is pleasant or painful, as when animals hiss, purr, and bark, but they don't have "speech" (*logos*), with which free men are "making clear what is beneficial or harmful, and hence also what is just or unjust."[65] In Aristotle's terms, then, the stoker is restricted to the senseless racket of a non-human "voice."

In general, rhetorical figures shape the way the fictional characters construct images of the community. Once again, the social imaginary is, first of all, a swarm of terms of abuse, often of nationalistic and chauvinistic character. To name just a few examples, Karl describes all the subordinate persons present in the head cashier's office as "just chaff,"[66] the German "Spreu" being a pejorative term for allegedly inferior people. The stoker refers to the Romanian Schubal as a "dirty dog" and complains that he is himself seen as a "shirker" who deserves to be thrown out.[67] The uncle narrates that Karl has been tossed out by his parents, "the way you kick out a cat that has begun to make a nuisance of itself."[68]

Yet Karl not only interprets how the others construct images of communal life aboard the ship; he also questions these images. Once Schubal has delivered his "beautiful" speech, Karl puts it through a meticulous textual analysis, claiming to detect "holes" that the gentlemen are unable to see: "Of course they did not notice that even his beautiful speech had holes in it. [. . .] Trickery, nothing but trickery! And these gentlemen tolerated it, even acknowledging it to be correct behavior?"[69] In German, "Trickery, nothing but trickery!" is "Gaunerei,

---

64 "nutzlosen Lärm" (DzL 87; SS 23).
65 Aristotle, *Politics*, 1253a7. For a contemporary discussion of the relationship between extra-political *phonē* and political *logos*, see, for instance, Bonnie Honig, *Antigone, Interrupted* (Cambridge and New York: Cambridge University Press, 2013), 142–7; Rancière, *Disagreement*, 21–52.
66 "Und alle anderen Leute hier sind Spreu" (DzL 106; SS 13).
67 "Lumpenhund" and "Faulpelz" (DzL 71, 72; SS 15, 16).
68 "wie man eine Katze vor die Tür wirft, wenn sie ärgert" (DzL 96; SS 28).
69 "Sie bemerkten freilich nicht, daß selbst diese schöne Rede Löcher hatte [. . .] Gaunerei, nichts als Gaunerei! Und die Herren duldeten das und anerkannten es noch als richtiges Benehmen?" (DzL 92; SS 26).

nichts als Gaunerei!" where the word "Gaunerei" issues etymologically via "Jauner" from "Zigeuner" ("gipsy" or "roma"). It is worth noting that Hans Gross, Kafka's professor of criminal procedure and law at the Charles University, includes an entire chapter "Über die Gaunersprache" ("On Criminal Slang") in his 1893 book *Criminal Investigation*. This chapter is really a small dictionary of the language of the Romani which, Gross argues, it is important for any young investigating judge to become acquainted with.[70] In any case, Karl's exclamation "Gaunerei, nichts als Gaunerei!" uses the pejorative figure of the gipsy in order to locate Schubal outside the civic community.

Thus, if the construction of images of the events in the head cashier's office rests on a swarm of imaginative figures, most of them chauvinistic terms of abuse, the stereoscopic style applies this swarm in two conflicting ways, thereby highlighting its inherent contrasts and incoherences. In so doing, the binocular style makes the reader notice the holes in the social imaginary. True, Schubal is a "peaceful fellow" able to speak convincingly before the authorities,[71] but truer still, or at least equally true, he is a "Gauner." And true, the stoker is "a hard worker, devoted to the job," but truer still, he is a "shirker" and a "well-known troublemaker."[72]

By comparing the two dissimilar images of the same situation, the reader's aesthetic reflection leads to a disfiguration of the chapter's configuration of communal life. As we have seen, a disfiguration is, according to Paul de Man, a disruptive mediation of a representation.[73] Thanks to the chapter's stereoscopic setup, the reader becomes aware of the acts of figuration that underlie the images of the community.

A Higher Forum

The chapter's third and last turning point is another *Rechtswendung*, this time a turn from human to divine justice. Before Schubal's witnesses swamp the room, and even before the chief engineer begins to speak, the idea of divine justice plays an important role in Karl's understanding of the proceedings in the office:

> Now, there might be a chance that the effect that this confrontation of the stoker and Schubal would have before a higher forum would not be lost on human beings; for even if Schubal were to

---

70 Gross, *Handbuch für Untersuchungsrichter*, 284; *Criminal Investigation*, 350.
71 "diesen ruhigen Menschen" (DzL 82; SS 21).
72 "fleißig, meint es mit seiner Arbeit gut" (DzL 80; SS 20); "Faulpelz" and "ein bekannter Querulant" (DzL 82; SS 21).
73 de Man, *The Rhetoric of Romanticism*, 110.

succeed in acting a part, he might still not be able to keep it up to the end. A single flash of his vileness would be enough to make it evident to the gentlemen, something that Karl intended to see to.[74]

The gentlemen in the cashier's office are only able to see the operations of human justice, which is why the chief engineer is able to fool them with his lucid, manly speech. By contrast, the judges of a "higher forum," Karl imagines, apparently a forum of divine justice, would be able to see through the beautiful speech and perceive the vileness hiding behind it.

This shift from a human to a higher forum seems to take place when Schubal's witnesses show up in the head cashier's office to sabotage the serious negotiations with their jocularity. The chapter's final pages articulate a rather puzzling idea of divine justice that hinges on the story of the crossing of the Red Sea as described in the Book of Exodus.

When the Jews, on their flight from Pharaoh's army, reached the Red Sea, the Lord "drove the sea back by a strong east wind all night, and turned the sea into dry land; and the waters were divided."[75] Likewise, when the uncle and Karl leave the crowded head cashier's office, the people present in the room are divided: "The sailor asked the senator's permission to lead the way and then divided the crowd for the senator and Karl, who passed easily along the bowing rows."[76] Kafka's phrase about the division of the crowd echoes the biblical translation he used, that of Martin Luther (Kafka: "und teilte dann die Menge für ihn"; Luther: "und die Wasser teilten sich voneinander"). Moreover, the German word for sailor, "Matrose," is phonetically close to Moses, who, by stretching out his hand, made the waters divide.

Later, when the Israelites had reached dry ground having made their way through the parted waves, Moses stretched out his hand once again and "the waters returned and covered the chariots and the chariot drivers, the entire army of Pharaoh that had followed them into the sea;

---

74 "Nun konnte man ja vielleicht noch annehmen, die Gegenüberstellung des Heizers und Schubals werde die ihr vor einem höheren Forum zukommende Wirkung auch vor den Menschen nicht verfehlen, denn wenn sich auch Schubal gut verstellen konnte, er mußte es doch durchaus nicht bis zum Ende aushalten können. Ein kurzes Aufblitzen seiner Schlechtigkeit sollte genügen, um sie den Herren sichtbar zu machen, dafür wollte Karl schon sorgen" (DzL 90; SS 25, translation modified).

75 Ex14:21 (NRSV).

76 "Der Matrose bat den Senator, vorausgehen zu dürfen und teilte dann die Menge für ihn und Karl, die leicht zwischen den sich verbeugenden Leuten durchkamen" (DzL 109; SS 35, translation modified).

not one of them remained."[77] The figure of the inundation plays a central role in the chapter. After having analyzed the trickery of Schubal's speech, Karl says to himself: "And so, Karl—hurry, at least make good use of the time before the witnesses appear and swamp the whole thing!"[78] When, on the last page of the chapter, the uncle and Karl leave the ship in a dinghy, it looks as if the whole legal process were already underwater. Sitting closely together in the boat, they look back at the windows of the head cashier's office: "All three windows were filled with Schubal's witnesses, who were shouting goodbye and waving in the friendliest manner [. . .]. It was really as if there were no longer a stoker."[79]

At the beginning of the twentieth century, of course, passengers did not disembark from steamships in small boats. Holitscher, for instance, offers a meticulous description of how he left the ship in the harbor of New York via a gangway.[80] However, Kafka wrote the chapter only a couple of months after the sinking of the *Titanic* in April 1912. I contend that both this famous modern disaster and the legendary tale of the drowning of Pharaoh's chariots and horsemen inspired the final pages of the chapter. In the words of Johannes V. Jensen's description of the Mourning March, the stoker's case has, at the end of the day, "only formed another eddy in the human whirlpool of Manhattan."

In the biblical story, the drowning of Pharaoh's army is an act of justice from which the Lord, as he declares himself, will gain honor. Thus, based on the story of the crossing of the Red Sea, divine justice is to be understood as the inundation and dissolution of a well-organized hierarchic community, be it Pharaoh's army or the captain's ship. A similar dissolution is caused by the merry foolishness of Schubal's witnesses who, after having swamped the head cashier's office, are unable to take anything seriously: "It looked as if these basically good-natured people considered the quarrel between Schubal and the stoker a joke, and the ridiculousness of it did not end even in front of the captain."[81] After the "Rechtswendung" from human to divine justice,

---

77   Ex14:28 (NRSV).

78   "Also Karl, rasch, nütze jetzt wenigstens die Zeit aus, ehe die Zeugen auftreten und alles überschwemmen!" (DzL 93; SS 26).

79   "Alle drei Fenster waren mit Zeugen Schubals besetzt, welche freundschaftlichst grüßten und winkten, [. . .] Es war wirklich, als gäbe es keinen Heizer mehr" (DzL 110; SS 35).

80   Holitscher, *Amerika*, 43.

81   "Es schien, daß diese im übrigen gutmütigen Leute den Streit Schubals mit dem Heizer als einen Spaß auffaßten, dessen Lächerlichkeit nicht einmal vor dem Kapitän aufhöre" (DzL 109; SS 35).

the stoker's case is not solved at the court but, rather, dissolved together with the entire court.

To complicate things further, the final pages of the "The Stoker" allude not only to Exodus but also to the concluding scenes of Abraham Scharkansky's play *Der Meschumed*, which Kafka saw staged by Yitzhak Löwy's theater troupe at Café Savoy a year earlier (as discussed in Chapter 5 above).

The villains in the chapter and in the play, Schubal and Seidemann, like Shakespeare's Shylock, are capable of thwarting the practice of human justice by their well-formulated speeches. "[B]y his fluent, decisive speech, by his reasonable bearing, by correctly addressing the presiding judge in contrast to the former witnesses," Seidemann, the renegade murderer, "makes a good impression which is in terrible contrast to what we know of him."[82] Both Kafka's chapter and Scharkansky's play end with a courtroom scene in which the villains treacherously prop up their case via a group of naïve witnesses who have absolutely no understanding of the seriousness of the legal proceedings. Like Schubal's witnesses, the two in caftans cannot help making fun of everything.

However, at the very end of the courtroom scene in *Der Meschumed*, Seidemann's vileness is revealed, at which point he takes poison and confesses his misdeeds to the Jewish God. It is evident that Karl hopes that something similar will happen in the head cashier's office. When listening to Schubal's beautiful speech, he feels a strong urge to disclose the vileness that the gentlemen in the office are unable to see, focused as they are on the justice of this world: "Everything was clear, had even unwittingly been presented as such by Schubal, but it had to be offered in a different way, made absolutely obvious to the gentlemen. They needed to be shaken up. And so, Karl—hurry, at least make good use of the time before the witnesses appear and swamp the whole thing!"[83] Apparently, Karl dreams of a defamiliarizing experience, a much-needed shake-up ("Aufrüttelung"), that would reveal that the chief engineer is, in fact, not a peaceful fellow but a "Gauner." Unconcerned with the dispute between the stoker and Schubal, such an aesthetic experience would make it absolutely obvious how the individuals

---

82 "[Seidemann] macht durch seine fließende bestimmte Rede, durch seine verständige Haltung, durch richtige Ansprache des Gerichtspräsidenten gegenüber den frühern Zeugen einen guten Eindruck, der in einem schrecklichen Gegensatz ist zu dem, was wir von ihm wissen" (T 65–6; D 69).

83 "Alles war klar und wurde ja auch von Schubal wider Willen so dargeboten, aber den Herren mußte man es anders, noch handgreiflicher zeigen. Sie brauchten Aufrüttelung. Also Karl, rasch, nütze jetzt wenigstens die Zeit aus, ehe die Zeugen auftreten und alles überschwemmen!" (DzL 93; SS 26).

stand in relation to each other, how they fit together, how they relate to other groups and to the surrounding world.

Karl on the Balcony II

Near the end of *Amerika*, Karl is standing on a balcony belonging to a retired female opera singer, the statuesque Brunelda. With growing excitement, he watches a chaotic demonstration for the election of a judge in the district:

> At first Delamarche stood behind Brunelda with his arms crossed, and then he ran into the room and brought out opera glasses for Brunelda. Below, behind the musicians, the main section of the parade had appeared. Seated on the shoulders of an enormous man was a gentleman of whom all one could see from this height was a faintly glistening bald spot and a top hat perpetually raised in greeting. All around him people carried wooden signs that seemed completely white—at least as seen from the balcony; the signs were set up in such a way that they were literally leaning on the gentleman, who towered up in their midst. Since everything was moving, the wall of signs was continually loosening up and continually arranging itself anew. The gentleman's supporters surrounded him, filling the entire width of the street—but only for a relatively short distance, at least insofar as one could make out in the dark—all of them clapped their hands and probably proclaimed his name in a rhythmic chant, which, however, was short and quite incomprehensible. Cleverly scattered about in the crowd, several of them carried car lamps with extremely strong lights, which they slowly trained up and down the houses along both sides of the street. At Karl's height the light was no longer bothersome, but one could see the people on the lower balconies that it had briefly illuminated putting their hands over their eyes.[84]

---

84 "Delamarche stand zuerst mit gekreuzten Armen hinter Brunelda, dann lief er ins Zimmer und brachte Brunelda den Operngucker. Unten war hinter den Musikanten der Hauptteil des Aufzuges erschienen. Auf den Schultern eines riesenhaften Mannes saß ein Herr, von dem man in dieser Höhe nichts anderes sah, als seine matt schimmernde Glatze, über der er seinen Zylinderhut ständig grüßend hoch erhoben hielt. Rings um ihn wurden offenbar Holztafeln getragen, die vom Balkon aus gesehen ganz weiß erschienen; die Anordnung war derartig getroffen, daß diese Plakate von allen Seiten sich förmlich an den Herrn anlehnten, der aus ihrer Mitte hoch hervorragte. Da alles im Gange war, lockerte sich diese Mauer von Plakaten immerfort und ordnete sich auch immerfort von neuem. Im weiteren Umkreis war um den Herrn die ganze Breite der Gasse, wenn auch, soweit man im Dunkel schätzen konnte, auf eine unbedeutende Länge hin, von Anhängern des Herrn angefüllt, die sämtlich in die Hände

The description of the demonstration, which continues over several pages, focuses equally on the political rally taking place on the street and on Karl's aesthetic experience of it. The wooden signs seem completely blank, at least as seen from the balcony; the supporters follow the candidate, at least insofar as one could make out in the dark; and the extremely strong lights are far enough below not to trouble Karl in his vantage point.

It is not difficult to see that Kafka models Karl's violent aesthetic experience on the balcony on his own experience in the Kaiserpanorama in Friedland. In the passage above, Brunelda's opera glasses allude to the binocular optics of the stereoscope. "Don't you want to look through the glasses?" she asks,[85] upon which she forces Karl to look through the binoculars by embedding his head between her colossal breasts. Apart from these glasses, the stereoscopic character of Karl's aesthetic experience is auditory rather than visual. In his description of the Mourning March in New York, Johannes V. Jensen underlined the "shrill disharmony" produced when brass bands marched so close to each other in the procession "that one muffled psalm mixed its lamentation with the next one." In *Amerika*, Kafka describes a similar conflict between the song of the candidate's party on the balconies and the countersong from the balconies of the opponents:

> On the balconies occupied by members of the candidate's party, everybody began to shout out his name, and their hands, which hung far out over the balustrades, began to clap like machines. On the other balconies, which were in fact in the majority, there arose a powerful countersong that, however, failed to produce a coherent effect, since the people singing were supporters of different candidates. Still, all the enemies of the present candidate came together in a general round of whistling, and one could even hear numerous gramophones being switched on again.[86]

---

klatschten und wahrscheinlich den Namen des Herrn, einen ganz kurzen, aber unverständlichen Namen, in einem getragenen Gesange verkündeten. Einzelne, die geschickt in der Menge verteilt waren, hatten Automobillaternen mit äußerst starkem Licht, das sie die Häuser auf beiden Seiten der Straße langsam auf- und abwärts führten. In Karls Höhe störte das Licht nicht mehr, aber auf den unteren Balkonen sah man die Leute, die davon bestrichen wurden, eiligst die Hände an die Augen führen" (V 323–4; A 219–20).

85 "Willst du nicht durch den Gucker schauen?" (V 327; A 222).

86 "Auf den übrigen Balkonen, die sogar in der Mehrzahl waren, erhob sich ein starker Gegengesang, der allerdings keine einheitliche Wirkung hatte, da es sich um die Anhänger verschiedener Kandidaten handelte. Dagegen verbanden sich weiterhin alle Feinde des anwesenden Kandidaten zu einem·allgemeinen Pfeifen und sogar Grammophone wurden vielfach wieder in Gang gesetzt" (V 326; A 221).

The result of this stereoscopic juxtaposition of song and countersong seems to be a perpetual destruction and reconstruction of the events in the street. This constructive destruction of the urban world is the shared theme of the two balcony scenes in *Amerika*.

On the one hand, this specific kind of aesthetic experience entails a destruction of the well-ordered world of New York. When Karl looked at a street from the balcony outside his uncle's flat at the beginning of the novel, it felt to his dazzled eye "as if a glass pane [. . .] were being smashed again and again with the utmost force."[87] Similarly, standing on the balcony outside Brunelda's flat, Karl hears the crash of splintering glass from the street when the opponents of the candidate succeed in smashing all the supporters' car lamps to bits.[88]

On the other hand, the aesthetic experience also seems to set in motion a process of construction that recreates the world anew. When Karl perceived the cityscape from his uncle's balcony, it appeared—as noted above—according to a complicated sentence, as "a mixture, thrown together in ever new beginnings [*aus immer neuen Anfängen*], of distorted human figures and of the roofs of all sorts of vehicles." Likewise, from Brunelda's balcony, as we saw in the quotation above, the wall of wooden signs under the candidate is recreated again and again: "Since everything was moving, the wall of signs was continually loosening up and continually arranging itself anew [*ordnete sich auch immerfort von neuem*]."

In the election scene, Kafka also establishes a more direct link between stereoscopic style and political import. As the election develops, "political arguments erupted" between the members of the candidate's party and the members of the opposing party.[89] At first, people on the balconies resemble the audience of a theater piece or an opera, but after a while they have to run down into the street to participate in the demonstration themselves. The shrill disharmony creates a political space: "even the people in the houses had been unable to resist the temptation to get directly involved; only women and children mostly were left behind on the balconies and at the windows, the men surged out from the gates of the houses."[90] Thus, the conflictual

---

87 (V 55–6; A 33–4, translation modified).
88 (V 334; A 227).
89 "Zwischen den einzelnen Balkonen wurden politische Streitigkeiten mit einer durch die nächtliche Stunde verstärkten Erregung ausgetragen" (V 326; A 221).
90 "und selbst die Leute in den Häusern hatten der Verlockung nicht widerstehen können, in dieser Angelegenheit mit eigenen Händen einzugreifen, auf den Balkonen und in den Fenstern waren fast nur Frauen und Kinder zurückgeblieben, während die Männer unten aus den Haustoren drängten" (V 332; A 226).

aesthetic experience urges the audience to leave behind aesthetic contemplation and engage in the acting in concert.

In "The Stoker," the political thinking effected by the stereoscopic style can be seen as a political moment in this Arendtian sense of the term. As we have seen, the chapter makes two images of the events on the ship grind against each other in a frightful manner: order and disorder, legal scene and family scene, matter of justice and matter of discipline, *polis* and *oikos*. The shrill disharmony produced by this juxtaposition confronts the reader with a question of justice, which has to do neither with the distribution of goods nor with retribution for transgressions but, more fundamentally, with the configuration of the community. Put differently, the "higher forum" of divine justice, so feverishly hoped for by Karl, assembles itself in the reader's aesthetic experience.

Eight I Speak for Them, Not for Myself

Josef K. as Popular Speaker: The Trial

The day before Easter Sunday 1899, the 19-year-old tailor's apprentice Agnes Hruza was found murdered in the forest of Brezina close to the Bohemian town of Polna, around 130 kilometers southeast of Prague. The Czech and German nationalist newspapers were quick to present the crime as a ritual murder, committed in order to use the victim's blood in the traditional matzo balls made for the Jewish Passover. Allegedly, the evidence for this was that the murdered girl had a large gash in the throat and that a surprisingly little amount of blood was found at the scene of crime. A couple of days later, the 22-year-old Jewish shoemaker Leopold Hilsner was arrested. Even if the evidence was rather thin owing to sloppy forensic work, Hilsner was found guilty and sentenced to death in the subsequent trial, essentially as a result of the way in which the examining magistrate and the prosecutor described his personality. The intellectually disabled Hilsner's clean criminal record counted for nothing, it was intimated: he was Jewish, had no regular work, and "vagabondized," often close to the forest of Brezina.[1] Moreover, the lawyer of the victim's family, a certain Dr. Baxa, alluded to medieval blood libel myths in his highly dramatic description of the murder. Seen from the point of view of the victim, the court and the jurors were made to understand how three unknown persons, belonging to "a race disgusting to her [. . .] threw themselves over her as over a sacrificial animal."[2]

The Hilsner trial took place just as the Dreyfus case reached its anti-Semitic climax in France, and in the Bohemian case, Émile Zola's part

---

1 Maximilian Paul-Schiff, *Der Prozess Hilsner: Aktenauszug* (Vienna: L. Rosner, 1908), 17, 33. For further discussion, see Michael Curtis, "The Hilsner Case and Ritual Murder," in *Jews on Trial*, ed. Bruce Afran and Robert A. Garber (Jersey City, NJ: Ktav, 2005).
2 Paul-Schiff, *Der Prozess Hilsner*, 38.

was played by Tomas Masaryk, professor of ethics at the Charles University in Prague and later president of Czechoslovakia. In his pamphlet *Notwendigkeit der Revision des Polnaer Processes* (*The Necessity of Revising the Polna Trial*, 1899) he offered a detailed critique of the evidence, among other things pointing out that the murder was committed *after* Passover so that it could hardly be understood as a preparation for the ritual. In the introduction, Masaryk criticizes the entire legal proceeding:

> In my analysis of the Polna trial, I will try to make up for the shame of our national journalism that by its slanderous and hate-mongering coverage of the Hilsner affair has created a Bohemian and Austrian Dreyfusiade for us. [. . .] So much lack of judgment and consideration, so much inhumanity on the verge of cruelty—such a phenomenon can only be explained by the nervous over-excitement and the abnormal situation of our Bohemian and Austrian life in general. For those who observe this situation with only a little attention, the Polna trial is a bloody memento.[3]

Although Masaryk's pamphlet led to a reopening of the case, the second trial saw Hilsner reconvicted and sentenced to life in prison. A year later, Masaryk published another pamphlet about the Hilsner trial (or the Polna trial, as he called it) in which he described how his critical evaluation of the trial had given him a "painful and depressing insight into our Bohemian-Austrian situation in general, into the moral and the education of the population, among lawyers, judges, doctors, and especially in journalism."[4]

In his two pamphlets, Masaryk approaches the Hilsner case as both a legal and a political matter. Not just an isolated murder case, the case is a "bloody memento" of the abnormal situation in Bohemia and Austria in general, a testimony of the "political misery" of the times.[5]

The Hilsner trial took place when Franz Kafka was a 16-year-old high school student, and Kafka's father, like Max Brod's, Franz Werfel's, and Felix Weltsch's, took a keen interest in the "Austrian Dreyfusiade." A whole series of cases about alleged ritual murders fueled the anti-Semitism emerging at the turn of the century: 1883 in Hungary, 1891 on

---

3 Tomas G. Masaryk, *Notwendigkeit der Revision des Polnaer Processes* (Vienna: Die Zeit, 1899), 3. I gratefully reuse the English translation from Wagner, "No one indicates," 311.

4 *Die Bedeutung des Polnaer Verbrechens für den Ritualaberglauben* (Berlin: H.S. Hermann, 1900), 80, my translation.

5 *Bedeutung des Polnaer Verbrechens*, 80, my translation.

Corfu, 1903 in the Russian town Kishinev, and finally 1912–13 in Kiev.[6] All of these incidents received enormous media attention and were represented on postcards, posters, leaflets, cartoons, and even in stereoscopic panoramas of the same type as the Kaiserpanorama in Friedland. The latter case, against another Jewish shoemaker, Menachem Mendel Beilis from Kiev, was discussed so intensively in Prague that it was referred to simply as "the trial" ("der Prozess").

"I don't understand how whole nations of people could ever have thought of ritual murder before these recent events," Kafka writes to his Christian pen friend Milena Jesénska in the summer of 1920 with reference to these cases.[7] What most terrifies him about the Hilsner story is the strong "conviction" of the Christian population "that the Jews are necessarily bound to fall upon you Christians, just as predatory animals are bound to murder."[8] Earlier, the anti-Semitic affect was just a diffuse feeling of anxiety and envy toward the Jews, Kafka notes in the letter, but now it takes shape as a graphic conviction: "but here there is no question, we see 'Hilsner' committing the crime step by step; what difference does it make that the virgin embraces him at the same time?"[9]

There are no direct references to Jewish ritual murders in the unfinished novel *The Trial*, on which Kafka started to work in August 1914. Structurally, however, there are a number of striking similarities between the trial of the protagonist Josef K. and the contemporary trials about alleged ritual murders. Like Hilsner, Josef K. is a victim of a false accusation: "Someone must have slandered Josef K.," the novel begins, "for one morning, without having done anything wrong, he was arrested."[10] Both cases are, to all appearances, miscarriages of justice,

---

6   For Kafka's relation to the Hilsner trial and to other alleged ritual murders, see Bruce, *Kafka and Cultural Zionism*, 12–33; Sander L. Gilman, *Franz Kafka: The Jewish Patient* (New York: Routledge, 1995), 101–56; Michael Löwy, "Franz Kafka's Trial and the Anti-Semitic Trials of His Time," *Human Architecture: Journal of the Sociology of Self-Knowledge* VII, no. 2 (2009); *Franz Kafka: Subversive Dreamer*, trans. Inez Hedges (Ann Arbor, MI: University of Michigan Press, 2016); Christoph Stölzl, *Kafkas böses Böhmen: Zur Sozialgeschichte eines Prager Juden* (Munich, 1975), 67–123.

7   "Ich begreife überhaupt nicht wie die Völker ehe es zu solchen Erscheinungen der letzten Zeiten kam auf den Ritualmordgedanken kommen konnten" (B4 189; LM 51).

8   "Das für mich zunächst Schrecklichste an der Geschichte ist die Überzeugung wie sich die Juden notwendigerweise, so wie Raubtiere morden müssen" (B4 189; LM 51).

9   "hier aber ist doch der eindeutige Anblick, hier sieht man 'Hilsner' die Tat Schritt für Schritt tun; daß die Jungfrau ihn dabei umarmt, was bedeutet das" (B4 189; LM 51).

10   "Jemand mußte Josef K. verleumdet haben, denn ohne daß er etwas Böses getan hätte, wurde er eines Morgens verhaftet" (P 7; Tr 3).

based on the perception of the victim's character in the collective imagination.

Like Masaryk, K. reacts to the false accusation by approaching the legal matter as a political issue. When K. appears at the initial inquiry, he doesn't behave as if he were defending himself at session of a court but, rather, as a speaker at a political assembly: "what has happened to me is merely an isolated case and as such of no particular consequence, since I don't take it very seriously, but it is a sign of the proceedings being brought against many people. I speak for them, not for myself."[11]

I return to K.'s ill-fated attempt to make a political speech in the second half of this chapter. For now, it must suffice to point out that K. describes the case against him as "a sign" ("ein Zeichen") of a wretched state of affairs, the same way as Masaryk described the Hilsner trial as a "bloody memento" of the abnormal situation in Bohemia and Austria in general.

After having returned from his work as chief financial officer of a bank, K. immediately pays a visit to his landlady in order to talk through the events of the morning. It seems to him that the events have "caused great disorder throughout Frau Grubach's apartment," and "that he was the one needed to restore order."[12] Since K. views the case as a political matter rather than as a legal matter, restoring order is not only an act of retribution but also an act of reconfiguration, a political action that can change the corrupted order of things. K.'s attempt to restore the order of things fails miserably, however. In the last chapter of the novel he is simply picked up at his home by two men who take him to a stone quarry outside the city and execute him "like a dog."[13] Just as in *Amerika*, the political moment is conspicuous in the novel by its absence. In this chapter I will show how K.'s attempt to restore the social order plays an important role at the level of the aesthetic experience of the novel.

The "Most Risky" Moment

Normally Frau Grubach's cook brings K. breakfast each morning at around eight o'clock, but, on the first page of the novel, she does not

---

11   "was mir geschehen ist, ist ja nur ein einzelner Fall und als solcher nicht sehr wichtig, da ich es nicht sehr schwer nehme, aber es ist das Zeichen eines Verfahrens wie es gegen viele geübt wird. Für diese stehe ich hier ein, nicht für mich" (P 64; Tr 46–7, translation modified).

12   "ohne genau zu wissen, was er meinte, schien es ihm, als ob durch die Vorfälle des Morgens eine große Unordnung in der ganzen Wohnung der Frau Grubach verursacht worden sei und daß gerade er nötig sei, um die Ordnung wieder herzustellen" (P 30; Tr 21, translation modified).

13   "Wie ein Hund" (P 312; Tr 231).

appear. When K. rings for her, there is immediately a knock at the door and a man K. has never seen before enters. The man is the guard Franz; accompanied by another guard, Willem, he informs K. that he has been arrested. A short while later, K. is called to the room of a certain Fräulein Bürstner where he has a short conversation with an inspector who seems to be the guards' superior. While arranging the objects lying on Fräulein Bürstner's nightstand, the inspector asks K. how he has experienced the morning's events. In the last version of the unfinished novel, K. merely answers that, even if he does not think the whole thing's a joke, he does not take it too seriously either.[14] However, in a remarkable deleted passage, he sketches a short theory in order to explain his experience of the morning:

> Someone told me—I can't remember who it was—that it was remarkable indeed that, when one wakes up early in the morning, one finds, at least in general, everything in the same place where it had been in the evening before. One has been after all in sleep and dream, at least apparently, in a condition essentially different from waking; and one needs, as that man remarked quite rightly, an immense presence of mind or rather a quickness of repartee in order to grasp, when one opens one's eyes, whatever there is, so to speak, at the same place where one left it [*unverrückt*] in the evening. Therefore, the moment of waking up is the most risky moment of the day; if one has gotten over it without having been pulled away from one's place, one can be confident for the rest of the day.[15]

The moment of waking up is located at the point of intersection between sleeping and waking. Without the presence of mind or quickness of repartee that it takes to restore a familiar reality, one perceives the world

---

14 (P 21; Tr 13).
15 "Jemand sagte mir, ich kann mich nicht mehr erinnern, wer es gewesen ist, dass es doch sonderbar sei, dass man, wenn man früh aufwacht, wenigstens im allgemeinen alles unverrückt an der gleichen Stelle findet, wie es am Abend gewesen ist. Man ist doch im Schlaf und im Traum wenigstens scheinbar in einem vom Wachen wesentlich verschiedenen Zustand gewesen, und es gehört (wie jener Mann ganz richtig sagte) eine unendliche Geistesgegenwart oder besser Schlagfertigkeit dazu, um mit dem Augenöffnen alles, was da ist, gewissermaßen an der gleichen Stelle zu fassen, an der man es am Abend losgelassen hat. Darum sei auch der Augenblick des Erwachens der riskanteste Augenblick im Tag, sei er einmal überstanden, ohne dass man irgendwohin von seinem Platze fortgezogen wurde, so könne man den ganzen Tag über getrost sein" (PA 168); I gratefully reuse the English translation from Rainer Nägele, *Benjamin's Ground: New Readings of Walter Benjamin* (Detroit, MI: Wayne State University Press, 1988), 36.

in a stereoscopic mixture of two dissimilar states of consciousness.[16] The risk in this double exposure proceeds from the possibility that the experience might dislocate things from the place one left them the previous evening, and from the possibility that one might have even been pulled away from one's rightful place—as, for instance, K. is dragged away to his death by the two executioners at the end of the novel.

In a sense, the stereoscopic moment of waking up is extended to the entire novel, given that people and things tend to look as if they have been moved from their proper place. After his first conversation with the two guards, K. reflects that he has to "bring this show to an end."[17] The German "Schaustellung" is a name for shows, spectacles, and visual attractions such as, for instance, the Kaiserpanorama in Friedland. Remarkably, the people and things represented in *The Trial* look as if they were seen in a stereoscopic show.

In his diary entry from Friedland, Kafka noted: "People inside like wax figures, their soles fixed to the ground on the pavement."[18] Entering Fräulein Bürstner's room, K. meets three junior clerks from his bank, all "uncharacteristically anemic young men,"[19] who more than anything resemble pale and immobile wax figures. One of them is described as "stiff," while another has an annoying smile, "produced by a chronic muscular twitch,"[20] as if the movements of his body were frozen in the immobility of the wax figure. In a later chapter, K., in the company of his uncle, pays his first visit to the lawyer, Huld. Here they are received by the maid Leni, who has "a round, doll-like face" and "pale cheeks"[21] and who, in a later chapter, as if to underline the connection to wax figures, kneels down beside someone "to scratch away some wax that had dripped onto his trousers."[22]

---

16 For an eminent analysis of the dual vision of the risky moment, see Gerhard Neumann, "Der Zauber des Anfangs und das 'Zögern vor der Geburt': Kafkas Poetologie des 'riskanten Augenblicks'," in *Nach erneuter Lektüre, Franz Kafkas "Der Process,"* ed. Hans Dieter Zimmermann (Würzburg: Königshausen & Neumann, 1992). For a discussion of the intellectual background to this passage, see Joel Morris, "Josef K.'s (A+x) Problem: Kafka on the Moment of Awakening," *German Quarterly* 82, no. 4 (2009).

17 "K. mußte dieser Schaustellung ein Ende machen" (P 15; Tr 9).

18 (T 936; D 430).

19 "so uncharakteristischen blutarmen jungen Leute" (P 27; Tr 17).

20 "mit dem unausstehlichen durch eine chronische Muskelzerrung bewirkten Lächeln." A similar observation is made by Carolin Duttlinger: "even once K. has recognized the three as his colleagues, their appearance still maintains a photographic character." Duttlinger, *Kafka and Photography*, 180. I contend that their character is not only photographic but also stereographic.

21 "ein puppenförmig gerundetes Gesicht" and "bleichen Wangen" (P 130; Tr 97).

22 "um etwas Wachs wegzukratzen, das von der Kerze auf seine Hose getropft war" (P 244; Tr 180).

As always in Kafka, the stereoscopic "Schaustellung" is closely connected to questions of normative order and disorder. If we look at the orderly image, the fictional characters of *The Trial* act in their official capacity, complying with the laws of the community. If we look at the disorderly image, on the other hand, the characters can be seen not as rule-bound officials but, rather, as unruly private persons who bend the universal laws to their own particular interests, either because they are friendly or because they are corrupt, or both.

"I'm exceeding my instructions by talking to you in such a friendly way," the guard Willem explains to K. "But I hope no one hears except Franz, and he's being friendly too, although it's against all regulations."[23] In short, K. has woken up in a local state of exception in which the laws of the community are suspended: "After all, K. lived in a state governed by law, there was universal peace, all laws were in force; who dared assault him in his own lodgings?" he thinks at first.[24] In the disorderly image, however, the laws are no longer in force, so that the guards are being friendly against all regulations and so that K. no longer possesses "the right [. . .] over the disposal" of his things.[25]

We have encountered the double exposure of order and disorder, of public and private several times in previous chapters. In *The Trial*, however, the stereoscopic style stands out for its sexual or even pornographic character. At times, K.'s interaction with the two guards has echoes of sexual intercourse, maybe even homosexual rape:[26] "the belly of the second guard—they surely must be guards—kept bumping against him in a formally friendly way, but when he looked up he saw a face completely at odds with that fat body: a dry, bony face, with a large nose set askew, consulting above his head with the other guard."[27]

The second guard, Willem, turns away his dry, bony face and looks at the other guard, Franz, over K.'s head, just as the uncle, discussed in the preceding chapter, cast a knowing look at the captain over Karl's

---

23 "Ich gehe über meinen Auftrag hinaus, wenn ich Ihnen so freundschaftlich zurede. Aber ich hoffe, es hört es niemand sonst als Franz und der ist selbst gegen alle Vorschriften freundlich zu Ihnen" (P 9; Tr 5).
24 "K. lebte doch in einem Rechtsstaat, überall herrschte Friede, alle Gesetze bestanden aufrecht, wer wagte ihn in seiner Wohnung zu überfallen?" (P 11; Tr 6, translation modified).
25 "das Verfügungsrecht über seine Sachen" (P 11; Tr 6).
26 For this allusion, see Anderson, *Kafka's Clothes*, 161.
27 "immer wieder stieß der Bauch des zweiten Wächters—es konnten ja nur Wächter sein—förmlich freundschaftlich an ihn, sah er aber auf, dann erblickte er ein zu diesem dicken Körper gar nicht passendes trockenes knochiges Gesicht, mit starker seitlich gedrehter Nase, das sich über ihn hinweg mit dem andern Wächter verständigte" (P 11; Tr 6, translation modified).

head in the head cashier's office in *Amerika*.[28] At the same time, however, Willem repeatedly bumps his belly against K. as if they were engaged in sexual intercourse. The belly is described as bumping against K. "in a formally friendly way" ("förmlich freundschaftlich"), an oxymoronic expression that captures the stereoscopic juxtaposition of formality and friendliness, of procedure and sex.

Far Too Corporeally

Before I detail K.'s attempts to deliver a political speech at the initial inquiry, I will take a brief look at his visit to the same courtroom the following Sunday. Expecting a second round of questioning, he is disappointed to find the courtroom empty, and so that his long walk to the suburb be not entirely wasted, he persuades the court usher's wife to show him the books that lie on the table of the examining magistrate:

They were old dog-eared books; one of the bindings was almost split in two at the spine, the covers barely hanging by the cords. "How dirty everything is," said K., shaking his head, and before K. could reach for the books, the woman wiped at least some of the dust off with her apron. K. opened the book on top, and an indecent picture was revealed. A man and a woman were sitting naked on a divan; the obscene intention of the artist was obvious, but his ineptitude was so great that in the end there was nothing to be seen but a man and woman, emerging far too corporeally from the picture, sitting rigidly upright, and due to the poor perspective, turning toward each other with difficulty. K. didn't leaf through any further, but simply opened to the frontispiece of the second book, a novel entitled *The Torments Grete Suffered at the Hands of Her Husband Hans*.[29]

---

28 (DzL 107; SS 33–4).

29 "Es waren alte abgegriffene Bücher, ein Einbanddeckel war in der Mitte fast zerbrochen, die Stücke hiengen nur durch Fasern zusammen. 'Wie schmutzig hier alles ist,' sagte K. kopfschüttelnd und die Frau wischte mit ihrer Schürze, ehe K. nach den Büchern greifen konnte wenigstens oberflächlich den Staub weg. K. schlug das oberste Buch auf, es erschien ein unanständiges Bild. Ein Mann und eine Frau saßen nackt auf einem Kanapee, die gemeine Absicht des Zeichners war deutlich zu erkennen, aber seine Ungeschicklichkeit war so groß gewesen, daß schließlich doch nur ein Mann und eine Frau zu sehen waren, die allzu körperlich aus dem Bilde hervorragten, übermäßig aufrecht dasaßen und infolge falscher Perspektive nur mühsam sich einander zuwendeten. K. blätterte nicht weiter sondern schlug nur noch das Titelblatt des zweiten Buches auf, es war ein Roman mit dem Titel: 'Die Plagen, welche Grete von ihrem Manne Hans zu erleiden hatte'" (P 76–7; Tr 57, translation modified).

This *ekphrasis* (a linguistic representation of a graphic representation) describes the man and the woman represented in the obscene image while offering a careful description of K.'s aesthetic experience of it—an experience shaped by the "ineptitude" of the artist and the "poor perspective" of the image. Due to this failed aesthetic experience, the man and the woman look as if they were "emerging" or "protruding" ("hervorragten") far too corporeally from the picture. A couple of years earlier, Kafka experienced a similar three-dimensional effect in the Kaiserpanorama in Friedland which made the smooth floor of the Italian cathedrals emerge from the image plane as if located "in front of

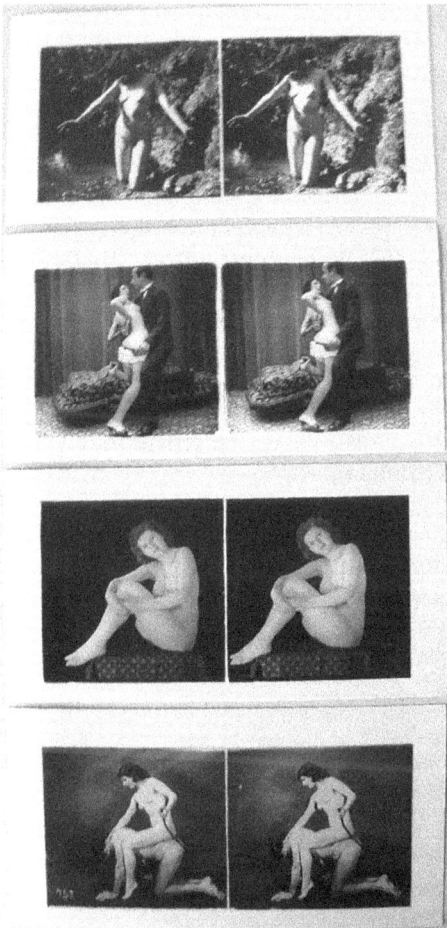

Figure 8.1 Pornographic stereoscopic slides from the early twentieth century.

our tongue."[30] In other words, K. experiences the indecent image in the
law book as if it were a pornographic stereograph.

People and things emerging from the image plane is a recurring
motif in the novel. Later, when K. pays a visit to the lawyer Huld, he
notices a large and pompous painting on the wall in a dark room:

It showed a man in a judge's robe; he was sitting on a throne, its
golden highlights sticking out from the painting in several places.
The strange thing was that this judge wasn't sitting in calm
dignity, but instead had his left arm braced against the back and
arm of the chair, while his right arm was completely free, his hand
alone clutching the arm of the chair, as if he were about to spring
up any moment in a violent and perhaps wrathful outburst to say
something decisive or even pass judgment.[31]

The golden highlights on the throne protrude from the painting in
several places ("hervorstach"), and the judge himself looks on the verge
of springing up ("aufspringen"). Later again, when visiting Titorelli,
the artist who painted the picture of the judge, K. notices a third picture
with the same three-dimensional effect. This time, the painting
represents the goddess of Justice: "But, except for an imperceptible
shading, brightness still surrounded the figure of Justice, and in this
brightness the figure seemed to protrude strikingly."[32]

Returning to the indecent image on the table of the examining
magistrate, its three-dimensional effect seems to be produced by a
juxtaposition of two dissimilar perspectives. In any case, K. interprets
the image in two different ways separated by the words "but . . . in the
end" ("aber . . . schließlich"). While K. can see the clearly obscene
intention of the artist, in the end, he cannot see more than a man and a
woman sitting rigidly upright.

This is a pornographic version of the juxtaposition of orderly and
disorderly image. The *ekphrasis* begins with the disorderly and indecent

30 (T 936–8, D 429–31).
31 "Es stellte einen Mann im Richtertalar dar; er saß auf einem hohen Tronsessel,
    dessen Vergoldung vielfach aus dem Bilde hervorstach. Das Ungewöhnliche
    war, daß dieser Richter nicht in Ruhe und Würde dort saß, sondern den linken
    Arm fest an Rükken- und Seitenlehne drückte, den rechten Arm aber völlig frei
    hatte und nur mit der Hand die Seitenlehne umfaßte, als wolle er im nächsten
    Augenblick mit einer heftigen und vielleicht empörten Wendung aufspringen
    um etwas Entscheidendes zu sagen oder gar das Urteil zu verkünden" (P 141–2;
    Tr 105, translation modified).
32 "Um die Figur der Gerechtigkeit aber blieb es bis auf eine unmerkliche Tönung
    hell, in dieser Helligkeit schien die Figur besonders vorzudringen" (P 197; Tr
    146, translation modified).

image which, at least according to K.'s idea of the artist's intention, depicts a man and a woman engaging in sexual intercourse. In this image, then, the rules of decency are not in force.[33] By contrast, the orderly image is one of a man and a woman sitting beside each other in full compliance with the rules of decency. Seen this way, the two bodies are not in any erotic interrelation, belonging to two separate and autonomous persons who turn toward each other only with difficulty.

We have already seen this connection between ambivalent vision and ambivalent bodily posture in the scene of arrest. Here, the guard Willem turned his body toward K. by bumping his belly against him while, at the same time, turning his head away from him, "with a large nose set askew,"[34] a kind of chronic turning-away. The opposition between turning toward and turning away also plays a role the night after the arrest when K. visits, and in a sense assaults, Fräulein Bürstner in her room. This time, the sexual interaction takes place on an ottoman rather than on a divan. Avoiding turning her gaze toward K., the Fräulein stares silently at the floor in front of her for the entire conversation, "without changing her posture."[35] K. tries to turn toward her with difficulty, but he fails: "Then he kissed her on the neck, right at her throat, and left his lips there for a long time. [. . . .] She nodded wearily, allowed him to take her hand for a kiss as she was already half turned away [*halb abgewendet*], as if she were unaware of it, and entered her room with bowed head."[36] Thus, in *The Trial*, the stereoscopic style is used to create a number of hybrid bodily postures that are simultaneously half turned on sexually, and half turned away.

Court and Apartment Building

A couple of days after the arrest, K. is informed by telephone that a short inquiry into his alleged crime will take place the following Sunday. K. is to appear in a building on a street in a distant district he has never been to before, and since he is given neither the specific hour nor the precise address of the building, he has to run around searching in a run-down apartment building filled with children and

---

33 It is worth noting that the artist's intention is obscene or base ("gemeine Absicht") according to K.'s interpretation of it. In principle, the image might be a highly cultivated croquis that becomes pornographic only thanks to K.'s excited projections. For further discussion, see Ronald D. Gray, *Franz Kafka* (Cambridge: Cambridge University Press, 1973), 109.

34 "mit starker seitlich gedrehter Nase" (P 11; Tr 6).

35 "in unveränderter Haltung" (P 47; Tr 32).

36 "Schließlich küßte er sie auf den Hals, wo die Gurgel ist, und dort ließ er die Lippen lange liegen [. . .] Sie nickte müde, überließ ihm schon halb abgewendet die Hand zum Küssen, als wisse sie nichts davon und gieng gebückt in ihr Zimmer" (P 48; Tr 33).

women who are cooking while holding their babies. Finally, after knocking on a random door, K. is told that the initial inquiry is meant to take place in the very room behind. The courtroom is a medium-size hall packed with onlookers both in the main hall and upstairs on a elevated gallery close to the ceiling. The entire inquiry in this hall comes into view in a "formally friendly" mixture of public order and private disorder.

First, the hall itself hovers between an orderly and a disorderly image in so far as it is located in a building referred to both as a "court" and as an "apartment building."[37] The little room in front of the hall is, simultaneously, an official office and a private room in which a young woman is washing nappies in a bath.[38] The following week, when K. visits the court again, the room has turned into "a fully furnished living room."[39] And the young woman in the little room, the wife of the court usher, as it later occurs, is at the same time a court official and a washerwoman who points with a wet hand toward the open door of the hall.

Likewise, the conversation between K. and the examining magistrate is, at the same time, orderly and disorderly. A red-cheeked small boy leads K. along a narrow path through the crowd toward the other end of the hall, where a small table is placed on a low platform. When K. reaches the platform, the examining magistrate says that he should have been there an hour and five minutes earlier, but that, on account of K.'s supposed unpunctuality, the inquiry is to be a special case with only semi-official status: although he is "no longer required to examine" K., "I'll make an exception for today."[40]

Incidentally, the semi-official conversation between K. and the examining magistrate reveals the strong influence of Dostoyevsky's *Crime and Punishment*, where the three interrogations in Rodion Raskolnikov's murder case take place in a gray zone between public and private, between the formal and the intimate.[41] By coincidence, the examining magistrate, Porfiry Petrovich, and Raskolnikov have friends in common, and this means that, had Raskolnikov not fallen ill after having murdered the pawnbroker and her sister, they would have met

---

37 "Gericht" and "Mietshaus" (P 52, 53; Tr 37, 38).
38 (P 57; Tr 41).
39 "ein völlig eingerichtetes Wohnzimmer" (P 74; Tr 55).
40 "ich bin nicht mehr verpflichtet, Sie jetzt zu verhören" and "ich will es jedoch ausnahmsweise heute noch tun" (P 60; Tr 43).
41 See my "Das Recht zu Athmen: Existenzberechtigung und Anerkennung bei Dostojewskij und Hegel," *Internationales Archiv für Sozialgeschichte der Deutschen Literatur* 36 (2012).

at a party the evening before the first interrogation. This is the reason why the interrogation takes place in Porfiry's private home and why he repeatedly stresses their personal relationship. The examining magistrate assures Raskolnikov that he regards him "simply as a visitor," addresses him with the cozy Russian "little father," and refers to the interrogation as spending "five minutes with a friend."[42] As an intimate trump card, Porfiry even mentions his hemorrhoids that force him, he confides, to walk up and down without pause during the interrogation.

Third, and most importantly, in *The Trial*'s "Initial Inquiry," the crowd of people in the hall come into view in a dual vision. In the orderly image, the crowd is configured as a political assembly; in the disorderly image, to which K. suddenly shifts at the end of the chapter, the crowd is configured as a private organization. As we shall see in the following sections, this opposition between political assembly and private organization shapes the entire chapter.

Political Assembly

After being shown the way to the crowded hall by the wife of the court usher, K. "thought he had walked into an assembly [*Versammlung*]."[43] When passing this judgment on the community's mode of being, K. is a little confused by the long, loose, formal coats that the people are wearing, but had it not been for these coats, "he would have taken it all for a political precinct assembly."[44] In the manuscript, Kafka originally wrote "a socialist precinct assembly."[45]

Accordingly, K. views the narrow path through the crowd as a line "that possibly divided two parties."[46] The right-hand side of the hall is, as K. sees it, filled with his supporters who murmur disapprovingly when the examining magistrate speaks. The left-hand side is occupied by a small party that seem hostile to K. and which he, therefore, seeks to win over. Standing on the low platform, as described above, K. acts as if he is a politician addressing two antagonistic parties: "[W]hat has happened to me is merely an isolated case and as such of no particular consequence, since I don't take it very seriously, but it is typical of the proceedings being brought against many people. I speak for them, not

42 Fyodor Dostoyevsky, *Crime and Punishment*, trans. Oliver Ready (New York: Penguin Books, 2015), chapter 5.
43 "K. glaubte in eine Versammlung einzutreten" (P 57; Tr 41, translation modified).
44 "sonst hätte er das ganze als eine politische Bezirksversammlung angesehn" (P 58; Tr 42, translation modified).
45 "eine socialistische Bezirksversammlung" (PA 188).
46 "der möglicherweise zwei Parteien schied" (P 58; Tr 42).

for myself. [. . .] What I seek is simply the public discussion of a public disgrace."[47]

In accordance with the judgment of the crowd as a political assembly, K. approaches what happened to him the morning of the arrest as a political rather than a legal matter. This is why his speech is a contribution to "the public discussion of a public disgrace." On the face of it, K.'s political aim is to halt the scandal of the arrest of innocent people and the imposition of senseless proceedings against them. On closer examination, however, K. seems to also have something more fundamental in mind: the constitution of a political community in which such collective decisions can be made. Indeed, he appears to be less interested in the specific content of the laws of the community than in the very establishment of a common will in the hall.

At one point, the crowd in the hall suddenly falls quiet. According to K.'s interpretation, probably a misinterpretation, the silence is a sign that he is winning over the crowd: "There was an immediate silence, so completely did K. now control the assembly. People weren't shouting back and forth as they had at the beginning; they no longer even applauded but seemed by now convinced, or on the verge of being so."[48] An early draft of this passage focuses in the same way on K.'s sovereign power over the people gathered in the hall by asserting that he already had "such a power over the assembly in which he, in so short a time, had introduced a clear and uniform need to abolish the great misconduct."[49] Clearly, K.'s aim here is not only to bring an end to a great wrong but also, more fundamentally, to establish a unified common will. When he first entered the hall, the community is described, seen through his eyes, as a "crowd of the most varied sort."[50] Out of this disorderly multitude he imagines that he is able to make an organized and uniform political community. In fact, K.'s appearance before the court can be said to go wrong precisely because he is seduced by his feeling of exerting sovereign power over the crowd.

---

47 "was mir geschehen ist, ist ja nur ein einzelner Fall und als solcher nicht sehr wichtig, da ich es nicht sehr schwer nehme, aber es ist das Zeichen eines Verfahrens wie es gegen viele geübt wird. Für diese stehe ich hier ein, nicht für mich [. . .] Was ich will, ist nur die öffentliche Besprechung eines öffentlichen Mißstandes" (P 64–5; Tr 47, translation modified).

48 "Sofort war es still, so sehr beherrschte schon K. die Versammlung. Man schrie nicht mehr durcheinander wie am Anfang, man klatschte nicht einmal mehr Beifall, aber man schien schon überzeugt oder auf dem nächsten Wege dazu" (P 68; Tr 50).

49 "[. . .] Versammlung, in die er in so kurzer Zeit ein deutliches und einheitliches Verlangen nach Abstellung der grossen Misstände gebracht hatte" (PA 191–2).

50 "ein Gedränge der verschiedensten Leute" (P 57; Tr 41).

The imaginative figures used for his attempt to institute a political community are drawn from the biblical story of the crossing of the Red Sea. In "The Stoker," as we saw in the last chapter, the sailor leads the way out of the head cashier's office, dividing the crowd for the senator and Karl as Moses divided the waters for the Jews.[51] In "Initial Inquiry," the little boy leads K. along a narrow path through to the platform, dividing the crowd of people into two antagonistic parties.

In general, Moses plays an important if inconspicuous role in *The Trial*. After the two visits to the hall of the initial inquiry, K., in the home of the lawyer Huld, notices Titorelli's painting of a man in a judge's robe. As we saw above, the man in the painting is sitting with his left arm braced against the back and arm of the chair and with his right hand clutching the arm of the chair, "as if he were about to spring up any moment in a violent and perhaps wrathful outburst to say something decisive or even pass judgment."[52] The model for Titorelli's painting is, very probably, Michelangelo's famous statue of Moses, showing the lawgiver sitting as if he too were on the point of jumping up, with one arm resting on the tablets of the law and the other arm free.[53]

Interestingly, Kafka uses the story of the crossing of the Red Sea for different purposes in *Amerika* and in *The Trial*. In "The Stoker," the focus is on the Jews' crossing of the sea and on the drowning of Pharaoh's chariots and horsemen. "Initial Inquiry", meanwhile, alludes to the events that take place after the Jews have reached the coast with dry shoes and have gone into the wilderness of Shur. In other words, the biblical story is not used as an image of the practice of divine justice, that is, an image of God's saving the Jews and drowning the Egyptians, but, rather, as an image of the institution of human justice. When the Jews have gone three days in the wilderness, Moses steps up, for the first time, as a lawgiver who mediates between God and humans: "There the LORD made for them a statute and an ordinance and there he put them to the test. He said, 'If you will listen carefully to the voice of the LORD your God, and do what is right in his sight, and give heed to his commandments and keep all his statutes, I will not bring upon

---

51 (DzL 109; SS 35).
52 (P 141–2; Tr 105, translation modified).
53 For Kafka's inspiration by Michelangelo's statue (and by Freud's essays on this statue), see Malcolm Pasley, "Two Literary Sources of Kafka's Der Prozess," *Forum for Modern Language Studies* 3, no. 2 (1967). For the Moses figure in Kafka more generally, see Bertram Rohde, *Und blätterte ein wenig in der Bibel: Studien zu Franz Kafkas Bibellektüre und ihre Auswirkungen auf sein Werk* (Würzburg: Königshausen & Neumann, 2002), 221–32.

you any of the diseases that I brought upon the Egyptians; for I am the LORD who heals you.'"[54]

Reflecting on the Book of Exodus, Jean-Jacques Rousseau characterizes Moses as one of the three principal lawgivers in world history (the two others being Lycurgus and Numa) who, with a sovereign *fiat*, instituted a political community. What happened in the desert, according to Rousseau, was "the astonishing enterprise of founding into the body of a nation a swarm of unfortunate fugitives without arts [. . .]. Moses dared to make out of this wandering and servile troop a body politic, a free people."[55]

The inconspicuous allusions to Moses in "Initial Inquiry" underline that what is going on in the hall—or, rather, what is on the verge of happening in the hall—is not the application of law to a concrete case but, rather, the institution of a political community to which the laws can be applied—the sovereign making of a statute and an ordinance for the people.

Yet the people are not merely pliable material for the sovereign decisions of the lawmaker. When the examining magistrate contends that K. should have appeared an hour and five minutes before, a general murmuring or muttering ("ein allgemeines Murren") is heard from the right-hand side of the hall, the one occupied by K.'s supporters, as he sees it.[56] This general murmuring is mentioned twice in the following passage, and the last time it is unclear whether the discontent is directed toward the examining magistrate or toward K., or toward them both.

This general murmuring, too, alludes to Exodus. When the Israelites had crossed the Red Sea and gone three days in the wilderness without finding water, the people "murmured against Moses, saying, 'What shall we drink?'"[57] In the Bible translation which Kafka used, Martin Luther uses the German word "murren": "Da murrte das Volk wider Mose." In fact, the Jewish people are repeatedly murmuring in Exodus. According to rabbinic commentary, this continual murmuring is not only to be understood as the people's materialistic longing for Egypt, where they sat by the "fleshpots" and ate their fill of bread.[58] At issue also is a more fundamental resistance to the application of the laws that

---

54   Ex 15:25 (NRSV).
55   Jean-Jacques Rousseau, *The Plan for Perpetual Peace, On the Government of Poland, and other Writings on History and Politics*, trans. Christopher Kelly (Hanover, NH: University Press of New England, 2005), 171–2.
56   (P 59; Tr 43).
57   Ex 15:24 (RSV). NRSV has "complained against" rather than "murmured against."
58   Ex 16:2–3 (NRSV).

Moses introduces. The Jews, a "stiff-necked" people "running wild,"[59] are murmuring because they do not want to listen to Moses's commandments and to comply with his laws. In other words, the murmuring is the sound of the extra-political. Seen this way, the Israelites' slavery in Egypt was a free, ungoverned life that was subject to no law, whereas their political life in the desert must conform to the law.[60] In Rousseau's terms, the servile troop murmur because they resist becoming a body politic.

While the Hebrew word for the murmuring of the Jews, *va-yilonu*, simply means to complain or to wail, Luther chooses a word with clear connotation to animal sounds. According to the Grimms' *Deutsches Wörterbuch*, the word "Murren" is used for the sounds "of animals, of dogs" such as growling and purring. But the word can also be used figuratively for human sounds, in this case referring to the expression of "rage, dissatisfaction, bad temper with muffled, restrained sounds." The murmuring in the hall, then, is a rhetorical description of the crowd not only as inarticulate but also as non-human, as opposed to the clear and distinct speech of K. and the examining magistrate.

In the previous chapter, we saw the same figuration at work in the distinction between, on the one hand, the chief engineer Schubal's lucid, manly speech, "the first human sounds" the people in the head cashier's office had heard in a long time,[61] and, on the other, the stoker's "senseless racket."[62] In Aristotelian terms, the figural distinction between "voice" (*phonē*) and "speech" (*logos*) draws a line between those who are able to speak about what is just or unjust and those whose are unable to.[63] If we insist on interpreting the figure of murmuring on the background of Exodus, however, we can add that the animal *phonē* of the crowd is not just an expression of dissatisfaction with a specific law but, rather, an expression of the resistance to the application of laws in general, an auditory sign of a general inapplicability of law to an extra-political world.

Private Organization

While K. is busy accusing the corrupt organization that arrests innocent people and introduces senseless proceedings against them, he is suddenly disturbed by a shriek from the other end of the hall.

---

59   Ex 32:9, 25 (NRSV).
60   I am drawing on Michael Walzer, *Exodus and Revolution* (New York: Basic Books, 1985), 43–55.
61   (DzL 92; SS 26).
62   (DzL 87; SS 23).
63   Aristotle, *Politics*, 1253a7.

Recognizing the washerwoman engaging in what looks like sexual intercourse, K., deeply disturbed, recklessly springs from the platform and stands eye-to-eye with the crowd. At close range, K. notices the tiny black eyes of the men in the crowd, the cheeks drooping like those of drunken men, and the stiff and scraggly beards. Suddenly he realizes— or believes he does—that the crowd in the hall is not a political assembly at all.

> Beneath the beards, however—and this was the true discovery K. made—badges of various sizes and colors shimmered on the collars of their jackets. They all had badges, as far as he could see. All belonged together, the apparent parties on the left and right, and as he suddenly turned, he saw the same badges on the collar of the examining magistrate, who was looking on calmly with his hands in his lap. "So!" K. cried and flung his arms in the air, this sudden insight demanding space; "I see you're all officials, you're the corrupt band I was speaking about; you've crowded in here to listen and snoop, you've formed apparent parties and had one side applaud to test me, you wanted to learn how to lead innocent men astray."[64]

According to K.'s sudden insight, the crowd is, in fact, a private organization in which the individuals are not equal citizens, but rather subordinate employees that all have the same badges ("Abzeichen"). The political space collapses when it appears, or seems to appear, that the two antagonistic parties on the left and right are only "apparent parties," and that everyone in the hall "belonged together" in one single organization. To the extent that the crowd of people are configured as a "corrupt band," their concern is not the just but, rather, the useful and the profitable. K. emphasizes this by finishing their denouncement by sarcastically wishing them luck with their "trade" ("Gewerbe").

In other words, the turning point in "Initial Inquiry" is the moment of recognition in which K. suddenly flings his arms in the air and

---

64 "Unter den Barten aber—und das war die eigentliche Entdeckung, die K. machte—schimmerten am Rockkragen Abzeichen in verschiedener Größe und Farbe. Alle hatten diese Abzeichen, soweit man sehen konnte. Alle gehörten zu einander, die scheinbaren Parteien rechts und links, und als er sich plötzlich umdrehte, sah er die gleichen Abzeichen am Kragen des Untersuchungsrichters, der, die Hände im Schooß, ruhig hinuntersah. 'So!' rief K. und warf die Arme in die Höhe, die plötzliche Erkenntnis wollte Raum,—'Ihr seid ja alle Beamte wie ich sehe, Ihr seid ja die korrupte Bande, gegen die ich sprach, Ihr habt Euch hier gedrängt, als Zuhörer und Schnüffler, habt scheinbare Parteien gebildet und eine hat applaudiert um mich zu prüfen, Ihr wolltet lernen, wie man Unschuldige verführen soll'" (P 71; Tr 52, translation modified).

switches from the orderly to the disorderly image of communal life. This turning point is closely related to the moment of recognition in "The Stoker" in which the uncle identifies Karl as his nephew and changes the configuration of the group of people in the head cashier's office from a legal scene into a family scene.[65] In both cases, the protagonist is suddenly incorporated into a community to which universal rules do not apply. According to K., the problem is not only that the laws of the community happen not to be applied to the mafia-like organization that arrested him. Rather, the problem is that the private organization is incompatible with law altogether; the community is senseless in a way that makes legal sense-making impossible: "Given the senselessness of the whole affair, how could the bureaucracy avoid becoming entirely corrupt? It's impossible, even the highest judge couldn't manage it, even for himself."[66]

The Stereoscopic Inquiry

In summary, the stereoscopic style of "Initial Inquiry" contrasts an orderly image of the crowd in the hall configured as a political assembly with a disorderly image of the same crowd configured as a private organization. The aesthetic experience of the chapter is reflective in so far as the literary stereoscope challenges the reader to move back and forth between the two incompatible images of the same crowd and, consequently, to turn back from the images in themselves to the construction of the images. The way that K. constructs an image of the perplexing crowd in front of him is carefully staged so that the reader is made aware not only of the differences between the two images of communal life but of the difficulties of forming these images, too. "K. had decided to observe more than speak,"[67] we learn when the protagonist reaches the platform, and even if he does not stick to this decision, his political speech is repeatedly interrupted by brief moments of observing the crowd:

K. interrupted himself and looked down into the hall.[68]

"What has happened to me," K. continued, somewhat more quietly than before, and constantly searching the faces of those in the front row, which made his speech seem slightly disjointed,

---

65 (DzL 94; SS 27).
66 "Wie ließe sich bei dieser Sinnlosigkeit des Ganzen, die schlimmste Korruption der Beamtenschaft vermeiden? Das ist unmöglich, das brächte auch der höchste Richter nicht einmal für sich selbst zustande" (P 69; Tr 50).
67 "K. hatte sich entschlossen mehr zu beobachten als zu reden" (P 60; Tr 43).
68 "K. unterbrach sich und sah in den Saal hinunter" (P 62; Tr 45).

"what has happened to me is merely an isolated case and as such of no particular consequence."[69]

As K. interrupted himself at this point and glanced at the silent magistrate, he thought he noticed him looking at someone in the crowd and giving him a signal.[70]

Like the passage with the indecent image in the examining magistrate's book, this scene offers both a representation of a community and a representation of K.'s efforts to construct an image of this community. At the end of his political speech, K. realizes that his judgment on the basic shape of the crowd might be wrong: "he sprang from the platform recklessly. Now he stood eye-to-eye with the crowd. Had he misjudged these people? Had he overestimated the effect of his speech?"[71]

Characteristically, K.'s way of constructing an image of communal life is guided by a hierarchical notion of order. Standing on the low platform, K. starts out by explaining to the crowd that he happens to be "the chief financial officer of a large bank."[72] Later, he refers to Fräulein Bürstner as "a young lady,"[73] to the landlady Frau Grubach as "a very simple person,"[74] and to the two employees from the bank whom he met in Fräulein Bürstner's room at the morning of the arrest as "low-ranking employees."[75]

Since order is an abstract phenomenon, imagination plays an important role in K.'s construction of an image of the order of things. Indeed, his political speech contains a swarm of imaginative figures that orchestrate his underlying idea of order. I will focus on the first judgment K. passes on the nature of the proceedings against him. Curiously, this act of judging is modified by a reflection on its rhetorical status: "I'm not saying these proceedings are sloppy, but I would like to propose that

---

69 "'Was mir geschehen ist,' fuhr K. fort etwas leiser als früher und suchte immer wieder die Gesichter der ersten Reihe ab, was seiner Rede einen etwas fahrigen Ausdruck gab, 'was mir geschehen ist, ist ja nur ein einzelner Fall und als solcher nicht sehr wichtig'" (P 64; Tr 46).
70 "Als K. sich hier unterbrach und nach dem stillen Untersuchungsrichter hinsah, glaubte er zu bemerken, daß dieser gerade mit einem Blick jemandem in der Menge ein Zeichen gab" (P 67; Tr 49).
71 "er sprang rücksichtslos vom Podium hinunter. Nun stand er Aug' in Aug' dem Gedränge gegenüber. Hatte er die Leute nicht richtig beurteilt? Hatte er seiner Rede zuviel Wirkung zugetraut?" (P 71; Tr 51).
72 "erster Prokurist einer großen Bank" (P 61; Tr 44).
73 "eine Dame" (P 65; Tr 48).
74 "eine ganz einfache Person" (P 66; Tr 48).
75 "niedrige Angestellte" (P 66; Tr 48, translation modified).

description for your own personal consideration."[76] According to K., he is not making a literal proposition about the sloppy nature of the proceedings; rather, he is indirectly or improperly proposing this expression so that the examining magistrate can reflect on it himself.

The sloppy proceeding is, in the German original, "ein lüderliches Verfahren." Even if the rare word "lüderliches" is fully legible in Kafka's handwritten manuscript, Max Brod, in the first edition of *The Trial*, chose to replace it by the more common and synonymous "liederliches."[77] At the level of semantics, both "lüderlich" and "liederlich" means dissolute, wanton or slutty. A "Luder," for instance, is a woman living a debauched and immoral life. At this level, describing the proceeding as "lüderlich" is only figurative to the extent that the word, in its literal sense, is most often used to describe an individual or a way of life—and not a court proceeding. This socially derogatory sense of "lüderlich" connects the word to the terms of abuse that K. uses later in his speech, for instance when describing the two guards as "unprincipled riff-raff" and the organization as a "corrupt band."[78]

At the level of etymology, however, there are important differences between "lüderlich" and "liederlich." According to the Grimm brothers' *Deutsches Wörterbuch*, a "Luder" is a dead animal used by hunters as "a bait for carnivores." The reason why a slutty woman is called a "Luder," then, is that she attracts men in the same way as a carcass attracts animals of prey. In fact, Kafka was a frequent user of the Grimms' dictionary, Brod has informed us,[79] so he might in fact have studied the dictionary's detailed etymology of "lüderlich." As is often the case in Kafka's literary works, the dead metaphor is woken to life by its context. In a sense, Kafka's prose is characterized by a *lüderliche* attraction to the carcasses of metaphors.

In the remaining part of K.'s political speech, the figurations develop the sensible image hidden in the etymology of "lüderlich." When describing the nature of his arrest, K. tends to use violent figures of hunting and preying. "I was assaulted [*überfallen*] in the morning in bed"; an arrest like that "means as little as a mugging [*ein Anschlag*] on the street by teenage hoodlums"; and—after the turning point—the crowd in the hall has allegedly "crowded in here as eavesdroppers and

---

76   "Ich sage nicht, daß es ein lüderliches Verfahren ist, aber ich möchte Ihnen diese Bezeichnung zur Selbsterkenntnis angeboten haben" (P 62; Tr 45).
77   (PGS 50). For a facsimile of Kafka's handwritten manuscript, see (PFE 65).
78   "demoralisiertes Gesindel" and "die korrupte Bande" (P 65, 71; Tr 47, 52, translation modified).
79   See Max Brod, *Über Franz Kafka. Franz Kafka, eine Biographie. Franz Kafkas Glauben und Lehre. Verzweiflung und Erlösung im Werk Franz Kafkas* (Hamburg: Fischer, 1966), 213, 110.

snoopers."[80] The German "Schnüffler" ("snooper") issues etymologically from a hunting dog's sniffing for prey. It could be that the original sense of "Luder," as bait for carnivores, also plays a role for the figure of pollution and despoiling that K. uses when he claims that the room of Fräulein Bürstner "was defiled [*verunreinigt*], so to speak, by the presence of the guards and the inspector."[81]

In conclusion, "Initial Inquiry" not only offers two disjunct images of the community in the hall; it also offers an image of K.'s construction of these images—an act which is, in its essence, one of figuration. As it turns out, K.'s images of order and disorder hinge on a swarm of sensible figures such as, for instance, "lüderlichkeit," "assaulting," "snooping," and "defiling." The figuration has important consequences for the reader's interpretation of the chapter.

On the one hand, the reader's process of reflection moves back and forth between the two juxtaposed images of the same crowd, comparing the image of the crowd as political assembly to the image of the crowd as private organization, or, in the terminology of Hobbes, of comparing a people to a multitude.[82] As I suggested in Chapter 4, this movement back and forth creates an awareness of the limitedness of both images. The two images of the same group of people decenter each other in so far as their juxtaposition exposes that neither can have unlimited access to the truth.

On the other hand, the chapter's focus on K.'s peculiar way of constructing images of the crowd means that, in the reader's process of reflection, thought not only moves back and forth between the two juxtaposed images; it also turns back from these images to the construction of these images. As we have seen, this recoiling back upon the construction of the images affords an awareness of their constructedness. The images of the crowd are denaturalized when they are no longer perceived as natural and unalterable facts but, rather, as produced by K.'s rather idiosyncratic projection of imaginative figures.

Taken together, the reader's aesthetic experience of the chapter involves what I suggested calling, in line with Paul de Man, a disfiguration of the images of communal life.[83] Due to the stereoscopic style, the representation of sociality comes into view as limited to

---

80   "Ich wurde früh im Bett überfallen," "nicht mehr bedeutet, als ein Anschlag, den nicht genügend beaufsichtigte Jungen auf der Gasse ausführen" and "durch die Anwesenheit der Wächter und des Aufsehers gewissermaßen verunreinigt wurde" (P 65, 66, 71; Tr 47, 48, 52, translation modified).

81   "durch die Anwesenheit der Wächter und des Aufsehers gewissermaßen verunreinigt wurde" (P 66; Tr 48).

82   See, for instance, Hobbes, *Leviathan*, 94.

83   de Man, *The Rhetoric of Romanticism*, 110.

contingent points of view and as constructed on the basis of contingent social imaginaries. In the vocabulary of the researcher dog, this disfiguration leads to a loosening-up or slackening-off of the edifice of communal life.[84]

An Essential Disturbance

As noted above, K.'s political speech is cut short by an indecent situation at the other end of the hall:

> K. was interrupted by a shriek from the other end of the hall; he shaded his eyes so that he could see, for the dull daylight made the haze whitish and dazzled him. It was the washerwoman, whom K. had sensed as an essential disturbance from the moment she entered. Whether or not she was at fault now was not apparent. K. saw only that a man had pulled her into a corner by the door and pressed her to himself. But she wasn't shrieking, it was the man; he had opened his mouth wide and was staring up toward the ceiling. A small circle had gathered around the two of them, and the nearby visitors in the gallery seemed delighted that the serious mood K. had introduced into the assembly had been interrupted in this fashion.[85]

Evidently a precursor to the indecent image on the table of the examining magistrate in the following chapter, this passage describes an act of sexual coupling that emerges "far too corporeally from the picture." The sexual character of the scene is underlined in a deleted passage about the undressing of the washerwoman (in the next chapter referred to as the wife of the court usher): "Now K. saw that her unbuttoned blouse hung down around her waist, and that a man had pulled her into a corner by the door and there pressed the upper part of her body, only covered by a petticoat, against himself."[86]

---

84 (NS2 456; SS 148).
85 "K. wurde durch ein Kreischen vom Saalende unterbrochen, er beschattete die Augen um hinsehn zu können, denn das trübe Tageslicht machte den Dunst weißlich und blendete. Es handelte sich um die Waschfrau, die K. gleich bei ihrem Eintritt als eine wesentliche Störung erkannt hatte. Ob sie jetzt schuldig war oder nicht konnte man nicht erkennen. K. sah nur, daß ein Mann sie in einen Winkel bei der Tür gezogen hatte und dort an sich drückte. Aber nicht sie kreischte sondern der Mann, er hatte den Mund breit gezogen und blickte zur Decke. Ein kleiner Kreis hatte sich um beide gebildet, die Galleriebesucher in der Nähe schienen darüber begeistert, daß der Ernst, den K. in die Versammlung eingeführt hatte, auf diese Weise unterbrochen wurde" (P 70; Tr 51, translation modified).
86 "dass (ihre aufgeknöpfte Bluse in der Taille rings um sie hinunterhieng und dass) ein Mann (ihren nur mit dem Hemd bekleideten Oberkörper) sie in einen Winkel bei Tür gezogen hatte und dort an sich drückte" (PA 192).

K. immediately senses that the washerwoman is "an essential disturbance" ("eine wesentliche Störung"). Just as the expression "in a formally friendly way" ("förmlich freundschaftlich"), "an essential disturbance" is an oxymoron that condenses the dual vision of Kafka's stereoscopic style. If we look at the orderly image, the washerwoman is a disturbance because she does not belong in the all-male political assembly; but if we look at the disorderly image, she is somehow essential anyway. The oxymoronic quality is owed to the juxtaposition of two conflicting images of what is essential and what inessential.

In the previous chapter, we saw a serious legal process disturbed when Schubal's "crazy" witnesses suddenly swamped the head cashier's office in "The Stoker," unable to take anything seriously: "It looked as if these basically good-natured people considered the quarrel between Schubal and the stoker a joke, and the ridiculousness of it did not end even in front of the captain."[87] The sexual behavior in the hall is a similar interruption. According to the passage quoted above, the visitors in the gallery "seemed delighted that the serious mood K. had introduced into the assembly had been interrupted in this fashion." In other words, to interrupt the solemnity introduced by K. is to disfigure the act of figuration by which he tried to create order and uniformity in a "crowd of the most varied sort."[88]

The disturbance at the other end of the hall, however, equally disfigures and transfigures K.'s images of the crowd. Given that the disturbance is essential, it alters the border between essential and inessential, between important and unimportant. In fact, the essentiality of the disturbance is underlined by the chapter's biblical figures. When Moses went to Mount Sinai to receive the Commandments, there was thunder and lightning and a thick cloud as the Lord descended on the mountain.[89] A similar white and dazzling haze hides the commotion, forcing K. to shield his eyes. If K. had convinced himself that he played the role of Moses the lawgiver, he now realizes that the divine light does not shine over the low platform on which he stands but over the disturbing sexual acts at the other end of the hall, possibly a kind of provocative gold calf that challenges K.'s sovereignty.

K. is so shocked by the sexual behavior because it disfigures his images of order and disorder. In the German original, the man emits a "Kreischen," a word referring to the cries of humans and the howls of animals alike. Just as the crowd's dissatisfied "Murren" a little earlier, this shrieking is located at the border between human and animal. The

---

87   (DzL 109; SS 35).
88   (P 57; Tr 41).
89   Ex 19:9–16 (NRSV).

important difference, however, is that the unarticulated and inhuman voice is no longer an inessential background noise, instead becoming suddenly audible in the foreground by interrupting K.'s political speech. Thus, once again, the stereoscopic style brings about a transfiguration in which a figure of marginality and inessentiality moves into the center of the community.

The Man from the Country

Ever since Orson Welles's 1962 screen version of *The Trial*, practically every attempt to understand law in Kafka's oeuvre has begun with "Before the Law." However, if we begin with the legend of the doorkeeper, originally a part of the chapter "In the Cathedral", at the end of *The Trial*, we are likely to end up with the standard "Kafkaesque" picture of Kafka and the political. According to this picture, there is a sharp border between the powerless single individual and the meaningless objective powers, all of them sinister relatives of the doorkeeper.

In Kafka's legend of the doorkeeper, the man from the country does not know who intended the door for him, nor why he cannot gain admittance, nor when he will be able to enter. "I am powerful," the doorkeeper merely says, and adds that he is just the lowliest doorkeeper: "outside each hall stands a doorkeeper, each more powerful than the last."[90] Hence, the legend seems to take place in a world where no political deliberation is possible and where political moments will never occur. Over the years, the doorkeeper asks questions about many things, but "these are uninterested questions, such as higher-ups ask."[91] The man from the country can do nothing but sit down at one side of the door and curse his miserable luck.

Admittedly, "Before the Law" would seem to test my approach to Kafka and the political. Casting a glance at the legend's historical background, however, we can see that the political moment does indeed play an important role here. It is highly probable that Kafka was inspired by a midrash (an early rabbinic narrative interpreting the Written Torah) that he either read in German translation or heard from some of his more religious friends, such as Yitzhak Löwy.[92] In this midrash from the collection *Pesikta Rabbati*, Moses ascends Mount Sinai and enters the cloud "in order to receive the law [*der Thora*] for

---

90 "Ich bin mächtig. Und ich bin nur der unterste Türhüter. Von Saal zu Saal stehn aber Türhüter, einer mächtiger als der andere" (DzL 267; SS 68).
91 "teilnahmslose Fragen, wie sie große Herren stellen."
92 This historical background of "Before the Law" was brought to light by Ulf Abraham, "Mose 'Vor dem Gesetz': Eine unbekannte Vorlage zu Kafkas 'Türhüterlegende'," *Deutsche Vierteljahrsschrift für Literaturwissenschaft und Geistesgeschichte* 57 (1983).

Israel."[93] On his way, he meets the "angels of service" Kemuël, Hadarniel, Sandalfon, Rigjon, and Gelizur, and, somewhat later, also a band of "angels of corruption." Moses kills the first angel he meets, but those following are so terrible to look at that God, in a variety of ways, must help him to pass. Once the angel Hadarniel has led Moses some of the way, he takes his leave with the words: "Thus far I am permitted to go, from here I am not permitted to go, Sandalfon's fire would burn me up."[94] The doorkeeper in Kafka's legend says the same thing, nearly verbatim, to the man from the country: "I am powerful. And I am only the lowliest doorkeeper. But outside each hall stand a doorkeeper, each more powerful than the last. The mere sight of the third one is more than even I can stand."[95]

Interestingly, the midrash establishes a connection between Kafka's doorkeeper and the Moses motif explored in this chapter. If the man from the country is in fact a modified Moses, the question of admittance to the law is to be understood as a question of admittance to the political space where the law can be given to Israel. Of course, the Moses of "Before the Law" is much less energetic than the Moses of *Pesikta Rabbati*. The man from the country sits down quietly on a stool to one side of the door, whereas the Moses of the midrash readily kills an angel to fulfil his mission as a lawgiver. In Kafka's legend, the political moment remains a non-realized possibility.

In the above analysis of "Initial Inquiry," we have seen how K. emulates Moses by trying to introduce in the hall "a clear and uniform need to abolish the great misconduct."[96] In this sense, K. behaves not as a lawyer who pleads in a case of private law, but rather as a lawgiver who founds a political community. In fact, K. is seduced by his feeling of being admitted to a political space where he, like the Moses of the midrash, can receive the law of the people. To be sure, K.'s attempt to bring about a political moment fails miserably when he suddenly understands, or believes that he understands, that the crowd in the hall is a private organization rather than a political assembly. Yet, as this chapter has demonstrated, thanks to its stereoscopic style, the novel about K. is able to do what K. himself was unable to do: to reconfigure the image of communal life.

---

93 Jacob Winter and August Wünsche, *Die jüdische Litteratur seit Abschluss des Kanons: Eine prosaische und poetische Anthologie mit biographischen und litterargeschichtlichen Einleitungen* (Trier: Sigmund Mayer, 1894), 450, my translation.

94 *Die jüdische Litteratur seit Abschluss des Kanons*, 451

95 "Ich bin mächtig. Und ich bin nur der unterste Türhüter. Von Saal zu Saal stehn aber Türhüter, einer mächtiger als der andere. Schon den Anblick des dritten kann nicht einmal ich mehr ertragen" (DzL 267; SS 68).

96 (PA 192).

Nine As If the Whole of Existence Were Transformed

K. as Liberator of Girls: The Castle

"One must take the world as it is—this is the substance of the lives and doings of these millions, the copy-people. They find everything given: concepts, notions, thoughts, as well as customary behavior—in short, everything is given—the copy-person brings nothing with him."[1] According to Søren Kierkegaard's short text "One Must Take the World as It Is," written in his diary *Journalen* in autumn 1854, a year before his death, the "copy-man" ("Exemplar-Mennesket") is a man who takes the world as it is. This copy-man can be likened to a stickleback, Kierkegaard argues, because he passes freely through the fishing net that has been set for "larger fish," such as, for instance, the "man who brings with himself a primitivity":

> On the other hand, as soon as there comes a man who brings with himself a primitivity, so that he therefore cannot be said to take the world as it is (the license to pass through it like a stickleback), but says, However the world may be, I relate to something original that I do not intend to change in accordance with the whims of the

---

1 "*Man maa tage Verden som den er*, dette eller: Verden er som man tager den, vel at mærke forstaaet saaledes: man maa tage Verden som den er, er Gehalten af disse Millioner, Exemplar-Mskets Liv og Levnet. De forefinde Alt givet, Begreber, Forestillinger, Tanker, ligesaa Skik og Brug kort alt er givet— Exemplar-Msket bringer Intet med sig." Søren Kierkegaard, *Journalerne*, ed. N. J Cappelørn, et al., Søren Kierkegaards skrifter (Copenhagen: Søren Kierkegaard Forskningscenteret, Gad, 2009), NB 32:127, vol. 26, p. 214. Bruce H. Kirmmse has kindly provided his (as yet unedited) English translation of the journal entry to be published in *Kierkegaard's Journals and Notebooks*, ed. Niels Jørgen Cappelørn, et al., vol. 10 (Princeton, NJ: Princeton University Press, forthcoming). In the following comments on Kierkegaard's diary entry, I quote from this translation.

world. The moment these words are heard, it is as if the whole of existence were transformed. As in the fairy tale: when the word is spoken, the castle that had been under a spell for a hundred years opens up and everything comes alive—thus does existence become transformed into sheer attentiveness. The angels get busy and pay curious attention to where all this is heading, because it concerns them. On the other side, dark, sinister demons who had long been sitting and gnawing their fingernails—they jump up, stretching their arms and legs—because, they say, Here there is something for us, and they have been waiting for it a long time [. . .].[2]

The man who brings with himself a primitivity ("Primitivitet") relates to something original with which he can correct the ethical and political order of the community. A note in the margin makes clear that Kierkegaard is referring to his concept of faith understood as trust against all odds: "And, as I have pointed out elsewhere, ethical primitivity is to stake everything, to venture everything, *first* the kingdom of God."[3]

When the young prince arrives at the sleeping castle in the Grimms' fairy tale "The Briar Rose" (or "The Sleeping Beauty"), the hundred years of enchantment have come to an end and the castle comes alive: "Indeed, the fire flared up and cooked the meat until it began to sizzle again, and the cook gave the kitchen boy a box on the ear, while the maid finished plucking the chicken."[4]

Kierkegaard refers explicitly to "The Briar Rose" in the journal entry: "As in the fairy tale: when the word is spoken, the castle that had been under a spell for a hundred years opens up and everything comes alive." This opening up and coming alive of the castle Kierkegaard conceptualizes as a "transformation" or a "metamorphosis" ("Forvandling") which

---

2   "Saasnart der derimod kommer et Msk, som fører en Primitivitet med sig, saa han altsaa ikke siger man maa tage Verden som den er (dette Tegn til som Hundesteile at passere frit) men som siger, hvordan Verden saa end er, jeg forholder mig til en Oprindelighed, som jeg ikke agter at forandre efter Verdens Forgodtbefindende: i samme Øieblik dette Ord er hørt, foregaaer der som en Forvandling i hele Tilværelsen. Som i Eventyret—naar Ordet siges, det i hundrede Aar fortryllede Slot, aabner sig og Alt bliver Liv: saaledes bliver Tilværelsen idel Opmærksomhed. Englene faae travlt, see nysgjerrige efter, hvad dette vil blive til, thi dette beskjeftiger dem. Paa den anden Side mørke, skumle Dæmoner, som længst have siddet uvirksomme og gnavet paa deres Fingre—de springe op, rette Lemmerne—thi her bliver Noget for os, sige de, og det have de længst ventet paa [. . .]."

3   "Og ethisk Primitivitet er, som andetsteds paaviist, at sætte Alt ind, vove Alt, *først* Guds Rige."

4   Jacob Grimm and Wilhelm Grimm, *Original Folk and Fairy Tales of the Brothers Grimm*, trans. Jack Zipes (Princeton, NJ: Princeton University Press, 2014).

seems to have taken place in the whole of existence.[5] In a parallel phrase, he writes that the arrival of the man who brings with himself a primitivity sets "both heaven and earth in motion."[6]

It is worth noting that Kierkegaard describes the transformation in the whole of existence in both religious and political terms. The stickleback-man finds everything given, including "customary behavior."[7] To take the world as it is, then, is to accept the written and unwritten laws that govern human life. By contrast, the man who does not take the world as it is performs a revolutionary act that contests the given order of things. Drawing on St. Paul the Apostle, Kierkegaard writes that the man who brings with himself a primitivity does not struggle "against enemies of blood and flesh, but against the rulers, against the authorities, against the cosmic powers of this present darkness."[8]

Franz Kafka quotes the above passage from Kierkegaard's journal entry about the enchanted castle in the last of two letters on the Danish philosopher which he sent to Max Brod in March 1918. During the winter, after having been diagnosed with tuberculosis and moving to Zürau, a village in the Bohemian countryside, to convalesce from his hemorrhage, Kafka, in his own words, "possibly really lost his way in Kierkegaard."[9] He started out by reading *Either-Or*, the first volume of which he confided to Brod that he could not read "without repugnance."[10] In February 1918, he went on to read *Fear and Trembling*, *The Repetition*, and the polemical broadsheet *The Moment* (or *The Instant*). Kafka must have found the journal entry about the enchanted castle in a somewhat chaotic selection of Kierkegaard's papers in German, *Buch des Richters*, which he read in 1913 and again in the first months of 1918.[11]

---

5   "en Forvandling i hele Tilværelsen."
6   "sætte baade Himmel og Jord i Bevægelse."
7   "ligesaa Skik og Brug."
8   Eph. 6:12 (NRSV).
9   "In Kierkegaard habe ich mich möglicherweise wirklich verirrt" (B4 30–36; LFFE 199–203, translation modified). In the following analysis of Kafka's letters on Kierkegaard, I quote from these pages.
10 "kann ich aber noch immer nicht ohne Widerwillen lesen."
11 In a diary entry from August 1913, Kafka notes: "Today I got Kierkegaard's *Buch des Richters*. As I suspected, his case, despite essential differences, is very similar to mine, at least he is on the same side of the world. He bears me out like a friend" ("Ich habe heute Kierkegaard Buch des Richters bekommen. Wie ich es ahnte, ist sein Fall trotz wesentlicher Unterschiede dem meinen sehr ähnlich zumindest liegt er auf der gleichen Seite der Welt. Er bestätigt mich wie ein Freund" [T 578; D 230]). For the German translation of the enchanted castle diary, see Søren Kierkegaard, *Buch des Richters: Seine Tagebücher 1833–1855, im Auszug aus dem Dänischen*, ed. Hermann Gottsched (Jena; Leipzig: Eugen Diderichs, 1905), 160. Hermann Gottsched only translates a part of Kierkegaard's journal entry, and Kafka, again, quotes only a part of the German text.

Kafka's interest in this journal entry is not surprising given that the transformation in the whole of existence can be understood as a political moment. Unfortunately, he simply quotes Kierkegaard in his letter to Brod, and adds no further comment. After March 1918, however, Kafka starts writing about castles in his notebooks and diaries, until he finally sets out to write *The Castle* in January 1922. In this chapter, I will approach Kafka's third unfinished novel as his elaborate response to Kierkegaard's journal entry

The Arrival of a Land Surveyor

In the village below the castle, the villagers take the world as it is. Frieda, the barmaid who quickly becomes the girlfriend of the protagonist K., has "intimate knowledge of local affairs" in comparison to him, being so newly arrived.[12] The other villagers, not least Gardena, the innkeeper's wife, also keep stressing that to them, the order of things is a matter of course. Their taking the world as it is has made the world fall asleep like the castle in "Briar Rose." Most villagers are fast asleep as K. arrives in the novel's opening pages. Throughout, the castle authorities have a remarkable habit of lying in bed when negotiating with him.[13]

K.'s appearance transforms life into sheer attentiveness (as Kierkegaard phrased it), however. On the night of his arrival, he is awakened by the young Schwarzer, the son of a castle sub-steward, who, on account of his unpleasant behavior and ominous name, is easy to identify as one of the dark, sinister demons from Kierkegaard's enchanted castle journal entry. The following day, K. encounters the angelic messenger Barnabas, who is "dressed almost entirely in white" and is flying at high speed when he walks.[14] At the end of the novel, K. inadvertently enters the room of the castle official Bürgel, who, waking from sleep, immediately sets about giving a detailed account of the castle's bureaucratic procedures. While K. is falling asleep, Bürgel offers his private version of Kierkegaard's enchanted castle journal entry with angels and demons waiting for the word that could awaken the castle. According to Bürgel, the desperate castle official "sits there waiting for the party's plea, knowing that one must grant it as soon as it is uttered, even if it should, at any rate insofar as one can perceive this oneself, literally tear apart the official system."[15]

---

12 "Frieda, die doch mit den hiesigen Verhältnissen so vertraut sei" (S 198; C 125).
13 This goes for the village council chairman in Chapter 5, for the innkeeper's wife in Chapter 6, and for the castle official Bürgel in Chapter 23.
14 "fast weiß gekleidet" (S 38; C 25).
15 "auf die Bitte der Partei wartet und weiß daß man sie, wenn sie einmal aus-gesprochen ist, erfüllen muß, wenn sie auch, wenigstens soweit man es selbst übersehen kann, die Amtsorganisation förmlich zerreißt" (S 422; C 269).

Unlike the villagers, K. does not say that one must take the world as it is. Instead, he keeps asking annoying questions about things that the villagers perceive as matters of course. In the words of the enchanted castle journal entry and its allusion to St. Paul the Apostle, K. is battling with principalities and powers. On the night of his arrival, he claims to be the land surveyor sent for by the Count who owns the castle. In this context, it is important to note that land surveying is a politically charged work to the extent that a surveyor does not take the spatial distribution of the world as it is. This political aspect of land surveying is made clear in the novel's first pages: "He watched the peasants gathering timidly and conferring, the arrival of a land surveyor was no trifling matter."[16]

Remarkably, some of the villagers seem to have high hopes for the deeds of the land surveyor. From her tiny, dark chamber, the low-ranking barmaid Pepi, for instance, perceives K. as "a hero, a rescuer of maidens."[17] His capacity to prompt a transformation in the whole of existence is also underlined by the fact that in Hebrew the word for Messiah, *mashiah*, is very similar to an (infrequently used) word for land surveyor, *mashoah*.[18] Yet, as in *Amerika* and *The Trial*, the political moment does not take place in the fictional world of the novel. K. never gets to survey land or to rescue maidens but ends up in the lowly position of stableman. According to Brod's afterword to the first edition of the novel, Kafka planned that K. should die soon after.[19]

Kafka researchers disagree on how to understand politics in *The Castle*. On the one hand, K. is most often interpreted as an apolitical figure; in his afterword, for instance, Max Brod suggests that the castle is "precisely what the theologians call 'grace,' the divine guidance of human destiny (the village)."[20] On the other hand, K. has also been viewed as a revolutionary hero. Hannah Arendt, for instance, argues *pace* Brod in an essay from 1944 that K. teaches the villagers "that human rights may be worth fighting for, that the rule of the Castle is not divine law and, consequently, can be attacked."[21]

---

16 "Er sah die Bauern scheu zusammenrücken und sich besprechen, die Ankunft eines Landvermessers war nichts Geringes" (S 10; C 3).

17 "ein Held, ein Mädchenbefreier" (S 453; C 290).

18 This relation was originally pointed out by Evelyn Torton Beck, *Kafka and the Yiddish Theater: Its Impact and his Work* (Madison, WI: University of Wisconsin Press, 1971), 195.

19 Max Brod, "Nachwort," in *Franz Kafka, Das Schloss* (Frankfurt am Main: S. Fischer, 1946), 347.

20 "Nachwort," 349, my translation.

21 Hannah Arendt, "Franz Kafka: A Revaluation," in *Essays in Understanding, 1930–1954*, ed. Jerome Kohn (New York and London: Harcourt, Brace & Co, 1994), 73. For further discussion, see the influential interpretations by Wilhelm Emrich, for instance *Franz Kafka* (Bonn: Athenäum, 1958); "Franz Kafka Ost und West," in *The Literary Revolution and Modern Society, and Other Essays* (New York: Ungar, 1971).

As I see it, however, what is important here is not what K. does in the novel but, rather, what the novel about K. does. To the extent that the enchanted castle opens up and everything comes alive, it is an event that should be located in the aesthetic experience of the novel. In other words, if *The Castle* is not *about* a political moment taking place in the world of the fictional characters, it *brings about* such a moment in the mind of the reader.

Apparent Village Worker

On his second day in the village, the messenger Barnabas seeks out K. to deliver him a letter of employment from the high-ranking castle official Klamm. Written in inconspicuous officialese, it is easy to overlook that the short letter is in fact one of the novel's important turning points:

> "Esteemed Sir! As you know, you have been accepted into the Count's service. Your immediate superior is the village council chairman, he will furnish you with all further details concerning your work and terms of employment, and you, in turn, will be accountable to him. Nevertheless, I too shall keep you in mind. Barnabas, who brings you this letter, will occasionally call on you to ascertain your wishes and relay them to me. You will find that I am always ready, insofar as possible, to oblige you. Having satisfied workers is important to me."[22]

After a short conversation with Barnabas, K. withdraws to his room at the inn in order to reread the letter. At a second reading, the letter seems contradictory to K.:

> It wasn't consistent [*einheitlich*]: some passages treated him as a free man and conceded that he had a will of his own, such as the initial greeting and the passage concerning his wishes. There were other passages, though, that treated him openly or indirectly as a lowly worker who was barely noticeable from the director's post, the director had to make an effort to "keep him in mind," his superior

---

22 "'Sehr geehrter Herr! Sie sind, wie Sie wissen, in die herrschaftlichen Dienste aufgenommen. Ihr nächster Vorgesetzter ist der Gemeindevorsteher des Dorfes, der Ihnen auch alles Nähere über Ihre Arbeit und die Lohnbedingungen mitteilen wird und dem Sie auch Rechenschaft schuldig sein werden. Trotzdem werde aber auch ich Sie nicht aus den Augen verlieren. Barnabas, der Überbringer dieses Briefes, wird von Zeit zu Zeit bei Ihnen nachfragen, um Ihre Wünsche zu erfahren und mir mitzuteilen. Sie werden mich immer bereit finden, Ihnen soweit es möglich ist, gefällig zu sein. Es liegt mir daran zufriedene Arbeiter zu haben.'" (S 40; C 22–3, translation modified).

was only the village chairman, to whom he was even accountable, his only colleague was perhaps the village policeman. Undoubtedly these were contradictions, so obvious they must be intentional.[23]

On the one hand, K. finds that Klamm is talking formally to him as to a subordinate; this is the case in the letter's first half and concluding sentence. On the other hand, Klamm also addresses K. in a more personal way, as if he were not a professional but a free private person whose wishes somehow mattered to him; this is the case in the second half of the letter after the word "Nevertheless" ("Trotzdem") and in the address "Esteemed Sir!" ("Sehr geehrter Herr!"). In other words, the letter is a stereoscopic setup that juxtaposes two dissimilar images of communal life. K. is viewed as a "lowly worker" subject to the rules of the village and, simultaneously, as an "Esteemed Sir" with a will of his own.

Near the novel's end, as K. sits sleepily at the foot of Bürgel's bed, the official gives an account of the difference between daytime and night-time interrogations. During the day, the secretaries interrogate their subjects with "iron-clad pursuit and performance of duty,"[24] Bürgel explains, but at night, they tend to view them in a different light: "At night one involuntarily inclines to judge matters from a more private point of view."[25] Likewise, Klamm's letter of employment juxtaposes a professional and a more private point of view on K.

K. interprets these two points of view as two job descriptions between which he can choose. The first half of the letter seems to offer him a position as a "village worker with a distinctive but merely apparent connection to the Castle." In contrast, the second and more personal half offers him a job as an "apparent village worker who in reality allowed the messages brought by Barnabas to define the terms of his position."[26] The nearly identical job descriptions can make it almost impossible to

---

23 "Er war nicht einheitlich, es gab Stellen wo mit ihm wie mit einem Freien gesprochen wurde, dessen eigenen Willen man anerkennt, so war die Überschrift, so war die Stelle, die seine Wünsche betraf. Es gab aber wieder Stellen, wo er offen oder versteckt als ein kleiner vom Sitz jenes Vorstandes kaum bemerkbarer Arbeiter behandelt wurde, der Vorstand mußte sich anstrengen „ihn nicht aus den Augen zu verlieren", sein Vorgesetzter war nur der Dorfvorsteher, dem er sogar Rechenschaft schuldig war, sein einziger Kollege war vielleicht der Dorfpolicist. Das waren zweifellose Widersprüche, sie waren so sichtbar daß sie beabsichtigt sein mußten" (S 41; C 23).

24 "eiserne Befolgung und Durchführung des Dienstes."

25 "Man ist unwillkürlich geneigt, in der Nacht die Dinge von einem mehr privaten Gesichtspunkt zu beurteilen" (S 411–2; C 262).

26 "Dorfarbeiter mit einer immerhin auszeichnenden aber nur scheinbaren Verbindung mit dem Schlosse" and "scheinbarer Dorfarbeiter, der in Wirklichkeit sein ganzes Arbeitsverhältnis von den Nachrichten des Barnabas bestimmen ließ" (S 42; C 24).

distinguish between the two positions. But the difference is important, and according to K., it has something to do with the distance from the castle. As "village worker," K. will be "as far from the Castle gentlemen as possible"[27] and his work will be defined by the village council chairman and the other low-ranking village officials. As "apparent village worker," on the other hand, he will have a much more direct connection to Klamm through the letters brought to him by Barnabas.

K. does not hesitate to choose the first of these two job descriptions, or these two "paths" leading to Klamm, as he later calls them.[28] His decision to follow the indirect path as a village worker, however, becomes less firm after the appearance of Barnabas, who makes K. think that he can access the castle directly. And in the following chapter, K. changes his mind when he meets the barmaid Frieda and they end up rolling around together in puddles of beer and other rubbish on the floor of the taproom at the Gentlemen's Inn. Frieda claims to be Klamm's mistress, so K. imagines that an intimate relationship with her will facilitate direct access to Klamm and, thus, a position as "apparent village worker."

In one of the novel's many deleted passages, K. considers that the relationship with Frieda has given him "an almost bodily relationship with Klamm, almost like a close whispering conversation."[29] But earlier in the same passage, K. regrets that he chose this intimate path to the castle: "His first intention regarding Klamm's letter, namely to become a simple and unattended worker in the village, had been very sensible. But he had had to change it when Barnabas's deceptive appearance had made him think he could come as easily into the castle as, for example, one conquers a hill on a Sunday stroll."[30]

The fundamental structure of the novel is stereoscopic. The two paths to Klamm lead through two different spheres most often referred to as "office" and "life" ("Amt" and "Leben") where the word "Amt" is also present in the noun "official" ("Beamter") and in the adjective "official" ("amtlich"). Thus, K.'s hair's-breadth distinction between "village worker" and "apparent village worker" points toward a much deeper difference between public and private sphere, between *polis* and *oikos*. In the "amtlich" sphere, K. interacts in a formalized and

27 "möglichst weit den Herren vom Schloß entrückt."
28 (S 177; C 112).
29 "eine, fast körperliche, bis zur flüsternden Verständigung nahe Beziehung zu Klamm" (SA 263, my translation).
30 "Seine erste Absicht angesichts des Klammschen Briefes, einfacher unbeachteter Arbeiter im Dorf zu werden, war sehr vernünftig gewesen. Aber er hatte doch notwendiger Weise von ihr ablassen müssen als die trügerische Erscheinung des Barnabas ihn hatte glauben lassen, er könne so leicht ins Schloss kommen, wie man etwa auf einem kleinen Sonntagsspaziergang einen Hügel bezwingt" (SA 262–3, my translation).

rule-bound way with his male superiors and subordinates; in the private sphere, he has a close, whispering contact with a large number of village women: Frieda, Gardena, Hans's mother, Pepi, and the landlady at the Gentlemen's Inn. On the one hand, the circulation of signs consists in an endless stream of case files and protocols; on the other, the signs are made up by women's clothes.

Even if the binocular structure of the novel is fundamental, it is also strangely indistinct. K. is a land surveyor and, simultaneously, "a liar and a common tramp, and probably worse still."[31] K.'s two assistants are "of course, Klamm's emissaries," Frieda admits, "but even if they are, they're still clumsy youths whose education could profit from a beating."[32] For the short span of time where K. works as a school janitor, the schoolroom is his workplace and, simultaneously, an interim home where he lives his family life with Frieda and the child-like assistants. At his first meeting with the village council chairman, K. reflects upon the blurred border between public and private sphere:

> Nowhere else had K. ever seen office and life [*Amt und Leben*] so intertwined as they were here, so intertwined that it sometimes seemed as though office and life had switched places. How great, say, was the power, so far only formal, that Klamm wielded over K.'s service compared with the power Klamm possessed in actual fact in K.'s bedroom.[33]

Unbotmässig

Barnabas's sister, Olga, offers one of the most detailed accounts of the novel's stereoscopic style when describing Klamm's servants:

> While at the Castle, where they must move about under its laws, they are calm and dignified, I have heard various reports confirming this, and even among the servants here you find traces of it, but only traces, because in the village the laws of the Castle are no longer entirely applicable to them, they seem transformed, having turned into a wild, unbiddable people, governed not by the laws but by their insatiable drives. Their shamelessness knows

---

31 "ein gemeiner lügnerischer Landstreicher, wahrscheinlich aber ärgeres" (S 12; C 4).
32 "Abgesandte Klamms" and "so sind sie doch auch gleichzeitig läppische Jungen, die zu ihrer Erziehung noch Prügel brauchen" (S 218; C 138).
33 "Nirgends noch hatte K. Amt und Leben so verflochten gesehen wie hier, so verflochten, daß es manchmal scheinen konnte, Amt und Leben hätten ihre Plätze gewechselt. Was bedeutete z.B. die bis jetzt nur formelle Macht welche Klamm über K.s Dienst ausübte, verglichen mit der Macht die Klamm in K.'s Schlafkammer in aller Wirklichkeit hatte" (S 94; C 58, translation modified).

no bounds, it's lucky for the village that they can leave the Gentlemen's Inn only upon orders.[34]

Here Olga passes two opposing judgments on the same group of people. In the orderly image, the servants are judged to be calm and dignified and, first of all, conforming to law: they move about "under the laws of the Castle." In the disorderly image, on the other hand, the community of servants is judged to be configured as a wild, unbiddable people ungoverned by law. Thus, Olga's judgments do not apply the specific laws of the castle to the servants. Rather, they are concerned with the very applicability of these laws; in the village, she states, the laws "are no longer entirely applicable" to the servants.

"A wild, unbiddable people" is, in the German original, "ein wildes, unbotmäßiges Volk." Like the English "unbiddable," the rare word "unbotmäßig" contains a negation of "Bot" ("command" or "order"). According to the Grimms' *Deutsches Wörterbuch*, the word means "insubordinate, difficult to bring under control, without discipline and obedience." Kafka might have stumbled across it in Theodor Mommsen's *Römisches Staatsrecht* (*Roman Constitutional Law*, 1876) which he read as a law student, as discussed in Chapter 1. Here, Mommsen uses the word to describe moments of insubordination in Roman institutions, such as when soldiers disobey the officers.[35] What is important to realize is that, unlike "unlawful," "unbotmäßig" does not characterize individual actions but, rather, the underlying configuration of communal life.

In the opening chapter of *Amerika*, the group of people present at the cashier's office of the Hamburg–America Line was configured, simultaneously, as a legal scene and as a family scene. As noted in Chapter 7, Karl's uncle made a distinction between a matter of justice and matter of discipline.[36] In *The Castle*, we find a very similar distinction between office and life.

First, just as in "The Stoker," the contrast between orderly and disorderly image can be understood as an opposition between freedom and submission. At the Gentlemen's Inn, Frieda exceeds her instructions as a barmaid by inviting K. to stay at the taproom during the night.

---

34 "sie [. . .] sind im Schloß, wo sie sich unter seinen Gesetzen bewegen, still und würdig, vielfach ist mir das bestätigt worden und man findet auch hier unter den Dienern noch Reste dessen, aber nur Reste, sonst sind sie dadurch, daß die Schloßgesetze für sie im Dorf nicht mehr vollständig gelten, wie verwandelt; ein wildes, unbotmäßiges, statt von den Gesetzen von ihren unersättlichen Trieben beherrschtes Volk. Ihre Schamlosigkeit kennt keine Grenzen, ein Glück für das Dorf, daß sie den Herrenhof nur über Befehl verlassen dürfen" (S 348; C 222, translation modified).

35 Mommsen, *Römisches Staatsrecht*, 349.

36 (DzL 105; SS 32).

Cunningly hiding him behind the counter, she puts her little foot on his chest in what looks like a sadomasochistic posture of domination.[37] And at the end of the novel, Pepi, Frieda's replacement, invites K. to move into the narrow, subterranean room she shares with two of her female workmates. Since he has no right to be there, he will have to subject himself to the authority of the girls completely: "you must naturally be careful while you are with us and not go showing yourself anywhere unless we've said that there's no danger there, and in general you must follow our advice," Pepi explains, "that's the only thing that binds you."[38]

Second, the opposition between orderly and disorderly image is an opposition between the universal and the particular. Viewing a human being through the lens of bureaucracy, one notices the universal features that make up the legal and political existence of the person, as opposed to the multitude of particularities of the single individual. In his interpretation of Klamm's letter of employment, K. imagines that a position as village worker will make him "indistinguishable" from the other villagers.[39] As their "fellow citizen," not as their "friend," he will have the same parcel of universal and abstract rights as any other villager. "Member of the community—rights and duties—no stranger," K. meditates in the deleted passage quoted above.[40]

By contrast, viewing a human being through the lens of non-bureaucratic life, one sees only the individual's private existence. In the disorderly image, communal life is not a matter of justice but rather a matter of sex, friendship, trust, and care—in other words, of intimate interactions directed toward the single individuals with their myriad agreeable and annoying oddities.

Thus, the novel is structured by a fundamental opposition between "achtungswert" and "liebenswürdig," between being worthy of respect and being worthy of love.[41] Affects play a crucial role in both images of the community but circulate in two dissimilar affective economies. Whereas the orderly image is characterized by feelings of respect, awe, admiration, and fear, the disorderly image features affects such as desire, bliss, attraction, and repulsion. On the one hand, awe of the

---

37   (S 67; C 40).
38   "auch sonst mußt Du natürlich, wenn Du bei uns bist, vorsichtig sein, Dich nirgends zeigen, wo wir es nicht für ungefährlich ansehn und überhaupt unsern Ratschlägen folgen" and "das ist das einzige was Dich bindet" (S 488; C 311).
39   "ununterschiedbar" (S 42; C 24).
40   "durch die Heirat gewann er eine andre besserer Sicherheit—Gemeinde-mitglied—Rechte und Pflichten—kein Fremder!" (SA 264, my translation).
41   (S 37, 463; C 21, 296).

authorities is innate in the village;[42] on the other, all the young women in the village love the castle officials: "Love is never lacking here."[43]

Thirdly and lastly, the opposition between orderly and disorderly image is an opposition between right and grace. As one of the complicated philosophical and religious thematic strands in *The Castle*, this demands a more detailed account. When K., after having interpreted the terms of employment in Klamm's letter, chooses to become a village worker and not an *apparent* village worker, one of his important arguments is that the apparent village worker would be relying solely "on the gentlemen above, on their good graces."[44] A little later, during the meeting with the village council chairman, K. again refers to the concept of grace: "what I want from the Castle is not gifts of grace, but my rights."[45]

On the whole, the novel frequently alludes to the Christian doctrine of grace as formulated, for instance, in Romans and Galatians. It is no coincidence that the messenger of the good graces of the gentlemen above is called Barnabas, like St. Paul's companion in Romans, and that one of the castle officials is named Galater. After having lost his way in Kierkegaard in the beginning of 1918, Kafka not only delved into Judaism but into Christianity, too, not least the Christian doctrine of grace. We know that he read St. Paul and St. Augustine, and even Ernst Troeltsch's well-known book on Protestantism and modernity.[46] Another important book for Kafka's understanding of Christian grace was his friend Felix Weltsch's *Gnade und Freiheit* (*Grace and Freedom*), which he read in proof in 1920.

For Kafka, as for Weltsch, the opposition between right and grace is the defining difference between Judaism and Christianity. According to St. Paul, the Jews imagine that a human being is justified by works of the law, meaning that the glory of God is a matter of who deserves what. Christians, on the other hand, imagine justification as undeserved grace: "since all have sinned and fall short of the glory of God," St. Paul writes in Romans, "they are justified by his grace as a gift, through the redemption which is in Christ Jesus."[47] Put differently, in *The Castle*,

---

42 (S 288; C 182).
43 "Hier fehlt es an Liebe nie" (S 310; C 196).
44 "wenn es nur auf die Herren oben und ihre Gnade angekommen wäre" (S 42; C 24).
45 "ich will keine Gnadengeschenke vom Schloß, sondern mein Recht" (S 119; C 74, translation modified).
46 Ernst Troeltsch, *Luther, der Protestantismus und die moderne Welt*, vol. 4, Gesammelte Schriften (Tübingen: Scienta Verlag Aalen, 1912).
47 Rom 3:23 (NRSV).

Kafka articulates the opposition between the orderly and the disorderly image as a clash between Judaism and Christianity.

If we look at the orderly image, human interaction takes shape as a fair exchange in which the human being gets what she deserves. The teacher underlines that K. is being awarded the post as school caretaker "as a favor,"[48] because the authorities need a school caretaker as little as they need a land surveyor, but that he is sure that K., given that the position will assist him in time of need, will therefore discharge his "duties well, with great energy."[49]

Yet if we look at the disorderly image, human interaction does not consist in barter deals but, rather, in undeserved and groundless acts of grace. In reply to the letter of employment from Klamm, K. asks Barnabas to convey his thanks for the acceptance, but remarks that the job offer is an "exceptional kindness" because he has not proved himself yet.[50] Similarly, K.'s intimate relations with the women of the village are exchanges of gifts and undeserved favors. As K. tells Frieda after the end of their relationship: "on the whole I have been constantly inundated with gifts ever since you first turned your eyes toward me, and of course it isn't all that difficult to get used to receiving gifts."[51]

Since grace is undeserved and groundless, the individual human being can do nothing to influence its course. Here Kafka agrees with his friend Felix Weltsch, according to whom the "believer in freedom is an activist. The believer in grace is consistently a quietist."[52] To the extent that K. chooses to be an apparent village worker, the position that relied on the good graces of the gentlemen above, he can only wait for Barnabas to appear.

As a consequence of their lack of transparent grounds, gifts of grace are entirely random. The letters that Barnabas brings, K. thinks, might be pulled out from a pile of letters, "indiscriminately, and with no more sense than that employed by canaries at fairs who pick somebody's fortune out of a pile."[53]

---

48 "eine Gefälligkeit" (S 152; C 95).
49 "mit allen Kräften bemühen werden, sie gut auszufüllen" (S 146; C 91).
50 "besondere Freundlichkeit" (S 45; C 26).
51 "ich bin ja im Grunde immerfort beschenkt worden, seitdem Du Deine Augen zum erstenmal mir zuwandtest und an das Beschenktwerden sich gewöhnen ist nicht sehr schwer" (S 397; C 253).
52 Weltsch, *Gnade und Freiheit*, 141, my translation.
53 "wahllos und mit nicht mehr Verstand, als die Kanarienvögel auf den Jahrmärkten aufwenden, um das Lebenslos eines Beliebigen aus einem Haufen herauszupicken" (S 290; C 184).

The novel's fundamental opposition between right and grace is condensed in a description of the official Momus who, on one occasion, is working on a deposition over which he "broke a salted pretzel, which he enjoyed with his beer, sprinkling all his papers with salt and caraway seeds."[54] This emblematic image is a double exposure of deposition and pretzel, of the duties of the official and the food of the individual, of Jewish law and Christian supper.

Yet this is the kind of religious allusion that has made *The Castle* and Kafka's oeuvre in general susceptible to profound misreadings such as Brod's claim that the castle is "precisely what the theologians call 'grace.' "[55] To my view, it would be misguided to hold tightly (as it were) to Momus's salted pretzel and insist on interpreting the novel as an allegory of the Christian doctrine of grace. Kafka is not a religious thinker; he is a literary writer using Jewish and Christian symbols in the same way as he manipulates the stories and figures of Greek mythology in literary texts such as "Prometheus," "Poseidon," and "The Silence of the Sirens." As we have seen, Kafka had begun to juxtapose orderly and disorderly images in his literary works after his visit to the Kaiserpanorama in Friedland in February 1911; it was only in the last years of his life that he began approaching the stereoscopic style in the language of right and grace.

The Stereoscopic Village

We might understand 1920's "Fellowship," discussed in Chapter 1, to be an early draft of *The Castle*. Seen this way, the superfluous sixth individual is a prefiguration of the land surveyor who intrudes where he is not wanted, and the union of friends is a model of the village community who do not want to accept him. As demonstrated above, the novel, just like the short parable, juxtaposes two dissimilar images of the unwelcoming community. As a literary stereoscope, *The Castle* challenges the reader to compare the two conflicting images of communal life in the village, configured as either office or life, either biddable or unbiddable.

Interestingly, a similar process of reflection is staged in the novel itself. During his meeting with the bedridden village council chairman, K. produces Klamm's letter of employment in order to discuss its meaning. The chairman reacts by calling his wife: the letter "is valuable and even venerable because of Klamm's signature, which appears to be

---

54   "über dem jetzt gerade Momus ein Salzbrezel auseinanderbrach, das er sich zum Bier schmecken ließ und mit dem er alle Papiere mit Salz und Kümmel überstreute" (S 184; C 116).

55   Brod, "Nachwort," 349, my translation.

genuine, but otherwise—still, I wouldn't risk saying anything about it on my own. Mizzi!"[56] After having whispered together with his wife Mizzi for a while, the chairman is keen on underlining that he is in perfect agreement with her, thereby implying that the interpretation of the letter is conditioned by an alliance between the official and the private image of the case.

The novel consists, to a large extent, of such collective processes of reflection. In the second half of the book, narration tends to be replaced by interpretation. As K.'s efforts to enter the castle come to nothing, the novel instead focuses on his endless conversations with Olga, Pepi, and Frieda about how to interpret the events narrated in the novel's first half and other events that took place before K.'s arrival.

The fictional characters' collective construction of an image of communal life is shaped by their imaginative figurations of Klamm and the other castle officials. The signature on the letter of employment is not legible, "but printed beside it were the words: The Director of Bureau X."[57] Here, "X" is not just a Roman numeral but also a mathematic variable for unknown concepts. Throughout the entire novel, K. and the villagers try to form an image of the unknown X by incessantly telling each other what is referred to as "castle stories" and "new stories about Klamm."[58] On one occasion, Olga gives a detailed account of these stories about Klamm:

> [Klamm's] appearance is of course well known in the village, some have actually seen him, everyone has heard of him, and what emerges from this mixture of sightings, rumors, and distorting ulterior motives is an image of Klamm that is probably correct in its essential features. But only in its essential features. Otherwise it is variable and perhaps not even as variable as Klamm's real appearance [. . .]. And even within the village there are some rather significant differences in the reports, differences in size, posture, corpulence, beard, and only concerning the coat do the reports happily agree [*einheitlich*].[59]

---

56 "ist wertvoll und ehrwürdig durch Klamms Unterschrift, die echt zu sein scheint, sonst aber—doch ich wage es nicht mich allein dazu zu äußern. Mizzi!" (S 112; C 69).

57 "Der Vorstand der X. Kanzlei" (S 40; C 23).

58 "Schloßgeschichten" and "Geschichten von Klamm" (S 323, 464; C 205, 296).

59 "natürlich ist sein Aussehn im Dorf gut bekannt, einzelne haben ihn gesehn, alle von ihm gehört und es hat sich aus dem Augenschein, aus Gerüchten und auch manchen fälschenden Nebenabsichten ein Bild Klamms ausgebildet, das wohl in den Grundzügen stimmt. Aber nur in den Grundzügen. Sonst ist es veränderlich und vielleicht nicht einmal so veränderlich wie Klamms wirkliches

Since Olga hasn't seen Klamm herself, she can only describe the swarm of stories and images that condition the villagers' experience of him. In other words, what Olga refers to as "an image of Klamm" ("ein Bild Klamms") is what I suggest calling a social imaginary. In Kantian terms, the castle officials are schematized by this art hidden in the depths of the villagers' souls. Since the villagers always see Klamm with eyes "blind from excitement,"[60] the image of him, just like the letter from him, is not consistent ("einheitlich"). According to Olga, "a man such as Klamm, who is so often the object of yearning and yet so rarely attained, easily takes on a variety of shapes in the imaginations of people."[61]

As the individual's position in the community is defined by his or her distance from the castle officials in general and from Klamm in particular, the act of imagining Klamm shapes the way the villagers view themselves. The flickering collective image of Klamm, in other words, is to be understood as a condition of possibility for constructing images of the village community. The desirability of the women in the novel, for example, seems to be based not on their psychological or physical features but solely on their imagined closeness to Klamm. At the beginning of the novel, K. is drawn toward the barmaid Frieda because she claims to be Klamm's mistress, even if she is "an unattractive, oldish, thin girl with short, sparse hair."[62] And at the end, he is tempted to embrace Pepi for similar reasons, regardless of her "small, fat, slightly round-backed body."[63]

The reader of the novel is assigned a task comparable to the fictional characters'. In both cases, the construction of an image of communal life demands a process of reflection in which the two incompatible images of the same events are compared. The constitutive split between "Amt" and "Leben," between office and life, calls on the work of reflection.

It is important to add that this process of reflection takes place at the level of the social imaginary rather than at the level of specific social rules. The novel has very little to say about the legal precepts that define the professional duties of a land surveyor or the sexual behavior of a

---

Aussehn [. . .] Und es sind schon selbst innerhalb des Dorfes ziemlich große Unterschiede, die berichtet werden, Unterschiede der Größe, der Haltung, der Dicke, des Bartes, nur hinsichtlich des Kleides sind die Berichte glücklicherweise einheitlich" (S 277–8; C 176, translation modified).

60   "vor Aufregung blinden Augen" (S 289; C 183).

61   "ein so oft ersehnter und so selten erreichter Mann wie es Klamm ist nimmt in der Vorstellung der Menschen leicht verschiedene Gestalten an" (S 286; C 181).

62   "ein unhübsches, ältliches, mageres Mädchen mit kurzem, schütterem Haar" (S 454; C 290).

63   "dieses kleinen dicken ein wenig rundrückigen Körpers" (S 160; C 101).

village girl. By contrast, it offers a detailed overview of the "mixture of sightings, rumors, and distorting ulterior motives" that make up the collective image of Klamm, according to Olga. In other words, the aesthetic reflection, orchestrated by the stereoscopic style of the novel, is to be understood as a reflective working through of the social imaginary.

The Tower

After his first night in the village, K. wakes up at the village inn, opens the door, steps out into the fine winter morning, and sees the castle for the first time. I quote the entire description of the castle, which is one of the novel's core passages:

> Now he saw the Castle above, sharply outlined in the clear air and made even sharper by the snow, which traced each shape and lay everywhere in a thin layer. Besides, there seemed to be a great deal less snow up on the hill than here in the village, where it was no less difficult for K. to make headway than it had been yesterday on the main road. Here the snow rose to the cottage windows only to weigh down on the low roofs, whereas on the hill everything soared up, free and light, or at least seemed to from here.
>
> On the whole the Castle, as it appeared from this distance, corresponded to K.'s expectations. It was neither an old knight's fortress nor a magnificent new edifice, but a large complex, made up of a few two-story buildings and many lower, tightly packed ones; had one not known that this is a castle, one could have taken it for a small town. K. saw only one tower, whether it belonged to a dwelling or a church was impossible to tell. Swarms of crows circled round it.
>
> Keeping his eyes fixed upon the Castle, K. went ahead, nothing else mattered to him. But as he came closer he was disappointed in the Castle, it was only a rather miserable little town, pieced together from village houses, distinctive only because everything was perhaps built of stone, but the paint had long since flaked off, and the stone seemed to be crumbling. Fleetingly K. recalled his old hometown, it was scarcely inferior to this so-called Castle; if K. had merely wanted to visit it, all that wandering would have been in vain, and it would have made more sense for him to visit his old homeland again, where he had not been in such a long time. And in thought he compared the church tower in his homeland with the tower up there. The church tower, tapering decisively, without hesitation, straightaway toward the top, concluded by a wide roof with red tiles, was an earthly building—what else can we build?— but with a higher goal than the low jumble of houses and with a clearer expression than that of the dull workday. The tower up

here—it was the only one in sight—the tower of a residence, as now became evident, possibly of the main Castle, was a monotonous round building, in part mercifully hidden by ivy, with little windows that glinted in the sun—there was something crazy about this—and a terrace-like conclusion, whose battlements, uncertain, irregular, brittle, as if drawn by the anxious or careless hand of a child, serrating the blue sky. It was as if some melancholy resident, who by rights ought to have kept himself locked up in the most out-of-the-way room in the house, had broken through the roof and stood up in order to show himself to the world.[64]

---

64   "Nun sah er oben das Schloß deutlich umrissen in der klaren Luft und noch verdeutlicht durch den alle Formen nachbildenden, in dünner Schicht überall liegenden Schnee. Übrigens schien oben auf dem Berg viel weniger Schnee zu sein als hier im Dorf, wo sich K. nicht weniger mühsam vorwärtsbrachte als gestern auf der Landstraße. Hier reichte der Schnee bis zu den Fenstern der Hütten und lastete gleich wieder auf dem niedrigen Dach, aber oben auf dem Berg ragte alles frei und leicht empor, wenigstens schien es so von hier aus./ Im Ganzen entsprach das Schloß, wie es sich hier von der Ferne zeigte, K.s Erwartungen. Es war weder eine alte Ritterburg, noch ein neuer Prunkbau, sondern eine ausgedehnte Anlage, die aus wenigen zweistöckigen, aber aus vielen eng aneinanderstehenden niedrigem Bauten bestand; hätte man nicht gewußt daß es ein Schloß ist, hätte man es für ein Städtchen halten können. Nur einen Turm sah K. ob er zu einem Wohngebäude oder einer Kirche gehörte war nicht zu erkennen. Schwärme von Krähen umkreisten ihn./ Die Augen auf das Schloß gerichtet, gieng K. weiter, nichts sonst kümmerte ihn. Aber im Näherkommen enttäuschte ihn das Schloß, es war doch nur ein recht elendes Städtchen, aus Dorfhäusern zusammengetragen, ausgezeichnet nur dadurch, daß vielleicht alles aus Stein gebaut war, aber der Anstrich war längst abgefallen, und der Stein schien abzubröckeln. Flüchtig erinnerte sich K. an sein Heimatstädtchen, es stand diesem angeblichen Schlosse kaum nach, wäre es K. nur auf die Besichtigung angekommen, dann wäre es schade um die lange Wanderschaft gewesen und er hätte vernünftiger gehandelt, wieder einmal die alte Heimat zu besuchen, wo er schon so lange nicht gewesen war. Und er verglich in Gedanken den Kirchturm der Heimat mit dem Turm dort oben. Jener Turm, bestimmt, ohne Zögern, geradenwegs nach oben sich verjüngend, breitdachig abschließend mit roten Ziegeln, ein irdisches Gebäude— was können wir anderes bauen?—aber mit höherem Ziel als das niedrige Häusergemenge und mit klarerem Ausdruck als ihn der trübe Werktag hat. Der Turm hier oben—es war der einzige sichtbare—, der Turm eines Wohnhauses, wie sich jetzt zeigte, vielleicht des Hauptschlosses, war ein einförmiger Rundbau, zum Teil gnädig von Epheu verdeckt, mit kleinen Fenstern, die jetzt in der Sonne aufstrahlten—etwas Irrsinniges hatte das—und einem söllerartigen Abschluß, dessen Mauerzinnen unsicher, unregelmäßig, brüchig wie von ängstlicher oder nachlässiger Kinderhand gezeichnet sich in den blauen Himmel zackten. Es war wie wenn irgendein trübseliger Hausbewohner, der gerechter Weise im entlegensten Zimmer des Hauses sich hätte eingesperrt halten sollen, das Dach durchbrochen und sich erhoben hätte, um sich der Welt zu zeigen" (S 16–8; C 7–8; translation modified).

The tower up here [had] a terrace-like conclusion, whose battlements, uncertain, irregular, brittle, as if drawn by the anxious or careless hand of a child, serrating into the blue sky. It was as if some melancholy resident, who by rights ought to have kept himself locked up in the most out-of-the-way room in the house, had broken through the roof and stood up in order to show himself to the world.

The "melancholy resident" has by rights—"gerechter Weise," that is, according to the local version of justice—kept himself locked up in an out-of-the-way room. This passage supports the interpretation of the castle tower as an image of modern art in general and of Kafka's writing in particular. In "The Metamorphosis," for instance, Gregor Samsa is also by rights kept locked up in his room so as not to bother the family members and their tenants with his disgusting beetle form. In general, the motif of being locked up in a distant room is prominent in Kafka's autobiographical and fictional writing.

Interestingly, however, the melancholy resident also alludes to "Briar Rose" and hence to Kierkegaard's enchanted castle journal entry. In the Grimms' fairy tale, the princess pricks herself on a spindle when visiting an old woman locked away in a little room at the end of a narrow staircase in an old tower. In fact, we are never told whether the old woman is the fairy who was excluded from the feast at the beginning of the tale, and who cast her spell over the new-born baby. In any case, the melancholy resident in Kafka's novel is kept locked up in an out-of-the-way room similar to the old woman's. Just like her, the melancholy resident challenges the given order of things, in this case the understanding of justice that determines where he "by rights" should be located in the community. He does this by standing up in order to show himself to the world, and like the English "standing up," the German "sich erheben" not only refers to a physical movement (in Latin *tollere*, according to *Deutsches Wörterbuch* by the same Grimm brothers), but also to a political movement (*surgere*), of the kind through which a people claim their rights.

As we have seen in this chapter, the political moment does not take place in the fictional world of *The Castle*. K. can also be seen as a melancholy resident dweller who by rights is locked up in the most remote room but who, in this scene as in the remaining chapters of the novel, has come to a standstill in the deep snow where he can do nothing but look at the castle. The transformation of the whole of existence, in Kierkegaard's words, simply never occurs. However, a surprising transformation takes place in K.'s aesthetic experience in the passage analyzed above: the castle opens up and comes alive when the melancholy resident breaks through the roof. Seen this way, the political moment is a kind of three-dimensional effect, an event not represented in the novel but produced by its stereoscopic style.

An End or a Beginning

A week before writing the first Kierkegaard letter to Brod, in a notebook entry dated February 25, 1918, Kafka compares his own literary writing to Kierkegaard's religious output:

> The slight amount of the positive, and also of the extreme negative, which capsizes into the positive, are something in which I have had no hereditary share. I have not been guided into life by the hand of Christianity—admittedly now slack and failing—as Kierkegaard was, and have not caught the hem of the Jewish prayer shawl—now flying away from us—as the Zionists have. I am an end or a beginning.[72]

According to Kafka, Kierkegaard was "positive" because he was guided by the hand of Christianity, even if this hand was already slack and failing, just like Kafka's Zionist friends were "positive" because they had managed to catch the hem of the Jewish prayer shawl, even if this positivity, too, was already vanishing.

In this diary entry, then, Kafka refers to as "the positive" what Kierkegaard called "a primitivity" in the journal entry about the enchanted castle. In a difficult phrase, Kafka characterizes Kierkegaard's version of the positive as an extreme negativity that has somehow capsized or tipped over ("umkippenden") into the positive. In fact, this idea is explained in some detail in the letters written to Brod about Kierkegaard in which Kafka touches upon the Danish philosopher's concept of incommensurability: "For the relationship to the divine evades any outside judgment, as K[ierkegaard] sees it," Kafka writes. "Consequently the present external image of the religious relationship has no significance."[73] In perfect accordance with Kierkegaard's idea of

---

72 "an dem geringen Positiven sowie an dem äußersten, zum Positiven umkippenden Negativen hatte ich keinen ererbten Anteil. Ich bin nicht von der allerdings schon schwer sinkenden Hand des Christentums ins Leben geführt worden wie Kierkegaard und habe nicht den letzten Zipfel des davonfliegenden jüdischen Gebetmantels noch gefangen wie die Zionisten. Ich bin Ende oder Anfang" (NS2 98; BON 98–9, translation modified).

73 "Denn das Verhältnis zum Göttlichen entzieht sich zunächst für K. jeder fremden Beurteilung" and "Darum hat das gegenwärtige Außenbild des religiösen Verhältnisses keine Bedeutung."

an incommensurable religious interiority, Kafka here asserts that the interiority of the Christian is impossible to judge from the outside, even if it is Jesus who is judging. In the following sentence, however, Kafka reverses the Kierkegaardian negativity into positivity. Even if there is no positive answer to the question of the individual's relationship to the divine, Kierkegaard's trick is to somehow "capsize" the negativity into positivity:

> However, the religious relationship wishes to reveal itself, but cannot do so in this world; therefore the striving man must oppose this world in order to save the divine element within himself. Or, what comes to the same thing, the divine sets him against the world in order to save itself. Thus the world must be violated by you as well as by Kierkegaard, in one place more by you, in another place more by him.[74]

Kafka uses a remarkably strong word for this positivity through provocation: the striving man is constrained to "overpower" or even "violate" the world ("vergewaltigt") in order to save the divine element within himself. The monstrous positivity is an abusive positivity because it has to do violence to the world.[75]

If this is so, one might expect that Kafka would finish the notebook entry by describing himself as a historical endpoint: "Ich bin Ende." If the striving man must violate this world in order to save the divine element within himself, the evident solution would be to simply stop striving.

Yet, emulating the Christian God of the Book of Revelation, Kafka writes "I am an end or a beginning"—more insecure and ambivalent than God, to be sure, but also more self-confident than we normally imagine him. According to Kafka, modern literature could also function as a beginning. Using Arendt's phrasing about the miraculous political

---

74 "Nun will sich allerdings das religiöse Verhältnis offenbaren, kann das aber nicht in dieser Welt, darum muß der strebende Mensch sich gegen sie stellen, um das Göttliche in sich zu retten oder was das gleiche ist, das Göttliche stellt ihn gegen die Welt um sich zu retten. So muß die Welt vergewaltigt werden von Dir wie von K., hier mehr von Du, hier mehr von ihm" (B4 33; LFFE 203, translation modified).

75 It is highly probable that Kafka found this idea of the negative capsizing into the positive in a famous essay on Kierkegaard by the Catholic essayist and novelist Rudolf Kassner, whom we know he read. According to Kassner, "the beauty and the goodness of the individual is of its own kind, and therefore he lives against the opinion of the others. The individual is his form, but the form in which the others understand him, is the contradiction, the paradox." Rudolf Kassner, "Sören Kierkegaard – Aphoristisch," in *Sämtliche Werke* (Pfullingen: Neske, 1969), 93.

moment, he perceives literature as able to bring about "the birth of new men and the new beginning, the action they are capable of by virtue of being born."[76]

In contrast to Kierkegaard's self-confident view of the mission to transform the whole of existence, Kafka perceives his role as a modern writer as being the instigator of a different transformation, a political moment not dependent on a striving man who relates to some positive original principle. Instead of Kierkegaard's decisive, immediate movement toward the top, Kafka depicts a melancholy resident who breaks through the roof to show himself to the world. It is important to note that the castle tower, even if the stone is crumbling and the melancholy resident is destroying its roof, is still moving upward. With a remarkable formulation, the castle tower is serrating or zigzagging "into the blue sky,"[77] an oxymoron that synthesizes the destructive jagged movement with the constructive, transcendent movement into the blue heavens—perhaps one of Kafka's finest descriptions of his stereoscopic style.

76 Arendt, *The Human Condition*, 247
77 "in den blauen Himmel zackten."

Conclusion

Worthy of the Law: "On the Question of the Laws"

"Unfortunately, our laws are not generally known; they are the secret of the small group of nobles who rule us. We are convinced that these ancient laws are being strictly upheld, but it is still an extremely tormenting thing to be ruled by laws that we do not know."[1] Even if nothing is said of the nationality of the people and of the nobility who rule them, the parable "On the Question of the Laws" ("Zur Frage der Gesetze"), written in 1920 and published posthumously, must be understood as a part of the so-called "China complex," a group of texts in which Franz Kafka takes issue with political questions. Like the Chinese narrator of "Building the Great Wall of China," analyzed in Chapter 6, the narrator of this short parable offers an ethnographical account of the political order of his own society.

Interestingly, the question of the laws is not a question regarding those laws' content. As one of the people, the narrator is unable to specify what the secret laws say. In fact, the laws discussed in the parable could equally be interpreted as juridical laws, moral laws, natural laws, and even religious laws. As in the literary works explored in the previous chapters, what is at stake is rather the configuration of the community to which the laws are applied, in this case the basic shape of communal life that draws a line between the nobility and the people. For the people, it is extremely tormenting that they are ruled by

---

1   "Unsere Gesetze sind leider nicht allgemein bekannt, sie sind Geheimnis der kleinen Adelsgruppe, welche uns beherrscht. Wir sind davon überzeugt, daß diese alten Gesetze genau eingehalten werden, aber es ist doch etwas äußerst Quälendes nach Gesetzen beherrscht zu werden, die man nicht kennt" (NS2 270–3; SS 129–30). In the following analysis of "On the Question of the Laws," I quote from these pages, in some cases modifying the English translation slightly.

laws they do not know and that only a small, noble, party "may participate in the interpretation" of these laws.[2]

Further down in the short text, the narrator formulates the same problem by saying that the people, as opposed to the nobility, "cannot yet be deemed worthy of the law." The German sentence is slippery: "weil wir noch nicht des Gesetzes gewürdigt werden können." By introducing the concept of dignity ("Würde") as a verb ("würdigen," "appreciate" or "acknowledge"), the text underlines the act of judging that categorizes a group of people as either worthy or unworthy of the law.

When the narrator complains that only certain individuals and not the entire people may participate in the interpretation ("Auslegung") of the laws, the parable clearly alludes to Talmudic interpretation. The political conflict between nobility and the commons can be understood as the religious conflict between traditional orthodox Judaism and Hasidism, a Jewish revivalist movement from the last half of the eighteenth century which continued to play an important role in the first decades of the twentieth century. In Meyer Isser Pinès's 1911 Yiddish literary history, *Histoire de la littérature judéo-allemande*, which Kafka devoured immediately upon publication, the orthodox rabbis are characterized as "intellectual aristocracy." On the other hand, Hasidism is labeled as a "democratic movement" because it understood the interpretation of the Law as a job for the entire religious community and not only for the rabbis.[3]

It is worth noting, however, that the question of the laws is a more fundamental question than religious practices in Judaism. In a sense, Kafka uses Jewish theology in the same way that he uses Greek mythology or the Protestant doctrine of grace (as we saw in a previous chapter): as a theological language with which to address a political question concerning the configuration of the community.

In this book, I have explored a number of fictional and real communities in Kafka's writings that were judged to be at one and the same time worthy and unworthy of the law. "Fellowship" simultaneously depicts a circle of friends and a crowd of strangers. The diary entry

---

2   Here I agree with DeCoste's perceptive interpretation of the extremely tormenting thing: "The people's pain arises [...] from the very disjunctiveness of the law. For the law at once separates the people from the nobility and, in so doing, detaches them from themselves." Frederick C. DeCoste, "Kafka, Legal Theorizing and Redemption," *Mosaic: A Journal for the Interdisciplinary Study of Literature* 27, no. 4 (1994): 163.

3   See Meyer Isser Pinès, *Histoire de la littérature judéo-allemande* (Paris: Jouve et Cie, 1911); Hans Dieter Zimmermann, "Jüdisches, unjüdisches: Zur Frage der Gesetze bei Franz Kafka," *German Life and Letters* 49, no. 2 (1996): 227.

about the asbestos factory describes the employees as grown-up women entitled to polite treatment, and, simultaneously, as non-humans. "The Judgment" represents Georg's communal life as a circle of friends and a true family and, simultaneously, as a crowd of non-friends and a non-family. "Researches of a Dog" offers an account of a dog people who live in warm togetherness and who are, simultaneously, widely dispersed. The diary entries on the Yiddish theater performances reflect on dramatic characters who are complying with the laws of the Jewish village, but simultaneously dancing around as light as a feather, seemingly exempt from human and natural laws. "The Stoker," the first chapter of *Amerika*, simultaneously depicts the events in the head cashier's office as a legal and a family scene. In *The Trial*, the chapter "Initial Inquiry" simultaneously pictures a group of people as a political assembly and as a private organization. And in *The Castle*, the villagers are legal persona in the official sphere of the castle administration and, simultaneously, individuals in the private sphere of affective and erotic interactions. In each of these fictional and non-fictional communities, Kafka's stereoscopic style offers two disjunctive images of how the individuals stand to each other, how they fit together, how they relate to other groups and to the surrounding world.

In this short concluding chapter, I will argue that Kafka's topicality today is owed to his distinctive way of posing the question of the laws: by focusing on a judgment of the configuration of the community to which the laws are applied.

The Character of the Laws

As we have seen, judgments on the configuration of the community in Kafka are most often passed from a generalized and depersonalized position, in some cases attributed to the indefinite pronoun "one" ("man"). This was the case even in Kafka's very personal meditations on the literary wishes of his own youth discussed in Chapter 3. According to the hopeful young writer, the literary work should be able to represent, for instance, the hammering together of a table "in such a way that *one* could say [. . .] 'Hammering is a real hammering to him, but simultaneously also nothing.' "[4] Similarly, in "On the Question of the Laws," the central judgment on the legal and political status of the people is formulated in the passive so that the reader has no chance to tell whether it is the nobility or the commons who pass judgment: "we cannot yet be deemed worthy of the law."

Based on the narrator's formulations, it seems in fact to be the laws themselves that make this decision about their secrecy. To be more

---

4   (T 854; GWC 108–09, translation modified, my italics).

precise, the reason for the inaccessibility and secrecy of the laws is what the narrator suggests conceptualizing as their character: "the character of these laws also demands that their continued existence be kept secret."[5] The little word "also" ("auch") is crucial here since it intimates that the character of the laws does more than just demand their own secrecy. In general, the word "character" denotes an essential quality or a distinctive nature, in this case that of the laws. In his brief commentary on Kafka's parable on the question of the laws, Jacques Derrida suggests the character of the laws might be interpreted as "law's essence" and "the being-law of these laws."[6] In the terminology of the legal philosopher H. L. A. Hart, on which Derrida draws here, the character of the laws is defined by the secondary rules of recognition used as authoritative criteria for identifying primary rules of obligation.[7]

However, the narrator's statement about the character of the laws is not a literal proposition, but rather a rhetorical figure that describes the laws as if they were human beings with the capacity of making demands: "the character of these laws also demands [*verlangt*] that their continued existence be kept secret." This anthropomorphizing figure is recurrent in the short text. A few lines earlier, the narrator argues that "the law seems to have put itself exclusively into the hands of the nobility. In this, naturally, there is wisdom—who doubts the wisdom of the ancient laws?—but equally misery for us as well."[8] Thanks to the imaginative figures, it appears not that the hands of the nobility have grasped the law, but, inversely, that the law has acted to put itself into those noble hands on its own account. Likewise, the wisdom is imagined not as the wisdom of the human beings who created the laws but as the wisdom of the ancient laws in themselves.

In other words, the narrator's statements about the laws are shaped by the social imaginary of the people, a collective repertoire of figures, metaphors, symbols, narratives, and other forms of imagination with which they construct images of the configuration of the community. Thanks to this web of imaginative figures, the configuration of the community, even if it is "tormenting," seems natural to the narrator: "In this, *naturally*, there is wisdom" (my italics).

The narrator's name for the social imaginary is "tradition" and "popular tradition" ("Volkstradition"). The second and last section of

---

5   "der Charakter dieser Gesetze verlangt auch das Geheimhalten ihres Bestandes."
6   Jacques Derrida, "Before the Law," in *Acts of Literature*, ed. Derek Attridge (New York: Routledge, 1992), 205, 192.
7   H. L. A. Hart, *The Concept of Law* (Oxford: Clarendon Press, 1961), 79–99.
8   "deshalb scheint das Gesetz sich ausschließlich in die Hände des Adels gegeben zu haben. Darin liegt natürlich Weisheit—wer zweifelt die Weisheit der alten Gesetze an?—aber eben auch Qual für uns, wahrscheinlich ist das unumgänglich."

the short text describes how the people have been attentively following the actions of the nobility from the most ancient times, and how they, based on observations of innumerable facts, are able to surmise the laws and so to "make some little arrangements for our lives for the present and the future."[9] It is possible, the narrator speculates, that the people's collective imagination about the laws is the only thing there is:

> By the way, the existence of these apparent laws can only be surmised. It is a tradition that they exist and have been entrusted to the nobility as a secret, but this is not nor cannot be anything other than an old tradition to which age lends credence; for the character of these laws also demands that their continued existence be kept secret.[10]

It is important to note that the social imaginary of the people is not concerned with the content of the laws but solely with their existence and the character. In the narrator's own words, the old tradition provides a "belief in the laws."[11]

One can see how the narrator lends credence to the laws in the many provisos that take the edge off his initial assertion about the extremely tormenting thing. First, what is so tormenting is not that the laws are being ignored, the narrator notices, because the people are "convinced that these ancient laws are being strictly upheld." Neither, second, is it the disadvantages arising from the laws being interpreted in different ways. "These disadvantages are probably not so great," the narrator speculates, since the freedom of interpretation is very limited after "centuries have labored over their interpretation."[12] Nor, third, is the extremely tormenting thing that the laws are being manipulated by the particular interests of the nobility, since, as the narrator surmises, the nobles have no need to manipulate: "the nobles apparently have no reason to allow their personal interests to influence their interpretation to our disadvantage, since from the very beginning the laws have been determined for the nobility."[13]

---

9 "für die Gegenwart und Zukunft ein wenig einzurichten suchen."
10 "Übrigens können auch diese Schein-Gesetze eigentlich nur vermutet werden. Es ist eine Tradition, daß sie bestehn und dem Adel als Geheimnis anvertraut sind, aber mehr als alte und durch ihr Alter glaubwürdige Tradition ist es nicht und kann es nicht sein, denn der Charakter dieser Gesetze verlangt auch das Geheim-halten ihres Bestandes."
11 "dem Glauben an die Gesetze."
12 "Diese Nachteile sind vielleicht gar nicht sehr groß. Die Gesetze sind ja so alt, Jahrhunderte haben an ihrer Auslegung gearbeitet."
13 "Außerdem hat offenbar der Adel keinen Grund sich bei der Auslegung von seinem persönlichen Interesse zu unsern Ungunsten beeinflussen zu lassen, denn die Gesetze sind ja von ihrem Beginne an für den Adel festgelegt worden."

These three provisos are based on the people's conjectures about the laws rather than their knowledge of the laws. The people are *convinced* that the ancient laws are being upheld, the disadvantages are *probably* not so great, the nobles *apparently* have no reason to bend the law. In consequence, it is the people who judge themselves as unworthy of the law. This is why it is only logical that they don't hate the nobility but hate themselves instead: "This statement is certainly not made with hatred of the nobility, not in the least and not by anyone; we are more readily inclined to hate ourselves because we cannot yet be deemed worthy of the law."[14] It is the imaginary conjectures of the people that determine the configuration of the community. Formulated with Kant's famous definition of enlightenment, the political emancipation of the people would be their emergence from the self-incurred immaturity caused by their own stubborn belief in the laws.[15]

On Three Questions of the Laws

Like the concept of the "Kafkaesque", a number of well-known themes in Kafka research are presently approaching their expiration date. This is the case for the absurd bureaucracies, the authoritarian fathers, and the guilt-ridden sexuality. Today, much is said and written about the horizontal, non-bureaucratic organization of work life, about the problematic lack of paternal authority in family life, and about the permanent injunction to enjoy. In the remaining sections of this chapter, I will (in broad strokes) approach Kafka's topicality today by briefly sketching out three contemporary versions of the parable's question of the laws.

First, Kafka and the rest of his family worshipped in the Pinkas synagogue in Prague's Jewish ghetto. The collapse of the multi-ethnic empires of Russia and Austria-Hungary after the First World War was followed by mass denaturalizations of unwanted minorities in the interwar years, among them the Jewish community in Prague, turning statelessness into a mass phenomenon. Millions of refugees, expatriates, deported aliens, stateless persons, and displaced persons were deemed unworthy of the law. After Kafka's death in 1924, many of his friends and family members were expelled from the legal and political community and subsequently murdered in the death camps. According

---

14 "Das wird nicht etwa mit Haß gegen den Adel gesagt, durchaus nicht und von niemandem, eher hassen wir uns selbst, weil wir noch nicht des Gesetzes gewürdigt werden können."

15 Immanuel Kant, *Political Writings*, trans. Hans Siegbert Reiss (Cambridge and New York: Cambridge University Press, 1991), 54.

to Hannah Arendt, herself forced to flee Germany in 1937, these allegedly superfluous persons were deprived of their "right to have rights (and this means to live in a framework where one is judged by one's actions and opinions)."[16]

Seen in this light, the question of the laws is a question of the exclusive nature of the legal and political community. This question continues to torment us. Compared to the interwar years, a much larger group of people are currently deprived of their right to have rights and, hence, to live in Western national states without the benefits of full citizenship.[17] We tend to imagine citizenship as hard on the outside and soft on the inside, but in a world of porous borders, the judgment on who is worthy and unworthy of the law is not passed at the hard edge of the community alone. Today, rather, we witness what has aptly been called an "introgression" and an "introprojection" of borders.[18] Within the confines of the nation state, certain groups of people are configured as non-members of the civic community. Viewed through the lens of contemporary migration politics, then, Kafka's parable, and Kafka's work in general, can be interpreted as a story about citizens and non-citizens of a legal and political community.

Second, from 1908 until his retirement in 1922, Kafka worked as an insurance assessor at the Workmen's Accident Insurance Institute for the Kingdom of Bohemia. During the war, as we saw in Chapter 6, Kafka was charged with the health care of disabled veterans returning from trenches. In peacetime, his professional tasks were the legal aspects of accident prevention in and risk assessment of the factories of Northern Bohemia. In other words, Kafka the official played an active role in the establishment of the modern social state, a project seen by many historians as a response to the 1871 workers' revolution

---

16 Hannah Arendt, *The Origins of Totalitarianism* (San Diego: Harcourt Brace Jovanovich, 1979), 296.

17 This is probably why Arendt's chapter on the calamity of the rightless right plays a central role in recent political philosophy. For further discussion, see, for instance, Giorgio Agamben, *Homo sacer: Sovereign Power and Bare Life* (Stanford, CA: Stanford University Press, 1998); Michel Agier, *Managing the Undesirables: Refugee Camps and Humanitarian Government* (Cambridge: Polity, 2011); Benhabib, *The Rights of Others*; Judith Butler, *Notes Toward a Performative Theory of Assembly* (Cambridge, MA: Harvard University Press, 2015); Nancy Fraser, *Scales of Justice: Reimagining Political Space in a Globalizing World* (Cambridge: Polity, 2008).

18 Etienne Balibar, *We, the People of Europe?: Reflections on Transnational Citizenship* (Princeton, NJ: Princeton University Press, 2004), 1; Linda Bosniak, *The Citizen and the Alien: Dilemmas of Contemporary Membership* (Princeton, NJ: Princeton University Press, 2006), 5.

in Paris.[19] In the years following the Paris Commune, important laws on social security were passed not only in France but also in Germany and Austria-Hungary, whereby political questions about the relation between workers and employers were transposed into technical questions about risk management. Thus, in the early social state, the question of the laws was depoliticized and neutralized. "How modest these men are," Kafka remarked about the workers that enquired at the Workmen's Accident Insurance Institute, according to Max Brod, "instead of storming the Institute and smashing it to little pieces, they come and beg."[20]

Through the lens of risk management, the question of the laws is a question of the defensive nature of the legal and political community. Again, this remains a pressing question. Kafka was an early professional actuary, although today calculating probabilities is a field with a significantly bigger and more influential reach, and is concerned with much more violent accidents such as terror attacks and climate-related disasters. The "directives and warnings" ("Weisung und Warnung") the narrator discussed in "Building the Great Wall of China" have become an important way of governing contemporary social life.[21] In other words, modern disaster management, with its advanced technologies of algorithmic modeling, scenario planning, risk profiling, and data analysis, brings about a specific configuration of the legal and political community. In the anticipation of future disasters, it seems more important to defend the given order of things than to transform it. According to the contemporary social imaginaries of disaster, the community consists of passive victims who have a right to be protected by the state rather than by active citizens who have a right to participate in the governance of that state.[22] From the perspective of contemporary disaster management, then, Kafka's parable can be understood as a story about security experts and vulnerable bodies.

---

19 For further discussion, see Greg Eghigian, "The German Welfare State as a Discourse of Trauma," in *Traumatic Pasts: History, Psychiatry, and Trauma in the Modern Age, 1870–1930*, ed. Mark S. Micale and Paul Frederick Lerner (Cambridge: Cambridge University Press, 2001); François Ewald, *L'État providence* (Paris: Grasset, 1986); Michel Foucault, *Sécurité, territoire, population: Cours au Collège de France, 1977–1978*, ed. Michel Senellart, François Ewald, and Alessandro Fontana (Paris: Gallimard, 2004).
20 Max Brod, *Franz Kafka: A Biography* (New York: Schocken, 1960), 82
21 (NS1 354; SS 122).
22 For further discussion, see Louise Amoore, *The Politics of Possibility: Risk and Security Beyond Probability* (Durham, NC: Duke University Press, 2013); Fassin, *Humanitarian Reason*; Honig, *Emergency Politics.*

Third, between the autumn of 1911 and the beginning of the First World War, Kafka was the co-manager of the Prague Asbestos Works Hermann & Co. In Chapter 2, we saw how he, in this professional capacity, treated female employees as if they were not rational beings on an equal footing. "They are not human beings," Kafka noted in his long diary entry about the asbestos factory, thereby explaining why he could have the feeling that he was under no obligation to treat the women politely and respectfully.

Against the background of the capitalist economy, the question of the laws is a question that touches on the insular nature of the legal and political community. This problem is probably even more frustrating today. Neoliberalism is most often defined as the expansion of the market economy's power structures to other societal institutions and practices. According to a number of contemporary political philosophers, neoliberalism is not only a way of organizing the economy, but also a way of configuring communal life—a certain governmentality, as it were.[23] According to the social imaginary of neoliberalism, social life is constituted by rational entrepreneurs who compete with each other in the marketplace rather than by political subjects who make decisions in common. Thus, in the light of a contemporary mode of capitalism, Kafka's parable can be understood as a story about corporate CEOs on the one hand, and workers and consumers on the other.

It is possible to imagine other contemporary versions of Kafka's question of the laws, and it is tempting to go into detail with the complicated intertwinements of migration politics, disaster management, and neoliberal economics. I restrict myself to these three questions because I have experienced them as being urgent. In the years I have spent working on Kafka, political responses to migration have decided the outcome of elections in Denmark and in other Western nation states. During those same years, the warnings about terror attacks and climate disasters have come to play an ever more prominent role in the way we imagine our common future. Simultaneously, Western welfare states have either delegated tasks to private companies or emulated the economic rationality of the private sector.

Taken together, the three contemporary versions of the question of the laws point to an overarching problem. If the nature of the legal and political community today can be said to be exclusive, defensive, and

---

23 For further discussion, see Wendy Brown, *Undoing the Demos: Neoliberalism's Stealth Revolution* (New York, and Cambridge, MA: Zone Books, 2015); Sheldon Wolin, *Democracy Incorporated: Managed Democracy and the Specter of Inverted Totalitarianism* (Princeton, NJ: Princeton University Press, 2008).

insular, this is a sign of what has been called the retreat of the political. "There is no alternative," Margaret Thatcher liked to say, and the so-called TINA principle is an updated belief in destiny according to which the political moment is, and should be, unable to reconfigure the community.

The retreat of the political is a recurring theme in contemporary political philosophy and cultural theory. Current discussion draws heavily on Carl Schmitt and Hannah Arendt, both of whom have played an important role in the discussion of the political moment in this book. According to Schmitt, the "neutralization" of the political is caused by our tendency to perceive the modern state as a lifeless machine made up of abstract legal rules, forgetting that political decisions created— and keep *recreating*—that machine.[24] According to Arendt, the "withering away" of the political realm is to be explained by the expanding social sphere, understood as the various forms of bureaucratic, economic, and technological management serving to undermine the political space where citizens can meet and make decisions about collective life.[25] And according to the narrator of "On the Question of the Laws," finally, the political sphere becomes inaccessible when it is only certain individuals, rather than the people, who may participate in the interpretation of the laws.

A Sigh of Relief
The narrator of Kafka's parable does more than explain how extremely upsetting it is for the people to be deemed unworthy of the law; he also expresses how extremely encouraging it is that one day the people will, in fact, become worthy of it. Centuries will still have to pass while the people patiently research the huge body of material constituting the popular tradition, he imagines. But even if this seems to be an endless and hopeless endeavor, it is driven forward by a utopian dream:

> What is dismal at present in this prospect is brightened only by the belief that one day the time will come when both the tradition and our research of it arrive, with a sigh of relief, so to speak, at their conclusion, when everything has become clear, when the law belongs to the people, and when the nobility disappears.[26]

---

24 Carl Schmitt, *The Concept of the Political*, trans. George Schwab (Chicago: University of Chicago Press, 1996), 61–3.
25 Arendt, *The Human Condition*, 60.
26 "Das für die Gegenwart Trübe dieses Ausblicks erhellt nur der Glaube, daß einmal eine Zeit kommen wird, wo die Tradition und ihre Forschung gewissermaßen aufatmend den Schlußpunkt macht, alles klar geworden ist, das Gesetz nun dem Volk gehört und der Adel verschwindet."

Here the narrator offers a magnificent description of a political moment: a utopian moment in which the people finally put an end to the tradition ("den Schlußpunkt macht"), breathe a sigh of relief, and begin their shared life anew.

It is worth noting that this description of a political moment is concerned with the character rather than with the content of the laws: what is at stake is the configuration of the community to which the laws are applied. In the political moment, everything becomes clear, the narrator imagines, and here the word "everything" ("wo ... *alles* klar geworden ist") does not refer to the political constitution of the community but, rather, to the swarm of imaginations that make up the popular tradition. When the imaginative figurations become clear, the people will no longer lend credence to the secret and inaccessible laws. In Hobbes's phrasing, the "ghostly power" underlying the legal and political order will be exorcised.[27] This critical awareness of the social imaginary will transform the oligarchy into a democracy: from the very beginning the laws have been determined for the nobility, but from this future moment, the laws are to be determined by the people themselves.

In this book, I have explored Kafka's dream of a political moment. Beyond the beautiful passage from "On the Question of the Laws," the most striking examples are perhaps the researcher dog's vision of the transformation of the edifice of dogdom, and Kierkegaard's parable, quoted by Kafka, on the transformation of existence. According to the dog, as we saw in Chapter 4, the miraculous moment was possible at the time of the first generations of dogs: "at that time the true word could still have intervened, determined the build, changed its tune, changed it at will, turned it into its opposite."[28] And according to Kierkegaard, as we saw in Chapter 9, the moment of awakening will occur upon the arrival of a man who does not take the world as it is: "the moment these words are heard, it is as if the whole of existence were transformed. As in the fairy tale: when the word is spoken, the castle that had been under a spell for a hundred years opens up and everything comes alive."[29]

Yet, as we have seen, the political moment takes place not only in the world of Kafka's fictional characters, but also in the mind of Kafka's readers. The literary stereoscopes are the apparatuses via which Kafka challenges his readers to rethink and reshape the hidden art of the social imaginary.

---

27 Hobbes, *Leviathan*, 172.
28 (NS2 456; SS 148, translation modified).
29 Kierkegaard, *Journalerne*, NB 32: 127, 26, 214.

According to what I refer to above as the "Kafkaesque" picture of Kafka, his works bear witness to a petrified and unalterable world in which tradition never fades and the law never belongs to the people. My contention is that this picture of Kafka focuses on his problem and forgets his *project*, which can be described as a version of the classical Enlightenment project of emerging from self-incurred immaturity, as Kant had it. Kafka's literary stereoscopes have the creative and beneficent force to prompt political thinking. A century after "On the Question of the Laws," these literary apparatuses still have this force. As long as the judgment deeming some groups of people worthy and others unworthy of the law continues to hold sway, Kafka's project will continue to be relevant. That is to say: we can attribute the enduring topicality of Kafka's works to his posing the question of the laws as a question about the configuration of the community to which the laws are applied. This is why his literary stereoscopes still promise to bring about political moments in which everything will become clear, the law will belong to the people, and the nobility will disappear.

Bibliography

Abraham, Ulf. "Mose 'Vor dem Gesetz': Eine unbekannte Vorlage zu Kafkas 'Türhüterlegende'." *Deutsche Vierteljahrsschrift für Literaturwissenschaft und Geistesgeschichte* 57 (1983).

Abraham, Ulf. *Der verhörte Held: Verhöre, Urteile und die Rede von Recht und Schuld im Werk Franz Kafkas*. Munich: W. Fink, 1985.

Adorno, Theodor W. *Prisms*. Translated by Samuel Weber and Shierry Weber. Cambridge, MA: The MIT Press, 1981.

Adorno, Theodor W. *Aesthetic Theory*. Translated by Robert Hullot-Kentor. Minneapolis, MN: University of Minnesota Press, 1997.

Agamben, Giorgio. *Homo sacer: Sovereign Power and Bare Life*. Stanford, CA: Stanford University Press, 1998.

Agier, Michel. *Managing the Undesirables: Refugee Camps and Humanitarian Government*. Cambridge: Polity, 2011.

Allison, Henry E. *Kant's Theory of Taste: A Reading of the Critique of Aesthetic Judgment*. Cambridge and New York: Cambridge University Press, 2001.

Alt, Peter-André. *Franz Kafka: Der ewige Sohn. Eine Biographie*. Munich: Beck, 2005.

Amoore, Louise. *The Politics of Possibility: Risk and Security Beyond Probability*. Durham, NC: Duke University Press, 2013.

Anderson, Benedict. *Imagined Communities: Reflections on the Origin and Spread of Nationalism*. London: Verso, 1983.

Anderson, Mark. *Kafka's Clothes: Ornament and Aestheticism in the Habsburg Fin de Siècle*. Oxford: Oxford University Press, 1992.

Appadurai, Arjun. *Modernity at Large: Cultural Dimensions of Globalization*. Minneapolis, MN: University of Minnesota Press, 1996.

Arendt, Hannah. *Between Past and Future: Eight Exercises in Political Thought*. New York: Viking Press, 1968.

Arendt, Hannah. *The Origins of Totalitarianism*. San Diego: Harcourt Brace Jovanovich, 1979.

Arendt, Hannah. "Franz Kafka: A Revaluation." In *Essays in Understanding, 1930–1954*, edited by Jerome Kohn. New York and London: Harcourt, Brace & Co, 1994.

Arendt, Hannah. *The Human Condition*. Chicago: University of Chicago Press, 1998.

Arendt, Hannah. "Introduction *into* Politics." In *The Promise of Politics*. New York: Schocken, 2005.

Arendt, Hannah. *On Revolution*. New York: Penguin Books, 2006.

Aristotle. *Politics*. Translated by Richard Kraut. Oxford: Clarendon Press, 1997.

Aristotle. *Poetics*. Translated by Anthony Kenny. Oxford: Oxford University Press, 2013.

Aristotle. *Nicomachean Ethics*. Translated by C. D. C. Reeve. Indianapolis, IN: Hackett, 2014.

Baioni, Giuliano. *Kafka: Literatur und Judentum*. Translated by Gertrud Billen and Josef Billen. Stuttgart: Metzler, 1994.

Bal, Mieke. *The Mottled Screen: Reading Proust Visually*. Stanford, CA: Stanford University Press, 1997.

Balibar, Etienne. *We, the People of Europe?: Reflections on Transnational Citizenship*. Princeton, NJ: Princeton University Press, 2004.

Beck, Evelyn Torton. *Kafka and the Yiddish Theater: Its Impact and His Work*. Madison, WI: University of Wisconsin Press, 1971.

Beicken, Peter. "Kafka's Visual Method: The Gaze, the Cinematic, and the Intermedial." In *Kafka for the Twenty-First Century*, edited by Stanley Corngold. Rochester, NY: Camden House, 2011.

Benhabib, Seyla. *The Rights of Others: Aliens, Residents and Citizens*. Cambridge: Cambridge University Press, 2004.

Benjamin, Walter. *Illuminations*. Translated by Harry Zohn. New York: Schocken, 2007.

Binder, Hartmut. *Kafka-Kommentar zu sämtlichen Erzählungen*. Munich: Winkler, 1975.

Binder, Hartmut. *Kafka-Handbuch in zwei Bänden*. Stuttgart: Kröner, 1979.

Binder, Hartmut. *Kafka: Der Schaffensprozess*. Frankfurt am Main: Suhrkamp, 1983.

Blanchot, Maurice. *La part du feu*. Paris: Gallimard, 1949.

Bloom, Harold. *Ruin the Sacred Truths: Poetry and Belief from the Bible to the Present*. Cambridge, MA: Harvard University Press, 1989.

Boa, Elizabeth. *Kafka: Gender, Class and Race in the Letters and Fictions*. Oxford: Clarendon Press, 1996.

Bosniak, Linda. *The Citizen and the Alien: Dilemmas of Contemporary Membership*. Princeton, NJ: Princeton University Press, 2006.

Bottici, Chiara. *Imaginal Politics: Images Beyond Imagination and the Imaginary*. New York: Columbia University Press, 2014.

Brod, Max. "Axiome über das Drama." *Die Schaubühne* 7, no. 2 (1911): 227–99.

Brod, Max. "Panorama." In *Über die Schönheit hässlicher Bilder*. Leipzig: K. Wolff, 1913.

Brod, Max. *Franz Kafka: Eine Biographie: Erinnerungen und Dokumente*. New York: Schocken, 1946.

Brod, Max. "Nachwort." In *Franz Kafka, Das Schloss*. Frankfurt am Main: S. Fischer, 1946.

Brod, Max. *Franz Kafka: A Biography*. New York: Schocken, 1960.

Brod, Max. *Streitbares Leben*. Munich: Kindler, 1960.

Brod, Max. *Über Franz Kafka. Franz Kafka, eine Biographie. Franz Kafkas Glauben und Lehre. Verzweiflung und Erlösung im Werk Franz Kafkas*. Hamburg: Fischer, 1966.

Brown, Wendy. *Undoing the Demos: Neoliberalism's Stealth Revolution*. New York and Cambridge, MA: Zone Books, 2015.

Bruce, Iris. *Kafka and Cultural Zionism: Dates in Palestine*. Madison, WI: University of Wisconsin Press, 2007.

Buck-Morss, Susan. *The Dialectics of Seeing: Walter Benjamin and the Arcades Project*. Cambridge, MA, and London: The MIT Press, 1989.

Burke, Kenneth. *A Grammar of Motives*. Berkeley, CA: University of California Press, 1969.

Butler, Judith. *Precarious Life: the Powers of Mourning and Violence*. New York: Verso, 2004.

Butler, Judith. *Frames of War: When is Life Grievable?* London: Verso, 2009.

Butler, Judith. *Notes Toward a Performative Theory of Assembly*. Cambridge, MA: Harvard University Press, 2015.

Calhoun, Craig. "The Idea of Emergency: Humanitarian Action and Global (Dis) Order." In *Contemporary States of Emergency: The Politics of Military and Humanitarian Interventions*, edited by Didier Fassin and Mariella Pandolfi. New York and Cambridge, MA: Zone Books, 2010.

Casanova, Pascale. *Kafka: Angry Poet*. Translated by Chris Turner. London and New York: Seagull Books, 2015.

Castoriadis, Cornelius. *The Imaginary Institution of Society*. Translated by Kathleen Blarney. Cambridge: Polity, 1987.

Caygill, Howard. *Kafka: In Light of the Accident*. London and New York: Bloomsbury, 2017.

Colebrook, Claire. *Irony*. London and New York: Routledge, 2004.

Connolly, William. *Pluralism*. Durham, NC: Duke University Press, 2005.

Corngold, Stanley. *Lambent Traces: Franz Kafka*. Princeton, NJ: Princeton University Press, 2004.

Corngold, Stanley, and Benno Wagner. *Franz Kafka: The Ghosts in the Machine*. Evanston, IL: Northwestern University Press, 2011.

Crary, Jonathan. *Techniques of the Observer: On Vision and Modernity in the Nineteenth Century*. Cambridge, MA, and The MIT Press, 1990.

Crary, Jonathan. *Suspensions of Perception: Attention, Spectacle, and Modern Culture*. Cambridge, MA, and London: The MIT Press, 1999.

Curtis, Michael. "The Hilsner Case and Ritual Murder." In *Jews on Trial*, edited by Bruce Afran and Robert A. Garber. Jersey City, NJ: Ktav, 2005.

Danius, Sara. *Prousts motor*. Stockholm: Bonnier, 2000.

Därmann, Iris. *Figuren des Politischen*. Frankfurt am Main: Suhrkamp, 2009.

de Man, Paul. *The Rhetoric of Romanticism*. New York: Columbia University Press, 1984.

DeCoste, Frederick C. "Kafka, Legal Theorizing and Redemption." *Mosaic: A Journal for the Interdisciplinary Study of Literature* 27, no. 4 (1994): 161–78.

Degner, Uta. "What Kafka Learned from Flaubert: 'Absent-Minded Window-Gazing' and 'The Judgement'." In *Kafka for the Twenty-First Century*, edited by Stanley Corngold. Rochester, NY: Camden House, 2011.

Deleuze, Gilles, and Félix Guattari. *Kafka: Toward a Minor Literature*. Translated by Dana Polan. Minneapolis, MN: University of Minnesota Press, 1986.

Derrida, Jacques. "Before the Law." In *Acts of Literature*, edited by Derek Attridge. New York: Routledge, 1992.

Dodd, William John. "The Case of a Political Reading." In *The Cambridge Companion to Kafka*, edited by Julian Preece. Cambridge and New York: Cambridge University Press, 2002.

Dodd, William John. "Kafka's Russia and Images of War in 1912 and 1914." In *Kafka, Prag und der Erste Weltkrieg = Kafka, Prague and the First World War*, edited by Manfred Engel and Ritchie Robertson. Würzburg: Königshausen & Neumann, 2012.

Dostoyevsky, Fyodor. *Notes from Underground: A New Translation, Backgrounds and Sources, Responses, Criticism*. Translated by Michael R. Katz. New York: Norton, 1989.

Dostoyevsky, Fyodor. *Crime and Punishment*. Translated by Oliver Ready. New York: Penguin Books, 2015.

Dowden, Stephen D. *Kafka's Castle and the Critical Imagination*. Columbia, SC: Camden House, 1995.

Duttlinger, Carolin. "Die Ruhe des Blickes: Brod, Kafka, Benjamin and the Kaiserpanorama." In *Science, Technology and the German Cultural Imagination*, edited by Christian Emden and David R. Midgley. Oxford and New York: Peter Lang, 2005.

Duttlinger, Carolin. *Kafka und Photography*. Oxford: Oxford University Press, 2007.

Edschmid, Kasimir. "Deutsche Erzählungsliteratur." In *Franz Kafka: Kritik und Rezeption zu seinen Lebzeiten 1912–1924*, edited by Jürgen Born. Frankfurt am Main: Fischer, 1979.

Eghigian, Greg. "The German Welfare State as a Discourse of Trauma." In *Traumatic Pasts: History, Psychiatry, and Trauma in the Modern Age, 1870–1930*, edited by Mark S. Micale and Paul Frederick Lerner. Cambridge: Cambridge University Press, 2001.

Emrich, Wilhelm. *Franz Kafka*. Bonn: Athenäum, 1958.

Emrich, Wilhelm. "Franz Kafka Ost und West." In *The Literary Revolution and Modern Society, and Other Essays*. New York: Ungar, 1971.

Engel, Manfred. "Entwürfe symbolischer Weltordnungen: China und China Revisited. Zum China-Komplex in Kafkas Werk 1917–1920." In *Kafka, Prag und der Erste Weltkrieg = Kafka, Prague and the First World War*, edited by Ritchie Robertson. Würzburg: Königshausen & Neumann, 2012.

Engel, Manfred, and Ritchie Robertson. *Kafka, Prag und der Erste Weltkrieg = Kafka, Prague and the First World War*. Würzburg: Königshausen & Neumann, 2012.

Esposito, Roberto. *Immunitas: The Protection and Negation of Life*. Cambridge and Malden, MA: Polity, 2011.

Esposito, Roberto. *Terms of the Political: Community, Immunity, Biopolitics*. New York: Fordham University Press, 2013.

Ewald, François. *L'État providence*. Paris: Grasset, 1986.

Fassin, Didier. *Humanitarian Reason: A Moral History of the Present Times*. Berkeley, CA: University of California Press, 2012.

Foucault, Michel. *Sécurité, territoire, population: cours au Collège de France, 1977–1978*. Edited by Michel Senellart, François Ewald and Alessandro Fontana. Paris: Gallimard, 2004.

Fraser, Nancy. "Abnormal Justice." In *Justice, Governance, Cosmopolitanism, and the Politics of Difference*. Berlin: Der Präsident der Humboldt-Universität zu Berlin, 2007.

Fraser, Nancy. *Scales of Justice: Reimagining Political Space in a Globalizing World*. Cambridge: Polity, 2008.

Gilman, Sander L. *Franz Kafka: The Jewish Patient*. New York: Routledge, 1995.

Glinski, Sophie von. *Imaginationsprozesse: Verfahren phantastischen Erzählens in Franz Kafkas Frühwerk*. Berlin and New York: De Gruyter, 2004.

Goebel, Rolf J. *Constructing China: Kafka's Orientalist Discourse*. Columbia, SC: Camden House, 1997.

Göhler, Hulda. *Franz Kafka: Das Schloss, "Ansturm gegen die Grenze," Entwurf einer Deutung*. Bonn: Bouvier, 1982.

Gray, Richard T. *Constructive Destruction: Kafka's Aphorisms, Literary Tradition, and Literary Transformation*. Tübingen: M. Niemeyer, 1987.

Gray, Richard T., Ruth V. Gross, Rolf J. Goebel, and Clayton Koelb. *A Franz Kafka Encyclopedia*. Westport, CT: Greenwood Press, 2005.

Gray, Ronald D. *Franz Kafka*. Cambridge: Cambridge University Press, 1973.

Grimm, Jacob, and Wilhelm Grimm. *Original Folk and Fairy Tales of the Brothers Grimm*. Translated by Jack Zipes. Princeton, NJ: Princeton University Press, 2014.

Gross, Hans. *Criminalpsychologie*. Graz: Leuschner & Lubensky, 1898.

Gross, Hans. *Handbuch für Untersuchungsrichter als System der Kriminalistik*. Munich: J. Schweitzer, 1904.

Gross, Hans. *Criminal Investigation: A Practical Handbook for Magistrates, Police Officers, and Lawyers*. Translated by John Adam and J. Collyer Adam. London: The Specialist Press, 1907.

Grøtta, Marit. *Baudelaire's Media Aesthetics: The Gaze of the Flâneur and 19th Century Media*. New York: Bloomsbury Academic, 2015.

Hanney, Roxanne. *The Invisible Middle Term in Proust's* A la recherche du temps perdu. Lewiston, ME, and Lampeter: Mellen, 1990.

Haraway, Donna. "A Manifesto for Cyborgs: Science, Technology, and Socialist Feminism in the 1980s." In *Feminism/Postmodernism*, edited by Linda J. Nicholson. New York: Routledge, 1990.

Hart, H. L. A. *The Concept of Law*. Oxford: Clarendon Press, 1961.

Hasselblatt, Dieter. *Zauber und Logik: eine Kafka-Studie*. Köln: Wissenschaft und Politik, 1964.

Hegel, Georg Wilhelm Friedrich. *Aesthetics: Lectures on Fine Art*. Translated by T. M. Knox. Oxford: Clarendon Press, 1975.

Heidsieck, Arnold. "Kafka's Fictional and Non-Fictional Treatments of Administrative, Civil, and Criminal Law." http://www.usc.edu/dept/LAS/german/track/heidsiec/KafkaLawsources/KafkaLawsources.pdf.

Heilmann, Hans. *Chinesische Lyrik vom 12. Jahrhundert v. Chr. bis zur Gegenwart*. Munich: Piper, 1905.

Hermsdorf, Klaus. "Franz Kafka und die Arbeiter-Unfall-Versicherungs-Anstalt." In *Kafkas Fabriken*, edited by Hans-Gerd Koch and Klaus Wagenbach. Marbach am Neckar: Deutsche Schillergesellschaft, 2002.

Hermsdorf, Klaus, and Benno Wagner. "Schreibanlässe und Textformen der amtlichen Schriften Franz Kafkas." In *Amtliche Schriften: Schriften, Tagebücher, Briefe*, edited by Klaus Hermsdorf and Benno Wagner. Frankfurt am Main: Fischer, 2004.

Hildebrand, Adolf. "The Problem of Form in the Fine Arts." Translated by Harry Francis Mallgrave and Eleftherios Ikonomou. In *Empathy, Form, and Space: Problems in German Aesthetics, 1873–1893*, edited by Robert Vischer. Santa Monica, CA, and Chicago: University of Chicago Press, 1994.

Hobbes, Thomas. *Elementa philosophica de cive*. Amsterdam and Lausanne: Françiscum Grasset, 1760.

Hobbes, Thomas. *Leviathan*. Translated by J. C. A. Gaskin. Oxford: Oxford University Press, 1996.

Hobbes, Thomas. *On the Citizen*. Cambridge and New York: Cambridge University Press, 1998.

Holitscher, Arthur. *Amerika heute und morgen: Reiseerlebnisse*. Berlin: S. Fischer Verlag, 1912.

Holm, Isak Winkel. *Tanken i billedet: Søren Kierkegaards poetik*. København: Gyldendal, 1998.

Holm, Isak Winkel. "Verkörperlichung der Symbole: Franz Kafkas Metaphern zwischen Poetik und Stilistik." *Hoffmansthal-Jahrbuch*, no. 10 (2002): 303–26.

Holm, Isak Winkel. "Monstrous Aesthetics: Literature and Philosophy in Søren Kierkegaard." *Nineteenth-Century Prose* 32, 1 (2005): 52–74.

Holm, Isak Winkel. "Das Recht zu Athmen: Existenzberechtigung und Anerkennung bei Dostojewskij und Hegel." *Internationales Archiv für Sozialgeschichte der Deutschen Literatur* 36 (2012).

Holm, Isak Winkel. *Stormløb mod grænsen. Det politiske hos Kafka*. Copenhagen: Gyldendal, 2015.

Honig, Bonnie. *Emergency Politics: Paradox, Law, Democracy*. Princeton, NJ: Princeton University Press, 2009.

Honig, Bonnie. *Antigone, Interrupted*. Cambridge and New York: Cambridge University Press, 2013.

Hug, Arnold. "Der Doppelsinn in Sophokles Oedipus König." *Philologus*, no. 31 (1872).

Hutcheon, Linda. *Irony's Edge: The Theory and Politics of Irony*. London and New York: Routledge, 1994.

Huyssen, Andreas. *Miniature Metropolis: Literature in an Age of Photography and Film*. Cambridge, MA: Harvard University Press, 2015.

Jahn, Wolfgang. *Kafkas Roman "Der Verschollene" ("Amerika")*. Stuttgart: Metzler, 1965.

Janouch, Gustav. *Gespräche mit Kafka: Aufzeichnungen und Erinnerungen*. Frankfurt am Main: Fischer, 1981.

Janouch, Gustav. *Conversations with Kafka*. Translated by Goronwy Rees. New York: New Directions, 2012.

Jensen, Johannes V. *Hos fuglene*. Copenhagen: Gyldendal, 2001.

Kafka, Franz. *The Blue Octavo Notebooks*. Translated by Max Brod, Ernst Kaiser, and Eithne Wilkins. Cambridge: Exact Change, 1991.

Kafka, Franz. *The Castle: A New Translation Based on the Restored Text*. Translated by Mark Harman. London: Folio Society, 2011.

Kahn, Paul W. *Finding Ourselves at the Movies: Philosophy for a New Generation*. New York: Columbia University Press, 2013.

Kant, Immanuel. *Political Writings*. Translated by Hans Siegbert Reiss. Cambridge and New York: Cambridge University Press, 1991.

Kant, Immanuel. *Lectures on Logic*. Translated by J. Michael Young. Cambridge and New York: Cambridge University Press, 1992.

Kant, Immanuel. *Lectures on Metaphysics*. Translated by Karl Ameriks and Steve Naragon. Cambridge and New York: Cambridge University Press, 1997.

Kant, Immanuel. *Critique of Pure Reason*. Translated by Paul Guyer and Allen W. Wood. Cambridge and New York: Cambridge University Press, 1998.

Kant, Immanuel. *Critique of the Power of Judgment*. Translated by Paul Guyer and Eric Matthews. Cambridge and New York: Cambridge University Press, 2000.

Kantorowicz, Ernst. *The King's Two Bodies: A Study in Medieval Political Theology*. Princeton, NJ: Princeton University Press, 1957.

Kassner, Rudolf. "Sören Kierkegaard – Aphoristisch." In *Sämtliche Werke*. Pfullingen: Neske, 1969.

Kierkegaard, Søren. *Buch des Richters: Seine Tagebücher 1833–1855, im Auszug aus dem Dänischen*. Edited by Hermann Gottsched. Jena and Leipzig: Eugen Diderichs, 1905.

Kierkegaard, Søren. *The Concept of Irony, with Continual Reference to Socrates.* Translated by Howard V. Hong and Edna H. Hong. Princeton, NJ, and Oxford: Princeton University Press, 1989.

Kierkegaard, Søren. *Journalerne.* Søren Kierkegaards skrifter. Edited by N. J Cappelørn, Joakim Garff, Anne Mette Hansen and Johnny Kondrup. Copenhagen: Søren Kierkegaard Forskningscenteret, Gad, 2009.

Kierkegaard, Søren. *Kierkegaard's Journals and Notebooks.* Edited by Niels Jørgen Cappelørn, Alastair Hannay, Bruce H. Kirmmse, David Possen, Joel Rasmussen, and Vanessa Rumble. Vol. 10, Princeton, NJ: Princeton University Press, forthcoming.

Kilcher, Andreas B. "Geisterschrift: Kafkas Spiritismus." In *Schrift und Zeit in Franz Kafkas Oktavheften*, edited by Caspar Battegay, Felix Christen, and Wolfram Groddeck. Göttingen: Wallstein, 2010.

Kittler, Wolf. "Schreibmaschinen, Sprechmaschinen: Effekte technischer Medien im Werk Franz Kafkas." In *Franz Kafka: Schriftverkehr*, edited by Wolf Kittler and Gerhard Neumann. Freiburg im Breisgau: Rombach, 1990.

Kittler, Wolf. "Heimlichkeit und Schriftlichkeit: Das österreichische Strafprozessrecht in Franz Kafkas Roman Der Proceß." *Germanic Review* 78 (2003): 194–222.

Kittler, Wolf. "In dubio pro reo: Kafkas 'Strafkolonie'." In *Kafkas Institutionen*, edited by Oliver Simons Arne Höcker. Bielefeld: transcript, 2007.

Koch, Hans-Gerd. "Nachbemerkung." In *Reisetagebücher, Kritische Kafka Ausgabe.* Frankfurt am Main: Fischer, 1994.

Kolesch, Doris. *Aufbauende Zerstörung: Zur Paradoxie des Geschichts-Sinns bei Franz Kafka und Thomas Pynchon.* Frankfurt am Main and New York: P. Lang, 1996.

Kracauer, Siegfried. *The Mass Ornament: Weimer Essays.* Translated by Thomas Y. Levin. Cambridge, MA, and London: Harvard University Press, 1995.

Lange, Wolfgang. "Über Kafkas Kierkegaard-Lektüre und einige damit zusammenhängende Gegenstände." *Deutsche Vierteljahrsschrift für Literaturwissenschaft und Geistesgeschichte* 60, LX (1986).

Lehmann, Hans-Thies. "Der buchstäbliche Körper: Zur Selbstinszenierung der Literatur bei Franz Kafka." In *Der junge Kafka*, edited by Gerhard Kurz. Frankfurt am Main: Suhrkamp, 1984.

Leslie, Esther. *Walter Benjamin: Overpowering Conformism.* London and Sterling, VA: Pluto Press, 2000.

Liska, Vivian. *When Kafka Says We: Uncommon Communities in German-Jewish Literature.* Bloomington, IN: Indiana University Press, 2009.

Long, J.J. "Photography." In *Franz Kafka in Context*, edited by Carolin Duttlinger. Cambridge: Cambridge University Press, 2018.

Longuenesse, Béatrice. *Kant and the Capacity to Judge: Sensibility and Discursivity in the Transcendental Analytic of the Critique of Pure Reason.* Princeton, NJ, and Chichester: Princeton University Press, 1998.

Löwy, Michael. *Franz Kafka: Rêveur insoumis.* Paris: Stock, 2004.

Löwy, Michael. "Franz Kafka's Trial and the Anti-Semitic Trials of His Time." *Human Architecture: Journal of the Sociology of Self-Knowledge*, 7, no. 2 (2009): 151–58.

Löwy, Michael. *Franz Kafka: Subversive Dreamer.* Translated by Inez Hedges. Ann Arbor, MI: University of Michigan Press, 2016.

Marchart, Oliver. *Post-Foundational Political Thought: Political Difference in Nancy, Lefort, Badiou and Laclau.* Edinburgh: Edinburgh University Press, 2007.

Masaryk, Tomas G. *Notwendigkeit der Revision des Polnaer Processes*. Vienna: Die Zeit, 1899.

Masaryk, Tomas G. *Die Bedeutung des Polnaer Verbrechens für den Ritualaberglauben*. Berlin: H.S. Hermann, 1900.

Massino, Guido. *Kafka, Löwy und das Jiddische Theater*. Frankfurt am Main: Stroemfeld, 2007.

Meltzer, Françoise. *Seeing Double: Baudelaire's Modernity*. Chicago: University of Chicago Press, 2011.

Meng, Weiyan. *Kafka und China*. Munich: Iudicium Verlag, 1986.

Menke, Christoph. *Tragödie im Sittlichen: Gerechtigkeit und Freiheit nach Hegel*. Frankfurt am Main: Suhrkamp, 1996.

Menke, Christoph. "The Presence of Tragedy: An Aesthetic Enlightenment." *Neue Rundschau* 111, no. 1 (2000): 85–95.

Menke, Christoph. "Ästhetik der Tragödie: romantische Perspektiven." In *Tragödie – Trauerspiel – Spektakel*, edited by Christoph Menke and Bettine Menke. Berlin: Theater der Zeit, 2007.

Mommsen, Theodor. *Römisches Staatsrecht*. Basel: S. Hinzel, 1876.

Mommsen, Theodor. *The History of Rome*. Translated by William P. Dickson. London: Macmillan & Co., 1908.

Monaco, C. S. *The Rise of Modern Jewish Politics: Extraordinary Movement*. New York: Routledge, 2013.

Morris, Joel. "Josef K.'s (A+x) Problem: Kafka on the Moment of Awakening." *German Quarterly* 82, no. 4 (2009): 469–82.

Musil, Robert. "Literarische Chronik." In *Gesammelte Werke*. Reinbek bei Hamburg: Rowohlt, 1978.

Nägele, Rainer. *Benjamin's Ground: New Readings of Walter Benjamin*. Detroit, MI: Wayne State University Press, 1988.

Neumann, Gerhard. "Nachrichten vom 'Pontus'. Das Problem der Kunst im Werk Franz Kafkas." In *Franz Kafka: Schriftverkehr*, edited by Wolf Kittler and Gerhard Neumann. Freiburg im Breisgau: Rombach, 1990.

Neumann, Gerhard. "Der Zauber des Anfangs und das 'Zögern vor der Geburt': Kafkas Poetologie des 'riskanten Augenblicks'." In *Nach erneuter Lektüre, Franz Kafkas "Der Process"*, edited by Hans Dieter Zimmermann. Würzburg: Königshausen & Neumann, 1992.

Neumann, Gerhard. "Wahrnehmung und Medialität." In *Franz Kafka: Eine ethische und ästhetische Rechtfertigung*, edited by Beatrice Sandberg and Jakob Lothe. Freiburg: Rombach, 2001.

Olson, Kevin. *Imagined Sovereignties: The Power of the People and other Myths of the Modern Age*. Cambridge and New York: Cambridge University Press, 2016.

Pasley, Malcolm. "Two Literary Sources of Kafka's Der Prozess." *Forum for Modern Language Studies* 3, no. 2 (1967): 142–47.

Pasley, Malcolm. "Semi-Private Games." In *The Kafka Debate: New Perspectives for Our Time*, edited by Angel Flores. Staten Island, NY: Gordian Press, 1977.

Paul-Schiff, Maximilian. *Der Prozess Hilsner. Aktenauszug*. Vienna: L. Rosner, 1908.

Pinès, Meyer Isser. *Histoire de la littérature judéo-allemande*. Paris: Jouve et Cie, 1911.

Pippin, Robert B. *Kant's Theory of Form: An Essay on the Critique of Pure Reason*. New Haven, CT, and London: Yale University Press, 1982.

Plato. *Ion, Hippias Minor, Laches, Protagoras*. Translated by Reginald E. Allen. The Dialogues of Plato. Vol. 3, New Haven, CT: Yale University Press, 1984.

Plato. *The Republic*. Translated by Tom Griffith. Cambridge: Cambridge University Press, 2000.

Puchner, Martin. "Kafka's Antitheatrical Gestures." *Germanic Review* 78, no. 3 (2003): 177–93.

Rancière, Jacques. *Disagreement: Politics and Philosophy*. Translated by Julie Rose. Minneapolis, MN: University of Minnesota Press, 1999.

Rancière, Jacques. *Dissensus: On Politics and Aesthetics*. Translated by Steve Corcoran. London: Continuum, 2009.

Ricoeur, Paul. "Le paradoxe politique." In *Histoire et vérité*. Paris: Éditions du Seuil, 1966.

Ricoeur, Paul. "The Function of Fiction in Shaping Reality." *Man and World* 12, no. 2 (1979): 123–41.

Ricoeur, Paul. *From Text to Action: Essays in Hermeneutics II*. London: Continuum, 2008.

Robert, Marthe. *Seul, comme Franz Kafka*. Paris: Calmann-Lévy, 1979.

Robertson, Ritchie. *Kafka: Judaism, Politics, and Literature*. Oxford: Clarendon Press, 1985.

Rodway, Allan. "Terms for Comedy." *Renaissance and Modern Studies* 6, no. 1 (1962): 102–25.

Rohde, Bertram. *Und blätterte ein wenig in der Bibel: Studien zu Franz Kafkas Bibellektüre und ihre Auswirkungen auf sein Werk*. Würzburg: Königshausen & Neumann, 2002.

Ronell, Avital. *The Telephone Book: Technology-Schizophrenia-Electric Speech*. Lincoln, NE: University of Nebraska Press, 1989.

Rousseau, Jean-Jacques. *The Plan for Perpetual Peace, On the Government of Poland, and other Writings on History and Politics*. Translated by Christopher Kelly. Hanover, NH: University Press of New England, 2005.

Schlegel, Friedrich von. *Philosophical Fragments*. Minneapolis, MN: University of Minnesota Press, 1991.

Schmitt, Carl. *Politische Theologie: Vier Kapitel zur Lehre von der Souveränität*. Munich: Duncker & Humblot, 1934.

Schmitt, Carl. *Political Theology: Four Chapters on the Concept of Sovereignty*. Translated by George Schwab. Cambridge, MA: The MIT Press, 1985.

Schmitt, Carl. *The Concept of the Political*. Translated by George Schwab. Chicago: University of Chicago Press, 1996.

Shattuck, Roger. *Proust's Binoculars: A Study of Memory, Time, and Recognition in* A la recherche du temps perdu. London: Chatto & Windus, 1964.

Siegle, Robert. *The Politics of Reflexivity: Narrative and the Constitutive Poetics of Culture*. Baltimore, MD, and London: Johns Hopkins University Press, 1986.

Sokel, Walter. *Franz Kafka: Tragik und Ironie*. Frankfurt am Main: Fischer, 1983.

Sokel, Walter. "Beyond Self-Assertion: A Life of Reading Kafka." In *A Companion to the Works of Franz Kafka*, edited by James Rolleston. Rochester, NY: Camden House, 2002.

Spector, Scott. *Prague Territories: National Conflict and Cultural Innovation in Franz Kafka's Fin de Siècle*. Berkeley, CA: University of California Press, 2000.

Stach, Reiner. *Kafka: The Decisive Years*. Translated by Shelley Laura Frisch. Princeton, NJ: Princeton University Press, 2013.

Stach, Reiner. *Kafka: The Years of Insight*. Translated by Shelley Laura Frisch. Princeton, NJ: Princeton University Press, 2013.

Stach, Reiner. *Kafka: die frühen Jahre*. Frankfurt am Main: S. Fischer, 2014.

Stach, Reiner. *Kafka: The Early Years*. Translated by Shelley Laura Frisch. Princeton, NJ: Princeton University Press, 2016.

Stölzl, Christoph. *Kafkas böses Böhmen: Zur Sozialgeschichte eines Prager Juden*. Munich, 1975.

Strathausen, Carsten. "The Return of the Gaze: Stereoscopic Vision in Jünger and Benjamin." *New German Critique* 80 (2000): 125–48.

Taylor, Charles. "The Nature and Scope of Distributive Justice." In *Philosophy and the Human Sciences*. Cambridge: Cambridge University Press, 1985.

Taylor, Charles. *Modern Social Imaginaries*. Durham, NC: Duke University Press, 2004.

Todorov, Tzvetan. *Introduction à la littérature fantastique*. Paris: Éditions du Seuil, 1970.

Todorov, Tzvetan. *The Fantastic: A Structural Approach to a Literary Genre*. Translated by Richard Howard. Cleveland, OH: Press of Case Western Reserve University, 1973.

Troeltsch, Ernst. *Luther, der Protestantismus und die moderne Welt*. Gesammelte Schriften. Vol. 4, Tübingen: Scienta Verlag Aalen, 1912.

Trotter, David. "Stereoscopy: Modernism and the 'Haptic'." *Critical Quarterly* 46, no. 4 (2004): 38–58.

Tucholsky, Kurt. *Gesammelte Werke*. Reinbek bei Hamburg: Rowohlt, 1975.

Virno, Paolo. *A Grammar of the Multitude: For an Analysis of Contemporary Forms of Life*. Cambridge, MA, and London: Semiotext(e), 2003.

Vogl, Joseph. *Ort der Gewalt: Kafkas literarische Ethik*. Munich: Fink, 1990.

Wagenbach, Klaus. "Kafkas Fabriken." In *Kafkas Fabriken*, edited by Hans-Gerd Koch and Klaus Wagenbach. Marbach am Neckar: Deutsche Schillergesellschaft, 2002.

Wagner, Benno. "'Ende oder Anfang?': Kafka und der Judenstaat." In *Kafka, Zionism, and Beyond*, edited by Mark H. Gelber. Tübingen: Niemeyer, 2004.

Wagner, Benno. "Insuring Nietzsche: Kafka's Files." *New German Critique*, 99 (2006): 83–119.

Wagner, Benno. "'No one indicates the direction': The Question of Leadership in Kafka's Later Stories." In *Kafka's Selected Stories: New Translations, Backgrounds and Contexts, Criticism*, edited by Stanley Corngold. New York: W.W. Norton, 2007.

Wagner, Benno. "'Zuerst die Mauer und dann den Turm': Der Widerstreit zwischen Biopolitik und Ethnopolitik als berufliches Problem und schriftstellerischer Einsatz Franz Kafkas." *brücken: Germanistisches Jahrbuch* 15 (2007): 89–99.

Wagner, Benno. "Kafkas 'vergleichende Völkergescichte'. Eine Skizze zum Verhältnis von Litteratur und kulturellem Wissen." *Aussiger Beiträge* 2 (2008): 89–99.

Wagner, Benno. "Kafka's Office Writings: Historical Background and Institutional Setting." In *Franz Kafka: The Office Writings*, edited by Stanley Corngold, Jack Greenberg, and Benno Wagner. Princeton, NJ, and Oxford: Princeton University Press, 2009.

Wagner, Benno. "Beim Bau der chinesischen Mauer." In *Kafka-Handbuch: Leben, Werk, Wirkung*, edited by Manfred Engel and Bernd Auerochs. Stuttgart: Metzler, 2010.

Wagner, Benno. "'Lightning No Longer Flashes': Kafka's Chinese Voice and the Thunder of the Great War." In *Franz Kafka: Narration, Rhetoric, and Reading*, edited by Jakob Lothe, Beatrice Sandberg, and Ronald Speirs. Columbus, OH: Ohio State University Press, 2011.

Walzel, Oskar. "Logik im Wunderbaren." In *Franz Kafka: Kritik und Rezeption zu seinen Lebzeiten 1912–1924*, edited by Jürgen Born. Frankfurt am Main: Fischer, 1979.

Walzer, Michael. *Exodus and Revolution*. New York: Basic Books, 1985.

Weber, Max. "Die protestantische Ethik und der Geist des Kapitalismus." *Archiv für Sozialwissenschaft und Sozialpolitik* 21, no. 1 (1904/5): 1–110.

Weltsch, Felix. *Gnade und Freiheit: Untersuchungen zum Problem des schöpferischen Willens in Religion und Ethik*. München: Kurt Wolff, 1920.

Winter, Jacob, and August Wünsche. *Die jüdische Litteratur seit Abschluss des Kanons, eine prosaische und poetische Anthologie mit biographischen und litterargeschichtlichen Einleitungen*. Trier: Sigmund Mayer, 1894.

Wirkner, Alfred. *Kafka und die Aussenwelt: Quellenstudien zum "Amerika"-Fragment*. Stuttgart: Klett, 1976.

Wolf, Burkhardt. "Die Nacht des Bürokraten: Franz Kafkas statistische Schreibweise." *Deutsche Vierteljahrsschrift für Literaturwissenschaft und Geistesgeschichte* 80, no. 1 (2006): 97–127.

Wolin, Sheldon. *Democracy Incorporated: Managed Democracy and the Specter of Inverted Totalitarianism*. Princeton, NJ: Princeton University Press, 2008.

Zimmermann, Hans Dieter. "Jüdisches, unjüdisches: Zur Frage der Gesetze bei Franz Kafka." *German Life and Letters* 49, no. 2 (1996): 225–35.

Ziolkowski, Theodore. *The Mirror of Justice: Literary Reflections of Legal Crises*. Princeton, NJ: Princeton University Press, 1997.

Ziolkowski, Theodore. "Law." In *Franz Kafka in Context*, edited by Carolin Duttlinger. Cambridge: Cambridge University Press, 2018.

Zischler, Hanns. *Kafka Goes to the Movies*. Chicago and London: University of Chicago Press, 2003.

Index

Abraham, Ulf 29 n.13, 219 n.92
accident insurance, *see*
    Workmen's Accident
    Insurance Institute for the
    Kingdom of Bohemia
Adorno, Theodor, W. 2, 76,
    105 n.49
aesthetic experience 4–6, 14, 23, 28,
    30, 62, 71–2, 79–81, 100, 115,
    119, 123, 127–30, 170–3, 183,
    189, 191–3, 198, 203, 213,
    216, 225–6, 240, 243
aesthetic reflection 14–15, 28, 66,
    71–5, 78, 83–4, 100–1, 105–7,
    184, 186, 213–14, 216, 234–7,
    241
Amerika heute und morgen:
    Reiseerlebnisse (*America Today*
    and Tomorrow, Holitscher)
anti-Semitism 104, 195–8
Apostate: A Comic Picture of Life
    with Song and Dance, The
    (Scharkansky), *see Der*
    Meschumed. Komisches
    Lebensbild mit Gesang und
    Tanz
Appadurai, Arjun 51
Arendt, Hannah 13–15, 29, 88, 95,
    98, 160, 163, 193, 225, 245,
    252–3, 256
Aristotle 30–2, 37, 45–6, 119, 122,
    163, 185, 211

asbestos factory, *see* Prague
    Asbestos Works Hermann &
    Co
Augustine, St. 232
Aurelius, Marcus 56
"Axiome über das Drama" (Brod)
    123–7

Balibar, Etienne 253 n.18
Bauer, Felice 67, 103, 114, 134
Benjamin, Walter 2, 8, 56
Binder, Hartmut 38, 100 n.34,
    169 n.7
Book of Exodus 187–9, 209–11
Book of Revelation 245
Bosniak, Linda 253 n.18
"The Briar Rose" ("The Sleeping
    Beauty", Grimm), 222–4, 243
Brod, Max 1–3, 5–6, 43–4, 54, 80,
    95, 113–14, 123–7, 147–8,
    160, 215, 223–5, 234,
    244–6
Burke, Kenneth 72

Castoriadis, Cornelius 49–51
Chinese Poetry from the Twelfth
    Century BCE *to the Present*
    (Heilmann), *see Chinesische*
    Lyrik vom 12. Jahrhundert v.
    Chr. bis zur Gegenwart
Chinesische Lyrik vom 12.
    Jahrhundert v. Chr. bis zur

Gegenwart (Heilmann)
138–9, 150–1, 154 n.69, 156–7
Christianity 115, 232–4, 244
citizen, citizenship 17, 81, 84,
135–9, 163, 212, 253–6
civil state, *see* state of nature
configuration of community
11–15, 24–5, 29, 34–7, 42,
46–7, 52–3, 58–9, 62, 66–9,
93–8, 102–5, 122–3, 130, 138,
146–7, 152, 176, 186, 193,
230, 234, 247–9, 257
Connolly, William 35 n.31
Corngold, Stanley 8 n.12, 63 n.2,
139 n.14
Crary, Jonathan 5 n.7, 23 n.5
Crime and Punishment
(Dostoyevsky) 206–7
Criminal Investigation (*Handbuch
für Untersuchungsrichter*,
Gross) 53, 186
Critique of Pure Reason (*Kritik der
reinen Vernunft*, Kant) 52–3,
100–3
Critique of Judgment (*Kritik der
Urteilskraft*, Kant) 72

de Man, Paul 7, 101–2, 154, 186,
216
DeCoste, Frederick C. 248 n.2
defamiliarization 127–8, 173, 189
Degner, Uta 66 n.7, 75 n.41
Deleuze, Gilles, and Félix Guattari
2, 15
Derrida, Jacques 250
destiny, *see* fate
Deutsches Wörterbuch (Grimm) 84,
96, 211, 215, 230, 243
disfiguration 6, 101–5, 154–5, 186,
216–7
distribution of the sensible, *see*
Rancière, Jacques
divine justice 122, 186–8, 193, 209
Dodd, William John 12, 160 n.81

Dostoyevsky, Fyodor 21–4, 206–7
Dowden, Stephen 239 n.65
dramatic theory 123–8, 239
Duttlinger, Carolin 6 n.8, 8 nn.12
and 13, 55 n.44, 170 n.10,
200 n.20

Edschmid, Kasimir 76–9
Embattled Life (Brod), *see Streitbares
Leben*
emergency powers, *see* state of
exception
Esposito, Roberto 11 n.16

*Fantastic: a Structural Approach to a
Literary Genre, The* (Todorov)
77–9
fate 38, 97, 163, 258
Fear and Trembling (Kierkegaard)
79–80
First World War 1, 45, 95, 133–8,
252, 255
Franz Joseph I 160
Fraser, Nancy 31 n.15, 253 n.17

Gnade und Freiheit (*Grace and
Freedom*, Weltsch) 95, 232–3
grace 135–6, 182–3, 225, 232–4,
248
Grace and Freedom (Weltsch), *see
Gnade und Freiheit*
Great Risk, The (Brod), *see Das
grosse Wagnis*
Greek mythology 234, 248
Gross, Hans 53–5, 186
grosse Wagnis, Das (*The Great Risk*,
Brod) 95

Handbuch für Untersuchungsrichter
(Gross), *see Criminal
Investigation*
Hart, H. L. A. 250
Hegel, Georg Wilhelm Friedrich
80, 106 n.50

Heilmann, Hans 138–9, 150–1, 154 n.69, 156–7
Hermann, Elli (or Gabriele, born Kafka) 39, 56–9, 68, 179–83
Hermann, Karl, 39, 45
Hildebrand, Adolf 5
Hilsner, Leopold, the Hilsner case, the Polna case 195–8
Histoire de la littérature judéo-allemande (Pinès) 114 n.7, 248
Hobbes, Thomas 32–5, 32–5, 140, 146, 150, 157, 216, 257, *see also* state of nature
Holitscher, Arthur 169–72, 188
Human Condition, The (Arendt) 98, 160 n.90, 246 n.76

inspiration 126–8, 240
insurance, insurance institute, *see* Workmen's Accident Insurance Institute for the Kingdom of Bohemia
"Introduction *into* Politics" (Arendt) 98
irony 72–4, 105–6, *see also* aesthetic reflection

Janouch, Gustav 78–9, 82
Jäsche Logic (Kant) 71, 100–3
Jensen, Johannes V. 167–70, 188, 191
Jesénska, Milena 36–8, 197
Judaism 114–15, 232–4, 248, 252
justice 30–2, 45–6, 136, 174–6, 181, 231–4, 243
Justitia, goddess of Justice 45, 181–2, 204

Kafka, Elli, *see* Elli Hermann
Kafka, Franz, works
    "A Page from an Old Document" ("Ein altes Blatt") 138

Amerika: *The Missing Person* (*Der Verschollene*), 17, 38, 75, 167–93, 198, 202, 209, 213, 218, 225, 230, 249
"An Imperial Message" ("Eine kaiserliche Botschaft") 143
"The Appeal" ("Der Aufruf") 160–3
"Before the Law" ("Vor dem Gesetz") 31–2, 41, 54–5, 175, 219–20
"Blumfeld, an Elderly Bachelor" ("Blumfeld, ein älterer Junggeselle") 118
"Building the Great Wall of China" ("Beim Bau der chinesischen Mauer") 17, 96 n.23, 133–63, 247, 254
Castle, The (*Das Schloss*) 18, 88, 118, 136, 182, 224–44, 249
Diaries (*Tagebücher*) 1, 3–9, 11, 15–17, 39–45, 61–3, 67–8, 81–8, 108–9, 113–28, 189, 239–42
"Fellowship" ("Gemeinschaft") 17, 21–37, 41, 55, 92, 94, 234, 248
"Help Disabled Veterans! An Urgent Appeal to the Public" ("Helfet den Kriegsinvaliden! Ein dringender Aufruf an die Bevölkerung") 133–7
"In the Penal Colony" ("In der Strafkolonie") 35
"The Judgment" ("Das Urteil") 9–11, 13–15, 17, 26, 36, 63–71, 73–5, 78, 90, 103, 105, 107, 146, 168–70, 249
"Letter to his Father" ("Brief an den Vater") 45–8, 55–7, 159
Letters to Felice (*Briefe an Felice*) 67 n, 12, 103, 114, 134 n.3, 138 n.10

Letters to Friends Family, and Editors (*Briefe*) 7, 43 n.8, 56–9, 68, 81 n.59, 179–80, 183, 223–4, 244–6

Letters to Milena (*Briefe an Milena*) 36–8, 197

"The Metamorphosis" ("Die Verwandlung") 47, 76–9, 243

Office Writings (*Amtliche Schriften*) 133–7, 140 n.16, 145 n.38, 160–3

"On the Question of the Laws" ("Zur Frage der Gesetze") 18, 139, 247–58

"Researches of a Dog" ("Forschungen eines Hundes") 17, 85–100, 114, 118, 148–9, 249, 257

"Speech on the Yiddish Language" ("Rede über Jargon") 128–31

"The Stoker" ("Der Heizer") 17, 75–6, 173–90, 193, 209, 211, 213, 218, 230, 249

Trial, The (*Der Proceß*) 18, 23, 26 n.8, 31, 54, 197–219, 225, 242, 249

"Workforce without Possessions" ("Die besitzlose Arbeiterschaft") 2

Kafka, Hermann 45–7

Kafka, Ottla 139

"Kafkaesque" 38, 41, 55, 219, 252, 258

Kaiserpanorama 2–9, 16, 23, 42, 115, 137, 170–2, 191, 197, 200, 203, 240, 242

Kant, Immanuel 14, 48, 51–4, 56, 59, 71–2, 100–3, 236, 252, 258

Kassner, Rudolf 245 n.75

Kierkegaard, Søren 73, 79–81, 109, 221–4, 232, 243–6, 257

Kracauer, Siegfried 147 n.44

Kritik der reinen Vernunft (Kant), see *Critique of Pure Reason*

Kritik der Urteilskraft (Kant), see *Critique of Judgment*

law 24, 29–36, 41, 53–5, 62, 77–8, 91–5, 118–19, 157–8, 175–6, 201, 208–13, 218–20, 229–30, 241–2, 247–58, 201, 213, 241–2, 247–58

Lehmann, Hans-Thies 28 n.11, 75 n.42

Leviathan (Hobbes) 32–5, 140, 146, 157, 216, 257

Liska, Vivian 15, 27–8

"Little Ahasuerus" (Jensen) 167–70, 188, 191

Löwy, Yitzhak 15–17, 46–7, 99, 113–18, 128–31, 168, 189

Luther, Martin 187, 210–11

Marschner, Robert 135 n.7

Masaryk Tomas 196–8

Menke, Christoph 73, 106 n.50

Merchant of Venice, The (Shakespeare), 121–3, 189

mercy, *see* grace

Meschumed. Komisches Lebensbild mit Gesang und Tanz, Der (*The Apostate: A Comic Picture of Life with Song and Dance*, Scharkansky) 115–23, 126–7, 129, 189

metafiction, *see* self-reflection

Michelangelo 209

miracle 76–9, 98–102, 245

Mommsen, Theodor 33–5, 176–7, 230

Moses 187–8, 209–11, 218–20

Musil, Robert 75–6, 137

natural state, *see* state of nature

Nichomachean Ethics (Aristotle) 30

Notes from Underground
(Dostoyevsky) 21–4
*Notwendigkeit der Revision des
Polnaer Processes* (*The
Necessity of Revising the
Polna Trial*, Masaryk)
196–7

On the Citizen (Hobbes) 33 n.24,
150
"One Must Take the World as It
Is" (Kierkegaard) 221–5,
243–4

patriotism 135, 150
Paul the Apostle, St. 223, 225,
232
Pesikta Rabbati (midrash) 219–20
Pinès, Meyer Isser 114 n.7, 248
Plato 30, 81–4, 126
poetic justice 120
Poetics (Aristotle) 119, 122
Pogroms 167–8
polis and *oikos, see* public and
private
political moment 13–5, 29–30,
87–8, 95–100, 102–4, 123,
131, 138, 160–3, 193, 198,
219–20, 224–6, 243–6, 256–8,
see also Arendt, Hannah
Political Theology (*Politische
Theologie*, Schmitt) 34, 93
Politics (Aristotle) 185, 211
Politische Theologie (Schmitt), *see*
Political Theology
Prague Asbestos Works Hermann
& Co 17, 39–45, 47–55, 62–3,
78, 94, 146, 249, 255
private, *see* public and private
*protestantische Ethik und der "Geist"
des Kapitalismus, Die*
(Weber), *see* Protestant
Ethics
prosopopoeia 153–7

Protestant Ethics (Weber) 138
public and private, *polis* and *oikos*,
Amt and *Leben* 45, 48, 162,
174, 177–9, 181–3, 201, 206,
208, 228–9, 236

Rancière, Jacques 12–13, 49–50,
141 n.23, 152, 185 n.65
reflection, *see* aesthetic reflection
Republic, The (Plato), 81–4
Ricoeur, Paul 13 n.24, 102, 107
ritual murder cases 195–8
Robertson, Ritchie 239 n.65
Römisches Staatsrecht (*Roman
Constitutional Law*,
Mommsen) 33–5, 176–7, 230
Rousseau, Jean-Jacques 140 n.18,
146, 210–11

Scharkansky, Abraham 115, 189
schema, schematization 52–3, 101,
236, *see also* Kant
Schlegel, Friedrich 74
Schmitt, Carl 34–5, 93, 256
self-reflection, self-referentiality,
self-thematization,
metafiction 28, 74–5, 105
Shakespeare, William 113, 121–2,
189
Social Contract (Rousseau) 146
social imaginary 14, 25–6, 28, 32,
48–53, 59, 71, 75, 93–4, 101,
106, 123, 135–8, 145–6,
150–7, 185–6, 214, 236–7,
250–2, 254–7
Socrates, *see* Plato
Sokel, Walter 1–2, 11, 38, 73, 139
Spector, Scott 148 n.47
state of exception, emergency
powers, state of war, 32–4,
118, 183, 201
state of nature, natural state 27,
32–5, 146, 148, 150
stereoscope, *see* Kaiserpanorama

Streitbares Leben (*Embattled Life*,
    Brod) 113
Swift, Jonathan 56

Talmud 248
Taylor, Charles 14, 31, 49–51
Todorov, Tzvetan 77–9
tragic irony, *see* irony
transfiguration 101–3, 106–7,
    218–19
Trial, The (Welles) 219
Troeltsch, Ernst 232
Tucholsky, Kurt 76

Vogl, Joseph 158–60

Wagenbach, Klaus 240
Wagner, Benno, 134–8, 140–1

Walzel, Oskar 76
Weber, Max 138
Welles, Orson 219
Weltsch, Felix 95, 196, 232–3
Workmen's Accident Insurance
    Institute for the Kingdom of
    Bohemia 1, 13, 39, 134–8,
    160, 253–4

Yiddish 114–15, 128–31
Yiddish theater, Yiddish theater
    troupe 17, 46, 99–100,
    113–23, 128–9, 189

Ziolkowski, Theodore 26 n.8,
    55 n.44
Zionism 2, 86, 95, 108, 11–14, 128,
    140–1, 244

.

9 781501 378362

Tales of
Whortle Manor

Gripping yarns of golf by Patricia Armstrong
and others.

Edited by Ben Clingain

MAVERICK

First published in the UK 1995 by Maverick Sporting Publications
an imprint of Midlands MAC (PUBLISHING)
65 St. Giles Street, Northampton NN1 1JF
Tel: 01604-232262 Fax: 01604-232126

British Library Cataloguing-in-Publication Data.
A catalogue record for this title is available from the British Library.

ISBN 1 899078 02 9

Typeset by Midlands MAC
Northampton NN1 1JF

Printed and bound in Great Britain by
J. B. Offset Printers (Marks Tey) Ltd
Marks Tey, Colchester, Essex

WHY LIFE BEGINS ON THE FIRST TEE

Countless millions have wondered why golf has such a hold on us. When we get up at dawn in the rain to knock a little white ball around in the middle of nowhere, we must all seem pretty daft.

But we choose the stroll on a spring fairway over the raucous shouts of the football fan. We prefer to smell the flowers in the rough, where we spent a fair amount of time, rather than the hamburger and onions of a rugby ground. There is a tone to golf, a feeling of lasting worth, not transitory passion. If golf is a long hike as opposed to a quick fix, so be it. In today's world, you feel the need to fence off a few golf courses where there is some reward for skill and decency, and where the lout and the absurd hardly ever invade. It is cloistered, warm and familiar.

And once you start a love affair with golf, it's an obsession, a nagging sore if your swing's off, or a sweet life if your putting's in the groove. Those of us who participate in this love affair at any level never want it to end.

It's difficult to communicate this love to a non-believer. But, for those who hibernate during the winter, the feeling on the first tee of the first game in early spring is an experience to be treasured. The colours, the fresh smells, the white ball daring you to hit it properly, the intense joy of your first par after an idle winter, only other golfers understand this kind of love. That's why many believe that life begins on the first tee. And so, for all golf fanatics, we have created Whortle Manor Golf Club, and the characters therein. . .

The Whortle Manor club can be found in leafy Pottershire amid the rolling hills and majestic oaks dating from the time of Henry VIII. Whortle Manor itself, home of the eighth Earl of Perth, and an historic Jacobean house, can be seen from the course, and is set in two thousand acres of ancient unspoilt woodland, split in two by the upper reaches of the river Sal. The golf course is one of the prettiest in Europe and was created at the turn of the century by the then Earl and his friend Muir Ferguson of St Andrews who helped design the Windsor Castle course for King Edward VII. It boasts magnificent views while demanding thought and accuracy at every hole. Tree lined fairways with liberal sprinklings of gorse to trap the unwary and demanding approach shots to the narrow greens offer a stern challenge to golfers of all abilities.

Spring Lake, some 19 acres of rippling water, provides a stunning centrepiece for the course and comes into play on five holes. There are two old-fashioned, deep timbered bunkers - Braid's and Tolley's - which are famous throughout the golfing world, a deep pond beside the 13th green and a large mound fronting the 14th. With various other traps and hazards, Whortle Manor is not a course to be taken lightly......

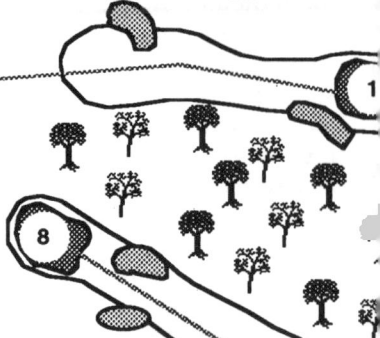

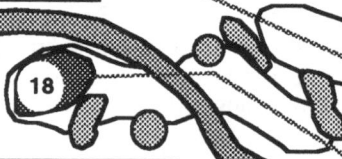

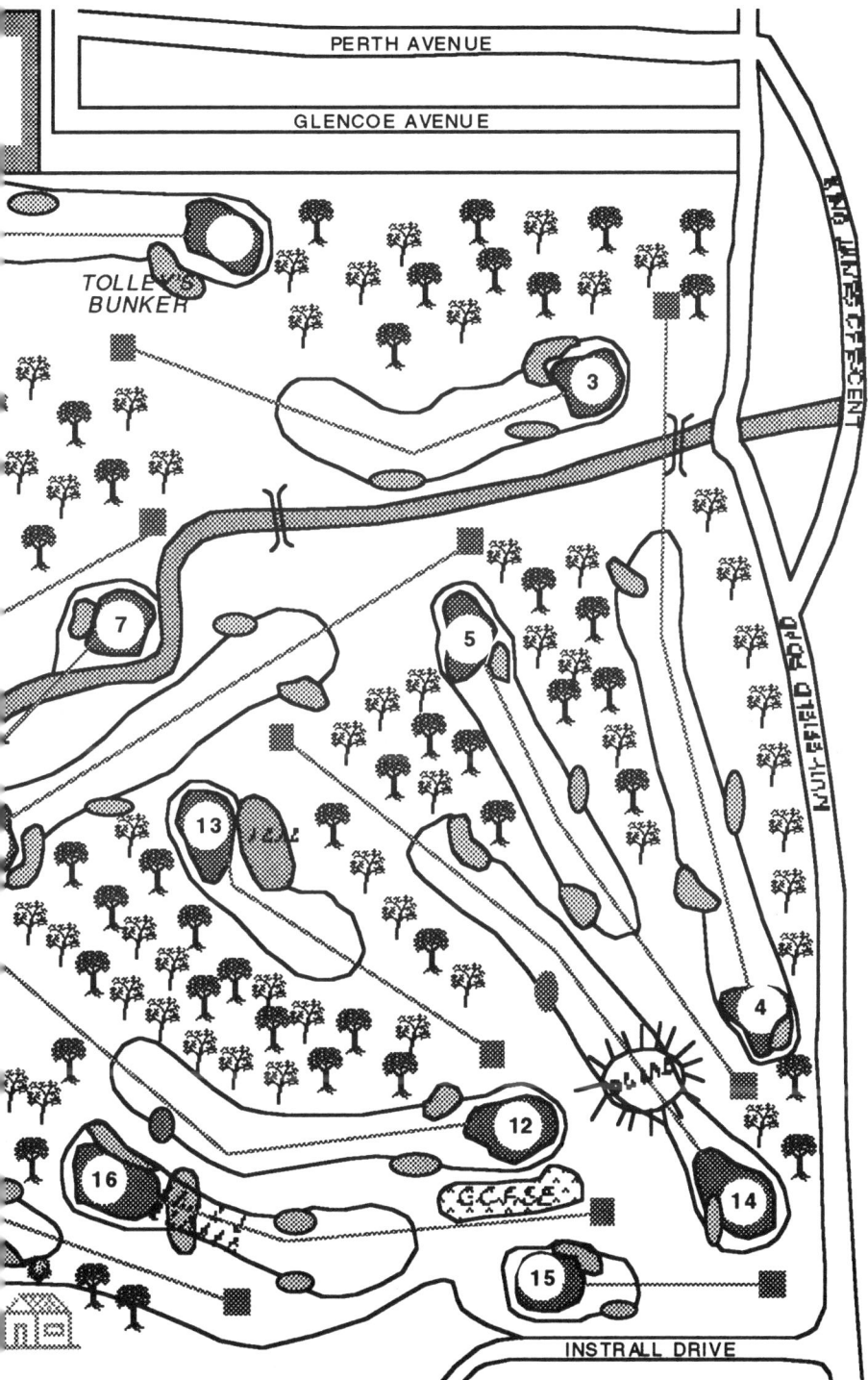

PERTH AVENUE

GLENCOE AVENUE

KING JAMES CRESCENT

TOLLE
BUNKER

3

MUIRFIELD ROAD

7

5

13

4

BLIND

12

16

G.C.F.S.E.

14

15

INSTRALL DRIVE

WHORTLE MANOR GOLF CLUB

S.S.S. 73

Competition.....................................

Player...

Date.................................   Exact Handicap..................   Strokes Received..................

Marker	Hole	White Tees	Par	Stroke Index	Player A	Player B	+/−/0
	1	415	4	7			
	2	351	4	15			
	3	403	4	9			
	4	568	5	3			
	5	422	4	6			
	6	474	4	1			
	7	175	3	5			
	8	540	5	11			
	9	318	4	18			
	OUT	3666	37				

Marker	Hole	White Tees	Par	Stroke Index	Player A	Player B	+/−/0
	10	370	4	14			
	11	180	3	8			
	12	473	4	2			
	13	301	4	17			
	14	515	5	10			
	15	178	3	13			
	16	390	4	12			
	17	524	5	4			
	18	377	4	16			
	IN	3308	36				
	OUT	3666	37				
	TOTAL	6974	73				

Marker's Signature.......................

Marker's Signature.......................

HANDICAP

SCORE

CONTENTS

JOSH'S WINTER *Patricia Armstrong* 9

EPIDEMIC *Patricia Armstrong* 13

THE MAN WHO KNEW TOO MUCH *Ben Clingain* 19

THE GREEN DIVIDE *K. D. Knight* 29

THE GRANDFATHERS' TANTALUS *Patricia Armstrong* 37

TAKE YOUR PARTNERS *Patricia Armstrong* 43

ON HIS OATH *John Pollitt* 49

METAMORPHOSIS *Patricia Armstrong* 55

EUNICE TAKES UP GOLF *Ben Clingain* 63

THE FIVE HOUR MAN *Patricia Armstrong* 71

THE VISIT *Patricia Armstrong* 77

THE TRIP TO SYDNEY *Philip Cannell* 83

GREAT BALLS OF FIRE *Tony Turner* 89

THE MATRIMONIAL BOWL *Patricia Armstrong* 95

THE COLONELS' TEWT *Patricia Armstrong* 103

THE VARDON CURE *Patricia Armstrong* 111

MISUSE OF THE PUTTER *Philip Cannell* 123

BLUE BUTTERFLIES *Patricia Armstrong* 129

A MATTER OF LUCK *Sybil Josty* 135

THE THURSDAY CLUB *Belinda Brett* 141

GOLF CAN BE MURDER *Don Powell* 151

THE COME UPPANCE *Philip Cannell* 155

THE GLASS EYE *Peter Sydenham* 163

THE THIRTEENTH HOLE *Terence Wright* 169

ABOUT THE AUTHORS 172

ACKNOWLEDGEMENTS 175

On the practice ground, Annie was a revelation

JOSH'S WINTER
Patricia Armstrong

When Josh Miller declared that the winter was going to be 'a reet booger' he was taken very seriously. Asked on what, exactly, he based his predictions he would simply say 'Ah knows.'

Local farmers always heeded Josh's long-range forecasts, experience having shown him to be far more accurate than any meteorologist. They arranged for extra deliveries of animal feed and got as much of their stock as possible under cover. Even the Council had gritting machines and snow ploughs serviced and at the ready.

Clive Daley had his own worries about prolonged bad weather. His reasons might have seemed trivial compared with the survival of livestock or getting to work, but they were of very real concern to him, for Clive was a golf nut of the first order.

He lived for the weekends, when he and his cronies played two rounds a day at Whortle Manor and perhaps a few extra holes after tea in the summer. His office carpet was of suitable texture for putting practice. The putter, and a shortened, weighted club - which he swung at regular intervals during the day - lived in a false filing cabinet. The notepad on his desk was always covered with little doodles of flags, and bunkers, and stick-men playing golf.

Over the years Clive's secretary had become so used to his antics that she scarcely noticed them. She was adept at keeping well out of the way of practice swings, and knew that on Monday mornings his temper was likely to be a bit uncertain if the weekend competitions had gone badly.

At home Clive had innumerable 'how to' books and videos, but if ever there was a whole weekend when he couldn't get out on the golf course he was like a caged animal.

One might imagine that with such single-mindedness, such dogged determination, Clive would be a first class golfer, but this was far from the truth. He had developed and nurtured a spectacular slice, so that he was a regular visitor to every hazard on the right of the fairways. He was not sought after as a foursome partner, and his handicap remained depressingly near the upper limit. However, in spite of all these vicissitudes he remained dedicated to the game.

Concerned about the bad weather report, he arranged a consultation with Josh, which took place in The Three Bells in Winster. This business could not be rushed, the sage being a dour character with a capacity for the local ale that had seen many a good man under the table.

After a full hour Clive was finally getting somewhere:

'Bad, you say, Josh?'

'Aye.'

'When, about, would you say?'

'Come January.'

'How long d'you reckon it'll last?'

There was a long pause before Josh pronounced the dreadful verdict. 'Weeks,' he said.

Annie Daley should have heard warning bells when her husband arranged an ad hoc meeting with members of his regular fourball and Scottie McLeod, the club Assistant Professional. As she dispensed coffee and sandwiches she was aware of an air of suppressed excitement, and wondered vaguely what they were up to. When they went to measure the cellar it finally dawned on her what they intended to do.

'An indoor golf school,' Clive confirmed. 'Just think, I'll be able to practice at home. The boys will help to set it up, in return for being able to use it themselves, of course.'

Within a week the cellar was ready. Scottie supplied practice balls and heavy rubber matting. Mirrors on stands were bought from an old-fashioned gentleman's outfitters. Great folds of netting hung from the ceiling, and extra lighting and electric fires were placed strategically.

It began to snow on the evening of the 4th of January, and for many weeks there was no let-up in the big freeze. Josh's reputation was enhanced and all contingency plans for man and beast ran smoothly.

The converted cellar was a hive of activity every evening and at weekends, Clive and his friends taking it in turn to hit balls into the net. It was judged a huge success and one of Clive's better ideas.

In an idle moment, when he had gone one morning to hit some balls in the cellar to keep his hand in, Scottie McLeod said to Annie: 'Haven't you ever thought of taking up golf yourself?'

'Gracious no,' she laughed. 'One addict in the family is quite enough. Anyway, I'd be bored paralytic with all that technical stuff. Clive is always tinkering with his grip, or making adjustments to his stance, or fretting about his putting stroke. It would drive me mad. I couldn't be bothered with worrying where the club was at the top of the backswing and all that nonsense.'

Scottie said it was a pity, because she looked athletic and he knew she had played hockey and tennis. She probably had a good eye for ball games. He'd always had an ambition to teach someone absolutely from scratch; someone who had never had a club in their hands, had never been on a golf course. Someone with no preconceived ideas, no ingrained faults to be ironed out. With the indoor net it seemed the ideal opportunity.

Annie really wasn't interested. Now that the children had left home she had plans for her spare time, which did not include stupid games. However, it seemed churlish not to humour Scottie, so she agreed to have just a couple of swings.

He showed her how to grip the club, and demonstrated with a seven iron how to hit the ball.

The first time Annie looked up too soon and missed completely. The next few balls shot off at odd angles, but then she connected with one which flew straight into the net with a most satisfying 'thunk'.

An hour later she was exhausted, but hooked. Scottie called a halt; he didn't want Annie getting blisters from the unaccustomed grip, nor did he want her so tired that she couldn't concentrate. 'Little and often,' he told her. He promised to return the next morning with some gloves and suitable clubs - there was always a good selection of ladies clubs in the 'reject bin' in the pro's shop at Whortle Manor - and to give her another lesson.

After that Annie crept down to the cellar at every available opportunity. She devoured golf books and magazines, put Clive's teaching videos on slow motion to see every nuance of the experts' swings, and made a long list of check-points. She studied the rules, moved furniture and putted across the sitting room. She chipped into a basket.

Scottie was astonished at her progress, and at the intensity with which she approached the game. Washing, ironing and hovering were all done to a mantra: 'Slow -and smooth-and wait- and SWISH.

Annie longed for the thaw so that she could get out to the practice ground, see the ball soar into the air and feel proper grass under her feet. Scottie could hardly contain himself. 'Ye'll go through the ladies' section like a hot knife through butter,' he told her. 'Ye've the bonniest swing I've ever seen.'

Clive, strictly forbidden to interfere with Scottie's experiment, felt left out of things and became morose and dismissive. With ill-concealed resentment he told Annie how much more difficult it was on the course, where one had to contend with wind and rain and dubious lies.

'And anyway,' he said spitefully, 'Forty plus is too late to start playing any sport, except perhaps bowls.'

Stung, Annie retorted that she was not decrepit yet. She could hit the ball perfectly well and Scottie was very pleased with her.

'Wait 'till spring,' she said. I'll show you.'

Bent on having the last word, Clive said loftily: 'Oh, it's easy enough indoors, in neutral conditions, on square mats, with mirrors, but it's an entirely different proposition when it's the real thing.'

Josh's winter finally relinquished its hold at the end of March. Snow melted, lambs were born, birds sang, and Annie sallied forth.

On the practice ground, she was a revelation. All the indoor teaching paid off.

In no time at all she was in the Silver Division, and progressed steadily to a single figure handicap, collecting prizes and acclaim as she went. Scottie was delighted; he was hailed as the local guru because of what he had done for Annie, and ladies flocked from other clubs for lessons. His only regret was that he hadn't had her much earlier. No doubt about it, she'd have been a County player, probably an International.

But Clive was not happy. Some thought he was jealous of Annie's success, and it is certainly true he was offended when she criticised his swing. He complained that the house, which used to shine, with not a speck of dust anywhere, now looked rather neglected; in the once-immaculate garden weeds abounded, and there were ugly divot marks on the lawn where Annie practised pitching.

The Daleys used to entertain a lot, but then Annie said she hadn't time to waste in the kitchen when she could be out playing golf.

Josh's winter has already passed into legend; it really was a record-breaker. The last time I saw Clive I asked him how his golf was going.

'Given it up,' he said with some asperity. 'I'm much too busy at work. Have to travel abroad a lot these days. And anyway, one addict in the family is quite enough.'

EPIDEMIC
Patricia Armstrong

When Archie Lewis told me he was retiring, I said it was bound to be a bit of a wrench, leaving Whortle Manor after all those years as a Professional.

'In a way it will be, Doctor,' he said. 'But I've been here nigh on 40 years, and to be honest it's time I went. Things are so different now. In my day we were craftsmen as well as golfers. We made clubs and took pride in our work. Now it's all carbon shafts and metal heads. Machine made.'

I remember Archie's workshop. Obsolete now, of course, but it seemed a magical place then. My father took me there when I was 12 and said diffidently to Archie, 'Boy needs a proper set of clubs. Can you fix him up?'

I was measured as well for those clubs as I would have been for a new suit. I can even recall the smell of Archie's workshop. There were bottles of varnish and glue, strips of leather for grips, and lead for weighting clubheads. He had blocks of persimmon and rows of shafts. His tools were arranged neatly, and on his workbench stood a newly finished club, beautifully whipped and polished.

'And then there's the teaching,' Archie said. 'Quite different now. All Method teachers. Takes them half-an-hour to dismantle a swing, and two years to put it back together again, in lessons at 20 quid a time.'

He reckoned television had a lot to answer for. People with the physique and co-ordination of Charlie Chaplin expected to be taught to play like Seve Ballesteros.

I laughed. 'I remember asking you how to get more length once. You told me it was easy: I should do as James Braid had suggested and hit the ball a bloody sight harder.'

Archie's teaching had been basic, but effective. No frills. No gimmicks. You swung up past the right ear going back and past the left ear going through, and kept looking at the ball while you did it.

We gave Archie a good send off. At his farewell party he was presented with a handsome cheque, and the Chairman made a fulsome speech. He said Archie had served the Club faithfully and well for many years and would be greatly missed. We were reminded that he had played regularly in the Open Championship in his heyday, finishing respectably in the middle of the field on each occasion. The Chairman said Archie's retirement marked the end of an era. They didn't make them like that any more. He was irreplaceable.

Two days later Archie's replacement arrived.

The Committee were pleased with their choice. They had selected a youngish man - fit, energetic and full of ideas. He had spent time with one of the leading instructors and was keen to teach his unique method, which was guaranteed to improve anyone's golf. Asked why he wanted to be Professional at our Club, he said he had been attracted by the excellence of the course, and by the first-class practice ground; ideal for teaching.

And so Simon Warrener was installed. Before long he had persuaded the Committee to invest in a covered bay - complete with heating and lighting - at one end of the practice ground so that he could teach in all weathers. He set up video equipment. Pupils were encouraged to bring their own cassette, which they could take home for further study.

Juniors were taught for a nominal fee. High handicappers of both sexes had group tuition. Our more promising single-figure golfers had individual coaching. Simon and his two specially trained assistants were kept busy from dawn to dusk. He was a most industrious new broom.

Mention the word Epidemic and people immediately think of influenza, or measles, or something more esoteric - like cholera or smallpox. In fact, many quite common minor epidemics are mechanical in origin. Although not life-threatening, they can be painful and incapacitating, and it is important to spot the cause as quickly as possible. Every suburban doctor has had to treat outbreaks of 'tennis elbow' in the hedge-trimming season. But things are not always so clear-cut.

Will Pargetter was the first to consult me with a sore shoulder. 'More than sore, damned painful, Doctor,' he complained. 'Can't comb my hair, or even put a jacket on in any comfort.'

He swore he hadn't been doing anything unusual. Certainly he'd been playing a lot of golf recently, but then he always did.

Will was only the first. During the next few weeks my partners and I saw first a trickle and then a torrent of painful shoulders. We became glib at explaining how the small tendon lying over the shoulder joint was in contact with both the top of the humerus and part of the shoulder blade above, and how normally it slid quite happily between the two when the arm moved. However, if it was bruised by unaccustomed, vigorous movements, or by injury, it became inflamed and swollen so that it hurt when rubbed between the bones. Treatment was rest and application of ice.

We had to order a large supply of slings, and the local chemist got hold of some American made, artificial ice packs which, kept in the freezer, could be used repeatedly. They sold like hot cakes.

My partners and I, all keen golfers, met to discuss the possible causes of the unusual epidemic. One thing was clear: the victims were also all golfers. Even unable to play, they did not stay away from the Club. Wearing their slings, they sat about, gloomily discussing their symptoms and comparing progress. Doctors were not very popular just then, and we tended to avoid the clubhouse.

One of the younger doctors remarked, 'Come to think of it, all these people seem to have been taking lessons. Perhaps we should investigate Simon Warrener's famous Method more closely.'

For some reason it was suggested that I was just the person to conduct a little Market Research. I was elected to go for a lesson to gather data at first hand. Reluctantly I booked a time and went.

On my arrival, Simon said, 'Let's see you hit a few shots first, Doctor.'

Self-consciously I demonstrated my narrow 'staying in the barrel' swing which had served me so well over the years, propelling the ball fairly straight down the middle.

'Good gracious, Doctor,' he said, tutting with disapproval. 'You're all stuck. Come on, SEPARATE. Move the arms. Away. Away. Stretch them out.'

15

The new swing method was undoubtedly vigorous. I was exhorted to 'Get The Arms Away From The Body. Separate.' Simon was determined to get the left arm moving - something I had never attempted before. He insisted that although the body must turn to some extent, it did so only to make room for the wide arm swing.

It felt different, no doubt about it. My difficulty in making contact with the ball at all left Simon completely unfazed. As I topped and socketed he said, "Don't worry about where the ball goes. Just get those arms moving away from the body. SEPARATE."

My old, faithful, consistent swing was apparently Out. Gone was my wrist-cock, my nifty transference of weight. I was put into positions previously undreamed of, and at the end of half-an-hour I was exhausted. Simon invited me to see the video of myself performing these incredible movements, and he tried to make another appointment for the following week.

'Got to get you loosened up, Doctor,' he said enthusiastically. 'Might take a few lessons to get you sorted out, but we'll do it, don't worry.' Pleading that my own appointment book was back at the surgery, I told him I would ring about a further lesson. I was about to make my escape when he said, 'Pop into the shop before you go. I've got a marvellous teaching aid and some exercises you can do at home.'

And by God, he had. I seem to remember in the days of my extreme youth there was a vogue for swinging Indian Clubs. Simon had 'rediscovered' them. He had also produced a sheet of instructions and diagrams for their use, swinging and twirling the confounded things in the air.

I made no comment, just paid my money, collected a pair of Indian Clubs and the instructions, and mumbled something about trying them out later.

At lunchtime I met my partners to display the clubs and the exercise instructions. I also played them the first five minutes of the video showing Simon demonstrating his Method, before pocketing the tape so that they were spared the undignified spectacle of my lesson. 'There, gentlemen,' I said with some satisfaction. 'There is the cause of our epidemic.'

The cure was not so simple. Getting rid of a Professional is a tricky business. Fortunately the thing solved itself; Simon resigned of his own volition. His appointment book was no longer full; the practice ground was deserted. He soon applied for the post of Professional to a new club several hundred miles away, where he could expound his Method afresh. We gave him a sparkling reference to speed him on his way.

By pulling a few strings, I got myself on the Committee appointed to make the final selection for the post of our new Professional. We questioned the short-listed applicants closely about their teaching methods.

The one we liked best assured us he was a back-to basics sort of chap. A little old-fashioned perhaps, but he advocated using the big muscles of the body to get a really good turn. This generated centrifugal force without straining. The arms must remain connected. "Turn and Connection' were his watchwords. On no account must the arms be allowed to function independently.

This was music to our ears. We appointed him and he flourished. The practice ground was filled with golfers playing 9 iron shots with a towel across their chests, the ends under each armpit. Everyone seemed happy.

Will Pargetter was again the first to present with symptoms. 'Got terrible backache, Doctor,' he said. 'Never had backache in my life before.'

He denied doing too much gardening, or stooping, or lifting heavy weights. Yes, he had been having a few lessons from Andy Burrows, the new Professional, and very good he was too. None of that crippling arm stretching nonsense. Andy was a great body man. Made you practise with a towel tucked under each armpit. Really made you turn or you couldn't hit the ball.

It wasn't long before other members drifted into the surgery complaining of back pain.

I rang my friend, an orthopedic surgeon. 'Tell me where I can get a quick supply of good surgical corsets,' I said. 'I think we're about to have another epidemic.'

Stanley was a nightmare, and fast becoming the worst sort of bore

THE MAN WHO KNEW TOO MUCH

Ben Clingain

I was sitting with Colonel Fortescue in front of the cosy fire after a morning round. It had been a crisp fresh October day and I had broken 100 for the second time in the week, thanks to a twelve foot putt at the last. It was an unexpected treat for me to be able to play during the week, but the wretched rail strike made a nonsense of trying to battle with the M1 and the convoys of trucks carrying cod roe and the cars full of double glazing salesmen. Railtrack, or whatever they were called these days, had really botched it up this time. But I shouldn't complain, I was getting to play on a weekday. To make it even better, I had beaten Alan Upwood, my bank manager and taken delivery of my winnings, a Topflite Magna ball, guaranteed to give me even greater distance, not to mention accuracy. As you can imagine, I was telling old Fortescue all about it when a breathless girl of wondrous looks rushed in and kissed the old buzzard on both cheeks. 'I beat him again with a bogey on the 18th,' she said in obvious rapture. A tall, burly young man, obviously her victim, joined us. He was smiling broadly, unlike anyone who's ever been beaten by a slip of a girl. And by a bogey into the bargain.

Fortescue did the honours introducing Stanley Clarke and his wife Nancy, who were quite charming. They were clearly captivated with each other and, they said, played golf together as often as possible. 'Her chip shots are usually unpredictable, but today they were quite unbelievable,' he beamed. We spent a happy ten minutes talking about their game and then they went off hand in hand for lunch.

'What a lovely couple,' I remarked. 'But one thing puzzles me.'

'What's that?'

'Well, he seems very taken with her.'

'He is.'

'And they've not been married long.'

'No, a few years. And they had the reception here in the club one Friday.'

'I've not seen them around.'

'You only play weekends. They play twice a week, usually on Mondays and Wednesdays.'

'But. .' I paused. 'But. . . why is he so delighted when he's been beated by a mere girl? And by a last-hole bogey, too.'

'Well,' said Fortescue, 'he wasn't always like that. In fact, he was really quite insufferable at times. Thinking about it,' he leaned back in his chair, 'he was probably the most boring, insufferable, pompous ass in the whole of Whortle Manor. And all because of those damn lessons.'

'Lessons?' I gasped. 'You mean golf lessons?'

'No, not quite. I'd call them memory lessons.'

'Memory lessons?'

Fortescue motioned to the steward and held out his glass for another gin. 'Ah, yes the memory lessons. It happened like this. . . .

Stanley Clarke was one of life's great golfers. Not that is to say, one of the greatest players of the game, but one to whom golf was an adventure. He never knew where his ball was going to end up. He'd play some shots that Faldo would have been proud of, then follow it with a duffer. He'd sink an eighteen foot putt, then miss an eighteen incher for the match. Playing with him wasn't just an adventure, it was an experience. And he had such enthusiasm for the game, it infected everyone. Stanley was an editor with the family book company, which specialised in military history books. He was especially kind to the old colonels who were members, bringing them the latest books on military manoeuvres and the like. His big problem, as he would admit with a grin, was his memory. He'd often forget his tee time, and the delightful Nancy, then his fiancee, often chided him for forgetting their dates altogether. There wasn't a red-blooded man in the club who would have dared forget a date with such a beautiful girl. But somehow Stanley's engaging manner made one forget his faults.

The beginning of the change came when Nancy persuaded him to go to the theatre where Leslie Welch, the world-famous Memory Man, was giving a performance. Stanley was enthralled.

'I just couldn't believe it,' he told me the next evening at the club. 'There must be a way I can improve my memory.'

'Look no further,' I said, showing him an advertisement in the Daily Telegraph. He read the ad, mesmerised. IMPROVE YOUR MEMORY, it read. YOU'LL BE A NEW MAN, it went on, promising no more missed appointments, and the ability to quote whole passages of Shakespeare without notes. For only £4.99 they would send full details and a booklet. 'I'll send off for it straight away.' He rose suddenly in haste. 'I forgot, I'm supposed to be at Nancy's parents for dinner,' and rushed away.

I was away in the Algarve for a month and consequently didn't see him again for some time. The change was marked, or so Nancy told me. She came into the dining room, sat down and burst into tears. 'I'm calling it off,' she cried.

'What?'

'The engagement, of course. He's insufferable.'

'Who?'

'Stanley. He's changed.'

'In what way?'

'This morning,' she began, 'I was having trouble with my driver. Stanley began quoting verbatim from Alex Hay's book, "Confidence on the Tee." Then my putting was a bit off and he started to quote from "Swing Through the Putter" by Ian Woosnam.'

'Well, perhaps he was only trying to help,' I offered.

She looked at me in desperation.

'Forty pages of Alex Hay, however nice he may be, and twenty pages of Ian Woosnam is not my idea of helping. And we held up two fourballs behind till he'd finished reciting.'

I thought about the problem. 'Would it help if I played a round with him tomorrow?'

'Oh, would you? It would be such a help.'

'Shall we say ten, and make sure he doesn't forget?'

'Forget? Forget? That's the problem. He doesn't forget anything now. I'll caddy for you if you like.'

I gladly accepted the offer and arrived on the tee in good time. They were already there, and I could see that all was not well. Nancy looked strained, and as I drew closer, I could hear Stanley.

'And did you know that last winter in Torquay they had to close a course for five weeks. Do you know how many gallons of rain fell in that time?'

Nancy looked ashen. 'Well, I'll tell you. 63.8 MILLION GALLONS. How about that?'

'How do you know that?' she asked.

'The International Golf Almanack. We produced it. It'll be in the shops soon. It's a work of genius.'

Stanley turned his attention to his drive, after welcoming me. I raised an eyebrow, nodding at him. 'I only said it looked like rain,' she whispered, 'then he gave me a lecture about last winter and how wet it was.'

I began to understand the severity of the problem when I hooked my 3-wood off the tee into the nearby trees.

'Where you went wrong there,' offered Stanley, 'was allowing your right heel to point down the fairway at the top of your backswing. Also your left knee collapsed too soon. And your right shoulder wasn't quite at right angles.'

'Good heavens,' I gasped, 'how can you see all that?'

'It's in Nick Faldo's book, "The Essential Golf Guide for Sun Readers", just published by Clarke and Clarke. I proof read it some months ago. I

21

must say Faldo's a very decent chap, offered to give me some private lessons. We met last week and I was able to straighten out his putting problems.'

'His putting problems?' I wasn't aware that Nick Faldo was experiencing any problems on the putting green.

'Well, he does have a tendency to stop his motion as he strikes the ball. I told him to carry on the stroke till he gets to nine o'clock.'

'Morning or afternoon?' I enquired.

Stanley rolled his eyes toward the sky. 'Don't be frivolous. The swing is like a clock, and so is the putting motion. . . .'

Ten minutes later, he was quoting from the David Leadbetter book, "How to Modify Your Swing if You're Over Sixty", as we finally reached the first green. This, I discovered, was to be published by Stanley's company, Clarke and Clarke, in a few months.

On the short seventh, I was unsure which iron to use. 'You're my caddy, what do you think?' I asked Nancy.

'Seven, I think,' she ventured.

'Six,' snapped Stanley. 'Wind against from the left, you've got to be long on this hole. Short is touble. The essence of good caddying is to know the course and to be able to assess the conditions, especially wind speed, carry, and the strength of the player.'

'Good Heavens, how do you know all this?'

'We're publishing Fanny Sunesson's book soon, "My Life with Nick." I proof read it last month. I was able to give her some advice on her back problems, because of the size of Nick's bag.'

'How do you know about back problems?'

'We're publishing Doctor Vernon Coleman's book, "How to Play golf Without Suffering a Bad Back", any day now. Did you know that most back problems are caused through incorrect posture? Even sitting at the dining table properly can help. And pulling a golf trolley must be done a certain way, did you know that?'

'No, but I'm sure you're going to tell us,' I muttered darkly.

And he did, at length, great length. I wondered if there was any subject he didn't know a lot about. It was now obvious to me that Nancy's problem was practically unsolvable.

At the ninth green, which we reached three hours later, I begged off, pleading a cold.

'Your blood thins down when you visit hotter countries, like Spain and Portugal,' Stanley advised as I took my leave. 'This is on account of the colour of the dominant corpuscles, which are mostly. . .' His voice faded as I quickly hurried into the clubhouse, and a stiff gin and tonic. Perhaps a double.

Now one of our members, Doctor Puri, is an eminent psychologist. She spent many years in the United States, and usually gives her advice without what her fellow-Americans call "bull". She happened to be in the lounge and I explained the problem in as few words as possible and she listened intently, making notes all the while.

'I'll need to think about this a little,' she finally said, ' but it's similar to the Extremities Theory, expounded by Professor Broady of NYU a few years ago. Basically it's the conversion from one extreme in behaviour to another. The simplest example is the man whose wife leaves him. He goes from a twice a day shaver to a once a week shaver, from a snappy dresser to a slob. Then he meets someone else and reverts back as quickly as the first time. Or the absent-minded professor, which is perhaps more relevant here. This type can remember college lectures from 20 years ago, or what was said at a conference back in 1973, but ask him where his car keys are, or the date of his wife's birthday, and he's stumped.'

'That sounds like Stanley in reverse. His memory was always bad until he took that memory course.'

'What memory course?'

'The one advertised in the Telegraph. It's in every week.'

'And that's what's caused the change?'

'As far as I can see. He can remember passages of Nick Faldo's book, and half a dozen other blasted books his company's producing. Recites golf lessons at the drop of a hat. And the silly blighter has started holding golf clinics on every tee. If you shank, he'll tell you what to do. If you talk about the weather, he'll tell you how many millions of gallons fell on some Godforsaken place near Torquay.'

Doctor Puri smiled sadly. 'I can't offer you any hope. If it's the Extremities Theory, there's no known cure.'

'No cure?'

'None.'

A little while later, Nancy joined me, as I was on my fourth gin and tonic.

'Now do you see?' she said desperately.

'I do. He's become a nightmare. But there's no cure.' I told her of my discusion with Doctor Puri.

'No cure?'

'Nothing. Psychiatry has no known remedy. Where's Stanley?'

Her eyes filled. 'He had an important meeting in the City. Then he's off to Frankfurt for the Book Fair.'

I bought her a stiff brandy and Moussec. She needed it, and shortly after she went home, as if the weight of the world was on her shoulders.

23

I didn't see her again for almost a month. But Stanley was everywhere. If a member was there to be upset, Stanley upset him. His newly found confidence extended to his golf, and he was now a self-confessed expert on the Vardon Grip, graphite shafts and the relative merits of the new Ping Zing metal woods. He had attacked the Greens committee for daring to reject his proposal to change the character of the 18th hole and introduce an island green.

'The finishing hole is all important,' he'd thundered at a meeting. 'It must be memorable. We can engineer it so that the green can be a floating island, to be moved every week. There is a book on the subject. . ..' And he'd talked for ten minutes non stop without notes. He was a nightmare, and fast becoming the worst sort of bore. On the tee he'd lecture his opponents, so much so that nobody would play with him. Nancy had begun staying away from the club, feigning headaches.

Unfortunately, she was committed to play with Stanley in the annual mixed partners championships in a few days. There was no way out of that one, and when she asked me to walk around with them, I reluctantly agreed, only out of thought for her sanity. She had lost all her natural ebullience, and was looking pale and drawn.

The day dawned, bright and frosty. Stanley and Nancy were drawn first to play, and a small crowd had gathered on the tee. Nancy was limbering up with her three wood. Her swing, even to my eyes, looked stiff and awkward. She had the look of a golfer who wanted to be somewhere else, anywhere else. Stanley looked at her thoughtfully.

'Darling,' he intoned. I knew the sound, as did all the long suffering Whortle members. A lecture on the relative merits of her stance and address position was about to commence. 'Darling, you're not applying the dynamics of golf properly. Your address position is all wrong. Look at your feet. . .'

He moved behind her as she swung the three wood, too close, as her near perfect backswing - a touch too fast, I must confess - came around swiftly and caught him just above the left ear. He crumpled to the ground as Nancy shrieked and the busy throng of members looked on in silent horror.

Despite the feelings that had festered in the past few months that the only way to cure Stanley was to kill him, we rushed to the poor man's rescue. Not a muscle moved, not a twitch twitched. For the first time in ten or more weeks, Stanley Clarke was silent.

His voice was still, and a trickle of blood could be seen heading due south toward his ear lobe.

'I've killed him. My God, I've killed him,' shrieked Nancy.

Now all policemen and army personnel above the rank of major know that the first thing you do at the scene of an accident is to remove, forcibly if necessary, all the hysterical women. Only then is it deemed safe to check the corpse. Once Nancy and three other distressed women, including the Lady Captain, had been escorted to the clubhouse, and an ambulance called, we turned our attention to poor Stanley. The tickle of blood had turned east, away from his ear lobe, and was heading for his chin. A good sign. I checked his pulse. Weak. Still no sound came from him, another good sign, many of his erstwhile victims would have said.

But golfers are basically kind hearted. They hold few grudges, and when it is a matter of life or death, they all tend to remember bits of their St John's Ambulance training.

As I placed him in the recovery position, helped by Chris Ross, he groaned. A good sign.

'What make are Nancy's woods?' I asked no-one in particular. 'And don't touch the evidence.'

'Ram Tour steel shafts,' I was told, as the murder weapon still lay nearby.

'Good.' I said smugly.

'What difference does that make?' young Ross asked.

'Simple. If they'd been McGregor or Cobra with graphite shafts, or, God forbid, a Wilson Firestick, they might have caused untold severe contusions.'

The murder victim groaned again, then sat up, shaking his head.

'What happened?' His voice was back, and a dozen Whortle members groaned too, for by this time the crowd had swollen.

'Stand back. Give him air.' The ambulance had arrived, and the professionals had taken over. We amateurs stood well back as the unfortunate was loaded onto a stretcher and carefully inserted into the ambulance. Apart from two words, Stanley Clarke hadn't uttered a word in fifteen minutes. The ambulance drove off, narrowly missing churning up the putting green, as the Captain said, 'Well we must get on. I suppose I'll have to scratch Stanley and Nancy.'

We all supposed so too, and the competition resumed. I made my way slowly to the clubhouse, to find Nancy still in distress, and I drove her to the hospital.

An hour later, he'd had X-rays and scans, but pronounced alive, and, apart from a headache and a slight cut, able to go home.

'But what happened,' he said, still dazed.

'I hit you, my darling.'

'When?'

'Beside the first tee.'

'What were we doing there?'

'Playing in a competition.'

'Which one?'

Nancy described what had happened. She was full of remorse and abject apology. It was obvious Stanley had no recollection whatever about the attempted murder. They took him home and put him to bed. Nancy stayed with him and read him stories and chatted. She had been warned to try to keep him awake for a few hours and not to let him sleep for a few hours. Mild concussion could be dangerous, hardly ever fatal.

A few days later, they came to join me for lunch at the club. Stanley had made a remarkable recovery, and Nancy looked relaxed and happy.

'We want you to be the first to know. We've set the date,' she said.

'We thought we'd have the reception at the club. Will you come?' said Stanley.

Considering the events of the past few months, I was surprised they were still engaged. As lunch progressed, I began to lose the feeling that I had come to expect every time Stanley opened his mouth. In a word, dread. There was no lecture on the origin of the mackerel, or the peculiar mating habits of the Atlantic prawn, or the family history of the Morellis who supplied the club with ice cream. In short, it was a relaxed and pleasant lunch. Everything a lunch should be, when confronted with two thoroughly nice people in love.

'We thought we'd quite like nine holes this afternoon," said Stanley. "Would you like to join us?'

The dread returned. Nancy pressed me, and I agreed.

Stanley seemed very relaxed on the first tee, the scene a few days before of his attempted murder. His drive was straight, and found the centre of the fairway, mine was shorter, but equally straight. We walked to the ladies' tee and Nancy topped her drive and it landed 30 yards away.

'Bad luck, darling,' said Stanley, sympathetically.

Stanley's second shot to the green caught on the wind and ended up in the bunker, mine found the green. 'Good shot,' applauded Stanley.

He took three to get out of the bunker, and the last stroke skied the ball out of bounds on the left.

'Watch out, Glencoe Avenue. I'll get your windows next time,' he grinned ruefully.

Nancy in the meantime had finally reached the green in six, and three putted for a nine. I had managed a bogey five.

On the second tee, we had both managed respectable drives, but Nancy looked uncertain. 'I'm not hitting my three wood very well, Colonel. What do you think I should use?'

I had to smile. She had used it well enough a few days before on the side of Stanley's head.

'Darling. Guess what?' Stanley's brow was furrowed.
'What?'
'I've just remembered.'
'What?'
'We're due at your parents for tea at five.'
'No, darling, that's tomorrow.'
'Oh good. Thank heavens for that.'

For the rest of the round, Stanley's game resembled Seve Ballesteros' at his best. Without the recovery shots, of course. He was hitting the ball well, though erratically, visited the woods often and dipped his ball more than once into Spring Lake. He was, in a word, the same old disastrous Stanley, the delightful scatterbrain that everyone at Whortle knew and loved. Over the next few weeks members who had sworn never to play with him again sought him out for a game.

They were married some months later, with the reception at the club. Stanley, of course, had forgotten the notes for his speech and had to adlib to great applause. Doctor Puri had missed the great change due to a prolonged lecture tour in the United States. I related the story to her one evening at the club, and she was relieved that it had all turned out so well.

'I'd have preferred a scientific solution,' she said, 'but I suppose a crack on the head is as good a result as you could have hoped for. The only trouble now is, you'll have to take good care to see he gets no more blows to the head.'

'You mean... you can't mean?"
'I do.'
'Oh no.'
'Oh yes...'

Until her 46th birthday, Betty remained indifferent to the whole idea of golf

THE GREEN DIVIDE
K. D. Knight

'Isn't that Betty Walker, the Ladies champion?' I asked Colonel Fortescue, as we watched an attractive lady cross to the putting green.

'Yes, she's been Ladies Champion now for two years in a row', said the Colonel. 'A very fine golfer, too. That's her husband Goerge, with her. He caddies for her every time she plays in a major tournament. He's found a new lease of life, went through a sticky patch a few years ago with his heart. Fit as a fiddle now.'

I looked over towards the couple. 'Is he caddying today?' 'No. She's playing with a couple of her Children's Society Committee, Rita Wilson and Peggy Leno. But she calls George her good luck charm. When he caddies, she wins. But it wasn't always like that.'

'What do you mean?'

Colonel Fortescue leaned back in his chair. I knew the signs. There was a story coming up, so I offered to replenish his gin and tonic. He nodded and I signalled for the waiter.

'Well' he began, settling back in the comfortable armchair,

'Until her forty-sixth birthday Betty's idea of exercise had been to take a walk to the bottom of the garden and peg the washing to the rotary clothes line. Though that is not to imply that she was an idler. In fact George, her husband of twenty-five years, had always been keen to entertain clients at home, rather than at a fancy restaurant, so that he could show her off to a wider audience. No, Betty's aversion to organised exercise had been merely that it appeared to be an indulgence, an activity only to be participated in by women with nothing more substantial to occupy their minds.

The change that unexpectedly took place was brought about simply. George had been too busy and too flummoxed, to know what to buy Betty for her forty-sixth birthday and their 25th anniversary. In the end, and in total exasperation, he took the advice of his accountant partner and surprised her with a set of golf clubs.

If he had not been under so much strain at the time perhaps he would have doubted the wisdom of such advice. But with the hours ticking by and a sports shop so close to his office, it seemed to George

29

a logical solution to the annual dilemma.

And so began the train of events that led to Betty viewing life in a different way and for George to wonder if his wife was the same woman he had wooed, doggedly courted and finally won, all those years ago.

Enforced early retirement, due to heart trouble a year later, (angina had been diagnosed), rendered George only fit for gardening duties and light manual work. Once the initial nursing stage was over, he was now under and around Betty's feet all day. Aware of the tribulations that such situations had caused to the marriages of friends and acquaintances, George decided that it would be beneficial to them both if Betty redeemed the neglected birthday present from the storage space in the garage and gave the game of golf a chance.

So the tartan bag was brought once more into the light and its contents, virginal and dulled from non-use, were polished and made presentable - though Betty remained indifferent to the whole idea. She suspected that George had an hidden agenda, and that he wanted her out of the way because of some nefarious scheme, doubtless concerning food that was not on his prescribed diet or involving actions that he knew she would frown upon. So despite her own need to shed poundage she could see no semblance of merit in this.

To his credit George tried every argument to persuade her, though it should be added that he did not believe for one moment that Betty would have the slightest aptitude for golf. His motivation was one of devotion towards their marriage, coupled with a wish for her to be independent in case his angina overcame him and left her prematurely a widow. And the golf clubs were there, taking up space and unused.

He informed her that Lady Antler, a woman whom Betty admired and considered well worth imitating on other matters, played golf regularly. He told her that the mysterious Persian women Zuleika Trout, who adorned the village with her Porsche, fur coats, diamonds and plentiful supply of young escorts, dined most evenings at the golf club. He also reminded her how often in the past her closest friends Bernice and Isla had tried to tempt her into joining them for a round.

Finally Betty decided that perhaps George's heart was in the right place after all, even if it was only kept functional by a daily intake of pills and bi-monthly monitoring, so she arranged for her friends to take her on their next jaunt to the course.

What no one could have imagined, especially Betty herself, was that a rare and wonderful talent had lain dormant, and when the club professional recognised this, the sight so captivated his imagination that he instantly vowed to return himself to a temperate and sober way of life. Betty possessed a completely natural swing. So natural, that after only half a dozen lessons she had no further need of professional advice, and he sadly reaquainted himself with the bottles of Johnnie Walker and Jack Daniels that once cured him of the yips and twitches.

Her friends were staggered, and they gave her loads of encouragement. She spent more and more time at the club. So, with a startling switch in their roles, George obediently swallowed his medication and perfected the use of hoe, secateurs and sit-on mower, whilst his dear wife dedicated herself to perfecting her approach shots to the greens and, because it was a real weakness, the bane of many beginners, her putting. This situation existed quite cozily for twelve months; George content with the excellence of his horticulture and Betty happy with her sport. But as she became more and more afflicted by the torturous golfing bug, and progressed from playing one round once a week to playing whenever she could get a tee-off time in the busy club schedule, the more excluded from her new world George became.

Spring, summer and autumn kept George's frustrations at bay. The garden during these seasons demanded so much of his energy. He kept thinking how much his life had changed, but winter denied him the opportunity to work off the feelings of neglect that pulled and tugged at his every fibre. His love for his wife weakened to suspicion and this created scenarios that frightened him. It was all too easy to see the differences in Betty since golf had so passionately seduced her. She had become frenetic in her dispensing of household chores, to the point where tasks which had become ritually observed during the years were now allowed to lapse or at best were only superficially attended to.

More significantly, perhaps, she could no longer be described as being chubby, the excess poundage having fallen away. In fact George looked at her in awe. She had the same youthful exuberance that she had when they had first met. But worse, and George found this particularly irritating, Betty had become very flip,using witty and unintelligible ripostes whenever he asked seriously-minded questions. This modernness that she had suddenly adopted only fired up his imagination even more and promoted even stronger suspicions. George now suspected that it was not only golf that galvanised her thoughts and disposition.

And in all, and whether or not there was any foundation to his suspicions, despite the doctor's assurances that his heart condition had stabilised and that he was as fit and healthy as could possibly be expected, Betty's deviation from the norm left George listless, deadened by the encroachment of an old age that appeared to have nothing to offer him but uselessness and daily visits by the meals-on-wheels lady. George was fast approaching the stage of serious depression.

He missed Betty's everyday endearments and could not prevent himself from speculating upon the possibility that another man was now the recipient of her affections. Other than the shift from her well-honed routine and her lessening interest in his health, he had no proof that Betty was being unfaithful, and he certainly had no intention of risking allegations of advancing senility by confronting her with his suspicions. So he promised himself not to overtip the apple-cart, hoping that the future was not as black as his dreams were forecasting.

But despite his determination to remain silent on the matter Betty's unhidden pleasure at having met Arthur Goss-Havelock brought things to a head. His name seemed to crop up in every conversation and this only served to heighten George's jealousy and he knew in his heart that decisiveness was called for, if only to demonstrate to his wife that he was not the sort of husband to stand idly by and allow a man notable only for his adulterous reputation to take her from him.

On his own George could not decide upon the most effective course of action he should take and after considerable thought he chose to take into his confidence Rupert Whiteladies, an old friend since their army days and an ally on the tennis court in civilian days.

'Look George, old thing, Betty isn't the type to fall for the swollen charm of someone like Goss-Havelock. She is much too level headed for that kind of behaviour. Are you sure that you are not making a mountain out of a molehill?' Rupert said as they sipped a beer in the lounge bar of The Minster Arms. But George repeated his fears and asked Rupert for any suggestions he might have on how the situation could be remedied.

'George, old chap, Betty isn't up to anything. All her life she has been viewed simply as a wife and mother. Her life has been domesticity. Cooking, cleaning, ironing, shopping and the like. Now, thanks solely to you, she has been liberated. I for one am pleased for her. Let things ride, George, old chap, that is my advice.'

But George remained unconvinced and he almost pleaded with Rupert to investigate the matter on his behalf.

'No I will not, George. To my mind Betty is above suspicion. If anything has changed, or anyone, it is you George. You used to be so steady and rational. If you want me to advise you, old thing, then I suggest that you volunteer to caddy for her in the Spring Tournament. Perhaps then you will regain your pride in her and see that her seducer is the golf course and not Goss-Havelock.'

Rupert's spirited defence of Betty's fidelity pricked at George's conscience, and though still racked by doubt, he realised that without any other alternative, his best option was to follow his old friend's advice.

Betty greeted George's request to caddy for her with muted appreciation. The rules of the competition did not exclude the assistance of a caddy, she told him flatly, but she did not want it to appear that she was getting ideas above her station.

'No-one else will have a caddy, dear. I don't want the club to think I'm getting big-headed. Of course, I'd love you to, but...'

George persisted, however, and to appease him Betty offered a compromise. If, before he even picked up her golf bag, he consulted a doctor as to whether his health was up to it, she would allow him to caddy for her, adding, in a tone that was so indicative of the change that had come about in her, that if he were to collapse halfway around the eighteen holes it might conceivably put her off her game.

George passed his medical with flying colours, then immediately upgraded Betty's golfing equipment by buying her a trolley. This further reduced the possibility of his falling down on the job.

But he soon recognised that to simply pull a golf trolley around eighteen holes of a golf course, and to witness his beloved wife enjoying a sporting contest would not be enough to return their marriage to its snug comfort zone.He was the one who had recklessly persuaded her to follow in the footsteps of aristocratic ladies, bejewelled gay divorcees and the like who fitted in their golf whenever weather and social commitments allowed. The day of the spring tournament had to be a catalyst. Something had to change because of it. It was not his intention to take golf away from Betty, he just wanted her to be around him more. He needed her to notice him again.

He considered presenting her with a good-luck bouquet of red roses on the first tee, but dismissed the thought, as it did not seem adequate enough to express the depth of his feelings. Similarly a jerobeom of champagne on the last green or a candlelit dinner for two at a voguish French restaurant also did not seem right. He sought something intimate, something that was personal and unifying. But the solution eluded him. So once more he approached Rupert.

'Well, old thing, if roses, champagne or a candlelit dinners are not up to it I cannot think how I can be of help to you,' Rupert told him candidly.

George poured Rupert another glass of wine.

'I want to make Betty see me once more as the man I was before angina struck me down and made me into a man of enforced leisure.'

'George, why make life so much more difficult than it is already?' Rupert implored. 'Plotting the obscure and pretty route is fine if you have the time to enthuse about the scenery, but you, old chap, do not. The tournament is tomorrow, so why not just buy her a small trinket to wish her luck and then take her to a nice restaurant afterwards. She will be just as pleased.'

George adamantly refused to be swayed from his opinion that the situ-

33

ation required a somewhat more intricate strategy.

'Old thing, even Goss-Havelock is not this dedicated when he is on the prowl for fresh skirt,' Rupert reproved.

The two sat around the kitchen table and chatted about this and that. Like any ageing friends they remembered the past with varying degrees of reflective glory and tossed verbal rocks at the unsteady and unbalanced world that now surrounded them. Away from the prickly topic of Betty their conversation was easy and without any particular link between one debate and the next.

As they drained a second bottle of Beaujolais, Rupert recalled, for no reason at all, Pinkie Fothergay and the twenty-first birthday party they had all attended in their youth. In an instant George was reformed, animated and alert to all manner of possibilities. His mind was racing. He knew what he had to do. . .

Unlike the preceding days that had been cold, drizzly with flurries of wet snow, the morning of the Spring Tournament dawned clear and bright, the sun enhancing the naturalness of the greenness of the fairways and highlighting the yellows and blues of the wild spring flowers. Betty stepped out of the club house, feeling bubbly, keenly anticipating the challenge ahead of her. When her opponent joined her they proceeded towards the first tee, waiting for George who had gone back to the car for the trolley.

As her start time drew nigh Betty grew impatient. She looked all over fro George, but to no avail. She felt so useless, having no clubs with which to practice her swing. Her opponent looked anxiously at her watch and Betty began to fear that the excitement of the day had over exerted George's heart and that he may be stricken in the car park; perhaps even feebly calling her name or gasping his last breath. As she finally took the decision to forfeit the game to go and search for him George came into view......

He was not attired in the usual dress of a caddy. He was dressed exactly the same as he had been on the evening of Pinkie Fothergay's twenty-first birthday party. The sight thrilled her, and she was suddenly transported back to the moment that George had proposed to her.

Like two long lost Hollywood lovers they dominated the moment. George, in his Fred Astaire outfit, top hat, white tie and tails, looking both absurdly and magnificently out of place as he walked boldly on to the tee, pulling the golf trolley behind him with as much aplomb as he could muster. Betty stood transfixed at the dream-like reality, not knowing how to react.

George took her hand and kissed it lightly, before dropping onto bended knee and pulling a silver eternity ring from his top pocket. He offered up the ring and Betty joyfully removed her glove and proffered a finger. He rose up and slipped the ring onto her finger and then once more lightly kissed her hand. 'Oh George,' she said, tears welling in her eyes. 'Pinkie Fothergay's twenty-first, you remember. Oh I should be Cleopatra, as I was then. This is so marvellous. But why, George, why?'

George could not explain, not then, not out in the open, with his profound love on open display. The rehearsed act completed, he felt suddenly foolish and swathed in guilt for doubting Betty. A tournament official appeared, suggesting that a start should be made, and George remembered how important the event was to Betty. He pulled a wood from the bag and handed it to her but Betty remained impassive.

The tournament official asked if she wished to scratch and give her opponent the match. Betty was unsure what golf's etiquette demanded of her. Finally George broke the impasse by telling her that though he may be unusually dressed he was wearing the correct footware, and that before leaving home he had cleared a space in the ornament cabinet in readiness for receiving the Spring Tournament Trophy, so in his opinion the game should commence. Betty looked at her opponent, who in response smiled broadly, bent down and pressed a tee into the ground.

Betty duly won the tournament, and attired in a more traditional style of clothing George caddied for his wife on a regular basis. So golf, which seemed to have divided them, now united themagain. Betty won many more tournaments, mostly with George as her caddy.

It was said that Flora had been piggy-backed off the green...

THE GRANDFATHERS' TANTALUS

Patricia Armstrong

After two blissful, restful weeks abroad - no newspapers, no television - I arrived back to the usual pile of letters, circulars and bills. There was also a copy of our local paper with the banner headline:

ELDERLY GOLFERS FIGHT OVER GLAMOROUS DIVORCEE

There followed an account of how two septuagenarians at the exclusive Whortle Manor Golf Club had come to blows. Mr Percy Allen and Mr Walter Somes had apparently both sustained minor injuries in a brawl on the course. The object of their passionate disagreement was a lady who had accompanied them round while they played in the Grandfathers' Tantalus. Tempers had festered for a couple of hours and had finally erupted in violence at the eleventh hole. Other competitors had raced to restrain the battling grandfathers and had themselves become embroiled in the fracas. The Secretary had been called from the clubhouse to quell the disturbance.

The whole tone of the report was mocking and salacious and I was appalled. I could just imagine what the Secretary would have to say, and I wasn't far wrong. I ran him to ground in his office, where he had been hiding from journalists since the incident, heavily guarded by his own secretary. 'What the hell's been going on?' I asked.

'You might well ask,' he replied bitterly. 'I'd like to get my hands on whoever tipped off the press. I've been besieged here. Even had photographers poking cameras through windows. The club's a laughing stock.'

I said it was difficult to believe that Percy and Walter had behaved so badly - they were usually such quiet men. It was even less credible that they had actually fought each other; they always played golf together perfectly amicably.

'Is it true?' I asked.

'Yes and no.' He sounded doubtful. 'It is, and then again it isn't. I suppose they did fight, although it was more pushing and shoving really. And in a way it was over some damned woman, but not for the reason the papers implied.'

The Secretary looked weary. He sighed. 'I'd better tell you right from the beginning,' he said. 'It took me a couple of days to piece the story together myself by the time I'd interviewed Percy and Walter and various other members who were involved. We've been crawling with reporters, mostly from the tabloids. You know what they're like. They followed Percy and Walter home, took photographs of their houses and cars, had everything costed. Made them out to be wealthy old lechers.'

It seems it all started with Percy Allen's visit to the dentist. While waiting his turn he flicked through a pile of magazines and found one specially for senior citizens. Quite apart from articles of interest - gardening tips for the stiff jointed, travel for the adventurous, how to make the most of retirement, and so on - there was a lonely hearts section. Percy had been a widower for several years and he was lonely. He read the advertisements, found them intriguing and finished up by buying a copy of the magazine on his way home.

He considered: 'Young-looking, unattached lady. 60. Non-smoker, wishes to meet professional gentleman', or - 'Widow. 66, with sense of humour, sincere, smart and active', or, 'Outgoing divorcee. 50s. Seeks friendship and shared interests'.

He couldn't bring himself to reply sending the necessary letter and photograph, but in the end he placed an entry himself, under the protection of a box number: 'Widower, early 70s. Non-smoker, seeks kind, sincere lady for companionship. Hobbies: golf and gardening'.

He had several replies, and felt a sense of panic at what he'd done. However, having got so far he thought he might as well pursue the matter and meet some ladies on neutral ground. He rang what seemed to be the most promising and they arranged to meet.

Her name was Flora and Percy found her quite attractive. She was cheerful and high spirited in a ladylike sort of way, very interested in him and all his doings. They went out a couple of times for a meal and a show.

Percy told the Secretary he was certain, well almost certain, that Flora had told him she played golf. Perhaps she had only said she was interested in golf, he couldn't really remember. At any rate he took her to mean she knew about golf. Flora wanted to see him again at the weekend. Percy said he was sorry, he couldn't manage Saturday because he had booked to play in an important golf competition with a friend and he couldn't let his partner down. Flora immediately offered to come and walk round with them while they played, pull his trolley for him if he liked.

Percy had his doubts about the wisdom of this, but he didn't like to put her off, so he rang Walter to ask if it would be all right. Walter didn't altogether approve of women on a golf course at the best of times and was not wildly enthusiastic, but he agreed. He told the Secretary he was a bit cross at being put in such an awkward position, but Percy had seemed set on it and he hadn't liked to refuse him. He understood she was a golfer and thought at least she would know how to behave while they were playing.

The first tee was reserved for the Grandfathers' Tantalus at 10 o'clock and Percy and Walter were first off. Flora drove up to the club at 9.45, and as soon as Percy saw her he had terrible misgivings. She was very well dressed, but for a garden party. He greeted her and ushered her towards the ladies' cloakroom in the hope that she would change into something more suitable for a golf course. She didn't. The first time Walter set eyes on Percy's new flame was when she teetered down to the tee wearing high heels and a flowery dress that billowed in the breeze.

With some foreboding Percy introduced Walter to Flora. Walter took in the blonde hair, the make-up and the unsuitable dress and shoes. He raised his cap ever so slightly.

Percy was worried. He hoped Walter wasn't going to be difficult. He thought he might have been a little more polite, a little more forthcoming.

Walter and Percy hit their usual drives, short but more or less straight down the middle. It was immediately obvious that Flora's acquaintance with golf was slight.

The Secretary said, 'Apparently she stood in all the wrong places. Kept getting in the way. And chatter! Walter says she didn't stop, not even when he was addressing the ball. The only effect Percy's frantic shushing had was for her to drop the decibels to a stage whisper. And she giggled

Flora didn't stop chattering, even when Percy was on the tee.

39

when either of them missed a putt.'

Walter put up with it for several holes, but by the time they got to the seventh he was near explosion point. Neither of them expected to win the Tantalus - that coveted trophy of two cut crystal decanters in a mahogany case, and the bottles that always went with them. It was usually carried off by some whippersnapper in his early fifties, but they both hoped that by some miracle their day might come and they always tried hard to win.

However, Walter's game was notoriously finely tuned, and when put off his doldrums were apt to last for several weeks. He began making furious asides to Percy: 'I thought you said she was a golfer,' he hissed. And: 'Can't you you keep that bloody woman quiet while I'm playing my shots?.' Percy, whose own game was disintegrating rapidly because of distraction by Flora, simply snapped back, 'That's no way to talk about a lady.' 'She's no lady, and I doubt she's ever been on a golf course before either,' said Walter. 'You're just a besotted old fool, Percy.'

They played on, the standard of play and the atmosphere getting steadily worse. Flora appeared quite unaffected, although she did remark that Walter seemed a grumpy old devil. Her chattering continued unabated.

Finally, at the eleventh, she committed the unforgivable sin: she pranced on to the green in her high heels, which immediately sank into the perfect turf, trapping her completely. Percy rushed to her aid. While he struggled to help her shed her tight shoes, as a preliminary to getting them unplugged from the green, Walter walked towards them in what Percy construed to be a threatening manner. Walter later maintained he was only going to help them, to hurry things along. Be that as it may, when he grasped one of her ankles there was a bit of a scuffle.

The 'minor injuries' were sustained when Percy overbalanced and fell into a deep greenside bunker. He was followed almost immediately by Walter, assisted by a push from Flora who had freed herself from her shoes and rushed to help Percy. Flushed at her success, Flora's high-pitched laughter rang out across the course. But to other competitors on adjoining holes it sounded like screams for help. At least four brace of grandfathers left their clubs and came running.

Perhaps if they had been alone Percy and Walter would have clambered out of the bunker, dusted themselves down and made their way back to the clubhouse. As it was, the presence of an audience acted like petrol on fire. When they had been dragged out of the sand - a matter of some difficulty - they attempted to resume hostilities and were restrained only by force. They then stood hurling insults at each other, still being held back by their friends. Walter shouted that there was no fool like an old fool. Percy, beside himself, shouted back that Walter was only annoyed because his golf was so bad he looked like the village idiot digging potatoes.

It was at this point that the Secretary arrived in a buggy. After some discussion he scooped up the antagonists, together with their clubs, and drove them in sullen silence back to the clubhouse. The others, the diversion over, wandered off and resumed their rounds.

While all this had been going on Flora had disappeared, and so had two of the other grandfathers playing in the Tantalus. It was said that someone had actually given Flora a piggy-back off the green, though nobody could confirm this. These enterprising gentlemen had retrieved her shoes, driven her back to the clubhouse in their buggy, fed her two large brandies to calm her nerves after a turbulent morning, and whisked her off to lunch.

The Secretary escorted Percy and Walter into the privacy of his office. At first there had been some talk of actions for assault and battery, but after the steward had produced double whiskies both calmed down. On reflection they realised that the least said about the whole affair the better for all concerned, and grudging apologies were exchanged.

What I found most puzzling was that Percy should have resorted to an advertisement in a magazine for a lady friend. There are umpteen unattached females in the club, most of them getting on a bit perhaps, but eminently presentable and very lively. I said as much to the Secretary.

'He was too shy to approach any of them.' he said. 'Wanted to keep it all private. Now look what's happened. But the whole thing might have blown over if some nark hadn't talked to the press. The tabloids just loved it.'

'Poor old Percy,' I said.

'Poor Percy?' the Secretary cried. 'What d'you mean, poor Percy? Don't waste your sympathy on him, he's never had it so good. The papers described him as "the gallant grandfather who fought for his blonde girl-friend". You should see his mail. Letters from all over the country, addressed c/o the club. Widows and divorcees want to meet him. He's had several offers of marriage. There was even a telegram saying, "Go For It Grandpa".

'And that's not all. In the club itself Percy's suddenly become very popular, particularly with the older, unattached ladies. Invitations to dinner, to dances and goodness knows what else. He's in great demand as a foursomes partner too. He loves it all. He's positively blossomed.'

For the first time in the whole narrative the Secretary smiled. 'Of course,' he said. 'Not everyone is happy. Percy's two daughters are as mad as wet hens. Came and interviewed me as if I were responsible for his behaviour. What's really bugging them is the thought that far from Percy's wealth cascading down the generations it might cascade sideways - to another wife.'

We both spoke together. 'Good luck to the old devil,' we said.

41

TAKE YOUR PARTNERS
Patricia Armstrong

It had rained all night and the course was already quite waterlogged by the time the first couples set out to play the Husbands and Wives Foursomes. By mid-morning the greens were swimming in water and unplayable and we had to abandon the competition.

The Secretary and I were sitting in the lounge watching the rain slant down out of dull pewter skies. The last unhappy stragglers were fighting their way back across the course, trying to stop umbrellas from blowing inside out and wrestling with their clubs and trolleys at the same time. At least the bar was open and there was a cheerful fire blazing in the hearth.

We looked round at various couples marooned with us in the lounge and the Secretary commented that golf seemed to bring some of the most improbable people together in the bonds of holy matrimony. I said it certainly did, and one of the most unlikely to have found a suitable partner was Daphne Martin.

Daphne was a perfectly nice girl in her late twenties; extraordinarily pleasant as a matter of fact. Nor was she plain; one might even have called her handsome. It was just that she was not exactly nubile. Daphne stood 6ft 2 in her golf socks and was large with it. Not fat, simply a very big girl. She could hump a full set of clubs round 36 holes without drawing a long breath, and had once been known to give a pickaback to one of our men members - all the way back to the clubhouse from the farthest point of the course - when he had sprained his ankle badly in a rabbit scrape.

The Secretary said, 'By God, she could wallop the ball. Out of sight.'

That she could. Mind you, it wasn't always in the right direction. There's something strange about tall people playing golf; you'd think that with all that extra leverage they'd be world beaters, but mostly it works against them. They have difficulty getting clubs to fit them properly, and for some reason they are never quite on balance. Daphne's short game was a bit suspect too - she seemed to have a problem getting down to the ball - but even so she was very useful off about ten handicap.

'Yes,' I said. 'When she hit the ball it stayed hit.'

43

The trouble was that from the ladies' tees she could rarely take a wood; she played mainly with irons, which must have been frustrating for her. Sometimes she would play off the men's tees with one of the assistant professionals - Scottie McLeod - so that she could really lash out with her driver, and even Scottie had trouble keeping up with her.

All her contemporary girlfriends had gradually dropped out of the golfing scene, getting married and starting families, but it looked as if Daphne would never marry. Not to put too fine a point on it, there was no one quite big enough for her.

Not, that is, until an American, Dwight Davis Carter IV arrived. Dwight had come to the British Isles for a month or two to see the country and 'play a little golf'. He'd done Scotland - St Andrews, Muirfield, Gleneagles, Turnberry - and had worked his way south, playing many of the famous courses as he came. He had played Sunningdale, Woburn, Wentworth, Walton Heath and The Berkshire, but now he wanted to spend the rest of his time in what he called 'real rural England' and play at Whortle Manor. Dwight was distantly related to our President and was granted temporary membership of the club while he visited our area.

The owner of our local hotel - The Whortle Arms - is a member so there was no difficulty in arranging suitable accommodation for him, although they had to send for an outsize bed and get in a supply of extra-large steaks.

Dwight was huge - a good 6ft 6 and broad with it. I was playing with Sam Johnson the first time I saw him. We were on the 6th fairway and he was on the 14th tee. He had obviously just driven and he blotted out a fair section of the skyline, standing with arms like tree trunks held high aloft, grasping his driver.

'Good grief,' I said. 'Who's that?'

Sam shaded his eyes and pondered for a moment. 'Not sure,' he said. 'Could be Zeus loosing a thunderbolt. Or his son, Hercules, having a good stretch after his Labours. Or even that chap Swartznegger, or whatever he's called, from Hollywood.'

When we were introduced later Dwight took my hand in his great paw and drawled, 'Ah come from Texas.' He volunteered the information that back home he had a li'l ole homestead with a few head of cattle, and a nine hole golf course.

He turned out to be a most pleasant, easy going chap; popular with the members and never short of partners.

I don't know whose idea it was to rope Daphne in to play with Dwight, but someone thought it appropriate to pair them together in a mixed foursome. After that Daphne and Dwight played together practi-

44

cally every day, and naturally enough there was some speculation. We thought Daphne was getting off and considered this a very good thing.

But absolutely nothing more happened in the next week or two, probably because they were both too shy. He did take her to the midsummer ball. This is an annual event - a formal do at the club - when everyone dresses up and dances the night away. It caused a bit of a stir when Dwight appeared in his tuxedo, accompanied by a radiant Daphne.

We didn't think Daphne danced; she had never before made an appearance at any of the social functions, but to our surprise she was very good, very light on her feet considering her size. Dwight said he was used to barn dances and square dancing but wasn't too sure about all this quickstep and foxtrot stuff, although he could manage a waltz. Daphne confided that she had been very fond of the old fashioned polka when at school and offered to teach him the steps. It was easy, she said, you just counted: Hop, one two three; Hop, one two three.

Dwight made his way through the throng and went up to have a word with the band leader. He slipped him a note and requested an old time polka 'for the little lady'.

The band struck up, the pair took to the floor and were soon well away. They took up so much room that other dancers stood back and clapped them as they whirled round the room.

We all hoped that after the ball something would happen, that there might be an announcement of their engagement. They seemed so well matched. But we were disappointed. Although Dwight seemed in no hurry to return to the States there was still no indication that they were anything more than congenial golfing partners.

Daphne was due to play her quarter final in a knockout competition - the Ladies Salver. It was important and she was expected to win, being the defending champion that year. She cancelled. Rang up her opponent and gave her a walk-over. Offered no excuses, just said she was sorry but she couldn't play and would be glad to concede the match.

On the afternoon that she should have been playing this match Daphne was out playing with Dwight. When they had finished their round and were enjoying tea in the dining room her erstwhile opponent appeared. Not being a lady of great sensitivity she went straight over to their table and asked Daphne why she hadn't played the match. Had she sustained some injury? Had their been some domestic emergency?

Daphne, crimson with embarrassment, tried to head her off, but the lady was persistent. 'I thought perhaps you were ill,' she said.

Dwight's great brow furrowed with concern. 'Ill,' he said. 'You're not ill, are you honey?'

Daphne mumbled that no, she was perfectly all right. Really.

Dwight wanted to know why she had given her opposition a walkover. At first Daphne was lost for words, but in the end she had to admit that she had wanted to play with him instead. His time in England was getting short and she hadn't wanted to miss any of their golf together. Dwight himself seemed to be struggling with strong emotions. His self-consciousness forgotten he at last spoke out. 'Aw shucks, honey,' he said. 'Marry me and come back to Texas. We can spend the rest of our lives playing together there.'

The table went flying as they fell into each other's arms. Daphne's answer was lost in the spontaneous applause that broke out from the other tables, but it was clear that she was in favour of the idea. Dwight wrapped his arms around her, using the Harry Vardon grip. Things moved quite quickly after that. There must have been a lot of string pulling because Daphne and Dwight were 'hitched', as he put it, in a surprisingly short time. He was determined that she should be married in 'the quaint little old church with her folks around her', and since both the local vicar and his bishop were members of Whortle Manor there was no impediment to setting up the wedding without delay.

The reception was held at the club. Dwight engaged a country and western group to play and champagne flowed. Never before, or since, has there been anything to beat that occasion. Everone agreed that she and Dwight were made for each other.

There were one or two things - it transpired afterwards - that Dwight had failed to mention. The li'l ole homestead and a few head of cattle turned out to be a vast ranch occupying a fair slice of Texas, with a herd of longhorns running into thousands. There was also the matter of a couple of highly productive oilwells. The nine hole course measured almost four thousand yards with plenty of room for them both to take full drivers at seven of its holes.

'Daphne landed right on her feet,' I observed.

The Secretary agreed: 'Just proves that there's someone somewhere to suit everyone.'

The Dwight Davis Carters now have a brood of sons. Goodness knows what size they'll eventually turn out to be. Still, there's plenty of room in Texas.

Everone agreed that she and Dwight were made for each other

ON HIS OATH

John Pollitt

'Is that the Rev. Spode over there?'

'Yes, his son is one of our finest players', said Colonel Fortescue.

'But he wasn't always like that. He was quite useless, but it all changed one day. Here's how it happened . . .'

George Spode joined the gathering for the Charity Lunch at Whortle Manor with low spirits. His was the duty visit in place of his father, the vicar of a neighbouring parish. Having reached the age of twenty-five George, who was unemployed and trying desperately to write good plays, was being asked increasingly to do good deeds of this kind.

Over the generous allowance of sherry he spied in the crowd a beautiful girl of about his own age, and although himself besieged by talkative friends he managed to glimpse her in action before the luncheon. It was apparent to him that she was a woman of poise. Bearing in mind his low spirits, the effect of finding that he was placed opposite this girl at one of the tables needs little imagination. By the time the table was rapped loudly for speeches which seemed unnecessarily long the effect of the sherry had prepared him to give his best.

After small talking for a few minutes to the overweight, bejewelled lady on his left and then to the rather quiet youth on his right, he managed to catch the eye of the girl opposite. Ignoring the attempts of her neighbours endeavouring to continue their own conversations with her, he opened with information about himself emphasising his literary hopes. She replied by changing the subject to golf and seemed relieved when he said he played. Anxious to impress her and feeling that she changed the subject from his writing because she was unimpressed by his efforts in that direction, he stressed his keenness on the game when, in truth, he was a poor player and badly out of practice. Believing that ends justify the means he thought no more about his distortion, particularly as he was soon engulfed in accepting some editing work from the fat lady and being inveigled into becoming Assistant Stage Manager for a production of "Ladies in Retirement" at the County Town Theatre.

The object of his admiration was collected by a uniformed chauffeur, but not before she had smiled invitingly at him and passed all the right words to the right people before departing. Noting from her place card her name as Lana Gamlin he left. He had already begun to feel downhearted, for although she seemed friendly she was clearly from a different social and financial class.

Three weeks later he was surprised to be invited to another charity function, this time at the Gamlin home. The invitation from her parents was to him personally, a fact which did not escape him, for clearly some money must be borrowed.

On this occasion he saw a great deal of Lana, and although she was busy as a 'hostess' she made a point of talking to him with golf as the main topic. This worried George partly because he regretted his enthusiasm for the sport at their last meeting, but mainly because the house and grounds seemed dedicated to the game. The long drive to the house passed through a good nine hole course which appeared to be private and for the family, and the front lawn contained a beautifully kept eighteen hole putting green. The inside of the house did nothing to dispel the impression that the family and their friends did little else but play golf extremely well. In the cloakroom of the hall a wooden affair intended for walking sticks and umbrellas was filled with putters of various kinds. There were six bags of clubs, several woods in a corner and several buckets brimming with golf balls. As one passed through the hall it was noticeable that the walls were covered with photographs of triumphant golfers all receiving trophies or poised at the top of a magnificent drive. The only exception was the occasional glass case exhibiting the trophies themselves.

Lana talked golf to him but he avoided asking questions relating to the family's prowess for fear of making a fool of himself. It was obvious to him that the family were steeped in it, and his chances of getting near to this enchanting girl were virtually nil. Again he left with a heavy heart.

Life continued in dull fashion for George. He could not concentrate on his new play. The publishers seemed incapable of of replying to his letters. Everyone around him seemed busy apart from himself. He felt isolated and a failure. Fortunately this sad state was not to last, but it was not from his work as a writer that success came.

Through the post arrived an invitation for a long weekend at the Gamlins' to join the family at golf. Delight at the implication in this invitation was dampened by the thought that he had been selected as a golfer of sufficient stature to match the family members, all of whom, he supposed, were master golfers. None of this "hacking round the course" stuff of his undergraduate days. His exposure was at hand: a poseur, golf-bluffer and deceiver of decent girls.

The next ten days were employed in golf practice and lessons from the pro. It is no exaggeration to say that George lived golf until the

Friday morning when he drove to the Gamlins' house. As he did so even his mini car caused him shame as he remembered the liveried chauffeur.

At eleven a.m. he joined Mr. and Mrs. Gamlin and Lana for coffee, meeting also a couple of elderly aunts who came in later. 'Just time for a look at the river from the bridge,' said Lana. George felt a sense of pure joy, and for the next three hours, which included lunch, he forgot his golf problems, his social inferiority and even himself. Then the blow fell. 'Would you like a round with Daddy and me, George?' she asked almost innocently. There was no turning back. Pity I can't last twenty-four hours, he thought. Yes, he'd brought his clubs . . . No, he had all his kit and gear, thank you . . . No, there's nothing he needed.

Fifteen minutes later, having been driven by Lana in her large saloon, they all arrived at the first tee. The three were alone. At least there were no caddies or other members of the public to watch his humiliation now that the truth was about to emerge.

'If you don't mind, Daddy and I will take alternate strokes as in a two-ball foursome,' said Lana, 'and we'll play you. This will save time, and we may be able to get in eighteen holes before tea.' George consented and they tossed. Mr. Gamlin and Lana won, and Lana teed off.

'She doesn't need the lady's tee,' commented Mr. Gamlin, and George replied that he was sure she didn't need any extra advantages with her standard of play.

She drove and the ball soared straight down the fairway landing a good iron shot from the green. George's hand was shaking as he teed his ball, feeling it could not be long before he was making excuses to drive home again on urgent business. As he straightened up he felt a click in his back and a twinge of pain. As he swung his driver the pain had the effect of slowing his usual impulsive lunge and he hit the ball fair and square. For once in his life he neither hooked nor sliced and the ball landed ten yards short of Lana's but 30 yards to the left. Thanking his maker he allowed Lana and her father to push on and take the next shot while he admired the view to the river. To his surprise he heard a shout which, had there been others on the course, he would have thought to be "Fore". Must have been shouting at an errant sheep or something.

He found that Mr. Gamlin's stroke had reached the green comfortably. George selected a number three iron and punished the ball in his usual way only to land it in a bunker short of the green. Here we go, he thought to himself.

'Bad luck,' said Lana.

Lana holed out easily and they marched to the next tee. George was not so lucky this time and he topped it badly sending his ball a mere fifty

51

yards. To his amazement Mr. Gamlin did the same, and George began to regain hope. Obviously this was a bad day for Papa. Perhaps they would allow him the same sympathy at the end of the day.

Cutting short a blow-by-blow version of this game, the events up to the climax can be summarised as George playing his usual poor standard up to the seventh hole and his opponents doing much better, although not nearly as well as he, George, would have expected from their obvious keenness.

Then, at the eighth hole, George drove into the rough, and in the search for his ball lost sight of Lana and her father. At his fourth attempt to extricate himself from a micro jungle, he made an excellent shot which landed him back on the fairway only a few yards from a deep bunker. As he neared his ball he heard sounds of raised voices. Mr. Gamlin was expressing every known expletive at the top of his stetorian voice while Lana, equally loudly and in tears, was attempting to quieten him.

'Of course you must score it at twelve to here,' she was saying, but her father's reply was unprintable - a sort of inflammatory version of "not on your life" or "over my dead body".

The truth began to dawn on George. He realised that Mr. Gamlin was no golfer. He had to be tactful. The least said the better. Only one more hole to go. Whether the relief of recognising a fellow 24 handicap man made the difference, who can guess, but George managed the last hole in five. Lana said they'd lost their ball and, anyway, it was time for tea. George changed into his only lounge suit.

Conversation was somewhat forced between sips of tea and cress sandwiches. Afterwards Lana suggested that they should walk round the formal garden, the herb garden and then the rose garden before drinks at 7p.m. George was full of questions but had to wait until she broached the subject.

'I owe you an apology,' she said. 'I was desperate and I just hoped it would work out. I knew you must have gathered that we are one of the keenest golfing families in the county, and we do a lot of entertaining based on the game.'

'Unfortunately, Daddy plays very badly and no amount of lessons - he's had hundreds - with professionals, or personal practice, seems to help. He was dyslexic as a child, and although you'd not believe it now he had several physical hang-ups. I'm sure I'm boring you, George. Shall we change the subject?'

George replied hastily, 'Not at all. I'm fascinated by what you're saying.' This was true in two senses but the subtlety was lost on Lana who was keen to get everything off her chest. She went on, 'Despite his difficulties he refuses to give up even after all these years. . . something about family honour and all that. So the family have always tried to help him but, frankly, they've got tired of it, and it's left to me to play with him and try to get others to give him a game. Unfortunately, all his friends have not only got tired of his poor play . . .they can forgive that. . . but whenever he muffs a shot he swears like a Major General at a Mess party, and this is not to everone's taste. . . I'm sorry.'

'But where do I come in?' gasped George. Lana was silent. Then, 'I guess it's confession time and I do owe it to you. I didn't invite you down

'Daddy plays very badly. No amount of lessons will help.'

for the golf, as such, although you had to be a player for me to invite you here. I'm looking for a manager in a business which I've started. We provide instruction booklets for foreign products. We write advertising material, read the proof of their own material and generally polish a whole range of written work before printing. That's where you come in.'

'Good Lord,' exclaimed George. 'Are you asking me or about to say it's off?'

'Don't be be silly . . . you've won hands down. Not only did you win the match by a good margin because Daddy also cheats on the score to lessen his shame, but you were able to understand the situation and cope with all the eventualities which you met. You're a bit inhibited, if I may say so, but you'll fit in well. I've got offices and computers and things in the stable block. It's not palatial but. . . come and have a look. Come on!' she said. 'I'll race you there.' So saying she pulled his arm and then ran ahead across the lawn and onto the stepping stones of the stream.

Running in your best suit does not always allow one the ideal degree of dexterity and George's lounge suit did not fit his body nor fit him for athletic performance. On the third stepping stone he slipped and fell, half immersed in the icy water. He sat there unsteadily, apparently unhurt, and then the stillness of a warm summer evening was broken by a bellow reminiscent of the expressed frustration of an angry bull. The air was filled with a steady, fluent cascade of florid epithets - an outpouring of oaths fully equal to the experience of a lifetime of casual converse in the Sergeants' Mess. It rolled on for two minutes. George stopped, spluttered and rocked with laughter.

Lana took his hand, helped him back onto the stones and then the path. 'Join the club,' she said. 'I thought you'd be the perfect partner, but I didn't realise you'd be the ideal companion as well. Come on . . . let's get you dry then discuss details and sign you up.'

'So what happened?'

'Well, young George never looked back. The business flourished, he and Lana married, and his golf improved. Strangely enough, so did Mr. Gamlin's and as his golf got better, so did his language. Strange how life goes, isn't it?'

METAMORPHOSIS

Patricia Armstrong

The two young men waited patiently behind, holding back, not pressing us, until we stood aside and waved them through. One, the nearest, doffed his visor and said, 'Thank you, Sir.' The other, striding down the far side of the fairway, raised a deferential cap in acknowledgment.

My guest was most impressed. 'Such polite young men,' he enthused 'What a refreshing change. At my club they'd drive into you as soon as look at you.'

It is encouraging to have one's course praised by a visitor, and having the behaviour of fellow members applauded is equally heartening. 'Oh yes,' I replied. 'Quite. Peter Furlow and John Statt are our two best players. Both 2 handicap. They hit the ball miles. Much better to have them in front and out of the way.'

What I could have said, but did not, was that it had not always been so. The pair was once as brash, as arrogant as any you were likely to meet on a golf course. But they became changed characters after the strange happenings following old George Tolley's death.

George was in his eighties. He no longer played a full round at Whortle Manor, just nine holes several days a week; sometimes early, before breakfast; sometimes in the late afternoon, but always on his own.

George was easily recognisable on the course. He was thin and bent; always wore old tweed plus-fours and carried a pencil bag containing four clubs and a putter. He could no longer see very well and he was getting deaf. He was also very slow, and for this reason tended to play before other golfers had started or after they had finished.

Unfortunately, Peter Furlow and John Statt also practised on the course at the same sort of times, before they went to work, or when they came home. Sooner or later they would happen on poor old George, pottering along by himself. They regarded him as a silly old fool and simply played straight through.

George, punctilious all his life about good manners on a golf course, could not help resenting being passed in this way, without so much as a 'by your leave'. Worse still, he sometimes overheard their remarks as they marched past. He often muttered about lack of respect in the youth of today, but never made any formal complaint for fear people would say he was past it, and wasn't it time he hung up his clubs for good.

I am the senior partner in a general practice near the golf club and many of the members are patients of mine. The Tolleys had been on our list for many years. My father in his time treated George, his wife Martha, and their children, so when Martha rang me to say George had died in his sleep, I went at once.

I signed the Death Certificate and made sure she understood about making funeral arrangements, and then we sat and talked for a while. I said it was sad for her, but a wonderful way for George to go, so peacefully like that. But Martha would not be comforted. 'He wasn't happy and peaceful, doctor,' she said, becoming more and more distressed.

Apparently, two days before, George had been out playing the back nine when a couple of young men, good golfers who had given him trouble before, had driven over his head. As they strode past him he heard them say that the dreary old sod shouldn't be allowed on the course.

'He came home very upset,' she said. 'Said if he couldn't play his golf he might as well be dead. Seemed obsessed with dying. Made me promise to scatter his ashes in the copse on the dogleg of the 17th when his time came. And now he's gone.'

That was odd. 'Are you sure he said the 17th?' I asked her. 'Sure it wasn't the pond in front of the short 13th, or the bunker on the right of the 2nd green?'

There would have been some sense in either of those. George had consigned several hundred balls to the pond over the years, and he had made that bunker his own. But he had not been in the copse to the left of the 17th in living memory. Not only was it about 180 yards from the tee - further than George could possibly hit a ball - but he had never been a hooker.

Martha insisted she was quite sure. George had definitely specified the 17th. In fact, he had repeated it several times. There was no way she could have made a mistake.

'I'd like you to come with me to scatter his ashes,' she said. 'I've never played golf and I don't know the course. I wouldn't know where to find George's copse. But I said I'd do it, just to humour him, and I must keep my promise.'

So, after the cremation, Martha and I went over and laid George to rest in a place where spotted orchids grew in the light shade of silver birch and hazel. Martha said she could quite understand why George had chosen this particular spot; it was like having your own bit of garden on your own golf course. I told her that in spring cowslips grew there, anemones and wild violets, and she was much happier after we had sprinkled George.

We didn't say a word to anyone else about it. Some people are squeamish about death and ashes, and I didn't want someone looking for a lost ball in the copse thinking about stamping on old George. So, I'm quite sure nobody else knew about his last resting place.

Being a Doctor of Medicine puts me firmly in the scientific lobby, among those who maintain that there is a rational explanation for everything. I do not believe in ghosts, but I must admit that the events which followed were decidedly strange. They were outside my previous experience and gave me cause for thought.

The story, as I gleaned it from both Peter and John - separately - when they consulted me a few weeks later, confirmed the accounts I had heard from other golfers, and was as follows:

The first time they saw George's ghost was when they stood on the 17th tee on the morning of the June Medal. The pair had each notched up a decent score, and it was nip and tuck as to which of them would win. On their way, as usual hitting the ball prodigious distances, glorying in their youth, their feeling of well-being and a perfect summer morning, they had gone through several pairs of middle-aged golfers, competent performers with useful handicaps in the low teens, but nevertheless called upon, somewhat brusquely, to give way. Higher handicaps scattered before the two, while the young tigers passed without deigning so much as a wave in acknowledgment.

All went well until the pair came to the long 17th. In the ordinary course of events they would have powered their drives past the copse, cutting the dog-leg corner, right up to the dewpond - which forms a convenient 250 yard marker. A really good tee-shot leaves a clear view of the flag, and a sweetly struck 3 wood gets such players well on to the green, setting them up for certain birdies, possibly eagles if the pin placing is not too severe.

Later, at a very private post-mortem in the bar, the pair went over the sequence of events. How, they asked themselves, could they possibly both have taken 13 at the 17th and wrecked their cards?

Peter had the honour. He took his stance, and as he looked down the fairway he suddenly felt cold and shivery, as if the sun had gone in - which it had not. As he addressed the ball his forward press tipped it off the tee, and he had difficulty replacing it because of an unaccountable twitching of the fingers. His legs felt weak and rubbery and he couldn't even waggle to get himself started. Finally, by dint of a quick lift, he heaved the club into some sort of tortured backswing, but then could only

57

get it down again by a quick, desperate yank. The clubhead plunged into the ground, cutting an enormous divot from the tee. The ball trickled feebly against the ladies tee-box some 30 yards ahead.

John fared little better. He was afflicted with the same sort of ague and had to grip the club very tightly to stop his arms trembling. In his anxiety to get the tee-shot over and done with, he swung the club at several times his normal speed, hitting a nasty snap hook into the copse and out of bounds. His second attempt was pushed out into the bunker on the right of the fairway. Although his first ball had been brand new, neither oug gested going into the copse to try to find it.

Each had made his way uneasily up the 17th, visiting the ditch on the left and trees and the bunker on the right in the process, aware that their shameful progress was being watched with a fair amount of schadenfreude and disbelief by the very members they had passed in such a superior fashion a short time before. They both three-putted the 17th green and were, in fact, fortunate to hole out in only 13.

Having gone over each wretched shot, they sat in miserable silence. Then Peter said, 'I know it sounds daft, but I'd swear I saw old Tolley standing on the edge of the copse, glaring at me, just before I drove. He had his old bag on his back and he was wearing his usual ghastly plus-fours. I know he's dead, but I can't think of anyone else it could be. That's when I came over queer.'

John then admitted that he too had thought he'd seen old Tolley. They parted and made their way home, very unhappy young men.

Much the same thing happened to them in the Stableford and the Foursomes competitions. Both swore to each other that they saw George before hitting their tee-shots, both felt cold and complained of uncontrollable shaking. They approached the 17th with dread and took treble bogies, or worse, every time.

It wasn't long before first Peter, then John, consulted me. Both were hollow-eyed from lack of sleep. Both begged for sleeping tablets, referral to a psychiatrist - anything. Each asked me not to mention his consultation to the other, I assured them both that my surgery was as sacrosanct as any confessional.

Hysteria can take many forms. It can produce temporary blindness, paralysis, and other manifestations of disease where none exists. In the case of Peter and John, I decided that their trouble was guilt-induced. It was no earthly use telling them that George's ghost was only a figment of their imaginations, because they were convinced they had seen him. I didn't want to start them taking pills at their age, and I certainly was not about to recommend any psychiatric mumbo-jumbo path.

58

To each I said their problem was unusual, but not unique. They had treated George badly and now he should be placated in some way. If they could make their own peace with him then he would rest and leave them alone. It was a good opportunity to tell them that I happened to know that not only George Tolley, but many other golfers in the club, had been annoyed by their lack of manners, their impatience in playing into people, not saying 'Thank you' when let through, and so on. In future a little more consideration for others might be wise.

They both seemed suitably chastened but said as far as George Tolley was concerned it seemed a touch too late.

To Peter I said perhaps he could write in the Suggestion Book that as Mr Tolley had been a member for well over half a century, and held in such high regard, the bunker on the right of the 2nd green should now be known as 'Tolley's Bunker'.

To John I suggested he start a club whip-round for a cup to be known as the 'Tolley Trophy' to be played for annually by all members.

I know I said I didn't believe in ghosts, and nor do I, but even so I reckoned it couldn't do any harm to go and have a quiet word with George.

It felt pretty ridiculous standing in the copse, talking, with nobody else there. I'd given a lot of thought to what I was going to say. He'd been a crotchety old devil and it was important not to take a hectoring tone; none of the 'What the hell d'you think you're playing at' sort of thing.

I said the boys were in a terrible state; it was making them ill, and didn't he think enough was enough? The Club Championship was coming up soon - 36 holes scratch medal - and it would just about break them if they had to play the 17th twice in one day with him appearing at the critical moment. I said they were sorry about spoiling his golf and were determined to mend their ways. Moreover, they were instigating the naming of the greenside bunker after him, and a 'Tolley Trophy' so that he would never be forgotten. Would he please think about it?. He'd had his revenge; the boys had had a hard time and I thought they'd suffered enough. Not only that, my professional reputation was at stake in the matter.

There was no sign that George had heard. No breath of wind - warm or cold. I felt no presence there in the copse, and I turned and made my way back to the clubhouse.

It goes down in my files as a case of the mind playing tricks; of the psyche getting the upper hand of a pair of impressionable young men. Whatever, they had no more trouble, and George was never seen again.

The greenside bunker to the right of the second green soon became known as 'Tolley's Bunker' and a plaque in the timber supports stated so. The Tolley Trophy is played for every year. Peter's name has been on it twice, John's once.

But it pleases me to see both boys give an almost imperceptible nod towards the copse whenever they play the 17th, and I can imagine old George smiling, now he has the respect he deserves.

EUNICE TAKES UP GOLF

Ben Clingain

'It can be a sad day for some men when their wives take up golf,' said old Colonel Fortescue, thoughtfully.

We were sitting in front of a roaring fire at Whortle Manor, sipping a pre-prandial drink, as Captain Harry Beecher came over to join us, accompanied by his wife, Eunice. They were a popular couple in their early sixties who had won the Seniors Matrimonial Bowl the previous year, and we made small talk for a few minutes before they went into dinner.

'What were you saying about women taking up golf?' I asked.

'I was thinking about Captain Harry and his wife,' the old man smiled. 'He was never the same after Eunice took up golf.'

'But they won the Matrimonial Bowl a few times, including the Seniors' one last year, so it couldn't have affected him that much,' I protested.

'Yes, but that was much later. A few years ago, Harry retired early from the Army. He'd never had much time for golf in the service, but he took to the game immediately. He'd spend two or three full days at the club, and, within six months had gotten down to a respectable fifteen. Within a year he was down to ten, and a fanatic. Very competitive, but nice with it. He was loving his retirement and his happiness was complete when he won the Whortle Matchplay Championship, beating my own grandson in law, Chris Ross, himself no mean player, 3 &2 in the final.

He was a proud man when he took the impressive silver trophy home to show Eunice. It must be said that she had been feeling a little left out in the past year. When Harry retired, she had been looking forward to spending lots of time together, but, with all his practising at the club, she had hardly seen him. Harry had the native cunning of so many army generals and politicians and bought her a Jack Russell early in his retirement. House training the thing consumed her time and countless copies of the Daily Mail. The only minor argument they'd ever had was over the dog, Doris, when Eunice had used Michael McDonnell's column to wipe up one of the dog's accidents in a corner of the kitchen, before Harry had read his remarks about Nick Faldo's views on the British press. But,

Every man knows you should never teach your wife to play golf

despite this distraction, she did miss Harry and she could easily, like so many wives, have slipped into sarcastic mode, made remarks about little white balls in little holes, commented on how the hedge at the bottom of their neat garden seemed to be getting closer, or remarked on the state of their little white picket fence which was still un-white. No, Eunice was above all that. When she listened to Harry talk about golf, there was an animation about him that had been missing since Army days.

'Well done darling, I'm really proud of you. You're a new man since you joined Whortle Manor.' She put her hand over his tenderly, as they sat having dinner.

Harry beamed. Good old Eunice. She wasn't a stick in the mud like some of the other wives, who were always moaning about the time their husbands spent at the club.

'I have some great news for you,' she continued. ' I think I'd like to learn to play.'

Harry gripped the end of the snowy tablecloth, his fork fell from his nerveless fingers, and upended the dish of new potatoes. There was a strangled moan from the Whortle Manor champion, Doris heard the noise and jumped on his lap, then on the table, knocking over the salt, pepper and the dish of asparagus spears.

Harry tried to save them, as they were his favourites, only succeeding in pulling off the tablecloth, and the asparagus, sweet corn and steak crashed to the floor.

Eunice fussed around, cleaning it all up, while Harry went to change. When, eventually, their meal was resumed and cold cuts had replaced the ruined repast, normal service was somewhat resumed.

'Well, what do you think, darling?'

'That dog's a menace. She oughtn't to be allowed on the table, at least during meals.'

'No, I meant about golf.'

Now Harry had been a life soldier. He'd faced the Mau Mau and the worst that Cyprus could throw at him and lived to tell the tale. But he was no match for a determined woman. Even one as gentle as Eunice.

'Yes, dear,' was all he could think to reply.

Eunice then, having slid the bayonet in under his ribs, proceeded to twist the said weapon. 'I don't think we need to go to the expense of lessons, darling. Your golf is so good at the moment, couldn't you teach me?'

Now even Harry knew that there are two laws of survival in any marriage. First, never ever teach your wife to drive. Second, never teach your wife to play golf. Both are recipes for disaster on a grand scale. Yet he nodded dumbly.

'Shall we have a little go tomorrow, darling?'

Another dumb nod.

'But..' Harry paused... 'I had a sort of arrangement to meet Colonel Fortescue and make up a foursome..'

' Oh, don't worry about him, it'd be much nicer for us to play together, just the two of us, don't you think?'

'But...you haven't got any clubs.'

She patted his hand tenderly.

'I've borrowed Betsy King's. She about the same size. She thinks it's a lovely idea.'

Her obvious joy was answered by another dumb nod, and she didn't see the abject misery in the captain's eyes. Had those same eyes been faced by ten thousand Zulus at Rorke's Drift, had they been facing torture at the hands of those horrible yellow men at the river Kwai, they would have looked fearlessly at death and yelled God Save the Queen. Faced with the prospect of a round with his novice wife, they lowered in surrender and listened as his voice said meekly, 'Yes Dear'

It was as bad as he could have imagined. 'Why can't I wear two gloves?' was her first question. 'Pink rather suits me, why can't I have a pink glove?' was her second. Worst, she waggled, wiggled, her left knee collapsed, her head came up, and her first effort at the tee ended in a trickle into a bush. She gave the second a white knuckle and it bounded sideways like a crab into another bush.

'Hee,hee,hee.' She also had the worst of all possible diseases, a giggle. No embarrassment, no swear words, just the giggles.

By the second green, she had taken thirty strokes, still giggling.

'Isn't this such fun? Aren't you glad I've taken up the game?'

Strangled, muffled reply.

Her divots were remarkable, and Whortle Manor was being ploughed up in no uncertain fashion. As they approached the fourth green, Eunice had taken her fiftieth stroke when Harry noticed Colonel Fortescue and his two partners - he would have been the fourth - close behind.

'Just wait a moment, dear. We'd better let the Colonel through.'

'Why?'

'We're holding them up. I'll wave them through.'

'No we won't. We were here first.'

'But..'

'The very idea. You wouldn't let them ahead of us in the Tesco queue would you?'

'No, but golf is..'

Unhearing, Eunice had addressed the ball, taken a huge lump out of the Whortle landscsape, and sent it in a long loop, over the fence into

Muirfield Avenue. The ball meanwhile, went the other way off the fairway to the right.

'What did I do wrong, darling?'

Everything, he wanted to say. Instead, 'You lifted your head too soon.'And at least a hundred other things, he thought. Eventually, he managed to persuade Eunice to stop and let the fuming Colonel and his party through. She glared at them, not returning their doffed caps, for, though fuming, they were too much like gentlemen to be rude to a lady, however bad her golf.

They finally finished, a six hour round. Harry's game, normally so steady, had gone to pieces. What made it so much worse was that when he duffed his drive at the 18th and went in the stream, Eunice was offering HIM advice on how to hold the club. It had been his worst nightmare.

'I did enjoy that. I feel so much better for the walk, as well.'

'Aren't you tired, dear.'

'Of course not, darling. We'll play again tomorrow.'

Harry Beecher didn't sleep a wink that night. Eunice, on the other hand, had curled up like a ball and instantly slept the sleep of the just and innocent. At the end of the week, after five days and one thousand and twenty four golf strokes by his wife, each one no better than the one before, Harry had reached crisis point. When Eunice mentioned that she missed Doris on their walks, and that they should take the dog on their rounds of golf, no amount of pleading with her, no amount of warning what the Committee - who didn't approve of dogs, apart from guide dogs, on the course - would do, had any effect, Doris was coming, and that was that. Harry was in despair. What could he do? So he did what other men have done when they can't cope with a home crisis. He went to the office.

The only problem was, he didn't really have an office. So he did what other men have done through the ages when they haven't got an office. He invented one.

Dinner on Sunday evening. Doris was nowhere near the table. That was because Harry, when Eunice was stirring the gravy, had managed to lock the animal in the downstairs cloakroom.

'Darling, light of my life....' Men talk to their wives like that when they a) have something to hide and b) when they're about to tell the most outrageous lie.

The gravy boat was being filled. It was cold cuts again. Eunice had learned her lesson.

'.......darling, do you remember old Colonel Biggs, Max Biggs?'

'No, darling, not really. Oh wait, was he the one who had the accident with the polo pony?'

'No, sweetheart. That was Percy Trumbell. Never been the same since, can't even look at a horse now.'

'Darling, what's that whining noise?'

'Must be the wind, dear.' He turned the television set up louder. Doris could wait.

'Well, Percy I mean Max called while you were in the garden. He wants me to go and see him tomorrow about a bit of consultancy work.'

'But I thought you'd retired, darling.'

'Well, yes, but I thought I'd do the old boy a favour. Something to do with M15, very hush hush, a bit poosh woosh, you know that sort of thing.'

'It won't be dangerous, will it?'

'Of course not, dear.'

'Will you be back in time for our game?'

'I doubt it, light of my life. Better postpone it for another day.'

She looked so crestfallen, he almost capitulated. Then he thought of the giggling and the redesigning of Whortle's sacred turf and steeled himself to go through with his plan.

At the end of the meal, he was feeling so magnanimous that he excused himself and freed Doris from her cloakroom prison. Eunice was moody and irritable for the rest of the evening, but he told himself that it would be better for his wife to feel miserable for a short while than for him to be suicidal all week.

Harry became a new man. He left for the office every day at eight and met some army friends who were members at the nearby Pinehurst club. After the first shaky nine holes when the horror of the previous week was all too fresh in his mind, he settled down and by the second day was back to his old self. The memory of the rounds with his wife kept him from feeling guilty. He was not a liar by nature, but had been in the Army and had done and seen things that would have made a normal man's hair stand on end. So he was not likely to suffer any torment because he was pulling the wool over the little woman's eyes. True, the odd pang came into view, then was summarily dismissed. Over the next few weeks, he continued to play every day at Pinehurst, and even entered the Pinehurst Open at the end of the month.

Four weeks after he had embarked on his office deception routine, he stood proudly holding the huge Pinehurst Open trophy, having scored 39 Stableford points, and won on a countback. His net score had been a hugely satisfying 79, the first time he had ever broken the magical 80 barrier. The only problem for him was that now he couldn't tell his wife about his wondrous achievement. It would have been his dearest wish to have demonstrated how he had send a screaming five wood on the par five last to just short of the green, then chipped stone dead for a magical birdie. But that was now out of the question for him.

The feeling of euphoria had evaporated by the time he got home, the giant trophy in the boot of his car. Elation had been replaced by a forlorn feeling. As he gazed at his beloved over dinner, he kept wanting to tell her.

'And how were things at the office today, darling?'

'Fine.' That was all he could think of to say.

'You shouldn't work so hard darling,' she said.

The pangs of guilt returned.

'You look a bit pale, darling. Are you having lunch every day?'

'Oh yes. Just a sandwich most days.' His appetite, like his putting and wedge shots, had returned since his visits to Pinehurst. The agony of his rounds with Eunice were now distant memories, thanks to Pinehurst.

'Are you going to the office tomorrow?'

'Yes.' He had promised the captain of Pinehurst a game at ten o'clock.

Her next words chilled him to the bone. It was the same feeling he had when missing a two foot putt. 'Max telephoned today.'

'Max?'

'Biggs, Max Biggs.'

'He did?" Suddenly flustered. "What did he want?'

'He thought he'd like a game of golf with you after all these years.'

'Oh, did he?'

'Yes.'

Wise men often say that when you find yourself in a hole, you stop digging. Lesser mortals say that you can lie your way out of any situation. Harry had never been a good liar, despite having been a career soldier. Had he been a company director, or an estate agent, he may have had the situation under control in seconds.

'Hmpphh.' That was all he managed to say.

Eunice looked at him sadly.

'I suppose it will all come out at the nasty court hearing.' Harry's heart sank. He felt worse than when he'd been beaten on the 18th when he had missed a four foot putt in the Whortle Matchplay Championship.

'Court hearing?'

'Yes. I suppose you want a divorce?'

'Divorce?'

'Who is she?'

'Who?'

'The woman, of course. You've been seeing a woman instead of going to the office. Max said he hadn't seen you in years. So who is she?'

'But there is no woman, dear.'

67

'So, where have you been going every day. What have you been doing?'

'Er - playing golf.'

'Playing golf.'

'Playing golf.'

'Explain yourself.'

Harry clenched his fists, hesitated. 'Well, I'm sure most men would enjoy playing golf with you.' This wasn't going to be easy. 'The fact is, I couldn't stand it. The fault, I'm sure, is entirely mine. But I couldn't bring myself to tell you the truth, you were enjoying it so much. So instead, I told you a lie. There is no office. I've been going to Pinehurst every day.'

Eunice sat, dumbstruck. 'You were there today?'

'Yes.'

'And the day before?'

'Yes.'

'And last week?'

'Yes.'

In spite of the agony of his confession, Harry was engulfed by a wild enthusiasm. 'Don't move. Stay right there.' He rushed out to the car, and returned with his giant Pinehurst trophy. 'See? It's all mine, I won the Pinehurst Open.' The words burbled out and he described how he had sunk a twelve foot putt on the third, then described in detail his stunning birdie at the final hole, and the tension of waiting for a countback before he was sure he'd won.

'Darling, you must forgive me. I didn't mean to deceive you. There is no other woman. Only golf.'

Eunice shook her head. "I shall never play again,' she said softly.

'But darling, you can play with the other girls. You'll love it.'

'Oh Harry, I'm so foolish. I suspected you. I thought there was another woman.'

'Never. Never.'

'I'm so silly. To think......'

'Oh, darling, can you forgive me?" Eunice folded him in her arms. "Of course, of course...'

'So that was that?' I said, motioning to the steward for another drink for the Colonel.

'Well, yes and no,' he said. 'What Harry didn't know was that Eunice wasn't as happy playing golf as she pretended. After the first few days, she was aching all over, but she thought that it would be a blow to Harry if she gave up the game, as he was enjoying teaching her so much. Or so she thought. When Harry started going to the office, she used her spare time wisely. She went to Scottie McLeod for lessons, and he soon told her that Harry was the wrong person to teach her. Harry, you see, has a very unorthodox swing, a bit like Lee Trevino only a lot worse. Trying to do it his way was giving her back ache. Scottie showed her how to do it right with a tighter swing and she was a lot more comfortable. She became quite useful.'

'So what happened?'

'Well, Harry thought she'd given up the game. He felt guilty about it, but Eunice didn't seem to mind. She carried on having lessons with Scottie for six months and swore him to secrecy. Then she persuaded Harry one night when they were out with a crowd for dinner at the club that they should enter the Matrimonial Bowl together. Harry was horrified, remembering what had happened when they'd played together. But he was persuaded, partly by his guilt pangs and partly by the wine he'd consumed. They entered and won it by a street. Harry was astounded by the transformation in her game.'

"Natural talent," was all she'd say when he complimented her on her straight drives and deadly chip shots.

She managed to keep a straight face until after the presentation dinner. Only then, as they cuddled the trophy, did she confess all. Harry roared with laughter. He'd been outfoxed and totally fooled by his wife. Now they play together as often as they can.

'Just never underestimate a woman', said Colonel Fortescue, 'especially one who's decided to take up golf'.

He sat down quietly and read his Jilly Cooper

THE FIVE HOUR MAN
Patricia Armstrong

We had our Invitation Meeting yesterday. My visitor remarked on the excellence of the greens, the well raked bunkers and the neatly cut fairways, but what seemed to impress him most of all was the speed of play. He said a fourball would have have taken half as long again at his club, and how pleasant it was to get round so fast. Much less tiring and plenty of time for lunch.

I explained that slow play had never been tolerated at Whortle Manor. During a round everyone was expected to keep his place, to proceed at a reasonable pace, and to let others through if necessary. People causing delay were left in no doubt about their unpopularity.

My visitor said it was a canker on his course, a small faction making life miserable for the rest. One young man in particular was painfully slow and set a bad example to his cronies. He got away with it because he was a good golfer and in the County side. He always started early at weekends and the whole place became snarled up behind him.

I said it reminded me of that business with Alex North and a chap called Toby Calder several years ago. . .

Alex was a personable young man with a pretty wife, two nice children and a good job with excellent prospects. There was only one thing he desperately coveted: he wanted to win the Scratch Matchplay Championship, to see his name in gold on the big board in the clubhouse.

Certainly he deserved success. He practiced hard, his drives were long and straight, his irons crisp and his short game deadly. That year he had won his matches in the earlier rounds with ease and he had reached the final comfortably.

The only cloud on the horizon was the presence in the other half of the draw of one Toby Calder, who had also sailed through all his matches on the way to the final.

Toby was a new member who had recently moved into the area. At first the club was pleased to have him, for he was undoubtedly a fine golfer - a scratch man. When the Committee received his application to join Whortle Manor they considered him an acquisition not to be turned down; he had, after all, been a semi-finalist in the Amateur Championship.

However, it soon became clear that he wasn't quite the catch we had all expected. His conceit didn't go down very well and he was also an excruciatingly slow player. Toby Calder turned out to be that most despicable species of golfer - a five hour man.

To begin with allowances were made, but there were so many complaints that he was warned by the Committee, without much obvious effect.

To the Starter he was anathema: 'Stands on the first tee as if he owns the place,' he said. 'Struts up and down like a peacock. Umpteen practice swings. Takes forever to get him off, then he ambles down the fairway as if all day will do.'

The Secretary and the Captain fielded the grumbling from members as best they could, but neither of them could stand the man.

Alex North had played with Toby just once, when he first arrived and was looking for 'suitable' partners. 'Never again,' Alex said when they eventually got back to the clubhouse. 'Tore up my card in the end. Couldn't concentrate with him prancing about addressing the ball for ten minutes every shot.'

Alex himself preferred a brisk round of two-and-a-half hours. Playing with someone so slow drove him to distraction. Toby had fiddled with his golf bag - constantly changing his mind about which club to use. He tossed grass into the air to test for wind direction, walked forward to pace distances, and he had a maddeningly long set-up ritual which, if interrupted, would be broken off and started all over again.

Alex met Toby's semi-final victim in the bar. He was only to pleased to regale Alex with his tale of woe: 'Impossible,' he said. 'Can't cope at that snail's pace. Forget what I've come about. Something should be done. Bloody man's a menace.'

Alex went home disconsolate. His wife Josie, spooning Heinz beef and mixed vegetables into the youngest child, made sympathetic noises in an absent minded sort of way. Josie didn't play golf, but she was pleased that Alex did - it was good exercise after being stuck in an office all day. She was delighted when he brought prizes home because it put him in such a fantastically good mood, but she had no real idea of what was involved. All she knew was that you hit a small ball with a club and tried to get it into a hole in fewer hits than anyone else.

So, when Alex moaned about his misfortune in meeting the execrably slow Toby Calder in the final of the Scratch Matchplay, she merely remarked, 'Why don't you take a book to read on the way round?'

Alex, who loved his rather scatty wife dearly, could quite cheerfully have strangled her at that moment. Tight lipped to avoid any unpleasantness in front of the children, he left the room.

In the garden he let off steam by doing some vigorous digging. Josie's words reverberated round inside his head: 'Why don't you take a book?'

'A book,' he said to himself. 'Women! Stupid creatures!' But as he dug a persistent little voice kept saying, 'Why not? Why not take a book?'

Finally he flung down the spade and went indoors. He kissed his wife: 'You're brilliant,' he told her. 'Absolutely brilliant.'

Alex confided his wife's idea to his friend, Roy, who had also fallen foul of the detestable Toby. 'I intend to take a book to read on the way round,' he said.

When Roy looked doubtful Alex asked anxiously, 'That'd be all right wouldn't it. I mean, you don't think it would be blatant gamesmanship?'

Roy, who considered that boiling in oil would be too good for Toby Calder said, 'No. It's fine as far as it goes, but you can't just stand there like a lemon reading your book while he plays. You'll have to have something to sit on.'

'Good idea,' Alex said. 'I can borrow my father's shooting stick.'

Roy shook his head. 'That's no good. You're not used to perching on one of those things. Damned uncomfortable if you ask me. I've got a much better idea. Here's what I think we ought to do . . .'

The first tee was reserved for half-an-hour on the morning of the match to let the contestants get well away. Competition finals at Whortle Manor always have a Starter in attendance, and an experienced umpire - usually a committee member. Both Toby and Alex had caddies and there was the usual small group of spectators. In addition Roy was there, carrying a hardback copy of Jilly Cooper's 'Rivals' and a collapsible chair.

Roy had thought of taking a proper deckchair, but it would have been cumbersome to carry and they were vicious things to put up and down - always snapping at your fingers. He had schooled Alex thoroughly, who had promised to carry out his instructions to the letter.

'Play it cool,' Roy said. 'He's bound to protest, but don't you get into any argument. The umpire will sort him out. You just concentrate on the job in hand and read Jilly between shots. Believe me, it's the only way you stand any chance of beating him.'

Toby was already on the tee, flexing his muscles and going through a complicated pre-play exercise routine for the benefit of onlookers. Alex had already been on the practice ground, working through his clubs, so he only needed a few desultory swishes to stay loose.

When Toby won the toss Roy put the chair up, facing away from the tee. Alex handed his driver to his caddie and sat down. Roy gave him the book. Alex opened it and began to read.

Toby regarded him with some surprise. 'Aren't you taking part in this match?' he asked sarcastically.

Without turning round or even looking up Alex replied, 'Yes, of course I am. Someone will tell me when it's my turn to play.'

Making no further comment, but obviously irritated, Toby went into his pre-drive rigmarole. At last he hit the ball, plum down the centre of the fairway, at which there was a lukewarm murmur of 'Good shot.'

Alex closed his book and handed it to Roy. He got up, took his driver from his caddie and teed up a new ball. After one languid practice swing he drove his ball with a nice bit of draw, just past Toby.

'Good shot,' everyone applauded.

The procession moved off down the first fairway, Roy carrying the book and the folded chair. When they came to Toby's ball Roy solemnly put up the chair and handed Jilly to Alex, who sat down with his back to Toby and proceeded to read.

Infuriated, Toby said, 'Hey, you can't do that, we're supposed to be playing a match.'

'Of course I can,' Alex replied, still with his back turned and without looking up. 'I'm not interfering with you in any way.'

Toby appealed to the umpire: 'You're only allowed one caddie,' he said.

'He's only got one caddie,' said the umpire. 'He's perfectly entitled to have other people following so long as they don't offer any advice or set foot on the greens.'

Toby continued chuntering. The umpire told him to get on with it or he would be penalised for undue delay.

Unusually for him, Toby's shot to the green finished well to the right, leaving him a nasty chip over a bunker on to a downslope. Someone in the gallery called, 'Bad luck.'

Toby glared.

Alex got up, stretched, took his club from his caddie, had a practice swing and put his ball in the middle of the green. He sat down again while Toby played his pitch - a mediocre shot which left the ball well past the pin. Alex rose and lagged his putt up stone dead. Toby missed and picked up.

'Mr North is one up,' announced the umpire.

The match continued. Roy didn't utter a word, he simply did his juggling act with the chair and the book. While Alex was very relaxed and playing well above himself, Toby became more and more angry, and more wayward with his shots. The umpire kept a firm grip of the situation, dealing dismissively with Toby's repeated complaints that Alex was deliberately trying to put him off, and that he was receiving outside aid.

The second and third were halved in par. At the par 5 fourth both hit long drives well over the stream, and seconds to within 40 yards of the green edge. Alex, playing first, put his shot 8 ft from the pin before sitting down and resuming his reading. Toby took even longer than usual to play; he walked forward to inspect the green carefully, walked back, addressed the ball, broke off, walked forward again, came back, addressed the ball and hit a full-blooded socket into the trees on the right. The ball was lost and Toby conceded the hole with bad grace.

The umpire announced that Mr North was two up after four.

The crowd of spectators, which had increased greatly as word of strange goings-on in the knockout final got around, were strongly pro-Alex. They applauded his good shots heartily.

The fifth and sixth were halved. At the seventh Alex, with the honour, played a superb shot which soared over the stream, landed on the green, bounced just once and came to rest quite close to the pin.

Toby snapped at his caddie for yawning and snatched the club out of his hand. He topped his ball into the stream.

Everyone - except Alex and Roy - went and peered into the water. While the ball was being located, dropped and played, Alex got through several more pages of 'Rivals'. Toby played on to the green and had a single putt, but Alex holed for a birdie.

'Mr North is three up after seven,' announced the umpire.

Alex increased his lead at the eighth when Toby, almost incandescent with rage, hooked into the lake. He dropped another ball beside the water, pushed his third and dunched his fourth. Alex, meanwhile, got a textbook par.

'Mr North is four up after eight,' droned the umpire.

At the 318 yard ninth Alex hit one straight down the middle before starting another chapter. Toby, obviously determined to drive the green, hit a terrific slice onto the clubhouse terrace - out of bounds.

The remnants of his self control finally snapped. He threw his driver down and shouted, 'I do not propose to continue with this travesty any longer. I shall lodge a strong protest with the Committee.' With that he stamped off the course.

The umpire proclaimed that, Mr Calder having abandoned the match, Mr North was the winner.

Toby wrote a long letter to the Committee, and a special meeting was convened to examine his complaints. Both competitors were bidden to attend.

Toby, called first, launched into a diatribe about how Alex had deliberately disturbed his concentration and play. Pressed for exact details of his opponent's conduct he said, 'He employed an accomplice to carry a chair and a book all the way round. Each time I played a shot Alex North was sitting with his back to me, reading.'

The Chairman asked exactly which rule Mr North was supposed to have broken. Toby didn't rightly know, but insisted there must be ample grounds for disqualifying him.

Questioned in his turn, Alex said that in order to maintain concentration in such an important match he felt it necessary to take rather unusual measures. He had been very careful not to infringe any rules or to interfere with his opponent in any way.

The Committee all knew about Toby Calder. Most had played with him and had suffered. For weeks they had been snowed under by complaints from members who had been held up by him on the course. They were unanimous in their verdict: there was no reason to uphold Mr Calder's protest. Mr Alex North was confirmed as winner of the Scratch Matchplay Championship.

My visitor wanted to know what happened afterwards. 'Was he cured of slow play, this Toby Calder?'

'I doubt it,' I said. 'He was extremely rude to the Committee; said the decision was disgraceful and he wished to tender his resignation forthwith. The Chairman asked him to put it in writing there and then. He stormed out, and that was the last time he was seen in the club.'

'Interesting, that,' my visitor said, looking thoughtful, 'I wonder if it would work again?'

THE VISIT
Patricia Armstrong

I've attended some pretty heated Committee Meetings in my time, and one that almost turned into a mutiny.

The Chairman had produced a letter from no less a personage than the Minister for Trade and Industry. It informed us that a Very Important Businessman from Tokyo was visiting the county of Pottershire, with a view to choosing a suitable site for a new electronics factory. Other parts of Europe were also under consideration, but if an English location were to be selected it could lead to hundreds of new jobs and an upswing in trade relations.

Apparently the businessman, one Mr Yukkimoto, had expressed a desire to play on our 'historic and renowned course', and the Minister had no doubt that we would be willing to accommodate him, together with two high ranking associates and a member of the Japanese Embassy, on the morning of Sunday, the 15th of June.

'Not Sunday,' we all cried, outraged. Sundays were sacred. Visitors of any kind were banned on Sundays, even when accompanied by a member. The thought of a Japanese fourball on the course at any time was bad enough; on a Sunday it was unthinkable.

'Afraid so,' the Chairman said, very glum. 'I'm not happy about it either, but it looks inevitable. I rang the Minister, and he was pretty terse. These politician chaps can be vindictive, and if we refuse they could make life difficult for the club.'

We knew what he meant. Environmental Health Officers arriving unexpectedly to inspect the kitchens; policemen with breathalysers sitting outside the gates waiting for weekend lunchers to start out for home, that sort of thing.

We all had a great deal to say on the matter, but nobody could come up with a decent excuse not to have Mr Yukkimoto's fourball.

The Chairman said, 'Perhaps we can make special arrangements, just this once. If members started their rounds extra early, they could get off before the Japs started at 10.30. And if the other members waited until after lunch to play, that should give enough time for the course to clear.

We decided to arrange for a small tent to be erected near the turn. A steward would serve light refreshments there to save the fourball leaving the course in the middle of their round. It would also avoid all the hassle of a formal meal in the clubhouse.

We insisted on providing caddies from the club. A quartet of Japanese was one thing; an octet, none of whom knew where they were going was quite another.

Sunday, the 15th of June, dawned bright and clear. The Embassy limousine whispered to a halt in front of the clubhouse, pennant fluttering in the light summer breeze. A uniformed chauffeur whisked open doors, bowing low as each of the occupants was decanted on the drive.

'Oh God,' the Secretary groaned. 'They've arrived.'

'Never mind,' I said. 'In a few hours it'll all be over, and we'll have done our bit for Queen and Country.'

'It's no joking matter,' he grumbled. 'Chairman should never have agreed to it. Thin end of the wedge, just you wait and see. Place'll be crawling with them before you can say Nip.'

As we watched, their luggage was unloaded from the boot, and four of our most stalwart caddies came hurrying forward to take charge of the enormous leather golf bags.

'Suppose I'd better go and meet them,' the Secretary said, and slunk out to the front hall, where there was much bowing and jabbering.

The Professional was pleased, at any rate. The Embassy Attaché had the foresight to invest in several dozen new golf balls, which were stowed away in their bags.

The oriental gentlemen, all immaculately turned out, emerged from the men's locker room, to be escorted towards the first tee and the Starter.

The Starter is one of our most important and conscientious employees. He is a stickler for punctuality, and his hut is festooned with notices exhorting players to replace divots, rake bunkers, have regard for other golfers and, above all, to AVOID SLOW PLAY. If there is anything that drives him mad it is lingering on the tee. He likes players to hit their balls, walk after them without delay and hit them again. He points out - often - that it is his job to keep things moving.

The Secretary and I watched from the terrace as the visitors made their way to the tee. Mr Yukkimoto, somewhat wizened and elderly, but spry enough, led the way; his Associates and the Attaché followed, two respectful paces behind him.

They all bowed to the Starter who, obviously surprised, bowed back. I expect he gave them his usual little spiel about having a nice round and not holding up the course, Sirs, as he does to us all; then they were off.

Well, almost. There was another little ritual of bowing before Mr Yukkimoto stepped up to address the ball.

The old boy swung, striking the ball a glancing blow so that it trickled gently off the tee. Another was teed up, which he squirted out to the right, about twenty paces. He played another, and another, and another. Still the first fairway stretched out before him, pristine and unsullied by any golf ball. We then saw the Starter intervene. He appeared to be having an animated conversation with the Attaché.

Later, he told us he couldn't believe his ears. The Attaché had explained carefully and patiently as to a child: 'Ah, Mr Starter. Velly solly, but we all wait till Honoluble Gentleman's ball on fairway.'

At the seventh attempt the Honoluble Gentleman's ball actually landed on the short grass, at which there were appreciative noises from his companions.

Fortunately the strange privilege of a stroke not counting until a ball reached the fairway applied only to Mr Yukkimoto. The others drove, in a manner of speaking, and the whole caravan moved off, but not before the Starter had been presented with a handsome tip for his trouble.

The first hole, one of the long par fours on the course, sweeps downhill away from the clubhouse. Progress down its wide fairway was slow and zig-zaggy, but eventually they dwindled into the distance.

The Starter, his duty done, tottered back to the terrace, where he was rewarded with a glass of beer by the Secretary who said, 'Well done. God, I thought they'd be there all day. What a performance. D'you suppose they go through that rigmarole at every hole?'

The Starter said he hoped not, or the round would take a week, and then some. Anyway, he was sure the hand-picked caddies would do their best to hurry things along.

A whole bunch of members ventured off at noon, in spite of the Secretary's warning that it was far too soon. It was. They caught Mr Yukkimoto and his entourage at the 4th - a long par 5 with the boundary hedge on its left and a rather fine wood of oak and copper beech on its right. More correctly, they came upon golf bags lying forlornly in the rough on the right, and there were rustlings and twitterings from the trees.

A caddie appeared from the undergrowth and waved them through. He was too far away for any exchange of views, but his demeanour said much. A couple of Japanese also fought their way back into the open, bowing and beaming as the members passed.

Later, - much later - we heard the whole story from the caddies, but there were frequent sightings during the day by members who caught them up and were bowed through with the utmost courtesy.

The fifth hole, with no real trouble except the lone bunker guarding the green, took only thirty minutes. The 6th is something quite else, a long par 4, with a stream running along its slice side, and dense woodland to trap the hooker on the left. It took best part of an hour.

The large lake on the left of the 8th is one of the most splendid features of our course. It is home to golden carp, water fowl and two resident swans. Who knows haw many balls rest on its gravelly bottom? Certainly there were a good many more by the time the Japanese fourball had passed.

They finally arrived at the turn by mid-afternoon. While they had a very belated lunch in the tent, the caddies staggered back to the clubhouse, gasping for beer and sandwiches. One went to the Pro's shop for more balls. 'We're running out of ammo,' he said. 'Better give me another four dozen. Charge it to the Embassy. Oh, and while you're at it, could you ring my wife and tell her to expect me when she sees me, probably not today at this rate.'

Fortified, the fourball set out to complete their odyssey. Members cut round them, or went through, and on returning to the clubhouse reported where the visitors from the East had last been seen. There was a time when they disappeared completely, but there is a lot of scrub and gorse at the far end of the course, and we knew they had to be there somewhere.

At 5.30 the Embassy car swept up to collect them, the chauffeur showing no surprise that they hadn't returned yet. By 6 o'clock, just as we were getting sufficiently concerned to talk about a search party, they hove into sight, straggling up the 17th. They were no longer playing, having run out of balls again. The caddies were incoherent with fatigue, but Mr Yukkimoto and company were still gabbling away happily.

It was another hour before we saw them off the premises. They showered and changed, and seemed as perky as when they had arrived in the morning. Actually, the caddies also recovered quite miraculously when they received their enormous tips.

The Attaché interpreted Mr Yukkimoto's speech of thanks to the Secretary and Captain for a most memorable visit. He had, he said, received much kindness and consideration from both club members and staff. He hoped very much to come and play again. The Captain said he was glad our distinguished guests had enjoyed themselves; it had been a pleasure to have them with us.

As the car disappeared the Secretary said, 'Again? Never. Over my dead body! God, I need a drink. A large one.'

Some months later, when the visit had almost faded from memory, the Chairman called an urgent meeting to discuss what he called 'The

Japanese Problem'. We were afraid Mr Yukkimoto was about to carry out his threat and come again, or, perish the thought, apply for membership. It was even worse than that.

'He,' said the Chairman, 'has made an offer to buy the Whortle Manor Club.'

Oh Cliste!

THE TRIP TO SYDNEY

Tommy Lawton was at the bar when I came into the clubhouse, surrounded by a group of friends, obviously just finished a round. Lawton was a big man, popular with the members and a good golfer. He had built a chain of garages in the county, and had a reputation for being a good man to deal with. Most of Whortle Manor had bought a car from him at one time or another. His wife Jane was a pretty fair player too. Although no looker, and built on Laura Davies lines, she was the apple of his eye and the centre of Tommy's universe. Apart, that is, from his three young grandchildren in Australia, none of whom he had yet seen.

They were, in fact, the topic of conversation at the bar. 'Another two weeks and we're off,' he was saying, 'Sydney here we come.'

Jane detached herself from the crowd around the bar, and came over to join me, as did Colonel Fortescue.

'He's been going on about them for months and months,' she said. 'I look out of the window sometimes when he's talking and I think he's looking at the Sydney Harbour bridge or the Opera House.'

'Aren't you looking forward to it?' asked the Colonel.

'Of course I am. As much as he is, maybe more. But I'm not that keen on flying, you see. I've persuaded him to break the trip in Singapore for a couple of days. Being up in the air for so long simply terrifies me.'

I couldn't imagine Jane being that terrified of anything. She was always first on the dance floor, despite her girth, and she seemed to lose her ungainliness in the polka or the foxtrot. Still you never knew. Her daughter Averil had fallen head over heels for a young Australian who had been playing in a pro-am at Whortle Manor. After a whirlwind courtship, they had married and returned to Sydney, where Gary had been trying to make a career on the Australasian Tour. A daughter was quickly followed by twin boys, just born, and the obvious delight of the Lawtons was tempered by the fact that the new family was on the other side of the world.

'I've got everything I need,' Tommy would often say. 'A lovely wife who actually enjoys her golf, a good business that's grown from nothing, a house right across from Whortle Manor and a handicap of eight. What more could a man want?'

'How long are you away?' I heard the steward ask.

'Seven weeks. We're going to do the grand tour, Ayers Rock, the Barrier Reef, Melbourne race track, and I'm going to give my son in law a good thumping at golf. But it's those little darlings I want to see. Imagine, twins in our family. Never been known before.'

I watched Jane's face. They had married just out of school, hadn't a brass farthing to rub together, and their only child, Averil, arrived soon after Tommy had found a job as a mechanic at the Ford garage in Minster. A few years later, he had the sense to start a partnership with two others and bought a run down old garage near his old firm. It was the sixties, the M1 had just been completed and their business boomed. Tommy didn't start playing golf till he was in his forties, and at first he struggled. But he persevered with Scottie Mcleod's lessons and gradually, as the business grew, and his time at the golf course lengthened, his handicap began to tumble. He and Jane competed in every Matrimonial Bowl, and, though enthusiastic players, had never won the event.

Now, as they had prospered, there was no reason they couldn't take a few months off and go to Australia. With Tommy, it had been a crusade. But Jane had needed a lot of persuading, and her fear of flying had finally, it seemed, been conquered by her desire to see their grandchildren.

But, though outwardly enthusiastic, she seemed more reticent about the trip, whereas it was all Tommy could talk about. Every brochure had been scoured and anyone who had been to Australia was buttonholed by Tommy, and he had picked their brains and developed an itinerary that any woman would have given her right arm for. Tommy walked over and gave her a big hug before disappearing off for a few minutes on the driving range before going home. Jane's eyes followed him as he went. She seemed a bit strained. Something was wrong.

'Everyone knows she's terrified of flying,' Colonel Fortescue murmured. 'The more he talks about it, the more time she's got to think about that flight.'

I nodded. Perhaps he was right. But they had been good to me and the children when my wife died, and she just wasn't herself. There was something behind her eyes that wasn't good old Jane. Perhaps they'd had a quarrel. But no, that was unlikely. It must be something else. I dismissed the thought.

I next saw them a week later, the day of the men's club championship. They had less than five days before they were to fly off to Australia. Some of the wags at the club suggested that Tommy had set the date in order to squeeze in the club championship. That way, if he won, he could take the trophy with him and show it off. It was one of those horrible muggy days, all the windows were open but there was no relief from the oppressive heat. Decidedly un-British, and the weatherman was forecasting more of the same, with thunderstorms.

'It's your weather, Tommy. You'll get lots of this in Oz,' said a wag at the bar.

'I don't care what the weather's like. I can't wait.'

Jane's face was grim, as if they had just had a major quarrel. Tommy's was a contrast, delight spread all over it.

'Let's have another pint. It'll be the last decent beer you get for seven weeks, Tommy,' said another.

'I'll be drinking amber nectar in my shirt sleeves while you boys are watching the autumn leaves fall and switching on your central heating. Isn't that right, Jane? We'll be having our barbies in the sun while you're all shivering.' He laughed.

'Not if it stays the way it is,' laughed another. 'This hole in the ozone layer is causing chaos. It'll probably be snowing when you get to Sydney, and we'll be still playing golf in shorts.'

'Dream on,' grinned Tommy, 'Come on, let's get to it before the weather changes.'

He kissed Jane goodbye tenderly. 'Wish me luck, sweetheart. I don't suppose I'l win this time, but you never know.' They embraced as he headed toward the first tee, and they walked arm in arm toward his opponent.

'You're not trying to psyche me out, Tommy,' said his opponent, the American Eddie McGraw, 'getting your wife to caddy for you?'

'No such luck,' smiled Tommy. 'She's back to the bar for bridge with the girls.'

'Good luck, my darling, give the Yank some stick for us girls.' Jane embraced him one last time and walked back to the clubhouse and the waiting bridge maniacs.

Rita, Peggy and Pam were waiting for her, impatient to get started.

'Did you give him a hug for luck?' asked one, teasing lightly. There was a faraway look in Jane's eyes, and she seemed preoccupied as the game started. The steward turned up the radio as the all-news station announced read the weather report.....''thunderstorms expected inland, high tides at the coast, and, unusually for the time of year, electric storms, followed by heavy rains.....'

Peggy caught Jane's anxious look at the ink-black clouds, and rose to close the windows. The mugginess had been replaced by a gathering wind, which was beginning to stir the curtains. 'Don't worry, dear, it never rains on a golf course. And if it does, the men won't admit it.

They'll play right on till they're soaked through. And your Tommy, he's the worst. He won't give up, especially if he's gotten a hole or two ahead of Eddie. He's not beaten him for a good few months.'

'Those men amaze me,' ventured Rita. 'Ask them to do a bit of gardening in the rain, and they look at you as if you're crazy. But they buy all the hats, trousers, umbrellas and the like, and they'll play golf in all weathers.'

'Yes, and when they come home, they might as well have bought a bucket and spade for all the good the waterproofs have done. They're soaked to the skin,' laughed Pam. 'Men are so useless.'

Reassured, they settled back into the game. The steward brought them tea in the gathering gloom. 'It's only four o'clock, it feels like...'

As the steward poured the tea, in the semi-darkness, the power suddenly went off and plunged the whole room into night. Just as suddenly, the lights came back on.

'Emergency generator,' explained the steward.

'Have you started packing, yet?' Jane was asked.

'We've filled two suitcases so far. They're full of Tommy's presents for the children,' she smiled, still tense. 'Would you believe it, he's bought a set of sawn off golf clubs for the twins, they're hardly a month old. Says they've got to start early, not like him.'

She paused, as tears suddenly filled her eyes. She stood up.

'I've got to find him, I've got to find Tommy.' The lights went off again.

The wind howled with a new force as the doors crashed open. Two men tumbled into the semi-dark.

'Lightning. It was lightning. Never saw anything like it.' They were both soaking, their waterproofs useless against the downpour. 'There was no warning. Just a rumble, then...' It was Eddie McGraw. 'Get us a couple of brandies, quick.' He looked wildly around, still mumbling. Then he saw Jane. Her eyes were wide with horror. 'Tommy!' she started to scream. As Eddie saw her, his face crumpled. He walked toward her as the room swam and she fell in a dead faint.

'It's Tommy. The lightning caught him. He had no chance,' he cried at their silent faces.

The girls gathered around Jane as the steward brought her a glass of water.

She slowly recovered. Eddie put his arms around her and she sobbed into his wet shoulder.

She could hear the ambulance siren dimly in the background. Eddie was holding her. The water from him had soaked her blouse and her hair. She stood slowly, holding onto a chair.

'Jane, are you alright? Jane?' The girls were around her, holding her up.

'It's my Tommy. Oh God, he only had a few months to live. Maybe less. I knew, but I made the doctor promise not to tell him. He wasn't in any pain. But there was no cure. He never would have come back from Australia alive. But this way, he died happy. He was on the golf course, thinking he was going to see his grandchildren. I couldn't tell him, you see. It was my way of thanking him for giving me such a wonderful life.'

GREAT BALLS OF FIRE

Tony Turner

'I remember the time they had a temorary green at the 18th for over a year' said old Colonel Fortescue.

'Why so long?' I asked, intrigued. I had been a member for almost ten years and the Whortle Manor greens were legendary throughout the country.

'It happened like this,' he said, settling back in his armchair, cuddling his gin and tonic.

Should Miles Taylor have so desired, began the Colonel, he could have been a Master Criminal instead of being just an eccentric schoolmaster. His devious brain was always working on ideas to put one over his fellow man. Indeed, people who crossed him, usually, after a time, got both barrels of whatever trick he had devised for them.

If the committee of Whortle Manor Golf Club had any sense, they wouldn't have blackballed his application! There may have been only one blackball, but as far as Miles was concerned, Sir James, and the whole committee needed teaching a lesson, and he was the man to do it.

His workshop consisted of the basement in the house where he had spent most of his fifty-two years of mischief making. His house was only 200 yards from the club.

"Balls," he said to his computer screen, "That's how I'll do it. Balls." He set about the mammoth task of redesigning the humble golf ball, by keying in a series of complicated instructions. That was the easy part. The electronics took all the drudgery out of the job. It would have taken days to work it out with pen and paper, but modern technology only took a few hours to complete the task.

Now he had the formula, his next task was to make the moulds. That proved more difficult and took all his spare time for weeks. He even used the schools craft room and their exact measuring equipment.

Now the moulds were ready, the mixture required making. This was the bit he liked best and used a food processor for the job. It was a good job he had no wife, as most of the kitchen equipment usually ended up in his workshop.

89

The liquid was then poured into the moulds to set, and he worked out that would take about six days. It would take that long to program the micro-chips and to work out his master control.

In an ideal world this type of work would be done by Robotic Machines instead of a middle-aged man with a fine soldering iron and magnifying glass.

Now that the half-globes were set and the micro-chips enclosed, the two halves needed sticking together with Miles's own version of Superglue.

When all this was completed, a final casing was needed, and that was a job in itself. Again a mould was required, along with a special compound. The final texture of the ball needed to look and feel perfect.

The whole process took almost three months, but now it was done. Fifty perfectly weighted golf balls stood in the cotton wool. All he needed to do was decide who was going to be his first victim, and what balls they usually played with. It was then he had the brainwave!

He could do them all at once!

Composing the letter was easy, what he needed now was a Post Office box in London to make it sound convincing. When that was done, the letter was posted.

Sir James Macman read the letter twice, unable to believe his luck. He chose a day in early August as the best day to carry out the trials for the new balls, and sent off the reply card. He fully understood the need for secrecy, as he always played his own cards close to the chest, but again read the final clause.

". . . . . should the trials be successful, and the new balls accepted by the Association, a Royalty of 15% of the wholesale price will be paid into an account of your choice for the first year's sales." It didn't sound much, but over a year it would add up, and of course, be tax free.

The morning of the trial saw a motor-cycle messenger riding up to the entrance of the club house with a package to be given to Sir James Macman in person. All the committee looked at the new balls with the look of a starving man finding a loaf of bread.

"I say, they all look normal," the captain said in his usual smarmy way. "Do we know who manufactured them?"

Sir James shook his head and fished out the accompanying letter, "No mention on here, it only states that there are eight sets of six balls, each set carrying its own number." He stuck out his chest "Naturally, I take number one and go first." He handed the box round to the others. "Two fours, yes?" the others nodded.

"Shall we say twenty pounds a point?" the treasurer asked, taking the number 'Two' balls. "Group total I mean." Again the others nodded in agreement.

Miles was sitting in the woods above the high part of the course with the control in his hand. He had programmed a mile range, and from his vantage point he could see over half the course – he was all set!

Sir James went through his usual warm-up routine, twirling his moustache before addressing the ball. With a resounding thwack, he forced the ball high in the air.

Miles pressed the white button, sending the ball accelerating forward, until it was high above the green. He then pressed the black, forcing the ball to drop like a stone. It landed not more than a seven feet from the flag.

"My God! Did you see that?" Old George cried, "I've been a member here for nearly fifty years and never seen anybody get so close with their first shot!"

A broad smile came on Sir James round face. "A fiver says you can't beat it!" All stayed silent.

The treasurer, with usual precision, selected a place to press in the tee, before he settled the ball upon it, with the red number 'Two' facing him.

"Get on with it Brian," the voice came from a red faced man at the back. 'We all want a go. You're all the same you accountants ditherers!"

The treasurer ignored the taunts of the junior member, and continued with his practice swing. When the ball eventually left the tee, Miles guided it to within six feet of the flag.

The accountant put back his driver and rubbed his hands together. "Did you say five pounds?"

One by one the same thing happened, Miles even managed to miss a hole-in-one by inches. He felt pleased with himself for that! Sir James was not!

By the fourth hole, the committee members were flying high. Now was the time for their first lesson.

Sir James fired from the tee, and when the ball was high over the pond, Miles pressed the black button.

"Plop!" it fell into the murky water.

"Oh. Bad luck, sir," a note of sarcasm came from young Giles. "It can be really tricky this hole."

The next player teed off with the same result.

"Plop!"

They all lost their first ball. Now for something completely different!

With Sir James's next shot, Miles just pressed the white button and watched the ball overshoot the green by almost a hundred yards.

"F..f..f..fore!" Sir James mumbled, not that he could be heard from where the ball finally landed.

"Play again, sir," this time it was the slimy vice captain who spoke up "It must have been a faulty ball."

"Little creep!" the captain whispered in his ear "You're not going to get my job by sucking up like that!"

Sir James grunted, before driving off the ball.

This time Miles directed it into a bunker, quickly followed by the seven other balls. He then left his hiding place and headed for his next vantage point.

He let them play the next hole without his help, then on the next he started having fun again.

Sir James placed the ball on his tee and started his swing. Miles pressed the green button just on the downswing, and the ball fell forward off the tee.

"Damn!"

Miles did this five times before allowing the red faced chairman to hit the ball. He then pressed the blue button and the ball swerved off to the right, and into the trees. "Damn and Blast!" Sir James yelled. "I'll never find that!"

"Play again then, sir" the vice captain said, much to the annoyance of the others. He did, and this time Miles directed it into the rough on the left side of the green, but still playable. The others, however, Miles put on the green, leaving Sir James visibly embarrassed.

Over the next few holes, Miles made sure that they all got similar treatment. He made the captain's ball hit a tree and come hurling back, hitting him in his rather fat stomach. The pompous club secretary's shot went two yards then stopped, as did his next few. Even Old George, whom Miles quite liked, didn't escape. His ball went off at an angle and straight into the hole on a neighbouring green.

As well as making fools of them, Miles also ensured that they all lost balls, until the final tee, where each committee member had only one ball left.

Aiming carefully, Miles ensured that each player scored a hole-in-one. Jubilation abounded as they walked the fairway towards the green.

Remarkable balls." Sir James stated.

"We should make a fortune." Brian said.

"We're just not used to them." the captain said, still rubbing his stomach.

Now every event usually ends with a fire work display. Miles, with theatrical flair, was ready for them.

When the group were a dozen yards from the green, he pressed the destruct button. One by one the balls flew out of the hole, high into the sky, and exploded into a splash of dazzling colours. The last ball exploded in the hole, sending tons of earth hurtling all over the unfortunate 18th green. The hole itself was now the size of a dustbin! The eight golfers threw themselves onto the grounds. Miles smirked and pressed the second destruct button, and all the lost balls followed suit.

Miles laughed all the way home, until he saw the fire engine pumping water onto his blazing house. He'd forgotten about the two spare balls in the cellar!

'What happened to him?' I gasped.

'Well the club wouldn't press charges. The poor man got pages of publicity in the national papers, but his house was destroyed. The insurrance company wouldn't pay up, so he lost everything. But it all ended happily enough. The Americans got hold of him offered him a job in rocket research, and he emigrated to Florida to work at NASA. He's happy now, given up golf, last I heard he'd taken up fishing. Strange how things turn out, isn't it?'

The
Matrimonial Bowl

THE MATRIMONIAL BOWL
Patricia Armstrong

The Matrimonial Bowl has caused more solid trouble in the club than any other competition. It has been directly responsible for at least two divorces, and when you consider that some fifty couples are involved annually, the marital tension and strife produced is incalculable.

Some say that is exactly what Aubrey Smith intended when he left the large, tasteless piece of silver to the club in his Will, his own marriage having been made contentious by his wife's insistence that they played mixed foursomes together on every possible occasion. He had set out both format and conditions for the Bowl carefully. It was to be husbands and wives, mixed foursomes, 18 holes MEDAL.

Unlike the less demanding Sableford, stroke play is not only a severe test of golf, but of temperament and self-control. Every shot counts. Every hole is played out to the bitter end.

This year there was a tie - even on countback of the last nine, the last six, and the last three holes. A nasty little sting in the tail of Aubrey's Will covered this eventuality: ties must be played off over another 18 holes, also Medal.

The opposing sides were the Fishers and the Brownes.

Jacintha Fisher - late 20's, blonde, slim, with very good legs. Wears short shorts and skimpy T-shirts which ride up on the follow through. Considered flighty. Handicap 20 (wobbly).

Piers Fisher - Early 30's. Lawyer. Stuffy; pedantic. Handicap 10 (plays to it about twice a year).

Muriel Browne - About 40. Large; thick ankles; bossy. Stridently argumentive. Handicap 16 (decidedly iffy).

Sidney Browne - 45ish. Wealthy. Quiet; deceptively mild. Handicap 14 (plays to it regularly).

The consensus was that the play off was unlikely to be either jolly or amicable. Betting at evens was brisk.

Club rules demanded a referee in such circumstances.

The Lady Captain said, "No way".

The Men's Captain refused rather more forcefully.

The Club Secretary said, that the great thing about Trouble was to see it coming, and No, thank you very much.

They put their heads together and decided they needed someone thick enough to take the job; someone who prided himself on knowledge of the rules. As one they chorused, 'Dudley Morris.'

Dudley was not the most popular person in the club. A pompous little man, his only claim to fame was that He Knew The Rules. More, he took every opportunity to pontificate on them. At home he had a whole shelf of books: The Rules of Golf; Rules Illustrated, Rules Explained; Interpretation of The Rules; Decisions on The Rules. Craving respect and attention as he did, he was delighted to be asked to referee the play-off, which was due to start at 1.30 on a Sunday afternoon.

Dudley arrived first, puffed up like a pouter pigeon. When the Secretary arrived there was immediate disagreement about a rule book. Dudley insisted it was quite unnecessary; the rules were all in his head. The Secretary was firm: players might want actually to see a rule. He presented Dudley with the book, a calculator and a clipboard. 'You'll need them all,' he said. 'Good thing their combined handicaps are the same; saves trouble counting.'

Some members who had played in the morning and lunched at the club arrived, forming a modest gallery.

Dudley was only a little put out when Jacintha elected to play the odds, and Muriel the evens. He checked - ostentatiously - that there were no more than 14 clubs in each bag, and that the balls to be used were different. Bristling with self importance, he made a ceremony of tossing for the honour.

Jacintha, with Dudley in close attendance, drove a low raker well down the fairway, to subdued applause. Dudley then scuttled back to the men's tee to supervise Sidney's shot, which also went straight down the middle.

But spectators expecting trouble hadn't long to wait. Both pairs were just short of the first green in two when Jacintha found their ball lying in a divot mark. She said to Muriel, 'God, what would you do with that?' and, quick as a flash, Muriel replied, 'I'd hit it hard with a sand wedge, and that's a two-stroke penalty for asking advice.' Jacintha, incensed, snapped 'Rubbish, it was only a casual remark.' At which Muriel appealed to Dudley, who, smirking, confirmed the penalty.

'Told you so,' Muriel gloated. But her triumph was short lived. Dudley declared that Muriel was also penalised two strokes for giving advice to an opponent. Muriel roundly abused both Dudley and Jacintha; Piers joined the fray to defend his wife, and Dudley, enraged, threatened further penalties for undue delay. Jacintha's comment: 'Silly old cow,' wafted over to a delighted gallery, who obviously were not going to be disappointed.

Subsequently there was some difference of opinion at practically every hole. By the time they reached the turn there had even been an argument over the nature of the earthworm. Muriel sliced into the right rough, and when Sidney came to play the ball his take-away was impeded by a huge worm cast, which he proceeded to brush aside. Piers objected on the grounds that worms were invertebrate annelids, not burrowing animals. The following argument and reference to the rules took a full ten minutes.

The first nine holes took the best part of two-and-a-half-hours. Golfers held up behind gave up the unequal struggle and joined the growing throng of spectators. Word got back to the clubhouse that the Matrimonial Bowl was providing excellent entertainment which would, with any luck, come to fisticuffs. Spectators now included dogs and children.

A large, unruly red setter made off with Jacintha's ball. Piers, thoroughly rattled, shouted, 'Leave it. Bloody dog's an outside agency. Drop another and play it, or we'll be here all night.'

Muriel turned to Dudley. 'Did you see that, Mr Referee? She dropped it nearer the hole.' Dudley made the baleful Jacintha re-drop.

It had become obvious to the onlookers that as well as ill-feeling between opponents, trouble was brewing on individual marital fronts. Jacintha and Piers bickered over every shot. Muriel, simmering, could be heard upbraiding Sidney. Snatches reached the crowd: 'Disgusting at your age.' 'Posturing Jezebel.' 'Flaunting herself.'

From his vantage point on the men's tees, Sidney could hardly avoid seeing Jacintha's spectacular legs as she bent down to tee up her ball, or her bare midriff, exposed when she held a finish reminiscent of Ajax Defying The Lightning. Nor could he be blamed when she turned and smiled sweetly at him.

It was also apparent that Dudley was losing his grip. His decisions were less confident and more confused. He eagerly grasped the lifeline thrown by Sidney, who suggested that one tricky point be decided 'in equity'.

But Dudley's composure finally cracked at the 14th. Here the green is approached over a large mound, which obscures it from view. Muriel drove, and Sidney really connected with a four wood, which sailed over the mound. 'Really caught that,' he said with satisfaction. 'Might be a bit strong through.'

The Fishers took three shots to reach the green, and when they arrived only their ball was visible.

'Damn,' Sidney said. 'Must be through.'

A four minute search in long grass behind the green revealed nothing. Chuntering, Muriel went back. She played short of the mound, and Sidney got on with a neat wedge. But when they came to putt, Sidney's first ball was found in the hole.

Piers, all smiles, said 'Dear me, what a pity we didn't think to look there before.'

'Doesn't matter,' replied Sidney. 'The score with the original ball counts - Rule 1. Our play was completed when that ball holed out.'

In the furious altercation that followed, both Dudley and Piers loudly maintained that Sidney was talking nonsense. They were only silenced when he produced a booklet: 'Help in Interpretation of The Rules' and made them read the appropriate section.

Play re-started, with the Fishers fizzing, and Dudley wilting visibly.

Ours is a very old course, and we have a couple of those deep bunkers faced with railway sleepers. One of these - said to have been designed by James Braid himself - lies in front of the green at the long par four 16th.

Sidney produced his usual straight drive, and Jacintha hit a long, low daisy-cutter just past him. Muriel socketed into a bush. Sidney took a penalty drop and put a good shot on the green edge. Piers, going for the carry, went into Braid's bunker.

As Jacintha approached the ball, Piers instructed her to play out backwards. 'I'll put you on the green,' he said. 'They've already taken four.'

She ignored him. Her full swing with a sand-wedge took the ball clean; it ricochetted from the sleepers, catching her in the middle, and landing back on the sand. Winded, she spun round, and fell on the ball, imbedding it deeply.

The crowd watched the ensuing chaos, mesmerised. Muriel burst into uncontrolled laughter; Piers smashed his club on the ground, breaking it; Dudley stood with his head in his hands. Sidney dashed forward to help Jacintha to her feet, enquiring anxiously if she was hurt.

Muriel turned to Dudley with obvious glee and said, 'That's two shots for stopping a moving ball, two shots for moving a stationary ball, and I can't wait to see how they get out of that lie.'

All five stood looking at the bunker, at the impression made by Jacintha's fall, under which, somewhere, the ball lay buried.

Sidney spoke, quite calmly. 'Actually, it's only three penalty shots. Two for the moving ball, but only one for the stationary. And that ball must be replaced.' He turned to Jacintha: 'That means you can smooth the sand and place the ball on top in a decent lie, my dear.'

This statement caused a riot. Muriel turned on Sidney, brandishing her wedge. 'Whose side are you on?' she screeched.

Piers told Jacintha, 'It's all your fault. Why didn't you do what you were told?'

Jacintha retorted, 'Who put me in the bloody bunker in the first place?' The crowd gathered round, offering unsolicited opinions and advice. The red setter bounded into the bunker and began digging for the ball.

It was all too much for Dudley. He hurled the rule book, clipboard and calculator on the ground and stamped on them, before heading for the clubhouse.

I'm sorry I missed all the fun, although it was described to me in minute detail later. I was called off the course where I was playing a few peaceful holes with a friend. We'd got as far as the ninth, when we saw the Secretary's car bearing down on us. 'Look out,' said my friend. 'Here comes trouble,' and how right he was.

Jumping from his car, the Secretary said, 'Can you come, please Doctor. Dudley Morris has had some sort of turn.'

On the way to the clubhouse, I gathered that the play-off had ended in total disorder, with Dudley walking off the course at the 16th. Since then he had been sitting in the Secretary's office, refusing to speak and just staring into the distance.

And that's how I found him; slumped in a chair, vacant-eyed and obviously not with us. He let me examine him without protest, and I could find no physical abnormality.

Pretty certain of the diagnosis, I rang a colleague, a Consultant Psychiatrist who ran a nice little private clinic nearby. 'Bill,' I said. 'I think I've got a genuine Fugue for you.'

When I described Dudley's condition, and the events leading up to it, he arranged to admit him forthwith, and we agreed to meet later at the clinic. Goodbye peaceful Sunday evening, and I wasn't even on call.

Strange things, Fugues. Very unusual. I've only seen a couple in my whole life. Faced with an intolerable situation, the mind simply switches off. There is subsequent amnesia, the patient remembering nothing of the unpleasant incident.

So it was with Dudley. He made a full recovery and returned to the club, but he never mentioned the rules again, and had no recollection of having refereed the Matrimonial Bowl - which, incidentally, was declared null and void by the Committee.

Some weeks later, the Secretary and I were chatting. He said he had been looking through the records, and it was most interesting: in the seven years it had been played, all winners of the Matrimonial Bowl had run into trouble of one sort or another - divorces, separations, and so on.

He thought old Aubrey must have jinxed his trophy, like the Curse of the Pharoahs. This year, with no clear winner, the misfortune seemed to have fallen on poor old Dudley too.

'And look at this,' he said, waving the draw for the Autumn Mixed Foursomes. Sidney Browne was partnering Jacintha Fisher.

THE COLONELS' TEWT
Patricia Armstrong

The Secretary and I spent the entire afternoon taking an inventory of the club trophies. It should have taken an hour at most, but we kept getting sidetracked. As we checked each piece we tended to reminisce. It was the 'Do you remember?' factor that held us up. The handsome mahogany box containing two crystal decanters reminded us of the near riot during a past Grandfathers' Tantalus, and handling the hideous Matrimonial Bowl we recalled the disastrous playoff and its repercussions.

Besides the usual cups, bowls, salvers, and so on, there were some interesting figurines. Once they would have been taken home by prizewinners and displayed proudly, but with burglaries and high insurance premiums they now remained under lock and key at the club.

A small bronze of three elderly gentlemen sitting scrutinising a large sheet of paper had a silver plate on its plinth bearing the legend 'The Colonels' TEWT'.

'You remember this,' the Secretary said. 'New members always ask what the devil it means.'

He and I certainly both knew, having been in at its conception. As we added it to our list we thought back to the afternoon when the colonels were closeted together behind locked doors with the Secretary. Outside there was a large notice - No Admittance.

Seen through the terrace window they - Willoughby, 4th Gurkhas; Anstruther, Welsh Guards; Fortescue, Royal Green Jackets, the youngest of them - were poring over a large sheet of graph paper. They were equipped with pencils, rulers, notepads, and small map-marking flags.

As I went past on my way to play nine holes they were completely absorbed, and were still hard at it when I came into the clubhouse a couple of hours later. I asked the Secretary what was going on. He smiled. 'The colonels requisitioned the small committee room for the afternoon to work on a TEWT,' he said. 'That's Army jargon. Means "A Tactical Exercise Without Troops"'.

'Sounds interesting,' I said. 'What sort of exercise exactly?'

'Top secret,' he said. 'But they've been cooking up something after that business this morning.'

'I missed it,' I said. 'What happened?'

Apparently the colonels had been sitting in their usual corner of the lounge with their pre-prandial drinks when there had been a bit of a ruckus outside.

Being high summer, and very hot, some young men in T-shirts and shorts were out on the terrace after their morning rounds, drinking beer and making a noise. This alone was enough to give the colonels grave offence; they were firm believers in being properly dressed and properly behaved at all times, even if the temperature was in the nineties.

Also, being Sunday when ladies were not allowed on the course until 12.30, several girls coming out of their locker room had to run the gauntlet of comments from the youths. The girls seemed not to mind this unduly, but that was not the point. In the colonels' view, ladies of any age should be treated with courtesy and, by Jove, this sort of thing was not to be tolerated. They strode out and berated the young men who, foolishly remained seated.

'Stand up, Sir, when I am speaking to you,' thundered Anstruther to one unfortunate youth. He stood, and the others followed suit sheepishly. They looked slightly bemused while the colonels took it in turns to upbraid them for bad manners and conduct unbecoming gentlemen. But it wasn't until Willoughby went too far that any of the young men dared to answer back.

'Furthermore,' he had declared, 'Not only are those young ladies better mannered, they're better golfers than any of you. Probably beat you level.'

Provoked, one youth said, 'Steady on, Sir. Off handicap perhaps, but not level. There's no real comparison.'

Fortescue, whose granddaughter - the current Ladies' Club Champion - was one of the girls in question, agreed with Willoughby. 'I'd back the gels against you any time,' he said.

Still fulminating, the colonels returned to their neglected drinks. Anstruther remarked that it was a pity the young puppies couldn't be taken down a peg. Willoughby said, thoughtfully, perhaps it might be possible. He remembered a golf club in India where they used to have cross country matches - officers versus ladies. The ladies always won because, although shorter hitters, they tended to play safe, whereas the men could never resist going for impossible carries and getting into awful trouble.

Fortescue and Anstruther thought a challenge match on those lines a capital idea, particularly if it could be organised so that the girls would have a good chance to win.

'Might work, y'know,' said Willoughby. 'Damn funny thing, cross country play. Completely disorientates some people. Like certain regiments we could mention going into action: start out not knowin' where they're going, arrive not knowin' where they are, and get back not knowin' where they've been.'

They got down to serious discussion, Willoughby suggesting a TEWT so that a suitable course could be selected. Obviously the first step was to decide the conditions of the proposed match, and then to choose some really tricky holes; the sort of thing that would provoke the boys into costly mistakes, leaving the girls to canter home the longer but safer way round.

They worked out the format very carefully: Two teams - men and ladies - six a side, with an age limit of 22. Play was to be sixsome medal. The two captains - playing number one - to drive off each tee, then a pre-determined rotation of play - two to six - continuing in the same order until the hole was completed. Tees and greens not on the prescribed course would be treated as Ground Under Repair. The three colonels themselves would act as Match Steward, Umpire and Scorer, and volun-teer ball spotters would be recruited. Competitors must carry their own clubs.

Once the match had started, interference or advice from anybody was strictly prohibited, and any infringement by a member of either side would incur a two stroke penalty.

The TEWT to map out 'the course' was a lengthy affair, and in its final form its only orthodox feature was that it started on the 1st tee and ended on the 18th green.

Four holes were chosen: 1st tee to 14th green; 15th tee to 8th green; 9th tee to 4th green, and 5th tee to 18th green.

The captain of each team would be presented with details of the course and conditions the evening before the match, but any reconnais-sance or practice was strictly forbidden.

The boys would play in the morning, the girls being banned from the club until lunchtime. In the afternoon, while the girls played, the club was out of bounds to the boys. The result and scores would be announced at a special tea hosted by the colonels, to which both teams, all helpers and such members as cared to attend were invited.

The challenge was issued and accepted, producing a surprising amount of interest in the club, and there was no shortage of volunteer help. Opinions on the outcome were sharply divided; the boys were con-fident of winning, but the girls were determined to teach them a lesson.

Carolyn, Fortescue's granddaughter, was to captain the ladies. He met her and her team the evening before the match to give them details of the course and conditions of play. He had also mapped out a safe route for the girls for each hole.

'If you stick to that and play carefully you have a good chance of beating the boys,' he said. 'Any short cuts are bound to land you in trouble.'

Carolyn was chagrined at his suggestion that the girls should play conservatively. 'That's feeble,' she complained. 'You want us to go the long way round. We'll be slaughtered. It'll take us far too many. The boys are boasting that they'll win easily. They will, too, if we don't cut a few corners.'

Carolyn had always been headstrong and wilful, and Fortescue was not sure he could persuade her to play safe.

'Now listen,' he said. 'I've played these things myself in the past, and I assure you, the easiest way to lose is to take chances. Let the boys get themselves into trouble, and believe me, they will.'

Carolyn grudgingly agreed to go over his plan with her girls, and Fortescue had to be satisfied with that.

However the boys had more sense than the colonels gave them credit for. When he received the course plan and rules Chris Ross, their captain, called his team together and left them in no doubt that the project was to be taken seriously.

'Those old boys are no fools,' he said. 'And they'd love to see us beaten. We will be, too, if we go at it like bulls at a gate. The course is dead cunning, and we must work out a way to use our length without taking too many risks.'

It took a couple of hours and a lot of argument, but eventually a plan was hammered out.

'That's it then,' Chris said. 'See you all tomorrow.'

At 10 o'clock the next morning the team, the three colonels complete with shooting sticks, several volunteer spotters and a surprising number of spectators had gathered around the 1st tee.

Chris Ross took his role as captain seriously. He reminded his team of their game plan: 'At the first hole I drive right - over the corner to the 9th fairway. Number Two pitches sharp left, short of the lake. Three carries the lake to the 11th fairway. Four hits an iron down to the dogleg on the 12th. Five puts us near the 12th green. Six pitches over the 13th tee to the 14th fairway. I play over the mound to the 14th green, and with two putts we have a nine.'

It started well enough. The first and second shots were as planned, but Three, famed for his prodigious length, pressed and topped into the lake. Unnerved, Four was fortunate to carry the water, but found thick rough. Five and Six, with the aid of alert spotters, were finally able to return to the fairway, but it took 13 shots to reach the 14th green. A single putt did little to cheer them.

The colonels were encouraged by events thus far; they thought things were shaping up nicely. If the boys panicked, or became dispirited, they were lost.

But Chris rallied his troops. 'Forget the first,' he said. 'We can afford it. Stick to our plan. The girls are bound to get into a dreadful muddle anyway,'

The 2nd hole - 15th tee to 8th green - went much better. A drive down 15; a second to the 16th fairway; a third right, over the 12th green; two decent shots along the 12th dogleg to the lakeside; a safe carry over the water; two reasonable irons up the 8th and on to the green, and a couple of putts. The only mishap was one ball lost in gorse between the 15th and the 12th, and the hole was completed in a respectable 12 shots.

'That's more like it,' Chris said on the 9th tee as they prepared to play the 3rd hole. 'Now remember: I play down the ninth; number 2 plays to just short of the stream where it runs into the lake; number three lofts over the stream and 10th green to the 11th fairway, and then we go down the 11th and 12th fairways, hop over the trees to the 13th, over the trees again to the 14th, and then a pitch will get us home on the 4th green. Shouldn't take more than ten.'

All was going so well that Five, without consulting his captain, conceived the idea of drawing a wood round the 12th dogleg with the intention of giving Six an easy short iron to the 14th. The draw turned into a colossal hook, the ball disappearing into the wood, going strong.

On sorties with his dog, Colonel Willoughby had come across an old disused hut deep in these trees, but had never imagined it could possibly come into play. It was with the greatest possible pleasure that he heard the 'clang' as the ball hit its corrugated tin roof, never to be seen again.

Thoroughly rattled, the team played a series of very shaky shots, encountering hazards and rough in their excursion towards the 4th green. They eventually holed out in fifteen.

On the last tee, the 5th, Chris tried to rally his dejected men. 'Come on,' he said. 'We can still do it. It's not so far to the 18th green, but there's a lot of rubbish in the way. The girls will have to go miles round. We can go straight for it so long as we don't do anything really stupid. We can pick up a handful of strokes on them here. Just keep your heads down and let every shot count.'

He himself hit a towering drive over the mound on the left, almost to the 12th green. His number Two played another cracker over the gorse to the 16th fairway. Here disaster almost struck: Three's attempt from a tight lie at a long carry to the 17th failed, and the ball came rest in Braid's Bunker, close to the wooden sleepers lining its steep face.

Four, a canny Scottish lad, cut short the ensuing discussion: 'I'm chipping out backwards,' he announced, 'Or we could be in this bluidy sand all day.'

'That's sensible,' agreed Chris. 'Then Five can play over the 16th green and the 17th tee onto the 17th fairway.'

Five hit an enormous shot which carried everything and put them well down the long 17th. Two more shots saw them beside the 17th green; another iron reached the edge of the stream crossing the 18th, and another put them into the heart of the 18th green. Two putts gave them an eleven.

The complexity of cross country play and the unusual course, not to mention penalty shots, had made scoring difficult to follow, and only the colonels were certain of the exact number of shots taken. The result was written down, placed in an envelope and sealed, not to be revealed until teatime.

The colonels had to admit that they had been impressed by the boys. They had played well and had made fewer gross errors of judgement than anticipated. Willoughby and Fortescue agreed when Anstruther remarked: 'It's going to be damned close.'

After lunch, as the girls' team walked to the 1st tee, Fortescue had a quick word with his granddaughter: 'Good luck, m'dear. Stick to your plan and you'll win.'

Carolyn reminded her girls to play by the book: 'No fancy improvisions,' she warned them. 'I've no idea what the boys scored, but we just play every shot as well as we can and hope for the best.'

The first went quite well. They played steadily down the 1st, 2nd and 3rd, then crossed the stream to the 4th without incident. Down the 4th fairway they went, then a neat pitch over to the 14th green and a couple of putts got them down in twelve shots.

The second - 15th tee to 8th green - also worked out nicely. They retraced their steps; back up the 4th, over the stream, back along the 3rd, across to the beginning of the 8th, up the fairway and on to the green. Two putts gave them another twelve.

Setting out from the 9th tee to play to the 4th green the ground seemed much more familier. From the tee they played backwards down the 8th, over the stream, back down the 6th and then the 5th. A good chip found the centre of the 4th green, and with another two putts they had a third twelve.

As they stood on the 5th tee preparing to play the final hole there were murmurings from some of the girls. According to their agreed plan it seemed an awfully long way round.

'Surely we can take a more direct route,' said one.

'Yes, come on, Carolyn,' urged the others. 'We're well played in, and we can save shots if we go straight for the 18th green.'

It was tempting, but Carolyn was adamant. 'No, we stick to the fairways,' she said. 'We haven't put a foot wrong yet, and we don't want to, not when we're in sight of home.'

Progress back along the 5th and 6th was fine, until a badly skimmed ball whistled over the 6th green, leaving them out of position far up by the lakeside. Young Katie, aged 16 and a strapping ten stone, was all for booming a wood straight over the water. 'I can carry it easily,' she said.

Carolyn paused for a moment. The colonels held their breath. But to their relief Carolyn made Katie chip back to the 6th fairway, ready for a safe pitch over the stream to the 8th fairway. They played down the 8th and on to the 9th fairway, just short of the green. Here Six played her best shot of the day - a glorious 5 iron which soared over the trees to the 10th fairway. Carolyn, playing the 13th shot, hit another perfect iron over the stream, to the middle of the 18th green.

There was an anxious moment when the first putt - a tricky left to right downhill - went 5ft past, but Katie, with the steely nerves of youth, rattled the return straight into the hole for fifteen.

As we closed the display cabinet and locked it the Secretary said, 'I can still see the colonels' faces as they came into the dining room to a standing ovation.'

'They were certainly surprised to find the boys all turned out in blazers and white shirts and club ties,' I said. 'And the girls all wearing dresses.'

As I remember it, tea was a pretty boisterous affair, and the colonels seemed rather overcome by all the attention. They went so far as to concede that perhaps the youth of the day wasn't so bad after all, and that chap, Ross, was good officer material; he'd kept remarkably strict control of his team.

Finally, Colonel Willoughby, as chief instigator, rose to announce the result of the match. With a fine sense of occasion he produced two score cards and waited for silence before speaking.

'Ladies and Gentlemen,' he said. 'The result of the four holes of the cross country match is as follows: Men — 14; 12; 15 and 11 — a total of 52.

When the babble had subsided he continued: 'The ladies were: 12; 12; 12 and 15 — a total of 51. I have great pleasure in declaring the ladies winners.'

When all the applause and noise had died down Chris Ross made a short speech. He congratulated the girls on beating the boys fair and square. He thanked the colonels for their brilliant idea of the cross country match and their choice of such a testing course. He hoped it might be possible to make the match a regular fixture.

Carolyn, speaking for the ladies, said perhaps they had been lucky to win - it had been a very narrow squeak - and she too would like to think the colonels' cross country could be played each year.

The rest is history. The club committee decided that in view of the obvious success of the competition it should be an annual event. On behalf of the club they commissioned and presented the trophy we had just been looking at - the bronze of the three colonels.

Colonels Willoughby and Anstruther are no longer with us; A Committee Member, Fortescue, very much still alive, and the Secretary work out the TEWT these days.

'How time flies,' he said. 'Must be all of twenty years since that first match. Carolyn and Chris Ross's eldest son is fifteen now; he'll be playing in the TEWT next year.'

I somehow think the colonels would all heartily approve.

THE VARDON CURE

Patricia Armstrong

Andy Burrows was not an ambitious man. He was, essentially, a club professional with a particular interest in teaching. When he first came to Whortle Manor he taught a 'method' but soon gave that up. Our members are like those of any golf club anywhere: all shapes and sizes, very different temperaments and degrees of intelligence, and with even greater variations of co-ordination and physical ability. Watch our first tee for an hour on a Saturday morning and you will see almost all the awkward movements the human body can perform. No one method could possibly suit them all.

While Andy had no aspirations to play on the tournament circuit he did have one secret, burning desire. He wanted to play in the Open Championship. Just once.

In 1984 it was to be played at St Andrews. Andy had cleared the first hurdle by surviving the pre-qualifying rounds at Camberley Heath, and even that had been a terrifying experience. Ordinarily, with friends or other club professionals, he would have expected to play to par or less with no trouble at all. But with such a goal in sight, when every drive had to be on the fairway, every approach shot close to the pin, every putt either dead or in, he was beset by unaccustomed anxiety. But he had succeeded and was now due to go north for the actual qualifying rounds which would really sort the men from the boys. He was to play at Ladybank, a course near St Andrews.

There were times when he wished he hadn't entered. The members all knew by then and their interest and support added to the pressure to do well. He practised hard and generally prepared himself for the ordeal. He was keen to work on his own rhythm and swing without the distraction of having to watch others, so he stopped giving lessons, leaving that to his assistants, who were perfectly able to teach and to help any members in trouble.

Rob Harris, that year's Captain, was not an easy man. In his year of office he had developed delusions of grandeur and he was not about to be fobbed off with any assistant. He had an 'important' match to play and, unfortunately, the wheels had come off. He needed some emergency

The wheels had come off the Captain's game, and he needed help, lots of it...

coaching and insisted that Andy Burrows personally should sort him out.

Scottie McLeod, the head assistant professional, relayed this message to Andy where he was trying to tidy up some paperwork in his office behind the shop.

Andy sighed. 'All right. I'll come and cope with Mr Harris,' he said.

As he appeared Rob Harris said briskly, 'Ah, there you are, Burrows. What's all this nonsense about not giving lessons before you go up to Scotland? Won't take a minute for you to come and have a look at me. Only needs a minor adjustment, I expect. Swing's usually pretty grooved, as you know.'

Andy did know. Pretty grooved for a ditch digger, perhaps. Reluctantly he followed the Captain out to the practice ground with a large bucket of balls.

'Let's see you hit a few, Sir,' Andy said. 'So that I can get some idea of the trouble.'

Watching the parody of a swing, Andy was overwhelmed by the impossibility of his task. Nothing was right; not that it ever was, but that day it was even more grotesque than usual. Grip, stance, takeaway, tempo, plane were all out of kilter. The Captain sprayed balls everywhere, most of them not even getting off the ground. He couldn't have hit a barn door at ten paces.

Andy decided to latch on to one fault, try to correct it and then beat it back to the haven of his office. No use tinkering with the grip - that way lay insanity. Getting him properly lined up would seem a good start, then perhaps trying for some position at the top of the backswing which would give him at least half a chance of getting the clubface back to the ball.

'We'll just put this club down across the feet to get your direction straightened out first,' he said. 'Then we can tackle the real problem.'

Rob Harris said, 'Knew you'd see straight off what had to be done, Burrows. Can't leave these things to the boys. All right for the hackers maybe, but not for serious golfers.'

'Right,' Andy said. 'Now we must get a good top of the backswing position so you have the right angle of attack coming down. At the moment you're much too flat.'

Easier said than done.

During the next fifteen minutes Andy found no way he could persuade, cajole, or even place Rob Harris into a position at the top of the backswing from which it was remotely possible to make a square contact with the ball. If urged to turn he swept the club round his ankles; if asked

113

to use his arms he plucked the club back with his right hand, leaning forward as he did so.

When they had run the whole gamut of possible contortions Andy knew the time had come for desperate measures. He took the club from the exasperated Captain and shook his head:

'I feared as much, Sir,' he said solemnly. 'But now I'm quite sure. I've only seen it half-a-dozen times in my life, but there's no doubt about it. It's the dreaded 'golfers ague' - a form of fatigue, Sir. It strikes active, intelligent men who've recently undertaken great responsibility. A good golfer suddenly finds his game has left him.'

Rob Harris looked extremely worried. 'Can't you do anything about it?' he pleaded. 'I've got this very important match next week, d'you see. All the club captains in the county are coming here and I can't afford to make a fool of myself, playing like an idiot on my own course. Must be something you can do.'

'Only one thing, Sir,' Andy said, 'The Vardon Cure. Very drastic though. Requires drastic changes. Only alternative is to give up golf for a month or two until the ague wears off.'

'Can't give up playing, but I'll do anything you say,' croaked Rob. 'Anything.'

Scottie McLeod was also out giving a lesson, and from his vantage point he could see Andy struggling with the Captain. Ohmygod, he thought, that's doing the boss no good at all. Scottie knew full well how vulnerable Andy was just then. He had offered to drive him up to Scotland so that he had a friend to look after his equipment and keep him calm. Scottie was taking his duties as minder very seriously, trying desperately to keep the more tiresome members off Andy's back before the great event. Now he was being scuppered by the bloody Captain.

Then Scottie saw Andy take the club from Rob Harris and proceed to teach him 'Vardon's Cure'. He grinned. It was going to be very interesting. His own pupil had left, but Scottie stayed to watch. He edged closer so that he could hear Andy's patter:

'Very severe remedy, Sir' Andy said. 'Requires a very different technique, but it usually works if you can master it.'

He had Rob's full and undivided attention. 'Yes, yes,' the Captain said impatiently. 'What do I have to do?'

First of all,' Andy said, 'We discard most of your clubs. Five will do. You only need a three wood, a five iron, a seven iron, a wedge and a putter. I'll find you a pencil bag to put them in. With a new method the fewer clubs to worry about the better.'

Rob agreed. He would have agreed to anything at that moment. "Right,' he said. 'Let's get on with the Cure.'

'Now,' Andy said, 'We start with the stance. . .'

For the next ten minutes Andy adjusted Rob's address position. He made him stand much more upright with his chin well away from its usual place on his chest. Knees very slightly bent; weight evenly balanced on feet placed shoulder width apart; right foot square to line of flight, left slightly out-toed; arms hung loosely - left straight but not rigid, right slightly bent with elbow pointing just behind right hip; hands a little in front of ball, palms facing and club held in a finger grip; everything loose and relaxed. When he had finished Rob looked more like a golfer.

But he was a bit tetchy with all this boring technical stuff. Said he had heard it all before - it was old hat - and when were they getting to the Cure?

'First step now, Sir,' said Andy. 'Only possible from a really good address position.'

He made Rob address a ball and then raise his arms and the club in one piece - straight in front - until his hands were level with his eyes. Andy repeated his instructions several times, demonstrating the while. 'Like this. Straight in front of you, in one piece.'

When Rob carried out this manoeuvre he found that the club was pointing just behind his right ear. Andy made him repeat the movement with each of his clubs until it had become smoother, less tortured.

'Very good, Sir,' Andy said. 'You're getting it nicely. Ready for the second step now.'

He put down a ball and asked Rob to address it and raise the club into position as before. 'Good,' he said. 'Now simply transfer your weight to the right foot and turn your back to the target.'

Andy demonstrated the smooth transition from hands in front at eye level to hands behind, with the club now pointing to the target and just short of the horizontal. He made Rob carry out the whole set of movements to a mantra: 'Address, relax, lift and turn.'

It was astonishing the way, quite suddenly, Rob's backswing position resembled that of a man who might well have played golf before.

'Perfect top of the swing position, Sir,' Andy said. 'You couldn't fail to hit it well from there. You've worked very hard and I think that's enough for today. Practice that as often as you can, at home in the garden will do, and we'll go on from there.'

Rob exploded. 'Good God, man,' he shouted. 'When do I get a crack at the ball? That's what I came for.'

'Not a crack, Sir,' Andy admonished. 'Never a crack. It must be a swish. Always smooth and easy. You can try just one shot, as you've done so well, but that's all for today.'

Andy handed Rob his three wood and teed up a ball. 'Now Sir. Address, loosen up those arms, chin up, then lift up in front, turn and swish. Have a couple of swishes first, then step into the ball and do exactly the same thing.'

Neither was prepared for what followed. Rob had a couple of swishes from his new position and then stepped up to the ball and did his thing. He addressed, lifted, turned and swished. There was 'click' as the clubface made contact with the ball - which soared away, dead straight, a good 200 yards. Rob stared after it. 'Did I do that?' he whispered, awed.

Andy knew when to stop. 'Well done indeed, Sir' he said. 'That's enough for now.'

He shook Rob's hand and picked up the scattered clubs, then propelled him, still bemused, towards the clubhouse, before making his escape while the going was good.

But the lesson had taken its toll. Andy spent a restless night in which his sleep was disturbed by dreams of golfers in a sort of hell of tormented backswings. He rose early and went out to the practice ground to make sure his own game was still intact. It was not.

Scottie found him in his office, haggard and with his head in his hands. 'I'll have to scratch from the qualifying rounds,' he groaned. I've been out for a few shots, and I can't hit my hat. It's gone. There's no way I can go up to Scotland now.'

Scottie was furious. All the good work of the past weeks wasted. What he said about the Captain was unrepeatable. But Andy, wallowing in his misery, said it wasn't all Mr Harris's fault:

'I was a fool to think I could do it,' he said. 'Haven't the temperament. Shouldn't have entered in the first place.'

'Course you can do it,' Scottie said. 'And I was looking forward to coming up home with you. Ladybank's a bonny course. You could sail round there, no trouble at all.'

Andy said no, he couldn't possibly. His game had gone. Scottie said it couldn't have gone far. Why didn't they go out to the practice ground and see if they couldn't get it right?

Eventually Andy agreed, and they went. Indeed it had gone. Completely. He couldn't even hit a seven iron to the guide post 150 yards away. They tried everything. Nothing worked. He wasn't comfortable standing to the ball, his usual fluid swing had become a nasty jerky action. No two shots were the same.

Scottie did his best, but if anything Andy got progressively worse. Finally he flung down the club and said, 'See? Hopeless. Might as well pack it in.'

'One last try,' Scottie begged. He gave the seven iron back to Andy and put down a ball. 'Now Andy, please. Address the ball, lift the club up in front of you, turn and swish.'

'Good God,' Andy muttered. He stepped up to the ball, casually addressed it, lifted the club to eye level, turned his back to the target and swished. The ball rose on a perfect trajectory and without a waver dropped within a yard of the guide post, backspin checking it where it fell.

Without a word Scottie put down four balls in a line, a few inches apart. Andy stepped up and, using the same method, hit them one after the other without even bothering to check their flight. The balls formed a neat group around the post, the last having actually struck it squarely.

'Great,' Scottie said. 'You were only off plane. That's cured it.'

During the next half hour they ran through all Andy's clubs, and it was the same story. When he used 'The Vardon Cure' he hit everything easily and well; when he tried to revert to his normal technique uncertainty and hesitation returned.

They went back to the pro's office to discuss the situation. Andy said it was all very well, but he couldn't play that way in public, he would be a laughing stock. Scottie said that was nonsense. All he had to do was say he'd injured his right shoulder and couldn't lift his arm sideways. He'd had to get round the problem by changing his swing temporarily.

'And anyway,' Scottie said, 'I doubt if anyone will notice if you do it smoothly, like a proper swing. It's only when you break it down into separate parts that it's obvious.'

That evening Scottie and Andy played nine holes to test the 'method'. It held up, Andy finishing two under par.

'The Vardon Cure' continued to work the next day, both on the practice ground and on the course. Andy was forced to admit that, although he might be sacrificing a little length, he had never bee so accurate in his life. He was finally persuaded to go ahead with the trip north. They set off at dawn on Friday morning, sharing the driving, and eventually reached the small hotel near St Andrews where Scottie had booked rooms.

For the Saturday morning practice round at Ladybank Scottie caddied for Andy. They played with a local lad, also there for the qualifying rounds. Scottie told him that Andy had injured his right shoulder and couldn't lift his arm sideways; he'd had to adopt his present method, but was sensitive about it - thought it looked foolish. After the round the young Scot remarked that if he could hit the ball as straight as Mr Burrows he'd stick to that swing for ever, no matter what.

117

At the clubhouse they met a large, rather elderly man in a long tweed overcoat. He greeted Scottie warmly, and Scottie introduced him: 'Angus Cameron,' he said. 'Going to caddie for you. Knows every hump and hollow on Ladybank and St Andrews.'

Angus, gratified by this testimonial, said he'd known Scottie since he was a wee lad and was glad to carry for his boss. Scottie drew Angus aside and explained about Andy's 'injury.' Angus, under no illusions about a golfer's ailments, didn't think Andy would be requiring his services beyond Ladybank's two qualifying rounds, but promised to look after him as best he could.

Next morning, after a very brief practice session, Andy and Angus were off with the dew sweepers. It was dull with little wind, and Andy was drawn with a Brazilian and a club professional from East Anglia. Scottie was the only spectator.

Angus steered Andy round unerringly: encouraging, warning of pitfalls and advising. The Cure worked as well as ever and, with the help of a few single putts, he finished in two under par. Angus, pleased with his charge, remarked to Scottie, 'He's a bonny golfer, yon. Crabbit shoulder or no.'

Latter, Scottie took Andy sightseeing round the Old Town and then watched him hit a few shots, just working through the bag to keep his muscle memory primed. Next morning they lingered over breakfast, went for a walk, then spent an hour on the practice ground at Ladybank before the second qualifying round.

After Andy's performance the previous day Angus was confident. 'Dinna fash yoursel', mon,' he said. 'We'll dae it easy. Just gang steady.'

And they did. Andy was round in par, his two under for the two rounds qualifying comfortably. Angus was delighted. To be carrying again in an Open Championship on the Old Course at St Andrews was something special.

On Tuesday and Wednesday Angus shepherded Andy round the Old Course; he also fixed partners, to whom he explained the 'injured shoulder'.

At first Andy found things difficult. Often fairways were not visible from the tees, hidden, cavernous bunkers lurked, huge undulating greens invited three putts and the unaccustomed wind troubled him. However, Angus showed him safe lines, pointed him at flags, always gave him the right club and remarked how fortunate there was no wind, 'just a bonny wee breeze.'

Gradually Andy settled down and began to enjoy himself. He now had complete confidence in Angus and the course seemed to become less formidable. No one appeared to notice his unorthodox swing.

With an early starting time for the first round on Thursday, Andy and Angus spent 20 minutes on the practice ground before making their way to the first tee. Here they met his drawn partners: a senior player, two years retired from the tour to be professional at a famous course, and a young Spaniard.

Standing on that hallowed spot, waiting for the starter to call his name, Andy felt acutely apprehensive. What was he doing at the Home of Golf, presuming to compete against all the best players in the greatest championship in the world? Angus sensed his anxiety and soothed him: "Dinna fret, lad. The Auld Lady likes ye. I can tell. Treat her w' respect, she'll look after ye."

Andy had a couple of practice swings; the starter called his name and home club. He stepped up, teed his ball and swung slowly and easily. His drive split the fairway and was a respectable length. The ball lay 130 yards from the flag. Giving him an eight iron Angus said, 'Weel up,' Mindful of the Swilken Burn, Andy carried the flag and finished on the far edge of the green. He was away. Angus looked over the line: 'Twa holes left,' he said, and went to the pin. A little tense, Andy hit the putt rather too hard. Angus whipped the stick out, the ball hit the back of the cup and stuck - a real gobbler. Angus whispered to him, 'I told ye. The Auld Lady's on ye're side.'

As they proceeded round the young Spaniard was a bit wild, but the senior professional played a rock steady game, hitting all the fairways and greens in regulation figures. His example helped to calm Andy. He too reeled off par after par, until the 13th when, keeping away from trouble on the right, he drove into a pot bunker and dropped a shot. Back to level par.

On 14, 'The Long', after a good drive down the Elysian Fields, he edged away from the notorious Hell Bunker and left himself with an awkward angle into the huge double green. Almost 20 yards past the pin, he three putted. One over par.

He parred 15. On 16, after a drive exactly on Angus's line, followed by a neat seven iron, he holed for his second birdie of the day. Level again.

On 17 Angus took no chances. Directed well left, Andy put his tee shot safely on the edge of the fairway, but a long way from the green. Angus again urged caution: 'An easy five iron short,' he said, and Andy obeyed. When they reached the ball Angus took out the wedge and said, 'Ye're 73 yards frae the hole into a wee breeze. Throw it weel up.' Andy took careful aim and swung smoothly. The sweetly struck ball hung high over the pin, dropped, checked with backspin and finished dead, three inches from the hole.

The formidable Road Hole negotiated, and still level, Angus and Andy approached the 18th confidently. Here a straight drive bounced merrily over Granny Clark's Wynd. As they walked up the wide fairway to the ball Angus said, 'Punch a shot over the Valley, straight for the flag. The slope'll stop it.' Andy did as instructed, keeping his follow through low. The ball lit on the green edge and rolled up to four feet below the hole. A single putt put him round in 71, one under par.

In the scorer's office Andy checked and double checked his card before signing it. Having confirmed his starting time for Friday, he joined Scottie and Angus for lunch. They spent most of the afternoon watching the golf on television.

On Friday, with a late starting time, Andy was much less nervous. After a thorough warm-up session, and taking no risks, he was round in a creditable 74. His total of 145 made the first cut with three strokes to spare.

Saturday remained relatively calm, and Andy was off early, paired with a young Swede. He played well, with a particularly hot putter, arriving on the 17th tee two under par. Angus allowed him a more adventurous line over the hotel corner so that he was able to put his second shot on the green with an iron, holing out in four.

At the 18th he drove well over the 'Wynd' and, on Angus's advice, pitched up over the Valley of Sin with a wedge. The ball landed beyond the pin and spun back, finishing eight feet above the hole. Angus studied the line long and carefully. Finally he said, 'Three inches right. Douce.' Andy lined up and swung gently. He kept his head down until he heard a clink, followed by cheering. The ball had dropped - round in 69 - and he was being applauded.

After the card had been checked and signed Angus went home to rest. Andy and Scottie watched golf on television until it ended. Andy's score of 214 for three rounds was well within the second cut, which fell at 219. Andy joined 63 other competitors for the final round. After the next day's starting times were posted he and Scottie went for dinner and early bed.

They woke to a strong wind. On the way to the first tee Angus said, 'It's bad noo, but the tide's on the ebb. When it turns it'll bring rain and mair wind. We'll be nearly in, it's those behind will suffer.'

Andy was paired with a Japanese who spoke little English. Setting off into the weather he remembered the adage: 'wind strong, swing easy'. He managed better than he expected. Playing into a stiff north-westerly he reached the turn in only two over par. He dropped another shot at 11 - three over.

On the 12th tee Angus said, 'It'll blae us hame noo.' The 12th and 13th were played in par, and Andy managed a good approach and a single putt for a birdie on the long 14th. Back to two over.

He parred 15 and 16 in spite of rising wind. At 17 Angus was adamant: 'Weel left. We'll play for five. Anything right the wind'll have.' Obediently Andy aimed well left and found the fairway. The Japanese put two drives out of bounds. With a following wind, Andy played a six iron short of all the trouble, then pitched on and holed out in two putts. Three over again.

The 18th was now familiar. A drive over the 'Wynd', a safe pitch on to the green and two careful putts saw Andy round in 75. Three over par.

Considering the weather, both he and Angus were well satisfied with the day. So was Scottie who, as usual, had walked round the whole way. He joined them looking, as Angus said, 'like a drookit corbie.'

When Andy had dealt with his card, they all got into dry clothes and went off for a hot meal and to watch the closing stages on television. There was an exciting finish in ever worsening weather.

Later they returned to the clubhouse for the final results and presentation. When the complete list was posted Andy's 71-74-69-75 - 289 - one over par, was surprisingly well up, the bad weather having played havoc with the final rounds. He had, in fact, tied for 32nd.

Ballesteros won with a total of 276 - 69-68-70-69, which was lower than any score previously recorded in an Open Championship at St Andrews. Bernhard Langer and Tom Watson were runners-up, tied on 278. Following them were Fred Couples and Lanny Wadkins, tied on 281, then Nick Faldo and Greg Norman, tied on 282. The first 30 players had broken par for the four rounds. The group on even par included the great Jack Nicklaus and Johnnie Miller. Among those tied with Andy on 289 were Nick Price, Mark James and Isao Aoki.

Reading this list Andy could not believe that he, Andy Burrows, was one of such an exalted company.

To his amazement Andy found that in due course he would receive an astonishingly large cheque. Up to that moment he hadn't considered money at all. His only ambition had been to play in the Open.

When he 'phoned his wife, she said she had been inundated with calls from members with their congratulations. Mr Harris, the Captain, had been particularly fulsome in his praise. The family had been glued to the television all weekend and had seen him several times.

Andy whisked Angus and Scottie away to the hotel most patronised by golfers. Here they found kindred spirits, and on this occasion drams weren't rationed. When Andy presented Angus with a cheque he protested, 'It's far too much, mon.' Andy itemised it - ten per cent of the prize money, eight days caddie fees and a small tip. He said that without Angus he probably wouldn't even have qualified. Angus staggered to his feet and proposed Andy's health. He said he had never carried for a nicer man, or a better golfer.

Andy's homecoming was quite an event in itself. His wife and two young sons had watched all the television coverage and recorded it. Apparently Andy's last two holes in the third round had been shown in full. The boys could both recite the commentator exactly: 'That's Andy Burrows, professional at Whortle Manor. Poor chap injured his right shoulder - can't lift his arm sideways - but he's adapted his technique wonderfully to compensate. Reminds me of Gene Littler. He couldn't lift his arm after an operation. . . Oh, good shot, well played.' And later: 'That's a 69 for Andy. Best round of the day so far.'

One Scottish paper had published a photograph of Andy and Angus - in his long overcoat - walking up the 18th, with the famous clubhouse and skyline in the background. It was in colour and the caption read: 'Andy Burrows and his caddie, Angus Cameron, on their way to a 69'. Scottie had procured six blown-up copies, complete with captions. He had sent one to Angus and two to the club Secretary, of which one was framed and presented to Andy at a special reception the weekend after the Open. The other hangs in the lounge at Whortle Manor.

MISUSE OF THE PUTTER

Philip Cannell

There have been several rows over the years amongst the Committee at Whortle Manor. The move to create a new nine hole course was probably the biggest I can remember. When a Japanese company offered a fleet of buggies - free - a few years ago, it also divided the committee. The purists, who believed that every golfer should carry, and that even trollies were to be barely tolerated, eventually won the day.

Eddie McGraw caused a row too. It became known in the Whortle Manor circles as the "Misuse of the Putter" row. It happened like this. . .

When Eddie McGraw first became a member, he was very popular. A native of Boston, Massachusetts, he was in his late thirties and the owner of a chain of print shops. He was a 18-handicapper who loved his golf, and had lived in Pottershire for almost 20 years. For an American, he was reasonably quiet and soberly dressed. He had married a local girl from Winster and they had three lovely children. He was an adequate golfer but had one horrendous weakness, seemingly uncorrectable. Bunkers. Shallow ones, deep ones, timbered ones, they were all the same. He couldn't play out of them.

It all came to head one Sunday in the medal. He had played a virtually faultless round, taking, I well remember only 70 strokes on 16 holes, a fair bit under his handicap. His putting as ever was deadly, and he was known as one of the best putters in the club.

On the long par 5 17th he'd driven well over the first bunker on the right. A massive drive, then a superb 5-wood near the bunker at the right of the green.

'I think you're just short' I said.

'I hope so,' he drawled. 'I hate the sand.'

I knew this was his Achilles heel, but he hadn't hit a single bunker all day. He'd also single putted eight or nine times that I could remember. At this rate, he'd be shooting a 79, six over par, probably the best round of his life.

When we got to his ball, he grinned ruefully. It had bounced and was sitting in the middle of the sand.

'There goes the round,' he laughed.

123

It was impossible to dislike him. He'd laugh at his own misfortune, but be the first to congratulate you on a good shot or console you on a bad one.

'Bad luck', I muttered, knowing his weakness.

The bunker was steep at the back but shallow at the front and the nearby green sloped downhill from right to left with the pin near the front. Eddie prowled around the bunker, looking for an escape.

'I was reading an article by Ian Woosnam last week,' he said. 'He claimed he'd putted out of bunkers once or twice. Would you object if I used my putter?'

'In a bunker?' I said incredulously. I thought for a moment. 'There's nothing in the rules about that,' I concluded. The other two players nodded. One was the secretary.

'I don't think so. A bit unorthodox, I suppose,' he said.

I could see a narrow neck at the front of the bunker that pointed up to the right hand side of the green, Eddie lined up carefully, making sure not to ground his putter in the sand, then struck it sweetly through the gap, up the right, where the ball swung left and ended up a few feet from the hole. It had been a putt all of 20 yards.

Eddie grinned as we all looked dazed.

'What a fluke!' he laughed.

The secretary was stunned. 'I've never seen a bunker shot like that,' he gasped.

Eddie sank the putt for a birdie four. 74 after 17 holes, he was ecstatic. He was still high as his tee shot on the 18th soared over the stream on the widest part of the fairway 250 yards away. But his chip was weak and landed in the greenside bunker, with the rest of us safely on the green.

Eddie studied the exit from the bunker.

'You need another miracle shot,' said the secretary, kindly. "I think I do,' said the American, reaching for his putter. The secretary frowned. I made a mental note to consult the rule book as he jabbed the ball out of the bunker, too hard this time, but it sprang up and rolled over the green, ending up just off at the back.

Eddie's flawless putting failed him this time. He left it short and two putted for a bogey five, and a round of 79, sensational by his standards, and beating all of us. I was nearest to him with a hard-earned 82, one under my handicap of 10. The secretary was one behind, playing to thirteen. 'Well done, McGraw. Most unusual,' said the secretary.

Eddie looked dazed. He kept shaking his head, as if unsure of what he'd seen and done.

In the clubhouse, he was exuberant. 'Doubles all round?' We shared his excitement, although the secretary was very thoughtful, and we parted soon after for our various Sunday roasts.

It was nine months before I played with Eddie McGraw again. His handicap had now been reduced to 12, on the medal cards he religiously handed in. His general play was the talk of the club. Everyone knew he had been a steady striker of the ball, his second shots were patchy, his putting brilliant and his bunker play horrendous. In short, a pretty typical 18 handicapper struggling to break 90. In nine months he had become the name on everyone's lips because of his all round skill with the putter.

In those nine months he managed to avoid the deep bunkers dotting the course. If he landed in a shallow one, he'd putt out. Once he'd gone into the notorious Braid's Bunker and got out left-handed, using the back of his Ping putter. That had been the talk in the clubhouse for weeks. I mean, who ever heard of using the back of a putter, left-handed, to get out of Braid's?

'Shouldn't be allowed', growled one of the older members, an ex-colonel in the Guards. 'Putters are for putting with,' agreed another, 'they're not bloody sand wedges'.

Eddie McGraw now had two strikes against him. He was American, and he used his putter to get out of bunkers. The club's Rules Committee eventually convened a meeting to discuss his unorthodox methods.

'I've looked in every Rule book I can find,' said the secretary, who had witnessed his metamorphosis nine months before. 'He can use a putter off the tee if he wishes.'

'Yes, but it's terribly un-golf like,' said the chairman. "What is he any-way, some kind of circus act?"

'There's nothing to stop you sinking a putt with a four wood, is there?' asked the secretary.

'That's hardly the point. You wouldn't do that would you?'

'No,' admitted the secretary, 'although Ben Crenshaw did use a three-iron to putt with in a Ryder Cup match not long ago.'

'That was an exception. He broke his putter in a temper and under the rules, couldn't replace it,' replied the chairman.

'I think we ought to give him a warning about etiquette,' said a com-mittee man. "And put up a warning notice about misuse of the putter."

'How can you do that?' enquired the secretary. 'He dresses properly, he plays quickly, he replaces his divots and he's a pleasure to play with. And as for the putter, I checked the article, and Woosnam did say that it was wise to use the putter in certain circumstances.'

'Look,' said the chairman, 'we've got to do something. The sand wedge and the pitching wedge have cost millions to develop. They're for playing out of bunkers. That's what golfers use them for. We'll be the laughing stock if another club finds out. Heaven help us if Pinehurst ever get to know about this. It's just not the way to play golf.'

'They will know soon enough,' said the secretary. 'We're playing them for the Tolley Trophy next week, and McGraw's in our team.'

The chairman put his head in his hands. 'Can you have a quiet word with him?' he asked the secretary.

'I will with pleasure, but what do I tell him? The first time he used his putter in a bunker, I was there and he asked me if I minded. I couldn't say I did. He played a truly amazing shot, made a birdie and his game has improved unbelievably. What do I say to him?'

The meeting broke up with no decision made. The match with Pinehurst was on all their minds. Pinehurst was seven miles away on the other side of Minster and there was great rivalry between the clubs. Friendly rivalry, to be sure, but they had won the Tolley Trophy two years in a row and were dropping broad hints about a hat-trick, laced with extra needle because they had three players in the county team. Whortle Manor had none.

The Tolley Trophy was played with twelve from each club, 18 holes of Matchplay. A light lunch was provided when the names of the players were drawn, Ryder Cup style, and the trophy was presented, complete with speeches, over dinner. This would be the third year and Whortle Manor had yet to win George's old trophy.

At lunch on the day of the trophy match, Eddie's name came out of the hat second last, followed by the secretary. I had volunteered to be a scrutineer on the last two matches so I'd be walking round with them. The secretary groaned when the draw was made. He and Eddie had drawn two of the current Pinehurst men recently picked for the County Second Team, one off 9, his opponent, and one off 8, Eddie's opponent.

Under the rules, they'd get three shots each. The match usually attracted a large crowd, and today was no exception. A mobile scoreboard was used to keep the players aware of the match situation and the Chairman was prowling around with his walkie-talkie, encouraging and motivating. There was no doubt, he wanted to win this one very badly.

Whortle Manor got off to a good start with the Captain and Vice-Captain both winning 3 & 2. Pinehurst struck back with four wins in a row, all by a single hole. 4-2 Pinehurst at the halfway stage. But Tom Billing won 2 - up, Chris Ross romped home 4 & 3 and the match was level. Alex North halved, thanks to a birdie on the 18th, and Percy Allen, the oldest man playing, missed his three footer on the final green for a win, and could only halve.

Eddie and the secretary, meanwhile were battling to stay alive. Eddie came back from three down after eleven to one down with one to play. The secretary see-sawed from two-up to two-down and was level as they came to the eighteenth. Both teams and all the spectators lined the last fairway and the green as they strode to the final tee. The scorecard showed all square and, under the Tolley Trophy rules, Pinehurst needed only to halve the match to retain the trophy. The Chairman fiddled with his walkie-talkie. The match was slipping away. Eddie could only hope to halve; it was all down to the secretary. Eddie's last drive had boomed over the corner, taking the tiger line on the last. His opponent found the middle of the fairway.

Eddie's opponent struck a seven-iron just over the back of the green. It would be a certain par if his putting nerve held. Eddie, just over 100 yards from the green, reached for his pitching wedge. It was an awkward approach with the pin at the back. He hesitated, replaced the wedge and drew out his eight iron. The crowd held it's breath as the ball arched to the right side of the green, found the slope and ran to the pin, then past to the left, twelve feet away. Eddie grinned ruefully at the scrutineer. 'That's what I get for changing my mind,' he said.

Meanwhile, back on the eighteenth tee the secretary's 3-wood also found safety, but his tall opponent followed Eddie's ball across the corner, some 50 yards ahead. What followed was the talk of Whortle Manor for some years.

The Pinehurst man, unfazed by all the drama, rolled his putt to less than a foot. Eddie picked it up and tossed it to him. Now Eddie needed to win the hole and ensure his half. He needed this birdie putt for a match half and a last chance to win the Tolley Trophy. It was a tricky length, twelve foot, with a slight left to right borrow. The crowd, now three deep around the green, watched Eddie's every move as he lined it up. The ball rolled slowly - too slowly - to the left of the hole, then seemed to gasp and fell in sideways as it ran out of breath.

The Whortle members cheered wildly. Their team still had a chance. The match was still delicately poised. If only the secretary could win...

Meanwhile, the Secretary wasn't happy with himself. His iron to the green was too soft and bounced into the bunker to the right. His opponent had found the front edge of the green, and his par looked certain.

Now the pendulum had swung inexorably toward Pinehurst. The secretary walked unhappily with the scrutineer toward the bunker. The ball lay in an identical position to Eddie's nine months before, near the shallow neck. The Secretary took out his sand wedge and examined the line from behind the bunker. Then he grinned at the chairman, 'I'll get hung, drawn and quartered for this,' he said and reached for his putter.

The Chairman glowered and the Whortle Manor members held their breath. Careful not to ground the putter, the Secretary struck the ball cleanly through the narrow exit, it scurried up the right side of the green, bent back sharply and came to rest against the flagstick, 20 yards away.

Whortle Manor erupted. Eddie pounded the Secretary's back and the two men embraced. Eddie grabbed the putter in one hand and raised the secretary's arm aloft with the other as wild applause broke out.

'Never seen a shot like that before,' mumbled the Chairman as he clapped both men on the back.

'I have,' said the Secretary, his eyes shining as he pumped Eddie's hand.

They waited, throats dry as the Pinehurst man studied his line. He needed to sink the put for a birdie, to keep the Tolley Trophy. The whole of Whortle Manor gasped in unison as the ball missed the hole by an inch and trundled a foot past.

Suddenly the green was full of cheering members, clapping Eddie and the secretary on the back. The trophy belonged to Whortle. In the crowd, the Secretary and the American embraced.

'What a game, well done, both of you', said the Chairman, an arm around each shoulder. 'And what a putt!'

Eddie looked at the Secretary.

'Which one?' he laughed.

Eddie needed this putt to drop to keep the Tolley Trophy hopes alive... . . . .

BLUE BUTTERFLIES
Patricia Armstrong

When Dr. Roly Adams, my most junior partner, asked to see me on a matter of some importance, I quite naturally assumed it was regarding a patient. In fact, he was due to meet Tom Billing in the Final of the Challenge Bowl and wanted to know what he was like.

A man enquiring about a prospective opponent doesn't want to be told his family history, or how many wives and children he has, or even what he does for a living. He is after inside information that might be of use to him in a tight match. He needs to know if a chap is steady off his handicap, or a bit of a hustler; whether he can be trusted by himself with a bad lie in the rough; whether there is any history of yipping three footers under pressure; that sort of thing.

'Good golfer off his handicap,' I said. 'Not particularly long, but very straight. Accurate short game. Fair bunker player. Takes the game seriously. Don't expect to be given any curly 18 inchers, but he won't expect any quarter from you either. Never talkative. Plays to win, but isn't unpleasant about it. Should be a good match with you both off 10.'

'Sounds a bit dour,' Roly remarked, and I agreed. Dour summed Tom up nicely.

Being a comparatively recent addition to our practice, and a newish member of the golf club, Roly couldn't have known of the unfortunate incident involving Tom Billing some years before.

It was when the extra nine-hole course was in the offing. Half the members were for it, the other half bitterly opposed. There were Extraordinary General Meetings, endless arguments about the layout, planning applications, and so on. The usual thing.

The club owned the land, so that was no problem. It had been leased out to local farmers who grazed cattle on it, and some parts had been used to grow cereals.

One faction argued that a nine-hole course would be an absolute money spinner. Not only would it relieve pressure and wear on the main course, but it could be used for extra green fees and small societies; an unmixed blessing in every way.

Others said it would be a crime to bulldoze open land, to spoil the view, and anyway it would cause chaos during construction, and subscriptions would have to go up to pay for it.

In the end, after all the skirmishing, the pros won the day, the antis were routed, planning permission was granted and work was about to begin. As a surveyor and low handicap golfer, Tom Billing was an obvious choice for the special ad hoc committee set up to oversee the project. He was more than enthusiastic, he was passionate about the scheme.

It was at this point that Tom found himself a girlfriend. Not an unusual state of affairs for a youngish man, you might think; particularly one who was dependable, honest, presentable in a gruff sort of way, and not short of a few bob. However, it was unusual for Tom, who was known to be terrified of women and thought to be a confirmed bachelor.

The first I knew of Tom being smitten was one summer Sunday morning when our regular fourball met. Usually Tom was a popular partner, being such a reliable performer, such a keen competitor, but Ian said he would like to partner Sam, and would I mind taking Tom. It soon became clear why.

For a man who usually focused on the job in hand, who always concentrated on what he was doing and gave of his best, Tom seemed curiously detached. The Irish call it 'throughother', which roughly translated means that someone is not entirely with us. Tom was wearing odd shoes and an unfamiliar, vague expression. In spite of winning the 6th - by a sheer fluke - Tom and I were 4 down by the time we reached the short 7th.

Now, men are not totally unappreciative of their surroundings. We do notice birds and flowers and trees and animals - we just don't go banging on about them, especially in the middle of a round of golf.

So when Tom stood looking dreamy on the tee, when he had the honour and the green had cleared, Sam said, 'Come on Tom, they've gone. Wake up. It's your shot.'

Tom appeared not to have heard him. He continued to gaze heavenward. 'Alauda arvensis,' he murmured reverently.

We all looked up to where a skylark trilled. 'Yes, very nice, I'm sure,' Sam said. 'But if you don't get on with it we'll have complaints from the people behind.'

By the time we finished the round - Tom and I having lost the match, the bye and the bye-bye - we had been treated to the undulating flight of a green woodpecker, badger sets in the woods and the subterranean goings-on of the mole. The last straw for Sam was a 'compare and contrast' lecture on adders and grass snakes.

Sam said to me through gritted teeth as we came to the 18th, 'I can't take much more of this.'

Ian was kinder. 'It makes fools of us all,' he said. 'Give him time. He'll get over it.'

Apparently Tom had fallen driver, wedge and putter, for a girl called Felicity, whose father was a famous naturalist. Like father, like daughter, and Tom, poor idiot, was wandering about in a wildlife reverie.

No one had actually seen Felicity - she was not a golfer - but it sounded as if she had her claws firmly into Tom.

Events might have run their course. Tom might have ended up with a wife and several children, much like the rest of us, if he hadn't taken his Felicity for an evening walk along the footpath through the site of the proposed new course. He was intent on telling her how it was going to be laid out: a tricky little par 3 here, a majestic dog-leg par 5 there. Trees would be planted, a lake created. It would be transformed. So keen was he to share his zeal with his love that he failed to notice how quiet she was.

When they reached the farthest point of the footpath she stopped, sniffing the air. 'Wild thyme,' she said, and Tom marvelled at the depth of her knowledge. She strode forward, searching for the source of the scent.

It came from a tumbledown cottage, whose garden wall was covered with the stuff. It had taken root in the crevices; it cascaded down, completely obliterating the brickwork; it had travelled from the wall along the pathside and the air was heavy with its perfume.

An old lady was in the garden, watering roses, when Tom and Felicity walked by. They passed the time of day, and Felicity remarked that the wild thyme was a picture, and so aromatic. The old lady said yes it was. She was afraid she had rather let it run riot, but she loved it, and so did the blue butterflies.

Tom said later that looking back he should have realised that Felicity was getting unduly excited about blue butterflies. She questioned the old lady closely. During the day, it seemed, the place was full of them. Bright blue they were when their wings were open; at rest, with wings erect, they were a sort of mottled brown.

On the way back Felicity said nothing much, but Tom went on enthusing about the nine-hole project. The cottage was to go to make way for the new course, but it was all right because the old lady was delighted at the offer of a small bungalow instead. It would be much more suitable for her arthritic knees. All things considered, the course was A Good Thing, since everyone was going to benefit.

But within 24 hours a preservation order had been slapped on the cottage. There were conservationists crawling all over the place with butterfly nets and cameras. The old lady was hopping mad - goodbye new bungalow with all mod cons, close to shops - and the golf club was in turmoil.

I found Tom nursing a double Scotch in the bar. "Oh God,' he moaned. 'The butterflies were Large Blues. Felicity went straight home and blew the gaff to Daddy. They sneaked back the next day there they were, hundreds of them.'

'So what?' I asked. 'What's so special about Large Blues?'

'Extinct in the British Isles,' he said. 'Or so everyone thought. Then we go for a walk and come on a damned great colony. It's put paid to all our plans. All work on the new course has been suspended.'

Felicity's father, scourge of despoilers of rain forests, was set to become the bane of our golf architects. Tom's infatuation went into sharp decline, became terminal and perished. He wanted nothing to do with someone who considered a butterfly more important than a golf course. How, he asked, could he have been such a besotted fool?

For a time arrangements for the nine-hole course were back in the melting pot, but eventually permission was given to go ahead - although the cottage and the path had to be bypassed. Proceedings were held up for months, and it cost the club a packet in revised plans and legal fees. We re-housed the old lady in her bungalow, and used the protected cottage for one of our greenkeepers.

The nine-hole course has still to be constructed.

Tom was pretty morose for a while, but his golf improved quite markedly once rid of the distraction of the treacherous Felicity. In time he made a complete recovery, but he never married.

The cottage is just visible from the 17th tee of the course, and if one really wanted to upset Tom's equilibrium in a finely balanced match it would only be necessary to mention blue butterflies at that point. But it's not something I'd be likely to tell anyone about to meet him in the Final of the Challenge Bowl, now is it?

A MATTER OF LUCK
Sybil Josty

Dai Rees had tried for years to win the annual Whortle Manor championship and this year he'd actually reached the finals. We rallied round to encourage him.

'Look here, Dai,' I said grabbing him by the lapels of his old tweed jacket, 'You know you can win if you want to. You hit the ball just as well as Gary.'

Someone gave a groan. 'Don't talk about Gary! He's won for the past two years. He'll be insufferable if he wins again.'

Dai's usually pleasant face creased into a scowl, 'It's all very well for you, but Gary's so damn confident he gives me the willies.'

'You'll walk away with it,' I said, crossing my fingers. 'We'll all be rooting for you. Besides, Gary's only a kid.' It rankled with some of us older ones that a youngster of eighteen had been able to win the club championship so easily.

Dai looked doubtful and my own confidence sagged as I watched him. He preferred a pint in the clubhouse to an hour on the practice ground. But Gary was always there whipping away piles of balls like an up and coming Nick Faldo.

'Besides,' I said, 'with a name like Dai Rees you've just got to be champion!"

Dai grinned. 'Okay, Bill. You win. I'll go into training. At least I'll give him a run for his money.'

At Whortle Manor the members are very friendly and that's part of thr reason why we couldn't stand Gary. He never mixed with us at the bar, and always seemed to be looking down his thin aristocratic nose. If you came across one of the older members snorting words like 'puppy' or 'whipper snapper' you could bet your last cent he was talking about Gary.

Dai put in a lot of practice in the next few days but still I wasn't really happy about his will to win. He needed an extra something to put him on his mettle. I said as much to Jean one evening.

My wife regarded me thoughtfully. ' He must pull it off this time,' she said. 'I couldn't bear to see Gary win again.'

135

From the expression on her face I knew she was thinking of those mixed foursomes recently. Jean and I had been drawn against Gary and his partner and Gary had made some pointed remarks about Jean's swing. It put her right off her game and the memory still rankled.

Then her eyes sparkled. 'We've got to find his Achilles heel.'

'Who do you mean, Dai?'

'Gary, you idiot. He's bound to have a weak spot.'

'Easier said than done,' I complained.

Jean was still cheerful. 'You never know, keep an eye on him. There's still a week to go before the championship.'

Afterwards I thought about her suggestion. It was worth a try.

I'd never studied Gary before, not surprising as it made my hackles rise to look at him, - but now I began to learn his habits. He always went to the club early on Saturday for a practice round, so I dragged myself out of bed and did the same.

Sure enough there he was on the first tee, warming up. I went across and joined him. We were the only two there so he said 'Want a game?'

'Righto,' I said.

I observed him carefully as he teed up. He went through a complicated rigmarole, waggling the club, hitching his trousers, putting his hand in his pocket. A few moments concentration then wham, the ball went soaring down the centre of the fairway.

'Nice ball,' I muttered as I teed up nervously. Gary stood there impassive as my ball curved into the trees, and I heard the splintering of wood as it caught an unlucky branch.

Gary watched as I put down a provisional ball, not bothering to hide his contempt. This time my drive was straight but short and we set off without a word.

His second shot landed on the green and he finished with a magnificent three. The best I could manage was a seven, and I was cursing inwardly for letting myself in for such humiliation. By the end of the game I knew what Dai meant when he said Gary gave him the jitters.

As I thanked him for the game I thought what a waste of time it had been. I was certainly no nearer to finding his weak spot. But there I was wrong.

As Gary turned away he pulled his handkerchief out of his pocket, and something fell to the ground. He picked it up in a flash, glancing at me to see if I'd noticed.

I pretended I hadn't, but I'd seen it all right. It was one of those rabbit's foot mascots some golfers think bring them luck.

I told Jean about it with relish. 'The great Gary is superstitious,' I said. 'He carries a rabbit's foot about with him.'

Jean had a faraway look in her eyes. 'There must be some way we can make use of that,' she said.

I felt alarm bells ring, and put up a warning hand. 'No, Jean,' I said. 'I can't pinch the thing. Dai wouldn't stand for it.'

'Need he know?' she asked wistfully.

I grinned. 'Come off it. He'd be bound to find out. I couldn't let him win like that. He's such a stickler for fair play.'

Jean didn't say anything, and I began to feel worried. 'I won't do anything underhand, do you hear?'

She patted my hand. 'Don't worry, Billy boy. This will be perfectly open and above board.' She put on an innocent expression. 'By the way what sort of rabbit's foot was it?'

The day of the championship was dry and clear. By the starting time, quite a crowd had collected and Dai was looking rather sick.

Everyone wished him luck, assuring him he could win but he did look a loser.

Gary was ice cool, accepting good wishes with a curt nod. They were about to begin when I went across to Dai and fumbled in my pocket. 'I almost forgot. Jean sent you something to bring you luck.' I pulled out a rabbit's foot and tossed it to him.

Dai relaxed and chuckled. 'That's jolly nice of Jean. I need all the luck I can get.'

He put the mascot away and patted his pocket, with a twinkle in his eyes. He wasn't a bit superstitious, but it tickled him that Jean had thought of it.

Gary stopped in the middle of a practice swing and stared at the mascot as it disappeared into Dai's pocket. He plunged his hand into his own pocket, looking far from happy. After all, what is the use of a lucky mascot if your opponent has one exactly the same?

Gary was to drive off first. He stood there, doing all the preliminaries, the waggle, the hand in the pocket, the hitch of the trouser leg. In spite of his confident bearing I got the strong impression that he was nervous.

Then he hit the ball and a gasp went up from the spectators. We all stared in disbelief as the ball curved into the trees on the left of the fairway and was lost to sight. Gary put down a provisional amid dead silence. It went straight but very unlike his usual powerful drive.

I glanced at Dai and was greatly cheered to see that the hangdog look had vanished. His drive soared down the fairway to admiring cries of 'Good ball!' He strode after it with the air of a man who has everything to win.

Dai won the first hole easily and went on to win two three and four. Gary was pale and wore a dogged look very different from his usual one of calm superiority.

137

By the half-way mark Gary was five down. As they crossed to the tenth I caught Dai's glance. 'Keep it up,' I said, and he nodded, smiling. But now Gary had got his second wind. He was so used to leading from the beginning that a bad start had thrown him completely. He pulled himself together and started to play with his old form, steadily winning holes back.

By the time they stood on the 18th tee they were dead level. So the outcome was all on the last hole. In spite of my dislike for Gary I had to admire his mulish persistence.

He drove first, a fine shot, long and straight. Dai matched it, and you could feel the tension in the air as we followed them down the last fairway.

Gary's second shot landed in the centre of the green, but Dai's touched the green then curved round and fell in the bunker. I stifled a groan as Gary strode forward with all his old cockiness.

Dai looked calm as he positioned himself in the bunker and there was an electric silence as he blasted the ball out. Gary looked on as if the result was only of academic interest.

The ball landed gently on the green, rolled towards the flag then dropped in the hole with the sweetest click imaginable. A burst of applause went up from the spectators and I could hardly stop myself myself from jumping in the air.

But the match wasn't over yet. If Gary holed his putt the game would be all square. You could hear a pin drop as he struck the ball. It was a good one, right on line but stopped an inch from the hole,

Gary picked up his ball and held out his hand. 'Congratulations, Dai,' he said. 'You played a good game.'

Dai's face was shining. 'Thanks, Gary. But that chip out of the bunker was sheer luck.'

I saw Gary blink at that, then we all went into the clubhouse. Dai bought drinks all round and basked in his newly won glory. Amid the buzz of talk and laughter he handed me a beer. 'Thank Jean for me,' he said with a grin. 'The mascot brought me luck all right.'

As I turned I met Gary's level gaze. I raised my glass. 'Hard luck,' I said.

He gave a twisted smile that seemed to me to sum me up.

Then he pulled the rabbit's foot out of his pocket and balanced it casually on his hand. 'Want it?' he said.

His tone made me uncomfortable, and I shook my head. I watched him as he strolled over to the wastepaper basket and carelessly flicked it in. Then he straightened his shoulders and came and sat opposite me, smiling.

'Funny things, mascots,' he said casually. 'A sort of crutch, really.' He grinned. 'Still, I must thank you. I can do without it now.'

He leaned over and patted my shoulder, as he said with a wry face, 'You'll really have to think of something better than that next year, Bill.'

THE THURSDAY CLUB
Belinda Brett.

In the Smoke Room the Thursday club prepared for the off. Puffing Billy knocked back the second of his pink gins and stowed his pipe in his trouser pocket.

'You're electronic now, I hear.' Shorty Harmer approached Cannonball Callick, who patted his chest and said, 'They say it'll last my time out.'

'Ah!' Shorty assumed a considering kind of expression as if he was listening to his own heart-beat and wondering if it, too, needed a bit of electronic assistance.

On the gravel outside the clubhouse the golf bags were ranged on their trolleys, guarded patiently by Cannonball Callik's arthritic springer spaniel and The Bull's hard of hearing yellow Labrador.

Martin, arriving at ten o'clock, passed the six trolleys and the two dogs on his way to the Smoke Room, where the old boys had got their spikes on and were sorting out the pairings. Watching them joke among themselves, Martin reflected that, in old age, the male body seemed to run to extremes: spindle-shanked, spare and stooping or purple-veined and corpulent. Which would it be for him? At thirty-five, straight-backed and athletic with no hint of a receding hair-line, he dismissed such fleeting thoughts from his mind, ordered a coffee from the steward and walked over to have a look at the trophies in their cabinet above the panelled lockers. The Wallace Cup, an elaborate silver chalice gleamed enticingly at him through the glass. He imagined his own name scored for ever into the soft silver, along with that of every winner since 1955. Josh's name was already there - three times over. He looked at his watch; ten-fifteen. They'd fixed to play at eleven: the semi-final. Josh would roll up at five to - full of good cheer, that laid-back exterior concealing a psyched up drive for victory. Gazing at the cup, Martin knew, if he could win today, the final would be a piece of cake. Josh was always the one to beat. Martin finished his coffee and went and changed his shoes. Then, he fetched his clubs out of the car, slung them over his shoulder and pushed open the tall wrought-iron gate to the practice ground, without glancing at the names enscribed on the stone obelisks either side: sombre reminder of all those club members lost in two

141

world wars.

He eased his golf glove onto his left hand, hit a few dozen balls into the distance with a five iron and then another dozen with his 3-wood. He then took his putter and one ball onto the practice green.

Josh arrived just as the last of the Thursday Club's pairs were driving off the first: Cannonball Callick, who lived up to his nick name and Permanently Straight who didn't.

'We'll give the old boys fifteen minutes to get away - don't want to be up their bums,' said Josh as he and Martin watched two old men and one old dog set off slowly but purposefully, Cannonball and the Springer Spaniel up the middle of the fairway, and Permanently Straight into the dunes on the left.

Josh's white golf bag, squatting on its trolley, bristled with the latest high-tec Cobra carbon fibre clubs, the woods protected by extra long scarlet woollen covers. He looked springy, confident, unbeatable. Martin's gut contracted.

'We'll toss shall we?' Josh spun a coin. 'You call.'

'Heads.'

'Heads it is.'

'I'll go first.' Martin hated that drive off the first tee. But no-one else was watching and to follow Josh's invariably cracking shot would make it marginally worse. "Titleist No. 3." In his cupped hand the dimpled 90 compression wound ball was blindingly white, pristine, No. 3 - in red - his lucky number. His steel-shafted driver was an old friend: its dark brown wooden head gleamed companionably in the sunshine as he got it out of his bag. He fitted the brand new ball onto a long blue wooden tee-peg, and holding it there, stuck the peg in the ground. He took the club in his hand, checked his grip, stood behind the ball, lined up on the left-hand edge of the bunker guarding the green over four hundred yards away, moved into the address position, flexed his knees, waggled the club a couple of times, thought "slowly back and follow through", and started his swing.

Overhead skylarks burst into song spiralling into the blue. But Martin didn't hear it. Club connected with ball and he knew immediately from the feel of it he'd struck it open-faced and off the toe. It shot way off to the right and disappeared into the trees near the eighthb green. Was it to be like this? With sinking heart, Martin watched Josh walk up the steps onto the tee.

'Bad luck,' Josh said. 'Pinnacle Gold No.2.'

He settled it in the ground on a short plastic tee-peg, lined up, addressed the ball and swung his graphite shafted driver. Seemingly without effort, the ball left the middle of the club-face with a sweet crack and whistled off into the distance two hundred and fifty yards up the fairway.

The rough seemed tall and tough as elephant grass and Martin's Titleist No.3 had buried itself in a kind of hollow at the base of some particularly thick and ugly stems. Resignedly, he hacked it out with his eight iron, jarring his left wrist in the process. His third shot pitched on the right edge of the green, hit a downslope and trickled back into the bunker. Josh, on the back of the green for two, was already lining up his approach putt by the time Martin had assessed the overhang from the bunker.

No point trying to come out sideways: this shot had to go down the hole and even then he'd only scrape a half: Josh would never three putt. He settled his feet, aimed at the pin, shielded by the lip of the bunker, and half blindly swung the club. Sand flew up into his face and when he opened his eyes he could just see the top of his ball which had plugged itself deeper in the soft sand. He waited for Josh to putt to within six inches of the hole, said 'That's it,' grabbed his ball, raked the bunker and moved on to the second tee.

From where they stood, it was possible to spot Cannon-ball and Permanently Straight on the green. Cannon-ball's well-trained Springer Spaniel was rooting near the fence for lost balls. Ahead of them the course unfolded like an undulating green blanket: inviting to Josh, intimidating to Martin. To the left of the second tee, beyond the fence, lay the exclusive houses on Glencoe and Perth Avenues. The sound of children laughing in the distance was unheard by the two men.

Josh lifted the club, turned his back to the hole, swung down, whipped his hands through, carried the great sleeper bunker - deep enough to hide a man in - and safe from the yellow chasm his Pinnacle Gold went hopping and skipping joyfully along the fairway. Martin, apprehensive of this daunting hazard, aimed right and his Titleist caught the short rough just encroaching onto the fairway, destined thus to trap the less courageous of the long hitters. Keep your head, he told himself. Josh had to give him a stroke on this hole. A fairly decent five wood out of the rough, a good chip and two shaky putts secured a half.

Josh had a bloody great bottom, thought Martin, an assertive, cocky looking buttocky ass, watching him hit a perfectly judged pitching wedge up over the bunker below the third green, to land within a foot of the pin. Sick with self disgust, Martin half shanked his third shot off the edge of the green into the stream on the right and lost the hole.

There was a bit of a wait at the fourth. 'The old Fox thought he'd lost his ball,' said Cannonball, 'but crafty old fox found the bugger down a rabbit hole, got a free drop, pitched on and holed out for only one over. Held us up a touch. You can go through if you like'.

'We're in no hurry,' said Josh. He and Martin sat down on the bench by

143

the tee with the spaniel and waited for the other two to play the long fourth.

'Cannonball still hits a good iron,' said Josh after they'd gone. 'A cricket stroke really - short back-swing, but struck out of the middle. Mostly the older they get the more woods they use. Shorty's got seven of 'em I believe and old Permanent's got five. Don't need the hand speed you see. Know why they call him Permanently Straight?'

Martin did, but he couldn't be bothered to say.

'Asked the Pro to give him the key to keeping his shots permanently straight. Ha! Ha!'

'You seem able to do it,' said Martin, watching Josh punch an eight iron to the heart of the fourth green. His own shot was pushed out to the hillock on the right as usual, and he scraped a six to Josh's par five.

By the time they got out to the ninth, Martin was four holes down. Here, the close proximity of Spring Lake had to be negotiated before the green was reached. Cannonball, Permanent, the old Fox, Shorty and the Springer Spaniel were scouting stiffly about on the edge of the lake searching for second or third shots while Martin and Josh waited on the tee.

In due course Josh sent his drive soaring up to pitch on the right hand edge of the fairway. He pocketed his tee peg and strolled to the left of Martin.

Way out on the Spring Lake the wind ruffled the water menacingly, and a pair of terns dived for fish. But Martin was only aware of the width of the marsh between him and the fairway, not of its flora and fauna. The white ball almost seemed to wink at him as he placed it on the tee. He took his old friend the driver into his hands and suddenly the distinctive weight of its slender shaft, and the familiarity of its shiny brown head, benevolent and strong, seemed to say, 'It's not too late. Trust me.'

The word "Pivot" came into his mind, and that was the last conscious thought he had had for all the remaining nine holes. From a suddenly perfect position at the top of his swing, the ball seemed to wink up at him again. His weight flowed through onto his left side as his hips turned naturally to clear the path for the descending club-head, powered by wrists unleashed with such confidence they might have been guided by some divine hand. The impact of the middle of the club-face, sweet and true into the back of the Titleist sent it soaring straight as an arrow to the left hand edge of the fairway just before the drop down into the lake.

'Good shot,' said Josh, as together they followed the balls down the fairway. It was Josh to play first. He sliced the Pinnacle Gold into a clump of of bull rushes near the edge of Spring Lake.

Martin selected his five-wood and struck a perfect shot which winged its way clear of all danger and pitched twenty yards short of the green.

144

Josh scuffled his ball out of the rushes and onto the fairway but arrived on the green one shot behind Martin, who eased a gentle little chip to within two feet of the pin and sunk the putt for a par.

'Back to three up.' Josh set his jaw.

Martin was in a trance, aware only of his swing, the ball, each shot as it came. As he selected a club, it seemed to live in his hands. The turf beckoned, 'Here ball - here - fly to the right of the black and white marker post and you'll catch the down slope and run another fifty yards - come to the lush patch of deeper green adjacent to the bent thorn bush from where you can reach the pin without rising over that bunker.' The ease of his body turn, free yet controlled, the grand sweep of his arms, the speed of his hands whipping through with the sweet crack of club-face against ball - its perfect trajectory zinging through the air - was like playing golf in heaven. Martin won three holes on the trot.

It was his long putt for a birdie three from off the green at the tenth which severely unsettled Josh, who ploughed his next drive into a forest of yellow ragwort. For Martin, lining up that putt was like being handed a present. He saw the borrow, clear as a diagram on the close-cut emerald turf. Strike the ball well left of the pin, hard enough to roll it to the small disk of paler grass where it will begin to lose speed, run down to the right a touch and hit the middle of the hole so that it can be gathered in with no chance of slipping by on the left, or rolling too far down on the right. The dark circle seemed big as a bucket, He knew, before he struck it, he would hear the ball drop with a satisfying clatter into the cup.

Josh watched Martin from under his eyes, bemused, as if his opponent had suddenly acquired a secret weapon. Martin, aware only of the mounting joy of sublime golf, parred the eleventh in three, unaffected by the cross wind from the lake, while Josh three-putted for a four. Martin's second shot at the par four twelfth was a beautifully judged six iron, rising sweetly over the bunker in front of the green, confirmed to be lying three feet from the pin when Martin breasted the slope while Josh was busy hacking his second shot out of the jungle below and to the right of the green.

Something happened on the thirteenth. Together they stood on the tee. Three hundred yards away lay the irregular cobalt oval behind which was a six foot drop to a sandy track before the 14th tee, an area that was alive with small rodents, birds and lost golf balls. Josh was still one hole up, but it was Martin to drive first. Boring into the head-wind, his ball powered its way towards the distant blue smear pitching on the upward sloping fairway thirty-five yards from the pin.

Josh, slow and deliberate, took out his driver and sent his Pinnacle Gold whooshing away to come to rest almost within an arm's length of

Martin's Titleist. Neither man spoke. And from then on they were silent, each cocooned in his own airtight bubble of concentration as, locked in combat, each played a low pitch, running their balls along the hard surface of the green to within inches of the hole, sinking their putts for threes. Still in silence they played the next two holes shot for shot, the par five fourteenth and the par three fifteenth, without dropping a shot. At the par four sixteenth, Martin was still one hole down but still the first to drive. And here they had to wait on the tee once more for the last two members of the Thursday Club. Cannonball was toiling up the slope to the dreadful Braids bunker below the green where his ball nestled, and Permanently Straight and the spaniel were looking for his ball up on the grassy slope on the left. And then the spaniel's old nose caught a whiff of rabbit and, ears pricked, nose down, he was off - following its scent as fast as his arthritic legs would carry him.

Ahead of Cannonball and Permanently Straight, the lean, bent figure of the Fox, two up and two to play, scented a win from his position near the green while Shorty disconsolately took his seven wood into the rough in search of his sliced drive. Reaching its close on the eighteenth, the match between The Bull and Puffing Billy was level. Puffing Billy, fingering his pipe in his pocket, examined the lie of his ball, sitting up on the fringe at the front edge of the green, and took out his jigger. The Bull, waiting for his opponent to play first, was poised for a charge at a fifteen footer. Next to his master's clubs, the old yellow Labrador sat down patiently to watch, ready for the signal to move off to the peace of the nineteenth hole. The clock on the clubhouse balcony showed two o'clock.

Back on the sixteenth tee, Martin and Josh waited for the two old boys to reach the green and then move off to the seventeenth tee. Martin still had the honour. Obediently, his ball traced the flight pattern drawn in his head and pitched to the right of the fairway within striking distance of the green with a seven iron. Josh's drive, longer than Martin's skipped past the right hand edge of the fairway bunker on the left. They both made the green with their second shots and then Martin sank a long curling putt for the supreme birdie three while Josh could do no better than the regulation par four, to bring them to all square at the seventeenth, which they halved in five.

Cannonball and Permanently Straight, the Springer Spaniel trailing behind them, exhausted by his fruitless pursuit of the rabbit, were making their way companionably down the eighteenth fairway as Josh and Martin set up for their last drives. Martin didn't think 'If I win this hole I'll beat Josh for the first time in my life'. He didn't think. Still guided by the mysterious hand of some benevolent god playing for him, he glanced briefly upwards before sending one last perfect drive whistling down the fairway. Neither he nor Josh heard the sharp bark of the Bull's old yellow Labrador somewhere in the vicinity of the club-house.

Wordlessly, Josh's drive followed and the two white balls could be seen way ahead, within feet of each other, in the middle of the fairway. The big bunker guarding the green was merely a blur of yellow to Martin as he swung his six iron. His shot bounced behind the bunker, took a crazy hop and finished a dozen feet from the pin. But it drew Josh's ball like a magnet and his Pinnacle Gold plummeted, dead as a shot pheasant, into the soft sand.

The Bull's Labrador was still barking, but neither Josh nor Martin heard a thing as Josh took out his sand-wedge and stepped down into the bunker. From his position in front of the green, Martin couldn't even see the top of his opponent's head. But after a while the ball shot up, fol-lowed by a shower of sand, and landed within a foot of the hole. Martin walked over to it, picked it up and gave it to Josh as he climbed up onto the green. Then, he took the pin out of the hole and walked back to his own ball twelve feet away.

Martin's putter had belonged to his father. Hickory-shafted, square-gripped, narrow-bladded, it fitted into his hands exactly right. The left lip of the hole tilted down. For six feet or so the ground sloped just percepti-bly up, then more gently down, only falling steeply away a couple of feet from the hole. He eased his putter back and felt it through, shoulders, arms, hands in one smooth movement, rhythmic as a line of poetry, a phrase of music and, as if answering a call, the ball rolled straight and to the right of the hole for ten feet, made a sharp left turn and dropped sweetly into the cup. Josh strode across the green, took Martin's hand, clapped him on the back, and neither of them could speak for the majesty of the golf they had played. And then Josh said in a hushed voice, 'Well done old chap - very well done!!'

Sight and sound came back. They saw the sunlight glinting the weath-er-vane on the clubhouse chimney, saw the swift darting flight of swal-lows swooping for insects in the clear air and they heard the howling of the Bull's Labrador as they closed the heavy iron gate behind them and made for the club-house.

Five old men and two old dogs, one of them howling pitifully, were grouped around the sixth old man who layed sprawled on the gravel by the club-house steps.

'I'm afraid he's a gonner.' said Puffing Billy to Martin and Josh. 'I said, I'll buy you a gin - loser buys the drinks - and he grabbed his chest and keeled over just like that.'

147

They were all breathing heavily, as if to make up for the one who had no breath left in him.

The Labrador stopped howling and lay down with his head in his paws.

Puffing Billy took his pipe out of his pocket and said, 'Poor old Bull. He holed a wonderful downhill putt on the eighteenth - right from the back of the green.'

The five old men and the two young men bowed their heads in silence.

GOLF CAN BE MURDER
Don Powell

The wind had began to howl again after lunch. We had cut short our game after nine holes, as it had been almost impossible to play in the conditions. Colonel Fortescue, not the longest hitter by any means, finally decided to quit after the wind caught his drive on the short seventh and blew his Titleist 3 into Spring Lake which was, from his position on the tee, behind his left shoulder.

Mine didn't fare much better, landing in a bunker on the edge of the eighth fairway.

'I haven't seen it blow like this since the great storm of 1987', observed Fortescue, as we sat around the roaring lounge fire, prior to lunch.

'Yes, we had most of the trees on the Minster road down then,' I remembered, 'and a lot of Whortle Manor was affected as well'.

'It was pretty awful. Course was closed for a week. Were you a member then?'

'No, I joined the following year.'

'So you wouldn't remember Clive Radley and Ralph Mason, would you?'

'Ralph Mason', I muttered. 'No, wait. Wasn't he the fellow . . .? Was he murdered?'

'You must have just moved here about then. Made all the local papers, and even the Daily Telegraph. Caused quite a sensation, local murder and all that.' Fortescue was well into his stride now. I knew the signs. There was a story coming up, whether I liked it or not. But I was fascinated. Golfers are not known for their murderous actions, despite what they sometimes do to the course and their clubs.

'How did it all happen?' I asked.

Fortescue signalled the steward to refill our glasses.

'I saw the fellow when he was on bail. Very remorseful, he was. And all because of his wife, Sonia.'

'His wife?'

'Yes, spot of marriage bother. But this is the version of events he told me. And he never would have been caught, if it hadn't been for the great storm of 1987' . . .

151

I meant to kill him on the thirteenth fairway and bury him in the pond but he was lucky, so Mason's story began. The golfers ahead of us were too close. So I had to kill him on the long sixteenth when he sliced his shot into the trees behind the green.

We searched for his ball and then I came up from behind. He half-turned in his stance to show a touch of grey at his temple and I hit him hard with an iron. In fact my faithful wedge with its thick flange. You might even crack a safe with it, I thought.

Everyone at the golf club knew that Ralph and my wife Sonia were having an affair. Everyone except me. The knowing glances and veiled remarks that passed in the bar had escaped me until recently.

I'd arrived home early one night and had found them together when I heard their whispers of love in our garden summer-house. I should have burst in and ended the affair right then. But shock strangled my passion. I wanted time to think.

A plan for revenge, and to get away with it, formed when Ralph and I had been drawn to play together in the club's Charity Cup over 18 holes one afternoon. It would be a special day to remember: my tenth wedding anniversary.

I brought our golf bags from the fairway and stayed in the cover of the trees. This remote part of the course was now clear and I had an hour before I was due back at the clubhouse.

Calmly, I searched through Ralph's pockets for his locker keys and then carefully cleaned my iron and wiped the bloodstains from my fingers. A slight movement in the bushes made my skin prickle. A policeman with his shiny buttons proceeding into the scene right now would have a lot of questions. A squirrel. It entertained me in the fading light while it nibbled through a scattering of fallen acorns. I took the border spade concealed in my bag. I'd intended burying Ralph deep in the soft earth back up the course. The ground about me was gnarled and difficult. So I dug into the sand and soft earth at the edge of a large bunker guarding the green.

Satisfied with the depth, I dragged Ralph over the lip of the bunker and pitched him into the hole. After filling in, I spread the sand evenly. Etiquette demanded it.

A chill came in the rising wind as I lugged the golf bags furtively over the course. Lights glowed in the club-house as I watched from the shadows until everything seemed quiet. I prayed I wouldn't be disturbed as I scampered into the changing rooms and put the bags in the lockers.

My mistake hit me: Ralph was still wearing his golf shoes. Someone would open his locker in time and wonder why his spikes weren't there if he had left the course. I took away his walking shoes to dispose of later.

I hurried to my car parked at the side of the clubhouse. I started it up and pulled away slowly. 'Aren't you coming in for a drink?' the club captain called, watching me from under the lamp at the top of the clubhouse steps.

'Sorry, Freddie,' I called back. 'Ralph here has an appointment. I'm dropping him off.' I knew Freddie couldn't possibly see into the passenger side of the car. 'See you tomorrow.'

I drove hard with Ralph's ghost beside me haunting my thoughts. Near home, headlights picked up the Horse and Groom. I pulled in for a strong drink and went over my plans for Sonia that night. She would end up under the summer house.

She put the telephone down quickly as I came into the hall. 'Who was that?' I asked casually.

'Hello, Clive. Oh, someone canvassing.' A flush came into her cheeks. Her uneasiness told me she'd tried to get hold of her lover. She ran a hand through her long red hair, her green eyes searching me. 'Enjoy your game with Ralph?'

'Pretty good. I won this time. I've just dropped him off.'

She busied herself in the dining room. I watched her rearranging the bouquet of red roses I'd sent her. I sank into my armchair as the telephone rang.

'I'll get it,' Sonia called, her steps hurrying into the hall.

'Someone for you, Clive. From the golf club.'

My mind shot back to the fairways and I hesitated before picking up the receiver. But it was just a friend wanting to fix up a game for the weekend. Reassurance filled me: no one would ever know what happened to Ralph.

Soft lighting gave the room a mood for romance; the candlelit dinner Sonia had prepared matched the sparkle of the champagne. 'Happy Anniversary, darling,' we whispered as we danced. She made a good pretence at happiness, I thought.

She opened my present. 'It's beautiful,' she breathed, holding up the gold cross and chain I'd bought. Her fingers fumbled with the clasp. 'Will you put it on for me?' Her voice was subdued.

I stood behind her and placed it round her soft neck. 'There!' I said and rested my hands on her bare shoulders, our cheeks touching as we looked in the mirror. I admired her attractive colour match. And when she half-turned to kiss me lightly her perfume and the bubbles of champagne made me feel giddy about my plans for this moment.

We went to bed. A strong wind made the curtains flap wildly. Howling wind scared Sonia and she drew close to me as the house quaked in the storm. I decided to reprieve her for the night. A disturbed night for both of us as the great October gale spread its havoc through the southern counties.

We walked down the garden in the pearl and charcoal of the morning. Many of the young trees in the bordering copse had cracked or fallen. Sonia pointed. 'Clive, look at the summer-house!' The grand silver birch planted on our wedding day had uprooted and crashed through the building.

Perhaps I should bury Sonia beside Ralph.

The telephone didn't work. I drove through the damage of the village to the clubhouse hoping to find there would be play that day. 'It's a shambles,' Freddie moaned repeatedly as we picked through the wreckage of the clubhouse roof. Later, we walked up to the ninth green where a swathe of fallen saplings covered our path. Further on, past the tenth green, Freddie pointed out more destruction. Torn-off branches and twigs littered the fairways and greens.

A line of rooks swept across the sky and took my gaze to the distant sixteenth fairway and to the people gathered there. We walked over.

Roots of the giant fallen oak trees had seared up through the woodland edge and the bunker and the fringes of green. Ralph's sand-caked body was spread-eagled on them with a firm grip. He always did get out of a bunker in a spectacular way - but hardly ever in one stroke, I thought.

Freddie positively identified the body and the knot of onlookers chipped in with comments. He accused me sternly. 'The man there on the tree - Ralph. You said you were dropping him off last night.'

I nearly fell about in the aisles of polka dots dilating before my eyes as the cars with flashing lights came up fast along the roadway.

Policemen tumbled out and came towards us....

THE COME-UPPANCE
Philip Cannell

Once a year, the local senior rugby club played for the Sinners Cup. All their members, supporters and players are eligible to compete for the annual trophy and there is usually a good turnout of at least forty. This year was no exception and the competition was a Stableford, off full handicap.

They had all teed off and I was playing a quick nine holes with Colonel Fortescue early on a blustery March afternoon when he motioned me over to the edge of the fairway near the trees on the fourth.

'We'll let them play through,' he signalled back down the fairway to where two golfers were already on the tee. 'The starter said there were two latecomers in the competition and would we let them go through?'

They drove, both very long and straight down the middle, far ahead of our humble efforts, and soon passed us, pleasant men in their late thirties, doffing their caps very politely. I had seen them around the club on a couple of occasions before, and asked the Colonel, usually the source of all wisdom, and himself an avid supporter of the rugby club.

'They're members of Pinehurst. Seem nice young fellows. Both very steady off 15. They're both long term members at Pinehurst, quite useful, it seems. One's a farming chappie, delivers milk all over the Minster area, the other one's something in sales. Designs bedrooms, I think.'

We watched their second shots, both to the heart of the green. 'Possible birdies, I should think. And on a pretty difficult hole, too.'

'They're long hitters,' said Fortescue. 'Those drives were almost to the 300 yard mark.' I was very impressed.

We resumed our game. I was going through a purple patch at the time thanks to a chance lesson with Scottie McLeod. He'd shown me Vardon's Cure, where you take the club and hold it straight out in front of you, then bring it back level as you turn. I had some initial problems getting it back down behind the ball properly, but plenty of practice and a few ugly divots later, my game had changed, and I was breaking ninety regularly. I was now down to 18, and my whole perspective had changed.

By the time we'd reached the fifth green, we could see them on the seventh green, both, it looked, putting again for birdies.

'Very impressive,' said Fortescue. 'We may have just seen the winners in action.'

I nodded. For fifteen handicappers, they were most impressive.

Later, in the clubhouse, we lingered over toasted teacakes as the players were filtering in.

'Thirty points,' said one, an England flanker, 'What a course!'

'You're lucky,' said another, 'That shaky par on the last gave me 29 points.'

The highest score seemed to be around 37 points, and the leader in the clubhouse was John Murray, the rugby club president, a solicitor who had been a past captain at Whortle Manor. He was a very steady seven handicapper.

'The course was playing long today,' he told us. 'That wind was playing havoc with the drives, especially on the last four holes.'

Sometimes the wind could be a real factor, especially if it was blowing from the clubhouse. At your back on the first three holes, you turned into the teeth of it on the sixth, and an errant drive on the eighth could leave your ball badly placed near the lake. But it was the last four holes where it could blow your ball all over the place.

'Thirty eight points will win it today,' said the England flanker, winking at the solicitor.

'I hope not. It'd be nice to win it for once. I was close the last two years. And it was a real struggle out there. Not an easy day by any means,' Murray replied.

We mentioned the two young men we'd seen, who'd played through.

'Ah, you mean Tweedledum and Tweedledee,' said the solicitor. 'They're a real threat. Good players. Very consistent. Usually play close to their handicap. Always seem to turn up late as well.'

'Why do you call them Tweedledum and Tweedledee?'

'They're inseparable. Enter competitions together, play at the club together. They've won quite a few of the Am-Ams around here. Always come in the top three or four. The prizes aren't great, though last year one of them won a weekend in Paris in a Holsten competition.'

'Sounds like they're not your favourite people,' Colonel Fortescue said mildly.

'Well...not exactly. They don't seem to mix very well, like most golfers do. They rarely play with anyone apart from each other. There's just something not quite right. Oh, it's probably nothing . . .'

I didn't think anymore about it till the dinner that evening. Old Fortescue, as the Whortle Manor president, had been invited, naturally, and was participating at the prize-giving. He had asked me to fill a seat because of a late cancellation, and I ended up sitting between him and the

Pinehurst club president, Ronnie Wilson, at the top table. Wilson had been the Rugby club's hooker for almost a generation some years ago, had played two dozen times for Scotland, and was very forthright with his opinions. Never one to shirk controversy, he had been a very active committee member during the club's rise from the depths of the third division to their position in the top five of the first division of the Courage League, and two appearances at Twickenham in the Pilkington Cup Final, both unfortunately lost. We had played golf several times together in tournaments, and against each other recently in the annual Tolley Trophy. He was a tough competitor and a long hitter.

'How's your game these days? I still have nightmares about that putt of yours in the Tolley.'

We had been level at the eighteenth, both putting for pars. Ronnie had missed an uphill six footer, I had sunk a twelve footer downhill for an undeserved win.

'Good and bad. The Vardon Cure has helped me a lot. But the putting's gone a bit cold.'

He laughed. 'It wasn't cold when I saw you last, unfortunately for me. That cost us the Tolley as well.'

And it had. Whortle Manor had been one down in the match. All we needed was for me to win to give us a half overall. As we held the trophy from the previous year, a half was enough to keep it, and in the years since old George Tolley's death, we now had two wins each and two halves. Things couldn't have been much closer.

'I saw two of your boys out there today, Ronnie,' said Fortescue, describing the players who had played through. 'Good players.'

'Oh them,' grimaced the president. 'Bloody pain in the arse.' He seemed to be about to say something else, but changed his mind.

Fortescue raised an eyebrow, but Ronnie shook his head. 'Later,' was all he'd say.

"Later" turned out to be the talk of the rugby club, and both golf clubs for years.

The highlight of this particular competition was the after dinner speeches and presentations. Whortle had invited Cliff Morgan, a more than useful player in his day, and a keen golfer, and he kept the audience entertained with a few well chosen insults about the England style of play which, though winning games, was often accused of being boring. Whortle Manor had invested in a large television wall screen complete with video a few years before to show, initially, Ryder Cup games. It was so popular with the members that it had been extended to rugby internationals, Cup Finals, World Cup football and cricket and the like. Morgan played his audience like fish on a hook with video clips to illustrate his points. Finally a few well chosen barbs about England's chances at Cardiff Arms Park in the forthcoming international drew the deserved catcalls and hoots of derision. He sat down to massive applause.

Next on the agenda was the presentation of trophies for the day's competition, and Colonel Fortescue rose to his feet. First prize was the large silver Sinners Cup and Waterford crystal whiskey glasses, plus tickets for the British Open. Well worth winning. Second place would get a golf trolley and bag, and the other prizes ranged down to a case of Carlsberg lager for tenth.

'In reverse order,' he boomed, to applause. The audiences nationwide always hoot and clap here, remembering Eric Morley's immortal Miss World finale.

'In tenth place is Eddie McGraw with thirty two points.'

The winner got to his feet to applause, shook Colonel Fortescue by the hand, and received his prize from the rugby club president. The Colonel, obviously enjoying his role, went down the list. A few players had tied on thirty three points, and again on thirty six. Reasonable scoring in the conditions.

'Now the top three.' The old boy was milking his audience, pausing for dramatic effect and lighting another cigar.

'In third place, with thirty seven points, your club president and a fine golfer, John Murray.' He led the applause, and the whole room stood, some shakily following the amounts of alcohol consumed.

'Now, gentlemen, we have a very unusual situation here, a tie for first place, a half, you might say. On forty two points, as well. Quite brilliant golf in the conditions. After a countback, in second place is Stewart McLean, therefore in first place and the winner of this year's competition is Robert Morris.' It was the two young men who had played through, Tweedledum and Tweedledee. They had won by five clear points.

There was lukewarm applause. Someone groaned across the table, 'Forty two bloody points. It's a disgrace.'

It was said loudly enough for at least two tables to hear. 'I bet they speak Mexican,' laughed another. But the laugh seemed hollow to me, and I remembered what John Morris had said earlier.

'Not those two again,' another muttered.

The two made their way through the tables toward Colonel Fortescue.

'Just a minute, gentlemen' said Ronnie Wilson beside me as he stood up.

'Before we present these two fine young men with their prizes, I have a little treat for everyone.' He motioned to Fortescue, who sat down, apparently surprised, and lit another cigar.

'As you know, this competition has been running for over ten years.

158

It's always a good turnout, this is a beautiful course, and we're invariably blessed with good weather. Today, despite the wind, has been no exception, and on behalf of the club I'd like to thank everyone who helped make it a special occasion.' He led the applause and Fortescue, on behalf of Whortle Manor, inclined his head in acknowledgement.

'And today has been significant in other ways,' he continued. 'There's been some great golf and some fine scores. May I say that forty two points is a stunning achievement.' He nodded toward McLean and Morris, still standing a few feet away.

'But the event is significant in another way. For the first time in the history of the competition, we had a go at filming the event, including the speeches tonight.' Ronnie pointed dramatically to the side of the room, where a figure stood pering into a video camera perched on a tripod.

'Say hello to our very own Cecil B. De Mille,' he demanded.

'Hello, Mr De Mille,' the audience chorussed obediently.

'And I hope he's got my best side.'

'You haven't got a best side, Ronnie,' a wag shouted.

'Yes, he has, it's his backside,' shouted another.

Ronnie held up his hands to stop the laughter.

'Seriously, folks, we appreciate just how much time Bob has put into this effort.' Bob was another ex-Sinners player, now on the committee.

'Jeremy Beadle convinced him to buy a camcorder and he's been driving us nuts at the club ever since. Mind you, he's got all the gadgets to go with it, zoom lens, built in editor, so he now wants to be Steven Spielberg.'

'He could make a movie about dinosaurs if he came to your house, Ronnie,' shouted another heckler.

'Yes, and he could make one about fairies if he came to yours,' retorted Wilson. It was typical good natured rugby club banter.

'Anyway, as I was saying before I was rudely interrupted, Bob's organised this video, and to raise money for the rugby club, these tapes will be available in a few weeks at only £10.99, so you can enjoy some of the golf and certainly you will enjoy hearing Cliff Morgan's expert analysis of the problems with English rugby.' The audience hooted in good natured derision.

'I hope you don't mind if I, in true British tradition, slip a little commercial in between the proceedings. Some of you will recognise yourselves on the eighteenth green, and there's some raw footage of some other holes. Please bear with us, as it's Bob's first commercial attempt, but I hope you enjoy the next couple of minutes.'

He sat down to great applause. All eyes were on the screen. Everyone had forgotten about the two winners, still standing by Fortescue.

159

The lights dimmed. For the next five minutes we were treated to the view of the eighteenth green, to groans as putts were missed, fists punching the air as they dropped.

'That's me, did you see that chip on to the green?'

'Christ, I look fat in that sweater.' Cheers were interspersed with insults and laughter.

Suddenly there was a view of a bunker. Braid's. The dreaded bunker on the sixteenth. In it were two balls, six feet apart.

Two pairs of feet entered the sand. Two pairs of hands lifted the balls, threw them, and the video camera panned as they landed on the green near the pin. The camera caught them as they raked the bunker clean and strolled toward the green. McLean and Morris. Tweedledum and Tweedledee.

Total silence from the audience, as the camera then revealed the seventeenth fairway. One of the balls had gone left and was nestling behind a sapling past the left hand bunker. A hand appeared, picked up the ball and threw it on to the fairway. As the camera moved up, it showed a profile. It was McLean.

On the seventeenth green, two balls lay at opposite ends, both twenty feet away from the pin. As one of the figures walked on to the green, he appeared to toss a coin over near the pin, then picked up his ball and placed it ahead of the coin. It was the face of Morris.

The film stopped suddenly, and the lights came on. Tweedledum and Tweedledee were still riveted to the spot.

We were all still stunned as Ronnie Wilson got to his feet again.

'I'm sorry to have taken up your precious time, gentlemen. There's more, obviously, but that was just a little taster and may I just remind you that it'll be available on sale in a couple of weeks. We shall be sending it to other rugby clubs and golf clubs all over the country to illustrate that a lot of money can be raised for the clubs with a little bit of imagination. We shall also send it to the local press so they can give our fundraising a bit of a plug. I think you'll agree it's got some fascinating views of Whortle Manor. Now where were we on your presentation, Colonel Fortescue?'

Colonel Fortescue stood, lighting another cigar.

As he stood, Tweedledum and Tweedledee took a few shaky steps toward the door.

'I'm sure you can't wait to go to the toilet, gentlemen,' said the Colonel, 'but if you would kindly bear with us a moment.' The pair froze. 'I think that a ten minute recess is called for, so that you can all recharge your glasses, gentlemen, don't you think so, Mr President?'

John Murray rose to his feet.

'I'd like to thank Ronnie for his news on the fundraising video. And great credit to Bob for making it. That was a complete surprise. Absolutely brilliant and very revealing. I will personally make sure that a copy is sent to every golf club and rugby club secretary in the Home Counties and the Midlands. I hope that you will all order your personal copy. And now I declare a ten minute recess. After that, I'd like the winners to return their prizes and we'll do the real presentation this time.'

A hand appeared and threw the ball onto the fairway.

He sat down to thunderous applause.

Tweedledum and Tweedledee, still thunderstruck, turned and walked quickly from the room. Without signal, the whole room stood in unison and total silence, watching them go.

As the door closed behind the pair, they remained standing, this time applauding and cheering wildly. The walls shook and Whortle Manor had never heard noise like it.

'How in God's name did you manage that?' I asked Ronnie later. Colonel Fortescue was beaming broadly. 'And did you know what he was planning?' I asked him.

'Do you think it was an accident that we were on the course this morning?' he gave me a broad smile.

'We've been trying to nail those two for years,' explained Ronnie. 'I hate cheats, we all do. Those two are the worst kind, but despite dozens of complaints, we've never been able to get any evidence. And that's the problem. Almost every club has at least one cheat, but you can't do very much about it. You know they cheat, but a lot of members won't complain because it sounds like whingeing, like sour grapes. But this time we got them, the act and the evidence. Our man hid over in the trees near Butterfly Cottage. He couldn't have had a better view. I was expecting to see Leslie Nielsen appear at any minute.'

'I think you nailed them pretty good. Do you think they'll ever play golf again?'

'Oh yes. Probably in Africa or South America. Not here. Not ever again,' smiled Colonel Fortescue.

THE GLASS EYE
Peter Sydenham

CRACK! The pistol shot rang out loud and clear in the cold crisp air. It was an early winter morning at Whortle Manor. For Colonel John Quinton Smythe it was most unfortunate. He heard the bang as he reached the top of his backswing, as he prepared to drive from the 11th tee.

It put him off his stroke completely. Not that much was needed to unnerve the good colonel when he was addressing the ball.

He was already off balance as he struck the ball, sending it from the heel of his club, arching it an angle of some 40 degrees to his left, away from the intended green towards the dreaded Spring Lake.

'Blast those bloody people!' he boomed, glad of the excuse to blame someone. 'They always seem to be out shooting when I'm playing.' He glared in the direction of Butterfly Cottage and the woods beyond.

'Yes,' sighed his playing partner, Neil Radford, whose ball was already safely on the par three green, 'I suppose we'd better go and look for it.'

For Radford it was another tedious journey into the rough to look for the colonel's ball for the umpteenth time that morning. It was just his bad luck to have been drawn against the pompous ass in the President's Winter Trophy. For Radford, though, it was an easy draw. After ten holes he was five up. But still, he would rather have played someone, anyone, else.

They walked toward the lake. 'Don't forget, Radford, you owe me another £500 by the end of the week,' said the colonel, as he thought of something to cheer himself up.

'You had £500 only two weeks ago,' his partner protested.

'I said by the end of the week, Radford,' as he lengthened his stride and moved ahead.

Radford grunted miserably and trudged after the colonel.

The early morning mist was clearing slowly to reveal another bright morning as the two men trampled through the wet grass toward the lake.

'I'll look down by those rushes,' said the colonel, as he reached the edge of the lake. He stormed off, not waiting to see what Radford was going to do. As he reached the bull rushes, he allowed himself a chuckle

163

of delight, as he saw a ball nestling on a muddy slope, just beneath the surface.

With some difficulty, for he was a large man, he stooped to pick it out, but, with typical clumsiness, only succeeded in pushing it further down into the water. He could still see it, however, and, not one to be deterred, decided to try again.

It was at this time that old Davy Jones, the caretaker at Whortle Manor, was tidying up in the Members' Club Room, on the second floor of the clubhouse. He was all alone in the room and decided to go out on the balcony and use the telescope to scan various parts of the course. He was pleased to see that the mist had lifted enough for him to see quite a lot of the course, but it was a relatively quiet morning and there weren't many players to be seen.

There was, however, the club captain, Tom Jackson and young Jim Brooks on the 18th tee across Spring Lake. As he scanned around to the near side of the lake he could see the colonel on his hands and knees. He chuckled at the thought of yet another fluffed shot. 'Serves the pompous old ass right,' he muttered to himself. 'I wonder who his unfortunate partner is?'

He quickly found Neil Radford, purposefully making his way up

'Don't forget, Radford, you owe me another £500'

behind the colonel, carrying a club in his hand as if it were an axe.

Later that day, the members' bar at Whortle Manor was awash with speculation, discussing the sudden departure of Colonel Smythe in the middle of his match with Neil Radford.

'Very unprofessional,' said the captain, Tom Jackson.

'Completely out of character,' said another.

'Not like him at all,' said old Colonel Fortescue, who sometimes played with Smythe, despite having little liking for the man.

Nevertheless, the facts were plain. He had left the course in the middle of his round and had disappeared. The fact that he was five down was irrelevant. His car had also gone from the carpark. Radford explained what had happened. He had been waiting on the 11th green to putt out while Smythe, having sliced the ball to the left toward the lake, had disappeared from view. He waited on the green for a while, then strolled back to the lake where he'd last seen the colonel.

'I thought at first he might have fallen in,' he said, 'But he was nowhere to be seen.'

An extraordinary business, everyone thought.

Mrs Smythe reported her husband missing later that afternoon, when he failed to appear for lunch. Radford repeated his version of events to the police and the committee. Most extraordinary, they all concluded. Colonel Fortescue suggested that they consider dragging Spring Lake, but, as it was now dark, no action was taken.

It was just gone midnight when Neil Radford drove his Four Track along the rutted track between the golf course and the edge of the woods near Butterfly Cottage. A full moon on a clear night gave him sufficient light to do without his headlights.

As the car bumped along, he kept going back over the events of the day. The increasingly unreasonable demands for more money from Smythe; the taking of the five iron from the colonel's bag; using it to strike him full on the back of his head as he peered down into the lake. Then the nightmare of dragging the heavy body into the woods, hiding it in the undergrowth along with the golf bag. It was dense in the woods, and he was terrified of being spotted. But the friendly mist came down soon after, and he had gone undetected. In reality it had been all over in minutes. He had been in the quietest part of the course, close to the woods, and the hardest part had been getting back to the carpark unseen. He had climbed the fence and approached the carpark from the road. There he had taken the colonel's car to the railway station, only minutes away from the club and left it in the deserted car park. He then walked back through the woods, over the fence beside Butterfly Cottage, back onto the course, collecting his own bag, and appearing much puzzled in

165

the clubhouse. The whole thing had taken less than an hour. The only person he'd seen was that old fool, Davy Jones, on the terrace as he returned to the locker room.

The police and the committee had swallowed his wide eyed innocence and his story. He felt confident that he was safe. All he needed to do was move the body to a safer place. He felt little guilt. The pompous ass had become too greedy, demanding more and more money. After all, Radford's affair with Tom Jackson's wife had been over for more than six months. But the colonel had found their letters and was now an expert blackmailer. Or had been before his encounter with his own five iron.

He reached the spot where he had dragged the colonel into the thicket. He had carefully covered the body and the golf bag with branches, bracken and leaves. Also an old sack which someone had thoughtfully left behind.

To his astonishment, there was no sign of body or bag. Panicking, he rechecked his bearings as best he could in the light. Stop at the double bar gate, walk twenty steps straight ahead. This was it. The right spot. He felt sick and uneasy. Had it been found and taken away? Had the police been tipped off? Had someone seen him? No, it couldn't be. He had not been seen. Hardly anyone came to that part of the woods. Butterfly Cottage was still unoccupied. After all, he'd been with the police only a few hours earlier, and there had been no mention of a body. They were still looking for a missing person.

He was suddenly aware he wasn't alone. He could make out a shadowy figure standing only a few yards away.

'Hello, Mr Radford,' said the shadow. 'I thought you might be along.'

'Davy, Davy, is it you?' Radford, petrified with fright, recognised the voice.

'Come for your body, have you?' The voice was taunting.

'What do you mean?' Play it cool. Buy some time, some thinking time.

'Don't be stupid, Radford. The body you dumped here this morning. That stupid old fool, Smythe.'

'What do you know about that?' Aggressive now. Regaining composure. Voice firmer.

'I saw you hit the old fool over the head down by the lake. You dragged him over here. Then you took his car to the station. Saw it all, Radford.'

'You couldn't have,' blurted Radford. 'There was nobody around. The course was empty.'

'I had a grandstand view, I did,' smirked Davy. 'Telescope on the balcony, watched it all, and very interesting it was too. Great things telescopes.'

'You saw it, all of it?'

'All of it. The whole thing.'

Radford shivered. Partly cold, partly fright. He had often used the telescope himself, and he knew it was possible to see well over Spring Lake. And how else could Jones have known where the body was, and that he would have to come back for it?

'What are you going to do about it?'

'Well, I thought you might like the body back. For a small consideration, of course.'

'And how much would that small consideration be?'

'Well, I reckon a couple of grand would see me all right.'

'How do I know you've got the body?' Radford's nerve was returning. It was only money, not the dreaded police and all the shame that would go with discovery. 'And what have you done with his clubs and bag?'

'I've got them safe, especially the five iron you hit him with. Left a nasty red stain on it, you did.'

'Well, my fingerprints won't be on it, I had gloves on.'

'That was a smart move, all right,' said Jones. 'So what about it? Do you want your body back?'

Radford thought for a minute. He had to gain some time, think things through.

'Okay, but I want proof you've got the body.'

'Why don't you get the money together and then contact me?' said Jones, as he began to move away.

'I'll need a day or two,' said Radford.

'Just don't take too long. Bodies have a funny habit of turning up.' Jones slipped away, back into the cover of the woods Radford watched him go, till he lost sight of him. He returned to his car. He had a great deal to think about.

It was later the following evening, as Radford sat at home, sipping a Scotch turning things over in his mind. He had no choice, he would have to pay up. And he knew well what blackmail was like, it never ended. A couple of grand would become five, ten or more.

He jumped like a nervous cat when the phone shrilled.

'Neil, it's Tom Jackson.'

Radford hesitated. "Yes, Tom. Nice to hear from you.'

'Didn't see you at the club today.' Jackson was as breezy as ever. Radford had spent the day at home, not daring to go out.

'I've been tied up all day, meetings, you know.'

'Well, I've been drawn against you in the next round of the President's Trophy. Wanted to fix a date.'

Radford groaned to himself. Jackson was a formidable opponent, difficult to beat.

'Well, does Sunday morning suit you, say around nine?' Jackson went on.

'Yes, that'll be fine, Tom. I look forward to it.'

'Good.'

'Any more news of the colonel?' Radford's voice was casual, his heart pounding.

'No, nothing. The police haven't come up with anything yet. The only thing that happened today was old Davy Jones.'

Radford sat bolt upright. 'What do you mean?'

'Died this afternoon. Heart attack. Cleaning out the boot room, keeled over just like that. Talking to one of the bar staff one moment, gone the next. What a way to go.'

His last words were lost as Radford dropped the phone on the floor.

'Neil, Neil, you there?'

Radford sank back in his chair and took a long draught of the Chivas Regal.

THE THIRTEENTH HOLE
Terence Wright

Henry Fairbanks had a few practice swings on the first tee, addressed the ball, and saw it land in the middle of the fairway with a good deal of relief. Not far, but far enough for seventy-five year old Henry. Much to his amusement Charles Arnold, his playing partner for the last forty-odd years, hooked his drive into the rough.

'Hard luck, old boy,' Henry said with a broad grin on his face.

'Just wait for the thirteenth,' Charles replied with a grimace, as they trudged off down the first fairway. Whortle Manor wasn't a steep course, but there were a few mounds and hills that would soon have the ancient pair out of breath.

'I've given up worrying about the thirteenth,' Henry muttered, as he helped look for Charles' ball. 'I can never get on in two, and then the ball won't go in the blasted hole.'

Charles fluffed his first shot out of the rough, then found the bunker to the right of the green. Henry grinned again as his second landed just short. A surefire bogey. Charles took three out of the bunker, sending sand flying everywhere. Henry chipped on to three feet, and sank the putt. Four on the first wasn't bad.

'You don't usually par the first,' Charles remarked.

'A good start, but, as you said, wait till the thirteenth.'

They played on slowly, two old men who loved the game and the course. Charles visited Tolley's bunker at the second, but splashed out to leave the ball dead, Henry had his usual bogey. Charles found his rhythm and extra distance but wildness came with the extra power, and he visited at least one bunker for the first twelve holes.

'What's the matter with you today?' asked Henry. 'You need a bucket and spade. I've never seen you in so many bunkers.'

'I thought I might take the wife off to Blackpool for a week,' mused Charles thoughtfully. 'But on second thoughts, I've seen enough sand for a while.'

Henry laughed. Charles was good company, they were evenly matched, and they'd had some great tussles over the years. The bets were always the same, one pound front nine, a pound back nine and two pounds the game. Matchplay of course, both off 21 handicap.

The dreaded hole, the thirteenth, arrived. A simple looking par four off the highest tee on the course. Stroke index 17, the only slight problem was the pond to the right of the green, although the green did severely slope from left to right. Behind the pond was deep gorse and heather. Today, as usual, the wind was across from Spring Lake, this time gusting sharply from the left.

'Your honour,' said Charles with a broad smile. He had lost the front nine by two, but was now one up. Henry's usual escapades with the thirteenth would square the match.

'I'll crack this hole if it's the last thing I do.' Henry teed up the ball, aimed well to the left into the wind and gave it everything he had. The ball arched beautifully toward the lake, held up in the wind and dropped like a stone two hundred yards away. Charles followed suit, a few metres ahead.

Henry was on the fairway, Charles in the rough.

A mere hundred yards from the green, Henry took his wedge, aiming for the back of the green and safety. The ball soared gently up, hit the green and bounded off into the deepest clump of heather on the course. Charles hit the green on the right and the ball fell into the pond. Henry was lucky to find his ball but took four shots to hack it out to the edge of the green. After four putts, he was finally down in ten. Charles found his ball underwater on the egde, took his penalty, chipped on and took a seven.

'In all the years we've been playing, Henry, I've never seen you take less than nine.'

'Always the same, always been the same,' replied Henry gloomily. 'After forty years, it's the same old story. I always end up in the gorse or heather. Never in the pond. Never on the green till it's too late.'

They were still discussing the thirteenth as they walked into the nineteenth, and Charles gleefully pocketing his winnings.

Henry died suddenly at the end of that week. His wife Meg sought advice from Charles.

'I don't know what you think,' she said with a frown. 'Henry left a note with his will. I knew he wanted to be cremated, but he says he wants his ashes....'she paused '...not scattered... He wants them poured into the hole on the thirteenth green.'

Charles consoled her, and said he would help her carry out his old friend's wishes.

It was a sunny day with only a light breeze. Charles, with Meg carrying the container, walked slowly to the thirteenth green.

There were no players approaching as Charles removed the flagstick.

'Do we say anything?' Meg asked.

Charles shook his head and smiled as he ceremoniously pulled the flag halfway down the stick. Meg knelt down and started to pour the ashes into the hole.

The sudden gust of wind took both of them by surprise and the contents of the urn were carried away....far away into the deepest clump of heather on the course.

ABOUT THE AUTHORS

PATRICIA ARMSTRONG's husband, James, a surgeon, taught her to play golf as a pre-condition to marriage, and introduced her to fishing on her honeymoon. The weather was kind, she caught a few salmon and she's been hooked ever since. He also encouraged her to play golf. Miraculously, some 25 years later, they are still together, although mixed foursomes have, on occasion, strained their devotion to the limit.

After living and working in London for many years, the Armstrongs now live in Surrey, where Patricia, an ex-county player, still has a respectable 9-handicap.

Her fishing stories have been pubished in The Field, Trout & Salmon, and in Salmon, Trout and Sea-Trout magazine. Her fiction stories have been featured in Writers News.

Patricia says that all her characters are imaginary and I suppose we must believe her.

BELINDA BRETT lives in Norfolk and is the author of one novel and several short stories. A keen, though moderate golfer, she inherited her love of the game from her father Frank Brett, who played off scratch and won the Gezira Sporting Club Championship while stationed in Cairo.

PHILIP CANNELL lives in the Midlands and has been writing sports poetry and stories since his days in university. His favourite targets are nosey journalists and cheats on the golf course. He is working on a screenplay about an ageing golf pro who quits the circuit, settles down at a course in Scotland, but hits the bottle. Then he meets a beautiful blonde caddy who straightens him out and convinces him to join the Seniors Tour. Sean Connery was asked to play the lead role but his reply is unprintable. He plays golf off 18.

SYBIL JOSTY started her career by writing articles and poetry, followed by short stories in numerous women's magazines. In the past few years she has had romantic novels published. She is also a member of St. Mellons Golf Club, Gwent, has had numerous golfing articles published and is secretary of the Cardiff Writers Circle.

K.D. KNIGHT lives in Gloucestershire and has had stories published in several literary magazines, winning a New Fiction Readers Award. He is secretary of Newent Writers Circle and organiser of the Little Acorns short story competition. Most of his friends play golf. He claims to be a starving writer and cannot afford the shiny sticks or fancy knitwear.

JOHN POLLITT lives in Kent. He has written many articles from history to romance, paints in watercolours and runs a small Letterpress printing business for pleasure. His fascination with golf began as a student when he played courses in Surrey and London. His play has improved little over the years, but he has become interested in the psychology of the game and its players.

DON POWELL has long enjoyed the game of golf, but the best he ever played off is a struggling 18. He made a hole-in-one on a San Diego course when on an aerospace trip to California in 1969. It was the wrong green. He has contributed articles to several countryside and other magazines.

PETER SYDENHAM lives in West Sussex and is a recently retired local authority entertainments and theatre manager. His two main interests in life are writing and golf. He is, however, an enthusiastic but frustrated 23 handicapper. "The Glass Eye" is his first golfing story and was inspired when his golf club opened a second course.

TONY TURNER is a prolific writer of short stories, many of which deal with sports. He admits to being a frustrated golfer who, due to disability, has to follow from the sidelines. He exercises his passion for basketball by following the Sheffield Sharks. He often walks the boundaries of his local course, seeking inspiration for his stories. Married with two teenage children, Tony is busy putting the final touches to his first novel, with plans afoot for a second.

TERENCE WRIGHT never wanted to be an author till he did a freelance writing course. Now, with one novel in the pipeline, he lives with his wife - four children having flown the nest - in a cottage in the East Lancashire hills. Ex-Royal Navy, he is a field service engineer with a computer company,but his golf is limited thanks to the inclement moorland weather.

BEN CLINGAIN, Editor of the TALES OF WHORTLE MANOR, emigrated from the United States at the time of the "Brain Drain" in 1972, and began working for Thomson Regional Newspapers in London. "I was the Dummy Drain," he claims proudly. By 1975, he had moved to Northampton to found his own newspaper and magazine chain. A self-confessed golf nut who plays erratically off 20, and a hopeless fan of the Boston Red Sox baseball team, he has contributed sports articles to magazines all over the world. Author of "Hunting Tales"(1994) and the "Ryder Cup Handbook"(1993), he edited the "International Golf Almanack 1995" for Blandford Press. His company, Maverick Sporting Publications, specialises in niche market sports books and will shortly publish Anthologies on fishing and greyhound racing. An offshoot company specialises in Applemac computer training for writers and journalists.

173

Acknowledgements

"Tales of Whortle Manor" could not have been produced without the great imagination and skill of several writers and a few golf nuts. I am indebted firstly to Writers News for spreading the word that I was on the lookout for original short stories about all aspects of golf while editing The International Golf Al;manack for Blandford Press. I was inundated with hundreds of short stories, some good, some brilliant, others less so. After months of sifting through these, I had a call from Patricia Armstrong who sent in a few stories, then some more, with the outline drawing of an imaginary golf course.

This was to become Whortle Manor Golf Club and that was when the real book began. Patricia's husband James helped with the redesign of the course, advised me on many points of clarification on the Rules of Golf. and the volume of stories began to take shape. Many had to be rewritten and adapted, as they mentioned specific holes at other courses, and to take account of the new location. The authors were very patient and understanding during the editing process.

The course was checked and rechecked by James Armstrong and Wing-Commander Bill McCrea DFC, himself an international golfer of some renown. Distances were measured, extra bunkers put in, and the stroke indexes worked out. All the while, Whortle Manor was feeling more and more like a real course, and as more stories arrived, the characters began to come alive. Colonel Fortescue was invented and emerged as the central character, around whom all good things at the club revolved. Any resemblance to the "Oldest Member" in the P.G. Wodehouse stories is entirely coincidental.

Kay Houghton graciously agreed to the use of some of her late husband George's brilliant cartoons to illustrate several of the stories, and Jim Watson used his fertile imagination to cartoonize others. Young Northampton student Rebecca Parry donated her talent to the creation of the cover, and Paul Instrall did the book formatting in his usual brilliant way. Many friends helped unwittingly, but any resemblance to persons living or dead is purely coincidental.

To all of the above I am deeply indebted.

Ben Clingain
Editor
Northampton
February 14th 1995

175